Gender, Ethnicity, and the State

SUNY series
in
New Directions in Crime and Justice Studies
Austin T. Turk, editor

Gender, Ethnicity, and the State

Latina and Latino Prison Politics

Juanita Díaz-Cotto

State University of New York Press

Published by
State University of New York Press, Albany

Printed in the United States of America

For information, address the State University of New York Press,
State University Plaza, Albany, NY 12246

Production by Cynthia Tenace Lassonde
Marketing by Theresa Abad Swierzowski

Library of Congress Cataloging-in-Publication Data

Díaz-Cotto, Juanita, 1953–
    Gender, ethnicity, and the state : Latina and Latino prison
politics / Juanita Díaz-Cotto.
        p.   cm. — (SUNY series in new directions in crime and justice
studies)
    Includes bibliographical references and index.
    ISBN 0-7914-2815-X (alk. paper). — ISBN 0-7914-2816-8 (pbk. :
alk. paper)
    1. Hispanic American prisoners—New York (State) 2. Women
prisoners—New York (State) 3. Corrections—New York (State)
4. Discrimination in criminal justice administration—New York
(State) 5. Green Haven Correctional Facility. 6. Bedford Hills
Correctional Facility (N.Y.) I. Title. II. Series.
HV9475.N6D53 1996
365'.6'089680747—dc20   95-16255
                                                          CIP

10 9 8 7 6 5 4 3 2 1

For Latina and Latino prisoners everywhere.

Until those of us who are indifferent or
vengeful realize that we too are being
dehumanized by what happens inside this
country's penal institutions, nothing of
significance will change.

Contents

PART I Challenging Custodial Hegemony

PART II Latino Prisoners: Green Haven Correctional Facility

PART III Latina Prisoners: Bedford Hills Correctional Facility

Tables

Acknowledgments

I would like to express my gratitude to the following persons for their support while I was writing this book:

All the prisoners and ex-prisoners who shared their painful experiences and memories with me. The example of their strength and courage in the face of widespread violation of their human rights will always serve as an inspiration to me.

All the community persons and penal staff who took time off from their busy schedules to allow me to interview them.

Doris Bonaparte Lee, who guides me in my spiritual journey and keeps me on the right path.

Rosalind R. Calvert, spiritual companion for fourteen years, who not only helped with the major editing of this book but also provided emotional support during the years the book was in development.

Darlene Desmond, who copyedited, gave editorial suggestions, and was a source of emotional support.

Attorneys Elizabeth Koob and Steve Latimer and Dr. Adalberto Aguirre Jr., Dr. Carole Boyce Davies, Dr. Deborah Britzman, and Dr. María Lugones who reviewed versions of the manuscript; Dr. Marilynn Desmond, who reviewed parts of the manuscript, provided much needed emotional support during the last weeks this book was in progress, and allowed me access to the Women's Studies office where I could work without interruption; Dr. Frank Bonilla and Camille Rodríguez, who not only granted me interviews, but also made the files and resources of the Center for Puerto Rican Studies accessible to me.

I would also like to thank Dr. Bonilla for his comments on the manuscript; and attorney Daniel Meyers and Dr. Edgar Rodríguez, who shared their personal files with me; Prisoners' Legal Services (New York City) and The Fortune Society (New York City) which allowed me to use their facilities to conduct research and xerox material.

Many thanks to Julanne Tyler, María del Carmen Díaz, and Steve Haweeli who copyedited different versions of the text; Xiomara

Torres, who researched newspaper articles; Jessica Rose, Dara Rose, Katherine Niles, David Stevens, Clyde Valentín, Alejandro Moya, Evelyn Erickson, Teresa Jiménez, Nandini Assar, Denise Copleton, Beatriz Aguirre, Xochitl Zuñiga and Margo Ramal-Nankoe, SUNY-Binghamton undergraduate and graduate students who did library research, proofread material and/or transcribed interviews. Nigel Ferguson, Wendy María, and Karen Lippitt who, as my teaching assistants, undertook a number of responsibilities which allowed me to devote a greater part of my time to revising the last draft of this book. Evelyn Tang and Holly Peacock for working on the index.

Friends and family members who offered emotional, spiritual, and/or financial support were Juanita Cotto Torres, Carmen Dolores Nieves Isern, Denise Devine, June Chan, and Mariana Romo-Carmona. Marcia Guardia kept me company at my office during several weeks of writing, encouraged me in times of great tension, and made sure I had a ride home whenever I stayed at the office working late.

Thanks are due to Rachelle Moore, SUNY-Binghamton librarian, who provided half of the book's title and whose conversations with me always inspire me to think of new projects; Phyllis Kuhlman, Sociology undergraduate secretary, and Steven Colatrella, who made last minute revisions on the manuscript; Carol Slavetskas, Women's Studies secretary, for her support during the final hours of writing; The Research Foundation of the State University of New York, which provided partial funding for travel and other research-related expenses; and finally, Lois Patton, Christine Worden, and Cindy Lassonde of the State University of New York Press, for their support in publishing the book.

Preface

My introduction to prisons occurred during the spring of 1980 when the director of an organization dedicated to the exhibition and sale of prisoner artwork asked me if I wanted to visit Bedford Hills Correctional Facility, New York State's maximum security prison for women. He specifically wanted me to meet the then-president of the formal Latina prisoner organization. Shortly afterwards, under the sponsorship of the same community group, I began recruiting women to take children to visit their mothers in prison. However, our group was soon canceled by the project's director, after a volunteer challenged one of the men in the organization about his sexism.

I then became part of a group of grassroots feminists who were conducting a support group for battered women imprisoned at Bedford Hills for killing their batterers. That was not a popular issue with prison administrators. Hence, we guarded against anyone other than prisoners, and a few trusted staff persons, knowing what the actual nature of the support group was, lest penal authorities interfere with our ability to conduct the group.[1]

My enthusiasm for joining the support group was motivated by my prior knowledge of the conditions prisoners were facing at the institution and the hope that there was something that we, on the outside, could offer our sisters on the inside that would make their lives more bearable. The fact that both the inside and outside support groups were interracial and interethnic made it quite interesting and satisfying. After almost two years of visiting the institution, our outside support work came to an abrupt end, the result of personal and political conflicts between two prisoner leaders and the administration's eagerness to use such conflicts to restrict the access of outside volunteers to imprisoned women. However, we continued to stay in touch with individual prisoners.

These experiences taught me valuable lessons. One was the fact that women on the outside who wanted to carry out support work for their sisters on the inside needed to create safe organizational spaces for themselves from which such support work could be carried out. Equally important was the realization that women prisoners felt, thought, and acted no differently than those of us on the outside, and that just as women in the outside community struggle daily to change conditions we perceive to be oppressive, there have always been groups of women who have organized within prison walls to try to change conditions. In fact, by the time our support group stopped visiting the institution, women prisoners, with the assistance of prisoners' rights attorneys, law students, paralegals, and women community activists, had managed to litigate several successful class action suits against prison administrators. These suits were instrumental in achieving the removal by the Department of Correctional Services (DOCS) of two prison administrations, and the issuance of a court order naming a Special Master to oversee certain areas of prison administration.

Through these experiences I also learned that coalitions among diverse groups of prisoners could take place even amidst intense rivalries. For although our outside support group ceased to visit the institution as a result of such tensions, Latina, African-American, and white women on the inside continued organizing joint groups and activities. I learned that perhaps the most important contribution prisoner support groups could make was to foster unity among prisoners.

In 1979, a colleague and I were asked by a church publication to edit an issue of their journal covering women in prison. While the issue did not materialize, I gathered enough data on women and the criminal justice system to submit a course proposal on Women, Crime, and Punishment to the Hunter College Women's Studies Program. I began teaching the course in the spring of 1982. The teaching was always complemented by presentations on women and the criminal justice system at academic and community organized events and conferences. These presentations eventually led me to publish the article, "Women and Crime in the United States."[2]

During the fall of 1987, through Marist College, I began teaching a one-year course in Latin American history at Green Haven, a maximum security prison for men. Through Hunter College, I was able to teach the course, Latin Women and Their Communities at Bedford Hills during the summer of 1989. Teaching both women and men allowed me to see just how much more stifled by their keepers women prisoners are; an assessment which was shared by many male and female prisoners and by penal personnel who have worked in both men's and women's facilities.

More and more I began to question the differing and similar ways Latinas[3] and Latinos have responded to their institutionalization. I knew both groups struggled to change prison conditions and mobilize sources of third party[4] and penal support. But I saw that these sectors responded differently to male and female prisoners' calls for help, and wondered why. How did conceptions of gender and ethnicity influence the response and treatment Latinas and Latinos received from third parties and penal personnel? I was particularly interested in exploring the conditions under which successful coalition-building efforts among these diverse sectors could take place. It was my interest in such issues that led me to write a doctoral dissertation for Columbia University on Latina(o) prisoners.[5] Subsequently, a grant from the Research Foundation of the State University of New York at SUNY-Binghamton, where I am an Assistant Professor of Sociology, allowed me to gradually expand my research interests to other areas of the criminal justice system and to Latina(o) prisoners outside New York State. *Gender, Ethnicity, and the State: Latina and Latino Prison Politics* is the result of such expanded research efforts.

As a Puerto Rican immigrant of working-class extraction I have always been aware of the problems confronted by poor and working-class people, particularly Latinas(os) who speak little or no English and are easily the victims of discriminatory practices by those who manage social institutions. Moreover, I have become keenly aware that unless one analyzes the disparate impact state policies have on women and men, one cannot understand the full effect these policies have on a community. As a result, one cannot discern clearly the tactics and strategies needed to change oppressive social conditions. While it is an underlying premise of my research that there is also a correlation between the experiences of Latinas and Latinos inside and outside the prison walls, this text will not directly draw such comparison points. It, nevertheless, provides fundamental information concerning the nature of the Latina(o) prisoner experience through which such similarities can and should be seen. The reader is asked to apply his/her own knowledge of the struggles of the Latina(o) community outside the walls, as well as his/her own knowledge of other community struggles, to draw the parallels.

As a community activist and academic, I am always interested in learning new ways alliances can be built among diverse groups. The fact that Latina and Latino prisoners could build coalitions under unrelenting state vigilance showed me that there was something I could learn from such efforts that would be useful to me in my outside work.

It was one of my goals to convey just how much of who we are as individuals is shaped by the same public policies that support the creation and continued expansion of penal systems. As a result, this book has been written with several audiences in mind: the academic community, which has historically ignored or distorted the experiences of male and female prisoners, particularly that of prisoners of color; Latina(o) and non-Latina(o) prisoners and ex-prisoners whose lives have been most affected by such experiences; community members interested in organizing to address criminal justice issues; state bureaucrats who are directly responsible for formulating and enforcing criminal justice policy; and lay people, whose interests in prison issues may be minimal but who are gradually becoming aware of how criminal justice policies are used by the state as the basis for maintaining social control.

NOTES: PREFACE

1. During the mid-1980s, a new prison administration in charge, imprisoned battered women were able to mobilize the support of professional women, women working within the state bureaucracy, and legislators in New York State, to hold hearings within Bedford Hills pertaining to the conditions encountered by battered women.

2. Juanita Díaz-Cotto, "Women and Crime in the United States," in *Third World Women and the Politics of Feminism*, ed. Chandra Talpade Mohanty, Ann Russo, and Lourdes Torres (Bloomington: Indiana University Press, 1991), 197–211.

3. The terms Latina and Latino refer to women and men of Latin American Spanish-speaking origin or parentage. The term Latina(o) is inclusive of both women and men. It includes persons born of mixed-parentage who identify as Latina(o). It includes the nineteen Spanish-speaking countries found in South America, Central America, and the Caribbean. The term Chicana(o) is used for Latinas(os) of Mexican origin or parentage or whose ancestors resided in states which formerly belonged to Mexico (i.e., Arizona, California, Colorado, New Mexico, and Texas). Although the Latina(o) prisoner population in New York State during the period studied was overwhelmingly Puerto Rican, the term Latina(o) is used throughout the text to include non-Puerto Rican prisoners.

4. Third parties are defined as individuals and organizations, not members of the penal bureaucracy or other state sectors (e.g., Legislature, Courts), whose mobilization is critical for prisoners to achieve educational, rehabilitative, ethnic/racial, and/or political goals. They include, among others: lawyers; paralegals; college professors; students; community activists; family members;

friends; and members of the mass media. For further discussion of the importance of third party support for resource-poor groups, see Michael Lipsky,
"Protest as a Political Resource," *American Political Science Review*, LXII
(1968): 1144–1158.

5. Juanita A. Díaz-Cotto, "Imprisonment and the State: The Political
Dynamics of Latino Men and Women in New York State Prisons, 1971–1987"
(Ph.D. diss., Columbia University, 1990).

1

Introduction

"The punishment of crime is a political act."[1] It is the state, through public policy decisions, that defines what actions are considered criminal and determines which types of crimes will be targeted for prosecution at a given point in time and the forms that punishment will take. The punishment of crime is also a political act in that it "represents the use of physical force by the state to control the lives of people the state has defined as criminal."[2]

The study of the penal system is of utmost importance if we consider that what distinguishes the state from other institutions of society is its claimed monopoly over the means of coercion. The state, as understood in this text, is composed of a series of administrative, legal, bureaucratic, and coercive organizations and relationships which reproduce political, socio-economic, racial/ethnic, gender, and sexual domination through repression, ideology, and struggles within and between classes and state actors.[3]

Within this context, the creation of the penitentiary as a form of punishment became an essential ideological and material component of the state apparatus which helped ensure its ability to exercise social control.[4] For without the threat of punishment, and ultimately imprisonment, the state's authority and legitimacy would continually be challenged by significant numbers of the population.[5] It is within penal institutions that we can observe, perhaps most clearly, the various mechanisms used by the state to quell rebelliousness. The fact that what occurs within prisons tends to reflect what is taking place on the outside makes the study of the impact of imprisonment on women and people of color all the more imperative.

Throughout United States history a variety of punishments have been used to penalize persons convicted of breaking the law.[6] The type of punishment applied has varied according to the social class, sex, age, sexual orientation, race/ethnicity and legal status (i.e., free versus slave) of the persons involved. Historically, public corporal and capital punishment as well as imprisonment have been used more

1

often to punish poor and working-class white and people of color.[7] The fact that Latinas(os) are disproportionately imprisoned makes the study of the penal system and the functions it serves all the more imperative for the Latina(o) community.

One of the major assumptions guiding this book is that to understand the Latina(o) prison experience, we need to reconceptualize the experiences of all prisoners taking into account differences in race, nationality, ethnicity, class, and gender, among them and between them and others. Further, unless one analyzes the disparate impact state policies have on women and men, one cannot understand the full effect these policies have on a community. As a result, one cannot discern clearly the tactics and strategies needed to change oppressive social conditions. Another assumption is that unless one understands the experiences of Latinas and Latinos inside and outside the walls, one cannot fully understand the Latina(o) experience in the United States.

While this text will not directly compare the outside Latina(o) community's struggles with those of their peers on the inside, the reader is reminded that this book should be read with the understanding that the struggles being waged by the Latina(o) community inside and outside the walls and the state's response to them, are not only similar but complement one another.

Issues of Gender and Ethnicity[8] in Prison Research

The past three decades have seen a flourishing within the social sciences of the literature on prisons and prisoners. With few exceptions, these studies have been written by white middle-class male academics,[9] and civilians working in penal institutions,[10] former guards,[11] and penal administrators.[12] Their focus has been almost exclusively on the male prisoner "society." Complementing these studies were the publications of the American Correctional Association, which concentrated on writings by prison administrators.[13] A few studies have been written by white middle-class women academics[14] and prison administrators.[15] These, with few exceptions[16] tended to focus on female prisoners. Until the 1970s, studies about prisoners were written as if the male and female[17] prisoner populations were racially and ethnically homogeneous.

Although since the mid-1960s, a few male and female prisoners and ex-prisoners have published autobiographies, essays, poetry, and so forth,[18] it has been the liberal and conservative studies carried out by academics and penal personnel that have gained the most recognition within the social sciences. This is so despite the fact that much of the growing interest in prison politics was motivated by the activities of prisoners who, beginning in the 1950s, called increasing national attention to their plight through strikes,[19] rebellions,[20] and litigation.[21] Prisoner interpretation of reality continues to be basically ignored or dismissed as the work of a few biased "radicals" or "revolutionaries" who should not be taken seriously.

Interestingly, while the concept of "power" is central to the field of political science, little attention has been paid by contemporary United States political scientists to the role of the penal system in society. This is so despite the fact that major European and United States political theorists of the eighteenth and nineteenth centuries devoted a great deal of time to discussing the roles punishment and imprisonment played in maintaining the social order and legitimizing the status quo.[22] While the academic literature on prisons, concentrated primarily in the field of sociology and criminology, has contributed to our understanding of some key aspects of prison life, the value of its theoretical contribution has been limited by the fact that the studies such literature was based upon were overwhelmingly biased in favor of state elites. One of the significant repercussions of such pro-status quo biases was that until the late 1970s, social scientists, with few exceptions,[23] avoided studying the dialectical relationship which existed between prisoners and penal personnel and the impact the actions of the latter had on the former. As a result, "By inadvertently stripping the social system of 'half' of its social action . . . the captives are left without captors to influence their social relationships."[24] The keepers, therefore, were exonerated from having to take responsibility for the manner in which their actions contributed to prisoner victimization.

A second consequence of the pro-elite bias was that the impact of third parties on prisoners tended to be ignored unless it was to argue (particularly after the emergence of various civil rights movements of the 1960s) that radical groups were "importing" their revolutionary ideas into prisons, thus disrupting the orderly process of prison administration.[25] This argument ignored the effect white supremacist ideology and activism within various sectors of the state, such as prisons, has historically had on the development of penal policies as well as prisoner/staff and intra-prisoner relations. Thus, for example, the implications of Ku Klux Klan recruitment of staff within penal institutions, as well as the preferential treatment white staff have generally accorded white prisoners, have been downplayed or ignored by students of northern prisons.

Furthermore, mainstream social scientists failed to analyze the differential impact of state policies on significant sectors of the prisoner population. This was particularly true in the case of women, people of color, and lesbian and gay prisoners. As a result, there was little or no recognition of how biases based on race, gender, nationality, ethnicity, class, and sexual orientation influenced the treatment given prisoners. Two of the significant political ramifications of such an oversight were that the concerns of women prisoners and male prisoners of color were basically ignored as penal policies and programs were primarily shaped by studies conducted about white male prisoners. The differential treatment accorded diverse groups of prisoners helped deepen existing differences and rivalries among a captive population competing for scarce resources.

Researching Women Prisoners

Women who break the law have been viewed in different ways depending on the nature of their crimes, their social class, their race and ethnicity, their sexual orientation, the historical period involved, their political persuasion, and so forth. Women offenders, however, share one thing in common; their actions have been perceived as the result of their inability to adapt to their socially-prescribed roles of dutiful wives, mothers, and daughters.[26] As such, women's crimes, by challenging the subordinate roles assigned to women in society, have been seen as threatening the foundations of the social, economic, legal, political, and moral order in ways that men's crimes have not.[27] Consequently, women offenders have not always been conferred the same treatment by the criminal justice system.[28] In many states discrimination against women was justified by legal statutes which, through the use of indeterminate sentencing, prescribed longer sentences for women than for men convicted of the same substantive offenses.[29]

Gender stereotypes, ultimately based on biological assumptions about the inherent nature of the sexes, have also been used to justify discriminatory policies. As a result, in many cases, women prisoners have been denied access to certain vocational programs available to male prisoners. In other instances, women in prison have been penalized for behavior, such as the use of profanity, generally expected of male prisoners. The result being that imprisoned women received a disproportionate number of misbehavior reports in comparison to their male counterparts.

Differential treatment has also been justified by social science studies on women prisoners that highlight the role played by women's prison family groups and kinship networks,[30] almost to the complete exclusion of other types of prisoner organization. By focusing on the dynamics of prison families, the studies reinforced *a priori* the assumption that the main concern of women in prison was to maintain their traditional roles. Hence, it was appropriate for penal elites to limit women's educational and vocational training to areas traditionally considered appropriate "women's" work, such as cooking, sewing, ironing, etc.

The bias in favor of highlighting prison family and kinship networks complemented those studies which portrayed women prisoners as "passive" and "apolitical," despite evidence to the contrary. By ignoring the various ways in which prison authorities hindered women's ability to organize themselves to pursue reforms, such as the use of male guards to physically subdue women prisoners, social scientists distorted the prison experiences of women and ignored important ways in which state sectors sought to maintain their continued subordination. Notwithstanding, women prisoners, as the current study will show, rebelled against traditionally imposed gender roles and oppressive penal policies in a number of ways. In addition to forming prison family groups and kinship networks, they created other informal and formal prisoner groups, participated in rebellions, work strikes and hunger strikes,[31] filed petitions and class action suits,[32] wrote for prisoners' rights newsletters,[33] published their autobiographies, physically resisted the attacks by their keepers, and escaped.[34]

In view of what has been discussed above, one of my objectives was to examine how major assumptions about women prisoners have influenced the treatment accorded Latinas in prison. While it is likely that a good deal of the information gathered by social scientists, private organizations, and government personnel on the problems encountered by Latinos throughout the criminal justice system are shared by both sexes, the fact that Latinas are also part of the women's prison population means that their needs have been ignored, not only because of their ethnicity but also because the concerns of women prisoners have generally been subordinated to those of their male counterparts. In light of prevailing stereotypes about women prisoners and the lack of data concerning the prison experiences of

Latinas in the United States, the current research examines how different the prison experience of Latinas was from that of Latinos as well as
what were their common experiences as a socially subordinate group.

As a partial study of the impact of ethnicity on prisoner organizing, however, we must start by identifying Latina(o) prisoner concerns. Since Latinas(os) co-exist with non-Latina(o) prisoners with
whom they share a number of interests, a distinction must be made
between those concerns which are perceived as specific to Latinas(os)
(e.g., end to discriminatory language policies, the implementation of
bilingual Spanish/English programs and the hiring of more bilingual
personnel)[35] and those which they shared with other prisoners (e.g.,
prison conditions, access to third parties).

Researching Latina(o) Prisoners: The Study

During the two hundred years penitentiaries have existed in the
United States, the experiences and concerns of Latina and Latino
prisoners have been virtually ignored by state elites, social scientists,
and third parties.[36] In New York State, it was not until the visible participation of Latinos in the New York City and upstate male prison
rebellions of the early 1970s that their presence within the state's
penal system was significantly acknowledged.[37] Even so, the plight of
Latina prisoners continues to be basically ignored.[38]

This study seeks to remedy the scarcity of data on Latina(o) prisoners in the United States in a number of ways. It examines and compares the experiences of Latinas and Latinos imprisoned in New York
State during the 1970s and 1980s. It explores the major conflicts
existing within the Latina(o) prisoner population. It analyzes the
nature of the relationship between Latina(o) prisoners, third parties,
and penal personnel. Moreover, it examines the confining conditions
under which members of the state as well as third parties provided
support. Lastly, it studies the combination of factors under which
Latina(o) prisoners obtained concessions from state elites.

By providing information not hitherto available about Latina(o)
prisoners and their relationship to other sectors of society, I offer a
more realistic interpretation of the relationship that exists between
prisoners, the state, and the civil society within which prisons operate. Through the lens of this illustration we can appraise the impact
of state policies on affected sectors of society, the manner in which
subordinate groups make demands on the state, and the ways in

which the state responds to such demands. Moreover, the data gathered challenges a number of widely accepted stereotypes about the behavior of imprisoned women. As a result, the book expands on current theories of gender, ethnicity, imprisonment, and the state.

The lack of data on Latina(o) prisoners led me to use a combination of methods for compiling the information encompassed in this text. Prisoner and mainstream English and Spanish language newspapers[39] were used as were books, articles, court cases, and government and private organizational reports. This data was complemented by private files made available to me by individuals and community groups. The latter included a variety of correspondence and position papers written by Latina(o) prisoners and their organizations as well as third parties. An additional source of valuable information was the newsletters published by community groups supportive of prisoners' struggles. However, the most exciting sources of information were the in-depth open ended interviews and oral histories conducted with Latina(o) and African-American ex-prisoners, prisoners' rights attorneys, community activists, and penal staff.

The fact that I had worked with prisoners and was eager to document their struggles made it possible for me to gain the trust of the ex-prisoners and third parties interviewed. Latina(o) penal personnel, generally marginalized within the penal bureaucracy as a result of racism and sexism, were also eager to talk about their experiences. Moreover, being Latina allowed me to approach the Latina(o) community with a deeper understanding, respect, and interest than mainstream white Anglo-European social scientists have historically shown it.

The importance of using oral histories and interviews when compiling information on Latina(o) prisoners cannot be overstated. With few exceptions, the material written by the prisoners themselves, which is difficult to come by, and oral histories and interviews have been, until recently, the only sources of information available on Latina(o) prisoners. One of the benefits of conducting oral history research is that it allows people to speak about their experiences from their own perspectives. One of the drawbacks is that human beings tend to forget even important events in their lives and sometimes simply distort reality. The fact that I interviewed a diverse number of ex-prisoners, penal personnel, and third parties about the same events allowed me to cross-check the information obtained. This information was then cross-referenced, wherever possible, with the written material available.

A case study approach was used to recreate and compare the experiences of Latina prisoners in Bedford Hills with Latino prisoners in Green Haven between 1970 and 1987. New York State was targeted as the site for the study because it has one of the highest concentrations of Latina(o) prisoners in the country. The period between 1970 and 1987 was chosen for several reasons. It was during the late 1960s that we began to see a steady increase in the number of Latina(o) prisoners in the state. The seventeen-year span studied allowed me to measure the impact the increasing number of Latina(o) prisoners had on the penal system. Moreover, it was after the Attica Prison Rebellion of September 1971 that widespread penal reforms emphasizing "rehabilitative" goals were carried out. These reforms created a new type of administrative organization, the Inmate Liaison Committees (ILCs),[40] and made it possible for prisoners to create formal prisoner groups[41] to pursue collective goals. The time span chosen allowed me to examine, not only the relationship between prison rebellions and prison reforms, but also the relationship between informal and formal prisoner groups. Additionally, I was able to explore the impact the post-Attica Rebellion reforms had on male and female prisoners, particularly Latinas and Latinos. Moreover, because the reforms allowed the entrance of a larger number of outside "volunteers" into the state's prisons, I was able to compare the type of support both penal staff and third parties offered male and female prisoners and the impact such support had on the framing of prisoner goals and the tactics and strategies prisoners pursued.

The broader historical questions that guided the chapters were: What impact did the post-Attica Rebellion reforms have on Latina and Latino prisoners? What constraints affected their ability to frame concerns, organize groups, mobilize support, and win concessions? What were the constraints under which third parties and penal personnel sought to provide support to Latina(o) prisoners? How did the nature of third party support, penal and non-Latina(o) prisoner response, affect the formulation of Latina(o) prisoner goals as well as the tactics and strategies they used? How did notions of gender and ethnicity affect the support given Latina(o) prisoners?

I show that while Latina and Latino prisoners tended to share the same concerns, substantial gender differences existed with respect to the manner in which they organized. The variation in organizing tactics was conditioned not only by the priority they assigned to diverse interests but also by the disparate treatment male and female prisoners have historically received from both penal personnel and third parties. Furthermore, the study concludes that the ability of Latina(o) prisoners to have their concerns addressed was affected by their level of organization and unity, the degree to which they were able to mobilize penal personnel and Latina(o) community members on their behalf, and their ability to secure the support of non-Latina(o) prisoners, or at least, neutralize their resistance to Latina(o) prisoner concerns.

The first section of the book discusses the conditions which gave rise to the Prisoners' Rights Movement of the late 1960s and 1970s and the response of penal personnel and third parties to prisoners' calls for reforms. Particular attention will be given to the response of the outside Latina(o) community to the plight of Latino prisoners. The second and third sections explore the impact of the post-Attica reforms on Latinos and Latinas imprisoned at Green Haven and Bedford Hills correctional facilities, two maximum security prisons in New York State from 1970 through 1987. The sections also explore the conditions under which Latina(o) prisoners organized themselves to achieve concessions from state elites and the manner in which third parties and sympathetic penal personnel provided support to Latina(o) prisoners. The concluding chapter compares and contrasts the experiences of Latina and Latino prisoners and offers a number of interpretations on the nature of the relationship between them, the state, and third parties.

Notes: Chapter 1

1. Erik Olin Wright, *The Politics of Punishment: A Critical Analysis of Prisons in America* (New York: Harper and Row, 1973), 22.

2. Ibid. This type of analysis, as Erik Olin Wright argues, does not find expression in United States political theory which, by calling those unjustly imprisoned or imprisoned for their political beliefs "political prisoners" and those breaking criminal laws "criminals," obscures "the meaning of punishment and the political functions it plays in society" (Ibid., 23).

3. For a discussion on theories of the state, see Ralph Miliband, *The State in Capitalist Society* (New York: Basic Books, 1969); Alfred Stepan, *The State and Society: Peru in Comparative Perspective* (Princeton: Princeton University Press, 1978); Theda Skocpol, *State and Social Revolutions: A Comparative Analysis of France, Russia and China* (Cambridge: Cambridge University Press, 1979); and Charles Tilly, *From Mobilization to Revolution* (New York: Random House, 1978).

4. For a discussion of the evolution of penal institutions and their role in helping maintain social control, see Harry Elmer Barnes, *The Story of Punishment: A Record of Man's Inhumanity to Man* (Boston: The Stratford Co., 1930); Idem, *The Evolution of Penology in Pennsylvania* (Montclair: Patterson Smith [1927] 1968); Georg Rusche and Otto Kirchheimer, *Punishment and Social Structure* (New York: Columbia University Press, 1939. Reprint ed., New York: Russell and Russell, 1968); Erik Olin Wright, *The Politics of Punishment: A Critical Analysis of Prisons in America* (New York: Harper and Row, 1973); Paul Takagi, "The Walnut Street Jail: A Penal Reform to Centralize the Powers of the State," *Federal Probation* 39, No. 4 (December 1975): 18–26; Michael Foucault, *Discipline and Punish: The Birth of the Prison* (New York: Vintage Books Edition, 1979); Estelle Freedman, *Their Sisters' Keepers: Women's Prison Reform in America, 1830–1930* (Ann Arbor: University of Michigan Press, 1981); Christopher R. Adamson, "Punishment After Slavery: Southern State Penal Systems, 1865–1890," *Social Problems* 3, No. 5 (June 1983): 555–569; and George C. Killinger and Paul F. Crownwell, Jr., eds., *Penology: The Evolution of Corrections in America* (St. Paul: West Publishing Co., 1983).

5. It was precisely this authority and legitimacy that was questioned by the social movements of the 1950s, 1960s, and 1970s, including the Prisoners' Rights Movement.

6. See Barnes, *The Story of Punishment,* 1930; Rusche and Kirchheimer, *Punishment and Social Structure* 1968; and Foucault, *Discipline and Punish,* 1979. Such punishments have included penance, fines, public corporal and capital punishment, draft, confiscation of property, probation, and confinement in houses of correction, reformatories, jails, and prisons.

7. Economically and socially, white-collar and corporate crimes are more costly to society than street crimes. However, it is the illegal actions committed by poor and working-class white and people of color in the United States which have been punished most frequently and severely, see Wright, *The Politics of Punishment,* 1973; Ian Taylor, Paul Watson, and Jack Young, eds., *Critical Criminology* (London: Routledge and Kegan Paul, 1975); Gilbert Geis and Robert F. Meier, *White Collar Crime: Offenses in Business Politics and the Professions* (New York: Free Press, Macmillan Publishing Co., 1977); Peter Wickman and Timothy Dailey, eds., *White Collar and Economic Crime: Multidisciplinary and Cross-National Perspectives* (Lexington, Mass.: D.C. Heath and Co., Inc., 1982); and David M. Ermann and Richard J. Lundmann, *Corporate and Governmental Deviance: Problems of Organizational Behavior in Contemporary Society,* 2nd ed. (Oxford: Oxford University Press, 1982).

8. It is difficult to speak about racial and ethnic identification because of the arbitrary nature of these categories and the manner in which they are used in the United States. For example, during much of United States history, the dominant categories for identification purposes were "racial" (e.g., black, white). Latinas(os) have generally been classified as white or black

depending on their skin color, place of birth, and/or Spanish surname. In reality, Latinas(os) are generally the product of the mixture of peoples of African, Indian and/or Spanish descent, with the Spanish itself being the result of a mixture of white European, Jews, and Arabs. Under these circumstances it is difficult to place "Latinas(os)" within a given racial or ethnic category. As a result, when I speak about ethnic and racial identification within the prison setting, I do so with the understanding that these concepts are insufficient to describe very complicated analytical concepts. In fact, the awareness of Latinas(os) that they were not all the same was reflected in the manner in which they tended to further subdivide according to: place of birth (nationality), language spoken, and/or racial identification. Racial identification led some dark-skinned Latinas(os) to identify as "Black" and to network primarily with African-American prisoners. It also led some light-skinned Latinas(os) to identify as "white" and to network primarily with white prisoners. English-speaking (e.g., Jamaican, Trinidadian) and French-speaking Caribbean peoples (e.g., Haitians), also tended to subdivide within the prison setting according to nationality and language even when they might all be labelled "Black" by prison staff and other prisoners.

9. See Gresham Sykes, *The Society of Captives: A Study of a Maximum Security Prison* (New Jersey: Princeton University Press, 1958); Richard A. Cloward, Donald R. Cressey, George H. Grosser, Richard McCleery, Lloyd E. Ohlin, and Gresham M. Sykes, *Theoretical Studies in the Social Organization of the Prison,* Pamphlet #15, Social Science Research Council, 1960; Erving Goffman, *Asylums* (Garden City: Doubleday, 1961); Theodore R. Davidson, *Chicano Prisoners: The Key to San Quentin* (New York: Holt, Rinehart and Winston, 1974); and Eric Cummins, *The Rise and Fall of California's Radical Prison Movement* (Stanford: Stanford University Press, 1994).

10. See Kenneth McColl Dimick, *Ladies in Waiting . . . Behind Prison Walls* (Muncie: Accelerated Development Inc., 1979).

11. See Leo Carroll, *Hacks, Blacks, and Cons: Race Relations in a Maximum Security Prison* (Lexington, Mass.: Lexington Books, 1974; repr., Prospect Heights, IL: Waveland Press, Inc., 1988).

12. See Donald Clemmer, *The Prison Community* (Boston: The Christopher Publishing House, 1940); Russell G. Oswald, *Attica—My Story* (Garden City, N.J.: Doubleday and Co., 1972); and Adolph Saenz, *Politics of a Prison Riot: The 1980 New Mexico Prison Riot, Its Causes and Aftermath* (Corrales: Rhombus Publishing Co., 1986). One exception to this is John Irwin who is both an ex-prisoner and an academic. See John Irwin, *The Felon* (Englewood Cliffs: Prentice-Hall, Inc. 1970); Idem, "Notes on the Present Status of the Concept of Subcultures," in *The Society of Subcultures,* ed. D. Arnold (Berkeley: Glendessary Press, 1970), 164–170; Idem, "Stratification and Conflict Among Prison Inmates," *Journal of Criminological Law and Criminology* 66 (1976): 476–482; and Idem and Donald Cressey, "Thieves, Convicts, and Inmate Culture," *Social Problems* 10 (1962): 142–155.

13. Its major publications are *Corrections Today* (formerly *The American Journal of Corrections*) and *Proceedings,* which publishes the yearly proceedings of the National Congress of Corrections.

14. See Rose Giallombardo, *Society of Women: A Study of a Women's Prison* (New York: John Wiley and Sons, 1966); Esther Heffernan, *Making It in Prison: The Square, the Cool, and the Life* (New York: John Wiley and Sons, Inc., 1972); Edna Walker Chandler, *Women in Prison* (Indianapolis: The Bobbs-Merrill Co., Inc., 1973); Joan W. Moore, *Homeboys: Gangs, Drugs and Prison in the Barrios of Los Angeles* (Philadelphia: Temple University Press, 1978); and Erika Anne Kates, "Litigation As a Means of Achieving Social Change: A Case Study of Women in Prison" (Ph.D. diss., Brandeis University, 1984).

15. Joy S. Eyman, *Prisons for Women: A Practical Guide to Administration Problems* (Springfield, Ill.: Charles C. Thomas, 1971).

16. Moore, *Homeboys,* 1978.

17. For studies that have recognized the existence of racial differences among women prisoners, see Margaret Otis, "A Perversion Not Commonly Noted," *Journal of Abnormal Psychology* 8 (June/July 1913): 112–114; Charles A. Ford, "Homosexual Practices of Institutionalized Females," *Journal of Abnormal and Social Psychology* 23 (January/March 1929): 442–444; Chandler, *Women in Prison,* 1973; Elouise Junius Spencer, "The Social System of a Medium Security Women's Prison," (Ph.D. diss., University of Kansas, 1977); Freedman, *Their Sisters' Keepers,* 1981; Nicole Hahn Rafter, *Partial Justice: Women in State Prisons, 1800–1935* (Boston: Northeastern University Press, 1985); James G., Fox, *Organizational and Racial Conflict in Maximum Security Prisons* (Lexington, Mass.: D.C. Heath and Co., 1982); and Candace Kruttschnitt, "Race Relations and the Federal Inmate," *Crime and Delinquency* 29 (October 1983): 577–592.

18. See Malcolm X with Alex Haley, *The Autobiography of Malcolm X* (New York: Ballantine, 1964); Frank Ellis, *The Riot* (New York: Avon, 1966); Piri Thomas, *Down These Mean Streets* (New York: Alfred A. Knopf, Inc., 1967); Eldridge Cleaver, *Soul on Ice* (New York: McGraw Hill, 1968); George Jackson, *Soledad Brother: The Prison Letters of George Jackson* (New York: Bantam, 1970); Angela Davis, *Angela Davis: An Autobiography* (New York: Random House, 1974; New York: International Publishers, 1988); Piri Thomas, *Seven Long Times* (New York: Praeger Publishers, 1974); Malcolm Braly, *False Starts: A Memoir of San Quentin and Other Prisons* (New York: Penguin, 1976); Jack Henry Abbott, *In the Belly of the Beast: Letters from Prison* (New York: Random House, Inc., 1978); Assata Shakur, *Assata: An Autobiography* (Westport, Conn.: Lawrence Hill and Co., 1987); Jean Harris, *They Always Call Us Ladies: Stories from Prison* (New York: Macmillan Publishing Co., 1988); Joyce Ann Brown, *Joyce Ann Brown: Justice Denied* (Chicago: The Noble Press, 1990); and Idella

Serna, *Locked Down: A Woman's Life in Prison, The Story of Mary (Lee) Dortch* (Norwich, Vt.: New Victoria Publishers, 1992).

19. Wright, *The Politics of Punishment,* 1973.

20. See Vernon Fox, *Violence Behind Bars: An Explosive Report on Prison Riots in the United States* (Westport, Conn.: Greenwood Press Publishers, 1956); Phyllis Jo Baunach and Thomas Murton, "Women in Prison: An Awakening Minority," *Crime and Corrections* (Fall 1973): 4–12; Burton M. Atkins and Henry R. Glick, eds., *Prison, Protest, and Politics* (Englewood Cliffs: Prentice-Hall, Inc., 1972); Wright, *The Politics of Punishment,* 1973; William D. Pederson, "Inmate Movements and Prison Uprisings: A Comparative Study," *Social Science Quarterly* 59, No. 3 (December 1978): 509–524; Saenz, *Politics of a Prison Riot,* 1986; Larry E. Sullivan, *The Prison Reform Movement: Forlorne Hope* (Boston: Twayne Publishers, 1990); and Bert Useem and Peter Kimball, *States of Siege: U.S. Prison Riots, 1971–1986* (New York and Oxford: Oxford University Press, 1989).

21. See George F. Murphy, "The Courts Look at Prisoners' Rights: A Review," *Criminology* 10, No. 4 (February 1973): 441–459; Ronald Berkman, *Opening the Gates: The Rise of the Prisoners' Movement* (Lexington, Mass.: D.C. Heath and Co., 1979); James B. Jacobs, *New Perspectives on Prisons and Imprisonment* (Ithaca: Cornell University Press, 1983); and Kates, "Litigation As a Means," 1984.

22. See Barnes, *The Story of Punishment,* 1930; and Idem, *The Evolution of Penology in Pennsylvania* (Montclair: Patterson Smith, [1927] 1968). A review of articles published in nine major U.S. political science journals between 1971 and 1987 revealed that when political scientists have addressed criminal justice issues their attention primarily focused on: the functioning of the courts; the relationship between crime and public policy; punishment as a deterrent to crime; methods of gathering criminal justice statistics; and juvenile delinquency. The few political scientists who have written about prisons have focused on prison conditions, penal policy (Philip Klein, *Prison Methods in New York State: A Contribution to the Study of the Theory and Practice of Correctional Institutions in New York State* [New York: Columbia University Press, 1920; repr., New York: Ames Press, 1969]; and Barbara Lavin McEleney, *Correctional Reform in New York: The Rockefeller Years* [Lanham, Md.: University Press of America, 1985]), and the relationship between the prisoner social system and the prison bureaucracy (Richard McCleery, "Communication Patterns As Bases of Systems of Authority and Power," in Cloward et al., *Theoretical Studies,* 1960).

23. See Sykes, *The Society of Captives,* 1958; and Cloward et al., Theoretical Studies, 1960.

24. Spencer, "The Social System," 6.

25. See James B. Jacobs, *Stateville: The Penitentiary in Mass Society* (Chicago: Chicago University Press, 1977); John Irwin, *Prisons in Turmoil*

(Boston: Little, Brown and Co., 1980); and Leo Carroll, *Hacks, Blacks and Cons: Race Relations in a Maximum Security Prison* (Prospect Heights, Ill.: Waveland Press, Inc., [1977] 1988).

26. See W.I. Thomas, *Sex and Society* (Boston: Little Brown, 1907); Ibid., *The Unadjusted Girl* (Boston: Little Brown, 1923); O. Pollack, *The Criminality of Women* (New York: A.S. Barnes, 1961); and G. Konopka, *The Adolescent Girl in Conflict* (Englewood Cliffs: Prentice-Hall, Inc., 1966).

27. For studies challenging traditional stereotypes of women offenders, see Laura Crites, ed., *The Female Offender* (Lexington, Mass.: D.C. Heath and Co., Inc., 1976); Carol *Smart, Women, Crime, and Criminology: A Feminist Critique* (London: Routledge and Kegan Paul, 1976); Carol Smart and June Kress, "Any Woman's Blues: A Critical Overview of Women, Crime, and the Criminal Justice System," *Crime and Criminal Justice* 5 (1976): 34–49; Carol Smart and Barry Kress, *Women, Sexuality and Social Control* (Boston: Routledge and Kegan Paul, 1978); Clarice Feinman, *Women in the Criminal Justice System* (New York: Praeger Publishers, 1980; Freedman, *Their Sisters' Keepers,* 1981; Kates, "Litigation As a Means," 1984); S. K. Mukherjee and Jocelynn Scutt, *Women and Crime* (Boston: George Allen and Unwin, 1981); Frances M. Heidensohn, *Women and Crime: The Life of the Female Offender* (New York: New York University Press, 1985); Ngaire Naffine, *Female Crime: The Construction of Women in Criminology* (Sydney, Australia: Allen and Unwin Australia Pty., Ltd., 1987); and Juanita Díaz-Cotto, "Women and Crime in the United States," in Chandra Talpade Mohanty, Ann Russo, and Lourdes Torres, eds., *Third World Women and the Politics of Feminism* (Bloomington: University of Indiana Press, 1991).

28. Although the legislative and executive branches of the state government form part of the criminal justice system by virtue of their ability to criminalize and decriminalize behavior (e.g., pass and abolish laws, issue executive orders, issue pardons, commute sentences, etc.), I am using the term criminal justice system here to encompass the areas of law enforcement, detention, prosecution, courts, penal institutions, probation, and parole.

29. See *United States v. York,* 281 F. Supp. 8, 16 (D. Conn. 1968); *State v. Costello,* 59 NJ 334 (1971); *Frontiero v. Richardson* (1973); *State v. Chamber,* NJ Supreme Court (1973); and "legal victory for n.j. sisters," *Midnight Special* 3, No. 11 (November 1973): 22, 23.

30. Prison families and kinship networks are groups in which women prisoners adopt the roles of mother, father, brother, son, daughter, cousin, etc. Perhaps the two best known examples of social science studies of prison families are David A. Ward and Gene G. Kassebaum, *Women's Prisons* (London: Weidenfeld and Nicolson, 1965); and Giallombardo, Society of Women, 1966.

31. "rikers women—'we're demanding now'," *Midnight Special* 3, No. 9 (September 1973): 1.

32. Kates, "Litigation As a Means," 1984.

33. Prisoners' rights newsletters, to which women prisoners submitted material, included *Midnight Special, The Outlaw,* and *No More Cages.*

34. "4 Women Flee Prison, Are Recaptured," *New York Times* (hereafter cited as *N.Y. Times*), 19 July 1976, 25; "Escapee Surrenders," *N.Y. Times,* 8 June 1977, II, 3; *N.Y. Times,* 3 November 1979; Robert Hanley, "Miss Chesimard Flees Jersey Prison, Helped by 3 Armed 'Visitors'," *N.Y. Times,* 3 November 1979, 1; *N.Y. Times,* John T. McQuiston, "'Squeaky' Fromme Sought After an Apparent Escape," 24 December 1987, 10; and Shakur, Assata, 1987. There were times when women's actions in self defense led to the murder of one of their keepers ("Joann Little," *Midnight Special* 5, No. 1 [January 1975]: 22).

35. This is not to say that other prisoners do not share the same concerns regarding the provision of bilingual personnel and services. In fact, as the number of non-Spanish-speaking prisoners of color increases in New York State's penal system (e.g., Haitians) so may the potential for them to unite with Latinas(os) to demand bilingual services and personnel.

36. Most studies of Latino prisoners in the United States have been written about Chicano prisoners. See Jorge H. del Pinal, "The Penal Population of California," in *Voices: Readings from El Grito, a Journal of Contemporary Mexican American Thought,* 1967–1973 (1973): 483–499; Davidson, *Chicano Prisoners,* 1974; Moore, *Homeboys,* 1978; Michael Belsky, "Mexican Nationals in U.S. Prisons," *Theme* 10, No. 3 (May/June 1980): 20–21; U.S. Department of Justice, Law Enforcement Assistant Administration, *National Conference on Law Enforcement and Criminal Justice* (Washington, D.C.: GPO, 1980); Adalberto Aguirre Jr., and David Baker, "The Execution of Mexican American Prisoners in the Southwest," *Social Justice* 16, No. 4 (Issue 38, Winter 1989): 150–161; and Idem., "A Descriptive Profile of the Hispanic Penal Population: Conceptual and Reliability Limitations in Public Use Data," *The Justice Professional* 3, No. 2 (1988): 189–200. A few studies have been published about Puerto Rican prisoners in New Jersey (see Robert Joe Lee, *Hispanics—The Anonymous Prisoners* (Trenton: Department of Corrections, 1976); Idem, "Profile of Puerto Rican Prisoners in New Jersey and Its Implications for the Administration of Criminal Justice" (M.A. thesis, Rutgers University, 1977); Maggie Agüero, "An Exploratory Profile of Puerto Rican Prisoners in New Jersey" (M.A. thesis, John Jay College of Criminal Justice, 1980); and Idem, *Hispanics in New Jersey Adult Correctional Institutions: A Profile of Inmates, Staff, Services, and Recommendations* (Trenton: New Jersey Department of Correction, 1981). Until the current book, no major study has ever been published about Latina prisoners in the United States.

37. See Thomas, *Down These Mean Streets,* 1967; Francis A.J. Ianni, *Black Mafia: Ethnic Succession in Organized Crime* (New York: Simon and

Schuster, 1974); Thomas, *Seven Long Times*, 1974; Agenor L. Castro, "Meeting the Special Needs of Hispanic Inmates," *Law and Justice* (September/October 1977): 37–41; Idem, "A Close Look at the Hispanic Inmates and Methods of Meeting Their Needs," *American Journal of Correction* 40, No. 2 (March/April 1978): 15, 16, 18; Idem, "The Case for the Bilingual Prison," *Corrections Today* 44, No. 4 (August 1982): 72, 74, 78; Idem, "Los hispanos en presidios EEUU buscan lograr mejor trato," *El Mundo,* 31 diciembre 1978; Puerto Rican Bar Association of New York, *A New Look at the Hispanic Offender: A Proposal by the Puerto Rican Bar Association of New York for a Study of Hispanic Prisoners* by Joseph L. Torres and Mildred R. Stansky, New York, September 1978; Agenor Castro, "Programming for Hispanic Inmates and Ex-Offenders," *Proceedings of the One Hundred and Eighth Annual Congress of Correction of the American Correctional Association,* Portland, Oreg., August 20–24, 1978 (College Park, Md.: American Correctional Association, 1979): 77–88; Peter L. Sissons, *The Hispanic Experience of Criminal Justice* (New York: Hispanic Research Center, Fordham University, Monograph No. 3, 1979); United States, Department of Justice, Law Enforcement Assistance Administration, *National Hispanic Conference on Law Enforcement and Criminal Justice* (Washington, D.C.: GPO, 1980); New York State Department of Correctional Services (hereafter cited as NYSDOCS), Division of Hispanic and Cultural Affairs, Hispanic Inmate Needs Task Force, *Report 1985 (Draft Action Plan for Hispanic Inmate Needs Programming)*, Albany, November 20, 1985; Ibid., *Final Report, "A Meeting of Minds, an Encounter of Hearts," 1986 (Action Plan),* Albany, 1986; NYSDOCS, Division of Program Planning, Research and Evaluation, *Selected Characteristics of the Department's Hispanic Inmate Population* by Charles H. Nygard, Albany, December 1986; Ibid., *Year-to-Year Changes in the Hispanic Under Custody Population 1986 and 1987* by Charles H. Nygard, Albany, August 1987; Migdalia de Jesús-Torres, "Profile of Puerto Rican/Latino Women Offenders in New York State Correctional Institutions: Program, Policy and Statutory Changes," Somos Uno Conference, March 1988, New York State Assembly Puerto Rican/HSP Task Force, The Hispanic Woman: Issues and Legislative Concerns, Albany, New York (unpublished paper); Israel Ruíz Jr., "New York State Department of Correctional Services, Hispanic Needs: Employment and Inmate Programs. Report," February 29, 1988 (xeroxed copy); NYSDOCS, Division of Program Planning, Research, and Evaluation, *Comparison of Male and Female Inmates Under the Department's Custody as of December 31, 1990* by Kathy Canestrini, Albany, September 1991; and Correctional Association of New York, *Not Simply a Matter of Words: Academic and Vocational Programs for Latino Inmates in New York State Prisons,* New York, July 1992.

38. Only a few brief references have been made to the plight of Latina prisoners in New York State. See Sissons, *The Hispanic Experience,* 1979; NYSDOCS, Division of Hispanic and Cultural Affairs, Hispanic Inmate

Needs Task Force, *Report 1985,* 1985; Idem, *Final Report,* 1986; NYSDOCS, Division of Program Planning, Research and Evaluation, *Selected Characteristics*, December 1986; de Jesús-Torres, "Profile of Puerto Rican/Latino Women Offenders"; NYSDOCS, Division of Program Planning, Research, and Evaluation, *Comparison of Male and Female Inmates,* 1991; and Correctional Association of New York, *Not Simply a Matter of Words,* 1992.

39. Researching New York City's largest Spanish language newspaper, *El Diario-La Prensa* (hereafter cited as *El Diario*), was particularly challenging because the periodical does not have an index. This meant that microfilmed copies of the newspaper had to be reviewed, page by page, for each of the years I selected for study. This time consuming process limited the amount of years I was able to focus on. The same process of page by page review had to be conducted in the case where prisoners' newspapers and prisoners' rights newsletters were available.

40. Administrative organizations, such as the Inmate Liaison Committees (ILCs) created in New York State prisons in 1972 and the Inmate Grievance Resolution Committees (IGRCs) created at the end of 1975, were groups whose existence was mandated by DOCS' directives and/or state laws. They could be comprised, as in the case of the ILCs, of prisoners, or, as in the case of the IGRCs, of prisoners and staff.

41. A prisoner group was composed of prisoners who had common goals and acted to further those goals. A formal prisoner group was one whose existence was officially recognized and authorized by DOCS. As such, it technically fell under the supervision of institutional personnel and/or outside DOCS approved volunteers. Informal prisoner groups were those whose existence had not been officially authorized by DOCS. Prisoner networks could include penal personnel and/or third parties who supported prisoner goals.

PART I

CHALLENGING CUSTODIAL HEGEMONY

2

Litigation, Rebellions, Reprisals, and Reforms

Neither slavery nor involuntary servitude, except as a punishment for crime whereof the party shall have been duly convicted, shall exist within the United States, or any place subject to their jurisdiction.
—*U.S. Constitution,* ARTICLE XIII, SECTION 4

In prison you could die. They put on your death certificate that you died of a heart attack after they beat the living crap out of you. There was a place that you look out over the wall and there was a graveyard, man, and they used to have white sticks shoved into the ground that were two inches thick and six inches wide, painted white with a number painted in black. They didn't even give them the dignity of putting their name.
—Piri Thomas, interview with author (1993)

Until the end of the 1960s, prison administrators and custodial personnel maintained almost complete control over penal institutions throughout New York State, partly because the courts and the legislature were hesitant to interfere in penal affairs. There was concern for maintaining the separation of powers. Judges and legislators argued that review of administrative decisions would undermine prison discipline and security. Prison administrators were seen as "the experts" in prison management. In 1969, the Federal Court (2nd District) of New York State recognized that:

We have consistently adhered to the so-called "hands-off" doctrine in matters of prison administration according to which we have said that the basic responsibility for the control and management of penal institutions including the discipline, treatment and care of those confined, lies with the responsible administrative agency and is not subject to judicial review unless exercised in such a manner as to constitute clear abuse or caprice on the part of prison officials.[1]

The burden of proof for such abuse was left up to prisoners who lacked the resources to legally document that such abuse existed.

21

Judicial and legislative noninvolvement also rested on the Thirteenth Amendment of the United States Constitution passed in 1865, which abolished slavery except in the case of persons convicted of a crime. The amendment read: "Neither slavery nor involuntary servitude, except as a punishment for crime whereof the party shall have been duly convicted, shall exist within the United States, or any place subject to their jurisdiction."[2] Using this Amendment as the basis for their decision making, some judges chose to ratify unchallenged penal authority by ruling that a prisoner was "a slave of the state."[3] As a result, prison administrators were accorded as much right to decide the fate of prisoners as slave masters had over slaves.

Although the provisions of the Thirteenth Amendment with respect to prison slavery were finally challenged in 1941,[4] it was not until the 1960s that federal and state courts gradually issued significant decisions supportive of prisoners. In *Sostre, Pierce, SaMarion v. LaVallee*, 293 F.2d 233 (2nd Cir. 1961) the court ruled that a suit could be heard in a federal court without having been previously litigated in a state court. In *Cooper v. Pate*, 378 U.S. 546 (1964); 382 F.2d 518 (CA7 1967) the U.S. Supreme Court held that under the 1871 Civil Rights Act, prisoners could bring lawsuits in federal court, as well as sue and claim damages from prison personnel. Other decisions recognized that prisoners retained "all the rights of an ordinary citizen except those, expressly or by necessary implication, taken from him by law."[5] In spite of such decisions, litigation had a limited impact on prisoners' lives.[6] At times, court rulings were applicable only to the institution from which the suit originated. At other times, decisions favorable to prisoners made by a lower court were overturned or modified by a higher court.[7] Moreover, decisions made by higher courts, short of the Supreme Court, had limited geographic impact. By and large, court decisions continued to grant deference to penal authorities.

The broad deference accorded penal administrators by legislative authorities in New York State was illustrated by the fact that the state's Penal Law, enacted in 1881, was not revised until 1965. Prior to 1967, chairpersons of the legislature's Penal Institutions Committee did not keep files of correspondence dealing with prisoner issues. This neglect resulted partially from the fact that legislators, oftentimes members of the monied elite, frequently tended to feel indifference or hostility toward criminal offenders. Further, prisoners were not a voting constituency. Nor did the sectors of the population prisoners tended to come from (e.g., poor and/or people of color) represent a significant voting block in the predominantly white upstate rural Republican areas which controlled the legislature after World War II.[8] Moreover, Latinas(os) and African-Americans were underrepresented in the state's legislature though they were precisely the sectors of the population overrepresented in state prisons. As a result, there was little motivation for legislative elites to address the concerns of the penal populations.

By the end of the 1960s, prisoner demands for better living conditions and greater access to community volunteers were heard repeatedly, but legislative bills proposing even minor changes either died in the Senate's Committee on Penal Institutions or were vetoed by Governor Nelson A. Rockefeller. The governor's reluctance to interfere with the policies pursued by his appointees meant that Paul McGinnis,[9] Commissioner of the New York State Department of Correction (DOC) from 1959 to 1970, had great control over what occurred in his Department. Under his direction, ". . . bureaucratic and administration policy were the same within the Correction Department, namely an overriding commitment to security and custody."[10] McGinnis' concern with security and keeping Department running costs low meant that rehabilitation programs that demanded expenditures and/or the liberalization of prison rules did not generally have his support.

McGinnis' response to a prisoners' rebellion at Auburn Correctional Facility in 1970, demanding an end to guard brutality, better conditions, and greater access to rehabilitation programs, was to place nearly all prisoners in keeplock[11] for three months and to lock others in solitary confinement indefinitely.[12] Once in their cells, many prisoners were tear gassed and subjected to severe beatings.[13] Many were transferred to Attica and other state facilities. Moreover, prisoners demanding reforms throughout the state were labelled "troublemakers"[14] and "revolutionaries."[15] DOC's practices were supported by the legislature, which in 1969 passed Chapter 319 of the New York State Corrections Law. This law allowed the Commissioner to transfer without restrictions prisoners protesting intolerable living conditions and/or attempting to organize other prisoners. This policy was designed to prevent reform-oriented leaders from forming bases of support within the prisoner population and from forging coalitions among prisoners. Furthermore, segregation and the frequent transfer of prisoners were used to interfere with prisoners' litigation efforts, which required prisoners to be housed in the institution in which the suit originated.

The mainstream media, owned and administered for the most part by wealthy white middle- and upper-class elements with close ties to state elites, tended to ignore or minimize prisoner concerns and protests. Penal matters became of interest only in times of crisis, such as rebellions, escapes, and other scandals. The few attempts made by the mass media to investigate prison conditions were resisted by penal authorities who feared that media coverage would invite increased public scrutiny, criticism, and demands for reforms, which would threaten the hegemony of prison administrators.[16]

Despite the nationwide resistance of penal administrators to calls for reforms, some minimal changes did take place in state prisons throughout the country after World War II. These changes occurred in the areas of facilities, job training, parole, health, psychological treatment, personnel, recreation, and revival of self-government and prisoner councils. Proponents of these reforms included members of the professional, legal, and academic communities. "With the maturation of the professions of social work, psychiatry and related disciplines, the forces of reform became truly national in scope and gained clear ascendancy on the intellectual plane as well as developing a body of potential prison administrators with a vested interest in reform on a practical level."[17]

In New York State, the debate between proponents of the traditional "custodial model" and reformers lobbying for greater prisoner access to rehabilitation programs continued to be decided in favor of the former. This imbalance was reflected by the fact that while personnel positions in the areas of rehabilitative services increased from 3 percent in 1960 to 6 percent in 1970, during the same period "custody-oriented personnel retained 73 percent of an increased total of the positions available."[18] The shortage in rehabilitation programs was most severely felt in the areas of counselling, vocational training, and education.

Reformism was debilitated by the fact that despite increasing prisoner unrest during the 1960s, traditional social/religious reformers were not effectively involved in the state's prison reform efforts in the legislative and fiscal arenas. Mainstream reform groups such as the Community Service Society, the Correctional Association of New York, and the National Council on Crime and Delinquency did testify at public hearings held by the governor's Special Committee on Criminal Offenders, established in 1966. There, they supported the expansion of "specific treatment programs such as: work release and furlough programs . . . halfway houses, conjugal visits and the amplification of educational programs within the institutions."[19] However, the committee's final report did not consider these recommendations important. Even when included in the work of the committee, these organizations generally had limited access to information discussed by state officials. And, in some cases, the national directors of reform groups failed to pass on information critical of prison security measures to their local directors. Summarizing New York State's prison policy during the 1960s, Barbara Lavin McEleney wrote:

> The reformers' lack of involvement, the bureaucratic concern for security and at the same time program economy, together with Rockefeller's lack of interest in this arena, contributed to a reinforcement of the status quo which may be viewed as a continuing tangible allocation of resources to the custodial interests of the correctional bureaucracy. . . .[20]

Thus, throughout much of the twentieth century, prisoners demanding reforms did not receive significant support from the courts, the legislature, penal authorities, mainstream social/religious reformers, community groups, or the mass media. It was not until the emergence of the first prisoners' rights movement that the hegemony of custodial elements began to be significantly questioned. This movement was spearheaded by: the litigation efforts of both individual prisoners (e.g., Martin Sostre) and of prisoners affiliated with the Nation of Islam; community actions opposing the imprisonment of grassroots activists; and the jail and prison rebellions of the late 1960s and early 1970s. It was the combination of third parties, reform-oriented state elites, and prisoners' individual and collective acts of resistance that characterized the first prisoners' rights movement.

Laying the Foundation for the Rise
of the First Prisoners' Rights Movement[21]

> . . . a prisoner movement is a fundamental agreement among prisoners that they have certain common goals and objectives and they have certain common ideology and that they are going to work in some concerted effort, however loosely organized it may be, towards the realization of these goals and objectives.
> —Eric Elliott, interview with author (1993)

In speaking of the prisoners' rights movement I refer to more than the sum total of court decisions affecting prisoners. We are dealing with a broadscale effort to redefine the status (moral, political, economic, as well as legal) of prisoners in a democratic society. The prisoners' rights movement, like other social movements . . . includes a variety of more or less organized groups and activities; there is also a wide variation in the extent and intensity of individual participation. What is decisive, however, is a shared sense of grievance and the commitment to enhanced rights and entitlements for prisoners.

—James B. Jacobs,
New Perspectives on Prisons and Imprisonment (1983)

What came to be known during the 1970s as the prisoners' rights movement emerged within a context of increasing demands for the extension of political and legal rights and economic benefits to sectors of the population theretofore marginalized. As James B. Jacobs observed: "Starting with the black civil rights movement in the mid-1950s, one marginal group after another—blacks, poor people, welfare mothers, mental patients, women, children, aliens, gays, and the handicapped—has pressed for admission into the societal mainstream."[22] These sectors sought to make their demands heard through social protest movements.[23] Some of these movements contained both civil disobedience and armed resistance components.

It was the violence against civil rights activists by rural and urban white populations as well as widespread police brutality in neighborhoods inhabited by people of color which had convinced many young Latinas(os) and African-Americans that armed resistance was the only way they could protect their communities from racial attacks and achieve significant societal changes. In 1966, the Black Panther Party was formed to offer an organized armed resistance against police brutality in the African-American community.[24] A year later, twenty-three rebellions broke out in major U.S. cities. The rebellions were a reaction to the increasing frustration and anger felt by African-Americans in the face of racial discrimination, police brutality, poverty, poor medical and educational services, and increased imprisonment, among others.

The disaffection of African-Americans was echoed by Chicanas(os) throughout the United States as well as the growing number of Puerto Ricans forced to immigrate to the United States during the 1950s and 1960s.[25] Once in the United States, Puerto Ricans joined with other people of color to demand better living conditions, an end to discrimination and police brutality, and the implementation of bilingual programs and services. Young Puerto Ricans, like young

African-Americans, formed groups such as the Young Lords Party (YLP) to express their ethnic pride, secure community control over local resources, and struggle for Puerto Rican independence.

The actions of Latina(o) and African-American community activists were complemented by the increasing number of young white women and men who throughout the late 1960s and early 1970s protested against the draft and the Vietnam War. Their use of civil disobedience was supplemented by the urban guerrilla tactics of the predominantly white Symbionese Liberation Army[26] and the Weather Underground.[27] Moreover, while white middle-class anti-war activists took over campuses forcing colleges and universities to close down, African-American and Puerto Rican students forced the closing of colleges and universities demanding the establishment of Puerto Rican and Black Studies Departments and the hiring of more Black and Puerto Rican staff. The latter efforts were duplicated by those of Latino and African-American prisoners who, through the use of rebellions and/or litigation, demanded criminal justice reforms, better prison conditions, the right to create formal racial/ethnic prisoner organizations, and the hiring of more staff of color.

Interestingly, the actions taken by Latino and African-American prisoners seeking reforms were not only examples of instances in which prisoners rebelled against their keepers but also, as was the case with outside Latina(o) and African-American community activism, occasions in which subordinate ethnic/racial populations challenged the hegemony of a dominant "white" state. The point that these populations were predominantly poor and working-class did not escape state elites. Furthermore, the fact that white women and women of color, as well as lesbians and gays, came to add their voices to these calls for reforms further brought into question the legitimacy of the heterosexual-dominated "male" state.

In the case of people of color, the white population and mainstream mass media responded to their numerous demands for social reforms with a cry for "law and order." This translated into calls for stiffer penalties for those who broke the law, larger police forces, and the construction of more prisons. The state responded with a combination of reforms and repression. The former included a number of anti-poverty programs designed to reduce discontent. The latter entailed blacklisting, framing, imprisoning, and murdering community activists[28] as well as legislating new and more punitive criminal laws. "Red Squads" formed within police departments to gather information on those considered "subversives" and to infiltrate and destroy their organizations.[29] In New York State, prisoners demanding reforms met similar fates. To many people of color and their white allies, the growing imprisonment of African-Americans and Latinas(os) itself demonstrated the continued unwillingness of the white-dominated state apparatus to seriously address the demands by communities of color for more civil rights and a redistribution of political power and economic wealth.[30]

Changes in the Prisoner Population

> Hispanics are disproportionately represented in numbers of arrests, numbers of convictions and by numbers of inmates in correctional institutions. They fail to receive appropriate support services while incarcerated and as a result have one of the highest recidivism rates among any ethnic group.
>
> —Homer F. Broome, Jr.,
> Address before the National Hispanic Conference (1980)

In 1963, the African-American prisoner population became for the first time the majority racial/ethnic group in New York State prisons.[31] At that time, Latinas(os) made up 11.5 percent of the total. This transformation in the racial/ethnic make-up of the prisoner population was accompanied by changes in the composition of the white prisoner population. The latter gradually came to include a significant number of anti-war activists and middle-class students imprisoned for drug offenses.

Diverse sectors of the prisoner population reacted and adapted differently to prison conditions. During the late 1960s and early 1970s some of the younger African-American and Latino prisoners, incarcerated for crimes not traditionally thought of as political in nature (e.g., burglary, larceny), began to see themselves as "political prisoners," victims of an unjust society which disproportionately imprisoned poor and working-class people of color. For these men, many of whom initially became sympathizers of the Nation of Islam and later of groups such as the Young Lords and the Black Panther parties, prison discipline and programming were seen as attempts to force them to accept the inferior and submissive roles assigned them by white society. They regarded their imprisonment as an extension of the same oppressive policies the state carried out against their communities on the outside and on Third World people around the world. This social/political analysis was supported by sympathetic whites and people of color on the outside as well as by the most politicized white prisoners.

Within the prisoner population, however, there remained many prisoners who feared becoming involved with reform-oriented activities, lest they risk further reprisals such as confinement in segregation, the loss of "good time," transfer to institutions located further upstate, and/or brutal repression at the hands of guards.[32] Nevertheless, by the end of the 1960s, a significant number of prisoners increasingly made demands for better prison conditions through the use of litigation, the mobilization of third party support, and/or prison rebellions.

> . . . up until that time we had prisoners who essentially felt that the treatment that was given them, there was nothing that they could do about it. They just had to suffer silently and accept it and try to be stoic and remain strong. Toward the end of the sixties and the early seventies we begin to see a prisoner now who's got a political consciousness and a social consciousness and begins to say that, "These are not acceptable conditions for any human beings to have to live under . . ." and begins to actively seek to make change. We see prisoners challenging their convictions and challenging prison conditions in the courts.[33]

The greatest threat to custodial hegemony posed by prisoner organizing efforts was attempts to forge interracial/interethnic alliances and/or mobilize third party support. Such alliances were facilitated by the emergence of a socially conscious white prisoner cadre and the oppressive living conditions to which all prisoners were subjected.

> . . . there are some progressive whites in prison who identify with the struggle for human rights. We have some whites in prison who were part of the Anti-War Movement. We have some whites . . . who are just, for lack of better terminology, "rebels," and threw their lot in with the Latinos and with the Blacks, not so much on the basis of race, but on the basis of the fact that the conditions are equally horrendous for Blacks, as well as whites. Although the whites are treated somewhat better because they're white . . . one of the favorite sayings of the guards during that time was, "Blue against green and clubs are trumps." And what they essentially meant was they wore blue uniforms, we wore green uniforms, so it was them against us and they had all the trumps because they had the clubs or the sticks, night sticks.[34]

That alliances between prisoners formed despite a history of interracial hostility and ethnic divisions served to further legitimize prisoner claims of exploitation. Thus, the treatment the penal system accorded prisoners, as a group, helped lay the foundations for the emergence of prisoner unity. Such unity allowed prisoners to organize collectively to demand changes in the terms and conditions of their imprisonment and to mobilize outside support.

The calls for third party support on behalf of prisoners in New York State during the end of the 1960s and the beginning of the 1970s were primarily answered by family, friends, students, attorneys, and other community activists in support of Puerto Rican "political" prisoners, such as Martín Sostre, and African-American prisoners affiliated with the Nation of Islam. A brief review of the events surrounding the conditions encountered by Sostre and members of the Nation of Islam will illustrate the manner in which the criminal justice system responded to attempts by communities of color inside and outside the walls to empower themselves.

The Impact of the Nation of Islam

The role played by prisoners affiliated with the Nation of Islam during the 1960s in the emergence of the first prisoners' rights movement cannot be overstated. By demanding the right to form groups to carry out collective goals, the Nation of Islam began to challenge the "do your own time" mentality encouraged by prison officials, substituting it with a disciplined organization. Collective organizing provided an alternative model to the informal prisoner cliques upon which prisoner society had been hitherto chiefly based.[35] Moreover, "With collective organization came the notion of collective oppression, which tended to blunt the individual pathology model."[36] The latter model, generally advanced by social scientists and penal personnel, argued that people who broke the law were mentally ill.

Moreover, the "Nation of Islam often promised a solution for personal problems like drug addiction as well as an aggressive political practice" which encouraged training in martial arts.[37] In an atmosphere charged with racism and violence perpetrated by white guards on prisoners of color, the latter training proved particularly attractive. African-American prisoners now had a collective way of physically protecting themselves from abuses by other prisoners and staff.

Furthermore, by asserting that, historically, all African-Americans shared a common enemy in whites, the Nation of Islam was able, during its early years of activism in prisons, to provide some measure of unity to an important sector of the African-American prisoner population. It was through contacts with the Nation of Islam in prison that future radical African-American political leaders such as Malcolm X, Eldridge Cleaver, and George Jackson became politicized. Furthermore, the Nation of Islam encouraged many Black Latino prisoners to develop a sense of racial as well as ethnic pride.

The impact of the Nation of Islam was also felt through court victories made possible by prisoners' rights attorneys and "jailhouse lawyers."[38] These victories showed other prisoners that they too could curtail the power of their keepers and achieve reforms through litigation. Such successes also illustrated how vital it was for prisoners to mobilize outside sources of support.

The demands of prisoners affiliated with the Nation of Islam to be able to freely exercise their religious rights and, therefore, have access within the prisons to outside religious leaders, religious literature, and places of worship, were met with severe repression on the part of New York State authorities. As early as 1960, Commissioner McGinnis asked prison officials to keep files on all those prisoners affiliated with or suspected of being "Muslims."[39] This information was turned over to the state police for placement in the "subversive file" for future reference.[40] Furthermore, prisoners affiliated with the Nation of Islam were locked in solitary confinement, transferred to other facilities, denied meeting space, and prohibited from wearing religious symbols. Nevertheless, litigation efforts by members and supporters of the Nation of Islam were successful in generating a series of favorable federal and state court decisions whose impact was felt at the institutional level.[41]

Complementing the efforts of members of the Nation of Islam were those of jailhouse lawyers such as Martín Sostre, a Black-Puerto Rican, who became a Muslim for a short period of time in order to carry out litigation efforts on behalf of Muslim prisoners denied the right to practice their religion.[42]

The Case of Martín Sostre

Martín Sostre's experience with the New York State criminal justice system exemplifies the treatment Puerto Rican community activists frequently received from state agencies.[43] The owner of an Afro-Asian bookstore in one of Buffalo's African-American neighborhoods at the end of the 1960s, Sostre was frequently harassed by FBI agents and local detectives for selling political literature by and about people of color and holding educational activities in the store.[44] In 1967, following a three-day rebellion in Buffalo's African-American community that summer,[45] Sostre was framed by police officers with the assistance of a community member and eventually arrested on charges of assault, arson, riot, and possession of narcotics.

> . . . first they accused me of teaching the youth how to make molotov cocktails and throw them to burn some of the businesses that were burnt. And then right after that, while they had me incarcerated . . . they changed that to selling drugs to some addict. Which later on this addict, several years later, he came back from California and recanted. In other words, he told the story as it happened, that the cops gave him the drugs when he came in the bookstore and the money . . .[46]

Sentenced for thirty years, Sostre was subsequently convicted of assaulting five prison guards and sentenced to an additional ten years. The conditions surrounding his conviction showed the dilemma prisoners of color faced at the hands of a white-dominated criminal justice system. "It's their word against me, you know, five guards. They're white and they're local. The judge is local, from that town, and me this Black Puerto Rican, you know. Who are they going to believe?"[47]

Sostre's political consciousness was sparked by the speeches of Paul Robeson, Malcolm X, and Vito Marcantonio[48] in the streets of Harlem and by his personal conversations while imprisoned in "The Tombs" (New York City House of Detention) with Puerto Rican nationalist Julio Pinto Gandia, himself imprisoned on false charges at the beginning of the 1950s. Sostre's own experiences in New York City jails and state prisons from 1952 to 1964[49] and his exposure to various civil rights and anti-colonialist movements in the United States and abroad (e.g., Vietnam, Puerto Rico) made him determined to resist the harsh treatment he received while imprisoned.

> They kept shifting me from prison to prison, and not only prison to prison, sometimes from the solitary confinement of one prison to another solitary confinement.[50]

> If you're in solitary confinement they take everything from you, you don't have anything. And yet, in order to humiliate you, every time you go out of solitary confinement, let's say to see a lawyer or visit or whatever, they make you strip. They make you bend over. They

make you open your cheeks and they look in your ass and they make remarks, you know, like, "I'd like to stick this club in there," and all that . . . So I just wouldn't submit to that. So they used to beat my ass and . . . put me on the ground, one used to . . . pull one leg one way and the other one way, you know. In other words, they used to force it themselves because I would never submit.

I always equated myself, compared myself to Vietnam, you know. I'd say, "Hell, if they can beat this country, I can beat these son of a bitches here. I don't care how many goons they have, what are the odds, how much time. I'm going to fight, just like the Vietnamese fought, and I'm going to win," which I did.[51]

While Sostre was older than most Puerto Ricans in New York State prisons at the end of the 1960s, he typified the politically conscious Latino prisoner present in New York jails and penitentiaries at the time. However, what is most instructive about the case of Sostre is how it resembled and, at the same time, differed from the experiences of Latino prisoners as a whole. Sostre's experiences in the criminal justice system (i.e., framing, imprisonment, physical abuse by guards, constant transfers, long periods in solitary confinement) have been shared by countless other Latino(a) prisoners throughout the United States, regardless of whether they have been labelled political prisoners or common criminals. However, few Latinas(os) have been able to mobilize the kind of local, national, and international support Sostre generated. Such support has generally been reserved for Chicana(o) political prisoners and Puerto Rican freedom fighters targeted, as was Sostre, by the United States government for persecution because of their political beliefs.[52]

Martín Sostre Defense Committees sprang up in major cities in the United States, Canada, and Europe and demanded his release from prison. These committees educated the public about Sostre's plight, distributed written material by Sostre,[53] held press conferences, picketed government offices, and carried out massive petition drives and demonstrations.[54] Additional support was generated by "the leftist newspapers, which were mostly [run by] whites . . . and publications like, *Palante* . . . and *Right On*, the Black Panther paper."[55] Support for Sostre's release was amplified during the early 1970s when he was declared a "prisoner of conscience" by Amnesty International. His case also motivated renowned foreign political figures, including Soviet dissident Andrei Sakharov, to rally to his support.[56] Sostre's outside support was matched by his own litigation efforts as a jailhouse lawyer. According to a *New York Times* article, "The name Sostre is tied to much of the legislation here involving the rights of prisoners to practice their religion, receive uncensored mail, obtain certain minimum conditions in solitary confinement and refuse rectal searches.[57]

Sostre's personal response to the treatment he received while imprisoned—his own use of physical resistance, the courting of third party support, and persistent litigation—differentiated him from the overall Latina(o) prisoner population which rarely used litigation as a strategy for changing prison conditions. Sostre attributes the lack of widespread litigation by Latina(o) prisoners to language barriers and the limited knowledge Latina(o) prisoners have about their legal rights and the workings of the legal system. An additional factor discouraging the use of litigation by Latina(o) prisoners has been the lack of access to legal personnel and concerned community members. In those cases in which legal support has been available (e.g., Puerto Rican Prisoners of War, Grand Jury resisters, Chicana(o) political prisoners), Latina(o) prisoners throughout the United States have been more than willing to use litigation as a tool of resistance.

In New York State, the relationship between prisoner litigation and DOC changes in policies was clearly evident. Frequently, DOC issued statewide directives modifying specific policies in response to litigation in progress at one of its facilities.[58] For example, it was in response to litigation filed by Sostre[59] that DOC issued a new directive, effective October 19, 1970, changing existing disciplinary procedures. Although the original court decision was modified on appeal to the state's advantage,[60] the DOC directive was not rescinded in the hopes that it would avert future litigation efforts.[61] By addressing issues which led to litigation before decisions were handed down, DOC hoped to avoid unfavorable and more far-reaching court decisions as well as precedent-setting cases which could be used by prisoners in other facilities to demand further changes.

Reforms initiated by Commissioner Russell G. Oswald[62] after his appointment on January 1, 1971, to the newly restructured Department of Correctional Services (DOCS),[63] clearly reflected not only his own liberal orientation, but the relationship he and other state elites perceived existed between litigation, reforms, and prison rebellions. Oswald's appointed by Governor Rockefeller to head DOCS, had itself served as a signal to custody-oriented personnel that the Governor was willing to address some of the demands for reforms from prisoners and their advocates inside and outside DOCS. Such reforms seemed especially urgent after the August and October 1970 New York City jail rebellions,[64] the strikes at Attica and Napanoch that same year,[65] and the November rebellion at Auburn Correctional Facility.[66] In all of these cases, Latino, African-American, and white prisoners had come together to demand changes just as they had done during the 1960s to demand the passage of a "good time" bill.[67]

Latino Prisoners, Their Allies, and the 1970 New York City Jail Rebellions

A prison riot explodes like a boiler that's built up steam from a long way back. When it comes, control is near impossible, especially if there's been no real planning, no prisoner unity, and only scattered, disorganized leadership.
          —Piri Thomas, Seven Long Times (1974)

. . . a rebellion is purposeful. A riot . . . has no particular rationale or if it does have a rationale the rationale is not to make change. . . . A rebellion seeks change and a rebellion comes at the end attempt of other ways of solving the problems.
          —Daniel Meyers, interview with author (1993)

The New York City jail rebellions which broke out in Manhattan, Brooklyn, and Queens during August and October 1970, were important to state authorities for several reasons. First, the fact that prisoners did not limit themselves to demands for prison reform but also encompassed issues pertaining to the broader criminal justice system (e.g., bail, trials), indicated their growing awareness of the interrelationship between state agencies.[68] Second, because a large number of prisoners held in New York City jails were state prisoners awaiting assignment to state facilities, the rebellions indicated the level of politicization and the concerns of a significant number of prisoners soon to be housed in state prisons.[69] Equally important was the fact that by questioning as a class the political system's right to institutionalize them, prisoners indicated their willingness and ability to form alliances across racial/ethnic lines. The newness of this solidarity was expressed by Victor Martinez, a Young Lords-identified prisoner leader, during the 1970 October rebellion at the Long Island Branch of the Queens House of Detention. Martinez himself had been chosen by his peers during the rebellion to serve as a representative in the negotiating committee of both Latino prisoners and the newly created Inmates Liberation Front. The latter was subsequently incorporated as a section of the YLP.[70] "Ayer los hombres aquí en esta prisión actuamos como verdaderos hombres y hermanos, y por primera vez hemos unido nuestras fuerzas para traer a la luz pública la horrible situación de injusticia, discriminación, abusos, suciedad y mal trato de que somos objeto por parte de los puercos."[71]

The solidarity of African–American and white prisoners with their Latino counterparts was demonstrated by the fact that the grievances put forth included concerns specifically pertinent to Latino prisoners. These included:

> a) que haya más intérpretes en cortes y prisiones;[72]
> b) más abogados puertorriqueños;
> c) comunicación en español con los familiares;
> d) que terminen las injusticias contra los boricuas por parte del "establecimiento"; y
> e) que les provea material de lectura en español, particularmente el periódico —*El Diario* totalmente gratis.[73]

An additional grievance Latino prisoners rallied to was the case of Efraín Hernández. At the time of the revolt, Hernández had been detained for three years pending his testifying as a material witness in a murder case.[74]

The support among Black and white prisoners for Latino prisoner concerns had also surfaced during the earlier August 1970 rebellion at The Tombs. At the time prisoners complained of, among other things, "'unnecessary brutality . . . directed against the black and Puerto Rican inmate population'."[75] Additionally, African-American and white prisoners supported Latino demands for a translator to be available on each floor on a twenty-four hour basis and for the provision of educational materials in Spanish and English.

Another aspect of the New York City rebellions which was of importance to state elites was the fact that Latino and non-Latino prisoners were able to mobilize third party support. For example, during the Long Island rebellion, Latino prisoners demanded and obtained the presence of reporters from *El Diario*[76] and the inclusion of Herman Badillo, then running for Congress,[77] in the Negotiating Committee. Latino prisoners also called for the creation of a "grievance committee" to which prisoners could submit their complaints. The committee was to include, among others, Herman Badillo and

Senator Robert García (District 30, Bronx-Manhattan).[78] By seeking the support of the Spanish-speaking press, Latino politicians, and radical Latina(o) groups, such as the Young Lords, Latino prisoners were indicating their willingness to court diverse sectors of the outside Latina(o) community to achieve their goals. Such support was needed both to publicize the plight of prisoners and to pressure penal authorities to make changes.

Prior to the late 1960s, the support of the Latina(o) community for prisoner concerns had been primarily limited to that of family members and a few radical political groups. The reasons for this were threefold. First, it was the Latina(o) community which bore the brunt not only of discriminatory criminal justice policies, but also of Latina(o) street crime. As a result, the outside community resented the actions of Latinas(os) who endangered the lives and property of those around them. Secondly, Latinas(os) internalized the arguments of social scientists, state and religious elites who labelled those who broke the law "sick," "immoral," and/or "deviant." Many came to believe that by imprisoning those who broke the law, the state was providing a valuable service to the community. Last, the outside Latina(o) community's day-to-day struggle for subsistence meant Latinas(os) had little time, energy, and/or few resources to support a prisoner population kept almost completely isolated by the state's procedures. It was those persons with close personal ties to Latina(o) prisoners (e.g., family and friends) or those who held a political view which emphasized the common experiences of Latinas(os) inside and outside the walls who were most likely to support Latina(o) prisoners.

Latina(o) families played a crucial role in providing their imprisoned kin much needed financial and emotional support. The type of support provided was, however, frequently constrained by limited economic resources, language and structural barriers (e.g., racial discrimination), and fear or lack of understanding of the workings of the criminal justice system. Nevertheless, it was family members who were the most likely to pool resources to hire an attorney for an incarcerated relative. It was also family members who were most likely to send prisoners much needed provisions or money. Contact with kin through visits, letters, and phone conversations helped break the isolation imposed by imprisonment and allowed prisoners to feel cared for. "We lived for letters from home. If a guard passed at night and he passed your cell and he didn't put a letter in your cell, you know, you didn't show it on your face, your face was "cara palo" but your heart almost wept. And then what would happen is we would let each other read our letters sometimes."[79]

Once Latina(o) prisoners became eligible for parole, work release and/or furlough programs, it became even more important for them to prove they had ties in the outside community, particularly with family members who could provide financial support upon release. Receiving frequent visits, mail, and packages from relatives were ways to prove such bonds existed.[80]

Latina(o) prisoners were well aware that those prisoners with few or no family ties were more likely to be mistreated by prison personnel.

> I think men with families do not suffer the victimization the men that don't have anyone suffer. . . . You can kill a guy if he doesn't have any family. Nobody is going to say anything to your questions. If a guy has got family and they care about that person, people are going to be asking questions and causing problems. Problems that you cannot answer.[81]

The "watchdog" functions family members exercised over penal authorities were essential. One's kin could write letters and/or make calls to prison authorities, attorneys, community organizations, and the mass media.

There were also times when family members provided support to prisoners engaged in activities for which they could be further punished by penal personnel. For example, on occasion, relatives became part of prisoners' reform-oriented networks.

> You get a manila envelope and put like ten letters in it, two of them just . . . [for] people you want to write, and you mail it to your family with a letter saying, "Please mail this out," you know, "We're having this and that problem." Or you get your family to call the prison or your family can get a lawyer and call your lawyer and ask them what's happening with you or with this group or with that . . . or you go to the media. You know, little things . . . [the] administration don't like any noise from the outside.[82]

The role of family members as sources of support for Latino prisoners was made evident during the 1970 New York City rebellions. Relatives and friends flooded DOC offices and *El Diario* with calls and letters inquiring about the status of imprisoned kin, some of whom had been transferred to other local or state facilities or who had been hospitalized as a result of guard brutality.[83] Families also held a vigil outside the Brooklyn House of Detention, protesting the conditions to which their loved ones were being subjected.[84] The inquiries of family members were frequently ignored and women asking about the fate of loved ones were at times physically abused by guards,[85] but such requests for information did help to further encourage public scrutiny of jail conditions.[86]

The actions of family members on behalf of imprisoned relatives were complemented by the calls of Latino politicians, such as Herman Badillo, for the formation of a poor people's bail fund and the creation of an impartial committee to investigate conditions in the city's jails.[87] Badillo felt the committee should include the input of lawyers from the YLP,[88] which had consistently supported prisoners' demands.[89]

At the time of the New York City rebellions, the Young Lords Party, in conjunction with prisoners' kin and grassroots organizations (e.g., Black Panther Party), held a series of demonstrations outside city jails[90] and other public buildings in an attempt to force government officials to carry out penal reforms. This included a demonstration organized in conjunction with women's, people of color, and other grassroots organizations, to highlight the conditions faced by the overwhelmingly Latina and African-American jail population at the Women's House of Detention in Manhattan's Greenwich Village. Prisoners' grievances included:

> 1) Basic necessities, such as toothbrushes, soap and deodorant are missing. 2) In order to get the basic necessities . . . inmates sometimes are forced to sell their bodies. 3) The sisters are paid only 3 cents to 10 cents an hour for work done inside (work in the laundry, kitchen, and library, etc.). 4) The allowance . . . is given only on request. 5) There is no instructive education taking place . . . 6) The most recent legal book in the prison library is dated 1950. All the Legal Aid lawyers are too busy and overworked now to handle the cases of our sisters properly. . . . 7) If women with money are picked up for shoplifting, they are dismissed as kleptomaniacs . . . If . . . arrested, they're usually let off with a much lesser penalty than if they were poor . . . 8) The cells inside the Women's House of Detention are divided racially—Black on one side and white on the other side. Sisters are encouraged to be antagonistic towards each other. . . . 9) Sisters from the streets are picked up for prostitution, yet the businessmen who buy and use their bodies are never prosecuted. . . ."[91]

It is clear from the description given in this quote, that the plight of Latinas in New York City jails was similar, if not worse, than that encountered by Latino prisoners during the New York City rebellions. However, aside from the support of family and friends, the attention given incarcerated Latinas by the outside Latina(o) community was scant. In fact, the demonstration organized in front of the Women's House of Detention, along with other activities held in support of African-American political activist Angela Davis during 1970,[92] and women members of the "Panther 21,"[93] was one of a few instances in which the plight of women in jails was highlighted by several outside Latina(o) community organizations.[94] This was so despite the fact that women held at the Women's House of Detention were as politically aware and as willing to support one another as their male counterparts.[95]

Several of the reasons the concerns of incarcerated women were ignored to such an extent by the Latina(o) community were the fact that women convicted of crimes were seen as being more morally corrupt than their male counterparts, women prisoners made up a small number of the jail population, and male prisoners, partly as a result of their larger numbers, were able to call attention to their plight through mass actions. However, as the New York City jail rebellions showed, even Latinos were only able to have their concerns acknowledged, though rarely adequately addressed, by penal authorities as a result of rebellions. Consequently, the importance for prisoners of having third party sources of support which could call attention to their plight on an ongoing basis.

In addition to sponsoring demonstrations, the YLP supported incarcerated Latinas(os) by holding press conferences and community forums attended by clergy, community members, politicians and other public figures interested in penal reform.[96] Perhaps one of the most significant actions carried out by the YLP was the takeover of the Primera Iglesia Metodista de Harlem (First Methodist Church of Harlem) on October 18, 1970.[97] The takeover, which had been carried out by an armed YLP, was a response to the death of Julio Roldán, a YLP member who died while being held at The Tombs. The YLP demanded that the church be turned into a legal center and that members of the clergy be allowed to begin an investigation into the penal system.[98] This demand seemed particularly urgent in view of the recent jail rebellions and the alarming number of "alleged" suicides among Puerto Rican and African-American prisoners in the city's jails.[99]

The response of the Latina(o) community to the takeover reflected conflicting political opinions concerning the appropriate tactics and strategies to pursue while seeking redress from state elites. For example, Hector L. Vázquez, executive director of the Foro Puertorriqueño, Inc., also called for an investigation into the death of Roldán.[100] However, Vázquez's declarations were aimed at reducing the increasing support for radical groups, such as the YLP, within the Latina(o) community.

> En estos momentos en que la atmósfera emocional de nuestra nación y de los países vecinos están preñados de violencia y temor, nos sentimos extremadamente alarmados por las recientes expresiones peligrosas de la creciente militancia en la comunidad puertorriqueña. Este se debe a las frustraciones causadas por el sentimiento de impotencia que sufre dicha comunidad . . ."[101]

Vázquez's statement was designed to make a comparison between the revolutionary violence occurring within the United States and Latin America at the time and to counteract the YLP's call to the Puerto Rican community to arm itself for the purpose of self-defense.[102] According to the YLP:

> The murder or "suicide" of a Puerto Rican or black in the prisons of amerikkka and Puerto Rico is not unusual. . . . For years, revolutionaries, servants of the poor, fighters for freedom, have been killed in the streets, houses, mountains. For years our people have been killed by the yanki . . .

> Our nation is a colony. Whether in Bridgeport or Fajardo, we are controlled by the yanki. . . . That is why on October 18, when 2,000 people from El Barrio marched in Julio Roldán's funeral, we seized the People's Church for the second time. This time, though, we took the church with arms, with shotguns, rifles, everything we could find, and prepared to defend it.

> We said, two LORDS are dead. We are not going to wait for the third, the tenth, the twentieth. . . . We have no choice, at this time, but to pick up those guns and say to all of our nation—ARM YOURSELVES TO DEFEND YOURSELVES. . . .[103]

Other public figures such as Councilman Carter Burden and Herman Badillo condemned the use of weapons but at the same time demanded an investigation of the unusual number of suicides.[104] William J. Vanden Heuvel, president of the Board of Prisons of the

City of New York, partly attributed the alarmingly high rate of suicides among Puerto Rican male prisoners to language barriers and
the cultural alienation they faced once incarcerated.

> No sé de ningún programa en los establecimientos de detención del
> Departamento de Prisiones de la Ciudad de Nueva York además de
> la que empezaron y operaron los mismos reclusos, donde los adultos
> que hablan o lean poco o ningún inglés sean adiestrados en idioma o
> literacía. Los pocos programas para los reclusos de habla española
> que existen o han existido, son generalmente de naturaleza reli-
> giosa, conducidos por ministros voluntarios, como las clases de
> Biblia en español. En Las Tumbas, según el Alcalde, hay ocho o
> nueve oficiales de habla español entre 240.[105]

Heuvel recommended hiring Spanish-speaking personnel and
interpreters, teaching literacy and English-as-a-second-language
courses, and providing cultural programs and events in Spanish that
would involve the participation of the Latina(o) community on the
outside.[106]

In summary, the support for incarcerated Latinas(os) within the
Latina(o) community at the end of 1970 was limited to: the individual
and collective actions of family, friends, and grassroots radical community activists; calls for reforms from a few Latino and Anglo politicians;
and coverage offered by *El Diario* and *Palante*. With few exceptions,
these calls for reforms centered around the conditions and needs of
Latino prisoners, the plight of Latinas in jail being generally ignored.[107]

Penal Responses to Calls for Reforms

The reaction of local and state elites to the New York City rebellions were varied. While New York City authorities named Latinas(os)
to the revitalized Board of Corrections,[108] the state singled out for prosecution a small number of predominantly Latino and African-
American prisoners involved in the revolts. Moreover, following the
rebellions, prisoners continued to be physically abused and were
denied basic services by custodial personnel. A former Latino prisoner
described the treatment prisoners at the Brooklyn House of Detention
received once the uprising had ended.

> "En la Sección A-B-C- y D en el cuarto piso, los presos han sido cas-
> tigados sin piedad con macanas, hierros y pedazos de maderos. Todo
> porque están protestando de la escasa comida—dos rajas de pan por

la mañana, dos por el mediodía y dos por la noche—que se les da, y porque hace más de 3 días que no se les suministra agua que beber. Otra cosa inhumana que han hecho"—nos sigue diciendo Miranda— "es que le han quitado 'frizas' y sobre todo que no les quieren llevar al médico sin antes no firman un papel que dice que han tenido esos golpes por un accidente sufrido."[109]

The response of local and state elites was seen by critics as an attempt to both intimidate reform-oriented prisoners and to "cover up the popular nature of the prison rebellions."[110] However, the response of most penal administrators was exemplified by New York City DOC Commissioner George McGrath, who declared that the rebellions were planned and directed by a small group of militant radicals inside and outside the jails.[111] These accusations were reiterated by then New York State Commissioner of Corrections Paul McGinnis.

> . . . inmates today are younger, organized, more militant, more vio-lent and more demanding. They don't consider themselves thieves, rapists or murderers. Today they feel they are political prisoners jailed by a repressive society . . . Black Panthers and Young Lords (a militant Puerto Rican group) are the most vocal and violent of the militant groups inside prison walls . . . There have been indicators that . . . disturbances are planned for other institutions within the system. There is reason to believe that inmates received instructions from outside.[112]

These arguments were the same ones used by Commissioner McGinnis to justify the breakout of rebellions in state facilities dur-ing 1970.

While local government officials resisted the calls for reforms, they quickly addressed the demands of the New York City Cor-rectional Officers Benevolent Association for more training, the pay-ment of overtime wages owed to guards, the hiring of more guards, new riot equipment, and the introduction of additional security measures.[113]

State elites also transferred six hundred of the sentenced prison-ers who had participated in the jail rebellions to state penitentiaries, despite the objections of Commissioner McGinnis. McGinnis's own replacement on January 1, 1971, by Russell G. Oswald, a liberal, was itself a response to growing tensions within state prisons that had become even more acute after prisoner actions at Attica, Napanoch, and Auburn at the end of 1970.

Once Oswald was named DOCS Commissioner, he began carrying out a number of reforms intended to reduce prisoner discontent. The reforms included the recruitment of a small number of Latina(o) and African-American guards and the involvement of more community volunteers in state prisons. The presence of volunteers was expected to lessen prisoner discontent because the former sponsored a number of programs that allowed prisoners to leave their cells for a greater number of hours each day. This helped ease tensions resulting from overcrowding. Oswald also upgraded the quality of the food and gave prisoners additional access to telephones. Equally important was the fact that he carried out reforms in areas already under litigation. "He granted mail and visiting privileges to inmates' common-law spouses; revised censorship procedures to permit inmates to correspond privately with attorneys and public officials; and allowed greater accessibility of news media to prisons to increase public knowledge of conditions."[114]

The impact of Oswald's initiatives, however, was hampered by the state's budget crisis at the time and the fact that, although Governor Rockefeller recognized the need for prison reforms, penal matters were never a budgetary priority of his or of the Office of the Budget. Moreover, custody-oriented personnel continued to resist the implementation of rehabilitation programs and the granting of more privileges and rights to prisoners. For example, when Oswald tried to liberalize the censorship of newspapers, guards responded by cutting out articles they felt prisoners should not read, especially those about rebellions in other facilities.[115]

By the time the Attica Rebellion occurred in September 1971, conditions throughout the state penal system were so tense from years of penal neglect and prisoner discontent that a major disturbance seemed imminent. Writing about the prevalent mood in the state's six maximum security prisons in the early 1970s, Oswald stated: "All of these were powder kegs in the fall of 1971 and, before Attica, we did not know which one, or which ones, would be ignited."[116]

Ironically, one of the final incidents that contributed to increasing tensions before the Attica Rebellion, the murder of African-American prisoner leader George Jackson, occurred not in a New York, but in a California prison. The important role Jackson played in awakening the political consciousness of African-American, Latino, and even white prisoners was described by former New York State prisoner, Eric Elliott.

. . . there's a direct relationship between what happened in Attica on September 9th and George getting killed. I think that kind of dramatized for prisoners all over the country, but particularly in New York State . . . how callous the administration was, how little regard they had for human life. . . . George . . . represented leadership in the prisons. He represented Black manhood. . . . He . . . was the first . . . national prison voice that really spoke to our issues and our concerns and defined us in terms of who we were. And when they murdered him, I think that . . . a little bit of us guys died with him, and a little bit . . . wanting to strike back, occurred.[117]

In summary, following World War II, prisoners' ability to have their concerns addressed was hindered by the lack of widespread third party support and the refusal of legislative and judicial elites to interfere in penal affairs. Third party support was generally limited to the actions of family members, a few radical organizations, and the limited actions of traditional social/religious reformers.

As a result of the emergence of various civil and human rights movements during the 1960s, Latina(o) and African-American prisoners and progressive forces on the outside began to question the role imprisonment played in helping maintain the status quo. Such questioning led to the growing support of prisoners by third parties and members of the non-penal state bureaucracy (e.g., judges, legislators). Such backing, in turn, allowed prisoners, individually and sometimes collectively, to challenge penal policies through successful litigation efforts.

Increased social awareness also allowed prisoners to become more conscious of the similarities they shared, as prisoners. This awareness, coupled with the limitations of litigation in achieving desired reforms, led Latino, African-American, and white prisoners to make their concerns heard through a series of rebellions in local and state penal institutions.

The New York City jail rebellions of 1970 represented one of the many attempts by prisoners since the nineteenth century to have their grievances acknowledged and addressed by state elites. The major differences between the earlier rebellions and those of the late 1960s and early 1970s were that Latino and African-American prisoners had come to regard their imprisonment as part and parcel of the oppression to which their communities of origin were subjected by those in power. Moreover, prisoners had developed a clearer understanding of how their grievances related to those decried by contemporary social movements. This led them to pursue coalitions with progressive social forces within and outside the penitentiaries. For Latino prisoners, such political awareness led to an identification with radical grassroots community groups such as the Young Lords Party, and demands for access to the Latina(o) media and the outside Latina(o) community during the 1970 August and October New York City jail rebellions.

Conservative state elites initially responded to prisoners' isolated calls for reforms with repression. However, once the latter demonstrated they could mobilize outside support, state elites countered with a combination of repression and reforms. The reforms were designed to reduce prisoner discontent or, at least, to intimidate prisoners into compliance. Additionally, the reforms were aimed at reducing the support for prisoners' rights among third parties and reform-oriented state sectors. However, as the September 1971 Attica Prison Rebellion demonstrates the reforms came too late to achieve any of these goals.

Notes: Chapter 2

1. *Bethea v. Crouse,* 417 F.2d (10th Cir. 1969).

2. *U.S. Constitution,* art. XIII, sec. 4.

3. *Ruffin v. Commonwealth,* 62 Va. (21 Gratt.) 790, 796 (1871).

4. As Erika Anne Kates noted: "In 1941 a landmark suit, *Ex Part Hull,*" (312 U.S. 546. 61 S. Ct. 640, 85 L. Ed. 2d. 1034 [1941]) "prisoners regained some Constitutional rights; and in 1944, *Coffin v. Reichard*" (143 F.2d 443 [6th Cir. 1944]) "they regained all rights except those expressly taken from them. However, almost all states still have Civil Death or Disability statutes which act to constrain prisoners and ex-offenders from holding specific types of employment, holding public office, jury duty and other responsibilities" (Erika Anne Kates, "Litigation As a Means of Achieving Social Change: A Case Study of Women in Prison" [Ph.D. diss., Brandeis University, 1984], 171). See also Alvin Bronstein, *Representing Prisoners* (Washington, D.C.: Practical Law Institute, National Prison Project, American Civil Liberties Union Foundation, 1981).

5. Kates, "Litigation As a Means," 1984. See *Jackson v. Goodwin,* 400 F.2d 529, 532 (5th Cir., 1968); *Sewell v. Pegelow* 291 F.2d 196, 198 (4th Cir. 1961); *Washington v. Lee* 262 F. Supp 327, 331 (M.D. Ala. 1966), aff'd per curiam 390 U.S. 333, 88 S. Ct. 994, 19 L. Md.2d 1212 (1968) ("Federal Remedy for Violation of Prisoner's Rights," *Midnight Special Prisoner News* 3, No. 3 [March 1973]: 21n2).

6. As a result of court intervention, "By 1980, twenty-nine states had been directed to undertake either partial or total overhaul of their penal systems. Most of these decrees were in response to suits alleging overcrowding, lack of adequate medical facilities, disregard of due process rights, inhumane or arbitrary staff practices, and lack of access to the courts" (Kates, "Litigation As a Means," 177). In some cases, court masters and monitors were appointed to oversee compliance with judicial decisions. (For more information on these cases, see Bronstein, *Representing Prisoners*, 1981). The most common legal methods invoked by prisoners are Habeas Corpus and Section 1983 of Title 42 of the United States Civil Rights Code. The former, used to challenge imprisonment, concerns itself with issues regarding trial and appeal procedures. It requires that all state and administrative channels be exhausted before a federal court hearing is granted. Section 1983, used to challenge prison conditions, claims a violation of civil rights. The amendments most widely invoked in prisoner litigation included: the First; the Eighth, which prohibits cruel and unusual punishment; and the Fourteenth, which guarantees equal protection under the law (Kates, "Litigation As a Means," 172–176). Although the Supreme Court was more willing to involve itself in prisoner litigation during the 1960s and 1970s, its decisions, even when considered favorable, have not, for the most part, constituted clear victories for prisoners. While in *Wolff v. McDonnell*, 418 U.S. 539, 94 S.Ct. 2963, 41 L. Ed. 2d 935 (1974), the Supreme Court held that, pending severe disciplinary measures, penal authorities must give prisoners written notification of disciplinary infractions within a twenty-four hour period as well as allow him/her to present witnesses before an impartial hearing, in 1976, the court held that, "states have absolute discretion in reclassifying and transferring prisoners without procedural protection (*Meachum v. Fano*, 427 U.S. 215 [1976]), unless prisoners were engaging in a constitutionally protected activity (*Montanye v. Haymes*, 427 U.S. 236 [1976])" (Kates, "Litigation As a Means," 175). Additionally, although the Supreme Court has declared entire prison systems in violation of Eighth Amendment rights (e.g., Arkansas), it has refused to set acceptable standards for prison officials to follow (*Pugh v. Locke*, 406 F. Supp. 318 [M.D. Ala. 1976]). Moreover, in *Pugh v. Locke*, 406 F. Supp 318, M.D.Ala (1976) the Supreme Court held that the right to "rehabilitative" programs itself was not established, only that once programs are available they must be available to all inmates" (Kates, "Litigation As a Means," 174). Once again, during the 1980s, state and federal courts became increasingly hesitant to involve themselves in penal matters or file decisions on behalf of prisoners.

7. An example of this conflict between various court jurisdictions involving prisoner litigation in New York State was illustrated by the decisions in *Sostre v. Rockefeller*, 312 F. Supp. 863 (S.D. N.Y. 1970), modified subnom, *Sostre v. McGinnis*, 442 F. 2d 178 (2d Cir. 1971), cert, denied, 404 U.S. 1049, 92 S.Ct. 719, 30 L.Ed.2d 740 (1972). In the first case, the District Court ruled

that prior to placing a prisoner in segregation, prison officials had to follow due process in disciplinary hearings (e.g., "notice, impartial hearing examiner, right of cross-examination, right to present witnesses, right to counsel or counsel substitute, written decision with reasons for finding and disposition") (Sheldon Krantz, *Corrections and Prisoners' Rights*, 2nd ed. [St. Paul: West Publishing Co., 1983], 112). The District Court also found that holding a prisoner in solitary confinement for over a year was cruel and unusual punishment. In order to insure that prison officials would obey the decision, Judge Motley retained jurisdiction over penal officials. However, in *Sostre v. McGinnis,* the court modified Judge Motley's opinion, claiming that although prisoners needed to be assured minimum protections these should not be determined by the courts (Ibid., 113). Both decisions refused to hold that confinement in punitive segregation was per se cruel and unusual punishment.

8. Barbara Lavin McEleney, *Correctional Reform in New York: The Rockefeller Years* (Lanham, Md.: University Press of America, 1985), 32–33. Underlying this situation was the fact that discriminatory economic, social, legal, and political policies and practices had historically prevented many people of color from exercising such constitutional rights as the right to vote.

9. Paul McGinnis was a former New York State trooper who had risen through the ranks. As such, he was widely supported by the penal bureaucracy and institutional custodial elements who saw him as "one of their own" (Ibid., 22–23).

10. Ibid., 94.

11. Confinement of a prisoner to his/her cell.

12. McEleney, *Correctional Reform,* 85–86.

13. Elmer Daniels [pseud.], interview with author, New York, N.Y., 15 and 16 April 1993.

14. See New York State Special Commission on Attica (hereafter cited as NYSSCA), *Attica: The Official Report of the New York State Special Commission on Attica* (New York: Bantam Books, Inc., 1972), 121.

15. McEleney, *Correctional Reform,* 86.

16. Such fears had been expressed as early as 1914. As a *New York Times* article reported, "The prisoners in the penitentiary have been agitated by newspaper stories and investigations. These stories have done immeasurable harm; so has the grand jury investigation which took place that year. In that investigation several indictments were found, and an inquiry was directed at certain prison officials and keepers. The prisoners got the idea that they were just as good as their keepers and they have taken advantage of what they thought was an opportunity to flaunt insults at the keepers" (David G. Garson, "The Disruption of Prison Administration: An Investigation of Alternative Theories of the Relationship Among Administrators, Reformers,

and Involuntary Social Service Clients," *Law and Society Review* 6, No. 4 [May 1972]: 531–560, 535–536 quoting *New York Times* [hereafter cited as *N.Y. Times*], 14 July 1914, 1, 6). Increasing prisoner access to books, radio, television, and newspapers throughout the twentieth century was blamed for the "contagion" effect observed during the 1970 New York City jail rebellions. At the time, prisoners in one facility appeared to rebel upon finding out that prisoners in other institutions had already rebelled or were about to do so (Garson, "The Disruption of Prison Administration," 543).

17. Ibid., 540–541.

18. McEleney, *Correctional Reform,* 64.

19. Ibid., 58.

20. Ibid., 34.

21. According to former prisoner Eric Elliott and prisoners' rights attorney Elizabeth Fink, New York State has experienced two distinct prisoner movements. The first movement emerged in the midst of, and was an extension of, widespread community activism during the 1960s and 1970s for civil and human rights. This movement found a cadre of politicized prisoners forming alliances with third parties seeking to wrestle significant concessions from the state (Eric Elliott [pseud.], interview with author, New York, N.Y., 15 April 1993; and Elizabeth Fink, interview with author, Brooklyn, N.Y., 20 March and 17 April 1993). The second prisoners' rights movement began to emerge during the first half of the 1980s and formulated a "clearly defined ideological base" by the beginning of the 1990s. Unlike the first movement, it finds itself in a societal context in which there is little basis of community support for prisoners' rights issues (Elliott, interview with author, 1993).

22. James B. Jacobs, *New Perspectives on Prisons and Imprisonment* (Ithaca: Cornell University Press, 1983), 35.

23. These social movements included the Black civil rights, the welfare rights, the women's rights, the anti-war, and the lesbian and gay rights movements. The definition of "protest movement" used here is that outlined by Frances Fox Piven and Richard A. Cloward who argue that, "The emergence of a protest movement entails a transformation of both consciousness and of behavior. The change in consciousness has at least three distinct aspects. First, 'the system'—or those aspects of the system that people experience and perceive—loses legitimacy . . . Second, people who are ordinarily fatalistic . . . begin to assert 'rights' that imply demands for change. Third, there is a sense of efficacy; people who ordinarily consider themselves helpless come to believe that they have some capacity to alter their lot . . ." This change in behavior according to Piven and Cloward, has two components, "First, masses of people become defiant; they violate the traditions and laws to which they ordinarily acquiesce, and they flaunt the authorities to whom they ordinarily defer. And, second, their defiance is acted out collectively, as

members of a group, and not as isolated individuals" (Frances Fox Piven and Richard A. Cloward, *Poor People's Movements: Why They Succeed and How They Fail* [New York: Pantheon Books 1977], 3–4).

24. White supremacist groups (e.g., the Ku Klux Klan and the Minutemen) had already been publicly exercising their constitutional right to bear arms (NYSSCA, *Attica*, 115).

25. This "forced immigration" was the result of a combination of economic factors and public policies pursued by the United States and Puerto Rican governments. These policies were designed to reduce social discontent and public support for the growing independence movement on the island. This would be accomplished by reducing the island's population by encouraging both the mass sterilization of Puerto Rican women and the immigration of massive numbers of Puerto Ricans to the United States. These policies were complemented by the repression of pro-independence sectors and the trans-formation of Puerto Rico from an agrarian to an industrial economy. See Manuel Maldonado Denis, Puerto Rico: *Mito y Realidad* (Barcelona: Ediciones Península M.R., 1969); Peta Murray Henderson, "Population Control, Social Structure and the Health System in Puerto Rico: The Case of Female Sterili-zation" (Ph.D. diss., University of Connecticut, 1976); Adalberto López, *The Puerto Ricans: Their History, Culture and Society* (Cambridge: Schenkman Books, Inc., 1980); Annette B. Ramirez de Arellano, *Colonialism, Catholicism, and Contraception: A History of Birth Control in Puerto Rico* (University of North Carolina Press, 1983); and Emilio Pantojas-García, *Development Strategies as Ideology: Puerto Rico's Export-led Industrialization Experience* (Río Piedras, P.R.: Editorial de la Universidad de Puerto Rico, 1990).

26. See Eric Cummins, *The Rise and Fall of California's Radical Prison Movement* (Stanford: Stanford University Press, 1994).

27. See Sam Melville, *Letters from Attica* (New York: William Morrow and Co., 1971).

28. Examples of such types of nationwide government repression against community activists during the late 1960s and early 1970s included the cases of Eduardo Cruz, Carlos Feliciano, Los Siete de la Raza, Reies Tijerina, Martín Sostre, Angela Davis, Fred Hampton, Assata Shakur, Malcolm X, George Jackson, The Panther 21, Connie Tucker. See Angela Davis, Ruchell Magee, the Soledad Brothers, and Other Political prisoners, *If They Come in the Morning* (New York: New American Library, 1971); Idem, *Angela Davis: An Autobiography* (New York: International Publishers, [1974] 1988); Assata Shakur, *Assata: An Autobiography* (Westport: Lawrence Hill and Co., 1987); and Martín Sostre, interview with author, New York, N.Y., 24 May 1993. During the 1980s, those selectively persecuted by federal authorities included Puerto Rican Prisoners of War Alejandrina Torres, Dylcia Pagán, Alicia Rodríguez, Haydé Torres, Ida Luz Rodríguez, Luis Rosa, Carlos Alberto Torres,

Alberto Rodríguez, Edwin Cortés, Elizam Escobar, Ricardo Jiménez, Oscar López-Rivera, Adolfo Matos, and Guillermo Morales. See Special Committee in Support and Defense of the Puerto Rican Prisoners of War, *The Puerto Rican Prisoners of War and Violations of Their Human Rights* (San Juan, P.R., 198?).

29. See Nelson Blackstone, *COINTELPRO: The FBI's Secret War on Political Freedom* (New York: Vintage Books, 1976); R. Samuel Paz, "Police Abuse and Political Spying: A Threat to Hispanic Liberty and Growth," *National Hispanic Conference on Law Enforcement and Criminal Justice*, U.S. Department of Justice, Law Enforcement Assistance Administration (Washington, D.C.: GPO, 1980), 215–267; Davis, *Angela Davis*, 1988; Shakur, *Assata*, 1987; and Ronald Fernández, *Prisoners of Colonialism: The Struggle for Justice in Puerto Rico* (Monroe, Maine: Common Courage Press, 1994).

30. See George Jackson, *The Prison Letters of George Jackson* (New York: Bantam Books, 1970); Davis et al., *If They Come in the Morning*, 1971; Daniels, interview with author, 1993; and Sostre, interview with author, 1993.

31. In 1963, there were 19,861 prisoners in DOCS facilities. Of these, 44.4 percent (8,810) were classified as Black, 43.5 percent (8,643) as white, 11.5 percent (2,278) Hispanic, 0.4 percent (85) as "other", and the remaining 0.2 percent (45) as "not stated." (New York State Department of Correctional Services [henceforth cited as NYSDOCS], "Ethnic Distribution of Inmate Population on December 31: 1960–1988," May 4, 1989).

32. See Piri Thomas, *Down These Mean Streets* (New York: Alfred A. Knopf, Inc., 1967); and Idem., *Seven Long Times* (New York: Praeger Publishers, 1974).

33. Elliott, interview with author, 1993.

34. Ibid.

35. See Thomas, *Seven Long Times*, 1974; James B. Jacobs, *Stateville: The Penitentiary in Mass Society* (Chicago: University of Chicago Press, 1977); Ronald Berkman, *Opening the Gates: The Rise of the Prisoners' Movement* (Lexington, Mass.: D. C. Heath and Co., 1979); and John Irwin, *Prisons in Turmoil* (Boston: Little, Brown and Co., 1980).

36. Berkman, *Opening the Gates*, 55.

37. Eric Cummins, *The Rise and Fall of California's Radical Prison Movement* (Stanford: Stanford University Press, 1994), 70.

38. According to James B. Fox 1961 and 1978, there were sixty-six reported federal court decisions dealing with prisoners affiliated with the Nation of Islam (Jacobs, *New Perspectives on Prisons and Imprisonment*, 36). The support of prisoners for the Nation of Islam began to dwindle as a result of conflicts between members who favored political activism (e.g., Malcolm X) and those who favored involvement in purely religious activities (e.g., Elijah Muhammad).

39. At Attica, followers of the Nation of Islam were "blacklisted" as early as 1957 (NYSSCA, *Attica,* 122–123).

40. Ibid., 121–123.

41. By the mid-1960s, traditional leaders within the Nation of Islam had decreased their support for African-American Muslim prisoner litigation efforts. In addition, the Nation of Islam lost followers because Allah failed to come to deliver them from the white oppressor. See Eldridge Cleaver, *Soul on Ice* (New York: McGraw-Hill, 1968); and Berkman, *Opening the Gates,* 1979.

42. Sostre, interview with author, 1993.

43. For a similar description of the experience of Chicana(o) community activists with the criminal justice system see: Davis et al., *If They Come in the Morning,* 1971; and Paz, "Police Abuse and Political Spying," 1980.

44. Sostre, interview with author, 1993.

45. During the rebellion, Sostre had allowed community members to use his store to cover themselves from the tear gas and firing of police officers. See *Angela Y. Davis, Ruchell Magee, the Soledad Brothers, and Other Political Prisoners* (Lagos, Nigeria: Third Press Publishers, [originally 1971], 2nd Printing, 1992), 83–84.

46. Sostre, interview with author, 1993. Sostre had been convicted by an all white jury in the spring of 1968 and sentenced to thirty years in prison. Prior to his trial, Sostre spent eight months in jail due to the excessively high bail set for him. Arto Williams first informed state authorities in 1971 that he had framed Sostre in 1968 to get himself released from jail. At the time, the courts refused to grant Sostre a mistrial. In a hearing held on May 30–31, 1973, in Buffalo's Federal Court, Williams once again recanted his testimony ("Sostre," *Midnight Special* 3, No. 8 [August 1973]: 21). During the spring of 1975, the Manhattan Second Circuit Court denied Sostre's appeal based on Williams' recantation ("Sostre," *Midnight Special* 5, No. 3 [May 1975]: 6).

47. Sostre, interview with author, 1993. On January 27, 1975, Sostre was found guilty by an all-white jury of three counts of second degree assault on three prison guards. Once the verdict was announced, twelve members of the Plattsburgh Martín Sostre Defense Committee were arrested on contempt charges for protesting the verdict while in the courtroom. See "Martín Sostre," *Midnight Special* 5, No. 2 (March 1975): 20; "Martín Sostre," *Midnight Special* 5, No. 3 (March 1975): 6; and Los 12 de Plattsburgh, "Saludos Revolucionarios," *Midnight Special* 5, No. 3 (May 1975): 6.

48. Italian radical supporter of Puerto Rican independence.

49. See Davis et al., *If They Come in the Morning,* 1971.

50. Sostre, interview with author, 1993. On May 14, 1970, Judge Constance Baker Motley awarded Martín Sostre $13,020 in damages. "Judge Motley

ruled that Sostre had been kept in solitary confinement for 372 days solely because of his Black Muslim activities. He had been segregated for more than a year because of his attempts to make legal motions for a co-defendant awaiting trial, for refusing to answer questions relating to the initials 'R.N.A.' (Republic of New Africa), for writing a letter to his sister setting forth certain political views, and for other less serious matters" (Herman Badillo and Milton Haynes, *A Bill of No Rights: Attica and the American Prison System* [New York: Outerbridge and Lazard, Inc., 1972], 168).

51. Sostre, interview with author, 1993. The international mobilization of support on behalf of Sostre as well as his legal victories led to his being granted clemency by Governor Hugh Carey in 1976.

52. Such was also the case of Carlos Feliciano, head of the Puerto Rican Nationalist Party, framed by government officials for his political beliefs (see, "the people will free Carlos Feliciano," *Palante* 2, No. 10 [28 August 1970]: 4; "Creen Probable Feliciano Salga Hoy de la Cárcel," *El Diario,* 23 septiembre 1971, 4; "Prosponen Juicio a Feliciano Para Octubre 18," *El Diario,* 28 septiembre 1971, 4; Mike A. Correa, "Carlos Feliciano Demanda Fiscalía Por Un Millón $," *El Diario,* 17 octubre 1971, 4; Alfredo Izaguirre Horta, "Feliciano en Libertad Bajo Fianza de $55 mil," *El Diario,* 29 septiembre 1971, 3; Eurípides Ríos, "Celebran Juicio Hoy a Feliciano," *El Diario,* 6 junio 1973, 4, 36; "Defensores Carlos Feliciano Convocan a Una Manifestación," *El Diario,* 11 octubre 1973, 4, 33; Antonio Gil de Lamadrid, "4 Años de Prisión Para Feliciano; Libre Bajo Fianza," *El Diario,* 14 octubre 1973, 3; and Information Ministry, Young Lords Party, "Libertad Para Carlos Feliciano," *Palante* 2, No. 17 [December 1970]: 8–9). Feliciano was subsequently absolved of all charges.

53. The Martín Sostre Defense Committee of Glen Gardner, New Jersey, distributed a pamphlet entitled *The New Prisoner* written by Sostre (Arthur Prince, "the new prisoner," *Midnight Special* 3, No. 11 [November 1973]: 23).

54. "Martín Sostre," *Midnight Special* 5, No. 3 (May 1975): 6.

55. Sostre, interview with author, 1993.

56. David Vidal, "A Freed Activist Sees No Change," *N.Y. Times,* 15 February 1976, 28.

57. Ibid. Law suits filed by Sostre included: *Sostre, Pierce, SaMarion v. LaValle,* 293 F.2d 233 (1961); *Sostre v. Mcginnis,* 334 F. 2d 906 (1964); *Sostre v. McGinnis,* 442 F.2d 178 (1971); *Sostre v. Otis,* 330 F. Supp. 941 (1971).

58. Stephen Latimer, interview with author, New York, N.Y., 16 March 1989.

59. Arnold J. Lubasch, "Court Extends Convicts' Rights," *N.Y. Times,* 25 February 1971.

60. *Sostre v. Rockefeller,* 312 F. Supp. 863 (S.D. N.Y. 1970), modified sub nom, *Sostre v. McGinnis,* 442 F. 2d 178 (2d Cir. 1971), cert. denied, 404 U.S. 1049, 92 S.Ct. 719, 30 L.Ed.2d 740 (1972).

61. The DOCS' directive issued on October 19, 1970, stated that an officer could keeplock a prisoner for only seventy-two hours pending a hearing to be conducted by the Adjustment Committee composed of one civilian and two security persons. At the hearing, the prisoner was to be asked his/her version of the incident. The accusing officer did not have to appear. On the basis of the officer's written report, the prisoner's version, and his/her past disciplinary record, the Committee made its final decision—dismiss the charges, defer action, loss of privileges, change of programs or facilities in the institution, keeplock, segregation or recommend a Superintendent's Hearing. At the Superintendent's Hearing, prisoners were allowed to be represented by an officer and written charges were given to him/her. The final disposition could result in dismissal of the charge, segregation or the loss of "good time." The decision could be reviewed by the Commissioner of Corrections.

62. Russell G. Oswald had been chairman of the New York State Parole Board during the previous twelve years. A former social worker, known for his support of rehabilitation programs, he was seen by custody-oriented sectors as being pro-prisoner.

63. On January 1, 1971, the Department of Correction and the Division of Parole merged under the new Department of Correctional Services (DOCS). This centralized "in one agency the custody of convicted felons from the time they entered prison until they were released from all state supervision, including parole" (NYSSCA, *Attica*, 19).

64. During the month of August 1970, male prisoners at "The Tombs" (the Men's House of Detention in Manhattan) rebelled on three separate occasions, taking guards hostage in each instance. On August 8, prisoners rebelled demanding the return of an African-American prisoner removed from their floor for hitting a guard (Badillo and Haynes, *A Bill of No Rights,* 13). On August 10, rebel prisoners demanded that their list of grievances be publicized over television. Grievances centered around "denial of preliminary hearings, excessive bail, delays of a year or more before trial, the suggestion given defendants by Legal Aid lawyers to plead guilty to 'lesser charges' even before these lawyers had asked whether they were guilty of the offenses charged. Inmates further complained of 'unnecessary brutality . . . directed against the black and Puerto Rican inmate population,' of insults and indecent proposals made by prison officers to women visitors, and of food 'not fit for human consumption'" (Ibid., 14). See also Young Lords Party, "Tumben las Tumbas," *Palante* 2, No. 10 (28 August 1970): 6. The third August revolt centered around lack of medication, overcrowding, unhealthy food, and living conditions (Badillo and Haynes, *A Bill of No Rights,* 14–15). In October, rebellions erupted in all of the city's detention facilities (e.g., the Long Island and Kew Garden branches of the Queens House of Detention, the Brooklyn House of Detention, and The Tombs). The major aims of the rebels were to gain the attention of the mass media, to publicize their demands, and to mobilize the

African-American and Puerto Rican communities on their behalf. Two of the main grievances were high bails and the lengthy time prisoners were held in detention while awaiting court appearances.

65. The Attica strike was to protest low wages in the printshop. The Napanoch strike was in response to the death of a prisoner who was left unattended while suffering a heart attack (Badillo and Haynes, *A Bill of No Rights*, 25).

66. The November 4, 1970 rebellion was touched off by the demand for the right to a day's vacation on Black Solidarity Day. Thirty-five guards were held hostage by four hundred prisoners. DOCS' response was to keeplock 1,600 men and give them two meals a day for three months (NYSSCA, *Attica*, 129–130). Other prisoners were held in segregation for indeterminate periods of time and several of those identified as leaders were transferred to segregation in Attica.

67. Francis A. J. Ianni, *Black Mafia: Ethnic Succession in Organized Crime* (New York: Simon and Schuster, 1974), 190–191. The strikes, which took place in 1960, 1962, 1963, and 1965, demanded that a specified amount of time be taken off a prisoner's sentence for good behavior. These actions, among others, led to the passage of a "good time" bill in 1967. The nation's first wave of prison riots/rebellions occurred during the 1929–1930 period. The main grievances voiced by the prisoners were overcrowding, bad food, protests over the deaths of prisoners caused by the negligence of prison authorities, and brutal discipline. The response of prison officials in New York State to the demands of prisoners at Clinton and Auburn that year was "to build the 'ultimate prison,' escape-proof and riot proof" (Bert Useem and Peter Kimball, *States of Siege: U.S. Prison Riots, 1971–1986* [New York and Oxford: Oxford University Press, 1989], 19). That prison was Attica. During the 1930s and 1940s prisoner grievances included unfair parole procedures and poor living conditions. Some riots, it was argued, were precipitated by racial mixing in federal institutions (Garson, "The Disruption of Prison Administration," 539). Between April 1952 and October 1953 there were forty prisoner riots/rebellions across the country. They demonstrated the increased ability of prisoners to plan and carry out collective actions and conduct negotiations (Ibid., 544). The prison rebellions of the 1956–1967 period included the demand for the establishment of inmate councils and involved primarily grievances concerning poor food, mail censorship, recreation policy, discipline, and medical care. According to Garson, almost 20 percent of these rebellions were related to African-Americans (Ibid., 545). Between 1968 and April 1971, on the eve of the Attica Rebellion, there were at least thirty-seven prison rebellions nationwide.

68. Badillo and Haynes, *A Bill of No Rights*, 1972; and McEleney, *Correctional Reform*, 1985.

69. An example of a prisoner who was identified by DOCS as being a prisoner leader in both the November 1970 Auburn Rebellion and the September 1971 Attica Rebellion was Richard L. Clark (Oswald, *Attica,* 21).

70. Gilbert Jiménez, "We Must Fight—To Be Free!," *Palante* 2, No. 4 (October 30, 1970): 15. The five main objectives of the Inmates Liberation Front were "1) To assure that no person be detained in jail because he or she is unable to make bail. 2) To investigate and act on the brutal, unjust, and inhumane treatment being executed on the inmates. 3) To assure that an inmate's committee be set up in the concentration camps, and that they be permitted to communicate with the outside world. 4) To insure that inmates are given speedy trials, and have access to counsel of his or her choice, and that none of the people's constitutional rights and basic human rights be violated. 5) To inact [sic] and provide the inmates, upon release, with jobs, education, housing and readjustment to the community" (Young Lords Party, "Frente de Liberación De Los Presos," *Palante* 2, No. 4 [October 30, 1970]: 14).

71. Esli Ramón González, "Relata la Suciedad, Abusos y Discrimen en Cárcel de Queens," *El Dario-La Prensa* (hereafter cited as *El Diario),* 4 octubre 1970, 4. Author's translation: "Yesterday, the men here in this prison acted like real men and brothers, and for the first time we have united our forces to bring out into the public light the horrible condition of injustice, discrimination, abuses, filth, and mistreatment to which we are subjected to by the pigs" (Ibid.). Prisoners' willingness to engage in coalition building efforts was also demonstrated by the fact that they tried to get the city to support their attempts to create the equivalent of a citywide Prisoners' Congress (Idem, "200 Heridos Motines Cárceles," *El Diario,* 5 octubre 1970, 1, 3, 33).

72. The need for Spanish-speaking interpreters was highlighted when the Federal Court of Appeals ruled that a new trial had to be held for a Latino agricultural worker who had been convicted of murder although he did not understand English, had not been provided with an interpreter during the trial, could not communicate with his English-speaking attorney for much of the trial, and twelve of the fourteen witnesses against him testified in English. A new trial was ordered with a translator provided for the defendant ("Por No Entender Inglés Haran Otro Juicio Acusado," *El Diario,* 10 noviembre 1970, 2).

73. Esli Ramón González, "Relata la Suciedad, Abusos y Discrimen en Cárcel de Queens," *El Diario,* 4 octubre 1970, 4. Author's translation: "a) that there be more interpreters in courts and prisons; b) more Puerto Rican attorneys; c) allow communication in Spanish with family members; d) an end to the injustices committed by the "establishment" against Puerto Ricans; and, e) that reading material in Spanish, particularly the newspaper *El Diario,* be provided totally free" (Ibid.). Other grievances included excessive high bails, long waiting periods before seeing a judge, and mistreatment.

74. Ibid.

75. Badillo and Haynes, *A Bill of No Rights,* 14. See also *N.Y. Times,* 11 August 1970. Esli Ramón González, "Fustigan a Lindsay Por No Acceder a Petición Presos," *El Diario,* 27 septiembre 1970, 2. Other demands included: continuous distribution of sanitary articles (e.g., soap, toothpaste, toothbrushes); a social worker on each floor to act as liaison between prisoners and family members; a phone on each floor to keep prisoners in communication with family members; the availability of spiritual leaders for all religious denominations; access to law books; dentists and doctors always available; change of diet to include more fruits; adequate clothing and shoe allowances; an hour of recreation; new tables and chairs in the mess hall; allow visits by children accompanied by adults; and more justice and equality for all (Ibid.).

76. Domingo Roche Jr., "Motín de Presos en Queens," *El Diario,* 2 octubre 1970, 1, 3, 33; and "Motín También en Las Tumbas, Apresan a Siete Guardias," *El Diario,* 4 octubre 1970, 4.

77. Badillo also acted as a translator for several of the prisoners whose cases were heard by judges during the emergency bail hearings held in the jail's yard (Badillo and Haynes, *A Bill of No Rights,* 19–20). Other Latinos present at the site of Long Island rebellion were State Senator Robert García and Manuel Casiano of the New York Office of the Commonwealth of Puerto Rico.

78. Esli Ramón González, "200 Heridos Motines Cárceles," *El Diario,* 5 octubre 1970, 1, 3, 33.

79. Piri Thomas, interview with author, Binghamton, N.Y., 19 April 1993.

80. Michael Armstrong [pseud.], interview with author, New York, N.Y., 22 April 1993.

81. Gregorio Palma [pseud.], interview with author, New York, N.Y., 16 April and 1 May 1993.

82. Ibid.

83. "Autoridades Controlan Situación en Cárceles," *El Diario,* 7 octubre 1970, 4, 34; Esli Ramón González, "Preocupa Familiares de Presos su Localización en las Cárceles," *El Diario,* 8 octubre 1970, 6; and Idem, "Investigan Presunta Golpiza a Recluso en Brooklyn," *El Diario,* 19 octubre 1970, 7.

84. Domingo Roche Jr., "Se Quejan de Que No Les Permite Visitar a Familiares Presos en N.Y.," *El Diario,* 7 octubre 1970, 2. One and one-half years later, Latino prisoners at the Brooklyn House of Detention continued to complain about: the lack of reading material in Spanish; lost correspondence; the monopolization of televisions by African-Americans; ill treatment of visitors; lack of bilingual programs; and the shortage of bilingual personnel. The latter made it virtually impossible for Latinos to communicate with staff members and to participate in the few available programs (Gil de Lamadrid, "Denuncían Tortura Sicológica Contra Presos Boricuas," *El Diario,* 1 May 1972, 2).

85. Alfredo Izaguirre-Horta, *El Diario,* 8 octubre 1970, 4.

86. "Trasladan a 435 Presos," *El Diario*, 13 octubre 1970, 4; "Young Lords Piden a Los Boricuas NY Que se Armen," *El Diario*, 20 octubre 1970, 10; Esli Ramón González, "Preocupa Familiares de Presos su Localización en las Cárceles," *El Diario*, 8 octubre 1970, 6, 39; and "Hallan Otro Preso Ahorcado en Celda, *El Diario*, 8 noviembre 1970, 3, 46. The inquiries of Latinas(os) outside the walls were frequently addressed by Agenor Castro, director of public relations for the New York City Department of Correction. Castro, himself a Latino, was responsible for acting as an intermediary between the penal establishment and the Latina(o) community. It was Castro who appealed in Spanish to Latino prisoners at the Long Island Branch of the Queens House of Correction to surrender to prison authorities (Badillo and Haynes, *A Bill of No Rights*, 23).

87. "Consejal Burden Pide Investiguen Cárceles de N.Y.," *El Diario*, 22 octubre 1970, 2, 35.

88. Esli Ramón González, "200 Heridos Motines Cárceles," *El Diario*, 5 octubre 1970, 1, 3, 33; "Acusan Depto. Corrección de 'Engañar al Pueblo'," *El Diario*, 22 octubre 1970, 4, 41; and Davis et al, *If They Come in the Morning*, 1971.

89. See Young Lords Party, *Palante—Young Lords Party* (New York: McGraw-Hill Book Co., 197?; Palante (Chicago); and *Palante: Latin Revolutionary News Service* (New York).

90. Esli Ramón González, "200 Heridos Motines Cárceles," *El Diario*, 5 octubre 1970, 1, 3, 33.

91. Mecca, "Free Our Sisters," *Palante* 2, No. 17 (December 1970): 19. The aims of the demonstration were to: "1) celebrate the 10th anniversary of the NLF (National Liberation Front of the People of South Vietnam. 2) To announce the beginning of a bail fund for the sisters inside the prison. 3) to demonstrate against the conditions in the prison" (Ibid.).

92. Angela Davis was held at the Women's House of Detention from October to December 1970 when she was extradited to California. See Davis, et al., *If They Come in the Morning*, 1971.

93. "On April 21, 1969, 21 members of the New York Chapter of the Black Panther Party were accused in a 30 count indictment of conspiracy" to bomb several public places (Ibid., 70). One of the defendants, Joan Bird, was beaten and tortured by police at the time of her arrest (Ibid., 70–71). Although the Panther 21 were eventually acquitted by a jury after only a two and a half hour deliberation, some of the defendants spent up to two years in prison while awaiting trial. Defendants were held at various New York City jails, including the Women's House of Detention.

94. Speakers at the demonstration included representatives from the YLP, the Women's Bail Fund, the Puerto Rican Student Union, and the Black Panther Party.

95. According to Angela Davis, "I have never encountered such an overwhelming warm and cordial welcome. Obviously the reason why prison authorities isolated me was the enthusiastic welcome I received. Each time I go from one area of the jail to another, the sisters hold up their clenched fists and convey expressions of solidarity. While I was in solitary confinement, the sisters on the floor conducted demonstrations in my behalf. When I embarked on a hunger strike, many of them joined" (Davis, et al., *If They Come in the Morning,* 188). The support for Davis continued despite the fact that penal authorities sought to hinder it. "After I was transferred into population, some of the sisters on my corridor with whom I had spent a great deal of time, were helping me answer letters from the outside. They were all immediately transferred to another floor but we still find ways to communicate with one another" (Ibid.).

96. Esli Ramón González, "Acusan Depto. Corrección de 'Engañar al Pueblo'," *El Diario,* 22 octubre 1970, 4, 41.

97. It was the second time the YLP had taken over the church. On December 28, 1969, the YLP, then called the Young Lords Organization, had taken over the church and set up a children's meal program, a liberation school, and free medical care (*Palante* [Chicago], Vol. 1, No. 5, [January 1970]: 20).

98. Richie Pérez, "Julio Roldán Center Opens," *Palante* 2, Vol. 14 (October 30, 1970): 4.

99. William J. Vanden Heuvel, "Tragedia en Las Tumbas: Muchos de los Suicidios en Cárceles de NY Han Sido Puertorriqueños; Destrucción," *El Diario,* 14 marzo 1972, Suplementario. Other community members, such as El Club de Mujeres de Todas las Naciones joined Agenor Castro in forming, albeit for a short period of time, El Comité de Ayuda a los Presos. The committee's purpose was to cooperate with Friendly Visitors, Inc., in the sending of clothes, toiletries, and Spanish literature to Latina(o) prisoners. Women prisoners were also sent cloth to make their own clothes (Luisa A. Quintero, "Marginalia," *El Diario,* 16 diciembre 1970, 24).

100. "Ocupan Young Lords de Nuevo Iglesia de Harlem," *El Diario,* 19 octubre 1970, 6; Esli Ramón González, "Acusan Depto. Corrección de 'Engañar al Pueblo'," *El Diario*, 22 octubre 1970, 4, 41; Denise Oliver, "Murder," *Palante* 2, No. 14 (30 October 1970): 2; and Richie Pérez, "Julio Roldán Center Opens," Palante 2, No. 14 (30 October 1970): 4.

101. "Piden que Aclaren la Muerte de Roldán," *El Diario,* 23 octubre 1970, 4. Author's translation: "In these moments in which the emotional climate of our nation and of the neighboring countries are permeated with violence and fear, we feel extremely alarmed by the recent dangerous expressions of the growing militancy in the Puerto Rican community. This is the result of the frustrations caused by the feeling of impotence this community is suffering."

102. Juan González, "Armense Para Defenderse," *Palante* 2, No. 14 (October 30, 1970): 12.

103. Ibid.

104. "Consejal Burden Pide Investiguen Cárceles de N.Y.," *El Diario*, 22 octubre 1970, 2, 35; and "Consejal Pide Investiguen Muerte de Roldán," *El Diario*, 27 octubre 1970, 10.

105. William J. Vanden Heuvel, "Tragedia en Las Tumbas: Muchos de los Suicidios en Cárceles de N.Y. Han Sido Puertorriqueños; Destrucción," *El Diario*, 14 marzo 1972, Suplementario. Author's translation: "I do not know of any program within the detention centers of the Department of Prisons of the City of New York, besides those begun and operated by the prisoners themselves, where adults who speak or read little or no English are taught language or literacy. The few programs in Spanish for prisoners that exist or have existed, are generally of a religious nature, conducted by volunteer ministers, such as Bible classes in Spanish. In The Tombs, according to the warden, there are eight or nine Spanish-speaking officials of 240."

106. Ibid.

107. In one of the few articles in *El Diario* that discussed a visit by members of the Latina(o) community to the Rikers Island women's section, the only grievances mentioned were poor food and clothing and the lack of radio and television programs in Spanish. The tour of the facility, headed by Agenor Castro, was taken by Latinos representing the: Proyecto Puertorriqueño de Desarrollo de la Comunidad, Organizaciones Unidas del Bronx, Corporación Comunal del Sur Del Bronx, and the Departamento de Higiene Mental del Centro de Servicios Múltiples del Bronx (Cesar A. Marín, "Dice es Lastimosa la Vida de Reclusas Hispanas en Rikers," *El Diario*, 22 marzo 1972, 2).

108. "Designan Nyrka Torrado Junta de Corrección de N.Y.," *El Diario*, 27 octubre 1970, 4; and "Heuvel Promete Investigar Suicidio en Cárceles," *El Diario*, 28 octubre 1970, 2. Three of the nine board members included Nyrka Torrado (sub-director of the Proyecto Puertorriqueño de Desarrollo de la Comunidad), Joseph J. De Monte (ex-councilman from Queens), and Gerald "Jerry" Rivera (attorney for the Young Lords Party). The board, conducted an investigation into conditions at the city jails and asked the district attorney to charge an African-American officer for the death of a Latino prisoner (Esli Ramón González, "Revelan Detalles en Nueva Muerte Prisión Las Tumbas," *El Diario*, 11 noviembre 1970, 4, 37).

109. Alfredo Izaquirre-Horta, "'Tenemos Hambre,' Gritan Presos Cárcel Brooklyn," *El Diario*, 8 octubre 1970, 4. Author's translation: "In Sections A-B-C- and D in the fourth floor, prisoners have been punished without pity with nightsticks, irons, and pieces of wood. All because they are protesting the small amount of food—two slice of bread in the morning, two at noon, and two at night—that they are being given, and because it has been more than

3 days since they have been given water to drink. Another inhumane thing they have done is that they have taken away the blankets and, above all, that they do not want to take them to the doctor without their having signed a paper saying that they received those "injuries" as a result of an accident."

110. "Tombs," *Midnight Special* 2, No. 6 (August 1972): 6. In The Tombs Rebellion, the state picked 7 out of 300 prisoners for prosecution. At least one of them, Ricardo de León, was Latino (Ibid.). He was subsequently acquitted of all charges.

111. "McGrath Ve Plan de Radicales en Motín Prisioneros," *El Diario*, 12 octubre 1970, 4. The argument that "militants" were behind rebellions in the city's jails was reiterated by Benjamin J. Malcolm after the February 1972 rebellions at the Rikers' Island Adolescent Remand Shelter for which 15 prisoners, among them 6 Latinos, were indicted ("Rikers Remand Rebellion," *Midnight Special* 2, No. 2 [April 1972]: 1, 4; and "Seis Hispanos Acusados por Disturbios Rikers Island," *El Diario*, 15 marzo 1972, 16). Malcolm had replaced McGrath as New York City's Commissioner of Correction on January 1, 1972. He was the first African-American to occupy that post ("Culpa Militantes de Motín en Rickers [sic] Island," *El Diario*, 29 febrero 1972, 3).

112. *New York Daily News*, 19 September 1970, 22 as quoted in McEleney, *Correctional Reform*, 82.

113. McEleney, *Correctional Reform*, 85.

114. Ibid., 91–92.

115. Ibid.

116. Oswald, *Attica*, 11. In 1971, the six maximum security prisons for men were: Great Meadow; Green Haven; Sing Sing; Clinton; Auburn; and Attica (Ibid.). Conditions at Great Meadow and Green Haven were so tense that Oswald was sure these facilities would experience a rebellion before Attica.

117. Elliott, interview with author, 1993.

3

The Attica Prison Rebellion and the Latina(o) Community Inside and Outside the Walls

The riot . . . started at about 9:15 . . . By 9:36 the gate was down. By 12 o'clock the riot had turned into a rebellion . . . and there was structure.
— Elizabeth Fink, interview with author (1993)

The entire incident that has erupted here at Attica is a result . . . of the unmitigated oppression wrought by the racist administration . . . of this prison. We are men. We are not beasts, and we do not intend to be beaten or driven as such . . . What has happened here is but the sound before the fury of those who are oppressed. We will not compromise on any terms except those that are agreeable to us.
— L.D. (James Elliott Barkley,
African-American prisoner leader
killed during the Attica Prison Rebellion) (1971)

I vividly recall talking at Attica Prison to a Spanish-speaking prisoner who had been there for five years and did not speak a word of English. In questioning him I found that no attempt had been made during his term to teach him English. I also remember . . . speaking to another prisoner who informed me that when the helicopter first came over the yard and ordered prisoners to lie down (in this way signifying to the state troopers that they had surrendered) some of the non-English speaking prisoners did not understand these orders and were shot as they remained standing.
— Louis Nuñez, "Rights of Spanish-speaking Minorities" (1973)[1]

On September 9, 1971, over half of the 2,243 prisoners at Attica Correctional Facility rebelled,[2] taking 39 security and civilian personnel hostage. The rebellion ended on September 13, with 32 prisoners and 11 guards dead and more than 80 wounded. The deaths resulted form the violent assault on the prison by state troopers, National

Guardsmen, and prison guards.[3] Five of the prisoners killed by the state were Latinos, at least four were Puerto Rican.[4] During the aborted negotiations between prisoners, negotiators, and prison administrators, then Commissioner of Corrections Russell G. Oswald had agreed, in principle, to twenty-eight ("The 28 Points") of the thirty-three demands[5] made by prisoners, thus recognizing the overall legitimacy of the grievances. Prisoner demands were basically paraphrased versions of the demands drafted less than a year earlier by California prisoners and known as "The Folsom Prisoners' Manifesto."[6] Together they represented the shared grievances and concerns of prisoners throughout the country.

The Attica demands were broad. They varied from reforms, which could be implemented solely with the authorization of DOCS administrators, to those which required legislative and/or other state intervention. Some of the demands reflected concerns common to all prisoners.[7] Others reflected the interests of a few.[8] Still others, such as demands 17, 18, and 20, reflected specific concerns of Latino and African-American prisoners.

> 17. Provide adequate medical treatment for every inmate; engage either a Spanish-speaking doctor or interpreters who will accompany Spanish-speaking inmates to medical interviews.
> 18. Provide a complete Spanish library. . . .
> 20. Institute a program for the employment of significant numbers of Black and Spanish-speaking officers.[9]

These demands echoed and/or complemented concerns voiced by Latino and African-American prisoners in local and state facilities during the 1970 rebellions. These included access to bilingual rehabilitation programs, the hiring of more bilingual personnel, and access to Latina(o) prisoners by members of the Latina(o) community.

Latino and African-American prisoner discontent was fueled by the racially and ethnically discriminatory practices of the overwhelmingly white custodial and civilian Attica staff. Such practices characterized the treatment received by prisoners of color throughout the state.

> Above all, for both inmates and officers, "correction" meant an atmosphere charged with racism. Racism was manifested in job assignments, discipline, self-segregation in the inmate mess halls,[10] and in the daily interaction of inmate and officer and among the inmates themselves. There was no escape within the walls for the growing mistrust between white middle America and the residents of urban ghettoes. Indeed, at Attica, racial polarity and mistrust

were magnified by the constant reminder that the keepers were white and the kept were largely black and Spanish-speaking.[11]

Latino prisoner discontent was also fueled by discriminatory treatment to which Latinos were subjected.

En Attica, si descubren a un boricua hablando español, lo castigan. Los tienen forzados a hablar inglés porque los guardias no entienden el español.

La correspondencia es muy mala. Muchas cartas no llegan . . . Confiscan las cartas que escriben en español, no las mandan. . . .

El pasado noviembre Victor Ortiz sufría por cinco meses un problema en el pecho. Luego de protestar lo llevaron al hospital de la cárcel y murió de una condición cardíaca. Si le hubiesen dado tratamiento a tiempo, Victor estuviera vivo hoy. . . .[12]

The extent of discontent among Latino and African-American prisoners at Attica was illustrated by the fact that their proportion among the rebels was 10 percent higher than their proportion within the overall prisoner population.[13]

The Attica Rebellion demonstrated, as had the previous rebellions in local and state facilities, that Latinos were willing to form alliances with African-American and white prisoners to demand reforms. Moreover, the active participation of Latinos in the events preceding the Rebellion, in the takeover of the institution, the formulation of demands, the formation of the negotiating committee, and the ensuing negotiations, underscored for penal administrators the extent to which Latino prisoners were willing to go to make their demands known and addressed.

Latino participation in the Rebellion also reflected the new collective posturing toward the outside Latino community that developed among Latino prisoners during the mid-1960s and was evident during the 1970 New York City jail and upstate prison rebellions. There was a clear acknowledgment that Latino prisoners were members of the larger Latina(o) community and that they needed to mobilize support within that community to pressure the predominantly white power structure to make reforms. By demanding the presence of Latino reporters and community members in the Attica negotiations, Latino prisoners once again demonstrated that they recognized the positive role third parties could play on their behalf.

It was the calls for community support by the mostly Puerto Rican Latino prisoner population during the Attica Rebellion, and the state's violent response to it, that led to the mobilization, albeit temporary, of important sectors of the (also overwhelmingly Puerto Rican) Latina(o) community in support of Latino prisoners in various parts of the state. The response of the outside Latina(o) community was also conditioned by existing personal and political rivalries. Such rivalries, to be discussed shortly, were reflected in conflicting opinions about the role played by Latino prisoners and outside Latino negotiators in the events which took place during the revolt.

Latino Prisoners as Leaders and Mediators

> The Young Lords Party were part of the overall coalition and they were considered comrades. They were part of the struggle. They were brothers.
> —Adam Turner, interview with author (1993)

> . . . you did have in Attica a very sophisticated, politically aware group of prisoners and it . . . was truly a rainbow in that sense. It was white. It was Latino. It was Black. . . . The Native American influence I'm not so sure of from a . . . prior political activism, but certainly because of the way the state targeted the Native Americans as . . . a primary focus of prosecution, it certainly politicized the Native American population in the prison and around the prison.
> —Daniel Meyers, interview with author (1993)

Until the eve of the Rebellion, Latino prisoner leaders at Attica who were predominantly identified with the Young Lords Party,[14] had been able to make few stable alliances with the overwhelmingly African-American prisoner population. Sectors of the latter were divided primarily into the Black Panther Party, the Nation of Islam, and the Five Percent Nation.[15] Until that time, alliances between Latinos identified with the YLP and prisoners identified with the Black Panther Party had been possible because of the overlapping political ideologies and the organizations' history of mutual support outside the walls. A number of Latino and African-American prisoners formerly affiliated with these organizations had also joined to form the "People's Party." The latter also included a number of progressive whites.[16]

In the weeks preceding the Attica Rebellion, Latino prisoner leaders had joined a small number of their African-American peers in an attempt to mediate between the Nation of Islam and the Black Panther

Party. Such mediation helped foster the creation of unity among prisoners.[17] Prisoner organization and unity were feared and opposed by
prison officials who did everything in their power to hinder the building
of such solidarity.[18] The motivation behind this fear was expressed by
former Latino prisoner Gregorio Palma:

> They do not like organization in prison because organization is
> something that can work against them. If men are organized they
> can stop some of the abuses or they can challenge their power. Of
> course, this is a positive mode, not a negative mode, but, nonethe-
> less, when men learn to organize they become a threat to the system
> because they can do constructive things to change their oppression.
> And I think any oppressor is afraid of organization.[19]

The importance of Latino prisoner leaders' mediation efforts lay,
not only in the role they played between rival African-American groups,
but also between Latino and African-American prisoners. The latter
frequently felt that Latinos were more inclined to identify with white
prisoners. In the words of former African-American prisoner leader
Elmer Daniels:

> And in prison I found, having been there so long, that [the] Puerto
> Rican or Latin was like a pendulum and when the system had a prob-
> lem, say [with] one pole, Black or white, the pendulum would swing
> one way or the other depending on what the onus was. So the Puerto
> Rican was either white or Black given the circumstances . . . And this
> was sort of a control mechanism because there was no unity . . . in
> that respect, you see? And by and large this existed in almost every
> prison that I was in. . . . There's a lot of fantastic guys that are excep-
> tions, who knew who they were, but I'm talking about generally.[20]

The ambivalent stance among Latino prisoners towards non-Latino
prisoners was viewed as the result of internalized racism and the state's
attempts to divide prisoners. According to former African-American
prisoner leader Angel Gear:

> . . . that was always a part of, I guess the underlying tensions . . . in
> the prisons, because for many years in prison . . . and I guess also in
> society at large, the society, you know, tried to separate Latinos . . .
> from African-Americans by classifying them as white . . . So like in
> prison they would have documents . . . [that] would have "White" or
> "White Hispanic" . . . and then "Black" . . . So that would cause a sep-

aration right then, okay. They would call Hispanics white but not white like other Caucasian folks but . . . certainly not Afro-Americans . . . Hispanic people would be very confused, you know, unless they really researched their history . . .[21]

Such tensions exemplified another one of the difficulties Latino prisoner leaders confronted when trying to make alliances with their non-Latino counterparts; the fact that the Latino prisoner body, although overwhelmingly Puerto Rican, was divided, like the Latina(o) community on the outside, not only by language barriers, political ideology, economic background, and ethnic rivalries, but also by skin color. Black Latino prisoners, such as Martín Sostre, felt that Black Latinos were more likely to engage in coalition-building efforts with African-American leaders than light-skinned Latinos.[22] Nevertheless, those Latinos who were the most willing to form alliances with African-American prisoners were those who, regardless of their skin color, had become aware, not only of the physical bonds shared by many members of the two groups but also of the common oppression Latinos and African-Americans historically were subjected to in the United States, Latin America, and the Caribbean. According to Gear:

> Those Latinos who . . . worked with . . . Blacks, you know . . . ran the whole gambit. But then again, I think that was because they were very progressive and . . . they had a sense of who they were, you know. So they could cut through . . . the . . . external appearance, stereotypes, okay, as compared to folks who didn't have any awareness, it didn't make any difference whether they was real light, light or dark, 'cause they was Latino and . . . they felt they was different, you know, in . . . maybe a superior type of way because of the orientation of the American society.[23]

To foster the building of unity within the Latino prisoner population and set the foundation from which coalitions could be built with non-Latino prisoners, Latino prisoner leaders frequently resorted to offering Puerto Rican/Latino culture classes. These classes, sought to educate Latinos about their common history as a people. Class sessions were conducted by prisoners identified with the YLP. Such prisoners became the Latino prisoner leaders during the Attica Rebellion.

Yet, there was another way in which Latino prisoner leaders at Attica, who tended to be bilingual, acted as mediators. The fact that a significant number of Latino prisoners had little or few English language skills meant that the leadership found itself mediating between them and the non-Spanish-speaking penal bureaucracy and prisoner population. The importance of such mediation was made apparent during the Attica Rebellion, when in the words of African-American Attica prisoner leader Adam Turner, "Each one of us would go to our respective groups explaining to the community what was going on. Blacks didn't speak Spanish so they couldn't go [to the Latinos]."[24]

The Latino prisoner leadership during the Rebellion was Puerto Rican, predominantly long-termers, and under the age of thirty. Their age differentiated them from the African-American prisoner leaders who tended to be older[25] and, thus, had been imprisoned for longer periods of time. As a result, African-American leaders also tended to be better acquainted with the inner workings of the penal system. Nevertheless, while the African-American prisoner leadership in the Rebellion was more pronounced and visible, the active participation of Latino (and white) leaders was significant and indispensable for the maintenance of prisoner unity during the Rebellion.

Latino Prisoner Participation in the Attica Prison Rebellion

The participation of Latino prisoners in the Attica Rebellion was evident in the incidents leading to the Rebellion. It was a Latino prisoner, William Ortiz, of "5 Company," who cut officer Tommy Boyle's head open with a full soup can on September 8, 1971.[26] It was Ortiz who was released from keeplock by prisoners from 5 Company the morning of September 9, 1971.[27] It was 5 Company (comprised of Latino, African-American, and white prisoners), that started the Rebellion on their way to being keeplocked as punishment for having released Ortiz that morning.[28]

African-American prisoner leaders attributed great importance to the active participation of Latino prisoners in the revolt. The regulations agreed to on the morning the Rebellion broke out, had been the result of negotiations between Latino and non-Latino prison leaders.[29] It was the concern with having Latino (and white prisoner) representation in the events taking place in the yard that led African-American prisoner leaders to support the former's inclusion in the "security guard." This body acted as an internal police force during the Rebellion.[30] Representatives of each racial/ethnic group were responsible for policing their own members and for keeping them informed of developments.[31] Moreover, it was the concern with having more Puerto Rican (and white) prisoner representation in the Negotiating Committee, which appears to have led prisoner leaders to hold block elections in the yard.[32]

Latino participation in the Rebellion was also evident in the list of "Immediate Demands," drafted by prisoners the first day of the revolt. These incorporated the demand to have representatives of *Palante,* the YLP newspaper, included in the Negotiating Committee.[33] The final list of thirty-three demands presented to Commissioner Oswald included demands by Latino prisoners for the hiring of bilingual personnel (particularly in the areas of security and medical services) and the provision of Spanish-language literature and educational materials.

What role did Latino prisoners play in the Negotiating Committee?[34] Approximately two to five of the ten to twelve prisoner leaders who negotiated with the state via the outside civilians who formed part of the Negotiating Committee were Puerto Ricans identified with the YLP.[35] They played a key role in the negotiations primarily by helping to maintain the overall unity of the prisoner coalition, by putting forth the specific concerns of Latino prisoners, and by demanding the presence of outside Latino civilians within the Negotiating Committee. It was expected that the latter would help sway DOCS prison administrators to listen to prisoners' demands as well as help mobilize public opinion in support of Latino prisoners.

Outside Latino Negotiators: Whom Did They Represent and What Role Did They Play?

The Latino civilians who ultimately took part in the Negotiating Committee represented a broader spectrum of political opinions than initially requested by prisoners. Originally, Latino prisoners demanded that negotiations between prisoners and DOCS personnel take place through representatives of *Palante* and African-American and white community members.[36] A few days later, Latino prisoners, along with their African-American counterparts, demanded the presence of additional Latina(o) and African-American media representatives because they felt coverage of the Rebellion by the white media was biased.

Ultimately, nine of the thirty-three outside negotiators were Latinos, all Puerto Rican. Juan ("Fi") Ortiz and José ("G.I.") Paris, representing *Palante* and YLP, were joined by Tom Soto,[37] of New York City's Prisoners' Solidarity Committee.[38] The other six outside Latinos who came to form part of the Negotiating Committee either invited themselves or were invited to participate in the Negotiating Committee by state officials. These included: liberal politicians such as Congressman Herman Badillo[39] and Senator Robert García; state and city employees such as Alfredo Matthew (Superintendent of Community School Board No. 3, Manhattan's West Side) and Alberto Cappas (Office of Minorities, SUNY-Buffalo); grassroots activists such as Domingo Rodríguez[40] (of BUILD, a Buffalo community organization); and *New York Daily News* reporter Rudy García (also brother of Robert García).[41]

The final composition of the outside civilian representation in the Negotiating Committee reflected the attempts of state elites to reduce the influence of those individuals and groups whose presence within the negotiating process had been the first requested by prisoners (e.g., the YLP, Prisoners Solidarity Committee, the Black Panther Party and attorney William Kunstler). These forces were seen as threatening the status quo, not only because they were known to be supportive of prisoners' reform efforts, but also because they were political radicals who questioned the very foundations on which the economic and political system were based. Thus, while representatives of the YLP were allowed to participate in the Negotiating Committee, as demanded by Latino prisoner leaders, Governor Rockefeller also sought the participation of liberal politicians such as Badillo. For while at the time, political support for both radicals and liberals within the Latina(o) community was strong, the latter's solution to the community's dilemmas was more acceptable to state elites. For example, while the YLP argued for Puerto Rican independence and the right of Puerto Ricans to arm themselves in self defense, Badillo contended that Puerto Rican independence was an issue for Puerto Ricans on the island to decide and that it was counterproductive for Puerto Ricans in the United States to arm themselves. By inviting government officials such as Robert García and Alberto Matthew to accompany him to Attica, Badillo, in turn, helped reinforce those elements within the Latina(o) community that government officials perceived as less threatening to the status quo. Ultimately, by appealing to the diverse constituencies represented by outside civilians on the Negotiating Committee, Governor Rockefeller hoped to reduce sympathy outside the walls for prisoners and at the same time address multiple political demands during an election year.

It is unclear from the media coverage provided in mainstream newspapers such as *El Diario* and the *New York Times,* and from published personal accounts of the Rebellion,[42] what role outside Latinos played in the negotiations as a whole. From the report issued by the New York State Special Commission on Attica,[43] it is clear that it was the Latinos affiliated with the YLP (i.e., Paris and Ortiz) and the

Prisoners Solidarity Committee (i.e., Soto) who spent the most time with prisoners in the yard. According to Tom Wicker one of the primary preoccupations of Paris and Ortiz was to ensure the continued autonomy of prison rebels. "Some observers, notably Franklin Florence and the Young Lords, Paris and Ortiz, insisted that the inmates form a political society capable of speaking and making decisions for themselves and that the observers must do nothing to commit the inmates to a position."[44]

However, it was Badillo's actions that received the most coverage in newspaper, book, and film accounts of the events. Badillo's main contributions were to publicize the plight of Latino prisoners and to try to mobilize the outside Latina(o) community to force Governor Rockefeller to meet with the outside community members on the Negotiating Committee. Badillo also warned Governor Rockefeller that if a massacre of prisoners took place in the facility during the takeover, widespread violence would break out in Latina(o) and African-American neighborhoods all over the country.

> An attack on Sunday afternoon, I told Rockefeller, would likely result in a massacre, which might in turn lead to widespread violence. People all over the country were watching their television sets. I told him to consider the impact of that news bulletin in Harlem, Bedford-Stuyvesant, the South Bronx, Buffalo, Rochester, Detroit, Cleveland.[45]

It is apparent that the role played by outside Latino liberals, although well intentioned, was ultimately an ambivalent one. On the one hand, by supporting prisoners' demands for reforms, they added their voices to those sectors within the state who supported the immediate implementation of such reforms. On the other hand, they cooperated in the state's efforts to introduce a placating influence into the negotiations and, thus, took the focus away from the more radical leadership within the prisoner population, the Negotiating Committee, and, ultimately, the outside Latina(o) community.

Outside Latina(o) Community Reaction to Events at Attica

Once the Rebellion had been quashed by the state's police forces, the Latina(o) community questioned the role played by Latino prisoners and outside Latino negotiators during the Rebellion. Politicians such as Assemblyman Manuel Ramos (District 79 of the South Bronx), who supported Governor Rockefeller's decision to retake the prison by force, argued that many Puerto Rican prisoners had been either duped or forced into participating in the Rebellion by African-American prisoners.[46] These statements were contradicted by outside members of the YLP who had participated in the Negotiating Committee.

After the Rebellion, YLP had continued to demand amnesty for rebel prisoners and to organize a series of demonstrations and press conferences to condemn the actions of Rockefeller, Oswald, and Attica Warden Vincent Mancusi. In a press conference held by the organization, José Ortiz, a member of the Attica Negotiating Committee and Chief of Operations for the YLP, argued that:

> . . . el gobernador Rockefeller está utilizando al asambleista Ramos para crear una desunión racial, clamando que los puertorriqueños no estaban envueltos y que eran manipulados por los negros . . . esto no es cierto, porque tanto los puertorriqueños como los negros y los blancos estaban unidos en Attica, y que ahora nosotros nos encontramos unidos para protestar esta masacre.[47]

In an interview with *El Diario* reporter Pedro J. Linares, Ortiz added that:

> Una de las cosas que están diciendo algunos políticos es que lo de Attica fue organizado por los negros, pero eso no es verdad. Yo estaba allá. Todo fue organizado por puertorriqueños, negros y blancos. Tenían un Comité Central que daba las instrucciones. Hablamos con un preso que se llamaba Che Santos y discutimos las condiciones, las demandas, y el racismo que los boricuas sufren.[48]

Nevertheless, Assemblyman Ramos continued to argue that "communists" had been behind the Rebellion and that Badillo had been supporting forces which had nothing to do with the interests of the Puerto Rican people. "Badillo vino a la prisión representando a fuerzas radicales que no tienen el bienestar del puertorriqueño en sus corazones . . . Badillo se prestó como mensajero y portavoz de ideales que son extranjeros a los puertorriqueños, que no tienen nada que ver con nuestras ambiciones como ciudadanos americanos."[49] The "forces and foreign ideals" Ramos had in mind were those of African-American "separatist nationalism."

> Indicó el asambleista Ramos "que existe la confusión debido a las demandas de los prisioneros de la raza de color cuyos líderes no representan al sentimiento puertorriqueño. . . ." Continuó diciendo

Ramos que, "el pueblo puertorriqueño se interesa en que se comprenda que existe una diferencia de opinión entre las demandas de los líderes negros, con su separatismo nacional, cuyas raíces son extranjeras a la cultura puertorriqueña."[50]

The implications of Ramos's arguments were that the forces and ideals of both African-American and Puerto Rican nationalism (i.e., Puerto Rican independence) supported by Latino prisoner leaders throughout the state and groups such as the YLP, with whom they identified, were foreign to the Latina(o) community. In an attempt to substantiate the validity of his comments, Ramos met with Latino prisoners at Attica after the Rebellion.[51]

The opinion that the goals of Puerto Ricans and African-Americans inside and outside the prison were somehow divergent, was supported by Latina(o) journalists such as Luisa A. Quintero of *El Diario*. Quintero argued that:

Como dice bien el Asambleista Manuel Ramos del Bronx, hay muchas cosas envueltas en los motines de las instituciones penales, algunas de origen político, en los cuales los puertorriqueños no tienen el mismo problema que los negros. Pero los que se hayan unido a ellos en la revuelta y hayan participado en los trágicos acontecimientos, van a ser juzgados de la misma forma."[52]

Other Latino politicians such as Assemblyman Armando Montano (District 77 of the South Bronx) blamed the outside Latinos on the Negotiating Committee, for their inability to convince Governor Rockefeller to meet with them at Attica during the Rebellion.[53] Reporter Gonzálo Jusino, writing in *El Diario*, went as far as to condemn Latino legislators for having participated in the Negotiating Committee.

Lo que pasó en Attica tiene que conmover a toda persona sensible, pero entre las cosas que se indican como causas de la tragedia, piénsese que quizás la más acertada es la de que en esa penitenciería se pasó más tiempo de la cuenta parlamentando con los rebeldes. . . .

¿Qué iban a hacer a Attica nuestros legisladores puertorriqueños? ¿A servir de conciliadores? La gran cosa. ¿A conocer las condiciones en que funciona la penitenciaría? Para eso tienen tiempo de más sin necesidad de aprovechar el momento de la desgracia. ¿A poner en dificultad a un gobierno que no es de sus simpatías aunque sea su gobierno y deba ser respetado?

... Entre las penas impuestas a estos confinados no estaba el morir trágicamente por circunstancias que podrían haber creado una media docena de criminales endurecidos, por quien no ha de sentir compasión alguna el resto de la humanidad.

Nuestros legisladores puertorriqueños y todos los puertorriqueños que puedan representarnos pueden hacer la obra meritoria de mejorar las prisiones desde el sitial a donde los ha llevado el pueblo mejor que desde el seno del motín que generan grupos disociadores y truculentos.[54]

Congressman Herman Badillo responded to criticisms by downplaying statements made by Latino politicians who were not present at Attica during the Rebellion. He also criticized those who, like Governor Rockefeller, claimed without foundation that radicals on the outside had contributed to the outbreak of the Rebellion. He supported the statements by the YLP that Puerto Rican prisoners had actively and willingly participated in the revolt.[55] Furthermore, Badillo demanded the immediate implementation of prison reforms and the creation of an independent body to investigate the Attica events.[56] He joined other Puerto Rican community leaders in forming the Comité Puertorriqueño de Ayuda a Presos de Attica (Puerto Rican Committee in Support of Attica Prisoners) whose primary function was to press for the implementation of prison reforms.[57] Badillo also joined Senator Robert García and other outside members of the Negotiating Committee testifying before the McKay Commission and the Judiciary Committee of the United States House of Representatives. In his testimony, Badillo criticized the discriminatory treatment to which Latino prisoners were subjected in New York State penal institutions.

A veces, el tratamiento que sufren los presos hispanos no está lejos del que reciben ciertos animales . . . Los esfuerzos para la rehabilitación de los presos hispanos es casi nula, ya que no se hace esfuerzo alguno para comprender al ser humano y permitirle que se exprese en su idioma vernáculo. . . . Además, esto parece ser un patrón de discrimen contra estos presos y existe un claro sistema de castas dentro de Sing Sing, Green Haven, Great Meadow, Attica y otras instituciones penales . . . Por ejemplo . . . no se les permite escribir en español a sus familiares—aun cuando sus padres y demás familia no sepan inglés . . . La excusa que me dan es que no tienen personas hispanas para censurar la correspondencia y no veo indicación alguna de que traten de remediar este mal. Este es un problema que tiene fácil solución."[58]

Badillo and Milton Haynes's book, *A Bill of No Rights: Attica and the American Prison System*,[59] while not discussing the specific nature of Latino participation in the Rebellion, remains the only book written by a Latino that discusses the events at Attica and the 1970 New York City and upstate prison rebellions. Badillo's support of prisoners was also exemplified by his introduction of legislation known as the "Prisoners Rights Act," designed to protect the basic rights of prisoners.[60]

Other Latino politicians such as Robert García and Luis Nine (South Bronx), called for the hiring of more Latino and African-American guards and the implementation of penal reforms. García also visited state prisons to investigate the conditions encountered by Latino prisoners.[61] Nine indicated that the lack of bilingual personnel created communications problems particularly between Latino prisoners and guards and Latino prisoners and medical personnel.[62]

Members of the Latina(o) community also took part in a number of committees created to investigate the events surrounding the Attica Rebellion and the conditions found in the state's prisons. For example, Louis Nuñez, National Executive Director of ASPIRA Inc., became one of the five members of the Goldman Panel, a "citizen's group which monitored the prison after the riot."[63] Amalia R. Guerrero, president of the Society of Friends of Puerto Rico, became one of the nine members of the New York State Special Commission on Attica (i.e., the McKay Commission), a "citizens committee" to investigate "the events leading up to, during and following the riot."[64] In addition, Robert García and Angel M. Rivera, regional director of the Office of Economic Opportunity, became two of the fifteen members of the Jones Committee. The Jones Committee was responsible for making recommendations to the governor on how to improve the state's penal system.[65] Other Latinas(os) were hired by these investigative bodies as clerical personnel, consultants, translators, and/or investigators responsible for interviewing Latino prisoners.[66]

In spite of Latino participation in these committees, the concerns of Latino prisoners were seldom addressed adequately. For example, Paul Roldán, chief investigator for the McKay Commission, resigned from the Commission claiming that the public hearings it held had ignored the needs and concerns of Latino prisoners. Roldán claimed that none of the Latino prisoners he interviewed over a period of three months had been given the opportunity to testify before the Commission.[67] Moreover, the request by Latino prisoners to be represented by Spanish-speaking Latina(o) attorneys seems to have been only minimally addressed.[68]

One of the most disturbing reactions to the Attica Rebellion within the Latina(o) community was the coverage offered by *El Diario* during the four days of the Rebellion. Coverage of the Attica Rebellion tended to portray prisoners as inherently violent because of their status as convicts: "Los presos, todos criminales convictos, se amotinaron el jueves. Hirieron a unos doce guardias, tomaron rehenes e incendiaron tres edificios."[69] Guards were portrayed as "victims" of prisoners' wrath.[70]

While reporters for the newspaper mentioned that Latino prisoners were involved in the Rebellion, at least one important photograph tended to highlight the participation of African-American prisoners demanding "Black Power."[71] This contributed to the erroneous impression that the Rebellion had been a "Black" affair. Moreover, of the thirty-three demands made by prisoners, the one El Diario chose to highlight was the one considered the most politically extremist: the demand for prisoners who wanted to leave the country to be allowed to go to a non-imperialist nation.[72] Hence, from the beginning, the paper's coverage downplayed prisoners' combined demands for reforms.

Furthermore, during the Rebellion, El Diario's coverage, like that of most of the English language newspapers, failed to question the veracity of the statements made by penal administrators.[73] On September 13, 1971, El Diario reported that guard William Quinn had died as a result of being thrown out of a second-story window.[74] On September 14, 1971, it reported that hostages had been brutally killed by prisoners: "Algunos de los rehenes fueron degollados. Otro murió de un tiro."[75] Both of these statements proved false. Even political progressives such as Luisa A. Quintero showed their political naiveté and biases by writing that: "El Comisionado Estatal de Corrección Russell Oswald, naturalmente siguió órdenes superiores cuando cesaron las negociaciones, pero se sabía que los rebeldes no iban a dejarse capturar sin arrebatar vidas."[76]

On September 14, 1971, El Diario published an editorial endorsing Governor Rockefeller's decision to retake the prison violently and endorsing his statements that the Rebellion had been planned by small groups of revolutionaries inside and outside the walls. The former, he argued, had committed grave acts of violence against the hostages. Governor Rockefeller's statements eventually took on an international slant when he declared before the McKay Commission that to have gone to Attica would have meant creating an international forum for political revolutionaries.[77] El Diario's initial endorsement of Governor Rockefeller stated:

> As Governor Rockefeller said: "The tragedy was brought on by the highly organized revolutionary tactics of militants who rejected all efforts at a peaceful settlement, forced a confrontation, and carried out cold-blooded killings they had threatened from the outset. . . ."

Attica is a prison of high security. Its inmates are dangerous criminals, repeaters, and many who are hard to handle. Their crimes put them in prison and they had no right to cast themselves as political prisoners by demanding that they should be sent to a "non-imperialist country," meaning Cuba or other Communist nation.

Our suspicion that the riots were promoted from the outside is evidently shared by Governor Rockefeller who said: "I have ordered a full investigation of all factors leading to this uprising, including the role that outside forces would appear to have played."

We are inclined to believe that political extremists are behind the riots, not only in our prisons but also in our colleges.[78]

El Diario's assertion that political extremists were creating chaos both in prisons and universities was repeated a few months after the Rebellion by Attica Warden Vincent Mancusi, who blamed the uprising on Marxist elements or elements of the extreme Left. "Definitivamente hay en nuestro país un movimiento para tumbar algunas de nuestras instituciones. Hemos visto esto en las universidades e instituciones penales para cuando fuera el momento propicio para golpear. No fue espontáneo. Estaban organizados para lograrlo . . ."[79]

Once it was revealed that the hostages had been killed by the state's police forces, *El Diario* continued to dwell on the theme that the Rebellion had been planned by Puerto Rican and African-American militants.[80] The paper supported the Governor's argument that visiting the institution during the Rebellion to meet with the Negotiating Committee would have looked like "el derrumbamiento de la ley y el orden."[81] It was not until the release of the McKay Commission's report that an editorial in *El Diario* recognized the validity of prisoners' grievances and the manner in which prisoners' rights had been violated.

It has been clearly established that the basic rights of the prisoners at Attica were ignored prior to, as well as during and after the disturbances. Among other important revelations, the McKay Commission reported that conditions inside Attica which led to the prisoners' revolt were dehumanizing, debasing and volatile almost to the point of inevitable conflict. Thus, this distinguished panel has affirmed the belief held by a great many that the Attica riot represented a desperate attempt by some of the more than 1,200 inmates to achieve a decent standard of survival and to secure basic rights of human dignity and just treatment.[82]

Ironically, this recognition also came after DOCS had begun to institute some of the reforms demanded by prisoners and their supporters. Outside Latina(o) community reaction to events at Attica was additionally apparent in the support given Latino prisoners by family members, friends, and grassroots community organizations. Such support had been apparent during the four days of the Rebellion, when supporters of both prisoners and hostages gathered outside the prison awaiting the final outcome. Once the Rebellion was quelled, family members participated in demonstrations organized by YLP and other progressive groups protesting what became known as the "Attica Massacre."[83]

Family members also forwarded the letters of imprisoned relatives to the Latina(o) news media and visited newspaper offices in an attempt to force coverage of problems encountered by kin.[84] These letters described the treatment to which prisoners were subject during and following the takeover of the institution. As one letter stated:

> A mí me han pegado un tiro en una pierna y me han dado una golpiza que ni yo mismo me reconozco. Leonor, yo quisiera que tú trates de venir aquí y que traigas a un abogado contigo para que demandes a esta prisión, porque aquí lo que hay es un abuso contra los presos. Por favor hazlo lo más pronto posible. Nos tienen encerrados todo el día y no nos dejan salir de la celda y yo con ésta pierna que ni la puedo mover.[85]

Another letter indicated that:

> ". . . los paquetes con ropa llegan a su destinación, pero los encargados de tramitarlos hasta nosotros, como en el caso mío, quieren hacernos firmar que nosotros reusamos aceptar algunos artículos en los mismos. . . ."

> Puntualizando, Héctor Manuel nos señala, en la carta que nos trae a la redacción de *El Diario-La Prensa* la autora de sus días, que le negaron entregarle unas botas color verde y unos "pantaloncillos" de rayas del último envío que le hicieron de su casa . . . como en su caso existen otros tantísimos que se encuentran impedidos de recibir frazadas, ropa de cama, etc., por el capricho de los guardias de dicho penal de Attica."[86]

When on December 18, 1972, thirty-seven prisoners, including William Ortiz, were indicted by a grand jury[87] for events occurring during the Attica Rebellion, family members joined Latina(o) organizations such as the Puerto Rican Socialist Party, El Comité, and El Comité de Solidaridad con los Reclusos to picket the offices of Governor Rockefeller.[88]

In conclusion, the reaction of the outside Latina(o) community to the Attica Rebellion varied depending upon political orientation and personal affiliations with Latino prisoners. On the one hand, *El Diario* and Latino politicians, supportive of the status quo, backed the actions of Commissioner Oswald and Governor Rockefeller and blamed the Rebellion on radical agitators inside and outside the prisons. On the other hand, liberal politicians, progressive community activists, and/or family members criticized the state's actions and pressured state elites to carry out much needed reforms as well as grant prisoners' demands for amnesty. The response of state elites to these conflicting interests was a combination of repression and reforms, aimed at reducing support for prisoners and their supporters outside the walls.

Reforms: The Other Side of Repression

During and immediately following the Rebellion, prisoners at Attica were beaten and tortured by guards, kept in segregation for long periods of time, and transferred to other state facilities.[89] Numerous prisoners were indicted for their participation in the revolt. At least six of the fifty-one prisoners held in segregation on suspicion of having helped plan the Rebellion were Puerto Rican.[90] However, according to Louis Nuñez of the Goldman Panel, not all Latinos held in segregation could have been leaders in the Rebellion because some of them barely knew how to speak English.[91]

Latino prisoners at Attica responded to such reprisals by writing letters and/or petitions to family members, politicians,[92] newspapers, and prisoners' rights newsletters exposing what was taking place at the facility. At least one Latino prisoner leader, Mariano González, joined African-American and white prisoners to file an injunction to stop the mistreatment of prisoners following the Rebellion.[93] Prisoners efforts were supported by the newly created Attica Brothers Legal Defense Fund (ABLDF). Other Latino prisoners subsequently joined a class action suit demanding, among other things, redress for injuries incurred during the Rebellion.[94]

The state's indiscriminate actions against Latino prisoners (and their African-American and white peers) can be better understood if they are interpreted as attempts to coerce the former into compliance.

Governor Rockefeller and Commissioner Oswald's decision, as well as the support they received from numerous local, state, and federal elites following the takeover, were designed to send a clear message to prisoners nationwide that collective reform-oriented efforts would be met with harsh repression at the hand of state elites. The concern about prisoner activism among political elites across the country had intensified as of 1968 when prisoners in California's San Quentin penitentiary had demonstrated they could join together, despite multiple cleavages, to demand reforms.[95] Disturbing to state elites was the fact that these actions were organized with the support of progressive and radical forces in the outside community, some of whom, like the Young Lords Party, the Black Panther Party, and the Weather Underground, backed their verbal support with more militant action.[96] Thus, the state's actions against Latino prisoners must be placed within a historical context in which political elites across the country, overwhelmed by demands for reforms from diverse sectors of the population, had become increasingly concerned with reducing support for prisoners and radical ideologies inside and outside the walls. Within this context, the ability of Latino prisoner leaders to play a mediating role between various sectors of the prisoner population gained additional importance.

Ultimately, the response of state elites to prisoners' demands for reforms was based on the recognition, shared by radical political prisoners and their New Left allies,[97] that prisons were one of the most important arenas in which the struggle between state elites and subordinate social groups was being waged. For prisons contained people who had dared, in one form or another, to challenge the status quo. It should, therefore, not come as a surprise that President Nixon also supported Governor Rockefeller and Commissioner Oswald's decision to retake the prison by force.[98] For if prisoners could organize, unite, and mobilize outside support to pressure state elites to redefine the conditions of their imprisonment, how much more would subordinate groups on the outside be able to achieve if they put their energies into forming alliances and challenging the status quo? Hence, the actions of local, federal, and state elites to reduce prisoner political activism should be seen as coincident with those taken by state elites to reduce political activism within the population at large. Ironically, imprisonment was one way state elites sought to deter outside political activism.

Another way state elites sought to reduce both prison activism and outside support for prisoners, was by carrying out a number of penal reforms (to be discussed further in parts 2 and 3 of this book). The calls for change came as much from prisoners and their advocates as from custody-oriented sectors. According to Oswald, ". . . we needed a meeting of the minds. The national debate was getting to us and we were under intense pressure."[99] As discussed earlier, one of the responses of political elites had been to create numerous local, state, and federal commissions and investigative committees to study the state's penal institutions. Additionally, between September 1971 and February 1972, almost one hundred prison reform bills were introduced in the New York State Legislature.[100] On May 23, 1972, eight prison reform bills, totalling 12 million dollars, were endorsed by Commissioner Oswald and signed into law by Governor Rockefeller.[101] Ironically, many of these changes did not require legislative action or the expenditure of significant amounts of money by the state.[102] In fact, DOCS had already begun to implement some of the reforms before the bills were signed into law.[103]

With the signing of the bills, however, state elites sought to accomplish several goals. For one, by "rubber stamping" actions already being undertaken by DOCS, both the governor and the legislature reinforced their support for the initiatives undertaken by penal administrators. Secondly, state authorities hoped to reduce prisoners' claims of deplorable prison conditions and outside support for such claims. Legislative action also seems to have been motivated by the desire, among some sectors of the state, to take the initiative for reform efforts away from prisoners and their supporters. State Senate Majority Leader Earl Brydges stressed that the government must not be seen as instituting new prison programs in response to prisoners' demands during the Rebellion.

> It was important, he felt, to separate the immediate needs of the cri-
> sis—and the longer-term needs of our prison programs. He was very
> concerned that if new programs were seen to be the result of the Attica
> uprising, then "people will say the action by the inmates was justi-
> fied." There would be an apparent incentive for new disturbances.[104]

The new legislation was only partially successful in achieving this last goal, as many of the reforms were clearly responses to prisoners' demands at Attica.[105]

Lastly, the legislation sought to satisfy the demands of the guards' union for additional resources and more stringent security measures. Nevertheless, custody-oriented sectors continued to resist reforms tailored to meet prisoners' demands arguing that they curtailed the power guards could exert over prisoners, allowed prisoners greater mobility within the institution, and increased the access of reform-oriented elements to state prisons.

As demonstrated in this chapter, Latino prisoners formed a small but significant component of prisoners participating in the September 1971 Attica Prison Rebellion. The presence of Latino prisoners made itself felt in the events preceding the Rebellion, in the takeover of the institution, the formulation of demands, the formation of the negotiating committee, and the ensuing negotiations. Most importantly, Latino prisoner leaders, identified with the YLP, played a vital role in helping maintain the overall unity of the prisoner coalition during the uprising.

While Latino prisoner leaders originally demanded and obtained the inclusion in the Negotiating Committee of members of grassroots organizations known to be supportive of prisoners' struggles (e.g., YLP), it was the actions of mainstream Latino politicians, invited by government elites to form part of the Negotiating Committee, that received the most attention in the mass media. The role played by the latter was an ambivalent one. On the one hand, they were asked to participate in the Negotiating Committee because they were mainstream politicians supportive of the status quo. On the other hand, they criticized harshly the state's penal policies and actions during the Rebellion.

The reaction of the outside Latina(o) community to the role played by Latino prisoners and outside Latino negotiators during the Rebellion was conditioned by personal rivalries and political ideology, and the nature of the relationship community members had with Latino prisoners prior to the Rebellion. Thus, while some supported both Latino prisoner participation in the Rebellion and the involvement of outside Latino Negotiators, others condemned the participation of both.

Following the Attica Rebellion, the state continued to pursue its combined tactic of repression and reforms in its attempt to reduce both prisoner unrest and prisoner activism.[106] State elites also sought to take the initiative for prison reform efforts away from prisoners and their advocates. The ultimate aim was to weaken prisoners' ability to organize and form coalitions inside and outside the walls.

It is the impact state policies had on Latina(o) prisoner discontent and the manner in which Latina(o) prisoners and their allies sought to attain concessions from the penal bureaucracy that will be discussed in the two case studies examined in parts 2 and 3 of this book.

In addressing these issues the case studies will primarily explore the types of groups Latina and Latino prisoners organized, the goals, tactics, and strategies they pursued, as well as the ways in which they sought to mobilize penal and third party sources of support. The questions guiding the chapters are: How effective was the state's tactic of combining repression and reform in curbing Latina(o) prisoner discontent and activism following the Attica Rebellion? What were the constraints under which third parties and penal personnel sought to provide support? How did notions of gender affect the support given Latina and Latino prisoners? Under what conditions were Latinas(os) able to win concessions from penal elites?

Notes: Chapter 3

1. For a discussion of diverse issues confronted by non-English speaking Latinos, see Louis Nuñez, "Rights of Spanish-Speaking Minorities," *American Journal of Correction* 34 (November/December 1972): 24. Latinos were not the only ones affected by the lack of translators. On September 13, 1973, Jonnie Barnes filed a lawsuit claiming that his son, a Haitian prisoner killed during the Rebellion, had not been given adequate notification of prison authorities' intention of assaulting the institution because he did not speak English (*New York Times* [hereafter cited as *N.Y. Times*], 13 September 1973, 57). It should be noted, however, that during the beginning of the assault state authorities also failed to adequately instruct English-speaking prisoners what was expected of them.

2. The number of prisoners involved in the Rebellion was 1,281 (New York State Special Commission on Attica [hereafter cited as NYSSCA], *Attica: The Official Report of the New York State Special Commission on Attica* [New York: Bantam Books, Inc., 1972], 194).

3. "Dice Usaron Rifles GN Sin Permiso Attica," *El Diario-LaPrensa* [hereafter cited as *El Diario*], 26 abril 1972, 12, 36; and "Alcaide Iba a Renunciar a Favor Rehenes de Attica," *El Diario*, 28 abril 1972, 8.

4. See NYSSCA, *Attica*, 496–506 for a list of the names of those killed. The five Latino prisoners killed were Raymond Rivera, Santiago Santos, Rafael Vázquez, José Mentijo, and Carlos Prescott (Mike A. Correa, "Boricua Renuncia de la Comisión Sobre Attica," *El Diario*, 30 abril 1972, 4, 47). At least one source also identified Michael Privitiera, a prisoner killed by peers during the Rebellion, as Latino.

5. NYSSCA, *Attica*, 251–257. See Appendix E for a complete list of the Attica prisoners' demands.

6. See Appendix D for a list of the Folsom prisoners' demands.

7. General demands dealt with: medical services; the quality of food; religious freedom; censorship; visiting policies; use of prisoner funds; prisoner wages; work release programs; greater access to educational and other rehabilitation programs; reduction of cell time; conditional release and parole regulations; availability of legal assistance; disciplinary procedures; training of guards; the right of prisoners to form groups and to engage in political activity; inmate grievance procedures; removal of the warden; and amnesty for prison rebels (NYSSCA, *Attica*, 251–257).

8. Demand 26 read: "Arrange flights out of this country to non-imperialist nations for those inmates desiring to leave this country" (NYSSCA, *Attica*, 255).

9. NYSSCA, *Attica*, 254–255. At the time of the Rebellion, 54 percent of the 2,243 prisoners at Attica were classified as African-American, 9 percent as Puerto Rican, and 37 percent as white. The only persons of color employed at the institution were a Puerto Rican guard and an African-American civilian teacher. At the time there were 500 security and civilian employees, twenty-eight of them women secretaries (Ibid., 28).

10. It is important to note that the much discussed practice whereby prisoners segregated themselves according to race and ethnicity was, in fact, preceded by de facto legal segregation. Once segregation in penal institutions was partially outlawed by the Supreme Court's *Lee v. Washington* decision, 390 U.S. 333, 334 (1968), prison authorities continued to encourage racial and ethnic divisions among prisoners. See Christopher R. Adamson, "Punishment After Slavery: Southern State Penal Systems, 1865–1890," *Social Problems* 3, No. 5 (June 1983): 555–569; The Editors of RAMPARTS Magazine and Frank Browning, eds., *Prison Life: A Study of the Explosive Conditions in America's Prisons* (New York: Harpers Colophon Books, 1972); Francis A.J. Ianni, *Black Mafia: Ethnic Succession in Organized Crime* (New York: Simon and Schuster, 1974); and NYSSCA, *Attica*, 1972.

11. NYSSCA, *Attica*, 4.

12. Pedro J. Linares, "Relata Condiciones de Vida a Que Someten Presos en Attica," *El Diario*, 19 septiembre 1971, 10, 44. Author's translation: "In Attica, if they discover a Puerto Rican speaking in Spanish, they punish him. They force them to speak in English because the guards don't understand Spanish. Correspondence is very bad. Many letters do not arrive . . . They confiscate letters written in Spanish, they do not mail them . . . Last November Victor Ortiz suffered for five months with chest problems. After protesting they took him to the prison hospital where he died of a cardiac condition. If they had treated him on time, Victor would be alive today . . ."

13. NYSSCA, *Attica*, 194. In addition, prison rebels "were slightly younger, had a slightly lower level of education, and included higher percentages of men from urban areas and recent arrivals into the prison system, than the overall population of the institution" (Ibid.).

14. The Young Lords was a Puerto Rican youth gang in Chicago, which in January 1969, became the "Young Lords Organization," a "revolutionary political party" (Central Committee, Young Lords Party, "Editorial," *Palante* 2, No. 4 [5 June 1970]: 11). A chapter of the organization was founded in New York in July of 1969. Its 13 point program advocated: self-determination for Puerto Ricans and all other Latinas(os), including independence for Puerto Rico; liberation of all Third World People; "true education of our creole culture and Spanish language"; "community control of our institutions and land"; freedom for all political prisoners; equality for women; fighting anti-communism with internationalism; armed self-defense and armed struggle as the only means to liberation; and socialism. It opposed racism, "the amerikkkan military," and "capitalists and alliances with traitors" (Young Lords Organization, "13 Point Program and Platform, Young Lords Organization, October 1969," *Palante: Latin Revolutionary News Service* 2, No. 2 [8 May 1970]: 19). In May 1970, the New York branch split from the Chicago national office and became the Young Lords Party (Central Committee, Young Lords Party, "Editorial," *Palante* 2, No. 4 [5 June 1970]: 11). Young Lords Party affiliates also formed in cities such as Philadelphia, Newark, and Connecticut. See "Young Lords in Philadelphia," *Palante* 2, No. 10 (28 August 1970): 10; Wilfredo Rolón, "Newark Rent Strike," *Palante* 2, No. 15 (20 November 1970): 17; and Bridgeport Branch, Young Lords Party, "Desayuno Gratis en Bridgeport," *Palante* 2, No. 17 (December 1970): 22.

15. NYSSCA, *Attica,* 107.

16. Angel Gear, [pseud.], interview with author, New York, N.Y., April 8, 1993. The *New York Times* described the People's Party as being a "loose coalition of former Black Panthers, Young Lords, and radical group members" (John Darnton, "Clash Among Inmates Reported at Green Haven State Prison," *N.Y. Times,* 16 September 1972, 13; and Idem, "Security is Tight at Green Haven," *N.Y. Times,* 17 September 1972, 21).

17. NYSSCA, *Attica,* 139; and Tom Wicker, *A Time to Die* (New York: Quadrangle, 1975), 7.

18. Elmer Daniels [pseud.], interview with author, New York, N.Y., 15 and 16 April 1993; Gregorio Palma [pseud.], interview with author, New York, N.Y., 16 April and 1 May 1993; and Martín Sostre, interview with author, New York, N.Y., 24 May 1993.

19. Palma, interview with author, 1993.

20. Daniels, interview with author, 1993.

21. Gear, interview with author, 1993.

22. Sostre, interview with author, 1993.

23. Gear, interview with author, 1993.

24. Adam Turner [pseud.], interview with author, New York, N.Y., 25 June 1993.

25. Elizabeth Fink, interview with author, Brooklyn, N.Y., 20 March and 17 April 1993.

26. NYSSCA, *Attica,* 152.

27. Ibid., 154.

28. Ibid., 155–156.

29. Ibid., 198.

30. Ibid.

31. Turner, interview with author, 1993.

32. Ibid., 240.

33. Ibid., 205.

34. The Negotiating Committee was composed of "citizen observers" and state legislators. Members of the mass media were also present as observers. While in the NYSSCA report the civilians who participated in the negotiations between prisoners and DOCS personnel as well as others who merely "observed" the events taking place in the yard were referred to as the "Observers' Committee," in this text the former are referred to as the Negotiating Committee because they did, in fact, carry on negotiations between prisoners and state authorities (NYSSCA, *Attica,* 242–247, 250–257, 273–274, 277–278, 280, 315–317).

35. According to former Attica prisoner leader Adam Turner, three of the ten rebellion leaders were Latinos, six were African-American, and one white (Turner, interview with author, 1993). Acccrding to Oswald, two of the twelve prisoner leaders were Latinos, three were white, and seven were African-American (Russell G. Oswald, *Attica—My Story* [Garden City, N.Y.: Double Day and Co., Inc., 1972], 21–28). One other confidential source stated that there were at least five Latino prisoners who played significant roles during the Rebellion.

36. NYSSCA, *Attica,* 205.

37. Tom Soto was a Puerto Rican community activist who had participated in the building takeover at City College in New York (Wicker, *A Time to Die,* 71).

38. The Prisoners' Solidarity Committee was affiliated with Youth Against War and Fascism.

39. According to Badillo, he was asked by Governor Rockefeller, via his counsel, to go to Attica and "bring some Puerto Ricans from the Buffalo and Rochester area because, after Attica was settled, they would need people to remain with the problem on a continuing basis" (Herman Badillo and Milton Haynes, *A Bill of No Rights: Attica and the American Prison System* [New York: Outerbridge and Lazard, Inc., 1972], 53). Badillo reported that he was also asked to "select someone who could relate to the more radical prisoners"

(Ibid.). Badillo was unable to contact any Puerto Ricans in the Buffalo area but he did invite Robert García and Alfredo Matthew to go to Attica with him. According to the NYSSCA report, however, Badillo volunteered to go to Attica when a representative of the governor's office called him to ask "whom he might be able to recommend that would be acceptable to the Young Lords" (NYSSCA, *Attica,* 233). At the time, Badillo represented Congressional District 21 ("Triboro"), which included parts of the South Bronx, Astoria, and East Harlem in New York City.

40. BUILD had been summoned to Attica by Arthur Eve.

41. Luisa A. Quintero, "Badillo Dice Que Tratan de Evitar 'Una Matanza'," *El Diario,* 13 septiembre, 1971, 3, 29.

42. See Badillo and Haynes, *A Bill of No Rights,* 1972; Oswald, *Attica,* 1972; and Wicker, *A Time to Die,* 1975.

43. NYSSCA, *Attica,* 1972.

44. Wicker, *A Time to Die,* 153.

45. Badillo and Haynes, *A Bill of No Rights,* 82.

46. "Ramos Pide al Gobernador se Reuna con los Presos Boricuas," *El Diario,* 14 septiembre 1971, 3; and "Boricuas Fueron Obligados a Unirse al Motín: Ramos," *El Diario,* 19 septiembre 1971, 2.

47. Eurípides Ríos, "'Young Lords' Piden Amnistía Para Presos," *El Diario,* 16 septiembre 1971, 2. Author's translation: "Governor Rockefeller is using Assemblyman Ramos to create racial disunity by claiming that Puerto Ricans were not involved and that they were manipulated by the Blacks . . . this is not true because Puerto Ricans, like Blacks and whites, were united at Attica, and we are united now to protest against this massacre."

48. Pedro J. Linares, "Relata Condiciones de Vida a Que Someten Presos en Attica," *El Diario,* 19 septiembre 1971, 10. Author's translation: "One of the things that some politicians are saying is that what happened at Attica was organized by Blacks, which is not true. I was there. Everything was organized by Puerto Ricans, Blacks and whites. They had a Central Committee which gave the instructions. We spoke with a prisoner named Che Santos and we discussed the conditions, the demands, and the racism suffered by Puerto Ricans."

49. "Asambleista Ramos Culpa a Comunistas de Crear Motín," *El Diario,* 16 septiembre 1971, 2. Author's translation: "Badillo came to the prison representing radical forces which do not have the well-being of Puerto Ricans in their hearts . . . Badillo lend himself to act as a messenger and spokesperson for ideals that are foreign to Puerto Ricans, that do not have anything to do with our ambitions as American citizens."

50. Eurípides Ríos, "Asambleista Ríos Gestiona Protección Especial Para Presos Boricuas," *El Diario,* 13 septiembre 1971, 3. Author's translation:

"Assemblyman Ramos indicated 'that there exists confusion because of the demands of Black prisoners whose leaders do not represent the Puerto Rican sentiment . . .' Ramos continued saying that, 'the Puerto Rican people are interested in letting others understand that there exists a difference of opinion between the demands of the Black leaders, with their national separatism, whose roots are alien to the Puerto Rican culture'."

51. Cesar A. Marín, "Participación Boricua en Motín Attica Fue Mínima," *El Diario*, 26 septiembre 1971, 3. Ramos also asked family members to call him with information concerning the treatment received by imprisoned relatives at Attica, and he announced his intentions of creating the Asociación Defensora Hispanoamericana to inquire into the possibility of suing prison authorities for damages ("Boricuas Fueron Obligados a Unirse a Motín: Ramos," *El Diario*, 19 septiembre 1971, 2).

52. Luisa A. Quintero, "Marginalia," *El Diario*, 14 septiembre 1971, 16. Author's translation: "Like Assemblyman Manuel Ramos of the Bronx well says, there are a lot of things involved in the riots of penal institutions, some of them of political origin, in which Puerto Ricans do not have the same problems as Blacks. But those who joined them in the revolt and participated in the tragic events, are going to be judged in the same manner."

53. Cesar A. Marín, "Dice Comité es Tan Responsable Como Rocky," *El Diario*, 22 septiembre 1971, 4. Montano argued that Governor Rockefeller should have sought the input of the state legislature's Black and Puerto Rican Caucus, which had been reviewing prison issues for months (Ibid.).

54. Gonzálo Jusino, "Columna Sin Nombre," *El Diario*, 23 septiembre 1971, 28. Author's translation: "What happened at Attica has to move all sensible people, but of those things indicated as having caused the tragedy, one has to think that maybe the most accurate one is the fact that more time than necessary was spent in the penitentiary politicking with the rebels . . . What did our Puerto Rican legislators go to do at Attica? To serve as conciliators? Big deal. To learn about the manner in which the prison functioned? For that they have more than enough time without having to take advantage of a tragic moment. To put at jeopardy a government that they do not sympathize with even though it is their government and it should be respected? . . . The punishment imposed on prisoners did not include dying tragically due to circumstances that could have been created by a half dozen hardened criminals, for whom the rest of humanity should not feel any compassion. Our Puerto Rican legislators and all other Puerto Ricans who can represent us could do the meritorious task of bettering the prisons from the seat to which the people have elevated them rather than from within the bosom of the riot generated by isolated and belligerent groups."

55. "Creen Que Motín Fue Planeado Con Cinco Semanas de Anticipación," *El Diario*, 15 septiembre 1971, 3, 41.

56. "Badillo Pide Una Pesquiza Completa," *El Diario,* 15 septiembre 1971, 3, 41; and "Badillo Pide se Implementen Reformas en las Cárceles," *El Diario,* 16 septiembre 1971, 3, 39.

57. Luisa A. Quintero, "Crean Comité Ayuda Presos Boricuas," *El Diario,* 22 septiembre 1971, 3, 28.

58. Idem, "Tratan a Presos Hispanos Como Animales: Badillo," *El Diario,* 11 noviembre 1971, 2, 39. Author's translation: "Sometimes, the treatment suffered by Hispanic prisoners is not that far off from that given to certain animals . . . The efforts to rehabilitate Hispanic prisoners are almost nil, since there are no attempts to comprehend the human being and allow him to express himself in his vernacular tongue . . . In addition, there appears to be a pattern of discrimination against these prisoners and there exists a clear caste system at Sing Sing, Green Haven, Great Meadow, Attica and other penal institutions . . . For example . . . they are not allowed to write in Spanish to their families—even when their parents and other family members do not know English . . . The excuse they give me is that they do not have Hispanic persons to censor the correspondence and I do not see any indication that they are trying to correct this wrong. This is a problem which has an easy solution."

59. Badillo and Haynes, *A Bil, of No Rights,* 1972.

60. "Editorial: Attica Aftermath," *El Diario,* 20 septiembre 1972, 23.

61. Cesar A. Marín, "Senador García Investiga Quejas Presos Attica," *El Diario,* 6 enero 1972, 2; and "Presos Podrán Celebrar Descubrimiento de Pto. Rico," *El Diario,* 5 noviembre 1972, 10.

62. "Piden Más Guardias Boricuas y Negros en Prisión Attica," *El Diario,* 20 septiembre 1971, 3; and "Asambleista Nine Aboga por la Implementación de Reformas Penales," *El Diario,* 21 septiembre 1971, 2.

63. NYSSCA, *Attica,* 438. On September 14, 1971, Governor Rockefeller asked Justice Goldman, presiding Justice of the Appellate Division's Fourth Department, to create a citizens' panel to investigate continued charges of reprisals against prisoners committed by DOCS personnel following the retaking of Attica (Ibid., 463). The Goldman Panel was at Attica from mid-September until early November 1971. Its report was issued on November 15, 1971. For a brief summary of the Panel's findings see Ibid., 463–466.

64. Ibid., xxiv. NYSSCA began to conduct its investigations at Attica shortly after the Goldman Panel had left the institution. The work of the McKay Commission lasted from November 1971 until May 1972 (Ibid., 466).

65. Oswald, *Attica,* 339–340.

66. Luisa A. Quintero, "Comienza Hoy Vistas en N.Y. Sobre Caso Attica," *El Diario,* 17 abril 1972, 2; and "Murieron Más en Attica por Lentitud Autoridades," *El Diario,* 21 abril 1972, 4.

67. Mike A. Correa, "Boricua Renuncia de la Comisión Sobre Attica," *El Diario*, 30 abril 1972, 4, 47.

68. After the Rebellion, progressive Jewish and white prisoners' rights attorneys and community activists gathered under the umbrella of the Attica Brothers Legal Defense Fund. The ABLDF filed a number of class action suits and injunctions protesting the treatment prisoners received during and following the Rebellion. None of the attorneys in the ABLDF were Latinas(os) (Fink, interview with author, 1993). While the Colegio de Abogados Puertorriqueños supported the implementation of penal reforms at the city and state levels and created a subcommittee to discuss such issues, it is unclear if the subcommittee provided any direct collective assistance to Latino prisoners at Attica. It is also unclear why these Puerto Rican attorneys did not become part of the ABLDF. The subcommittee included attorneys: Miguel Hernández, George Batista, Emilio Gautier, Cesar Perales, Austin López, and Roberto Lebrón (Luisa A. Quintero, "Marginalia: Comité de Abogados Boricuas," *El Diario*, 4 octubre 1971, 16).

69. "Presos Amotinados Piden los Envíen a País 'No Imperialista'," *El Diario*, 12 septiembre 1971, 3, 52. Author's translation: "The prisoners, all convicted criminals, rioted on Thursday. They injured twelve guards, took hostages, and set three buildings on fire."

70. "Presos Desnudan y Golpean Guardias, 'Arrestan' a 43," *El Diario*, 10 septiembre 1971, 4; and James Peppard, "Guardias Toman Attica 40 Muertos," *El Diario*, 14 septiembre 1971, 3.

71. *El Diario*, 12 septiembre 1971, 3.

72. "Presos Amotinados Piden los Envíen a País 'No Imperialista'," *El Diario*, 12 septiembre 1971, 3, 52.

73. Badillo and Haynes, *A Bill of No Rights*, 1972.

74. "Rehusan Amnistía a Amotinados en Attica," *El Diario*, 13 septiembre 1971, 3.

75. James Peppard, "Guardias Toman Attica, 40 Muertos," *El Diario*, 14 septiembre 1971, 3, 30. Author's translation: "Some of the hostages were beheaded. One was shot to death."

76. Luisa A. Quintero, "Marginalia," *El Diario*, 14 septiembre 1971, 16. Author's translation: "State Commissioner of Correction Russell G. Oswald naturally followed his superior's orders when the negotiations ceased. But it was known that the rebels were not going to allow themselves to be captured without taking lives."

77. "Rocky Dice No Fue Attica por Evitar se Hiciera Política," *El Diario*, 1 mayo 1972, 2.

78. "Editorial: Tragedy at Attica," *El Diario*, 14 septiembre 1971, 17.

79. "Superintendente de Attica Dice Extremistas Inspiraron el Motín," *El Diario*, 1 diciembre 1971, 2, 40. Author's translation: "There is definitely a

movement in our country to bring down some of our institutions. We have seen this in the universities and penal institutions waiting for the right time to strike. It was not spontaneous. They were organized to achieve it . . ."

80. "Cree Que Motín Fue Planeado Con Cinco Semanas de Anticipación," *El Diario,* 15 septiembre 1971, 3.

81. "Piden Más Guardias Boricuas y Negros en Prisión Attica," *El Diario,* 20 septiembre 1971, 3. Author's translation: "The collapse of law and order."

82. "Editorial: Attica Aftermath," *El Diario,* 20 septiembre 1972, 23.

83. A march on Albany was organized by the People's Coalition for Peace, a grassroots umbrella organization composed of representatives from the women's movement, the lesbian and gay movement, Prisoners' Solidarity Committee, Students for a Democratic Society, family members, and others (Richard Phalon, "800 in Albany Protest Attica Assault," *N.Y. Times,* 24 September 1971, 26). Demonstrations were also held whenever Governor Rockefeller, Commissioner Oswald, and Warden Mancusi showed up at public events.

84. Luisa A. Quintero, "Badillo y Heuvel Preparan Plan en Pro de Boricuas," *El Diario,* 8 diciembre 1971, 4; and "Preso Boricua en Attica Cuenta Injusticias Cometidas," *El Diario,* 1 febrero 1972, 11.

85. Mariano González, "Boricua Confinado en Attica Dice Fue Baleado Pierna," *El Diario,* 3 octubre 1971, 4. Author's translation: "They shot me in the leg and they gave me such a beating that I don't even recognize myself. Leonor, I want you to try and come here and bring an attorney with you so that you can sue this prison, because what they have here is an abuse against the prisoners. Please do that as soon as possible. They have us locked up all day and they do not let us go out of our cells and I with this leg that I can't even move it."

86. "Preso Boricua en Attica Cuenta Injusticias Cometidas," *El Diario,* 1 febrero 1972, 11. Author's translation: "'. . . the packages containing clothing arrive at their destination but those in charge of delivering them to us, as in my case, want to force us to sign a paper saying that we refuse to accept some of the articles contained in them. . . .' Emphasizing his point, Hector Manuel tells us, in the letter that was brought to *El Diario* by his mother, that they refused to give him a pair of green boots and a pair of striped underwear that was included in the last package sent to him from his home . . . as in his case there are many others who are prevented from receiving blankets, bed sheets, etc., because of the caprice of the guards of the Attica prison."

87. The grand jury had been created on November 29, 1971, after Governor Rockefeller named Deputy Attorney General Robert E. Fischer, a former state trooper, to "conduct a broad investigation into the events before, during, and after the rebellion in the Attica Correctional Facility" (*N.Y. Times,* 16 September 1971, 1).

88. "Alega Inocencia Hispano Involucrado Motín Attica," *El Diario,* 21 diciembre 1972, 4. By January 1973, 61 prisoners had been indicted by the grand jury, among them Mariano González, charged with murdering another prisoner during the Rebellion ("Acusan 61 Reclusos Participaron Rebelión Attica Que Costó 43 Vidas," *El Diario,* 4 enero 1973, 4, 37).

89. Fink, interview with author, 1993; NYSSCA, *Attica,* 1972; and Turner, interview with author, 1993.

90. Oswald, *Attica,* 347. These included: Mariano ("Dalou") González, Tuco Wilson Sánchez, Armando Rodríguez, Juan Soto, William Ortiz, and Pedro Crispín.

91. Luisa A. Quintero, "Reinician Mañana Visitas Reclusos en Prisión de Attica," *El Diario,* 28 septiembre 1971, 2. According to Nuñez, there were forty-six prisoners in segregation when he conducted his investigations. Five of these were Puerto Rican. Two of the Latinos held in segregation, Mariano González and Juan Soto, had been identified by Commissioner Oswald as having been leaders in the Rebellion (Oswald, *Attica,* 28). However, while Oswald lists one of the Latinos as being Juan Soto, Nuñez lists his name as Francisco Soto (Ibid.).

92. Luisa A. Quintero, "Badillo y Heuvel Preparan Plan en Pro de Boricuas," *El Diario,* 8 diciembre 1971, 4; and Mario González, "Afirma Tratan Presos Attica 'Como Animales'," *El Diario,* 26 octubre 1971, 13.

93. "Tribunal Prohibe Maltrato a Presos de Attica," *El Diario,* 2 diciembre 1971, 2, 32; *Inmates of Attica Correctional Facility, Mariano Gonzáles, Peter Butler, Herbert X. Blyden, Richard Clark, Roger Champen, William Jackson, Ernest Holley, On Behalf Of Themselves And All Other Persons Similarly Situated v. Nelson Rockefeller, Governor of the State of New York, Russell G. Oswald, Commissioner of Corrections of the State of New York, Vincent Mancusi, Superintendent, Attica Correctional Facility, Robert E. Fischer, Deputy Attorney General, State of New York.* Argued November 5, 1971, decided December 1, 1971, before Judges Lumbard, Mansfield and Oakes. U.S. Court of Appeals for the Second Circuit (New York City) Nos. 284,334 (Badillo and Haynes, *A Bill of No Rights,* 185fn31; NYSSCA, *Attica,* 463).

94. Fink, interview with author, 1993.

95. See The Editors of RAMPARTS Magazine and Browning, *Prison Life,* 1972); and Angela Davis, Ruchell Magee, the Soledad Brothers, and Other Political Prisoners, *If They Come in the Morning,* (New York: New American Library, 1971); Oswald, *Attica,* 28–29; and Eric Cummins, *The Rise and Fall of California's Radical Prison Movement* (Stanford: Stanford University Press, 1994).

96. On September 17, 1971 the Weather Underground, a radical white urban guerrilla group, bombed DOCS offices in retaliation for its handling of

the Rebellion ("Records of Judge Censured in 1971 Ordered Disclosed," *N.Y. Times,* 10 June 1973, 31). On September 24, 1971, the State Capitol building had to be cleared due to a bomb scare (Oswald, *Attica,* 320).

97. See Davis et al., *If They Come in the Morning,* 1971.

98. "Nixon Apoya Decisión Rocky en el Motín," *El Diario,* 14 septiembre 1971, 3, 30. After the Attica Rebellion, the federal government also granted New York State additional funds to purchase more sophisticated weapons for its guards. See "Attica," *Midnight Special* 2, No. 1 (March 1972): 8.

99. Oswald, *Attica,* 333.

100. Some of these had been prepared with the assistance of the American Civil Liberties Union (Alfonso A. Narvaez, "Legislature Gets 11 More Bills on Prison Reform," *N.Y. Times,* 3 February 1972, 37).

101. Idem, "Prison Reform Measures Are Signed by Rockefeller," *N.Y. Times,* 24 May 1972, 27. For a more detailed discussion of the reforms carried out, see Barbara Lavin McEleney, *Correctional Reform in New York: The Rockefeller Years and Beyond* (Lanham, Md.: University Press of America, 1985).

102. Idem, "Legislature Gets 11 More Bills on Prison Reform," *N.Y. Times,* 3 February 1972, 37.

103. Robert E. Tomasson, "Changes Pledged for State Prisons," *N.Y. Times,* 6 September 1971, 23; and William E. Farrell, "State Panel Issues Its Proposals for Prison Reforms," *N.Y. Times,* 17 March 1972, 24.

104. Oswald, *Attica,* 338. The creation of the Select Committee on Correctional Institutions, known as the Jones Committee, by Governor Rockefeller was an example of how state elites sought to change the focus of reform efforts to the state. The committee was to make "a searching examination into the problems affecting our correctional system . . . [and] make recommendations for improvements in the system along with short- and long-term priorities" (Ibid., 339).

105. Robert E. Tomasson, "Changes Pledged for State Prisons," *N.Y. Times,* 6 September 1971, 23.

106. Following the Attica Rebellion, Latino, African-American, and white prisoners in New York City jails also continued to make their demands for changes felt. On June 5, 1972, prisoners at The Tombs organized a work stoppage demanding: minimum wage; better food and sanitary conditions; better medical care; more hours for recreation; the availability of full-time attorneys; an end to indeterminate sentences; an end to the segregation of political prisoners; the creation of a committee to act as a liaison between prisoners and penal personnel; and that criminal charges be filed against guards found to have brutalized prisoners. Agenor Castro responded to prisoners' complaints by saying that meals and medical services were adequate (Pedro J. Linares,

"Presos Plantean Demandas, Quieren Aumento de Sueldos," *El Diario,* 6 junio 1972, 2, 11). On July 10, 11, and 12, 1972, prisoners at the Queens House of Detention in Kew Gardens held a hunger strike protesting: their transfer from the Brooklyn House of Detention, which was located closer to their families; the opening of their legal mail by prison authorities; and their inability to freely walk through the institution. On the other hand, prisoners at the Bronx House of Detention complained of the poor quality of the food frequently infested with vermin. Agenor Castro responded to the latter by stating that prisoners awaiting trial had been provided with telephones from which they could call their families, friends, and attorneys (Idem, "Termina Huelga de Hambre en Cárceles de NY," *El Diario,* 13 julio 1972, 4).

PART II

LATINO PRISONERS:
GREEN HAVEN CORRECTIONAL FACILITY

4

Latino Prisoners and the Institutional Context for Reforms

Prison riots and rebellions take place in male and female, juvenile and adult, local, state, and federal institutions. They occur for different reasons and under different circumstances.[1] What takes place depends primarily on the conditions at the institution, the political consciousness of prisoners, outside political events, and the relationship between these. The response of penal administrators, some argued,[2] is based on the relationship they perceive exists between prisoner uprisings and prison reforms.[3] They believed that statewide reforms carried out in New York State after the September 1971 Attica Prison Rebellion were designed to subdue the state's male prisoner population. Moreover, the current text argues that the prison reforms carried out by state elites following the Rebellion (the "post-Attica Rebellion reforms" or "post-Attica reforms"), were designed to reduce prisoners' litigation successes as well as the support of prisoners' rights issues within the prisoner and non-prisoner population.

The use of both rebellion and litigation had become widespread prior to the Attica Rebellion. Ironically, the Attica Rebellion was preceded by a number of reforms instituted by DOCS Commissioner Oswald at Green Haven and other state facilities in hopes of reducing tensions and avoiding a major prison revolt. Oswald's actions were also motivated by the desire to avoid legislative and/or further court interference in penal affairs. Interference had been provoked previously by a series of class action suits filed by prisoners seeking to redress prison conditions. The pressure on penal administrators to change their policies was also the result of prisoners' political underground organizing on a scale unparalleled in penal history. The Attica Rebellion showed state elites that reform-oriented policies could no longer be ignored when formulating penal goals. Moreover, by bringing to light conditions encountered by prisoners, the Rebellion and the state's response to it motivated increasing numbers of community members and reform-oriented sectors of the state to respond to prisoners' calls for support.

The years immediately following the Attica Rebellion found custody-oriented sectors at Green Haven Correctional Facility making a number of concessions to prisoners and their supporters both inside and outside the penal establishment. These concessions, made possible by the ever present threat of another Attica Rebellion, were exemplified by the penal reforms of 1972. Although these concessions were complemented by a number of repressive actions on the part of state elites, they did lead to a general redefinition of the conditions of imprisonment. This is not to say that custodial interests lost their control over penal institutions, but that the manner in which such control was exerted had to be modified.[4]

The chapters in this part of the book will explore: the institutional arena in which Latino prisoners sought to have their concerns addressed; the various types of formal and informal groups and networks they created to achieve diverse goals; and the ways in which they sought to mobilize the support of penal personnel and third parties in the Latina(o) community between 1970 and 1987. Particular attention will be paid in the last two chapters to the manner in which penal and Latina(o) third party support affected the formulation of Latino prisoner goals and the tactics and strategies they used. The ultimate aim is to explore the conditions under which Latina(o) prisoners were able, even if only temporarily, to wrest concessions from their keepers amidst widespread resistance from custodial sectors.

Institutional Setting and Post-Attica Reforms

Green Haven Correctional Facility was opened in 1949 as the newest maximum security prison for men. The institution is located 70 miles north of New York City. It is the maximum security prison for men closest to the city. It covers 50 acres and is surrounded by a wall one mile long, thirty feet high and two feet thick at the top. It has twelve gun towers. Although the prison's normal capacity is 1,868 prisoners, between 1970 and 1986 it frequently surpassed that amount (see Table 7).

Between 1970 and 1987, the custodial (i.e., security) and civilian staff[5] at Green Haven was overwhelmingly white, male, and suburban. While in 1976, 36.8 percent of the staff was comprised of civilians, by 1986, civilians made up only 28.9 percent of institutional employees. Throughout the period studied, most of the prison's civilian employees were kitchen workers, clerical staff, supervisors of industrial classes or assignments, and administrators. A small number of civilians provided teaching, religious, medical, parole, and counselling services.

In 1972, as one of the statewide post-Attica Rebellion attempts to decentralize administrative responsibilities and underplay the role of security concerns, the post of Deputy Superintendent was replaced by three new positions: Deputy Superintendent of Programs, Deputy Superintendent of Security, and Deputy Superintendent of Administration.[6] Additionally, the position of Coordinator of Volunteer Services was created by a federal grant designed to help DOCS involve community volunteers in the prison system. In 1972, Green Haven also experienced a change in superintendents. Leon Vincent, a thirty-six-year veteran of corrections and deputy superintendent at Attica at the time of the Rebellion, was named superintendent at Green Haven when the former warden chose to resign rather than carry out the mandated post-Attica reforms.[7]

Reforms carried out at Green Haven and other state facilities, particularly between 1972 and 1973, were a direct response to demands raised by Attica prisoners. In fact, according to the *New York Times*, a year after the Rebellion, all but four of The 28 Points agreed to by Oswald during the negotiations had been, in some manner, addressed by DOCS.[8] Dress codes were liberalized. Screens separating prisoners from visitors were removed from the visiting room. Censorship of incoming mail was relaxed and mail regulations were revised. Prisoners were allowed to call family and friends collect twice a month. A legal library was opened as a result of a federal grant[9] and recreation was expanded with the opening of a gym in 1973. The boredom prisoners experienced during their daily fourteen hours' lockup was reduced by allowing tape players and typewriters in cells. Moreover, cell time was reduced by allowing a greater number of community volunteers to enter the facility and conduct a variety of programs.

In addition to these changes, in January 1972, a DOCS directive mandated the creation of Inmate Liaison Committees (ILCs) in all state facilities. The ILCs were instituted as a partial response to the demands by prisoners during the Attica Rebellion for the establishment of inmate grievance delegations that would meet with administrators to discuss prisoner grievances as well as "develop other procedures for community control of the institution."[10] The importance of the ILCs was that they were the first formal groups established after Attica to act as liaisons between prisoners and institutional administrators. Prisoners were expected to see the ILCs as legitimate organizations because their members were elected by the general population and had access to prison administrators. However, according to Commissioner Oswald:

> The committees will not deal with grievances of individual inmates or have administrative or disciplinary functions. . . . Their role will be to "advance practical and constructive suggestions for custodial, housekeeping and treatment programs in each facility as well as an interchange of information and suggestions about the facility situation between inmates and the administrator."[11]

As a result of these stipulations, soon after their creation, the ILCs lost their credibility because they did not have the power to force prison administrators to make changes. For example, between 1970 and 1987, administrators at Green Haven allowed the ILC to carry out polls regarding "movie selection and radio/TV programming,"[12] the quality of food in the mess hall, whether soda machines should have cups or cans, etc.[13] A former ILC representative imprisoned at Green Haven during the late 1970s responded to the question, "What Does the Inmate Liaison Committee Mean to You?" with:

> Not too much. Reason? Well, there is no discussion. If the staff feel that they don't want something they say "no." That's final, and that's it. There's no vote, no discussion. The name I.L.C. is in itself a lie, because who do they liaison [sic] with. What committee? The staff that are supposed to be there seldom show, and all they come to the meetings with is, "I'll check on it." I've seen it go from "we can, together . . ." to virtually non-existent. I've been on it a year. We never got on any big issues, just token ones."[14]

Under these circumstances, prisoners who formed part of the ILCs came to be looked upon with suspicion by their peers. As Gregorio Palma, a former Latino prisoner leader at Green Haven, explained, "The Liaison Committee was looked upon as a group of individuals who just did what the administration wanted. If you disagreed with the administration, you were shipped out. . . . The individuals that were there were entrenched, like maybe old politicians and, you know, they didn't always work in the best interest of the population."[15]

For some prisoners, participation in the ILC was merely a means by which they acquired additional privileges within the institution, such as greater access to staff members and increased mobility within the institution.[16]

As a result of the ILC's failure to effectively represent prisoners' collective interests, throughout the period studied prisoners continued to call for the creation of a representative prisoner body that would have the authority to meet with penal administrators, discuss collective grievances, and help design and implement penal policy. When prisoner discontent began to mount during the mid-1970s, the state responded in August 1975 with the creation of yet another administrative group designed to elicit widespread support among prisoners at Green Haven and other state facilities. These were the Inmate Grievance Resolution Committees (IGRCs).[17] The IGRCs, composed of guards and prisoners elected by their peers, were more respected than the ILCs because they had the ability to make decisions concerning a number of grievances submitted to them by prisoners. Moreover, prisoners could appeal the IGRC rulings "to the superintendent, to a central office review committee in Albany and, finally, to the Commission of Corrections."[18]

According to Palma, a former Latino representative to Green Haven's IGRC, one of the most common ways in which Latino prisoners sought to change the conditions of their imprisonment was by filing grievances with the IGRC. Nevertheless, the credibility of the IGRCs also suffered as prisoners frequently complained that they failed to resolve grievances satisfactorily. Palma explained, "You have a hearing and it's by an officer and a civilian . . . but you really don't get nothing major out of that. It's really just a . . . place where you can, you know, blow off some steam and think you did something . . ."[19] In spite of such complaints, Latino prisoners continued to file grievances. Those who did not read or write English frequently asked Latino IGRC representatives to translate their grievances for them. Others sought the assistance of their English-speaking counterparts by writing letters and complaining to administrative personnel.

The effectiveness of the IGRCs was also hampered by the fact that the committees had authority to handle only individual prisoner complaints. Prisoners were thus prevented from submitting collective grievances. Perhaps one of the most serious drawbacks of the IGRCs was that their existence hindered prisoners' litigation efforts. Prisoners could not turn to the courts until they had "'exhausted' their administrative appeals, including the grievance process where relevant."[20] Thus, it became easier for DOCS' personnel to thwart prisoner reform efforts as the former controlled the institutions and the very process from which prisoners were to seek redress.

While the creation of the IGRCs was resented by guards because it allowed prisoners to question their actions, a DOCS employee assigned to Green Haven's IGRC stated that, "A lot of trouble can be avoided using this as an escape valve to air problems and bring them to the attention of the administration."[21] Thus, as in the case of the ILCs, one of the primary functions of the IGRCs was to act as a "troubleshooter" by bringing problems to the attention of prison administrators before they led to collective disturbances and/or prisoner litigation. As a result of these limitations, both the ILCs and IGRCs left prisoners with no means of making collective demands on prison personnel other than through the informal and formal groups they created for such purposes. In the meantime, the custodial staff continued to resist any new policies which appeared to give prisoners greater power to determine the course of their lives while imprisoned.

Guard Resistance to Reforms

Custodial personnel, which had condemned Governor Rockefeller, Commissioner Oswald, and outside negotiators for bargaining with prisoners during the Attica Rebellion, resisted the implementation of reforms that they felt were designed to "coddle" hardcore criminals. Guard hostility was deepened by the fact that many of the reforms were seen as having been forced on security personnel by agencies outside the penal bureaucracy (e.g., legislature, executive branch, prisoner advocates) and by Oswald, an unpopular liberal penal administrator. Oswald, in fact, went as far as to state that one of the things which prevented his implementing all of The 28 Points at once was guard resistance to them. According to Oswald: ". . . if we had put all twenty-eight points into effect in all of our institutions right now, there would have been a great deal of trouble. 'There would have been riots,' I said. 'The staff is not ready for us yet, for another thing, the staff still look on us as lax and lenient'."[22] Guard opposition to reform translated into harassment of prisoners, civilian penal personnel, visitors, community members, and even DOCS administrators like Oswald.

The intensity of custodial resistance to post-Attica reforms was evident in late September 1971, when the guards' union, Council 82 of the American Federation of State County Municipal Employees (AFSCME), threatened to keeplock prisoners indefinitely unless union demands were met.[23] Weeks earlier, guards at Green Haven had organized a six-hour work slowdown protesting what they perceived was the lack of swiftness in freeing the Attica hostages.[24] Once again, in March of 1972, the guards' union voted to strike at Green Haven and three other male facilities if their demands for increased wages and reforms were not implemented.[25] The result of these threats was that Council 82 was able to secure increased monies for operating expenses, new guard positions, salary increases, renovation or construction of buildings, new riot equipment, and the expansion of the training course for guards.[26] In fact, over half of the $12 million allotted for penal reforms in 1972 was allocated to increase and train penal personnel.[27]

Custodial discontent with post-Attica reforms, judicial decisions, and DOCS central office directives was once again expressed in April of 1979 when "nearly all of New York State's prison guards . . . walked off the job at the state's thirty-three penal facilities."[28] According to James B. Jacobs, guards were reacting to a perceived erosion of their authority.

> . . . court decisions have weakened the guards' disciplinary prerogative. Judicial involvement in the prisons these days severely restricts the guards' use of physical sanctions, requiring that any use of force be accurately documented. Line officers' decisions are subject to repeated review and are frequently reversed or modified. The extension of due process to inmates charged with disciplinary infractions means that prisoners can challenge a guard's version of the "facts."[29]

Moreover, guards argued that increased rights and privileges accorded prisoners complicated their job by increasing prisoner movement within the facility. This change, they felt, multiplied opportunities for assaults, drug usage, and other rules violations. Equally important was the belief that the reforms signified public sympathy for prisoners and corresponding antipathy for guards.[30] Ironically, reforms aimed at increasing the number of Latino, African-American, and women guards throughout the state met with similar hostility from the predominantly white male rural custodial staff.

The Dynamics of Prejudice: White Male Guards Versus Women Guards and Staff of Color

In 1973, Green Haven received its first three women guards. By 1981, there were fifty women guards working at the facility, though they made up less than 10 percent of the guard force.[31] In October 1976, twenty bilingual (mostly Puerto Rican) and seventy-five African-American guards were employed at the facility.[32] This increase in the number of guards of color and the introduction of women guards into male facilities was the result of state and federal efforts to diversify the guard force.[33] Moreover, the hiring of more Latina(o) and African-

American guards was a response to yet another of the Attica demands: "Institute a program for the employment of significant numbers of black and Spanish-speaking officers."[34]

Both the hiring of women guards and guards of color was resented by the white custodial staff.[35] White guards were indignant about the fact that DOCS had changed its regulations[36] and physical qualifications[37] to make it easier for Latinos and women to apply for guard positions. Additionally, they presumed and resented the solidarity Latina(o) and African-American guards would feel toward prisoners of color.[38] Some white guards believed that if a crisis were to develop between prisoners and guards, Latina(o) and African-American guards would side with "their own." This suspicion was strengthened by the fact that Latina(o) guards and Latino prisoners shared a common language few staff members understood.[39] Moreover, according to Danny Vázquez, a former civilian administrator at Green Haven, white guards tended to assume that all Latinos were Puerto Ricans and that, "Not only are they tecatos and criminals . . . they're foreigners. . . . And they come here to get on welfare."[40] Such biases demonstrated both the extent of racism prevalent among the white custodial staff and ignored the preferential treatment white penal staff had historically accorded white prisoners.

The hostility of white guards towards their Latina(o) and African-American peers was further intensified by the fact that in 1974 a federal district judge ruled in favor of 117 Latina(o) and African-American guards throughout the state who argued that the examination for the sergeant position was discriminatory, resulting in a situation in which all of the 122 permanently assigned DOCS sergeants were white.[41]

White guard resentment toward women guards and staff of color took several forms. They filed litigation challenging the new state and federal hiring policies.[42] They openly and quite frequently made racist and sexist remarks in which women guards were called "girls,"[43] African-Americans "niggers," and Latinos "spiks." Male guard hostility to women guards was as extreme as the former trying to humiliate the latter in the presence of and/or with the participation of male prisoners.[44]

Moreover, white guards segregated themselves in the prison dining room and in other work-related social activities.[45] Racial/ethnic tensions resulting from white guard racism were also apparent within the guards' union. The response of Latina(o) and African-American guards to such treatment was to create the Minority Correctional Officers Association (MCOA). The MCOA sought to "fight discrimination within the union and the DOCS."[46] However, when Latina(o) and/or African-American employees organized to provide one another support and/or counter discriminatory treatment, their attempts were frequently met with further hostility from both peers and supervisors.

> Attempts by Hispanic employees to form fraternal organizations reportedly have resulted in reprimands from superiors or harassment in the form of stricter enforcement of work rules and inflexibility in work schedules. Many new Hispanic employees also complain that these tactics are used to "weed them out" during probationary periods.[47]

The hostility of white security personnel toward guards of color was demonstrated by the fact that during the late 1970s, an African-American prisoner reported that between 1973 and 1977, at the insistence of white prison officials, he had attempted to entrap African-American guards at three state prisons as well as discredit an African-American counsellor. These efforts included framing five African-American guards at Green Haven in 1977 at the request of a white lieutenant.[48]

The harassment encountered by women guards and Latina(o) custodial and civilian staff made them hesitant to continue working in such environments. Furthermore, it was difficult to attract and/or retain Latina(o) staff because facilities tended to be located in rural areas with little or no Latina(o) community.[49] In addition to the isolation they experienced in such settings, Latinas(os) had to contend with the prejudices of the predominantly white conservative rural townspeople.[50] As a result of these difficulties, and the fact that the salaries offered by DOCS could rarely compete with those offered in the private sector, there was a high turnover rate in the Latina(o) custodial and civilian staff.[51] Those who stayed were faced with constant job insecurity and, in the case of Latina(o) civilian staff, the resulting inability to design and implement long-term bilingual programs and services.

The ability of Latina(o) civilians to implement and supervise programs effectively was also handicapped by their having to fulfill a number of functions for which they had not been hired.

> Hispanic staff are so few in the institutions that none of them has the time to fully engage in his or her respective profession. A teacher has to double as an interpreter, a social worker as a counselor. A psychologist has to be a social worker, an ombudsman, an advisor and an advocate. These are results of (1) lack of coordination and supervision, and (2) lack of staff.[52]

Latino guards were also frequently expected to act as translators. In view of what has been discussed above and the fact that staff of color preferred to transfer to facilities near New York City where most of them lived, by August 1986, only 3 of the 632 security staff and 11 of the 257 civilian staff at Green Haven were Latina(o) and/or bilingual (see Table 8).

The behavior of white guards towards Latino staff tended to mirror their behavior toward Latino prisoners. Guards' attitudes towards the latter were also affected by the changes which took place in the composition of Green Haven's guard and prisoner population during the period studied.

White Guards, Latino Prisoners

Immediately after the Attica Rebellion, a significant number of African-American and Latino prisoners involved in the Rebellion were transferred to Green Haven. These prisoners were considered by guards as threatening to institutional security. Moreover, as a result of post-Attica Rebellion reforms, prisoner movement throughout the facility increased. In response to these changes, more experienced guards began to request assignments to duties or shifts with little or no contact with prisoners (e.g., construction or transportation officers, evening or night shifts, tower duty). Additionally, veteran guards used their seniority to transfer to newer facilities requiring less security.[53] This left the younger and least experienced officers with the most day-to-day contact with prisoners. In 1978, "more than a third of Green Haven's 700 officers and civilians were usually trainees fresh from the correction's academy . . ."[54] As Green Haven became one of the state's "training facilities" for new officers during the 1980s, guard turn-over rates further increased and so did guard/prisoner tensions.

These changes in the composition of the guard force were occurring at the same time that the prisoner population was itself changing. During the 1970–1987 period, a significant shift took take place in the ethnic/racial composition of the prisoner population. While on December 31, 1970, Latinos comprised 18.7 percent or 358 of all prisoners at Green Haven, by May 5, 1986, this number had increased to 582 or 28.0 percent (see Table 7).[55] These changes were offset by a decrease in both the percentage of African-American and white males imprisoned at Green Haven.

The tensions created by the lack of Latino staff and bilingual programs were reflected in the fact that as the number of Latino prisoners increased so did the number of verbal and physical confrontations between them and the white custodial force. During the 1980s, these tensions were aggravated by the fact that a large number of the Latinos imprisoned during the 1980s (e.g., Dominicans, Colombians, Mariel Cubans, Puerto Ricans), were Spanish-monolingual. Under these circumstances, communication between Latino prisoners and staff members became virtually impossible. Prisoners who spoke Spanish were frequently harassed and penalized by security personnel. In addition, because Spanish is a language often spoken with the accompanying use of hand gestures, there were times guards claimed Latinos had threatened them physically when in fact they had just been expressing anger and frustration.

Latino prisoners were further handicapped by the fact that until the late 1970s, the DOCS rule book was written only in English. Thus, they were frequently penalized for breaking rules of which they were not aware.[56] As late as March 1986, a report published by the Correctional Association of New York (CANY) indicated that, "In many facilities that we visited, departmental and institutional rules and regulations had not been translated into Spanish."[57] An added problem was the fact that, particularly during the 1970s, the rules were formulated not only by institutional and central office administrators, but by guards as well. As a result, rules could vary from guard to guard and from day to day. The problem was especially acute in institutions with a high staff turnover, such as Green Haven.[58]

Perhaps one of the most threatening aspects of white guard (and white civilian) racism was the fact that Latina(o) and African-American prisoners at Green Haven and other state facilities felt physically threatened by the presence of guards who were rumored to be or bragged about being members of the Ku Klux Klan (KKK).

Guards and the Ku Klux Klan (KKK)

The extent of white guard racism within New York State's penal system was evidenced by the fact that, particularly during the 1970s, guards were recruited on the job by the KKK.[59] In fact, KKK activity in the prisons was so serious that on September 3, 1975, DOCS Commissioner Benjamin Ward issued a directive indicating that security personnel who did not resign their affiliation with the KKK by October 1, 1975, would be dismissed.[60] The directive was challenged in court by a guard who had been fired for being a member of the KKK. The guard's case was supported by Council 82, the KKK, and the American Civil

Liberties Union (ACLU). In April 1979,[61] the New York State Court of Appeals declared the DOCS directive unconstitutional. According to the court: ". . . the Department of Correctional Services had failed to offer enough evidence to show that the 'claimed detrimental impact of employee membership in the Ku Klux Klan (or even the perception thereof by inmates) upon the operation of correctional facilities' justified the suspension of the guard."[62]

While KKK activity at Green Haven has not been the object of widespread publicity, as has occurred with other New York State prisons (e.g., Eastern Correctional Facility in Napanoch), ex-prisoners and staff members interviewed (who wish to remain anonymous) claimed that the facility had its share of KKK membership among guards during the 1970s and 1980s. Regarding guard harassment of prisoners of color, Gregorio Palma claimed that:

> Most of these white guys that would come after us like that, in groups, they were all Clansmen. You know, they wouldn't talk about it openly but you would get the word here and there that they were down with Ku Klux Klan. And they would rally against you, you know, and they would tell their buddies, "Hey, hassle this guy for me. He did this or he did that" or "I don't like him." So all kinds of things would happen to you.[63]

The presence of KKK members among the Green Haven security staff seems to have been based on more than just rumors. For example, a guard suspended from Eastern following a March 17, 1976 incident in which he wore a Klan uniform (sheet and hood) in the lobby of a cell block and, along with other guards, burned a paper cross, was subsequently transferred to Green Haven.[64] Moreover, during the spring of 1978, two sergeants suspected of KKK membership while working at Eastern (one of whose removal had been demanded by prisoners protesting KKK activity at the institution during an August 1977 rebellion), were also transferred to Green Haven.[65] In 1978, the "Frank Khali Abney Defense Committee" claimed that, "Just recently in Green Haven prison, a Black prisoner was burned to death while held in solitary confinement. Earlier, he had witnessed a meeting of prison guards suspected of Klan membership."[66]

In addition to white guard hostility, Latino prisoners had to confront discriminatory treatment from the mainly white civilian staff who, along with administrative and security personnel, were responsible for overseeing prison operations.

The Politics of Discrimination and Language

Many Latino prisoners faced discriminatory treatment from the moment they entered the facility and met with the "classification committee"[67] responsible for distributing work, educational, and program assignments. In 1976, work assignments were divided into the areas of: kitchen and mess hall; porters; clerks; maintenance (painters, plumbers, masons, electricians, carpenters, sewermen, repairmen); prison hospital (nurses and technicians); runners (messengers); tailor shop and laundry; officers' mess hall; prison industry (knit shop, upholstery shop, optical and furniture shops); academic school (basic math and English, high school English and history, some college), vocational school (printing, drafting, welding); prison band; outside assignments (farm, garage, driving tractors); and one-man jobs (cobbler, identification room technician, gardener). These assignments remained fairly stable throughout the period studied except for the fact that by the late 1980s Green Haven's primary industries included an auto body shop, but not the optical shop.[68] According Domingo Morales, a former Latino prisoner leader at Green Haven,

> "Green Haven had . . . a furniture shop where they make a lot of office supplies. It's Corcraft. It's a billion dollar industry that they only sell to all state agencies. All the office furniture that you see in all the state agencies and city agencies, they sell. They have like contracts for them, for computers, for beds, or file cabinets . . ."[69]

The primary goal of Green Haven's industries was to, "provide services to the facilities and to the state. On the facility level by providing work programs for prisoners and, on the state level, by providing products the state can use in a profitable and cost-saving manner."[70] In fact, by 1986, the industries were profitable enough that they were able to cover their own security costs.[71]

Both Latino and African-American prisoners, particularly during the 1970s, were at a disadvantage in relation to white prisoners in the prison job market. However, the fact that many Latinos had few or no English language skills further limited the range of jobs and educational and vocational programs to which they were assigned. As a result, it was not uncommon to see Latinos working in the lowest skilled work areas such as porters. A porter's responsibility was to, "maybe clean the yard or you'll stay in the blocks of the prison and clean the . . . blocks, keep the alleyways clean and the stairways clean and clean the toilet bowls, stuff like that, regular porter jobs."[72]

Even in cases where Latino prisoners were skilled workers and literate in English, it was customary for white staff members to assign white prisoners to the most desirable jobs. According to Gregorio Palma:

> ... there are some jobs they get priority, like warden's runner, hospital workers, plumbing. Plumbing is a very elite, usually all whites. ... They clique together. ... electricians is the same way. You know, these are skilled laborers that a lot of them had when they came to prison. A lot of us didn't have any types of training.[73]

The most desirable jobs included assignments which allowed greater access to administrative personnel, information, higher pay, and/or fringe benefits. Preferred assignments included working as runners and clerks because they allowed prisoners greater mobility within the institution and greater access to administrative personnel. Those who worked in the administration building and offices throughout the facility also had the greatest access to information, typewriters, photocopy equipment, and sometimes telephones. Fringe benefits included access to information, equipment, and goods that were normally either rationed or not easily accessible. For example, kitchen workers had greater access to food, commissary workers to supplies, laundry and knit shop workers to clothing. Those working in the furniture shop had access to wood. All of these, as shall be shown in chapter 5, were bartered for other goods and services.

Although by law, prisoners had a right to receive education up to the high school level, the lack of adequate bilingual programs prevented many Latinos from receiving such education during much of the 1970s. In January 1982 the bilingual education program consisted of: basic education; high school; English-as-a-Second Language (ESL); and Marist College's one-year bilingual program, which began in the fall of 1979.[74] At that time there were over 500 Latinos in the facility.[75] During 1983, a Spanish language component was added to the Literacy Volunteer Program.[76] In March 1988, there were still no bilingual instructors in the vocational school.[77]

Additionally, many Latinos who spoke or read some English, but did not meet the grade 8.0 English reading level required by some instructors, were prevented from participating in educational and vocational courses and rehabilitation programs. Confronted with this situation and the fact that prisoners who attended school were paid less than those employed in industry,[78] most Latinos, when given a choice, opted for industrial assignments rather than educational or vocational programs. During the 1980s, this basically meant working in the furniture shop. At the end of 1987, Latino prisoners working in industry were still forbidden to speak Spanish during work assignments, even if that was the only language they knew.

Despite the fact that Latino prisoners were not responsible for penal policies limiting their access to bilingual programs, their lack of participation in programs created a disadvantage when they appeared before the Parole Board. The Board judged a prisoner's rehabilitation on the basis of program participation, especially school attendance. As Domingo Morales stated, "You gonna need programs . . . if you have a drug beef you're going to need a drug program. If you got a violent crime you're going to need 'Alternative to Violence.' You know, those are things that they're going to look at."[79]

One other major area in which the lack of bilingual services and staff persons was most severely felt was medical care.[80] In 1976, Green Haven had three doctors, seven nurses, two dentists, one pharmacist, and several part-time psychiatrists for a total of 1,855 prisoners.[81] None of them were Spanish-speaking. There was also the problem that many Latino immigrants suffered from tropical diseases, the diagnoses and cures for which were little known by doctors in the area. The lack of bilingual medical staff and insufficient medical knowledge prevented many Latinos from getting even the minimal medical treatment afforded prisoners by law. These limitations resulted in unnecessary physical hardships and even deaths of Latinos. In those cases where other Latino prisoners or non-medical personnel were used as translators, the privacy of patients was seriously compromised.

The need for bilingual medical personnel became more acute as the number of Latino prisoners diagnosed with Human Immunodeficiency Virus (HIV) and Acquired Immune Deficiency Syndrome (AIDS) increased during the 1980s. The high percentage of AIDS death among Latinos in the state's prisons was due primarily to the high number of Latino prisoners with a history of intravenous drug use, as well as HIV transmission through sexual activity between prisoners.[82] In spite of the large number of prisoners with HIV/AIDS, DOCS carried out few educational efforts concerning the disease.[83] The fact that DOCS refused to distribute condoms among its prisoner population and, until 1988, had not instituted permanent educational or training programs about HIV/AIDS within its prisons, also contributed to the transmission of HIV. The few educational programs, commonly initiated by individual staff members and/or prisoners, which were offered during the late 1980s, were generally conducted in English.

The lack of bilingual personnel affected Latino prisoners in other ways. Until November 1970, English was the only acceptable language for correspondence. After that date, prisoners were allowed to receive incoming mail in a foreign language. However, outgoing mail had to be written in English. This meant that prisoners not literate in English had to get other prisoners to translate their letters before they could mail them out. Incoming mail in Spanish was censored by bilingual staff members, when available, or by other prisoners.[84] Both of these stipulations compromised a prisoner's right to privacy.

Although access to the mass media in the form of television, radio, and reading material was limited to all prisoners, those with limited or no English language skills were most affected. Radio and television stations accessible through institutional channels were predominantly English-speaking. And while few of the books in the general prison library were in Spanish, none of the books in the law library were in Spanish.

The difficulties created by the lack of available legal material in Spanish were compounded by the lack of bilingual personnel in the law library. None of the twelve employees in Green Haven's prison library at the beginning of 1982 were bilingual.[85] Moreover, although the law library had been established in 1972, it was not until February 1982 that the first bilingual law class was taught, and then by a Latino prisoner.[86] The impact of this situation was twofold. While a number of prisoners (e.g., Martín Sostre) used their acquired legal knowledge to litigate for changes in prison conditions, the greater number used litigation to challenge the legal proceedings which led to their own incarceration (e.g., arrest and/or trial procedures). "A lot of them . . . felt that they got hung in court because they didn't speak English. The interpreters didn't speak their language and they got railroaded. . . . They would say one thing to the attorney and the attorney would do something else, would not mention certain things in their defense."[87] Consequently, Latino prisoners lacking access to Spanish legal materials and bilingual legal personnel were prevented from using the courts either to solicit a review of their individual cases or to challenge prison policies. Asked if Latino prisoners resorted to filing class action suits to redress their grievances during the 1980s, Palma responded:

> You don't hear class action anymore. You see, the Latinos of the seventies were more bilingual and were more acclimated to the system and knew how to write. You had a lot of legal minds. Not to say that

you don't have some legal minds today, but by and large, you have a lot of Latinos that are not bilingual. You have a growing majority of Latinos that are monolingual immigrants who don't feel they have any rights and don't want to start too much of a beef because . . . when they're finishing up their bids they're rounded up and put into one of these holding pen prisons, like Fishkill. That's for immigrants and then they're carted off to immigration and deported.[88]

The few Latino jailhouse lawyers and Latino clerks working in the prison's law library as of the mid-1980s primarily helped Latinos file motions and contact attorneys concerning individual cases. However, because they were few in number, they were unable to meet the multiple requests of Latino prisoners.

An equally serious area in which the lack of bilingual personnel affected Latino prisoners directly was in the proceedings of the Adjustment Committee, the body responsible for conducting disciplinary hearings. DOCS' regulations required that notification of charges, as well as prisoners' response to them, be written in English. Once again, Latino prisoners frequently had to depend on their peers for such translations. According to Palma, Latino prisoners who appeared before the Adjustment Committee, "would be treated a lot worse if they didn't speak English. They were always found guilty."[89]

Within this general context, it is clear that discriminatory policies and the lack of bilingual personnel and programs resulted in differential treatment towards Latino prisoners. Faced with these constraints, Latino prisoners increasingly demanded the implementation of bilingual services and the hiring of more bilingual personnel. A major assumption behind the latter demand was that Latina(o) staff would better understand the cultural values, non-verbal communication, and language of Latino prisoners and could, therefore, provide them better access to equal treatment under the law. A significant Latina(o) presence could also help reduce the existing tensions between Latino prisoners and non-Latino personnel. Moreover, it was expected that both Latino prisoners and non-Latino staff would benefit from seeing Latinos fulfill roles other than that of prisoner.[90] In spite of these expectations, however, Latino prisoners were aware that the presence of Latino staff did not, by itself, ensure them fairer treatment. In fact, it was as a result of the negative experiences that Latinos had also had with a number of Latino and African-American staff members that they considered the hiring of more Latina(o) personnel as only one means to achieve their goals.

To summarize, following the Attica Prison Rebellion, New York State elites implemented a series of penal reforms designed to address the conflicting demands of both custodial and reform-oriented interests. On the one hand, prisoners and their allies sought an improvement in the living standards and treatment accorded prisoners, the liberalization of prison conditions, and the sharing of decision-making power with penal authorities. On the other hand, custodial interests and their supporters demanded a tightening of security, which implied a greater restriction of prisoner movement within the facility, the further isolation of prisoner leaders, and a reduction of outside access to prisoners. The reforms failed to fully satisfy either set of demands.

Although more than half of the budget allocated to the penal establishment in 1972 went to addressing the calls of guards for increased security measures, security interests claimed that the liberalization of prison conditions diminished their authority and, as a result, made it more difficult for them to control prisoners' behavior. Prisoners argued that, despite the creation of the ILCs and IGRCs, the reforms were "cosmetic" in nature and did not affect the fundamental balance of power in favor of their keepers.

Latino prisoner discontent was further fueled by the fact that, despite the reforms, they continued to receive differential treatment as a result of discriminatory penal policies, the lack of bilingual programs and personnel, and the racism of the predominantly white institutional staff. The latter was also apparent in the continued harassment by white staff of Latina(o) and African-American civilian and custodial personnel. Within this context, Latino prisoners (a significant number of whom had little or no English language skills) were forced to compete for the few available resources with African-American prisoners, who were the majority, and with white prisoners, who received preferential treatment.

Confronted with this situation, Latino prisoners responded by intensifying their efforts at mobilizing third party support, solidifying underground interracial/interethnic prisoner coalitions, and participating in the formation of formal and informal prisoner and administrative groups. The motivations behind these efforts were twofold. On the one hand, Latino prisoners strove to force penal administrators to address a number of concerns shared by all prisoners (e.g., better medical care). On the other hand, Latino prisoners pursued a number of distinct concerns (e.g., bilingual programs). It is the nature of Latino prisoner concerns and the types of informal groups and networks Latinos created to address them that will be the subject of the next chapter.

Notes: Chapter 4

1. See Bert Useem and Peter Kimbal, *States of Siege: U. S. Prison Riots, 1971–1986* (New York and Oxford: Oxford University Press, 1989).

2. See David G. Garson, "The Disruption of Prison Administration: An Investigation of Alternative Theories of the Relationship Among Administrators, Reformers, and Involuntary Social Service Clients," *Law and Society Review* 6, No. 4 (May 1972): 531–560.

3. Social scientists and penal authorities have attempted to link the occurrence of prison reforms to riots in numerous ways. These arguments, as outlined by Garson, will be briefly summarized here. The "breakdown approach" argues that riots occur as a result of a breakdown in social control caused by reforms which "undermine the informal system of power headed by unofficial inmate leaders on whom guards rely to maintain social control in return for privileges." Riots occur when these informal inmate "leaders" are replaced by official prisoner representatives "working closely with a reform warden." The "rising expectations approach" argues that riots occur when reforms raise the level of expectations of prisoners and attack the legitimacy of prison administrators" (Garson, "The Disruption of Prison Administration," 533). The "deprivation approach" holds that prisoners are forced to riot by poor conditions. A fourth argument is that prison riots and reforms occur on a cyclical basis with each causing the other—reforms undermine informal controls, this leads to rioting, the rioting leads to a new tolerance for informal controls, which leads to massive corruption, and to new reforms, etc. Garson himself concluded that there is no given permanent relationship between riots and reforms. In addition, he expressed the relationship between riots and reforms in two other ways. One, riots in some cases "revived a moribund reform movement and mobilized prison opinion." Two, reforms may decrease the possibility of riots occurring if they succeed in diffusing discontent by meeting some of the prisoners' demands.

4. This research supports the arguments of Barbara Lavin McEleney that, in spite of the post-Attica Rebellion reforms, custodial elements continued as of 1973 to maintain firm control over penal institutions and, in fact, were the first to gain from such reforms. It also supports McEleney's claim that, "The benefits accorded prison inmates did not significantly alter their power position vis-a-vis the correctional bureaucracy" (Barbara Lavin McEleney, *Correctional Reform in New York: The Rockefeller Years and Beyond* [Lanham, Md.: University Press of America, 1985], 128).

5. The word civilian is used throughout this text to refer to non-custodial DOCS' employees.

6. In March 1980, the Deputy Superintendent of Administrative Services at Green Haven was responsible for, "Plant superintendent, services to the prison; plant maintenance (carpentry, plumbing, etc.); food services; the farm;

personal service to employees; institution business (institution steward, head account clerk, senior budget analyst, senior commissary clerk, storehouse, payroll [employee], inmate accounts, purchasing, travel vouchers); laundry services; housekeeping and health" (Tom Lewis, "The Monthly Interviews a Busy Deputy Superintendent," *Green Haven Monthly* [hereafter cited as *GHM*] 3, Nos. 3 and 4 [March/April 1980]: 19). The deputy superintendent of administrative services was also responsible for coordinating many duties with security personnel.

7. From 1949 to 1970, the facility had only two wardens. Both enjoyed considerable autonomy. Between 1970 and 1978, Green Haven had eight wardens. This high rate of turnover in wardens was the result of Albany intervention and the fact that when Benjamin Ward was appointed DOCS Commissioner in 1975 he convinced the state legislature to remove the warden's position from the civil service category. This allowed commissioners to appoint wardens at their discretion (Susan Sheehan, *A Prison and a Prisoner* [Boston: Houghton Mifflin Co., 1978], 40). In May 1972, DOCS also established the Inspector General Program designed to insure that prisons were "operating in compliance with the law and with the correction commissioner's directives" (Ibid.).

8. According to a *New York Times* (hereafter cited as *N.Y. Times*) article, of The 28 Points, "The four demands that have not received attention were that inmates be paid the state minimum wage, that a grand jury investigate use of profits from prison industries, that administrative resentencing of parole violators be ended, and that disciplinary segregation of inmates be stopped" ("Attica Prisoners Have Gained Most Points Made in Rebellion," *N.Y. Times*, 12 September 1972, 1).

9. See New York State Special Commission on Attica (hereafter cited as NYSSCA), *Attica: The Official Report of the New York State Special Commission on Attica* (New York: Bantam Books, Inc., 1972), 251–257; Sheehan, *A Prison*, 133; "Reforms Reported in State's Prisons," *N.Y. Times*, 11 September 1972, 47; and "Attica Prisoners Have Gained Most Points Made in Rebellion," *N.Y. Times*, 12 September 1972, 1.

10. NYSSCA, *Attica*, 255.

11. Alfonso A. Narvaez, "State Plans Reforms," *N.Y. Times*, 4 February 1972, 36.

12. Henry Burroughs, "ILC," *GHM* 2, No. 8 (August 1979): 14.

13. "I.L.C. Questionnaire," *GHM* 6, No. 9 (December 1983): 5.

14. "Question of the Month," *GHM* 2, No. 4(April 1979): 16.

15. Gregorio Palma [pseud.], interview with author, New York, N.Y., 16 April and 1 May 1993.

16. "Question of the Month," *GHM* 2, No. 4 (April 1979): 16.

17. Correction Law Section 139 created institutional grievance committees (The Correctional Association of New York, *AIDS IN PRISON: A Crisis in New York State Corrections*, by Cathy Potler, New York, June 1988, 2). According to Sheehan, the Inmate Grievance Resolution Committee was established at Green Haven in August of 1975 (Sheehan, *A Prison*, 133). According to the *N.Y. Times*, the first IGRC was established at Green Haven in October 1975 and was to be implemented in all twenty-six state facilities by February 5, 1976 ("Inmate Committee Present Grievances of Prisoners at Green Haven," *N.Y. Times*, 18 January 1976, 41).

18. "Inmate Committee Present Grievances of Prisoners at Green Haven," *N.Y. Times*, 18 January 1976, 41.

19. Palma, interview with author, 1993.

20. McEleney, *Correctional Reform*, 140.

21. "Inmate Committee Present Grievances of Prisoners at Green Haven," *N.Y. Times*, 18 January 1976, 41.

22. Russell G. Oswald, *Attica—My Story* (Garden City, N.Y.: Doubleday and Co., Inc., 1972), 336.

23. *N.Y. Times*, 23 September 1971, 66.

24. "Guards at Another Prison Protest Over Attica Death," *N.Y. Times*, 13 September 1971, 71.

25. "State Prison Guards Vote to Walk Out if Talks Fail," *N.Y. Times*, 16 March 1972. On the guard's union, see also *N.Y. Times*, 1, 2, 4, 6, 8, 14 April 1972.

26. The guards also demanded the creation of a "maxi-maxi" institution, that is, a maximum security prison for prisoners seen as being particularly troublesome (e.g., those labeled revolutionaries, militants, and troublemakers). DOCS backed down from the original maxi-maxi project as a result of resistance to it and because it feared that the courts would declare the maxi-maxi unconstitutional (McEleney, *Correctional Reform*, 97–99). However, although the maxi-maxi project was not officially endorsed by the legislature, a behavior modification program known as "Prescription (RX) Program," targeting the same prisoner population, became a temporary component of the Adirondack Correctional Treatment and Evaluation Center (ACTEC) in Dannemora, N.Y., during 1972–1973. (As-Allah, "X The Rx," *Midnight Special* 3, No. 8 [August 1973]: 5, 6; and Martín Sostre, "End to ACTEC?," *Midnight Special* 3, No. 9 [September 1973]: 10). Interestingly, it was Oswald who claims to have first put forth the idea for the opening of a maxi-maxi in a series of secret meetings held by top government administrators at the end of September 1971 (Oswald, *Attica*, 320–341). "Then I talked for a while about my concept of segregating troublemakers so that the rehabilitation of the majority of offenders might proceed at greater speed. 'The problem is so urgent,' I said, 'that we cannot wait for construction of a completely new facility. We will have to adapt existing

security institutions for this purpose. Then we can juggle around our popula-
tion. . . . These troublemakers ought to be selected by criteria, including their
willingness or unwillingness to conform to reasonable modes of conduct . . .'."
(Ibid., 335). Behavior modification programs targeting specific groups of pris-
oners have continued to exist in New York State and throughout the country.
For a discussion of modification programs in penal facilities outside of New
York State during the early 1970s, see "Head S.T.A.R.T.," *Midnight Special* 3,
No. 4 (April 1973): 1, 2; "Behavior Modification," *Midnight Special* 3, No. 6
(June 1973): 11; Prisoner, Marion, Ill., "CARE," *Midnight Special* 3, No. 10
(October 1973): 20; and "start's back," *Midnight Special* 5, No. 2 (March 1975):
17–18). For a discussion of the use of behavior modification programs during
the 1980s and 1990s, see Ronald Fernández, *Prisoners of Colonialism: The
Struggle for Justice in Puerto Rico* (Monroe, Maine: Common Courage Press,
1994); Eric Cummins, *The Rise and Fall of California's Radical Prison
Movement* (Stanford: Stanford University Press, 1994); and *Madrid v. Gomez*,
case no C-90-3094 [TEH] (Filed in 1992 in U.S. District Court for the Northern
District of California by Wilson, Sonsoni, Goodrich, and Rosati).

27. James F. Clarity, "State Senate Votes $12-Million to Improve and
Reform Prisons," *N.Y. Times,* 10 May 1972, 56.

28. James B. Jacobs, *New Perspectives on Prisons and Imprisonment*
(Ithaca: Cornell University Press, 1983), 142.

29. Ibid., 144.

30. Ibid., 143–145.

31. In 1981, there were 540 guards and 1,900 prisoners at the institution
(Robert D. McFadden, "Two-Time Murderer Accused of Slaying Prison
Guard," *N.Y. Times,* 7 June 1981, 37).

32. Sheehan, *A Prison,* 146–147.

33. At the end of 1971, the federal government awarded DOCS a grant to
increase the number of "black and Puerto Rican prison guards" in New York
State (Steven R. Weisman, "State Receives Grant to Hire More Minority Prison
Guards," *N.Y. Times,* 8 November 1971, 29). At the time, only 240 of the 4,000
state guards were Latina(o) and/or African-American. White guards responded
to such recruiting efforts by filing a "reverse discrimination" suit ("Suit Challenges Plan for Attica," *N.Y. Times,* 25 January 1972, 23). The court rejected
their claim (Murray Schumach, "Ethnic 'Must' Set for 19 State Jobs," *N.Y.
Times,* 8 March 1972, 46). For many years, discriminatory civil service regulations and union practices prevented Latina(os) from acquiring civil service jobs
(Agenor Castro, "Meeting the Special Needs of Hispanic Inmates," *Law and
Justice* [September/October 1977]: 37–41; and Mayor's Commission on Hispanic Concerns, *Report of the Mayor's Commission on Hispanic Concerns,*
December 10, 1986). More often than not, the federal programs under which
Latina(o) staff were employed (e.g., Title I, CETA) tended to be pilot programs
and/or temporary positions (New York State, Department of Correctional

Services [hereafter cited as NYSDOCS], Division of Hispanic and Cultural Affairs, Hispanic Inmate Needs Task Force, *Final Report, "A Meeting of Minds, an Encounter of Hearts," 1986 (Action Plan)*, Albany, 1986; and Agenor Castro, "A Close Look at the Hispanic Inmates and Methods of Meeting Their Needs," *American Journal of Correction* 40, No. 2 [March/April 1978]: 15, 16, 18). Once hired Latinas(os) might be denied promotions based on discriminatory work ratings. According to Agenor Castro, traditionally, "Poor central office planning and personnel directors" allowed local wardens to make arbitrary decisions which amounted to discriminatory hiring practices. Frequently, administrators made matters worse by penalizing Latinas(os) and African-Americans who complained about discriminatory treatment (Agenor Castro, "Programming for Hispanic Inmates and Ex-offenders," *Proceedings of the One Hundred and Eighth Annual Congress of Correction of the American Correctional Association*, Portland, Oreg., August 20–24, 1978 [College Park, Md.: American Correctional Association, 1979], 83).

34. NYSSCA, *Attica*, 255.

35. Interestingly, James G. Fox found that white male guards tended to resent women guards more than they did male guards of color (James G. Fox, *Organizational and Racial Conflict in Maximum-Security Prisons* [Lexington, Mass.: D. C. Heath and Co., 1982], 66).

36. Guards could now only take the civil service exam in the region where they resided and work in prisons within that region. Previously, guards could work in any region if their test scores were higher than those of persons from that region. Since Green Haven was located near New York City and most white guards lived further upstate, African-American and Latina(o) guards now stood a better chance of getting a job at Green Haven, which was closer to New York City where most of them lived.

37. The physical standards were changed so that Latina(o) and women guards, who tended to be shorter than white and African-American male guards, could enter the guard force.

38. The assumption by white guards that African-American officers would be more sympathetic to African-American prisoners seems to be based more on bias than on reality. A study conducted on white/Black guard attitudes in two Illinois facilities found that "there were no consistent differences in their attitudes toward prisoners, staff, correctional goals or their occupations" (James B. Jacobs and Lawrence Kraft, "Integrating the Keepers: A Comparison of Black and White Prison Guards in Illinois," *Social Problems* 25 [1978]: 316). Moreover, "Those black officers attracted to the prisoners and most antagonistic toward the prison regime either resign, are fired, or change their attitudes" (Ibid., 314).

39. The charge of being "too friendly" frequently found its way into negative job evaluations where Latina(o) staff members were judged as being unprofessional (Castro, "Programming for the Hispanic Inmate," 1979).

40. Danny Vázquez [pseud.], interview with author, New York, N.Y., 20 March and 17 April 1993.

41. Tom Goldstein, "Some State Tests Ruled Improper," *N.Y. Times,* 7 April 1974, 24. White guard hostility to the suit was deepened by the fact that when the litigation ensued in 1973, all guards were temporarily prevented from taking other examinations which would have allowed them to occupy positions above the sergeant level. Although the suit filed by African-American and Latina(o) guards was decided in their favor in 1974, in August of 1975 the United States Court of Appeals for the Second Circuit reversed the lower court's ruling, which had imposed a racial quota on promotions within DOCS. The Court of Appeals, however, did affirm the lower court's order, "for a fair job-related examination and it permitted a temporary racial quota for interim promotions to sergeant until the new examination was approved" (*N.Y. Times,* 10 August 1975, 21). African-American and Latina(o) guards were represented by the NAACP Legal Defense and Education Fund.

42. "Suit Challenges Plan for Attica," *N.Y. Times,* 25 January 1972, 23; and Murray Schumach, "Ethnic 'Must' Set for 19 State Jobs," *N.Y. Times,* 8 March 1972, 46.

43. Many male guards tended to question the ability of women guards to defend themselves and/or their male counterparts in times of crisis (Fox, *Organizational and Racial Conflict,* 68–72).

44. Fox described a situation in which male guards and their superior smirked while women guards frisked male prisoners, thus potentially undermining the former's authority as guards. As a result of this type of harassment, Fox found that the primary source of irritation for women guards came from male guards, not male prisoners (Ibid., 71–72).

45. Sheehan, *A Prison,* 146.

46. Jacobs, *New Perspectives,* 145–146. Other examples of organizations created by Latina(o) staff to counter discriminatory treatment by criminal justice personnel have been the National Hispanic Correctional Association (NHCA), founded in 1977, and the Mexican-American Correctional Association (MACA) (Castro, "A Close Look at the Hispanic Inmates," 1978).

47. Paul García, Jr., "Bilingual Programming: A Viable Alternative in Corrections—Part B," *National Hispanic Conference on Law Enforcement and Criminal Justice,* U.S. Department of Justice, Law Enforcement Assistance Administration (Washington, D.C.: GPO, 1980), 125.

48. The prisoner's charges were confirmed by African-American officers who had been the target of such actions. Although DOCS officials denied the charges, they admitted that the prisoner had been used as an "informant" in investigations of drug dealings ("Charge of Entrapment in 3 Prisons Under Inquiry by Albany and U.S.," *N.Y. Times,* 11 March 1979, 38).

49. Castro, "Meeting With the Special Needs," 1977. Traditionally, some of the reasons given by penal administrators to explain the virtual absence of Latina(o) staff, particularly at the upper levels of the administrative ladder, have been that: Latinas(os) are not interested in working for the government; they have an aversion to tests; and there are not enough qualified Latina(o) employees from which to draw personnel for supervisory positions (Robert García, Untitled, *National Hispanic Conference on Law Enforcement and Criminal Justice* [U.S. Department of Justice, Law Enforcement Assistance Administration, Washington, D.C.: GPO, 1980], 29–38).

50. Castro, "A Close Look at the Hispanic Inmates," 1978.

51. Ibid.

52. Robert Joe Lee, *Hispanics—The Anonymous Prisoners* (Trenton: Department of Corrections, 1976) 44.

53. Nathaniel Sheppard Jr., "Green Haven Reports Increase in Prisoner Clashes," *N.Y. Times,* 2 November 1976, 49.

54. Pranay Gupte, "Two Deaths and An Escape Raise Green Haven Tensions," *N. Y. Times,* 29 May 1978, II, 2.

55. By December 31, 1962, Latinos already comprised 12.8 percent of Green Haven's prisoner population. See NYSDOCS, Division of Research, *Characteristics of Inmates Under Custody of New York State Correctional Institutions,* December 31, 1962, Albany, December 20, 1963, 8).

56. Ironically, although the prisoners' handbook had been printed in English in 1961, it was not easily available to English-speaking prisoners or staff persons throughout much of the 1970s.

57. The Correctional Association of New York, *State of the Prisons: Conditions Inside the Walls* by Cathy Potler, New York, March 1986.

58. The high guard turnover rate was due to the geographic location of Green Haven and the place of residence of the guard force. While white guards took jobs at Green Haven only until they could transfer to prisons near their upstate home towns, African-American and Latina(o) guards took the assignments at the facility until they could transfer to prisons near New York City, where most of them lived.

59. Michael T. Kaufman, "Upstate Prison Teacher Defends His Klan Role," *N.Y. Times,* 23 December 1974, 24; and "Klansman Teacher is Ousted by State from Prison Post," *N.Y. Times,* 24 December 1974, 42.

60. The directive was issued after a six-month investigation of KKK activity within the state prison system ("State Assailed on Klan Ruling," *N.Y. Times,* 4 September 1975, 37). In spite of the directive, prisoners at Eastern Correctional Facility at Napanoch continued to assert that the ban was not being enforced. To counter KKK organizing, Latino and African-American

prisoners at the facility organized the John Brown Anti-Klan Committee. In June 1977, the committee issued a press release in which they named thirty-five guards who they claimed were either KKK members or sympathizers. During an August 1977 rebellion, prisoners demanded the transfer of two sergeants accused of KKK membership and brutality (Tom Wicker, "Catch-22 Behind Bars," *N.Y. Times,* 22 May 1979, 19). According to the Frank Khali Abney Defense Committee, the KKK particularly targeted Latino and African-American prisoner leaders at Eastern Correctional Facility. "For instance, in January 1975, all the officers of the N.A.A.C.P. chapter were thrown into segregation for one month immediately preceding their elections. On February 28, 1976, Joseph Kershaw, executive board member of the N.A.A.C.P. chapter, was beaten in his cell, segregated and beaten again . . . March 17, 1976, Correction Officer Dennis Lauria wore a Klan uniform (sheet and hood) in the lobby of a cell block; he and other guards burned a paper cross" (Frank Khali Abney Defense Committee, "Free Frank Khali Abney," Brooklyn, N.Y., 1978, 3) (pamphlet). Prisoners responded by filing lawsuits against the state and the KKK.

61. "State Assailed on Klan Ruling," *N.Y. Times,* 4 September 1975, 37; Tom Goldstein, "Appeals Court Backs Prison Guard Who refused to Reply on K.K.K.," *N.Y. Times,* 4 April 1979, II, 1; "The Klansman and His Prisoners," *N.Y. Times,* 13 April 1979, 26; and (Rev.) C. Herbert Oliver, "To the Editor," *N.Y. Times,* 25 April 1979, 22.

62. Tom Goldstein, "Appeals Court Backs Prison Guard Who Refused to Reply on K.K.K.," *N.Y. Times,* 4 April 1979, II, 1. According to a *New York Daily News* February 1979 article, the KKK's influence among both prisoners and staff persons in New York State prisons was most evident at Eastern, Wallkill, Attica, and Elmira penitentiaries (*New York Daily News,* 11 February 1979).

63. Palma, interview with author, 1993.

64. National Alliance Against Racist and Political Repression, "The Klan Presence at Napanoch," New York, N.Y. (loose sheets).

65. The Napanoch Brothers (private correspondence).

66. Frank Khali Abney Defense Committee, "Free Frank Khali Abney," Brooklyn, N.Y., 1978 (pamphlet). The incident took place on May 10, 1978 (The Napanoch Brothers [private correspondence]).

67. Sheehan, *A Prison,* 24, 25, 27, 29. The classification committee was comprised of one sergeant and two civilian employees, with the sergeant playing the dominant role.

68. Larry White, "Correctional Industry," *GHM* 8, No. 11 (February/March 1988): 8; and Kathleen Maguire, "Prison Industry: The Effect of Participation on Inmate Disciplinary Adjustment," (Ph.D. diss., State University of New York at Albany, 1992), 62. As of 1991, New York's prison industry

program, operated under the Division of Industries within DOCS and marketed under the label of Corcraft, employed 3,000 of the state's 45,000 prisoners. By 1991, there were at least thirty shops located in nineteen of the state's facilities (Ibid., 61). According to Maguire, "Sales have gradually increased from $12 million in fiscal year 1981 to over $58 million in fiscal year 1990. However, New York has only realized a net gain from its industry program since the mid 1980s. Division of Industries has operated at no net expense to the state since 1986" (Ibid.). The legal status of prison industries is determined by Articles II, Sec. 24 of the New York State Constitution and 170 of the New York State Correction Law (Larry White, "Correctional Industry," *GHM* 8, No. 11 [February/March 1986]: 8).

69. Domingo Morales [pseud.], interview with author, New York, N.Y., 6 April 1993.

70. Larry White, "Correctional Industry," *GHM* 8, No. 11 (February/March 1986): 8–9.

71. Ibid.

72. Morales, interview with author, 1993.

73. Palma, interview with author, 1993.

74. Robert Maldonado, "Nuevos Horizontes," *GHM* 2, No. 4 (April 1979): 19.

75. José Rodríguez, "Entrevista con el Profesor Rogelio Cuestas," *GHM* 5, No. 2 (February/March 1982): 17. At the time, Latino prisoners were also sponsoring a peer counseling group called Compadre Helper.

76. "L.V.A. 1983–1984," *GHM* 6, No. 9 (December 1983): 6.

77. José Rodríguez, "H.U.P. se Reune con Diana Correa," *GHM* 10, No. 2 (March 1988): 17–19. For an update of the academic and vocational programs available to Latina(o) prisoners in New York State as of 1992 see Correctional Association of New York, *Not Simply a Matter of Words: Academic & Vocational Programs for Latino Inmates in New York State Prisons*, New York, July 1992.

78. In 1977, there were four pay grades or "work incentives allowance" scales as they were called after 1974. Wages ranged from $0.35 to $1.15 (maximum) a day. Unemployed or physically disabled prisoners received $0.25 a day. Those refusing to work were housed separately and did not receive an allowance. Industry jobs paid between $0.625 and $0.2875 an hour. However, prisoners were expected to pay market prices for essential goods bought in the commissary (Sheehan, *A Prison*, 27–28). In 1982, a prisoner going to school received $0.50 a day, while one working in the furniture shop earned between $8.50 and $25 a week (José R. Rodríguez, "La Industria Vs. Escuela," *GHM* [March/April 1982]: 16).

79. Morales, interview with author, 1993.

80. Pranay Gupte, "Two Deaths and An Escape Raise Green Haven Tensions," *N.Y. Times,* 29 May 1978, II, 2.

81. Sheehan, *A Prison,* 52–53.

82. Male prisoners comprised 90 percent of the AIDS cases in New York State (Correctional Association of New York, *AIDS in Prison* by Cathy Potler, New York, June 1988, 11). In 1987, Latinas(os) and African-Americans comprised approximately 80 percent of the over 41,000 persons housed in fifty-two state prisons. At the time, DOCS estimated that 60–70 percent of all prisoners had a history of drug abuse (Ibid., 6). At least until March 1988, "The only existing policy on AIDS is the 12-page DOCS directive issued in December 1985" (Ibid., 24). However, according to the Correctional Association of New York, the directive was obsolete and full of inaccuracies.

83. According to CANY, the only consistent activity DOCS has carried out in relation to HIV/AIDS education has been the distribution, as of 1985, of a pamphlet entitled, "100 Questions and Answers" to staff members and prisoners in its facilities. The pamphlet was helpful to the 82 percent of the prisoner population which was literate (Ibid., 12).

84. NYSSCA, *Attica,* 60.

85. Cervantes Hernández, "La Librería de Ley & el Hispano," *GHM* 5, No. 1 (January/February 1982): 17.

86. Tony Rodríguez, "Clase Bilingüe de Leyes," *GHM* 5, No. 2 (February/March 1982): 16.

87. Palma, interview with author, 1993.

88. Ibid.

89. Ibid.

90. Castro, "Meeting with the Special Needs," 37–41.

5

Latino Prisoner Participation
in Informal Groups and Networks

Some people get through prison life by . . . staying by themselves,
reading books, staying in their cells. . . . People find what works for
them . . . you know. . . . Most prisons have football teams. They have
basketball teams. Some prisons have boxing teams. . . . In some prisons . . . there are school programs, there are some vocational training
programs. But, certainly, neither one are enough to really absorb the
amount of people who are in the prisons. . . . People sometimes have
jobs, okay, 'cause industry is a big thing in prison, working in sweat-
shops, making undergarments, making license plates or street signs.
                    —Angel Gear, interview with author (1993)

I always rebelled against the system. I wasn't violent, per se, but I
rebelled . . . challenged authority . . . One of the things that was very
rebellious for me was cooking. You're not allowed to cook. I became a
hell of a cook in prison. . . . You have little underground networks. You
study culture. . . . You read. You exchange. And I went to school. . . . I
would go to the law library and I was trying to fight my case. And
when that didn't work I tried for clemency.
                    —Gregorio Palma, interview with author (1993)

Latino prisoners at Green Haven created and/or participated in
informal prisoner groups and networks designed to address a wide
variety of concerns (e.g., social, economic, cultural, political, security).
The nature of such groups was determined primarily by the interaction of several factors. On the one hand, there were elements such as:
facility conditions; racial and ethnic discrimination by staff and non-
Latino prisoners; and the opportunities available within the prison
setting for prisoners to associate with one another. On the other
hand, there were influences such as: relationships established with
other prisoners prior to incarceration or during previous incarceration together; prisoners' individual interests and concerns; relationships with non-prisoners inside and outside the walls; and racial and

ethnic identification. Thus, while a significant amount of literature on prisoners has tended to describe the actions of prisoners as either the product of endogenous, internal to the prison) or exogenous factors (i.e., external influences)[1], this and the following chapters will demonstrate that in the case of Latino prisoners at Green Haven such influences were experienced simultaneously.

The major types of informal groups existing among prisoners during the period studied were those centered around homeboy networks and cliques[2] and those based on racial and ethnic identification. There were times when Latino-dominated informal groups included African-American and white members. However, white prisoners who joined prisoners of color were generally ostracized by other white prisoners and staff persons who labelled them "nigger lovers"[3] and "spik lovers." Additional subdivisions formed depending on prisoners' housing and work assignments, social and recreational activities, political interests, and prior experience of incarceration with other prisoners. Because at Green Haven, prisoners' ability to associate with one another was largely determined by housing and work assignments, attention will be given to this area first.

Housing and Work Assignments

Green Haven was divided into an "East Side" and a "West Side." These two sides were further divided into distinct "housing blocks." Generally, "The west side men stay on the west side—except for legal call-outs, interviews, regular assignments or programs—and the east side remains in its area, with similar conditions."[4] Each side had its own open yard which was used year-round. As former Green Haven prisoner Gregorio Palma explained:

> A, B, C, D, and J block were on the west side. On the east side you had E, F, G, and H. Basically, what we had on the east side was GED school, English-as-a-Second-Language, you had industry, you had east side plumbing, and you had the idle block, where guys didn't have jobs, they just, you know, refused to work or didn't want to work or couldn't get the kind of job they wanted, so they locked in that block.
>
> There's a west side dining area and an east side. . . . The guys on the east side sometimes never see the guys on the west side unless they go to church on Sunday together or something, and it's pre-planned that they're going to meet there. . . . They got different programs,

except for maybe college . . . [where] they would see each other at night. . . . now the school, there's a lot of people on the west side at school and there's a lot of people on the east side at school. That's something that was common.[5]

A limited amount of east side/west side contact was also made possible by the fact that while, "The school is located on the east side . . . the people that predominantly work in the school are all clerks from the west side."[6]

During most of the period studied, a prisoner's work assignment determined his place of residence. "Guys on the west side are all predominantly clerks. . . . They had the most prestigious jobs. . . . [Some] . . . work in the kitchen. . . . The kitchen had C block . . . and in that block it was always all kinds of food. Honor block was compiled of everyone who was on an honor roll."[7]

There were other characteristics that distinguished the east side from the west side. In 1976 prisoners on the west side earned "a bit more than $1 a day."[8] Prisoners on the east side worked the most difficult jobs (e.g., industry) and were paid lower wages. One prisoner described the east side as, "Here we have the east side, which is considered the working class, or poor side of town. . . . It has the toughest men and the toughest guards and the sweatshop jobs that pay 80 cents a day . . ."[9]

> The cells on the east side were small and plain, containing a sink, toilet, and small bed. Shower stalls were at the end of the cell block . . . The accommodations on the west side of the facility were noticeably different. The cells in the so-called honor blocks were larger than those on the east side and many were decorated with pictures and posters. The halls were much less littered.[10]

Furthermore, "On the honor blocks on the west side, inmates can move about their areas between 6 P.M. and 11 P.M., while on the east side the inmates remain locked in after the 5 P.M. head count, except on alternate nights when they are assigned to yard recreation."[11]

Within the west side itself, there was yet another distinction between prisoners who were locked in "J" and "R" blocks and the rest of the west side population. In J block, for example:

> . . . there were washrooms instead of cells. . . . You could take a shower whenever you wanted. In the regular blocks they let you take three showers a week. Every other day you would get a shower.

In J block the shower was open. You could take a shower all day.
You had a day room to watch television. You didn't have to go to the
big yard. You had a small yard in the back that was your own yard.
You could lift weights, run, or whatever you wanted there. You could
play handball. . . . You could watch different television programs.
Other than that, if you weren't in R block, who also had their own
recreation areas, you had to watch TV in the yards. And they would
lock the yards down at a certain time.[12]

Privacy in J block was enhanced by the fact that, "it's sort of away on
the west side. . . . It was on the extreme end of the prison. It was like
in a little corner of the prison by itself. . . . "[13] Guards on J block also
had better reputations than those in other blocks. "All the officers in J
block were usually mellow officers. They were very decent."[14] Prisoners
housed in these privileged blocks included: ". . . all those individuals
that were doing administrative work . . . doing clerical work, that ran
different programs, the colleges, everything else, all locked in these
blocks. That was a privilege. . . . clerical, law library workers, pre-
release workers, all of your major clerks."[15]

As a result of these distinctions in housing and work assignments, some prisoners complained that there was "a class structure
that favors some men against others . . ."[16] Superimposed on this class
structure were racial and ethnic differentiations favoring white prisoners throughout the period studied. According to Palma, "there's a
lot of white people in the west side. A lot of them were in the
kitchen."[17] The fact that an overwhelming number of Latino prisoners
were forced to take industrial assignments meant that they were
more likely to be housed on the east side.

In response to the structural conditions described above prisoners
tended to form cliques or subgroups based on their housing assignments and sometimes on the basis of the work assignments. Hence,
these two types of associations were framed by the opportunities available for prisoners to associate with one another.

On both sides of the prison, however, the personal preferences of
prisoners were made most evident in the two main yards. While much
has been said about the racial/ethnic subdivisions that take place
among prisoners in institutional mess halls and yards, the most interesting aspect of this phenomenon is that prisoners in the yards further
subdivide themselves according to a whole range of interests. It is in
the prison yards where one can observe most clearly how diverse prisoners' concerns are. Speaking about territorial divisions within the

Green Haven yards during the early 1970s, Eddie Rosa, a former bilingual education teacher at Green Haven, observed:

> The yard which is an area where they released several hundred men. . . . It was a highly structured, divided area by the prisoners themselves. African-American Nationalists were in one area. African-American Muslims were in another. The druggies were in another area. Whites were in one area, the Irish whites. . . . The Latinos were in another area subdivided by Cubans, Puerto Ricans and Dominicans. And areas for weight-lifting and a place for playing cards, etc. It was like walking through a maze. You had to be very careful. You couldn't step on people's territory. It would be viewed as an offense.[18]

In view of the existence of a wide range of groups among the prisoner population, it is clear that while structural constraints such as housing and work assignments, limited prisoners' ability to form affiliations, they found ways in which to create informal groups composed of similarly minded peers. It was within this context that homeboy networks and cliques as well as informal prisoner groups based on racial and ethnic identification came to constitute the dominant form of male prisoner organization.

Homeboy Networks and Cliques

Latino homeboy networks, like their non-Latino counterparts, were generally formed by prisoners who knew one another before imprisonment and/or came from the same cities or neighborhoods or sections of neighborhoods. Some homeboys were blood-related. In the case of Latino immigrants, some came from the same towns or from the same country. Others had family members who had emigrated from the same towns or countries. Cliques were formed by prisoners who shared similar interests but who were not necessarily homeboys. Homeboy networks and cliques were generally composed of members from the same racial/ethnic group although it was not uncommon for prisoners of other ethnic/racial groupings to be included in them. As former Green Haven prisoner Domingo Morales explained: "It was like you usually be more tight with somebody if you come from that borough . . . so no matter what color you are, you're still a homeboy . . . that's like the informal type of thing . . . a network . . . you know, where they support each other."[19]

Some of the primary functions of homeboy networks and cliques were to provide group members emotional, social, and economic support as well as protection from other prisoners and staff members. Being part of such groups reduced a prisoner's probability of being victimized by others. According to Morales:

> [In prison] . . . you always going to bump into somebody that's going to show you the ropes, you know. . . . But then you also got to be careful because some people will take advantage. . . . You think they're showing the ropes and in the long run they might trap you off where you will be in debt, you know . . . if they give you a carton, they might want two cartons, right? And if you can't pay it, they might want whatever you might have in your cell and then in the long run, it's a small percentage, but it might be even something sexual.[20]

A prisoner's incorporation into a homeboy network or clique was designed to sidestep these pitfalls. Eric Elliott, an African-American prisoner leader formerly at Green Haven described how the homeboy networks operated.

> Usually what happens when you come to a new prison, the homeboys in the prison who know you from the neighborhood or guys that know you from the street, will come look for you. They have what they call a "chain sheet" that comes out every day. The chain sheet records all the people who leave the prison and all the people who are newly arrived in the prison. . . . People are always looking at this chain sheet to see who of their friends are coming in and who of their friends are leaving. So once your name comes up on the chain sheet all the guys that know you come to see you. And . . . usually when you first arrive in a prison you're put in what they call a "reception status," and in reception you don't have your personal property. You don't have any soap, toothpaste, things of that nature that you're going to need for the next two or three days. So the homeboys come and they see you and they give you some soap and some toothpaste, and they might bring you some food, a couple of cans of soda, if you smoke they give you some cigarettes, just to hold you over until you get your personal property. . . . So when I first got there, you know, and the homeboys came to see me, they brought me all this stuff and then right from the beginning they begin to give you an orientation of who's here first of all, you know, "So-and-so's here from 116th Street and Joey's here from the Bronx and . . ."[21]

Once a new prisoner was released from reception, the homeboys continued to provide one another support.

Like if you . . . come in and you're from Brooklyn and I know you're from Brooklyn, if I have cigarettes, you don't have cigarettes, I'll give you some cigarettes. If you don't have tuna fish, I'll give you some tuna fish. If you don't have sneakers, I might have a pair of sneakers to help you out and stuff like that.[22]

Once the homeboy network was set up, its members used their work assignments within the institution to meet each others' material needs. According to Michael Armstrong, an African-American imprisoned at Green Haven during the 1970s and 1980s:

Say if I worked in the laundry, I did five or six of my homeboys' laundry. If you worked . . . say the commissary, when they went to the commissary you looked out [for] so many of your homeboys getting the packages on time when they go to the window. If another guy worked in the shoe shop or the brush shop, whatever they needed you had a homeboy. That would be the informal system in spite of the formal system . . . And then, outside of your homeboys, if you knew somebody else and they wanted something from your particular areas, then you had an opportunity to make a profit because this is outside of your circle.[23]

Sometimes prisoners became part of other prisoners' homeboy networks or cliques as a result of having shared a previous experience of incarceration with one of the members. At other times, such common experience led to the creation of a network of friends that complemented one's homeboy network.

. . . during my stay at the county prison I met Black and Latino guys . . . that I didn't know from the street but . . . we formed, you know, relationships over a year and got to be pretty close. And then some of them went upstate ahead of me. . . . Sing Sing was a reception center at the time . . . so they were already in Sing Sing when I came through and we formed our alliances and, you know, just picked up where we left off.[24]

For the purpose of the current research, one of the crucial questions asked was whether homeboy networks and cliques or other similar informal prisoner groups could play a politicizing role among prisoners. The answer provided by Angel Gear, a former African-American prisoner leader at Green Haven during the early 1970s, seems to illustrate the ambivalent feelings many prison leaders had toward such types of groups, although they too participated in them.

> Do they play a positive role? . . . Maybe only in the sense that they might help some people survive prison life. . . . But . . . in terms of people really . . . being willing to try to take a look at their life, maybe to bring about some qualitative change and all that other stuff, no, they don't. . . . If anything, all they do is hold people back, okay, and, in fact . . . probably make them worse 'cause not only now do they have the same negative attitudes that they had when they originally came in the prison . . . but being in prison for any number of [years] . . . would just make people worse.[25]

However, because prisoners in these types of groups and networks shared some common concerns with prisoners involved in other types of informal and formal groups, there were times when homeboy networks and cliques had the potential to play a politicizing role. According to Gear:

> Certainly . . . they can help, you know, because . . . usually those cliques, whether it's from people that came from the same city or came from the same neighborhood in the same city, you know, . . . in prison they . . . were . . . usually . . . very strong . . . loyalty bonds . . . so that when one thing happened with . . . somebody from the clan or . . . that network, then everybody else was pulled in . . . And too, if . . . you start educating or organizing . . . one or two of those people in those cliques . . . it can have . . . an impact, you know, like a ripple effect . . . Even though these people . . . usually in these cliques . . . these little courts . . . whether . . . it was the weight courts or basketball courts or whatever, the teams, right, but usually to some degree . . . they [Puerto Rican prisoners] related . . . to the Young Lords, and when the Young Lords would talk about, you know, the Puerto Rican liberation they can relate to it, you know, in terms of the pride, or if it was the Young Lords talking about . . . "Power to the people," you know, on the fringe basis . . . just the rhetoric, they could relate to it. Well, if push come to shove they . . . could even be pulled in even further. So there was potential there, certainly there was a lot of potential there but there was a lot of work there too.[26]

Interestingly, former prisoner Michael Armstrong argued that the primary function of homeboy networks was to organize. This organizing could take the form of underground activities proscribed by prison authorities or aboveground endeavors sanctioned by penal personnel. In fact, homeboy networks could form the core of both informal and formal prisoner groups. Armstrong described how such overlapping membership reinforced one another.

Say if I'm the leader of an organization [and] I need support, these
are my homeboys, all right, whoever can fight, I need security on me
. . . Then . . . whoever can speak, the speaker before I speak, I'm the
main speaker, my homeboy speaks to bring me on, bring me a round
of applause . . . Then the other guy goes and rally and keep pushing
in the people . . . Then the other ones might be the fundraisers. They
telling the guy, "Here, donate man, Michael's alright, man. He
gonna do the right things. ". . . Then I got another homeboy he might
be a lady's man, you know, so he's gonna bring all the ladies behind
the party or an event or something like that.[27]

As described above, homeboy networks and cliques were among the
primary vehicles through which prisoners organized themselves to address a number of social, economic, cultural, and security concerns.
Membership in these groups and networks coexisted and frequently
overlapped with membership in other types of informal and formal
prisoner and administrative groups, such as the ILC and the IGRC. As
a result, the concerns of prisoners involved in homeboy networks and
cliques were generally shared by prisoners in other groups and networks.

While some prisoner leaders argued that homeboy networks and
cliques tended to hinder prisoner politicization, others argued that such
groups formed the basis for most, if not all, types of prisoner organizing. In
either case, it is clear that homeboy networks and cliques had the potential
to contribute to prisoner politicization. In fact, because of the primacy of
homeboy networks and cliques within the overall prisoner body, it would
have been impossible for prisoner leaders to organize collective acts of resistance, such as work strikes, rebellions, and prisoners' unions, without the
active support and participation of such groups.

However, as fundamental as homeboy networks and cliques were
to prisoners' day-to-day survival, it is imperative to remember that
they existed within a larger context characterized by racial and ethnic
discrimination and rivalries. Moreover, homeboy networks were not
accessible to all Latino prisoners at all times. As a result of these factors and others which will be discussed below, Latino prisoners tended
to depend a great deal on informal groups formed on the basis of ethnicity; ethnic groups, in turn, tended to further divide themselves along
nationality, language, and sometimes color lines.

Ethnicity, Nationality, Language, and Racial Identification

The discrimination most Latino prisoners experienced, coupled
with their distinct language and cultural concerns, fostered a great
degree of solidarity among them.

> . . . It's my experience que, the Latinos always look out . . . for each
> other. When you coming into a new prison . . . there's always going
> to be a Latino there that's going to say, "Yo, what's happening?" He
> might not even know you but he just knows that you're Latino . . .
> He's always the first one to rap to you, "Where you come from? What
> you in prison for?" You know, "What other prison was you in?" Stuff
> like that . . .²⁸

Such support was vital in situations where, "you might not have a
homeboy network in that prison or . . . you might be in a block where
that homeboy network is not even there."²⁹

Latino prisoner solidarity was most evident during the 1970s, when
the Latino prisoner population was comprised almost entirely of Puerto
Ricans. Even then, however, Puerto Ricans born and raised in the
United States and those born and raised in Puerto Rico tended to form
subgroups on the basis of language spoken and experiences growing
up in two distinct societal contexts.

> Yeah, there's a split because . . . there's a language barrier, okay.
> The Puerto Ricans born, like me, if I'm born here, I can't speak to
> them. I don't know the language. I had to learn Spanish in prison so
> I could communicate with my people. But there's some Puerto Ricans
> born here that don't see the need to speak no Spanish and don't see
> the need to communicate period.³⁰

Differences in language skills also led Puerto Ricans born and raised
in the United States to have closer ties with African-American and white
prisoners than their non-English-speaking counterparts who gravitated
toward other Latino immigrants who spoke primarily Spanish.

> All the different groups are very . . . cliquish. I think Puerto Ricans
> are more broad in that they deal with everybody a lot more, but then
> Puerto Ricans have been here a lot longer. But, you know . . . there's
> a division in the Puerto Ricans also. The Newyorican and the Puerto
> Rican . . . I won't even say they don't get along, I'm just saying that
> the Newyorican can hang out more with the African-American,
> while the . . . monolingual Puerto Rican hangs out more with the
> other Caribbean people who are, you know, of monolingual descents
> also. They identify more.³¹

Variations in skin color also led some Puerto Rican prisoners to
identify more with African-American prisoners, while others gravi-

tated towards the white prisoner population. Morales summarized the long-term impact diverse interests and cleavages had on Latino prisoner solidarity. These differences were particularly evident in the prison yard.

> ... los colombianos or los mejicanos or the ones from Nicaragua ... they'll share like a space and they'll share food and stuff like that. They like to play soccer. . . . The Latinos, especially the Puerto Rican-born Latinos, or even the ones that don't play that much soccer, they're into baseball. . . . Not that they are against each other but after something more in common, so that's how they sit like that. . . . But usually the Puerto Ricans don't even be hanging like that. One is hanging thinking he's Italian, the other one se cree que es negro. . . . Pero, you know, *they* still have that brothership bond. The Puerto Ricans, we don't have that. . . . Before, it was there but they lost that.[32]

As the number of Mariel Cuban,[33] Dominican, and South and Central American immigrants increased at Green Haven during the 1980s, cleavages along national and linguistic lines became even more pronounced within the Latino prisoner population. Non-Puerto Rican Latinos first gravitated toward members of their own countries, then toward other recent immigrant groups, and finally toward Puerto Ricans.[34] According to Gregorio Palma, "Though they all got along with Puerto Ricans. . . . I did notice though that the Mariel Cubans . . . got along very well with Dominicans and Colombians and other foreign born individuals . . ."[35] The fact that most non-Puerto Rican Latinos were not United States citizens, meant that they shared additional concerns regarding immigration status and deportation. These issues oftentimes were not prioritized by Puerto Rican prisoners, themselves citizens by birth.

During the first half of the 1980s, such diverse experiences and concerns led Cuban, Dominican, South and Central American, and even Puerto Rican prisoners to create distinct informal prisoner groups based on nationality. During the 1980s, these groups competed for leadership with the only existing formal prisoner organization, which was Puerto Rican-dominated until the mid-1980s. The ways in which Puerto Rican and other Latino prisoner leaders involved in formal Latino prisoner organizations sought to overcome such tensions and cleavages will be discussed in chapter 8. Despite these divisions, however, Latino prisoners continued to provide one another support in a number of ways.

Social and Recreational Activities

Latino prisoners participated in a number of social and recreational activities centered around sports, board games, and music. Sports at Green Haven ranged from football, weight-lifting, boxing, volleyball, softball, and soccer, to track and field, table tennis, handball, paddle ball, boccie, and shuffle board.[36] While teams tended to be segregated along racial and ethnic lines, it was not uncommon for Latinos and African-American prisoners, particularly during the late 1970s and 1980s, to play together on some teams.[37] Such mixing was sometimes resented by other Latino and African-American prisoners.[38] Because Green Haven was divided into east and west wings, there were times when Latino prisoners had two sets of sports teams. For example, during the late 1970s, Latino prisoners on one side of the prison played on the Canecas softball team, while those on the other side played in the Borinquen Soul team.[39] Other recreational activities Latinos engaged in included table games of dominoes, chess, checkers, and pinochle as well as musical bands formed by Latino prisoners that played at institutional events.[40]

The role played by social and recreational activities, particularly sports, in helping build prisoner solidarity and leadership capabilities should not be underestimated.[41] Sports allowed prisoners to strengthen their self-esteem, vent their emotions, cultivate discipline, work collectively to achieve common goals, and remain occupied. The latter was particularly important during those times in which there was a high degree of overcrowding, prisoner idleness, and few programs available to occupy prisoners' time.

Another advantage of sports activities was that it took place in the yards, where the greatest degree of prisoner interaction took place and staff exercised the least direct control. As former African-American prisoner Elmer Daniels expressed: "I'd always try to carve out a space that uniquely I could operate in without running into that bureaucracy, and that was mostly sports, you know, if it was organizing a league or having a pitchers' class or something like that . . . it dealt with the yard and the teams primarily . . ."[42]

It was also in the yards, as will be shown further, that prisoner leaders educated their peers politically. In a setting in which such political discussion was frequently penalized, social and recreational activities provided safe covers. Most frequently, however, social and recreational activities allowed prisoners to share camaraderie and ease the tensions created by their captivity. Another of the ways Latino prisoners provided one another support and met their material needs, was through their participation in a wide range of underground economic groups and networks.

Latino Prisoner Participation
in the Underground Prison Market

The material deprivations prisoners endured in penal settings,[43] coupled with the fact that even ordinary actions, such as taking food to one's room, could be considered a violation of institutional rules, made it almost impossible for Latino prisoners to not participate in activities prohibited by DOCS. In addition, Latino prisoners, like their African-American and white counterparts, deliberately defied institutional rules and regulations to have access to a number of desired goods and services. Gregorio Palma describes some of the goods considered contraband.

> We would take can tops and turn them into a cutter. You fold one edge of the can top and you'd use that to cut onions. Everybody has a can top in their cell. Well, they would write you up for contraband. Sometimes the pots and pans they would catch you with, the stoves. If they found you with eggs, raw eggs, wire, some clips, any, you know, little tools. And, you know, prisoners are always making little tools to be able to do a little handiwork. If your radio breaks, you want to fix it so you take a clip and, you know, you try to turn it into a screw driver.[44]

Engaging in proscribed activities required prisoners to become more resourceful.

> You're not supposed to cook in your cell using electrical equipment . . . Well, I had to get a coil and I had to turn it . . . into a wheel with two ends and then I had to attach electrical wires to it, a resistance cord. And that gets so hot it's like a stove. . . . So I had to learn how to make that. And I had built all these little gadgets. And of course, all this stuff is illegal to have . . .[45]

To have access to proscribed goods and services, prisoners developed an underground economy. Anthony L. Guenther called the various types of activities at the center of this underground economy the "prisoner market system."[46] While I agree with Guenther that this type of underground network constituted a market, I hesitate to call it a "prisoner" market because of the frequent participation of staff in such networks. The term underground prison market more aptly describes these sets of relationships. The main currency used in this market was cigarettes, although at Green Haven drugs and money (considered contraband) were also used as currency.[47] At Green Haven there were Latino prisoners who engaged in gambling, loan sharking, and stealing or selling stolen goods. Others engaged in the production of alcohol, and the smuggling, distribution, and sale of drugs. "Personalized"[48] services included, among others, the sale and/or interchange of clothing, food, lumber, information, protection, sex, haircuts, laundry services, legal advice, letter writing and translating, and transporting goods from one section of the prison to another. Gregorio Palma, described the bartering system that developed as part of the underground prison market.

> Cigarettes is money in prison but also there's a bargaining system . . . everybody has a service they can provide. So guys work together, you know, "Whatever you need, I take care of. . . . For me, I never went hungry in prison because I could cook. There was a lot of guys who had big packages, they had all the connections in the mess hall, they can get anything they wanted, but they didn't know what to do with it, so they always called on me, so I could always cook . . .

> A guy that works in the laundry has access to pants and shirts, and he can also do your laundry every week. You see, we get contracts. . . . For a carton of cigarettes a month. . . . I would get a guy to wash my clothes once a week. He would take them to the laundry, put them in the washing machine and he'd bring them back folded. And all I had to do was iron them. And for a little more, they would even iron your shirts, but we always found a way of getting an iron.

> Okay, now the guy in the mess hall, he gets fish, chicken, onions, lettuce, tomatoes, all these things that you don't have access to unless you get it through a package, and you could only get two packages a month or one thirty-five pound package a month. So we would contract with the individual to have . . . all the ingredients. . . . You'd give them two packs of cigarettes and he would bring you all these things. And if you gave him a carton a month or every commissary, he would make sure that he gave you some chicken . . . and raw rice . . .

> . . . the plumbing shop could make pots and pans . . . So you would make contracts with all these different guys to have different things.[49]

Participation in underground economic networks also took place within the aegis of the new formal prisoner groups and programs created as a result of the post-Attica Rebellion reforms.

Now . . . a lot of us were clerical individuals and we would be in charge of all the events, festivities. Now, suppose you wanted to go to an event and only your family is allowed to come, but because I'm doing the call-out and I'm approving your family, I would put on the call-out your girlfriend who is not allowed to come because she is not a family member. . . . Or I would be able to get your name on a call-out for the festival that is happening that is already filled up. . . . And I would know all the people that were canceling out, so those slots would open up and I would get them. So now the guy in the mess hall would tell me, "I need two slots," and I'd be able to do that for him. Or in the Pre-Release Center we would invite guest speakers in or we would do legal motions. You know, if somebody needed an Article 78, one of us can do it up.[50]

Interestingly, Palma saw the bargaining skills acquired within the prison setting as a reproduction of similar skills highly valued outside the institution. "I tell you, prison made me a hell of a politician. . . . And it made me understand the political systems and how to work within the dynamics of these systems and how communities worked."[51]

While the exploitative nature of underground economic networks has been explored extensively by social scientists, the role such networks played in helping to build loyalty and solidarity among groups of prisoners (including prisoner leaders) has been underplayed.

And there was a bunch of us who were doing this and we would eat real good because the foods in the mess halls . . . were bland and they were not cultural. . . . As a matter of fact . . . if the guys remember me for anything, it was more for my cooking than anything else. . . . So these are little things that bring guys together, you know, this sense of camaraderie. A lot of the guys, like Eric Elliott . . . him and I cooked for years together.[52]

Participation in the underground economy generally took place within racial/ethnic groups because those were the bonds prisoners tended to trust most. There were exceptions to this. First, there were Latinos who sold goods and services to whomever paid the highest price. Secondly, there were Latinos who engaged in proscribed activities with homeboys and/or clique members. As stated earlier, such groups could include African-American and white prisoners as well.

Furthermore, Latinos who engaged in the smuggling, sale, and distribution of drugs frequently did so with the participation of non-Latino
prisoners and staff persons because this type of operation required the
existence of extensive contacts within and outside the institution.
During the 1980s, as the number of Latino prisoners increased so did
their control over the drug trade. According to Palma: "In New York, by
and large, the Latinos own the drug trade, Blacks are in it, too, but not
to the extent that Latinos are . . . Blacks originally had it, but . . .
Latinos who are coming to prison predominantly are all coming to
prison for drugs, so they're individuals that are connected and they
have the contacts." However, as the composition of the Latino prisoner
population experienced changes during the 1980s so did the control of
the drug trade. "I would say by and large the Dominicans have a
greater grasp of the drug trade now in the prison system but they basically have a lot of control over the cocaine. Heroin is still Puerto Rican
and Black."[53] Undoubtedly such struggles for control over the distribution and sale of drugs contributed to increasing nationality-based tensions and divisions among Latino prisoners.

Internal drug connections at times extended outside the prison. "If
you have people that will work with you, if you have a network of, you
know, homeboys or . . . gang or whatever . . . I've seen people . . . send
people to other's people's houses to collect money.[54]

Drug networks involved the participation of institutional personnel, particularly guards, because they were among the few persons
who could enter and leave the institution free of major searches. While
not all guards participated in underground economic networks, it was
not uncommon for them to turn their heads the other way when they
discovered prisoners engaging in such, and other less serious, rule
violations on a day-to-day basis. For example, prisoners who cooked
in their cells were generally able to do so because there were guards
who participated in such rule violations.

> You'd smoke cigar inside your cell, you know, throw . . . a towel over
> the door or something, so that, you know, they can't smell it. And
> then your friend is outside and might be a porter and he's smoking
> a cigar and they wouldn't smell it. Or when he's coming, you know,
> you would fan, or, you know, [use] baby powder or incense. But a lot
> of guards also like to eat and they knew that we were cooking. So
> you hit the guard with a plate and he turned his head. . . .[55]

At other times, guards were the initiators of such transgressions. "I
tasted deer meat for the first time in prison. A guard went hunting.

He caught a deer and, you know, brought in some deer steaks. I cooked them for him and he gave me half of the package. So there were little things that we did for each other."[56]

However, within the underground economy, Latino and African-American prisoners were generally at a disadvantage relative to white prisoners. Whites were disproportionately assigned to jobs which accrued the most privileges and, hence, the most access to supplies and services which could be sold on the underground market. Moreover, prison guards tended to sanction the actions of white prisoners more often. This was particularly true during the 1970s, when white prisoners, generally those with "organized crime connections," were frequently allowed by white guards to use drugs and alcohol and to visit prostitutes and criminal associates while on trips outside the facility. These favors were granted prisoners in exchange for cash and other material goods.[57]

Palma describes how the participation of racist white guards in underground economic activities produced a situation in which Latino and African-American prisoners were more likely to be penalized than white prisoners for similar transgressions.

> There was an officer once, his name was Deer. . . . He would let the whites cook but he was dead against the Blacks and the Latinos cooking. This was in J Block. And . . . everybody would lock in at 4 o'clock and you would not be released 'til 6 o'clock. . . . They call that, "the count." And he would let the whites out in fifteen minutes. . . . There was a room that was like a kitchen . . . and the whites would come with their, you know . . . stoves and they would cook in there and he would eat with them. But if a Latino was caught cooking in his cell, he would write him up, take the stove from them, take the pots and pans. And a lot of times the white guys would wind up with your pots and pans. . . . One day he caught me with a pan, I was making pizza and he took the pan and everything. I had borrowed the stuff. . . . I asked him, "Please, don't take this from me. I give you my word you won't catch me cooking again." He wouldn't let me go. He wrote me up and he took my pots and pans.[58]

As shown above, Latino prisoner participation in the underground prison economy was geared toward securing access to a number of desired goods and services. Such activities frequently took place with the active participation and/or encouragement of custodial personnel.[59] It was not uncommon, however, for prison guards, to penalize Latino and African-American prisoners for rule infractions while ignoring those of their white peers.

Guard victimization of Latino prisoners was exacerbated by the exploitation Latino prisoners experienced at the hands of one another. While underground economic networks helped prisoners meet each other's daily needs and wants, a discussion of the underground prison economy would not be complete without a brief reference to its more exploitative and volatile aspects.

> ... prisoners are only a microcosm of ... general society, you know, so ... the drugs, the violence, gangs, extortions, sexual relationships, prostitution, all of those things exist in prison ... the only difference is that they're closed in and so ... they're exacerbated by just the daily tension ... and the stress ... and the pressure of prison life, okay, with the potential threat always right there on the surface, of violence ... So people do network a lot of different ways. ... They recreate environments that ... they're more comfortable with ... that they're most knowledgeable about, okay? If it's swagging, which is like running little rackets of, maybe, how they can liberate food from the mess hall and then sell it ... that might be their means of survival on the inside. Or maybe making wine or ... getting drugs in and selling them, of course, at, you know, tremendously inflated prices. ... Having a chain of homosexual prostitutes or relationships, that might be their racket, you know, being a pimp on the inside. Yeah, so all those things are recreated in prison life, and ... they account for a lot of the actual violence of prison. Mostly ... the violence that takes place in prisons ... doesn't ... stem from ... the politically aware or the activists or the progressive people ... it stems basically out of people who are so caught up, you know, in all that bullshit, the same type of stuff they was involved with in the street. ... That's where the stabbings come from, most of the fights, and it's very much a part of prison life.[60]

A great deal of the violence prisoners perpetrated against one another was motivated by the need to survive imprisonment and/or acquire a number of desired goods and services. Survival entailed resorting to behaviors which were the most familiar and/or comfortable means available. While some of these behaviors were learnt prior to imprisonment, others were adopted upon incarceration. Within this context two of the goals of politicized Latino and African-American prisoner leaders, as will be discussed in the following chapters, were to encourage prisoners to change those behaviors which contributed to intra-prisoner victimization while highlighting the common ways prisoners were oppressed by their keepers.

While the mass media and the social science literature on prisons have tended to highlight this exploitative nature of prisoner society, the current study stresses how such victimization took place alongside the existence of numerous overlapping informal prisoner groups created for the purpose of providing members support. One of the ways in which Latino prisoners sought the support of their informal groups and networks to survive prison life was by using their support system to challenge discriminatory treatment by staff. Below, Palma describes the actions he took against the white officer who wrote him up and took his pots and pans for cooking in his room.

> I got very mad . . . so I told a few of my friends, "Watch, I'm going to get this guy." The next day I was out of my cell, and I remember I had a needle and I was sewing my shorts. . . . And I was just waiting because I knew . . . this guy would get a Kosher diet stolen from the kitchen every day . . . and that's illegal. Officers are not allowed to eat inmate food . . . at that time I was a grievance representative and I had . . . a lot of clout because I was sort of like a representative of the prison population. Well this guy got these two trays and. . . . I waited. . . . And when he got into eating them I ran up to the console where he was at and I pulled out my finger as if I was a cop and I said . . . "I'm making a citizen's arrest. You're in trouble . . . Now I want you to call the watch commander. He's waiting!" He bitched over me, "No, I don't want to!" Now all the tough guy that he was and all the abuses that he was doing everybody, all of that went out the window. . . . He was like a little kid. And so many guys got pleasure out of that 'cause . . . he was always writing everybody up and harassing and oppressing all the men on the floor, except for that little clique of white guys. . . . And I told somebody, "Call the sergeant for me," and they went and got me a sergeant. I showed the sergeant the two plates of food. Well, that guy disappeared. We never saw him again.[61]

However, not all Latinos were so situated within the facility's structure to enable them to confront the actions of guards directly. Generally, ". . . when you make the complaint about a cop . . . you just got to learn to accept it unless you got money to go to court . . ."[62] Prisoners like Palma, who was bilingual and an IGRC representative, were in a better position to confront the actions of guards. Although, even in his case, retaliating against a white guard brought the wrath of other guards on him.

> I paid hell for that because . . . all his buddies . . . started picking on me. . . . They started writing me up for every little thing and . . . they

would open all my dresser drawers and all my boxes, take all my shirts and throw them in the middle of the floor and walk on them. And they would pour baby oil on them and water. And . . . you know, in prison your belongings mean so much to you because they are so hard to come by. And I had to stand there and watch them abuse me like that. . . . And they were looking at personal items, private pictures from a girlfriend of mine who had sent me nude pictures and they were looking at them and joking. . . . They were just totally humiliating me, raped mentally. . . . And every day they would do this or every other day. . . . I learned to deal with that because what they wanted me to do was to make me react. If I said anything they would take me to the box. So I had to stand there and be quiet and take this. They would write me up for all these tickets. Anything in prison is contraband. . . . And they could write you up for a million things. And most of my tickets while I was in prison were for contraband, for little things like that.[63]

No area of a prisoner's life was spared harassment.

I had also gotten a job in the radio room as an announcer for the prison and the job was taken from me because of one of these guards. . . . During the time I was being harassed, he went up to the radio room and he found a whole bunch of legal stamps, they were there for years before I ever got there, and he said they were mine and I lost the job because of that.[64]

Faced with this situation Palma, once again, sought the support of other prisoners to counteract the actions of guards.

I belonged to a network where we never hassled the officers . . . but if there was an officer that was very abusive, was very racist, we would come together against him. And a lot of us knew how to write. We knew how to complain. We knew how to make things work.

And one day I started fighting back. And I had friends that would rally with me when I was trouble . . . and when they were in trouble I would rally with them against whoever was oppressing us 'cause most of us, by and large, we weren't troublemakers. . . . We had little things that were illegal, you know, but it wasn't nothing major. We were cooking and things like that. That was survival and you wanted to eat a good meal. So they rallied with me and I started writing these guys up, and they backed off for a little while. One day they come to my cell, and I had been in prison almost nine years. I'm going for clemency, and they found out. They'd read my papers. They threw them away . . . and they said, "We found two joints under your bed on the floor." . . . The thing is that they didn't even find the joints or they put them there themselves. I got locked up, big investigation and man, they really put me through changes but all this was behind that officer that we got rid of.

I was able through all these guys that were witnesses for me in showing what happened, they dismissed that case for me. But a lot of times I would get locked up for thirty days or twenty days or fifteen days in my cell, you know. And I couldn't go to work, couldn't come out, that type of stuff.[65]

In summary, Latino prisoners, with the support of informal groups and networks, were at times able to successfully counter the actions of guards they perceived as being particularly oppressive. However, the probability that penal administrators would consistently contradict the decisions of its own staff was not likely. Moreover, even when successful, Latino prisoners still had to contend with the retaliatory actions of other guards, and, at times, of the civilian staff as well.

It was partially a result of the consistent inability of Latino and non-Latino prisoners to openly confront both DOCS policies and the behavior of staff, which led them to form political underground groups for the purpose of achieving a redefinition of the terms and conditions of their imprisonment. While some of these political groups were organized along racial or ethnic lines, others were interracial/interethnic. In fact, right before and after the Attica Rebellion, political underground groups at Green Haven were forming interracial/interethnic coalitions that sought to challenge custodial hegemony. Such organizing was opposed by penal administrators who countered prisoners' political organizing efforts with a combination of reforms and repression aimed at reducing prisoner discontent and political activism. It is the diverse actions pursued by political underground prisoner groups and coalitions and the response of penal personnel to them that will be discussed in the following chapter.

Notes: Chapter 5

1. For such discussions, see Leo Carroll, *Hacks, Blacks and Convicts: Race Relations in a Maximum Security Prison* (Prospect Heights, Ill.: Waveland Press, Inc. [1974] 1988); Donald Clemmer, *The Prison Community* (Boston: The Christopher Publishing House, 1940); Richard A. Cloward, Donald R. Cressey, George H. Grosser, Richard McCleery, Lloyd E. Ohlin, and Gresham

M. Sykes, *Theoretical Studies in the Social Organization of the Prison,* Pamphlet No. 15, Social Science Research Council, 1960; R. Theodore Davidson, *Chicano Prisoners: The Key to San Quentin* (New York: Holt, Rinehart and Winston, 1974); James G. Fox, *Organizational and Racial Conflict in Maximum-Security Prisons* (Lexington, Mass.: D.C. Heath and Co., 1982); Rose Giallombardo, *Society of Women: A Study of a Women's Prison* (New York: John Wiley and Sons, 1966); Erving Goffman, *Asylums* (Garden City: Doubleday, 1961); John Irwin, *The Felon* (Englewood Cliffs: Prentice-Hall, Inc., 1970); John Irwin and Donald Cressey, "Thieves, Convicts, and Inmate Culture," *Social Problems,* Vol. 10 (1962): 142–155; James B. Jacobs, *New Perspectives on Prisons and Imprisonment* (Ithaca: Cornell University Press, 1983); Joan W. Moore, *Homeboys: Gangs, Drugs and Prisons in the Barrios of Los Angeles* (Philadelphia: Temple University Press, 1978); Gresham Sykes, *The Society of Captives: The Study of a Maximum Security Prison* (New Jersey: Princeton University Press, 1958); and David A. Ward and Gene G. Kassebaum, *Women's Prisons* (London: Weidenfeld and Nicolson, 1965).

2. According to Gregorio Palma, a clique was "a group of individuals who had something in common" (Gregorio Palma [pseud.], interview with author, New York, N.Y., 16 April and 1 May 1993). Francis A.J. Ianni prefers to use the term "courts" to "cliques." See Francis A.J. Ianni, *Black Mafia: Ethnic Succession in Organized Crime* (New York: Simon and Schuster, 1974). John Irwin spoke of the existence of cliques and "tips." He defined tips as ". . . extended social networks or crowds that were loosely held together by shared subcultural orientations or pre-prison acquaintances. Most of the tips were interracial, and they were overlapping and connected. Consequently, an individual could be involved in more than one tip and usually was related to other tips that connected with his own. . . . Prisoners formed smaller cliques within or across tips" (John Irwin, *Prisons in Turmoil* [Boston: Little, Brown and Co., 1980], 58–59).

3. This was also the experience of Piri Thomas while imprisoned in New York State during the 1950s (Piri Thomas, interview with author, Binghamton, N.Y., 19 April 1993).

4. Howell (Sonny) Williams, "The Ghetto Prison (as I see it)," *Green Haven Monthly* (hereafter cited as *GHM*) 3, No. 8 (August/September 1980): 10.

5. Palma, interview with author, 1993.

6. Ibid.

7. Ibid.

8. Nathaniel Sheppard Jr., "A Rare Inside Look at Green Haven Prison, Troubled but Innovative State Institution," *New York Times* [hereafter cited as *N.Y. Times*), 17 August 1976, 62.

9. Ibid.

10. Ibid.

11. Ibid.

12. Palma, interview with author, 1993.

13. Ibid.

14. Ibid.

15. Ibid.

16. Ibid.

17. Ibid.

18. Eddie Rosa [pseud.], interview with author, New Paltz, N.Y., 19 February 1989.

19. Domingo Morales [pseud.], interview with author, New York, N.Y., 6 April 1993.

20. Ibid.

21. Eric Elliott [pseud.], interview with author, New York, N.Y., 15 April 1993.

22. Morales, interview with author, 1993.

23. Michael Armstrong [pseud.], interview with author, New York, N.Y., 22 April 1993.

24. Elliott, interview with author, 1993.

25. Angel Gear [pseud.], interview with author, New York, N.Y., 8 April 1993.

26. Ibid. The political role Latino homeboy networks and cliques played in helping to organize collective acts of resistance in New York State prisons as early as the 1950s was described by Piri Thomas. See Piri Thomas, *Seven Long Times* (New York: Praeger Publishers, 1974), 183–192, 209–219.

27. Armstrong, interview with author, 1993.

28. Morales, interview with author, 1993.

29. Ibid.

30. Ibid.

31. Palma, interview with author, 1993.

32. Morales, interview with author, 1993.

33. Mariel Cubans were those who left Cuba through the port of Mariel during April 1980.

34. Palma, interview with author, 1993; and Rosa, interview with author, 1993.

35. Ibid.

36. Michael Armstrong and Elmer Daniels stated that the quality of the players in some of the teams (e.g., football, softball) was so high that it was not unusual for prisoner teams to play against outside non-prisoner sports teams. These games were also one of the few forms of entertainment available to much of the surrounding rural white population. Therefore, it was not unusual for prison guards and their families to provide the main audience for prisoner sports teams (Armstrong, interview with author, 1993; and Elmer Daniels [pseud.], interview with author, New York, N.Y., 15 and 16 April 1993).

37. See "Wild Bunch" (photograph), *GHM* 2, No. 9 (September 1979): 16; and Richard Montero, "1979 Green Haven Soccer Champions—The Warriors," *GHM* 2, No. 9 (September 1979): 19.

38. Daniels, interview with author, 1993.

39. Bob Maldonado, "Divisional Playoffs: Borinquen Soul vs. Canecas," *GHM* (September 1979): 14.

40. These bands included "Inspiración Latina," "Conjunto Le-Lo-Lai," "Conjunto Cristiano Salvación de Almas," "Conjunto Raíz," and "5–1" ("Hispanos en Acción," *GHM* [February/March 1982]: 18; and José R. Rodríguez, "Fiesta De San Juan Bautista," *GHM* 6, No. 6 [August 1983]: 11).

41. According to one person interviewed it was prisoners involved in sports (e.g., the coaches of the sports teams) who came to the forefront of the leadership during the Attica Rebellion.

42. Daniels, interview with author, 1993.

43. Gresham Sykes described such deprivations as encompassing: the deprivation of liberty (with its accompanying isolation from those on the outside, loneliness and boredom); deprivation of autonomy (with its accompanying attempt to control every minute detail in prisoners' lives); deprivation of security; deprivation of goods and services (including "amenities" such as cigarettes, drugs, alcohol, clothing and food of one's liking, etc.); and, deprivation of heterosexual relationships (Gresham Sykes, "The Pains of Imprisonment," in Robert G. Culbertson and Ralph Weisheit, eds., *"Order Under Law": Readings in Criminal Justice* [Prospect Heights, Ill.: Waveland Press, Inc., 3rd ed., 1988], 221–231).

44. Palma, interview with author, 1993.

45. Ibid.

46. Anthony L. Guenther, "Prison Rackets," in Culbertson and Weisheit, eds., "Order Under Law," 232–255.

47. Money could also be saved and sent home for use after one's release.

48. Guenther, "Prison Rackets," 242–244.

49. Palma, interview with author, 1993.

50. Ibid.

51. Ibid.

52. Ibid.

53. Ibid.

54. Ibid. Francis A. Ianni argued that the networks Latinos and African-Americans established inside prison opened the door to criminal activity on the outside once released because ". . . shared prison experience provides a basis of trust for risky activities outside . . . Not only do men learn to work together, they make contacts that will later afford them access to otherwise closed neighborhood networks" (Francis A.J. Ianni, *Black Mafia: Ethnic Succession in Organized Crime* [New York: Simon and Schuster, 1974], 155). Ianni held that this was not the case for Italians in prison whose contacts with organized criminal activities (e.g., Mafia) were established through family and kinship ties on the outside. Additionally, members of white organized crime were not as likely to be imprisoned as were Latinos and African-Americans.

55. Palma, interview with author, 1993.

56. Ibid.

57. E.J. Dionne, "In Green Haven Inquiry," *N.Y. Times,* 12 June 1981, II, 3. For a more detailed discussion of corruption at Green Haven, see New York State Temporary Commission of Investigation (NYSTCI), *Corruption and Abuse in the Correctional System: The Green Haven Correctional Facility,* May 1981. Interestingly, an investigation of Green Haven blamed the increase in guard corruption on the post-Attica reforms which had liberalized prison conditions (Ibid.).

58. Palma, interview with author, 1993.

59. Although the focus has been on custodial personnel, it should be made clear that civilian staff participate in such networks as well.

60. Gear, interview with author, 1993.

61 Palma, interview with author, 1993.

62. Morales, interview with author, 1993.

63. Palma, interview with author, 1993.

64. Ibid.

65. Ibid.

6

Political Underground Prisoner Groups and Coalitions

"... We don't belong to the state, we're the community folks ..."
—Angel Gear, interview with author (1993)

As the previous chapter showed, Latino, African-American, and white prisoners formed a series of informal prisoner groups to address a number of overlapping concerns. Differences in cultural heritage and language, as well as the discrimination they faced from non-Latino prisoners and staff, led Latino prisoners to form informal groups based on ethnicity. However, Latino prisoners in these groups further subdivided according to nationality, language spoken, immigration status, and color.

Although the general assumption is that members of most types of informal groups tend to be "apolitical," the distinction between what constituted political and apolitical activities was not always clear-cut. On the one hand, even the most radical prisoners participated out of necessity in activities organized by informal groups and networks otherwise considered apolitical.[1] On the other hand, as shall be discussed in this chapter, the treatment accorded prisoners by staff, sometimes led even the most apolitical prisoners to participate in reform-oriented coalitions.

Within this context, one of the goals of Latino prisoner leaders was to make Latino prisoners change those behaviors which contributed to the victimization of their peers both within the prison environment and their communities on the outside. A complementary goal was to highlight the common oppression to which prisoners were subjected by penal personnel and the manner in which Latino, African-American and poor whites were oppressed by the powers that be inside and outside the walls.

Although there were many reasons prisoners needed to be politically active, according to Angel Gear, African-American prisoner leader at Green Haven during the early 1970s, "the same thing that

153

was true for the majority of the Black prisoners in Green Haven . . . true for . . . Latinos was that . . . they was not politically involved."[2] One reason for this was that some prisoners preferred "doing their own time." For others, the support they received from the informal groups they participated in was enough to see them through their experience of incarceration. However, for many, it was prison authorities' response to prisoners' reform attempts that determined their political involvement. Speaking about the reasons for prisoners' fears at Green Haven during the early 1970s, Gear stated:

> . . . many prisoners were . . . afraid, you know, to be associated even with anybody that was talking about prisoners' unity or anything like that . . . because if you got branded "militant" or "revolutionary". . . you could kiss . . . your opportunity for parole goodbye, you know? And this is one of the . . . tactics that . . . prison officials tried to use to maintain some semblance of order or total control . . . to keep prisoners fighting at each other or afraid to come together . . .[3]

Other tactics used to prevent prisoner unification efforts included:

> . . . anywhere from being beaten, being . . . put in . . . keep-lock, being put in segregation, the box, to be, you know, shipped out to other institutions hundreds of miles away . . . in the middle of the night . . . and in those days particularly, if you ended up going to the box, you know, I mean, it was very likely . . . that you also ended up being beaten and . . . gassed . . .

> As a matter of fact, in those days, the New York State . . . they call themselves correctional officers, you know, still carried . . . batons . . . inside the prison . . . Because like in prison . . . wherever we went . . . from cell block to cell block to cell block, the mess halls, whatever, we marched in a line, alright? And the guards . . . used these . . . batons, they'd hit the wall, you know, one to stop and two to go . . . So there was still very much that whole physical attempt to intimidate, you know. And . . . people were being dragged out of their cell in the middle of the night 'cause they'd been identified as being a leader or a revolutionary or . . . they're . . . holding law classes or they . . . put in some class action suit or something against the institution . . .[4]

In spite of such intimidation, at the time of the Attica Rebellion, Green Haven's prisoner population contained a significant number of politically active prisoners. Shortly after the Attica Rebellion their ranks were reinforced by the transfer of over two hundred Attica prisoners to Green Haven.

As stated earlier, reform-oriented prisoners tended to form political underground prisoner groups because their ideologies and/or reform-oriented efforts were labeled "revolutionary" or "militant" by prison authorities and were thus heavily penalized. Undeniably, Latino, and some of the non-Latino prisoner leaders of the time considered themselves revolutionaries in the sense that they believed capitalism and U.S./European hegemony had to be overthrown to eliminate the exploitation of people of color by whites, and that of poor people by capitalists. However, what made an activity or a group revolutionary or militant, legitimate or illegitimate in the eyes of the penal bureaucracy depended more on DOCS' regulations and the personal idiosyncrasies of individual line staff and administrators. For example, according to Rule 105.10 in DOCS' *Standards of Inmate Behavior*, "The unauthorized assembly of inmates in groups is prohibited."[5] This regulation created a "catch-22" situation for prisoners. Many activities and groups were not recognized by penal personnel as legitimate. Hence, they were labelled militant or revolutionary. As a result, prisoners were not authorized to pursue those activities. Thus, the need to organize underground. Political underground activities at Green Haven, during the late 1960s, and early 1970s, included a broad range of issues such as: demands for better prison conditions; organizing a prisoners' labor union; advocating specific political beliefs (e.g., Marxism, Puerto Rican independence, racial/ethnic concerns); membership in the Nation of Islam; and, generally, any action seeking to empower prisoners. According to Gear:

> . . . just in terms of organizing on the inside with people who are about the same type of thing . . .whether it's the law library or a Black history class or a Latino history class could be called subversive, okay? It intends to cause some type of organizing. . . . It's a quote "a threat" to the system . . . and could cause a person to be put in keep-lock or in segregation for many days, weeks or months, you know . . . you might go to keep-lock or segregation for one thing but then once you get there you're . . . cited for two, three, four or five different other things, you know, so you don't never get out, you know . . .[6]

Asked where these organizing activities took place, Gear responded: "Well, we met in the yard . . . on the picnic tables and, you know, we were certainly under their watchful eyes. Which in those type of meetings and that type of being watched certainly caused . . . many of comrades to . . . like go to the box or be shipped out, you know . . ."[7]

While prisoners knew such meetings could result in reprisals, they continued to meet because:

> . . . part of the defiance and the confrontation was going ahead and meeting anyway, you know. . . . I guess it was . . . almost like a soldier . . . you expect all these other things to happen to you and you just had to bear up and . . . survive, you know, the best way you could . . . and it was happening from prison to prison to prison, so the network was when you went into another prison, you just gravitated to those that were doing the same thing there, you know, and this is how you became known all around the state.[8]

Asked how the leaders for the various political groups were chosen, Gear responded:

> . . . leaders aren't really picked, the leaders, you know, grow out of . . . or they rise up . . . People who exhibit consistency and commitment and dedication and insight and the foresight . . . and . . . showed the type of willingness . . . an ability to really, you know, motivate . . . usually are recognized by others, by their ability and willingness to sacrifice . . .[9]

The willingness of prisoner leaders to confront prison authorities at any personal cost motivated other prisoners to do the same. Hence, the multiple attempts by institutional personnel to persecute and isolate prisoner leaders from the general prisoner population.

> . . . the prison officials . . . they try to intimidate . . . the regular population . . . but actually the . . . prison population usually end up respecting the brothers that . . . go through the changes . . . even though they might call them crazy, whatever, but they end up really . . . respecting them a lot based on their willingness to stand on principles for the things that they believe in, you know, and to endure and to thrive . . . after going through so much.[10]

With few exceptions, political underground groups, like other types of informal prisoner groups and networks, were organized along ethnic or racial lines. African-American prisoners were subdivided mainly into the Black Panther Party, the Nation of Islam, the Sunni Muslims, the Five Percent Nation, and the African Revolutionary Movement.[11] While some of the above groups would define themselves as religious and not political, I have put them in the latter category because of the manner in which they sought to make their concerns heard and the way in which DOCS responded to their attempts.

Following the Attica Rebellion, Latino prisoner leaders tended to identify themselves with the Young Lords/Palante and the People's Party. There were also some Puerto Ricans who joined the Nation of Islam. A few white prisoners identified with radical white groups such as the Weather Underground. However, according to Gear, ". . . at least in Green Haven, for the most part, there wasn't any real strong, like, white socialist Weathermen . . . SDS type of presence. It was strictly, for the most part, a Latino and a Black . . . population struggle . . ."[12]

There were white prisoners who openly identified with the KKK and other white supremacist groups. Most white prisoner groups, ". . . were formulated around the fringes of organized crime or those . . . supposedly involved with organized crime . . . members or "wannabees," you know. And they were the basis of the . . . bulk group of whites in the prison, in terms of those who had any cohesiveness."[13] Writing about the early 1972 period at Green Haven, Francis A.J. Ianni (1974) stated:

> The Palante[14] is but one of the numerous political organizations that exist . . . Black Panthers, Black Muslims, Five Per Centers, Maoists, all have a political line and many believe they have a task to enlighten the inmate population as to their conception of political reality. Classes in Black history, Arabic and law are taught in the yard, even though all these activities are hated and feared by the administration and persecuted accordingly.[15]

Because the prison was divided into an east side and a west side, political underground prisoner groups had representatives on both sides of the institution. ". . . you had a group of Panthers or People's Party on the east side, you had another group on the west side, but they was part of the same party, you know, they just didn't interact every day . . . but that was part of the network, to get things happening on both sides of the prison."[16]

According to Gear, political identifications were generally adopted during imprisonment.

> . . . there was a few people who was involved in the movement before they came in the prison but most of the people that I've met, you know, who were involved with those organizations became involved while they were at the prison . . . So, as a result, . . . prison played a . . . very strong role in helping to . . . educate people in terms of . . .

changing their politics and changing some of their ideas about who they were.[17]

This held true for Latino,[18] African-American, and white prisoner leaders. In terms of political orientation, according to Martín Sostre, "Most of the political Puerto Rican prisoners and for most prisons, not only at Green Haven . . . were Puerto Rican nationalists."[19] The role Latino prisoner leaders played in coalition-building efforts was significant. "Latinos under the leadership of the Young Lords and . . . also the Latinos that was involved with the People's Party at the time . . . played a very strong leadership role in the prison."[20] As in the case of Attica, Latino prisoner leaders not only sought to create unity among Latino and non-Latino prisoners but to educate the Latino prisoner population as well. Sostre described some of the difficulties encountered when Puerto Rican prison activists attempted to politicize their peers.

> Naturally you couldn't get all of them because there's a lot of others that wouldn't participate in anything. You know, they were scared . . . they thought that by going along with the man and . . . being good model prisoners, that they would go home. So I don't care what you told them, you couldn't organize them, you know? Latinos, as well as Blacks. But the ones that were political, these were the ones that knew that regardless what you did . . . the authorities were going to treat you the same. You weren't going to get no favors, no favoritism. And they used one to undermine or maybe even snitch on the others.[21]

Informants were instrumental in fostering disunity among Latino prisoners.

> Then they had the snitches, the ass kissers, that were working for the man inside the prisons trying to persuade these Puerto Ricans and tell them, "Oye, esos tipos están locos. Déjate, no te metas con esos tipos. Mira. Te vieron ya jangueando con fulano y eso no te conviene porque cuando veas al parole board no te van a dejar salir."[22] You know, they would scare them . . . Let's say me or some other militant was coming down toward them and they would look the other way . . . like they don't . . . even see us, okay, because they don't want the man to even see them even talking to us. And they would shy away from us like we had the plague. But those that knew what was happening, we stuck together and we went on the strike and we did things together to demand our rights . . .[23]

Part of educating the mostly Puerto Rican Latino prisoner population at the time involved pointing out the similarities between the
treatment Puerto Ricans received from the white-dominated power
structure inside the prisons, outside in the ghettos, and in Puerto Rico.

> . . . they got groups that do nothing but bullshit. All they do is play
> dominoes and cards to pass time away . . . But there's a lot of groups
> there that become politicized and become aware as to the conditions
> that forced them to commit that crime that they were sentenced [for].
> And then, when they look around and it's pointed out to them that,
> "How come there's mostly Blacks and Hispanics there?" A lot of them
> are not even aware of that. They think that this is a natural state of
> affairs, you know, because . . . when you get arrested you are with the
> majority of Puerto Ricans and Blacks in prison . . . but the judges and
> the lawyers are white. So the average person, they consider this a
> way of life because that's all they know until it's pointed out to them
> by a political person, "Look, this isn't right. How come we're the
> minority here in this country and yet we're the majority in the pris-
> ons but when it comes to the jobs in Wall Street and comes to the
> good jobs and whatnot, we're the minority, you know, if any at all."

> Some were pro-United States . . . some were nationalists, some were
> neutral. So we used to get in arguments, I said, "You know some-
> thing? Here you are, you're for the United States. You're for Puerto
> Rico continuing to be a colony and if it's so good, how come you were
> forced out of Puerto Rico, your own country, to come here, live in the
> ghetto, where you couldn't make a living and then come to jail?
> There's your capitalism. . . . Another thing, all these other countries,
> they got countries that don't have not even a quarter of a million peo-
> ple yet they have their ambassadors. They're respected. They have
> the United Nations representatives. They have their own money. . . .
> You can't even do anything with foreign relations. You got to have
> boss man tell you what to do. You know, this is a colony!"[24]

Another aspect of politicizing Latinos was raising consciousness
about the role of racism and internalized racism.

> . . . a lot of light skinned Latinos were prejudiced, you know? . . . a
> lot of them want to be white and they think they're white. They don't
> know the mix that makes us . . . Some of them got kinkier hair than
> me and . . . all they are is just yellow, you know, grifo o mestizo, you
> know . . . "Oh, ¿tú eres Blanco? ¿Blanco? ¿Blanco? Shit, if you're
> blanco, how come you here in a Black ghetto?" . . . That's what I'd

tell them. "Yeah, tú eres blanco, ¿por qué tú estás en el Barrio? Mira, yo soy negro y tú está aquí conmigo. ¿Por que tú no estás allá con los blancos? . . . ¿Qué clase de blanco eres tú?"[25]

Such political discussions, often in Spanish, took place in the yards where these expressly political groups would compete with non-political ones for group membership.

> Well, when you first go in prison . . . most of the time you know some-one and whatnot. But if you don't know anyone there's usually Latinos there that will take you under their wing, so to speak. In other words, there's different groups of people, each one is like a clique . . . that hang out when it's yard time . . . just like out here, you know, as a group of friends . . . but only in prison it's even tighter . . . And eventually, you're going to gravitate to one of these groups. Of course, there's loners . . . but the majority . . . is a member of a group in prison . . . and you become one of the comrades, to use that term. And you play together, you talk together, you know, and you do your exercise together and whatnot. And if it's a political group, naturally we talk and politicize together and then we politicize some of the others. And when a young Puerto Rican comes in we try to bring him to our group, you know, so we can increase our numbers. Just like out here, you're recruiting.[26]

The process of political recruiting involved both one-to-one discussions and open discussions in the yard among Puerto Ricans of various political tendencies. Sostre described the conditions under which such discussions took place.

> Well . . . it was in a crowd, you know,. . . it was with the Puerto Rican nationalists who were arguing against some of these others . . . Some of these were for the Puerto Ricans continuing their colony status and others that were neutral that were listening . . . And that was very important because . . . most of the time we don't convince these diehard pro-colonists but we convince the ones listening . . . That's how we used to recruit. We used to engage them in rhetoric.[27]

One of the goals of such discussions was, ". . . to recruit members to our groups, so we'd have a group bigger and stronger and we would politicize more Puerto Ricans as to their status in this country, as to what's happening in this country."[28] Asked what was the ultimate purpose for such political education, Sostre responded: "Well, they're going out . . . most prisoners have very light sentences . . . So it's not just to stay in prison, it's for when they go out and they politicize others and they wake up maybe some of the members of their own families."[29]

Hence, while Latino prisoner leaders sought to educate their Latino peers about the need to change prison conditions, the ultimate goal of much of their political education was to contribute to the formation of political cadres who, upon release, would struggle to change disparate power relations at all levels (e.g., local, national, international) beginning with their Latina(o) communities on the outside.[30]

Latino prisoner leaders also encouraged their peers to join their African-American and white counterparts to demand changes in areas not addressed by the post-Attica Rebellion reforms. One of these common areas was work. The extent of prisoner discontent at Green Haven right before and after the Attica Rebellion with respect to work conditions and wages in the prison's industry was described by Gear.

Let me tell you what was happening at Green Haven just before Attica . . . if I say "we," I'm talking about . . . the Five Percenters, the Panthers, the Young Lords, the People's Party and progressive individuals, okay . . . we were in the process of organizing a prisoners' labor union . . . because of the . . . wages that was happening . . . in . . . the prisons . . . and also the working conditions . . . and just before Attica we were circulating petitions in all the cell blocks, you know, and . . . in fact, was trying to . . . petition the Public Employees Relation Board . . . and was planning to try to bring about a work stoppage in Green Haven . . . The prison so-called "officials" was aware of this, they tried to stop it. People were being keeplocked for this. People was going to the box for this. So the mood in Green Haven was very rebellious, very confrontational. There was a lot of stuff happening in the yards, and, so it's not surprising that Oswald and his people up in Albany thought Green Haven was going to blow instead of Attica.[31]

Building a Prisoners' Union

Prisoner leaders had begun their underground union organizing efforts during August of 1971. The creation of the Green Haven Prisoners' Labor Union (PLU), according to Gear, was a process which involved ". . . a lot meetings between the various groups . . . sitting down and agreeing that this is what we needed."[32] These efforts intensified after the Attica Rebellion because, "The Attica massacre . . . forcefully drove home the point that prisoners would have to organize as a simple matter of self-preservation."[33] By December 1971, the union had been

formed. On February 7, 1972, the PLU publicly announced its forma-
tion.[34] The union was supported by third parties such as the Young
Lords Party and other progressive and radical grassroots organizations,
Representative Herman Badillo, the New York Urban Coalition,
District 65 (Distributive Workers of America), and the Prisoners' Rights
Project of the Legal Aid Society. The latter represented the union.[35]

The PLU aimed to act as the "collective bargaining agent in all
matters referring to . . . wages, hours and conditions of employment."[36]
Prisoner unionization efforts were geared toward addressing another
one of the Attica demands: ". . . STOP SLAVE LABOR.[37] At the time,
prisoners working in Green Haven's garment shop earned 35 cents an
hour making "hospital gowns and bathrobes for men, women and children, slips, sheets, pillowcases, baby bibs, and United States flags, all
destined for state institutions."[38]

According to the PLU's constitution, its main goals included:

To seek, through peaceful and lawful means:

a. To improve the conditions of its members;

b. To equalize to the fullest extent possible the rights, privileges, and
protections of prison labor with those of free labor everywhere;

c. To advance the economic, political, social and cultural interests of the
prisoners at Green Haven;

d. To aid in the adoption of laws and to secure compliance with existing
laws, local, national, international, for the economic, political, and social
welfare of all prisoners . . .[39]

Equally important was the PLU goal of seeking to "advance the cause of
prison labor throughout the country, and promote unity between prison
labor and other sections of the people."[40] Thereby, the PLU's efforts were
directed not only at economic concerns, but also at coalescing with third
parties on the outside. While prisoners had different political ideologies,
they were able to come together in PLU because it gave them a common
voice with which to address the penal establishment. Between 1971 and
1972, union organizers were able to gather nearly 1,200 signed union
membership cards clearly demonstrating the support they had among
prisoners despite racial, ethnic, political, and class cleavages.

It was clear to the prisoners that meaningful change could come only
if they formed a strong organization comprised of prisoners only and
independent of control by prison authorities. The labor union con-

cept is a natural one for these purposes, for if a union is recognized, under the labor laws this would mean, hopefully, that prison authorities would be required to bargain in good faith with the union. In addition, recognition as a union would legally prohibit prison administrators from engaging in a wide variety of activities, which would be considered unfair labor practices.[41]

The threat posed to penal hegemony by the PLU's successful organizing efforts was heightened by the fact that PLU organizers tended to be the same prisoner leaders who sought to mobilize the support of radical and progressive forces on the outside. DOCS' initial response to union organizing efforts was to keeplock prisoners, lock them in segregation, and/or transfer them to other facilities further upstate. Sostre described some of the tactics used by DOCS personnel to harass union organizers.

> I was there while they had the strike in the . . . license plate shop. In fact, I helped organize that . . . they had slave labor like they . . . do in all the prisons, you know, they make you work for pennies a day. So the prisoners were trying to organize a union. And naturally, they didn't want to hear that so they had a strike, people refused to work. What they did is they . . . grabbed the strike leaders and they put them in the box, the hole, and then from there they shipped them out to different prisons. That's their methods that they use to break up any trouble in prison . . . When they see that you're growing and you're recruiting people and your group is getting larger, then they ship you out to another prison, you know?[42]

Sostre himself was sentenced to segregation by Green Haven administrators for 373 successive days as a result of his organizing activities.[43]

Speaking about the ethnic and racial composition of the strikers, Sostre added that, ". . . most of the prisoners is Blacks and Latinos, very few whites . . . So most of the ones that were in that strike were Black and Latinos."[44] Following the strike in the license plate shop, some of the prisoner leaders who had not been transferred joined new leaders who were emerging, to continue union organizing efforts. Prison authorities persisted in harassing union members and refused to deliver mail sent to them by their attorneys.[45]

In the end, the attempts to get the state to officially recognize the PLU as the prisoners' bargaining agent failed as a result of opposition, not only from DOCS, but from other state elites and state agencies such as the Public Employees Relations Board of New York. The latter denied the Green Haven local recognition as public employees (which they sought as members of District 65) on the grounds that the work performed by prisoners was not employment but rehabilitation.[46] As such, prisoners were not employees of the state and, therefore, did not have the right to organize and bargain collectively under the Public Employees' Fair Employment Act.[47] Others rejected the PLU because they saw District 65 as a "militant outside union."[48]

Clearly, one of the reasons state elites feared the existence of the PLU was because it unified prisoners, and thereby threatened custodial hegemony. Moreover, the continued existence of a prisoners' union would have resulted in significant financial losses for the state should workers demand increased wages, better working conditions, and/or go on strike. The official recognition of the prisoners' union in one facility also would have encouraged prisoners in other facilities to organize. In fact, male prisoners at Wallkill and women prisoners at Bedford Hills, both in New York State, attempted to form prisoners' unions following the PLU's example.[49] Ultimately, official recognition of PLU would have sent a message to other subordinate sectors of society from which prisoners came, that by uniting they too could force the state to make much needed reforms.[50]

As discussed above, the period immediately preceding and following the Attica Rebellion found Latino, African-American, and white prisoner leaders forming political underground groups along racial and/or ethnic lines. These groups tended to overlap, and at the same time, compete with other types of informal prisoner groups and networks for membership. Awareness of common grievances led political underground prisoner groups to form coalitions to demand changes in prison conditions and policies. The immediate response of Green Haven administrators to such efforts was to ignore prisoners' demands for reforms and to persecute prisoner leaders, particularly those involved in the PLU's organizing efforts. However, in spite of multiple attempts by the penal bureaucracy to discourage prisoner political activism and the failure of the PLU to obtain official recognition, prisoner leaders continued to meet underground and discuss ways in which they could collectively demand prison reforms. Such discussions led Latino, African-American and white prisoner leaders to create the Think Tank Concept (TTC) during the spring of 1972.

The Think Tank Concept

The TTC was comprised of the heads of political underground prisoner groups. According to Michael Armstrong, "Okay, there was groups that came together . . . and this was your Young Lords and your People's Party, the Five Percenters and . . . maybe some other . . . just newly formed groups, like the African Revolutionary Movement . . . they came together and formed an organization called the Think Tank . . ."[51] At least two members of the TTC identified with the Young Lords Party. The TTC was an elite group. "I think the idea was to represent the best and the brightest of the prisoners in some structured form where they could brainstorm and develop ideas for change within the prisons and within the communities from which most prisoners came."[52]

During the summer of 1972, the TTC officially announced its existence to prison authorities. At that time, according to Angel Gear, the TTC:

> . . . organized the first Prisoner/Community Dialogue in the state . . . We were able to send out invitations and have a dialogue with people from community-based organizations, some political people . . . There was a lot of prisoners, there was at least twelve or thirteen of us. We met with this large group of these outside folks and there was about twenty of them . . . And that was the first time anything like that happened in New York State . . . And that's when we formally started to . . . identify ourselves as the Think Tank. See, we was meeting in the yard as representatives of groups . . . but we actually became Think Tank Incorporated like after that . . . or almost simultaneously with that meeting with that community people.[53]

The purpose of this prisoner/community dialogue was, ". . . it's ironic because basically what we was asking for or talking about then is the same thing we are talking about now, [1993], okay, that there's a relationship between us and the community and that the community has a stake in what happens to us . . . We don't belong to the state, we're the community folks . . ."[54] The immediate significance of the prisoner/community dialogue was that, for the first time, prisoners were allowed to meet openly with community members to discuss a number of issues of concern to both communities. Such contact, nevertheless, took place under the ever watchful eye of custodial personnel.

At its peak during the second half of 1972 and 1973, the TTC devised a number of proposals, activities, and programs which set the precedent for others implemented in facilities throughout the state.[55] Thus, it was within the TCC that many of the programs which became the mainstay for New York's post-Attica prison policies were first formulated. These changes included: opening the prison doors to a greater and more varied number of community volunteers; developing new programs; and initiating the process whereby previously underground groups began to organize above ground with the approval of prison administrators.

> Out of these above ground prisoner organizations came the ability for people to begin to brainstorm and come up with all kinds of ideas. You know, somebody would come up with an idea that we need to have higher education in the prison system and a proposal was written and efforts and resources would begin to mobilize towards trying to realize that. . . . and then in a year or so later somebody came up with the idea that, you know, we're just taking these courses, they're not really leading anywhere, maybe we need to structure a formal program where guys could actually get these degrees . . . and . . . that became the first college program in the country . . . Some men came up with the whole question of family reunion, the idea of bringing men closer to their families . . . and as a result of that, a proposal was made that men be allowed to call their families . . . collect so it wouldn't cost the state anything . . . Out of the telephone home program came the . . . Family Reunion Program, which allows men who are married and have wives and family . . . to spend seventy-two hours with them in a relaxed residential kind of a setting divorced from the prison . . .[56]

Out of TTC also came the concept of establishing "pre-release" services. Eric Elliott describes the impact the new programs had on the development of penal policies.

> Prior to the Pre-Release Center . . . if you didn't have any way to get a job, you just had to sit in your cell and write as many letters as you could to as many people as you could and just hope that somebody would answer your letter and say, "Yeah, we have a job for you." And once you got that letter . . . you could then go to the Parole Board and they would release you. The Pre-Release Center brought in the idea of peer counselors who worked with men prior to them going to the Parole Board . . . who taught employment skills, how to fill out resumes, how to conduct interviews, how to search for jobs . . . In addition to that, they created a job skills bank where potential employers who were willing to hire ex-prisoners could register . . . And this just changed the whole face of how prisoners sought parole and . . . some of the things that parole began to look for in prisoners . . . Pre-release services became mandatory . . . It became one of the things that was required for parole.[57]

The TTC's ability to come above ground and influence the development of penal policy was the result of several major factors. After the PLU was denied official recognition, tensions within the facility remained high. Prisoners' calls for reforms could not be ignored much longer if another Attica-type rebellion was to be averted. Moreover, the TTC was influential also because it was organized at a time when New York State elites were under intense criticism due to existing prison conditions and the state's handling of the Attica Rebellion. (Such outside support for prisoner concerns had made themselves felt at Green Haven during the PLU's organizing drive). Under such pressures, Green Haven's warden and other sectors of DOCS' bureaucracy agreed to allow prisoners and third parties to experiment with a number of activities, programs, and prisoner groups. This experimentation, however, was closely monitored by custodial personnel. Ultimately, the programs proposed by the TTC became penal policy because they did not fundamentally threaten the hegemony of penal elites.

Moreover, such experimentation continued to take place alongside a number of actions by prison administrators designed to intimidate and/or remove from the general prisoner population some of the most radical prisoner leaders. For example, during September 1972, penal personnel used a violent confrontation between the People's Party and the Nation of Islam as an excuse to carry out a number of repressive actions.[58] After the incident, DOCS declared a state of emergency at the facility, keeplocked the population for two months, put prisoner leaders in segregation, and transferred some of the most politically active prisoners to other state facilities. Many of the transferred prisoners were sent to the newly created behavior modification unit for "incorrigible prisoners," opened in 1972 at the Adirondacks Correctional Treatment and Evaluation Center (ACTEC) in Dannemora. ACTEC, according to Gear who was transferred there for his organizing activities at Green Haven, was the state's response to Attica.[59]

> ... this was called the maxi, maxi, prescription program, RX. ... Prisoners ... were taken from all the prisons all over ... New York and placed in ... this unit. ... You was in your cell basically twenty-four hours a day ... They never allowed more than two people out of the cell at the same time in any common area ... The only thing you came out to do was take a shower ... I was there for six months ... all they did was end up sending me back to Green Haven and put me in population again ... .[60]

Thus, while penal administrators allowed the TTC, third parties, and liberals inside the penal establishment to experiment with new programs, groups, and activities, this experimentation took place alongside traditional forms of custodial control.

Nevertheless, the role prisoner groups, such as the TTC, played in helping to achieve a change in the conditions of imprisonment at Green Haven during the end of 1972 and throughout 1973, was significant. For the first time in Green Haven's history, prisoners had some, if little, say in how they were kept. And for the first time, third parties and liberal civilian personnel at the institutional level were allowed to join prisoners in such dialogue. One of the results of these combined efforts was the formalization or legitimation of political underground prisoner groups to be discussed below.

Administrative Formalization of Prisoner Groups

The formalization of political underground groups was made possible at the end of 1972 as a result of changes in prison policies carried out by the newly hired Deputy Superintendent of Program Services, Charles Burns, and the newly hired Coordinator of Volunteer Services, Danny Vázquez. Vázquez, a Puerto Rican, and Burns, an African-American, were both reform-oriented liberals. They were the only civilian administrators at Green Haven who were people of color. In fact, according to Vázquez, he ". . . was the only Puerto Rican in prison administration at any facility . . . anywhere in New York State at the time."[61]

According to Gear, the creation of Volunteer Services was designed to lessen prisoner discontent following the Attica Rebellion. "It was created with the mindset of like . . . 'Go give them what they want. Try to keep them quiet,' okay. That was a liberal approach . . . that's where Volunteer Coordinator Services came in. . . ."[62] Eric Elliott also argued that the post of Deputy Superintendent for Programs was designed to meet the conflicting interests of prisoners, liberals and conservative staff within DOCS.

> . . . for a couple of years Charles Burns had been advocating that . . . corrections needs to have a different kind of a vision, that correction needs to be more community-oriented, that prisoners need to have a greater sense of who they are and some measure of control over their own lives . . . After Attica now, these ideas become a little bit more attractive and because he's one of the leading proponents of these

ideas and he's in line for a promotion . . . he gets the opportunity to go to Green Haven and implement these things . . . Certainly there are several other agendas at work, one of which is, "Let's take Burns and let's put him in there and let's take some of his ideas and maybe . . . we can use them for some other things but certainly let's try it." So he gets an opportunity to go in there and do some of the things that he wants to do . . . He begins to make connections with the community people. He begins to bring them in but he doesn't do it on his own initiative solely. He does it at the request of prisoners.[63]

The fact that Burns and Vázquez were hired on the program level, however, which commands the least of status and resources within the penal bureaucracy, meant that the changes they promoted ultimately had to be approved by both custodial and administrative interests within the DOCS bureaucracy. However, conditions at Green Haven were so volatile, pressure for reforms so intense, and the memory of the Attica Rebellion so fresh in the minds of DOCS administrators that, between the end of 1972 and 1975, Burns and Vázquez were able to help prisoners and third parties carry out a number of reforms that changed the conditions of imprisonment throughout the state for almost twenty years.

As Deputy Superintendent of Program Services, Burns was responsible for the development of rehabilitation programs and, Vázquez, as the Coordinator of Volunteer Services, for developing ways to screen and process volunteers. Speaking about his responsibilities, Vázquez, hired in October 1972, asserted:

There was no job description . . . it was a very loose and broadly mandated job . . . My responsibility was to develop a process for the screening of volunteers that would work in the prison in a variety of different ways . . . We had in some cases 350 volunteers coming in and out of the prison for weeks and I had to devise a security process for screening them, getting their social security numbers, get some kind of an explanation of why they were coming into prison, and making sure they were affiliated with a reputable organization, reputable reflecting my own definition.[64]

Defining what was a "reputable" organization frequently brought Vázquez into conflict with other administrators, ". . . I frequently came up with organizations that the warden did not think so reputable but they were reputable nevertheless."[65] Some of these groups included "a couple of student organizations that were from . . . Hostos

Community College that he felt were "radical" because "some wore jackets and combat boots and looked like the common radicals of the day."[66] Thus, another of the roles Vázquez assumed was to act as a mediator between custody-oriented personnel and third parties seeking access to prisoners.

> I can't take a lot of credit for actually recruiting and bringing in the volunteers but what I could take credit for is establishing a process whereby they came into a facility where they would not have otherwise been welcomed . . . When I got there these inmate organizations had been in correspondence with lots of people on the outside already. What those people didn't have was access to the facility in a formal way. And I was able to establish access to the facility in a formal way and then help them structure their activities so that they were scheduled, that they had a place to meet, that they had some regularity . . . in some cases I had to find resources.[67]

Trying to implement changes frequently brought Vázquez into conflict with prison guards who resented not only the reforms but also civilian personnel they perceived as pro-prisoner.[68]

> In the beginning . . . we could not have a meeting without a guard there . . . So then . . . certain meetings couldn't be held because there was not enough guards. So some people would come to the prison and the security people would say, "Oh, they can't have their meeting because there's no guard I can assign to that meeting." I had to [go] up to the warden or whoever I had to talk to and say, "Listen, these people came 150, 200 miles, I'm not going to send them back. And I don't care how you do it but there's got to be a way to do it." . . . Eventually things relaxed to the point that, for the most part, it was left to my discretion. . . . I remember the first time when a guard didn't have to be present when a woman was present.[69]

Thus, at each step of the way, new security measures had to be devised to facilitate the systematic entrance of third parties into the facility. Latino prisoners and third parties were also affected by guard ignorance of Latino cultural habits.

> I remember one big issue I had with the superintendent because he was told by a probation officer that some of the volunteers I brought in were making out with the inmates. We called in the officer that made the allegations . . . and what he really saw was an "abrazo," two people met, both were Puerto Ricans . . . and they embraced . . .

and they pecked on the cheek. That's a culture custom. That's how we say hello.[70]

During the end of 1972 and the early part of 1973, Vázquez and Burns began to oversee the recognition or legitimation of political underground prisoner groups by prison authorities. One of the prisoner demands during the Attica Rebellion had been to, "allow all New York State prisoners to be politically active, without intimidation or reprisal."[71] As discussed earlier, before the arrival of Vázquez and Burns, political underground prisoner groups had generally been meeting in the prison's yard whenever they could. Vázquez and Burns believed these groups should be allowed to meet formally. They, therefore, began to allow the groups to meet officially and provided them regular meeting space. Groups were authorized to notify their membership of the time, place, and date of their meetings. The result of this process of formalization varied.

The fact that prisoners were allowed to organize above ground meant that certain things . . . came to them. For instance, they got a room to meet. They got the resources to work with in terms of, you know, just simple things like books, and pencils and pens. And they could use a blackboard and diagram stuff with chalk . . . Usually each prison organization was assigned a staff advisor. The staff advisor could . . . make calls out to other groups in the city or throughout the state. They were able to do networking. They were able to acquire information that previously had been, you know, prohibitive in terms of its ability to acquire it and access it.[72]

However, the process of formalization required political underground prisoner groups to change their names. According to Vázquez, there were two main reasons for this.

. . . you would have had a hard time getting the administration to recognize a group called "The Young Lords" as an inmate organization. In addition to that, while the central leadership of a group may have been Young Lords, the expanded membership would not have necessarily supported or wanted to be a member of the Young Lords . . . There was a sense that the groups wanted to be as inclusive as possible and, therefore, some names wouldn't have been inclusive as well as not acceptable to the administration.[73]

Other steps associated with becoming a formal prison organization involved delineating the types of activities the groups could engage in, the groups' structures, and the norms they were to be governed by. Vázquez described the process of formalization initiated during the spring of 1973:

> One of the things we did was to devise rules for their own self-governing. So, many of them created constitutions. They changed the names of their organizations, elected their own representatives, and focused on areas of rehabilitation and developed student-release programs, community work programs, community counselling programs and helped develop a higher education program at Green Haven, which at that time was very, very new for correctional settings.[74]

One of the consequences of becoming a formal organization was that formerly underground groups increasingly came under the jurisdiction of penal authorities. Many leaders, previously organizing underground, were now clearly identifiable and, as a result, more easily targeted for repression. Moreover, prison personnel could now contribute to the depoliticization of political prisoner groups by limiting the types of goals and activities in which organizations could engage. The fact that prison administrators could at whim withdraw privileges granted the groups (e.g., meeting space, ability to organize events, access to community groups, etc.) or disband organizations, reduced their attractiveness to members and/or potential members.

Prior to the process of legitimation, some prisoners in political underground groups felt they had less to lose. Once the groups became formalized, members were less willing to engage in organizing activities which could result in the withdrawal of their newly acquired privileges or in their being transferred to institutions further upstate. In fact, throughout the period studied, formal prisoner groups were continually forced to reconstitute, as leaders and members who stepped outside penal guidelines were segregated, prohibited from participating in the group's activities, transferred to other facilities, and/or released on parole. The response of some prisoners to such repression was to channel group activities into more "acceptable" areas, such as self-help programs, special interest groups, religious, and educational activities.

Another consequence of formalization was that prisoner groups such as the TTC began to lose their coalition character as some prisoners began to leave the organization to create formal prisoner groups along racial or ethnic lines. Additionally, with legitimation, Latino, African-American, and white prisoners began to compete for access to resources previously denied all prisoners. There were also now more groups competing for membership.[75]

The Think Tank was more, originally racially and ethnically representative of the groups. I think after the groups formed it became primarily Black . . . because the Hispanic leadership that was there had gone to formulate PUL . . . Everybody became more focused so that the core leadership became smaller and probably more exclusive . . .[76]

Within this context there were prisoners who saw the efforts of Vázquez and Burns to legitimize political underground groups as conscious attempts by penal bureaucrats to "co-opt" prisoners and further divide them. In fact, one of the objectives of Vázquez and Burns had been to, "devise programs to harness the interests and energy of the more politically conscious inmates to developing meaningful programs within the facility."[77] Nevertheless, Vázquez claimed that their objective was not to depoliticize prisoners. Moreover, according to Vázquez, immediately after Attica, DOCS had not developed a clear-cut, across-the-board policy delineating how the process of formalization should be accomplished. In fact, this process of legitimation did not take place at all state facilities at the same time. Green Haven, under Vázquez and Burns, was the precedent setting institution for what later became DOCS official policy toward formalizing prisoner groups

> . . . at different facilities things worked differently depending on the Superintendent, the Deputy Superintendent for Programs and the initiative of the Volunteer Coordinator . . . So that each of us defined our jobs as what we wanted them to be and what the circumstances permitted. So I was in a situation where the circumstances, along with my own personal convictions, resulted in trying to tap opportunities to first organize the inmate population in such a way that they could receive recognition from the prison officials and engage them in dialogue for the creation of programs that would help them upon their release. And that often required outside resources and outside contacts, meetings with . . . the community that would then [lobby] on their behalf . . . [with] elected officials . . . [with] prison officials, to get some of these programs done.[78]

Although efforts to formalize prisoner groups met with the resistance of security personnel, Superintendent Vincent gave Vázquez and Burns enough autonomy to carry out these changes.[79] It also helped that although the regional and statewide directors of Volunteer Services were "not necessarily supportive" at least, like Vincent, they were not "obstructive."[80]

The process of legitimation resulted in the creation of a wide variety of prisoner groups throughout the 1970s and 1980s. As the groups began to form, DOCS made a distinction between "inmate organizations" and "inmate programs." The basis for the distinction was not always clear even to institutional personnel interviewed. A group might be considered an inmate organization at one point but considered an inmate program at another (e.g., Alcoholics Anonymous). However, it was on the basis of this distinction that groups were granted distinct privileges. Thus, while inmate organizations and religious programs were allowed to sponsor one family day event a year, inmate programs were only allowed to organize seminars. Additionally, only members of formal organizations (restricted at first to 125 members, later to 150) were allowed to attend family day events and to invite family and community guests to them. What all of these groups had in common, however, was the fact that they were formally recognized by DOCS.

For the purpose of the current study, the major prisoner organizations (i.e., DOCS' "inmate organizations") that existed at Green Haven between 1972 and 1987 were divided into two categories: ethnic/racial organizations and special interest groups. The major prisoner programs (i.e., DOCS' "inmate programs") were also divided into two categories: self-help and religious programs. Self-help programs could be initiated by prisoners, third parties or penal staff. A list of the names of these diverse groups will provide a better idea of the types of prisoner concerns DOCS was more receptive to throughout the period studied. Ethnic/racial prisoner groups included:

National Association for the Advancement of Colored People (NAACP) (1972–present)[81]
Latin Think Tank Concept (February–March 1973)
Puente de Unidad Latina (March 1973–June 1977)
Hispanos Unidos Para el Progreso (1980–present)
Caribbean-African Unity (1985–present)[82]

Special interest groups encompassed:

South Forty Corporation (1971–present)[83]
Pre-Release Center (1972–present)
Community on the Move (1973–?)
Friends of Fortune (1970s?)
Think Tank Concept (1972–?)
Peregrine Jaycees (1972–present)
Creative Communications Committee (1975–?)[84]
Project Allied for a Calculated Transition (1980s?)[85]
Project Build (1970s–1980s?)[86]

Pinpoint (1980–present)[87]
Community Assistance and Prison Project (1970s–1980s?)[88]
Alcoholics Anonymous (?–present)
Open Gate (1973–1976?)[89]
Green Haven Monthly (1978–present)[90]

Of the groups listed above, those still existing in 1987 were:

NAACP
Caribbean African Unity
Hispanics United for Progress
Peregrine Jaycees
Pinpoint
Project Build
Project Allied for a Calculated Transition
Alcoholics Anonymous
Green Haven Monthly

Self-help programs created between 1972 and 1987 were:

Veterans Self-Help Project (1979–present)[91]
Alternative to Violence Program (1985–present)[92]

Religious programs existing between 1972 and 1987 included:[93]

Catholic
Jewish
The Protestant Center
The Sankore Masjid (Sunni Muslim)
American Muslim Mission (formerly World Community of Al-Islam
in the West)
Masjid Ut Taubah
Association for Research Enlightment
Jehovah's Witnesses
New York Theological Program
Seventh Day Adventists
Christian Science
Quaker
Residents Encounter Christ Council
Zen Buddhist Dharma Group

Self-help and religious programs existing in 1987 included:

Veterans Self-Help Project
Alternatives to Violence Program
Catholic
Jewish
The Protestant Center
Islamic
Zen Buddhist services

In addition to the formal prisoner groups mentioned above, in 1973, Italian prisoners formed an Italian Culture Class. While this group was not considered a formal prisoner organization, its existence is highlighted here because it appears that the class not only served as a rallying point for prisoners of Italian descent, but fulfilled some of the functions of a formal prisoner organization.[94] There seems to have been several reasons why white prisoners did not create formal prisoner organizations. For one, these types of groups were usually created by prisoners who felt they were at a disadvantage vis-à-vis other prisoners. As such, formal prisoner groups were designed to gain access to institutional resources and privileges. However, at Green Haven, white prisoners were generally given preferential treatment. Moreover, through the prison's Catholic chaplain many white prisoners, particularly Italians, had access to family and ethnic feast day events, seminars, etc. This led Latino and African-American prisoners to perceive the Catholic chaplain as acting as an "ombudsman" for white prisoners.

Other types of organizations which saw significant prisoner participation were administrative groups created by DOCS and composed either entirely of prisoners or a mixture of prisoners and staff:

Inmate Liaison Committee (1972–present)
Inmate Grievance Resolution Committee (1975–present)

Consequently, the process of formalization, begun during the second half of 1972 with the Think Tank Concept, had by 1987 given rise to a wide range of formal prisoner groups. While during the initial process of formalization Vázquez and Burns had been allowed to exercise some degree of autonomy by central office personnel, by the end of 1987, DOCS directives formed the basis for the legitimation of such groups. With time, DOCS' policies regarding the functioning of formal prisoner groups became more centralized and systematic. Furthermore, as DOCS sought to clarify its policies regarding the formation and privileges to be accorded these formal prisoner groups, DOCS central office directives began to categorize some as "inmate organizations," and others as "inmate programs." Both types of formal groups found themselves competing for a number of limited resources and privileges, not only with each other, but with also informal prisoner groups, and administrative groups.

In conclusion, the period prior to and following the Attica Rebellion found reform-oriented prisoners at Green Haven forming political underground prisoner groups and coalitions that sought to achieve a redefinition in the terms and conditions of imprisonment. As the process of formalization continued, both formerly political underground prisoner groups and new formal prisoner organizations found the range of acceptable activities constrained by DOCS guidelines. These guidelines outlined the privileges and penalties to be accorded prisoner groups. As a result, some of the most politicized Latino, African-American, and white prisoners saw the process of legitimation as an attempt to depoliticize and further divide the prisoner population. Faced with this situation some prisoner leaders withdrew from participation in formal prisoner groups while others continued organizing political underground prisoner groups and coalitions even as they continued to participate in formal prisoner groups.

What was the response of Latino prisoners to the process of formalization? On the one hand, they participated in the creation of the Think Tank Concept and other formal prisoner and administrative groups. On the other hand, as will be shown in the following chapter, they created a formal Latino prisoner organization at the beginning of 1973 and redoubled their efforts at mobilizing third party and penal support on their behalf. It is the nature of the formal Latino prisoner organization, the types of concerns it sought to address, and the manner in which prison personnel and third parties responded to their calls for support and demands for reforms that will be the main focus of the following chapter.

Notes: Chapter 6

1. Ianni argued that, "In their advanced stage, however, prison politics can and do pose a treat to hustling," because if a man engages in hustling, "which inevitably includes a certain amount of exploitation of others, his credibility as a political convert would have been difficult to establish" (A.J. Francis Ianni, *Black Mafia: Ethnic Succession in Organized Crime* [New York: Simon and Schuster, 1974], 189). This researcher argues that, as the case of Bedford Hills discussed in part 3 shows, there were times when the groups and net-

works developed by a "hustler" provided a fundamental source of support for prisoners organizing reform-oriented activities.

2. Angel Gear [pseud.], interview with author, New York, N.Y., 8 April 1993.

3. Ibid.

4. Ibid.

5. New York State Department of Correctional Services (hereafter cited as NYSDOCS), *Standard of Inmate Behavior, All Institutions (Inmate Rules, Penalties and Outline of Procedures)*, Albany, Revised June 1988, 12.

6. Gear, interview with author, 1993.

7. Ibid.

8. Ibid.

9. Ibid.

10. Ibid.

11. Two persons interviewed also mentioned the existence of a Pan-African group at Green Haven. According to Danny Vázquez and Mary Oxford, it was an attempt to form a broad coalition among all the African-American groups in the population (Mary Oxford [pseud.], interview with author, Ossining, N.Y., 10 February 1989; and Danny Vázquez [pseud.], interview with author, Bronx, N.Y., 20 March and 17 April 1989).

12. Gear, interview with author, 1993.

13. Ibid.

14. *Palante* was actually the name of the Young Lords Party newspaper.

15. Ianni, *Black Mafia,* 188. Ianni's description was based on two different accounts of prison experiences given to him by his two field assistants. Although the original accounts were based on Green Haven and Attica, according to Ianni, the events taking place in both institutions were so similar that he decided to write the narrative as if it were one institution (Ibid., 158).

16. Gear, interview with author, 1993.

17. Ibid.

18. This statement was also supported by former Young Lords' member Haydé Ortega [pseud.], interview with author, New York, N.Y., 12 and 28 February 1989 and 17 March 1989.

19. Martín Sostre, interview with author, New York, N.Y., 24 May 1993.

20. Ibid.

21. Ibid.

22. Ibid. Author's translation: "Listen, those guys are crazy. Leave them, don't get involved with those guys. Look, they saw you hanging out with so-

and-so and that's not good for you because when you go see the parole board they're not going to let you leave."

23. Ibid. In spite of these politicizing efforts, there was one area in which the overwhelming number of Latino prisoner leaders remained as traditional as their keepers. That was in the manner in which they defined masculinity as heterosexual. Unlike women's prisons, in which Latina prison leaders involved in lesbian relationships could gain the respect of both their peers and penal staff members, Latino and African-American males interviewed argued that in men's prisons it was not possible to be involved in such relationships openly and still be respected by one's peers. Thus, homophobia forced some Latino prisoner leaders to keep their intimate loving relationships with other men hidden. Moreover, as the quote included below illustrates, stereotypes about what gay males looked liked and acted like kept many Latino and African-American prisoner leaders from conceiving that one could be gay and politically committed at the same time. According to a former Latino prisoner leader, ". . . them guys tend to have their own agendas . . . They tend to be en la yarda, con . . . el tipo que es la mujer. Esta mas tiempo con esa persona and they're not really into positive things . . . They're more into la yarda . . . and they spend their time . . . making out and stuff like that. I never seen, since I've been there, you know, . . . ones that . . . got involved with positive things. They were more like in their own little world" (Domingo Morales [pseud.], interview with author, New York, N.Y., 6 April 1993). However, in spite of the rampant homophobia exhibited by Latino and African-American prisoner leaders, those interviewed conceded that during times of crisis (e.g., rebellions, strikes) even openly gay prisoners participated in such acts. Moreover, as the 1970s wore on, it was not uncommon to see gay prisoners openly struggle for gay rights within the prison. Such activism was made possible by the emergence of the lesbian and gay civil rights movement during the 1960s, and by outside lesbian and gay organizations that were openly supportive of their peers in prison. However, with the outbreak of the HIV/AIDS epidemic and the scapegoating of gay males as transmitters of the disease, many of the politically active gay males in prison were forced to go back into the closet as a result of retaliatory actions by other prisoners (and staff).

24. Sostre, interview with author, 1993.

25. Ibid. Author's translation: "Oh, you're white? White? White? Shit, if you're white, how come you here in a black ghetto?" . . . That's what I tell them. "Yeah, you're white, why are you in El Barrio? Look, I'm black and you're here with me. Why aren't you there with the whites? . . . What kind of white are you?"

26. Ibid.

27. Ibid.

28. Ibid.

29. Ibid.

30. Ibid.

31. Gear, interview with author, 1993.

32. Ibid.

33. Mark Dowie, "Unionizing Prison Labor," *Social Policy* 4, No. 1 (July/August 1973), 58.

34. See "Green Haven Prisoners Union," *Midnight Special* 2, No. 2 (April 1972): 5, 15; Emanuel Perlmutter, "Prisoners' Union Formed Upstate," *New York Times* (hereafter cited as *N.Y. Times*), 8 February 1972, 1; *N.Y. Times,* 9 February 1972, 27; Alfonso A. Narvaez, "Oswald Rejects Prisoners' Union, *N.Y. Times,* 11 February 1972, 76; "'Arise, Ye Prisoners . . .'," *N.Y. Times,* 12 February 1972, 28; and Gerald P. Hecht, "A Union for Inmates," *N.Y. Times,* 25 February 1972, 38. The prisoners' union at Green Haven was the first prisoner-based, as opposed to outside-based, union in the United States. Other states in which prisoners sought to unionize during the late 1960s and/or early 1970s were California, Ohio, Michigan (Marquette, Jackson), Delaware, Rhode Island, Massachusetts (Walpole), Maine, Wisconsin, North Carolina, Georgia, Kansas, Minnesota, Washington, and the District of Columbia. Such efforts also included women's prisons (e.g., the Women's Detention Center in Washington, D.C., Bedford Hills Correctional Facility, the Ohio Reformatory for Women in Marysville). For more on prisoners' union organizing efforts see, Dowie, "Unionizing Prison Labor," 1973; C. Ronald Huff, "Unionization Behind Walls," *Criminology* 12 (August 1974): 175–193; Idem, "The Prisoners' Union: A Challenge for State Corrections," *State Government* 48, No. 3 (Summer 1975): 145–149; "Sticking to the Union," *Midnight Special* 3, No. 4 (April 1972): 9–11; Committee for PLU in Jackson, "Prisoners' Strike: Greetings in Struggle," *Midnight Special* 3, No. 11 (November 1973): 4; and Terry Gallagher, "Prisoners' Strike: Lucasville," *Midnight Special* 3, No. 11 (November 1973): 4. The first successful prisoners' labor union in the world was created in Sweden in 1966 (Dowie, "Unionizing Prison Labor," 58).

35. According to Mark Dowie, the sequence followed by prisoners seeking to organize unions across the country was similar: organize a union along conventional lines, with signed union authorization cards; union attorneys on the outside received the cards and attempted to legitimize the union with employers; the employers resisted negotiations; and court procedures were then initiated (Dowie, "Unionizing Prison Labor," 59).

36. "Greenhaven Prisoners Union," *Midnight Special* 2, No. 2 (April 1972): 5. See also Paul R. Comeau, "Labor Unions for Prison Inmates: An Analysis of a Recent Proposal for the Organization of Inmate Labor," *Buffalo Law Review* (Spring 1972): 975.

37. New York State Special Commission on Attica (hereafter cited as NYSSCA), *Attica: The Official Report of the New York State Special Commission on Attica* (New York: Bantam Books, Inc., 1972), 253.

38. Emanuel Perlmutter, "Prisoners' Union Formed Upstate," *N.Y. Times,* 8 February 1972, 1.

39. "Union: Constitution of the Prisoners' Labor Union at Green Haven," *Midnight Special* 3, No. 4 (April 1973): 12.

40. Ibid.

41. "Greenhaven Prisoners Union," *Midnight Special* 2, No. 2 (April 1972): 5.

42. Sostre, interview with author, 1993.

43. Sostre's release from segregation was the result of a lawsuit he filed charging prison administrators with "cruel and unusual punishment." See *Sostre v. Rockefeller,* 312 F. Supp. 863 (S.D. N.Y. 1970), modified subnom, *Sostre v. McGinnis,* 442 F. 2d 178 (2d Cir. 1971), cert denied, 404 U.S. 1049, 92 S.Ct. 719, 30 L.Ed.2d 740 (1972). Sostre was awarded $13,000 in damages for the treatment he suffered while at Green Haven. Prison officials were also forbidden to censor his correspondence with attorneys, court and public officials.

44. Sostre, interview with author, 1993.

45. "Green Haven Prisoners Union," *Midnight Special* 2, No. 3 (May 1972): 10; and "Prisoners Union Update, UNITE!," *Midnight Special* 2, No. 7 (September 1972): 16.

46. Dowie, "Unionizing Prison Labor," 59-60.

47. Comeau, "Labor Unions for Prison Inmates," 975; and Huff, "Unionization Behind the Walls," 184.

48. "'Arise, Ye Prisoners . . .'," *N.Y. Times,* 12 February 1972, 28.

49. Prisoners at Wallkill unsuccessfully tried organizing a union along the lines of Green Haven's PLU. According to Martín Sostre, prisoners' objectives were: "a. To improve the conditions of Union members. b. To equalize to the fullest extent possible the rights, privileges, and protections of prison labor with those of free labor everywhere. c. To advance the economic, political, social and cultural interests of the prisoners at Wallkill. d. To aid in the adoption of laws and to secure compliance with existing laws, local, national, and international for the economic, political, and social welfare of all prisoners" (Martín Sostre, "Wallkill Union Struggle," *Midnight Special* 2, No. 6 [August 1972]: 1, 2). According to Dowie, women prisoners at Bedford Hills also tried unsuccessfully to organize a prisoners' union supporting at least the first two of the objectives listed above (Dowie, "Unionizing Prison Labor," 59). See also "Sticking to the Union," *Midnight Special* 3, No. 4 (April 1972): 9–11. Although union organizing efforts at Bedford Hills were mentioned in these sources the author was not able to find any other documentation supporting such claims. Readers with access to such information are encouraged to contact the author.

50. For additional discussion on why penal administrators object to prisoners' union organizing efforts, see Comeau, "Labor Union for Inmates," 1972.

51. Michael Armstrong [pseud.], interview with author, New York, N.Y., 22 April 1993.

52. Elliott, interview with author, 1993.

53. Gear, interview with author, 1993.

54. Ibid. In addition to the Prisoner/Community Dialogue, the TTC was responsible for organizing the first "festival" held in a New York State facility. According to Gear, it ". . . was like a festival . . . whereas the outside community came into the big yard and . . . brought dances, music, but it was very political . . . because we did it . . . in conjunction with this organization from Brooklyn called 'The East.' They brought up some African dances, you know, and the Think Tank emceed . . . there had to be like hundreds of prisoners, you know, because like it was under Think Tank's control . . . who could get on there . . . [and] we represented all the organizations, you know, . . . prisoners' families were there" (Ibid.). Equally significant was the fact that the event commemorated the birth of Marcus Garvey.

55. At least one ex-prisoner interviewed argued that the Think Tank Concept continued to exist in one form or another at Green Haven during the past 20 years (Ibid).

56. Elliott, interview with author, 1993.

57. Ibid.

58. According to Angel Gear, on September 15, 1972, "the Nation of Islam . . . attacked everybody in the [east] yard with bats, pipes, rocks . . ." (Gear, interview with author, 1993). The fight erupted because Norman Butler, a member of the Nation of Islam and one of three men convicted of the assassination of Malcolm X, felt that there was a conspiracy, particularly on the part of the People's Party, to kill him in retaliation for the murder of Malcolm X.

59. Ibid. For more information about ACTEC, see As-Allah, "X The Rx," *Midnight Special* 3, No. 8 (August 1973): 5, 6; and Martín Sostre, "End to ACTEC?," *Midnight Special* 3, No. 9 (September 1973): 10.

60. Gear, interview with author, 1993.

61. Vázquez, interview with author, 1989.

62. Gear, interview with author, 1993.

63. Elliott, interview with author, 1993.

64. Vázquez, interview with author, 1989.

65. Ibid.

66. Ibid.

67. Ibid.

68. The tensions between security and civilian penal personnel at Green Haven were so severe that during 1975 and 1976 "there were accounts of a half dozen guards and civilians who slugged each other in the prison." (Susan Sheehan, *A Prison and a Prisoner* [Boston: Houghton Mifflin Co., 1978], 129).

69. Vázquez, interview with author, 1993..

70. Ibid.

71. NYSSCA, *Attica*, 253.

72. Elliott, interview with author, 1993.

73. Vázquez, interview with author, 1989.

74. Ibid.

75. Ronald Berkman observed a similar process taking place in the California prison he studied during the 1970s. See Ronald Berkman, *Opening the Gates: The Rise of the Prisoners' Movement* (Lexington, Mass.: D.C. Heath and Co., 1979).

76. Vázquez, interview with author, 1989.

77. Ibid.

78. Ibid.

79. Vincent went as far as to partition his own office to create space for Burns and Vázquez and gave them daily access to him, thus increasing their visibility within the facility. Vázquez felt that one of the reasons Superintendent Vincent was not more obstructive of their reform efforts was the fact that he wanted to extricate himself for his actions while working as deputy superintendent at Attica during the Attica Rebellion (Ibid.).

80. Ibid.

81. "Present" in this context means that the organization existed at least until 1987.

82. The Organization of Caribbean African Unity was the first prisoner organization created in the United States to address the concerns of men from the English-speaking Caribbean. Its goals were: "1. To initiate and promote positive interactions between the organization and Caribbean community agencies, organizations and individuals . . . 2. To identify and implement special programs and services for Caribbean prisoners . . . 3. To provide Caribbean prisoners with the resources and program opportunities offered to other identifiable cultural and ethnic groups within the prison" (Organization of Caribbean African Unity, "Caribbean African Unity Organization at GHCF," *Green Haven Monthly* [hereafter cited as *GHM*] 8, No. 13 [June/July 1986]: 13). The CAU sponsored seven subcommittees including: religious; legal redress; political action; education; sports; arts and crafts; and music. The

CAU also sponsored a weekly history and culture class. In October 1987, the CAU organized the first annual Marcus Garvey Family Day event ("CAU Event," *GHM* 9, No. 1 [January/February 1987]: 8).

83. The South Forty Corporation, was a non-profit corporation which in June of 1971 began to sponsor programs for prisoners and ex-prisoners at Green Haven and other state facilities (Linda Charlton, "'South 40' Tries to Aid Convicts," *N.Y. Times,* 23 April 1972, 62). It was composed of a two-phase in-prison and out-prison rehabilitation program. The first phase sponsored "pre-release" programs aimed at helping prisoners prepare for their release. Programs and activities included father-son picnics, counseling, and a college study program. The second phase was geared toward reducing the recidivism rate by providing housing, work, counselling and other types of support for prisoners on their release. South Forty also sponsored a camp for prisoners' children (Paul L. Montgomery, "Inmates Romp and Picnic with Sons As Prison Offers Tokens of Family Life," *N.Y. Times,* 13 August 1973, 57).

84. The Creative Communications Committee (CCC) sought to "influence legislation beneficial to the lifer or long-termer with alternatives to life imprisonment" ("Creative Communication Committee Notice," *GHM* [March 1979]: 10). At the beginning of 1978, the CCC also identified itself as an "internal component of Prisoners' Accelerated Creative Exposure, Inc. (PACE)" (Ibid.). PACE was a prisoners' advocacy group. In January 28, 1979, the CCC held a legislative forum at Green Haven which was attended by legislators, third parties, and penal personnel (Ibid). In 1980, the CCC was also involved in issues concerning good time legislation, "juvenile crime prevention, progressive penal reform, and inequity of the 13th Amendment to the U.S. Constitution" (W. [Prince Allah] Brown, "C.C.C. Memo," *GHM* 3, No. 5 [May 1980]: 5).

85. Project Allied for a Calculated Transition was sponsored by Yale Law School (Randolph Jankins, "P.A.C.T. New Court Ruling," *GHM* 8, No. 2 [March 1985]: 4). P.A.C.T. sponsored the Caribbean Committee composed of men of English-speaking Caribbean, Central, and South American birth or parentage ("Caribbean Committee," *GHM* 8, No. 2 [February 1985]: 18).

86. One of the goals of Project Build was to counsel "delinquent youth" (Richard Montero, "Editorial: 'Scared Straight' Deserves a Try," *GHM* [April 1979]: 3). Other goals of the project were to help its members develop counselling skills ("Project Build Event," *GHM* 4, No. 7 [October/November 1981]: 8).

87. Pinpoint was Green Haven's official lifer's organization. Some of its programs included: "a Youth Development Project; an education committee for prisoners of Caribbean heritage; a legal research committee; and a Family Reunion Committee that offers various services to the Family Reunion Program here at Green Haven (Robert Green, "Pinpoint Interview," *GHM* 8, No. 12 [April/May 1986]: 4).

88. The Community Assistance and Prison Projects sponsored a criminal justice and drama workshop. It also supported "the good-time legislation, the Equity Parole Review proposal, and other alternatives to extreme imprisonment" (Gari Badi, "CAP Sponsors Musical Extravaganza," GHM [October/November 1981]: 7).

89. Green Haven's prisoner newspaper during the first half of the 1970s.

90. The *Green Haven Monthly* was founded in February 1978 by two prisoners, one of which was Latino (*"Green Haven Monthly* Wins Five Awards in Nationwide American Penal Press Contest," *GHM* [January 1979]: Supplement).

91. The Veteran Self-Help Project was established in February 1979 to provide a space, "where inmates could assist inmates in areas concerning benefits, education, employment and other veteran related matters" ("Veterans Self-Help Project," *GHM* 2, No. 11[November 1979]: 8–9; and Charles Siplin, "Veterans Self-Help Project," GHM [May 1980]: 8). At the time, 450 to 550 of Green Haven's prisoners were veterans, approximately 85 percent of them Vietnam War veterans.

92. Alternative to Violence was designed to help prisoners find non-violent ways to cope with conflict. The program was sponsored by the Society of Friends (H. Bial Panye, "Alternative to Violence," *GHM* 8, No. 2 [February 1985]: 16).

93. As late as the spring of 1980, the Five Percent Nation had been unable to get DOCS' authorization to become an "innate program." DOCS' objection was that penal personnel saw the group as being, at best, a Muslim sect and, at worse, a "gang" (Maurice Samuels, "The 'God' Nation, *GHM* 3, Nos. 3 and 4 [March/April 1980]: 15–16).

94. Paul L. Montgomery, "Inmates Romp and Picnic with Sons As Prison Offers Token of Family Life," *N.Y. Times,* 13 August 1973, 57); and Nathaniel Sheppard, "A Rare Inside Look at Green Haven Prison, Troubled but Innovative State Institution," 17 August 1976, 62). In 1973, the Italian Culture Class sponsored a family picnic for 500 people. Food and entertainment for the event was donated by the Italian-American Civil Rights League, which also issued Italian prisoners a charter granting membership in the organization (Paul L. Montgomery, "Inmates Romp and Picnic with Sons As Prison Offers Token of Family Life," *N.Y. Times,* 13 August 1973, 57).

7

Latino Prisoner Groups, Penal Personnel, and Third Parties

As discussed in the previous chapter, the post-Attica Rebellion reforms did not quell the discontent of Latino, African-American, and white prisoners who wanted the implementation of more substantial reforms and the ability to participate in the policy-making process. Prisoner attempts at empowerment were made through the activities of political underground prisoner groups as well as through the newly created formal prisoner and administrative organizations. Supporting them in these efforts were third parties, sympathetic penal elites, and other sectors of the state bureaucracy. Green Haven administrators responded to prisoners' continued demands for change with a combination of repression and liberalization.

In view of the fact that Latino prisoners had other concerns in addition to the ones they shared with African-American and white prisoners, this chapter explores the distinct ways in which penal elites sought to quell Latino prisoner demands for an end to discrimination, the implementation of bilingual programs, and the hiring of bilingual personnel. Additional questions asked were: How did conflicting interests within the Latino prisoner population affect their ability to collectively organize to demand reforms? Did Latino prisoners create formal Latino organizations to voice their concerns? How did the nature of third party support affect the formulation of Latino prisoners' goals as well as the tactics and strategies they used? Under what conditions were Latino prisoners able to wrest significant concessions from penal elites? To answer these questions it will be necessary to first explore how the process of formalization affected the manner in which politically conscious Latino prisoner leaders sought to frame Latino concerns.

The Latin Think Tank Concept (LTTC)

The first formal Latino prisoner group at Green Haven was called the Latin Think Tank Concept (LTTC). It was formed in February

187

1973 by Puerto Rican prisoners who sympathized with the Young Lords Party, some of whom had been involved in the reform-oriented activities of political underground groups and in the creation of the PLU and the multiracial/multiethnic Think Tank Concept. LTTC founders chose to begin the process of formalization because of the privileges that accrued from such legitimation and the need to form an organization which could make more direct demands on the state for changes. Formalization also made it easier for Latino prisoners to openly seek the support of third parties and sympathetic state elites.

LTTC founders were considered, by both their peers and sympathetic staff and third parties, to be intellectuals. This was so regardless of whether or not they had received any formal education. They were set apart by both their analysis of what needed to take place in order to achieve a redefinition of the terms and conditions of confinement and their analysis of the relationship between the inside and outside Latina(o) community. Arguing that traditional custodial approaches to prison management were based on keeping prisoners and staff members isolated from one another, the LTTC proposed the creation of "the collaborative institution" in which prisoners and staff would meet to discuss goals, resolve problems, and implement new programs. The ultimate aim was the "significant modification of institutional programs and practices."[1] This goal, shared by African-American and white prisoner leaders in the TTC and other political underground prisoner groups, required Latino prisoners to continue forming coalitions with their non-Latino peers. Consequently, many LTTC leaders continued to participate in both formal and informal coalition-building efforts.

The other major theoretical stance made by the LTTC concerned the relationship between Latino prisoners and the outside Latina(o) community. LTTC leaders saw the problems faced by Latinos within prisons as an extension of the problems confronted by the Latina(o) community on the outside. Such commonalities included discrimination, poverty, police/guard brutality, inadequate medical care and living conditions, the need for bilingual educational programs, and the need for more bilingual staff in public service agencies. In their perspective, the group's founders reflected the new type of politicized Latino prisoner who had emerged in New York State jails and penitentiaries prior to the Attica Rebellion.

At the same time, recognizing that Latino prisoners were not only victims of an oppressive political establishment but also perpetrators of crimes against their own community, the LTTC sought to help Latino prisoners develop skills which would allow their reintegration into the Latina(o) community as "active and constructive members of society."[2] Such rehabilitation would take place through counseling, family assistance programs, the acquisition of job skills, and access to basic education and college education in Spanish and English. Other goals of LTTC included increasing community involvement in developing alternatives to incarceration, and securing community assistance in helping prisoners find jobs and housing upon their release.

To accomplish these latter goals, the LTTC sought the support of Latina(o) community organizations and Latina(o) institutions of higher education. The objective was to involve them in the establishment of a "Latin Program" at Green Haven. These efforts proved successful when the Center for Puerto Rican Studies (CPRS or the Center) agreed to offer two bilingual college courses at Green Haven during the fall of 1972[3] for which students received credit through John Jay College of Criminal Justice. The importance of having outside sources of support was stressed by former prisoner Domingo Morales.

> What it shows is that at least there's people on the outside that are concerned. And having the outside communication, where it's not controlled by the Department of Corrections, at least it gives you some kind of hope that certain things could happen, you know. It gives you like a voice that you might . . . not have while you're dealing with the internal staff of the Department of Corrections.[4]

In addition to courting the support of community groups and outside educational institutions, the LTTC strove to mobilize the support of state penal bureaucrats, particularly Latinas(os) working inside and outside DOCS. The latter included judges, legislators, and agency administrators. A complementary strategy was to court the support of sympathetic institutional personnel, particularly civilian staff. Gaining such diverse types of patronage was vital because of the overwhelming resistance white penal staff throughout the state had to the implementation of bilingual programs and the hiring of bilingual personnel.

The LTTC's efforts bore fruit when in February 1973, representatives of LTTC were able to meet with Eddie Rosa and Juan Olmo, two bilingual education teachers, Herman Pena (Director of the Minority Recruitment Agency) and Ray Solar (in charge of Minority Recruitment at New Paltz College).[5] At that meeting it was agreed, at LTTC's request, that Rosa and Olmo would accept DOCS's offer to become the first official bilingual education teachers in New York State prisons. Until then, Latino prisoners had been unofficially filling this role in the prison yard. Such classes had been geared primarily toward non-English-speaking prisoners, illiterates, and those wanting to get a high school equivalency diploma in English or Spanish.[6] The importance of bilingual education for Latino prisoners was evidenced by the fact that such classes had been offered in prison yards throughout the state since the 1960s and became one of a series of services provided by formal Latino prisoner organizations in various institutions (e.g., Eastern, Great Meadow, Attica).[7]

At Green Haven, the LTTC's demands for the hiring of bilingual personnel had been motivated by the growing number of Latino prisoners who did not speak English and could not, therefore, continue their elementary and/or high school education while imprisoned nor participate in other programs being offered at the facility. Few penal administrators understood or supported the need for Latinos to have access to programs in Spanish. As a result, until then, DOCS had been unwilling to earmark funds for such programs. By hiring Olmo and Rosa, DOCS was for the first time, recognizing the need to address such concerns.

Latino prisoner requests for the hiring of bilingual personnel and bilingual education programs were made in a number of ways. Latino prisoner leaders wrote to DOCS administrators in Albany at the same time they mobilized the support of civilian institutional personnel such as Vázquez, the coordinator of volunteer services, Burns, the superintendent for program services, and Norman Bell, Green Haven's director of education. The LTTC also wrote to Latino legislators, community groups, and educational organizations such as Brooklyn College and the Center for Puerto Rican Studies, requesting that they pressure DOCS administrators to hire bilingual staff. Educational organizations were also asked to recruit personnel who would be willing to provide bilingual education classes and other services.

As a last recourse, Latino prisoner leaders threatened prison administrators with carrying out collective acts of resistance if their demands for bilingual staff and programs were not met.[8] Certainly, the fact demands for such services were being voiced in a facility that had been as tense as Attica during the late 1960s and early 1970s, gave DOCS the impression that Latino prisoners at Green Haven might take further steps to have their needs addressed. In the end, the LTTC's primary accomplishment was that it initiated the process, to be discussed later in this chapter, whereby Albany central office personnel, institutional civilian staff, and third parties in the Latina(o) community were mobilized, albeit temporarily, in support of several programs supported by Latino prisoners.

In spite of its successes, however, the LTTC confronted several limitations which reduced its ability to gain the support of the overall Latino prisoner population and eventually led to its dissolution. On the one hand, the LTTC was considered a highly intellectual and political group. This alienated the less educated prisoners as well as those who shunned the organization either because they did not agree with the political ideology of its members or because such ideology could lead to penal repression of members considered "militant," "radical" or "revolutionary."

On the other hand, several LTTC founding members were also members of several political underground prisoner groups as well as the interracial, coalition-oriented Think Tank Concept from which they had adapted their name. Such coalition-building efforts were opposed by many Latino prisoners on several grounds. Some were not generally inclined to form alliances with African-American and white prisoners by whom they felt oppressed. Others felt racial prejudice toward their African-American peers. Still others feared that by becoming involved in multiracial/multiethnic coalitions, Latino prisoners would be endangering the existence of the formal Latino prisoner organization. This fear was based on the belief that, ultimately, DOCS would be inclined to dissolve prisoner groups that became too threatening.

In response to these pressures, in March 1973, LTTC changed its name to Puente de Unidad Latina (PUL). This was done with the support of Vázquez, Rosa, and Olmo, the two bilingual education teachers. The name change represented a change in tactics. PUL was meant to become a mass Latino prisoner organization. However, in order to accomplish this, the group had to abandon a name associated both with a small group of radical Latino intellectuals and with an African-American dominated prisoner group (the TTC). LTTC also changed its name because, by having adapted the name of an existing prisoner organization, Latino prisoners had come into conflict with the African-American and white prisoners in it. However, not all Latinos agreed with this name change precisely because they felt that by using a name associated with a respected prisoner organization, Latinos would attract outside resources.

In addition to changing the organization's name, former LTTC leaders agreed to refrain from occupying leadership positions in non-Latino organizations. Only in this manner could they gain and hold the trust of the Latino prisoner population. As a result, during the first half of the 1970s PUL, as a group, became increasingly resistant to forming interracial/interethnic alliances with other prisoners, although individual members continued their involvement in such efforts.

Underlying the creation of PUL was also the recognition that, while the LTTC had the support of key civilian institutional personnel and community volunteers, without the existence of a strong, mass Latino prisoner organization, programs demanded by Latinos would either not be instituted by prison administrators or would be discontinued soon after their creation. Although not all members of LTTC agreed with this change in focus, they did agree that a change in tactics was needed if Latino leaders were going to obtain widespread support for specifically Latino goals among the general Latino prisoner population. A review of the membership lists of both the LTTC and PUL revealed that, in March 1973, all the major leaders of the LTTC joined other Latino prisoners to create PUL.

Puente de Unidad Latina (PUL)

During the 1970s, PUL was composed primarily of Puerto Rican prisoners, although Cubans, Colombians, and Dominicans were already visible minorities within it. While the organization's leadership fluctuated between ten and fifteen men, its call-out list ranged between sixty and eighty prisoners.[9] Initially PUL officers tended to be former LTTC members. This was so because these men were generally long-termers, bilingual, and more educated than the general Latino prisoner population.[10] This meant they were more acquainted with the workings of the penal system and, as a result of their English language skills, had easier access to institutional personnel, third parties, and African-American and white prisoners.

PUL's primary concerns were to organize Latino prisoners and mobilize sympathetic penal personnel and third parties, particularly within the Latino community, in support of various goals previously espoused by the LTTC. However, the conflict between PUL members who wanted to focus only on Latino concerns and those favoring coalitions with African-American and white prisoners continued to manifest. Vázquez recalls, "I remember one big argument we had with La Fiesta de San Juan Bautista where [some] Puerto Rican inmates didn't want anybody but Puerto Ricans to go to this event . . ."[11] Latino prisoners who advocated interracial and interethnic coalition-building tended to be former TTC members. These men were eventually forced to withdraw from the TTC altogether as a result of pressures from other Latinos who did not want them to be both leaders in PUL and visible members of a predominantly African-American group.[12]

Equally important was the fact that PUL was divided between those who wanted to engage in collective acts of resistance organized by political underground prisoner groups and those who wanted to limit themselves to using the new formal prisoner and/or administrative organizations (e.g., ILC) to pressure for changes. Such conflicts were evident in an internal PUL document dated March 23, 1973:

> There is rumors goin [sic] around that the Latin population is discontented . . . We must convince the population that to make a protest without investigating the possibilities for success is deadly. We are not here to do the work of the Liaison Committee. We are involved right now in making and establishing an educational program. And when this program gets of [sic] the ground, we will work to establish the Pre-Release Center in the Latin Community. My brothers, what's more important to you right now? To establish community relations or to get involved with the Administration about the discontents the population feels? Remember that some sacrifices have to be made in order to obtain our objective.[13]

Why did some Latino prisoners feel the need to make the distinction between Latino-oriented and coalition-oriented groups? And why did some Latino prisoners favor lobbying prison authorities only through the newly chartered formal prisoner and administrative organizations? Some of their reasons have already been discussed: resentment against white and African-American prisoners; racism towards the latter; or fear of reprisals. However, there was also the fact that PUL's reason for existence was to address the specific concerns of Latino prisoners. Furthermore, many Latino prisoners supported PUL because the group was able to deliver tangible benefits through the activities and programs it sponsored. Most Latinos had joined PUL for the same reason they participated in informal prisoner groups and networks, that is, for the fulfillment of individual rather than collective goals. Some of PUL's leaders had an added incentive in maintaining the organization, "The officers . . . had passes that would allow them access throughout the institution. It would allow them to ask for office space and to arrange for phone calls, stationery, to organize activities. So being organized legitimized them . . ."[14] As a result of these benefits, many Latino prisoners did not want to risk the existence of the organization over interests they felt could be fought for through the ILC, the prison's only formal administrative organization at the time.

Despite the resistance of Latino prisoners to PUL leaders having leadership positions in other formal prisoner groups, it should be clear that throughout PUL's existence, there were Latino prisoners who were members of PUL and active in other formal prisoner groups (i.e., inmate programs and organizations) sanctioned by DOCS. Some of these, listed in chapter 6, included: *Open Gate*, the Peregrine Jaycees, Community on the Move, the Pre-Release Center, and various religious denominations. Participation in PUL also overlapped with participation in sports teams and other forms of informal prisoner groups and networks.

As discussed above, Latino prisoners created a formal organization to achieve a number of diverse goals. Soon after its creation, however, Latino prisoners found themselves in the midst of a power struggle between those who favored pursuing specific "Latino" concerns through the formal organization and those who additionally wanted to openly pursue coalition-building efforts in an attempt to achieve additional reforms and a redefinition in the terms and conditions of imprisonment. By the end of 1973, some of PUL's leaders had been forced by their peers to abandon their leadership positions in the coalition-oriented TTC. These demands reflected both the hostility Latino prisoners felt toward their non-Latino peers and the fear that if Latino prisoners became involved with visible coalition-building efforts PUL would be disbanded. In spite of this turn of events, a number of radical Latino prisoners continued to participate in formal and informal reform-oriented efforts as well as in PUL. Nevertheless, they argued that PUL's leaders had been co-opted by prison administrators[15] and that the process of formalization contributed by design to the depoliticization of all prisoners.

In addition to these conflicts, throughout its existence, PUL's cohesiveness was also weakened by personality clashes. It was not uncommon for Latinos to drop out of the organization because of personal as well as ideological differences with other members.[16] These conflicts were frequently reflected in the fact that attendance at PUL meetings tended to fluctuate according to the issues being discussed and who raised them.

> PUL seemed to have one of the largest memberships of any of the inmate organizations. But the membership wasn't steady. You didn't see like the same people coming to the meetings every week . . . If they knew an issue would be discussed and they wanted it to go a particular way then they would get certain people to come to the meeting, you know, . . . sort of like lobbying in their direction.[17]

One of the other issues salient within PUL was whether or not Puerto Rico should be independent. While Puerto Rican prisoners tended to respond in the affirmative to this question, they disagreed on how this goal should be accomplished. According to Vázquez, ". . . I think that the left had a Marxist view of life . . . whereas the center firmly believed that there was substantial oppression in society and that it had to be changed . . . but not necessarily replaced with a Marxist system."[18]

Differences in opinion also surfaced with respect to the nature of the relationship PUL should have with prison administrators such as Vázquez. There were Latino leaders who were distrustful of Vázquez not only because he was "part of the system" but because they regarded his efforts to formalize prisoner groups as divisive.[19] As a result they preferred to associate with Rosa and Olmo, the two bilingual education teachers. Other Latino prisoner leaders, however, sought out Vázquez because he was Puerto Rican and/or had the potential to grant a wide range of privileges. The willingness of the latter Latino leaders to take advantage of the assistance provided by the few available sympathetic staff persons produced a situation in which, according to Vázquez, ". . . I helped them organize Puente de Unidad Latina . . . I'm not sure if I wrote the preamble in the constitution for them, but I was involved in its wording. I was involved in its structuring. I was involved in discussions about what's the appropriate procedure for conducting meetings."[20]

One of PUL's greatest difficulties was created, not by internal dissention, but by the strategies used by prison officials to discourage the formation of a strong and stable prisoner leadership. From the beginning, PUL was confronted with the dilemma that whenever its leadership gained the support of a large number of Latino prisoners, penal authorities would transfer some of the leaders to other prisons in the state. It was the fear of being transferred further away from New York City (where most of their relatives and friends lived), that kept many Latino prisoners from becoming involved in PUL's organizing efforts. The reasons given for these transfers varied; the prisoner had engaged in a fight with another prisoner or staff member, contraband had been found in his room, etc. As shown in the previous chapter, there were times when contraband was purposely planted by staff members and/or by other prisoners at the bidding of staff members in retaliation for behavior perceived to be threatening to institutional personnel. There were also times in which staff would try to provoke prisoners into engaging in behavior for which they could be further penalized. Another strategy used by penal personnel to disrupt PUL's leadership was to transfer Latino prisoners from other facilities to Green Haven in hopes that the newcomers would disrupt the group. There were also times in which DOCS would grant parole as a way of removing prisoner leaders from the population.

Then, too, Latino prisoner leaders would sometimes derail themselves by reverting to destructive behavior such as alcohol and drug abuse. The result of these externally and internally imposed setbacks was that PUL's leadership had to be reconstructed every few months.

Despite multiple internal conflicts and the constant harassment by penal personnel during the first half of the 1970s, PUL was able to mobilize the support of Latino third parties and civilian staff for the implementation of bilingual educational programs within the institution, a study-release program on the outside, and the organization of special events within the facility. Asked about the tactics and strategies used by Latino prisoners to achieve their goals, Rosa noted:

> Letters, petitions, meetings, activities to legitimize themselves before the administration . . . that was probably one of the key things that they had to do . . . And they were constantly trying to keep their forces together, organized, united, at the same time reaching out . . . against all odds. You know, by the time the letter got out and the person responded . . . weeks and months would go by. And they're isolated upstate. For anyone to connect with prisons is very difficult.[21]

Under what conditions then did third parties and civilian personnel form alliances with Latino prisoners? How did such support affect Latino prisoner organizing efforts? Before these questions can be fully addressed it will be necessary to explore the societal conditions under which third parties offered support to Latino prisoners. This will allow us to better understand the difficulties the former confronted that made it difficult to engage in long-term prisoner support work.

Latina(o) Third Party Support for PUL

A prime source of third party support for PUL, as it had briefly been for the LTTC, was the Center for Puerto Rican Studies (CPRS). The CPRS was technically a research center although, during its first years of existence, it operated much like a community organization. The center had been created as a result of coalition-building efforts within the Puerto Rican community of New York City.[22] As such, it acted as an umbrella group for students, professionals, college administrators, and community members, some of whom were activists in other struggles waged by the Latina(o) community during the 1960s and 1970s (e.g., bilingual education, an end to police brutality, adequate housing, etc.).[23] According to Carmen Roldán, CPRS administrator, the forces demanding the creation of the CPRS were, "a combination of students who were actively agitating within the [city] university [system] for Puerto Rican Studies programs and a research center. It was the few faculty we had within this university [system]. It was community groups like Evelina Antonetti and some of these leadership from our community agencies. And it was grassroots people."[24]

As a result of their diverse community involvement, many CPRS members were aware of the similarities in conditions encountered by Latinas(os) inside and outside the walls. There was a consciousness of the role prisons played in subduing the Latina(o) community and the importance of maintaining the links between those inside and outside. Moreover, there was the conviction that, ". . . for many of us during that time involved in all of these areas, prisons and schools were very similar."[25] According to Roldán:

> . . . a lot of the work revolved around the same kinds of issues that we found in our community; lack of bilingual services, lack of educational programs . . . I mean, it was sort of parallel with the school system, you know, fighting for bilingual education in the school system . . . whether they're free to communicate in their own language. Health services, I mean, all of those very basic issues that existed in the community were sort of exaggerated within the walls because . . . they were isolated and, were governed by even stricter rules, it was difficult to try to get those kinds of networks going."[26]

This awareness led the CPRS to create a Task Force on Criminal Justice and Correction,[27] hereafter referred to as the Prison Task Force (PTF or Task Force). The PTF was one of the Center's five research based task forces.[28] Its major goals were to "combine self training, research, services to inmates, and public education in its work."[29] While the PTF eventually also worked with Latina prisoners at Bedford Hills, it is the nature of their work with prisoners at Green Haven that will be discussed in this chapter.[30] The PTF's major goals were to provide Latino prisoners assistance on several levels:

a. Bilingual college level instruction;
b. Support for a high school equivalency program in Spanish in prison (materials and evaluation);
c. Lectures, seminars, and special events around themes of interest to inmates.[31]

The PTF presence was felt at Green Haven in numerous ways. Haydé Ortega, coordinator of the PTF, became the "community contact" or "inmate group coordinator" for PUL.[32] As such, she was authorized by DOCS to act as the liaison between PUL, PTF volunteers, and institutional personnel. While acting as mediators between prisoners and administration, PTF volunteers continually emphasized the need for the existence of strong prisoner organizations which could design, implement, and run autonomous programs. As CPRS Director Frank Bonilla explained, ". . . nuestra preocupación fue el no envolvernos sino a través de grupos organizados de presos. Es decir, no de servir las administraciones de las prisiones, aunque desde luego teníamos que entendernos con ellos, pero usar . . . como instrumento principal las organizaciones de los presos mismos."[33]

The regular presence of Ortega and other PTF members at the facility contributed to legitimizing PUL's activities and created the sense that the behavior of prison personnel was being monitored by outsiders. The consistent presence of community volunteers also provided prisoners much needed moral support in the face of continued harassment by the predominantly white penal staff. ". . . people from the Centro were there every week to give a class, to . . . read, to have meetings with the whole organization, with the inmates, and the prison staff."[34] Many prisoners began to feel that they were part of a community that cared about their welfare and was willing to lobby prison authorities on their behalf.

The PTF made itself responsible for providing PUL a series of support services pertaining to ethnic, social, and educational activities. Support services associated with ethnic and family day events included: meeting with PUL to organize, coordinate, and execute the events; providing transportation for family members and entertainers; organizing fundraising events; and soliciting donations of food, supplies, money, and entertainment. For example, in June 1973, the PTF helped PUL organize the first San Juan Feast Day event at the facility. These events were significant in that they not only commemorated holidays of importance to the Latina(o) community but, most importantly, allowed Latino prisoners to invite family and other community members to the facility. Hence, they allowed Latino prisoners to maintain ties with outside entities.

> They were important in that they gave you a day of Latinos and you could hear bands and, you know, it was all Latino families and . . . there was camaraderie. And . . . everybody shared and you could see your culture because all these people [were] coming from the street, you know, men, women, and children. And you'd hear of the . . . things that were happening in the community and what the street looked like. For men that have been incarcerated for a very long time, that means a lot.[35]

The PTF also provided support services for educational activities. These included conducting seminars, providing bilingual course materials, recruiting volunteers to teach classes, and helping PUL develop a bilingual higher education program. Latino prisoners, in turn, contributed to helping the CPRS achieve some of its educational objectives on the outside. For example, according to Carmen Roldán, ". . . when I was running the Early Childhood Program, we worked with inmates. They designed puzzles for us . . . in their woodworking shops that reflected Puerto Rican scenes so that we could take it to the children and use [them] in the classroom. So they sort of complemented the bilingual effort in early childhood."[36]

Volunteers affiliated with the PTF also assisted prisoners with individual problems and brought family members to visit. The latter service was important because mail in Spanish to and from family members was frequently censored and seized by prison staff. There were instances when Latino prisoners had to wait long periods of time to receive their mail because there was no bilingual personnel available who could screen the letters. In other cases PTF volunteers wrote letters of recommendation supporting prisoners' requests for parole. PTF efforts on behalf of Latino prisoners, according to Frank Bonilla, led to ". . . times at which inmates were paroled to us for weekends of meetings and conferences and activities."[37] On occasion, the CPRS itself hired prisoners upon their release. In addition to these activities inside the walls, the PTF conducted criminal justice seminars for the outside community.[38]

Two of the most far-reaching activities the CPRS helped Latino prisoner leaders implement were the initiation of a bilingual college program (begun at Green Haven during the fall of 1972 at the request of the LTTC) and the implementation of a bilingual study release program[39] at Hostos Community College during the fall of 1973 and spring of 1974. During the spring of 1973, at PUL's request, Frank Bonilla met with representatives of PUL, the Think Tank Concept, Malcolm-King College, Marist College, Duchess Community College, and the South Forty Corporation, to discuss creating a consortium of colleges that would allow prisoners to get a college education inside the facility. Bonilla describes the context in which third parties collaborated to support prisoner concerns.

> . . . within the prison there were always other organizations going in that we would join forces with. . . . There were people from . . . King College who were active in a parallel way with Black inmate organi-

zations that we were in touch with. And we did a lot of things together inside prisons. When it came time to negotiate some of these things in Albany we joined forces with the other organizations. . . . We had frequent meetings and we were often at the prison at the same time. We invited each other to each other's event . . . I would say it was more at that level than . . . a very formal interlocking coalition-building. It was based on a common interest in trying to help generate conditions inside the prison that gave the inmates some space to do things for themselves, principally with respect to education.[40]

Such combined efforts eventually led DOCS central office administrators to authorize the establishment of a college degree program at Green Haven. However, the concerns of Latino prisoners for the permanent establishment of a bilingual college education program at the facility were left unaddressed. While the CPRS had offered several bilingual college level courses during the fall 1972 and spring 1973 semesters, these classes had been offered on an ad hoc basis. In fact, the difficulties encountered while trying to offer the courses (e.g., recruitment of teachers, traveling to the facility, costs of educational materials for prisoners) led the CPRS to request that Hostos Community College[41] take over responsibility for offering them beginning in the fall of 1973. In the meantime, Hostos administrators had agreed, at the request of PUL and the CPRS, to participate in the implementation of a study release program at the college which was also scheduled to begin the fall of 1973. The Study Release Program would complement the bilingual higher education program Hostos would take over at Green Haven in the fall of 1973.

According to the original plans by PUL, the CPRS, Rosa and Olmo, the two bilingual education teachers, the recruitment for the Study Release Program was to be carried out primarily through PUL, Rosa, and Olmo at Green Haven although Latino prisoners throughout the state were eligible to participate in it. Prisoners transferred from other state facilities would then spend one semester at Green Haven getting acquainted with the goals of the program. Subsequently, program participants would be transferred to Ossining Correctional Facility (Sing Sing) where additional support would be provided to them by a sister PUL organization created for that purpose. From Ossining, participating prisoners would attend Hostos during the day, returning to the prison at night.

The Study Release Program, which was designed to encompass "the largest group of prisoners in any study release program in the state,"[42] was created as a result of negotiations between Hostos administrators,[43] Latino legislators and judges,[44] DOCS Commissioner and Deputy Commissioner for Program Services,[45] and Bonilla. Bonilla describes what such efforts entailed ". . . In the first year or so I put in a fair amount of time . . . going up there a good deal and negotiating, meeting . . . [with] PUL leaders and prison staffs and Albany, and . . . negotiating outside with . . . the president of Hostos, who was then Cándido de León, to get this program put in."[46]

These negotiations took place without the participation of top administrators at Green Haven. As a result, the latter came to see the Study Release Program as having been imposed from above. Moreover, the presence of Bonilla in the negotiations was resented by Green Haven administrators because while they were excluded from the process, PUL was seen as having been represented in the negotiations by Bonilla and the CPRS. Thus, from its inception, the program lacked the support of precisely those institutional sectors that held the responsibility for implementing it. In the end, final decisions about which prisoners would participate in the program were left to Green Haven's Temporary Release Committee.

The committee consistently rejected the suggestions made by the CPRS, PUL, and Hostos Community College administrators. While Olmo and Rosa had helped recruit Latino prisoners for the program and made some minor suggestions as to whom should be allowed to participate, these educators were not allowed to take part in the meetings of the Committee. Moreover, although the program had the support of prison administrators such as Vázquez, the coordinator of volunteer services, Burns, the superintendent of program services, and Bell, the director of education, they were not part of the committee that made the final decisions.

Furthermore, whereas PUL, the bilingual teachers, and the CPRS argued that anyone who qualified academically should be able to participate in the program, the final guidelines were determined by DOCS' security concerns.[47] "It was a very complex system in which really Correction had the final say so and a person's security status was a great determinant on whether they would be released or not, what type of crime they had committed, how much time they had to go. Then came the academic questions."[48] The message was clear that while the program was to be implemented, neither the Albany central office nor Green Haven's administrators were going to allow third parties, sympathetic civilian staff, or Latino prisoners to participate as equals in the decision-making process, or the program's implementation. DOCS' lack of support for prisoners participating in the Study Release Program was also apparent, according to George Soto, one of its participants, by the fact that ultimately, "DOCS didn't provide assistance for prisoners . . . just penalties."[49] In fact, it was Hostos' support which ensured Latino prisoners they would not be harassed by penal personnel while on campus.

> Hostos gave a lot of support. They had their two deans there who worked very hard for these guys. They fought to have them be treated like any other student . . . The prison wanted to bring the students up there just for their class and bring them back. They said, "No, the students have to be on the campus, have a chance to be part of extra-curricular activities and use the library. Have time to spend with fellow students." . . . The college fought with the Department of Corrections for them to have as normal as possible a student experience.[50]

Adding fuel to the fire was the fact that soon after its implementation non-Latino prisoners began to voice their objections to how the program was being executed. While the African-American dominated TTC had supported the Study Release Program in the hope that it would serve as a precedent that would eventually facilitate the release of large numbers of African-American prisoners back to community care, the overall African-American prisoner population, together with their white peers, began to object to what was perceived as the preferential treatment being given Latinos. According to Rosa, "Then there were the African-American Nationalist groups in the prison. Once that they found out about these programs they . . . started applying pressure that they also wanted programs because it meant getting out."[51] Consequently, though the creation of the program seemed to strengthen the position of Latino prisoners, albeit temporarily, within the facility, it also helped deepen existing rivalries between them and their African-American and white counterparts.

As a result of these obstacles and the growing tensions between DOCS and Hostos administrators, the Study Release Program at Hostos was terminated within a year of its creation.[52] In March 1974, Hostos announced its intention to discontinue the college program it had begun at Green Haven during the fall of 1973. By May 1974, the college had decided to discontinue participation in the Study Release Program as well.

As the discussion above shows, during the first half of the 1970s, third party support for PUL was felt primarily through the services provided by volunteers affiliated with the Prison Task Force of the Center for Puerto Rican Studies. Such services were designed to address a number of concerns voiced by Latino prisoners, including the implementation of bilingual college education programs. Ironically, while the PTF supported coalition-building efforts between prisoners, the support of the PTF for PUL strengthened those prisoner leaders within the organization who were less likely to risk the existence of the group in order to promote reform-oriented prisoner coalitions.

In carrying out its support activities, the PTF continually collaborated with institutional personnel and other third parties supportive of prison reform efforts. The ability to make such alliances was of the utmost importance since custody-oriented staff continually tried to thwart the efforts of reform-oriented prisoners, third parties, and DOCS civilian personnel. The efforts of the CPRS did, nonetheless, help to temporarily legitimize the demands of Latino prisoners and assured DOCS personnel that the latter did, in fact, have advocates who were monitoring DOCS' actions and policies.

While short-lived, the Green Haven Study Release Program demonstrated that Latino prisoners were able to secure the most from penal personnel when they were organized into a mass prisoner organization and were successful in mobilizing the support of third parties, non-Latino prisoner leaders, and DOCS personnel at the institutional and central office levels. Equally important was the fact that the experiment with the Study Release Program showed that it was when the DOCS bureaucracy, and by definition the state, was weakened by internal conflicts (e.g., reform-oriented versus custody-oriented sectors), that an opportunity or "opening" was created for Latino prisoners and their allies to achieve a number of limited goals. Such conflicts led Albany administrators to support the implementation of a program that was resisted by important sectors of the facility's staff. Still, such efforts could only go so far if they lacked the support of the overwhelmingly white institutional staff and the mass of the African-American and white prisoner population.

One of the primary motivations behind the supportive actions of central office personnel was the fact that state elites had been severely criticized for their treatment of Latino and African-American prisoners following the Attica Rebellion. It is safe to say that DOCS saw the Study Release Program both as a way to reduce Latino prisoner discontent and as a means of channeling Latino prisoner organizing into "acceptable" areas (e.g., educational and "Latino" issues).[53]

However, DOCS failure to include Green Haven administrators in the original negotiations undermined the implementation of the Study Release Program by intensifying the hostility of the white custodial and civilian staff toward it. Such hostility was not only due to security concerns, but was also a result of the ignorance of staff members concerning the purposes and goals of bilingual education. Confronting such attitudes became one of the primary tasks of Eddie Rosa and Juan Olmo, the two Latino bilingual education teachers hired during the spring of 1973. A review of some of Rosa's experiences with both institutional personnel and Latino prisoners will reveal some of the major problems confronting Latino civilian employees throughout the period studied.

The Dilemma of Latino Civilian Staff

Eddie Rosa's interest in the conditions encountered by Latino prisoners had been aroused by the Attica Rebellion.[54] Rosa found out about the availability of a bilingual education teaching position at Green Haven through a network of Latinas(os) working in the New York State college and penal systems. It was a point in New York State history when bilingual education programs were being developed and implemented throughout the state. These programs were resisted by the overwhelming number of white teachers and educational administrators working within the state's public school and college systems. This same resistance was encountered by Rosa and Olmo at Green Haven. It was this opposition which led Rosa to wholeheartedly support the transformation of the LTTC into PUL.

Rosa's support for the creation of PUL was motivated by the desire to insure the continued existence of the bilingual programs he and Olmo were developing at Green Haven. For one, a mass Latino prisoner organization could help recruit Latino students for the bilingual education programs. Secondly, it could serve as a support group for prisoners participating in the programs. Such support would encourage Latino prisoners to continue their education in spite of low self-esteem and reservations about the usefulness of educational programs. According to Rosa, ". . . I knew that educational programs often can be very farfetched for the inmates . . . they couldn't identify with it or perceive that they could do academic work. For people that were illiterate, people that had never done college work, this is often very remote for them . . ."[55]

The existence of a strong Latino prisoner organization was also expected to ensure, through the pressures it exerted on prison administrators, the continued existence of the programs.

> My agenda . . . was that . . . in order to have educational programs . . .
> I needed the support of the Latino community in the prison . . .
> because I knew that the innovations that I was presenting in the
> areas of bilingual education . . . would create conflict and did create
> conflict among my colleagues, co-workers, teachers, the educational
> administrators, the administration up front . . .[56]

Speaking about the resistance offered by white prison administrators, Rosa stated: "When I introduced the concept to the superintendent and the deputy superintendent . . . that these men would be studying in Spanish, it was the most foreign thing they had ever heard. They thought it was un-American. That these men . . . would be conspiring against them in Spanish."[57]

White educational personnel also showed their hostility to bilingual programs despite the support for them from Bell, Green Haven's director of education.

> They feared using Spanish in the curriculum when their goal was
> English. I had teachers who a couple of them were no better than the
> guards . . . people who had done ten, fifteen, twenty years in corrections as teachers, who were also not highly educated, not very articulate in English.

> They [were] constantly questioning what we were doing. Questioning
> that we weren't teaching as much as we should be teaching. When we
> first came in we were doing a lot of administrative work. We went
> through a process of a couple of months of trying to define what we
> would be doing . . . We were interviewing inmates, testing inmates,
> developing forms and curriculums and coordinating things up front.[58]

While Rosa and Olmo were continually criticized by colleagues for not teaching as much as was expected of them, prison administrators required them to fulfill additional duties not related to their educational responsibilities.

> We were constantly being pulled to do things that were not educational. We were being asked to interpret, to translate documents. . . .
> We were becoming . . . bilingual correctional counsellors combined
> with teachers, with psychologists, social workers . . . I was hired as a
> bilingual teacher but the prison didn't really know what that meant.
> They had no idea what bilingual education was. What they really
> wanted was somebody Latino, that spoke Spanish, that could deal
> with the inmates.[59]

The guards also resented the introduction of bilingual education and bilingual programs. "They did not think highly of inmates, let alone educated inmates. . . . They felt [that if] they didn't have a college education . . . these prisoners were not entitled to prison education."[60] The resistance of custodial personnel to Rosa and Olmo was expressed in several ways.

> They were not used to seeing professionals that were Latinos, and I would be harassed by the guards. I would be literally stopped when I walked down the corridor. I would be pulled into a room and threatened with a body strip search, meaning taking all my clothes and bending over. . . . They went as far as asking me to take off my jacket and my tie and my belt and my wallet and my shoes . . . and harassing me in the process of doing that . . . And they would sneer. . . . And I felt more threatened by the guards than by the inmates. . . . I really . . . feared for myself. I feared that if anything came down that I would be hurt physically by the white racist correctional guards at the time.[61]

In addition to the conflicts with white penal staff discussed above, Rosa and Olmo had to confront the hostility of those Latino prisoners who accused them of having played favorites during the selection process for the Study Release Program. As mentioned previously, Rosa and Olmo had been involved in the original formulation of the Study Release Program although their actual input in the final decision-making process was minimal. The creation of the Study Release Program had led Latino prisoners to argue with one another over who should participate in it. The program's desirability rested in the fact that prisoners would be able to leave the institution for part of the day. Tensions were so high that, according to Rosa, at least one stabbing took place over it. As a result, Rosa and Olmo felt the need to protect themselves from the actions of those Latino prisoners whom they felt joined the Study Release Program (and even PUL) for purely opportunistic reasons. These included prisoners who, "Wanted to use the programs so they could have access to the prison, so they could get a pass so they could smuggle contraband . . . whether it was booze they made in the facility or drugs or anything else that was considered contraband from weapons to materials, etc."[62] Rosa and Olmo also feared that opportunists, ". . . would use the office to store things, to communicate . . ."[63] Such actions would endanger the existence of the programs by giving prison administrators excuses to dissolve them. There was the additional danger that hostile personnel would try to use Latino prisoners to "... set us up with drugs, with contraband, letters ..."[64] in order to dissolve the programs and/or secure the dismissal of Rosa and Olmo. This situation led the two bilingual teachers to agree that, "We had to cover our backs all the time. That it was he and I first ... then we were in collaboration with the inmates in general, in principle, supportive of them as Latinos, as oppressed groups."[65]

Thus, Latino prisoner leaders and Latino civilians working at Green Haven needed each other's support to ensure the establishment and continued existence of bilingual programs at the facility. Once instituted, such programs had to be continually protected both from the disapproving predominantly white prison staff and from individual Latino prisoners who sought to use the programs for their own personal gain.

Despite the multiple obstacles discussed above during 1973, Rosa, together with Olmo, developed a Basic Literacy Program in Spanish, an English-as-a-Second-Language Program, and a High School Equivalency Program in Spanish. In the midst of such conflicts, what made it possible for Latino prisoners and their supporters to secure the implementation and continued existence of bilingual programs? Rosa described the combination of forces that made it possible for Latino prisoners to have these concerns addressed and the mediating role institutional civilian personnel played in this process.

> It was really ... Attica and the reform movement going on in corrections that propelled this forward. The pressure from the Latino inmates ... the outside people. And then myself, I was like a broker, if you will. I was with the men eight hours a day, five days a week. The outside people came in once a week or once every couple of weeks, for a couple of hours ...[66]

In addition to Rosa and Olmo, other important civilian institutional "brokers" included Vázquez, Burns, and Bell, who had also supported the implementation of bilingual programs. However, by 1975, PUL had lost not only the support of the latter three but that of Rosa as well. Rosa's resignation in September 1973 was followed by that of Vázquez in October 1974. By 1975, both Bell and Burns[67] had been promoted to other positions outside of Green Haven. Hence, within two years, PUL had lost the support of four civilian staff members who had been instrumental in facilitating both the organization's demands for bilingual services as well as the right of prisoners to create their own autonomous groups. Although Olmo continued working as a bilingual education teacher and another bilingual teacher was hired to replace

Rosa, the fact that these teachers could not mobilize significant sources of administrative and/or third party support limited their ability to influence penal policy on behalf of Latino prisoners. The loss of institutional support for PUL was further paralleled by the gradual decline of outside Latina(o) support for Latino prisoners.

The Decline of Latina(o) Third Party Support

In 1975, the Prison Task Force of the Center for Puerto Rican Studies began to undergo a transformation that resulted in its eventual dissolution and withdrawal from Green Haven. Since the PTF's creation in 1973, Haydé Ortega and Bonilla had been able to provide it with consistent guidance and leadership. However, in June 1975, Ortega left the CPRS and Bonilla, as director, was not in a position to assume the full responsibility that coordinating such a task force entailed. Thus, as in the case of PUL, the PTF found itself having to rebuild its own leadership.

Added to this situation was the fact that, as stated earlier, PTF members tended to be volunteers who were also active in other CPRS task forces. Each task force made equal demands for personnel, time, and resources. As time passed, the PTF's ability to compete in all of these areas declined. This was the result of several factors. First, were the growing difficulties encountered by the PTF when trying to recruit community volunteers. As mentioned previously, one of the reasons the Latina(o) community was hesitant to support Latina(o) prisoners was because it was the outside community which bore the brunt of Latina(o) crime. After the 1970 New York City jail rebellions, but particularly after the Attica Rebellion, the outside Latina(o) community had become more aware of the commonalities it shared with Latina(o) prisoners. As a result, it had been more willing to engage in prisoner support work. However, as economic conditions throughout the country worsened during the 1970s, it became increasingly necessary for people on the outside to focus on immediate survival issues (e.g., finding work, housing). Ironically, at the same time these developments were taking place, the material conditions of New York State prisoners seemed to be improving as a result of the post-Attica Rebellion reforms. This perception was reflected in the argument that, "You're coddling and trying to protect and give service to people that the community outside has not been able to get."[68] Such attitudes made it more difficult for the PTF to recruit volunteers.

Moreover, as economic conditions deteriorated, those community forces most likely to support prisoners were also the hardest hit by diminishing resources.

> ... community-based agencies ... had ... much more support en ese
> tiempo from, you know, government support of "The War on Poverty"
> ... and you had foundations ... Now foundations rather "write off"
> the Latino issue with less money in one swoop ... I mean, it's just a
> different economic environment that you're working in that makes it
> harder to ... pull together in the same way.[69]

Within this climate of diminishing resources, the costs of travelling to
the prisons while also having to provide educational materials and
other resources to prisoners made such support work difficult to sustain
on a permanent basis. The long trips to the institutions also demanded
great investment of physical and emotional energy as well as time.

However, what had made it possible for the PTF to support Latino
prisoners during the first half of the 1970s was its ability to mobilize a
wide variety of community support. As Carmen Roldán explained:

> ... it just didn't help just based on one group. It helped when it was
> a coalition of different forces. And it was much easier to pull off dur-
> ing that period because ... everybody ... networked in a very, very
> tight way. And if there was a problem, you know, you could pull off
> petitions or letters or that kind of thing much more easily than you
> could now.[70]

Another set of constraints encountered by PTF members were created by having to work with a population whose formal organization
and leadership had to be continuously recreated.

> ... poco a poco, nos fuimos alejando de la cuestión por una combi-
> nación de problemas, más bien de mantener el interés de gente fuera
> de la prisión, la dificultad de mantener relación con las organiza-
> ciones de los presos internas que desde luego son muy inestables y a
> la misma vez bastante vulnerables, que cada vez que comienzan a
> adquirir alguna solidez . . . pues la reacción muchas veces de la
> administración es de buscar manera de desmantelarlas.[71]

Added to the obstacles erected by institutional administrators were
the difficulties created by intra-prisoner rivalries and the personal setbacks experienced by prisoners.

The PTF's ability to support Latino prisoners was likewise affected
by the shift which took place in the CPRS during the mid-1970s
toward academic research. While the CPRS had been created as a
research center, since its inception it had successfully been able to

combine both academic activity and grassroots community activism. The shift in focus away from prisoner support work occurred at a time when it became more difficult to secure funding for prisoner support work but easier to obtain funds for academic research projects supported by other CPRS task forces. An additional factor that contributed to reducing the PTF's involvement at Green Haven was the fact that the work of the task force had lost some of its sense of urgency precisely because the PTF had been successful in generating other sources of support for Latino prisoners. According to Bonilla:

> I think that there was a shift but . . . some people were also taking over some of these functions . . . We more or less handed over the prisoner release program to Hostos Community College. Once that prison release program was in shape we stopped supporting the sending in of people to give courses which also . . . began to be a problem because for people to get up there each time and then sometimes they couldn't even get to the class because there was no guard to take them in . . . But I would say mainly the problems of working with the inmate organizations but also that the program evolved so that it had its own logic and weight.[72]

The PTF also helped colleges such as Marist develop its college education program in English. These programs were accessible to English-speaking Latinos. ". . . we worked with people at Marist. Marist sent faculty . . . and we helped get the local campuses for whom it was much easier to get to the prison to set up these courses . . . We worked and helped the prison organizations set up contacts with the local campuses and . . . to recruit faculty and so on."[73]

Ironically, as the PTF was undergoing these changes, some of its members came into contact with community persons who were working with Latino prisoners in other state facilities.[74] With these networking efforts came the conviction that what was needed was a strategy that would have an impact on policies toward Latino prisoners on a statewide level rather than on a facility-by-facility basis. In view of the PTF's decreasing ability to provide direct support to Latino prisoners, in 1975 the few remaining PTF members joined with other Latinos and a number of white and Jewish liberals to create the Ad Hoc Committee for Hispanic Inmates.[75] The primary aims of the Ad Hoc Committee were to engage DOCS central office personnel in negotiations to secure the widespread implementation of bilingual programs and the increasing recruitment and permanent hiring of Latina(o) personnel (particularly bilingual education teachers and counselors) within the state penal system.[76] The Ad Hoc Committee also lobbied state legislators to assure their support for such efforts.

At the same time that CPRS members helped form the Ad Hoc Committee, the CPRS tried to revitalize the PTF by hiring Martín Sosa, an ex-PUL member at Green Haven,[77] and Sally Stein, a former bilingual teacher at Elmira Correctional Facility, to coordinate the PTF. Stein's primary responsibilities were to raise funds for the PTF, network with person's interested in supporting Latino prisoners throughout the state, and coordinate the efforts of the Ad Hoc Committee. Sosa, on the other hand, was hired to, "Take the groups to the prison. To organize the events. [To] follow-up on relationships with particular inmate organizations and individuals"[78] at both Green Haven and Bedford Hills.

However, the work of Stein and Sosa was hindered by the fact that they had to carry out their responsibilities without access to the substantial number of volunteers and financial resources available to the PTF's previous coordinator. Once again, the inability to obtain support from outside sources of funding affected the ability of the PTF to fulfill its goals.

> . . . each Task Force in the Centro had its sort of core staff, which was usually somebody, a research director and an assistant. And then each is expected to develop and generate resources to enlarge itself and maintain itself . . . We brought Sally here with the hope that it would be possible . . . for her to enlarge that Task Force, make some money and . . . we just never got any kind of response to a whole bunch of proposals that she developed. . . . But I think there was also a kind of slackening off of interest in the foundations which is now reviving. But in that space of time they didn't seem to be much interest.[79]

To summarize, by 1975, Latina(o) third party support for Latino prisoners had substantially decreased. Resistance to such work was voiced by outside community members who resented advocating on behalf of persons who had victimized their own community. Others felt indignant about prisoners' increasing access to services, such as higher education, that seem inaccessible to Latinas(os) on the outside. Still others became discouraged by the long hours it took to travel to and from the facility and prisoners' personal setbacks and rivalries. Added to this were the constant attempts by custody-oriented personnel to disrupt prisoner organizations and keep their members isolated from the outside world. This translated into harassment of prisoners, reform-oriented personnel, as well as third parties.

Another set of factors contributing to the decrease in prisoner support work was the outside Latino community's growing inability in a period of worsening economic conditions, to invest time, energy, and resources in prisoner support work. This was reflected in the CPRS' shift in focus away from prisoner advocacy, partly as a response to the loss of outside sources of funding for both activist and research-related prisoner advocacy work and partly as a result of the PTF's success in passing on some of its projects to other third parties. The latter tendency had itself been a result of the PTF's inability to maintain ongoing prisoner support work in a time of diminishing resources.

The PTF's diminishing resources, particularly after 1975, was so acute that, as will be shown below, for Sosa to advocate on behalf of PUL between 1975 and 1977, he had to mobilize Puerto Rican community groups not directly affiliated with the CPRS. This change in the source of Latina(o) third party support affected both the nature of the support given PUL and the manner in which the organization sought to make the concerns of Latino prisoners heard. The shift in PUL's focus also reflected the changes the organization had undergone since the implementation of the Study Release Program in 1973.

PUL and the Changing Institutional Context

The participation of PUL members in the Study Release Program had created structural problems for the organization as some of its leaders and rank and file members were transferred to Ossining to participate in the program. Such transfers were complemented by DOCS' policies of segregating group leaders and/or transferring them to other housing units or facilities as soon as they seemed to be gaining a significant following. Consequently, as discussed earlier, PUL's leadership had to be recreated every few months.

As PUL began to experience the loss of significant sources of third party and institutional support, the organization began to experience yet another transformation in its leadership. This transformation, in turn, affected the organization's goals and tactics. The leaders who took over the organization after 1975 were more inclined to engage in both open and underground coalition-building efforts and collective acts of protest, such as strikes, than had their predecessors. This alienated Latinos who feared that such activities would invite the harassment of group members by prison administrators and would lead to the organization's dissolution but attracted others who were becoming convinced that Latino prisoners, by themselves, could not significantly alter the conditions of confinement.

The radicalization of PUL's leadership reflected not only the changing position of the organization within the institution but also changes
in the nature of third party support it received after 1975. While PUL
had enjoyed a number of privileges as a result of its alliance with penal
personnel and third parties, it had been hesitant to engage in underground coalition-building efforts that would endanger the group's existence. However, as PUL lost its major sources of institutional and third
party support, the concerns of Latino prisoners were increasingly
ignored by prison administrators. As a result, PUL leaders became
more frustrated with the discriminatory practices of institutional personnel. This turn of events coincided with the willingness of Martín
Sosa, co-director of the PTF, to support PUL's coalition-building tactics.

Added to this situation was the fact that PUL, along with other
Latino prisoner leaders throughout the state, had become more aware
that if Latino prisoners were ever to achieve any significant and long-
term changes in the treatment they received from penal elites they had
to unite, both at the institutional and statewide levels. Interestingly,
Latino prisoners were reaching this realization at the same time that
the Ad Hoc Committee was being formed to lobby on behalf of Latino
prisoners on a statewide level. PUL's awareness of the need to achieve
Latino prisoner unity across the state was made evident during its
Puerto Rican Discovery Day celebration, held in November 1975. The
event was planned with the support of Sosa and other Latina(o) community activists. However, unlike in previous years, the day's events
did not center around cultural activities, but on a series of workshops
aimed at confronting the problems of Latino prisoners throughout New
York State. One of the main objectives of the event was to unite the various Latino prisoner groups in the state. Green Haven administrators
responded to these unity efforts by increasing their persecution of PUL
leaders, placing some of them in segregation while transferring other
to facilities further upstate.

An example of DOCS' attempts to persecute PUL as an organization occurred in 1976, when the latter was informed that it would not
be allowed to invite visitors to the June San Juan Bautista Day
Festival that year. The harassment by administrative personnel lessened only after Italian prisoners, who had been granted permission to
invite visitors to their upcoming picnic, told prison administrators that
they, "would give up their visitors if the Puerto Ricans couldn't have
theirs."[80] According to Sheehan, white prisoners supported their Latino
peers because the two groups regarded each other as potential allies
against African-American prisoners who made up the majority of the

prison population.[81] However, it is also likely that Italian prisoner leaders were supportive of Latino prisoners because they were aware of the commonality of interests they shared as prisoners.

In fact, at the time of this incident, Latino prisoner leaders had been meeting with African-American and white prisoner leaders under the cover of a Puerto Rican Culture Class being sponsored by PUL, with the encouragement of Sosa. The class, which at its onset was the only higher education class offered for Latinos at Green Haven, had gradually become a multiracial/multiethnic "political education" class. As such, it lost its "Latino" character. This transformation was resisted by a number of Latino prisoners who wanted to continue focusing on "Latino" concerns.

The conflicts within the Latino prisoner population concerning the appropriate tactics and strategies to be employed to achieve Latino prisoner goals took place within an increasingly polarized institutional environment. The changes also occurred at a point in New York State's penal history in which custody-oriented sectors were increasingly demanding a return to the post-Attica emphasis on custody and an abandonment of reform-oriented goals. The response of African-American, white, and Latino prisoners to these changes was a renewed emphasis on the formation of political underground prisoner groups and a renewed commitment to engage in collective acts of protest.

On August 31, 1976, Latino prisoner leaders joined their African-American and white peers in a four-day work stoppage in which prisoners refused to go to work assignments or recreation.[82] The protest followed similar actions by prisoners at Attica and Great Meadow the previous week.[83] At Green Haven, the Inmate United Committee comprised of ten Latino, African-American, and white prisoner leaders demanded "better wages for inmates, improved health care, and promises that the state legislature consider restructuring sentencing, parole and temporary release programs."[84] Prisoners also requested to meet with legislators, penal personnel, and members of Governor Carey's prison task force. Other demands shared by prisoners in all three facilities included the hiring of more Latino and African-American guards and a liberalization of visitation policies.[85]

One of the reasons prisoners resorted to the work strike was because such actions had the potential to paralyze the institution, cause the state financial losses, and also attract media attention.

> . . . cause you can close a prison down like that . . . Prisoners do all the cooking, all the maintenance . . . the majority of the work in prison. If

men refuse to come out of their cells, who's going to feed them? . . . The administration suffers even more because now they got to change their whole routine. They got to get civilians and officers to cook the foods and they got to feed the entire population . . . And not only that . . . when guys do that they go out to the media, "Oh, there's a riot going on." The superintendent of the prison has to answer to Albany.[86]

One of the difficulties in organizing mass prisoner actions was the fact that it was difficult to get a large group of men to participate in them either as a result of the "divide and conquer tactics" of prison administrators or for fear of reprisals. In fact, the 1976 work stoppage at Green Haven led to the transfer of several hundred prisoners to other state facilities.

Prison authorities blamed tensions within the institution on over-crowding, the growing number of unseasoned prison guards, and the transfer in 1976 to Green Haven of "tougher prisoners" sent from other state facilities.[87] In view of the fact that DOCS personnel labelled the most politically aware and reform-oriented prisoners as "troublemak-ers," it is likely that during 1976, Green Haven also began to receive a larger number of these prisoners from other state institutions. As a result of guard harassment of prisoners and growing prisoner mili-tancy, violent confrontations between prisoners and guards increased. Moreover, during 1976 and 1977, institutional tensions were reflected in the continued rise of prisoner on prisoner assaults.[88] These con-frontations gave prison officials an excuse to lock up prisoners for long periods of time and prohibit regular visitation hours.

Tensions within the facility had escalated despite the fact that between August and October 1975, DOCS had introduced the Inmate Grievance Resolution Committees into Green Haven and other state prisons. The IGRCs, as discussed in chapter 4, provided prisoners a means through which they could voice their grievances. The inability of the IGRCs to lessen prisoner discontent was, on the one hand, due to the fact that they could only be used to file individual complaints. As a result, prisoners were still left without any means of filing col-lective grievances. On the other hand, many prisoners were indignant about the fact that with the introduction of the IGRCs prisoners could only seek recourse in the courts after all administrative appeals, includ-ing the grievance process where applicable, had been exhausted. This stipulation further allowed penal personnel to use institutional chan-nels to thwart prisoners' litigation efforts.

Notwithstanding these drawbacks, Latino prisoners continued to file frequent complaints with the IGRC. However, as the latter's inability to effectively address Latino prisoner concerns became apparent, more of them became convinced that they needed to use additional methods to make their interests heard by prison authorities. Consequently, they continued to participate in political underground prisoner coalitions seeking reforms.

In 1977, DOCS responded to continued prisoner militancy in its facilities with a number of policy changes which contributed to the strengthening of security interests in prisons throughout the state. The reemphasis on custody, which some argue had already become apparent by the end of 1973,[89] was made official on June 16, when Commissioner Benjamin Ward made a public speech in which:

> He instructed the superintendents to consider for elimination all full-time academic and vocational schooling, and all volunteer programs, which "have, in many cases, become very expensive because of necessary security coverage, limited inmate involvement, and 'call-out' from other programs. The superintendents should instead concentrate on expanding 'industrial programs' to help support the prison system and further reduce costs," he said. Then came an interesting sentence: "The alleged rehabilitative worth of such industrial programs should not be a prime consideration unless there is clear, documentable evidence of its nature."[90]

Thus, DOCS' apparent post-Attica Rebellion concern with rehabilitation had officially come to an end. While custody-oriented sectors had never lost their control over penal affairs, Commissioner Ward's declarations publicly endorsed the return to the "'get tough' policy on prison discipline."[91] Encouraged by these pronouncements, on June 26, 1977, Green Haven experienced what came to be known as "The Great Shuffle." The prison was locked down and 1,400 of its 1,800 prisoners were reassigned to different cells based on their job assignments.[92] The Great Shuffle was aimed at restoring guard control by reducing prisoner movement throughout the facility.

On July 7, 1977, Latino, African-American, and white prisoners at Green Haven organized yet another strike protesting the recent tightening of restrictions. Grievances voiced by prisoners included: a "12 hour-a-day forced lock-in"; "mandatory attendance at noon meals"; cutbacks in recreation time; a requirement for prisoners to march in pairs; and regulations prohibiting prisoners from receiving cooked food from relatives.[93] Prisoners were also indignant that the legislature was going to adjourn without acting on a "good-time bill." The bill would have granted "good behavior credits to reduce," not only maximum prison terms, as was the law at the time, but also minimum prison terms of prisoners serving 15 years or more.[94] Eric Elliott describes one of the major goals of strike leaders at the time. ". . . One of the goals was hopefully to set an example for other prisons in the state, they would also go out on strike. And the strike was essentially an attempt to focus attention on the question of good time so that the state legislature would act, and none of that happened."[95] Some of the reasons Elliott claims the strike was not successful in achieving its goals were that:

> . . . there were a lot of competing interests and a lot of hidden agendas . . . Some guys wanted to foment another Attica, you know, they thought that this was the best way to bring attention to our issues and things. And then other guys took a more moderate stand. And other guys thought that . . . protesting and striking and all that kind of thing really didn't mean a whole lot . . . What ultimately happened was that there was a small core group of guys who got together . . . and decided . . . that there was going to be a general strike in the prison and that everybody should lock in their cells . . . I think a lot of groups were excluded just organizationally from the decision-making process and they took offense to it . . . And even within groups, you know, some guys were down and some guys weren't down . . .[96]

The state's response to rumors that a strike was about to take place had also helped create dissention within the prisoner population.

> . . . in the course of organizing the strike and putting it together, a lot of people were identified as strike leaders . . . other people were identified as strike sympathizers. The administration . . . tried to pinpoint who these people were and get them out of the prison as soon as possible. A lot of other people were identified as either taking a neutral position and not getting involved one way or . . . actively working against it, and that created a tremendous amount of tension and conflict [within], you know, organizations and groups, that I think ultimately tore a lot of groups asunder.[97]

DOCS' immediate response to the strike was to transfer forty presumed Latino, African-American, and white strike leaders to other state facilities.[98] Soon after, PUL was dissolved.[99] Its office was closed and its funds were frozen. Most of its leadership was transferred to other facilities. According to several ex-prisoners interviewed, the organization was disbanded because it had participated in the strike.

According to an article that appeared in the *Green Haven Monthly,* "A mediados de los años [70] P.U.L. fue desintegrada a raíz de una huelga, sus principales dirigentes transferidos, cerrada su oficina y congelados sus fondos."[100] No other formal prisoner group was disbanded although, according to a *New York Times* article, an African-American Studies program, a photography program, and a bilingual studies program were discontinued.[101] Green Haven's deputy superintendent for programs claimed that the programs had been eliminated because, "Our finding was that there were too many independent programs and that certain of these had dubious worth."[102] It appears that one of the reasons PUL was disbanded was because of its leaders involvement in the organizing of the strike and the organization's ability to bring together Latino, African-American, and white prisoners, as demonstrated by their participation in the Puerto Rican Culture Class.

The disbandment of PUL ended Sosa's, and hence, the PTF's involvement at the facility. Shortly afterwards, the CPRS, some of whose personnel had also remained active in the Ad Hoc Committee for Hispanic Inmates, officially decided to withdraw from prisoner support work. According to Frank Bonilla, "We didn't have the resources or the right people to do the work . . . It was just a feeling that we couldn't do it seriously and well enough."[103] Nevertheless, Bonilla, Sosa, and Sally Stein, co-coordinator of the PTF, continued to be active for a while longer with the Ad Hoc Committee. The Ad Hoc Committee, was successful in advocating on behalf of Latina(o) prisoners statewide and even secured DOCS' commitment to hiring more Latina(o) bilingual personnel at both the central office and facility levels.

Thus, coinciding with the decrease of third party and civilian sources of penal support for PUL during the mid-1970s, was a change in the group's leadership, goals, and tactics. PUL leaders became more willing to use the organization to both foster the development of unity among Latino prisoners statewide and among Latino, African-American, and white prisoners at Green Haven. While many Latino prisoners opposed this turn of events, the fact that Green Haven administrators increasingly ignored the concerns of the former and that custodial elites were becoming more successful at thwarting reform-oriented actions by prisoners and their remaining allies, made PUL leaders more willing to openly engage in such endeavors than their predecessors. Although these changes in PUL alienated those Latinos who feared further harassment by custodial personnel, they attracted others who were convinced that Latino prisoners needed to unite both among themselves on a statewide basis and with their

African-American and white peers in order to achieve substantial changes in penal policy.

PUL's change in goals and tactics was supported by Sosa, co-coordinator of the Prison Task Force, and former member of PUL at Green Haven. Interestingly, it appears that the type of support provided by third parties affected the types of interests openly pursued by the formal Latino prisoner organization. During those times in which the PTF highlighted educational concerns (1972–1975), PUL leaders highlighted those issues. However, during those times in which the PTF supported leaders' aboveground (and underground) coalition-building efforts (1975–1977), Latino prisoners pursued those interests. While it is difficult to say that the actions of third parties determined those of Latino prisoners or vice versa, it is clear that at both points in time there was a convergence of interests.

Once PUL was disbanded other Latinos took the place of those leaders who had been locked in segregation or transferred to other state facilities. These men continued to demand the right to reform PUL or, at least, form another formal Latino prisoner organization. DOCS, as will be discussed in the following chapter, denied this request for over two years, allowing only the formation of Latino ad hoc committees for the organizing of the yearly ethnic feast day events.

It appears that DOCS' refusal to allow Latino prisoners to form another formal prisoner group was not only a response to the leadership role PUL had played in helping build prisoner solidarity at Green Haven, but also a reaction to the growing ability of Latino prisoners to assume leadership roles in prisoner struggles in other state facilities as well. In fact, as the incident described below demonstrates, less than a year after the dissolution of PUL, Green Haven administrators were reminded of how willing Latino prisoners were to form interracial/interethnic alliances and how third parties could be mobilized by prisoners to support such efforts.

On August 8, 1977, less than a month after PUL's disbandment, 200 Latino, African-American, and white prisoners at Eastern Correctional Facility in Napanoch, N.Y., took over part of the prison and seized eleven hostages. It was the most serious collective show of force by prisoners in New York State since the 1971 Attica Rebellion. Prisoners were protesting KKK activity at the facility as well as worsening prison conditions.[104]

State elites responded to the rebellion with the customary lockdown and/or transfer of prisoners to other state facilities, physical intimidation, and the convening of a grand jury. In March 1978, the all-white

Ulster County Grand Jury indicted 10 prisoners for their presumed leadership role during the rebellion. At least 6 of the 10 were Latinos active in Latinos Unidos (i.e., Eastern's formal Latino prisoner organization) and/or the institution's branch of the NAACP.[105]

Following the grand jury indictment, all ten Eastern prisoners, known as "The Napanoch Brothers" by their supporters, were transferred to Green Haven. Once there, they were subjected to continual harassment by prison guards. At least two of the latter were former Eastern guards who had been transferred to Green Haven following the August 8th rebellion, partly as a response to prisoners' charges that they were members of the KKK.[106]

The reaction of Green Haven prisoners and third parties to the indictment and subsequent transfer of the Napanoch Brothers to Green Haven was to hold a joint protest. On July 1, 1978, over 200 supporters of the Napanoch Brothers rallied and demonstrated outside Green Haven. In the meantime, according to a former Napanoch Brother, "On the inside we organized a silent noon meal protest to simultaneously coincide with the protest outside. It was more than 94 percent effective, having been organized with the help of inmate organizational leaders and political prisoners at Green Haven."[107] This joint protest had once again shown Green Haven and state penal elites, that prisoners were still capable of forming coalitions and mobilizing third party support despite constant surveillance and harassment by security personnel and intra-prisoner cleavages.

The response of Green Haven administrators to the joint protest came on July 25 when prisoners were placed in keeplock while Correction Emergency Response Teams (CERT) teams conducted a general search of the facility. Prior to that, guards had threatened to strike unless DOCS removed the Napanoch Brothers from the prison and allowed guards to conduct a cell-by-cell search for contraband and weapons. On July 27, all ten of the Napanoch Brothers were transferred to Ossining.[108]

The Napanoch incident was significant for several reasons. It showed the continual discrimination and racism to which Latino (and African-American) prisoners and their organizations were subjected by the predominantly white custodial staff throughout the state. It demonstrated the willingness of Latino prisoners to form interracial/ interethnic coalitions and resort to collective acts of protest to make their concerns heard. It highlighted the leadership role Latino prisoners were assuming in various prisoners' struggles. Equally important was the fact that it showed the manner in which DOCS responded to prisoners' calls for an end to discrimination and inhumane treatment.

Following the removal of the Napanoch Brothers from Green Haven, Latino prisoners continued to demand an end to discrimination against them as evidenced by DOCS' refusal to allow the formation of another formal Latino prisoner group. Equally important was the fact that Latino prisoners continued advocating for their concerns despite the lack of significant sources of third party and penal support.

As this chapter has shown, following the post-Attica Rebellion reforms Latino prisoners found themselves participating in the creation of a formal Latino prisoner group as well as a number of other multi-racial/multi-ethnic formal prisoner and administrative organizations. Soon after the creation of PUL, however, the organization became engrossed in a conflict between those Latino prisoner leaders who argued that the organization should focus primarily on "Latino" prisoner concerns pursued through formal prisoner and administrative groups, and those who argued that formal organizations, by themselves, were not enough to achieve substantial changes in the conditions encountered by Latino prisoners. While during the 1973–1975, period this conflict was settled on the side of those who wanted to focus on primarily Latino concerns, between 1975 and 1977, PUL became the voice of those Latino prisoners who favored using the organization also as a means of building coalitions among prisoners. DOCS responded to the latter approach with the dissolution of PUL, the transfer of its leaders, and the refusal to allow Latino prisoners to form another formal prisoner organization until 1980.

During the first half of the 1970s, Latino prisoners under the aegis of PUL, were able to mobilize the support of third parties and reform-oriented penal personnel for the implementation of a limited number of bilingual programs and the hiring of bilingual staff. The accessibility of prisoners to penal and third party support was made possible by the brief but significant pro-reform opening that occurred within the penal system following the Attica Rebellion. The post-Attica Rebellion reforms had allowed the hiring of civilian personnel who favored the liberalization of prison conditions and implementation of rehabilitation programs, the increased participation of community groups in the facility, and the creation of formal prisoner organizations.

However, as Latino prisoners lost their main sources of inside and outside support, by the mid-1970s, their ability to obtain concessions from custodial elites diminished. As a result, penal administrators increasingly began to ignore Latino prisoner concerns and the Latino prisoner population moved toward a more radical posture in response. This occurred at a time when institutions throughout the state were experiencing increasing prisoner/guard tensions as a result of inhumane prison conditions, harsh treatment by custodial personnel, and a more overt return to the pre-Attica Rebellion emphasis on repression rather than reforms.

PUL leaders responded by using PUL to pursue coalitions with Latino prisoners in other state facilities as well as with their African-American and white peers at Green Haven. Under the aegis of these coalitions prisoners sought, through a series of strikes, to pressure institutional as well as other state elites to make changes in the state's criminal justice system. Green Haven administrators responded to these calls for reforms with the segregation of prisoners, the transfer of prisoner leaders to other facilities, and the disbandment PUL. The dissolution of PUL reflected DOCS' awareness of the role Latino prisoners were playing in the forging of prisoner unity. This capacity was further demonstrated during the August 1977 Eastern Rebellion. Within this context, DOCS's refusal to allow Latino prisoners at Green Haven to form another formal Latino prisoner organization must be seen as one of its many attempts to prevent Latino prisoners from acting as effective coalition leaders and mediators within the overall prisoner population.

In view of DOCS' fears of Latino prisoner activism, how did departmental policies change during the 1977–1987 period to address the incessant demands for change by the increasingly diverse Latino prisoner body? How did DOCS's policies and fluctuations in the composition of the Latino prisoner population affect prisoners' ability to frame concerns and make collective demands on penal authorities? How successful were Latino prisoners in mobilizing effective sources of penal and third party support and securing significant concessions from penal elites?

Notes: Chapter 7

1. Latin Think Tank Concept (LTTC) (untitled xeroxed document), 1973.

2. Ibid.

3. Joseph Michalak, "60 Ossining Inmates to Study at Community College in Bronx," *New York Times* (hereafter cited as *N.Y. Times*), 23 August 1973, 40. While the initial contacts with the Latina(o) community had been made through the Brooklyn College Puerto Rican Studies Department, the initiative for prisoner support work soon passed to the emerging Center for Puerto Rican Studies (CPRS). This was partly the result of the fact that two of the LTTC's primary contacts, Haydé Ortega and Frank Bonilla, became staff persons at the CPRS. Although the CPRS was officially created in February 1973, it had

unofficially begun to exist at the end of 1972 and Latino prisoners at Green Haven had been in contact with it as of that time.

4. Domingo Morales [pseud.], interview with author, New York, N.Y., 6 April 1993.

5. All of the names given in this sentence are pseudonyms.

6. Interestingly, these educational efforts were being duplicated during the same period of time by Latinos in other New York State prisons and by Chicanos in California prisons such as San Quentin. See Joan W. Moore, *Homeboys: Gangs, Drugs and Prison in the Barrios of Los Angeles* (Philadelphia: Temple University Press, 1978).

7. Along with demanding the implementation of bilingual programs and the hiring of bilingual personnel, formal Latino prisoner organizations organized study groups, taught bilingual education and legal classes, as well as Puerto Rican and Latin American history, provided emotional and social support to Latino prisoners, pressured for authorization to celebrate ethnic feast day events, and/or sought to maintain contacts with the outside Latina(o) community (Center for Puerto Rican Studies, Untitled, 1978). At Elmira, classes called "Latin Dialogue" were created during the mid–1970s with the objective of bringing together selected Puerto Rican prisoners (Sally Stein [pseud.], interview with author, Ritchie, Md., 1989). The goals a particular organization advocated depended on the conditions at the institution, the group's membership and resources, and its ability to mobilize penal and third party support. For a summary of the objectives pursued by various Latino prisoner organizations during the early 1970s at Eastern, Great Meadow, Attica, and Elmira, see Appendix F.

8. Eddie Rosa [pseud.], interview with author, New Paltz, N.Y., 19 February 1989. At Elmira Correctional Facility, Latino prisoners were able to secure the hiring of a bilingual teacher (Sally Stein) in 1974 to conduct a High School Equivalency class only after they had repeatedly met with staff, submitted petitions to prison administrators, engaged in sit-ins and demonstrations, and continued to threaten prison authorities with carrying out further acts of resistance if their requests went unheeded. One of the initial responses of prison authorities was to lock Latino prisoners in segregation. Once the class began, prison personnel sought to sabotage it by providing inadequate classroom space, refusing to provide prisoners adequate educational materials, preventing certain prisoners from attending classes, and trying to intimidate Stein into not returning to the institution. Intimidating acts included sexist remarks and having guards trying to pinch Stein's buttocks and breasts. To overcome each of these obstacles, Latino prisoners had to continually engage in petition writing campaigns, meetings with administrative personnel, and collective acts of resistance. Stein found herself constantly confronting prison personnel about their harassment and discriminatory prac-

tices, and writing letters to administrators on behalf of Latino prisoners. Although both she and the prisoners had to work together in order to counteract the actions of institutional personnel, Stein concluded that, "I had no power . . . The only way to get things done was if . . . the . . . prisoners in the class would demonstrate or they would sit-in or write letters" (Stein, interview with author, 1989).

9. Rosa, interview with author, 1989.

10. Ibid.

11. Danny Vázquez, interview with author, Bronx, N.Y., 20 March and 17 April 1989.

12. The conflict between those interested in pursuing both coalition-building and the development of ethnic/racial organizations and those who wanted to focus almost exclusively on organizing along racial/ethnic lines was also observed by Eric Elliott within the African-American prisoner population. ". . . you have Blacks that are the same way, you know, who want to focus exclusively on Black issues . . . The feeling I think is that, 'We got enough issues to handle by ourselves without getting involved in somebody else's problems or without bringing somebody else into our problems,' you know, . . . you're always going to have that . . ." (Eric Elliott, interview with author, New York, N.Y., 15 April 1993).

13. Anonymous (untitled xeroxed document), 1973.

14. Rosa, interview with author, 1989.

15. Enrique Colón [pseud.], interview with author, New York, N.Y., 28 February 1990.

16. Ibid.; and Elliott, interview with author, 1993; and Domingo Morales, interview with author, New York, N.Y., 6 April 1993.

17. Vázquez, interview with author, 1989.

18. Ibid.

19. Colón, interview with author, 1990.

20. Vázquez, interview with author, 1989. Vázquez stated he provided the same services to all the other prisoner organizations at the time.

21. Rosa, interview with author, 1989.

22. According to Carmen Roldán, ". . . the Centro was created not because the University wanted it here but because everybody who was in the University and outside of the university from our community was saying, 'The University has to be made more relevant to Puerto Ricans.' And when the university finally conceded and said, 'Okay, we'll let you create a research center,' the next job was to sort of define areas of work" (Carmen Roldán [pseud.], interview with author, New York, N.Y., 8 February 1989). The manner in

which the CPRS initially defined the major areas of work was by, ". . . having a large conference and talking about what were some of the main issues in our community that we needed to look at from our perspective" (Ibid.).

23. For example, Haydé Ortega had been an active member of the Young Lords Party and Frank Bonilla, director of the Center for Puerto Rican Studies, had taught a seminar on Racism and Law Enforcement at Stanford University in 1970. The seminar was instrumental in helping organize Chicana(o), African-American, and white students in support of prisoners at Soledad (Haydé Ortega, interview with author, New York, N.Y., 12 and 28 February and 17 March 1989; and Frank Bonilla, interview with author, New York, N.Y., 10 March 1989 and 13 January 1990). For a discussion of the struggles being waged at the time by the Puerto Rican community and how various sectors joined their organizing experiences to achieve collective goals, see Alfredo López, *The Puerto Rican Papers: Notes on the Emergence of a Nation* (New York: The Bobbs-Merrill Co., Inc., 1973).

24. Roldán, interview with author, 1993.

25. Ibid.

26. Ibid.

27. Frank Bonilla, "Memorandum to Mr. Earl F. Cheit," 25 May 1973.

28. The CPRS' five major research areas were: History and Migration; Culture; Puerto Rican Studies; Language Policy; and Prisons.

29. Bonilla, "Memorandum to Mr. Earl F. Cheit," 25 May 1973.

30. For a discussion of PTF activities at Bedford Hills see part II of this book.

31. Bonilla, "Memorandum to Mr. Earl F. Cheit," 25 May 1973.

32. Ortega, interview with author, 1989.

33. Bonilla, interview with author, 1989 and 1990. Author's translation: ". . . our concern was not to get involved unless it was through organized groups of prisoners. That is to say, not to serve the administrators of the prison although, of course, we had to deal with them, but to use . . . as the principal instrument, the organizations of prisoners themselves."

34. Ibid.

35. Gregorio Palma, interview with author, New York, N.Y., 16 April and 1 May 1993.

36. Roldán, interview with author, 1989.

37. Bonilla, interview with author, 1989 and 1990.

38. For example, during the summer of 1973, the CPRS sponsored a seminar with Judge John Carro of the Criminal Court, to educate the Latina(o) community about criminal justice and prison issues.

39. Joseph Michalak, "60 Ossining Inmates to Study at Community College in Bronx," *N.Y. Times*, 23 August 1973, 40. Educational release programs allow prisoners to leave the facility for a certain number of hours during the day to attend an institution of higher education. Educational release was provided for under the first temporary release statute passed in New York State, ART. 26, CHAPT. 472 of the Correctional Laws of 1969 (New York State, Department of Correctional Services, "Administrative Bulletin No. 12," June 22, 1972). However, until September 1973, only a small number of white, African-American, and Latino prisoners had been allowed to participate in study release programs. According to Vázquez, "The idea of the Study Release Program began with the Black leadership of the Think Tank . . . and it really began with Malcolm King College in Harlem . . . but they were strapped for resources . . ." As a result, Malcolm King College could not afford to implement the program itself (Vázquez, interview with author, 1989).

40. Bonilla, interview with author, 1989 and 1990.

41. The 1970 opening of Hostos Community College in the Bronx had itself been the result of coalition-building efforts among diverse sectors of the Puerto Rican/Latina(o) community in New York City, which demanded greater access to institutions of higher learning geared toward addressing the specific needs of the Latina(o) community.

42. Joseph Michalak, "60 Ossining Inmates to Study at Community College in Bronx," *N.Y. Times*, 23 August 1973, 40. The total number of students targeted for participation for the 1973–1974 academic year was 60. At the time, this number was "twice as large as the present statewide total in all institutions of higher education—and perhaps the largest in the country" (Ibid.) During the spring 1974 semester, there were 34 prisoners participating in the program ("George Goodman, Jr., "34 Sing Inmates Come to City Daily for Bilingual Studies at Hostos College," *N.Y. Times,* 20 May 1974, 35).

43. Such as Cándido de León, President of Hostos Community College.

44. Congressman Robert García and Judge John Carro.

45. Commissioner Peter Preiser and Deputy Commissioner Ward W. Elwin.

46. Bonilla, interview with author, 1989 and 1990.

47. Prisoners excluded by legislation from participating in study release programs included those, "associated with organized crime, those convicted of violent crimes, escape risks, absconders from bail and parole supervision, those with long sentences or additional sentences, those known to have made threats against persons outside the institution and 'those who display undue emotional upset'" (Joseph Muchalak, "60 Ossining Inmates to Study at Community College in Bronx," *N.Y. Times,* 23 August 1973, 40). DOCS security concerns were also expressed by DOCS' initial insistence that prisoners wear their "prison greens" to the university. This policy was not instituted as a result of the combined opposition of PUL, third parties, and civilian penal personnel.

48. Rosa, interview with author, 1989.

49. George Soto [pseud.], interview with author, Beacon, N.Y., 9 February 1989.

50. Bonilla, interview with author, 1989 and 1990. According to Bonilla, During the mid–1970s, Latino prisoners who had participated in the Study Release Program showed their support for Hostos Community College by playing "a leading role in defending Hostos when they were threatened by major budget cuts and even a move to close the college. They provided the leadership for students resistance to that . . . (Ibid.).

51. Rosa, interview with author, 1989.

52. After the implementation of the Study Release Program at Hostos, DOCS began to explore the possibility of converting one of its facilities into a "prison college." Without consulting Hostos administrators, DOCS decided that the program would be transferred from the Hostos Bronx campus to Bedford Hills. In reaction to this and other problems encountered by Hostos administrators in their dealings with DOCS, Hostos decided to discontinue the Study Release Program after the spring 1974 semester.

53. An additional outcome of the implementation of the program was that it showed DOCS that it was feasible to use study release on a large scale basis. The success of the study release program begun at Green Haven during the fall of 1973 was demonstrated by the fact that in 1976, Vázquez was given the responsibility for helping to develop and implement a study release program at Lincoln Correctional Facility. The prison was to hold all prisoners on study release (Vázquez, interview with author, 1989).

54. Rosa's work history at Green Haven covered two historical time periods, the first of which will be discussed here. From March to September 1973, Rosa worked as a bilingual education teacher for DOCS. From September 1985 through July 1987 Rosa worked as the coordinator of the Bilingual College Program for Marist College at Green Haven. The latter program had been established during the late 1970s.

55. Rosa, interview with author, 1989.

56. Ibid.

57. Ibid.

58. Ibid.

59. Another difficulty encountered by bilingual teachers was that they could "be transferred to non-bilingual teaching positions at any time" (Ad Hoc Committee for Hispanic Inmates, "Letter to Mr. Victor Bahou," 22 February 1977).

60. Ibid.

61. Ibid. Sally Stein, who worked as a bilingual teacher at Elmira Correctional Facility during the 1970s, also noted that she was more afraid of the

guards, who continually harassed her sexually and verbally, than of the prisoners. In fact, Latino prisoners found themselves becoming involved in physical confrontations with the guards in an attempt to stop the latter's harassment of Stein (Stein, interview with author, 1989).

62. Rosa, interview with author, 1993.

63. Ibid.

64. Ibid.

65. Ibid.

66. Ibid.

67. Burns returned to Green Haven once again to work as deputy superintendent of programs, from the spring of 1980 to the end of 1984.

68. Bonilla, interview with author, 1989 and 1990.

69. Roldán, interview with author, 1989. While a discussion of the difficulties created by the loss of governmental and/or private foundation funding for grassroots organizing projects is not provided here, it is imperative to keep in mind the danger dependence on such types of funding poses to long-term community organizing goals.

70. Ibid.

71. Bonilla, interview with author, 1989 and 1990. Author's translation: "Little by little, we began to distance ourselves from the situation because of a combination of problems, keeping people outside the prison interested, the difficulty of maintaining relations with internal prisoner groups which are, of course, very unstable and, at the same time, very vulnerable. Every time they begin to acquire some solidity . . . the reaction of the administration many times is to look for a way of dismantling them."

72. Ibid.

73. Ibid.

74. Stein, interview with author, 1989; Bonilla, interview with author, 1989 and 1990; and Beth Fein [pseud.], interview with author, Buffalo, N.Y., 15 April 1989.

75. Members of the committee included: Frank Bonilla, director of CPRS; Martín Sosa, and Sally Stein, co-coordinators of the Prison Task Force; Judge John Carro; Rubén Franco, attorney with the Puerto Rican Legal Defense and Education Fund; Ruth Cubero, regional director, Eastern United States, United States Commission on Civil Rights; José Ortiz, president of Caribe Village; Cándido de León, president of Hostos Community College; Agustin Rivera, vice-president, Universidad Boricua; Ken Kimerling, attorney with the Puerto Rican Legal Defense and Education Fund; and Edgar Guerra. The committee also included ex-prisoners (Stein, interview with author, 1989; and Rubén

Franco, interview with author, New York, N.Y., 8 March 1989; and Ad Hoc Committee for Hispanic Inmates, "Letter to Commissioner Benjamin Ward," 22 February 1977).

76. Stein, interview with author, 1989; and Ad Hoc Committee for Hispanic Inmates, "Minutes," 21 January and 18 February 1977.

77. After his release from Green Haven, Rosa had been active in a PUL branch established at Hostos Community College.

78. Bonilla, interview with author, 1989 and 1990.

79. Ibid.

80. See Susan Sheehan, *A Prison and a Prisoner* (Boston: Houghton Mifflin Co., 1978), 64.

81. Despite such cleavages among prisoners, Sheehan states that, "The leaders understand the prison's tense racial situation and work with one another to keep things cool" (Ibid.).

82. One of the most consistently organized coalition activities was a day of silence held each year in prison mess halls throughout the state to commemorate the September 13, 1971 murder of prisoners by state police forces during the Attica Rebellion. While such an action generally did not lead to other collective acts defying penal hegemony, it did serve to remind DOCS of the ability prisoners had to unite despite multiple cleavages dividing them.

83. See "Protest Besets a 3d New York Prison," *N.Y. Times,* 1 September 1976, 44; Joseph B. Treaser, "Comstock Easing Prison Crowding," *N.Y. Times,* 2 September 1976, 29; "Legislators to Meet with Inmates," *N.Y. Times,* 4 September 1976, 23; C. Gerald Fraser, "'Strike' is Ended at Green Haven," *N.Y. Times,* 5 September 1976, 37; and "The Attica Idea Is Catching," *N.Y. Times,* 5 September 1976, IV, 4.

84. "Protest Besets a 3d New York Prison," *N.Y. Times,* 1 September 1976, 44.

85. "The Attica Idea Is Catching," *N.Y. Times,* 5 September 1976, IV, 4.

86. Palma, interview with author, 1993.

87. Nathaniel Sheppard Jr., "Green Haven Reports Increase in Prisoner Clashes," *N.Y. Times,* 2 November 1976, 49. DOCS transferred to Green Haven, Auburn, and Clinton, prisoners previously sent to Attica and Great Meadow. The July 1976 DOCS directive indicated that prisoners eligible for transfer to Green Haven would include those: "With a history of prior institutional confinement characterized by poor adjustments. With unsatisfactory performance to prior probation and parole supervision. With numerous conflicts with the law, which indicates aggressive and assaultive behavior. Who demonstrate poor motivation and response to previous treatment programs" (Ibid.).

88. Sheehan, *A Prison,* 148-151.

89. Barbara Lavin McEleney, *Correctional Reform in New York: The Rockefeller Years and Beyond* (Lanham, Md.: University Press of America, 1985).

90. Sheehan, *A Prisoner*, 160.

91. Ibid., 161.

92. Sheehan, *A Prison*, 161–162. According to Sheehan, part of the tensions at the facility had been created by the fact that prior to 1976 prisoners had been assigned to cells depending on their job assignments. For example, all kitchen workers might live in the same company and cellblock thus making it easier for guards to escort prisoners to and from their jobs. In late 1976, honor blocks were opened and prisoners were assigned to empty cells regardless of their job. This increased prisoner movement in the facility making it more difficult for guards to control interactions between prisoners (Ibid.).

93. Ronald Smothers, "Upstate Prison Inmates Strike Against Conditions," *N.Y. Times*, 18 July 1977, IV, 11.

94. Ibid. According to David Harris, Green Haven's warden at the time, the strike was not successful because only 600 of the 1,800 prisoners at the facility participated in it. Harris also claimed that the strike was only about the "good time bill" issue (Ronald Smothers, "Upstate Prison Inmates Strike Against Conditions," *N.Y. Times*, 18 July 1977, II, 4).

95. Elliott, interview with author, 1993. Elliott was correct in stating that right after the Green Haven strikes, similar actions did not erupt in other state facilities. However, the July Green Haven strike was followed a month later by prisoner strikes at Eastern, Auburn, and Woodbourne penitentiaries. In all three facilities, prisoners demanded the passage of a "good time" bill as well as prison reforms. The Eastern rebellion was also in response to KKK activity at the facility (David F. White, "Official Says Uprising at Upstate Prison Involved 2 Separate Incidents," *N.Y. Times*, 10 August 1977, 18; *N.Y. Times*, 12 August 1977, II, 3; "Prison Strike Deadline," *N.Y. Times*, 13 August 1977, 23; "A Short Prison Incident," *N.Y. Times*, 14 August 1977, IV, 4; and *N.Y. Times*, 17 August 1977, II 3).

96. Elliott, interview with author, 1993.

97. Ibid.

98. Ronald Smothers, "Upstate Prison Inmates Strike Against Conditions," *N.Y. Times*, 8 July 1977, 11.

99. According to an article that appeared in the *Green Haven Monthly*, PUL was disbanded on June 27, 1977 as a result of a strike (L. Lozano, "Hispanos Forman Comité," *GHM* 3, Nos. 3 and 4 [March/April 1980]: 26). However, the closest strike to that date that this author has been able to document is the one on July 7. Therefore, it is possible that PUL was, in fact, disbanded in July and not June of that year.

100. José R. Rodríguez, "Graduación del Programa Bilingüe," *GHM* 6, No. 7 (September 1983): 12. Author's translation: "During the mid-1970s, P.U.L. was disbanded following a strike, its main leaders transferred, its office closed, and its funds frozen."

101. Pranay Gupte, "Two deaths and an Escape Raise Green Haven Tensions," *N.Y. Times,* 29 May 1978, II, 2.

102. Ibid.

103. Bonilla, interview with author, 1989 and 1990.

104. For more on 1977 Eastern rebellion see page 123n. 60.

105. National Alliance Against Racism and Political Repression, "Who are the Napanoch Brothers?" (loose sheets).

106. The Napanoch Brothers (private correspondence).

107. Ibid. In 1979, Félix Castro, one of the Napanoch Brothers, was charged with "first degree rioting, attempted coercion and unlawful imprisonment stemming from events at the Eastern New York Correctional Facility at Napanoch on Aug. 8, 1977" (Tom Wicker, "Catch-22 Behind Bars," *N.Y. Times,* 22 May 1979, 19). When the rebellion began, Castro, then head of Latinos Unidos, was locked in his cell. During the rebellion he was released by other prisoners. He was then elected, along with three other prisoners, to represent his peers in the ensuing negotiations with DOCS. Castro was also given charge of the hostages until the rebellion ended. During the rebellion, Castro was not seen carrying weapons, damaging property or assaulting anyone. Nevertheless, DOCS' charges against him were supported by a judge who would not allow prisoners' attorneys to discuss prison conditions nor KKK activity at the facility, nor would the judge allow defense attorneys to question prospective jurors about KKK sympathies. Castro was found guilty on May 28, 1979, and given an additional sentence (Lynn Mulvaney, "Félix Castro Found Guilty," *Daily Freeman,* 29 May 1979, 1). On January 15, 1980, Eddie Pacheco, another one of the Napanoch Brothers was also found guilty of the charges against him.

108. The Napanoch Brothers (private correspondence).

8

Latino Prisoners Regroup, DOCS Reevaluates

Following the suspension of PUL in July 1977, Latino prisoners formed several informal prisoner groups to promote a number of common interests. Because of the goals these groups pursued and the manner in which Latino prisoners were singled out for persecution by penal elites at the time, they are here considered political underground Latino prisoner groups. Membership in these groups occurred alongside and, sometimes overlapped with other types of informal and formal prisoner and administrative organizations.

It is important to keep in mind that while Latino prisoners continued to lobby DOCS for the authorization to create another formal Latino prisoner group, they continued to disagree about the ultimate goals and tactics the new organization should promote. The old cleavage between those who wanted to pursue primarily "Latino" concerns through formal prisoner and/or administrative groups and those who favored using the formal organization to openly or secretly pursue coalition-building strategies with African-American and white prisoners continued to manifest.

Interestingly, although Latino leaders were not authorized to create a formal organization in the two and a half years following the suspension of PUL, DOCS did allow them to create "ad hoc committees" to organize the yearly ethnic feast day events. Participating in ad hoc committees allowed Latino prisoner leaders access to some of the privileges accorded members of formal prisoner groups. Privileges included a meeting space, supplies, and the ability to call prisoners to meetings and invite third parties to events. By allowing the formation of ad hoc committees, penal elites hoped to lessen Latino prisoner discontent without having to accept the existence of the more threatening political structure a formal prisoner group would have required.

Given the opportunity to form ad hoc committees, at least two political underground Latino groups decided to take on the characteristics of ad hoc committees between July 1977, when PUL was disbanded, and

February 1980, when a new formal Latino prisoner organization was created. The tasks assumed by ad hoc committees during these years varied. For example, on November 19 1978, Los Hermanos was authorized to organize the Puerto Rican Discovery Day event and invite community members to participate in it.[1] In addition to organizing the event, Los Hermanos tried unsuccessfully to be recognized as the institution's formal Latino prisoner organization. The fact that several former PUL members, including at least one of PUL's founders, were also active in Los Hermanos may have contributed to DOCS' denial of formal recognition to the group.[2] Los Hermanos' leadership seems to have been dominated by those Latino prisoners who favored coalition-building strategies.

In April 1979, Latino Americanos Unidos (LAU) was formed. The group included some former members of PUL and Los Hermanos. While LAU was authorized by DOCS to act as an ad hoc committee, it was in reality, "a coalition group established for improved Latin organization and prison conditions."[3] LAU brought together Latino prisoners involved in other formal prisoner and administrative organizations. Some of these were also members of political interracial/interethnic underground prisoner groups.

In addition to organizing the June 1979 San Juan Bautista Feast Day event[4] and the November 18 Puerto Rican Discovery Day event that year,[5] LAU sought the support of third parties in the Latina(o) community for the attainment of a number of goals. For example, throughout 1979, Latino prisoners renewed their efforts to secure the assistance of Hostos Community College and Boricua College for the implementation of a bilingual higher education program at Green Haven.[6]

Furthermore, LAU courted the support of the few Latinas(os) working at the institutional level. Latina(o) personnel, primarily male teachers and counsellors, did provide a number of services to Latino prisoners and sometimes lobbied on their behalf with white institutional personnel. However, the former's ability to effectively influence penal policy towards Latinos on a long-term basis was limited by the fact that they made up only a very small number of the staff and the positions they occupied within the institutional bureaucracy were generally not politically significant. As a result, Latino prisoners also solicited the support of the few Latinas(os) working at DOCS' central office in Albany. It was hoped that at least some of the latter would act as liaisons between Latino prisoners and institutional administrators. The hiring of a small number of Latina(o) central office personnel during the second half of the 1970s had itself been partially the result of the combined lobbying efforts of Latino prisoners and the Ad Hoc Committee for Hispanic Inmates.[7]

LAU members were given the opportunity to voice their concerns to Latina(o) DOCS personnel in April 1979, a few weeks after the group was founded. At that time LAU met jointly with institutional Latina(o) and non-Latina(o) civilian staff and Agenor Castro, head of Hispanic Affairs at DOCS' central office.[8] At the meeting, LAU members addressed the lack of bilingual education programs and the concern with hiring more Latinas(os) at the facility and central office levels. The need for bilingual personnel was becoming more pronounced as the number of non-English speaking Latino prisoners, primarily immigrants, continued to rise. LAU representatives also argued that it was essential to establish a liaison with Green Haven administrators in order to improve the latter's relationship with Latino prisoners and secure the recognition of a formal Latino prisoner organization.[9] According to LAU, the loss of civilian support for Latino prisoners was most apparent in the area of Volunteer Services. Since the resignation of Danny Vázquez in 1975 as coordinator of volunteer services, his successors had increasingly ignored Latino prisoner concerns. One of the ways in which such neglect made itself apparent, LAU argued, was the fact that non-Latino prisoners were frequently allowed to attend Latino ethnic events, although as a result of DOCS' quotas, this kept some Latino prisoners from participating.[10] Other issues of interest to Latino prisoners included the lack of adequate medical services, the inclusion of Latino foods and products in the prison's commissary, and improving communications with the mass media.

LAU's main accomplishments during its short period of existence were to organize the main ethnic feast day events that year, to try to mobilize sources of third party and penal support, and to let DOCS administrators know that Latino prisoners continued to be dissatisfied with the treatment they were receiving; and were capable of uniting, despite differences between them, to let their concerns be known.

In February 1980, Green Haven warden David R. Harris,[11] authorized (pending Albany's final approval) Hispanos Unidos Para el Progreso (Hispanics United for Progress, HUP) to become the facility-'s first formal Latino prisoner organization since the dissolution of PUL.[12] LAU and HUP shared two founding members.[13] While HUP's membership included Latino prisoners who favored coalition-building strategies, the organization was primarily the voice of those who preferred to focus on Latino prisoner concerns pursued through formal prisoner and/or administrative groups. This was the case until at least the end of 1987.

HUP's recognition occurred in a climate of escalating tensions within which a number of Latino prisoners were striving to build coalitions among prisoners.[14] In fact, the conflicts which erupted in February 1980 between the multiracial/multiethnic Creative Communications Committee (Green Haven's long-termers' group) and prison administrators[15] emphasized the need to address, even if minimally, some of the concerns of Latino prisoners. Given the "divide and conquer" tactics pursued by prison administrators, it is likely that DOCS allowed Latino prisoners to create a formal prisoner organization to counter the influence of those Latino leaders who favored coalition-building strategies. Moreover, by recognizing HUP, penal administrators gave Latino prisoners an organization in whose existence they had a stake in maintaining. Consequently, DOCS' recognition of HUP was designed, not only to reduce Latino prisoner discontent but also make Latinos more hesitant to engage in actions that could threaten the group's existence. Within this context, one of the motivations for granting HUP recognition, and not LAU, was precisely the fact that HUP's leadership was more moderate and its stated goals much more limited.

Hispanics United for Progress (HUP) and the Changing Latino Prisoner Population

HUP's initial goals were to form various subcommittees which would offer classes in music, culture, arts and crafts, and peer counselling. Other committees would publish a newspaper, offer orientation, and organize special events.[16] These services would address some of the concerns of the Latino prisoner population which at the time of HUP's formal recognition in 1980 comprised 25 percent of the 1,800 prisoners at the facility (see Table 7).

One of the most controversial aspects of HUP was that, from its inception the group declared itself to be "apolitical." This statement had several implications. One had to do with the nature of the Latin American political regimes and the relationship between them and the United States. In view of the various national liberation and anti-imperialist struggles which have characterized Latin American political development, and the multiple political opinions held by the increasingly diverse Latino prisoner population,[17] HUP's declaration meant that it was not taking sides with any particular political ideology. However, HUP's overwhelmingly Puerto Rican leadership, just like PUL's and the LTTC's before it, remained strongly supportive of Puerto Rican independence and Latin American revolutionary movements throughout the period studied.[18]

The other implication of HUP's statement that it was apolitical had to do with the prison environment itself. HUP's apolitical stance meant that it was going to prioritize educational goals and not become embroiled in conflicts with prison administrators which could lead to the harassment of group members and the dissolution of the organization. This stance was similar to that taken by PUL's leadership at the beginning of the 1970s. HUP's assertions were made within an increasingly tense prison environment.

During 1980, the number of prison escapes increased[19] and the number of intra-prisoner and prisoner/guard assaults rose. In July 1980, DOCS Commissioner Thomas A. Coughlin III responded to these events by replacing David Harris with Charles Scully, a twenty-four-year veteran of DOCS, as warden.[20] Scully was responsible for carrying out a reorganization of Green Haven's administration.[21] A week after Scully's appointment, nearly 80 percent of the approximately 1,800 prisoners at the facility refused to attend their morning programs to protest visiting restrictions and prison conditions.[22] Latino, African-American, and white prisoner solidarity and discontent once again threatened penal hegemony. Prison authorities responded to prisoner unity efforts by beating prisoners, transferring presumed leaders to other facilities, and vilifying these men as "terrorists." According to an article in the *Green Haven Monthly*: "A lawyer representing the inmates said correctional officers were provoked to beat the inmates after Coughlin and Scully disseminated information among the officers that the inmates were part of a terrorist group plotting to overthrow the prison."[23] Within this context, HUP's apolitical stance was interpreted as an indication that group leaders had been coopted by prison administrators. In spite of HUP's declarations, nonetheless, it is important to note that individual group members did participate in a number of reform-oriented activities such as the strike described above.

Within a couple of years after its creation, HUP once again came under criticism from both members and non-members, this time for being concerned primarily with organizing "parties."[24] HUP leaders responded by reiterating their earlier claim that it was an "apolitical" organization and by emphasizing HUP's educational orientation.

El objetivo central de H.U.P. siempre ha sido promover la integración de los hispanos en el campo de la educación. . . .

H.U.P es una organización apolítica, con principios democráticos, estructurada con el objetivo de ayudar al hispano a encontrar una solución apropiada a sus necesidades básicas: educación bilingüe, orientación legal bilingüe, aprendizaje del inglés como segunda lengua, servicios de orientación para aquellos de nuestros hermanos que no hablan inglés, clases para conseguir el equivalente de escuela superior. Estas orientaciones abarcan desde servirles de intérpretes hasta prepararlos para su cita con la junta de libertad condicional.[25]

The provision of these services seemed urgent because, according to HUP, in 1980 two-thirds of Latino prisoners had few or no English language skills.[26] While most of these prisoners were Puerto Rican immigrants, an increasing number were immigrants from Colombia, the Dominican Republic, Nicaragua, El Salvador, and Cuba. Many of the non-Puerto Rican prisoners were undocumented workers.

HUP's assertion that it was apolitical continued to bring it further criticism from those Latinos who felt there was a need to expand organizational objectives beyond social events and educational activities, and engage in more militant types of organizing to demand changes in prison conditions for all. The lack of widespread support for HUP was evidenced by the fact that at its January 1982 meeting, in which new officers were to be elected, only 26 of the 126 prisoners who had signed up to attend did so. As a result of the low turnout HUP decided to postpone its elections until February.[27]

An additional conflict that emerged within HUP was the fact that the organization was perceived as being "Puerto Rican." While the February 1982 election resulted, for the first time, in the election of an executive team that was interethnic,[28] the fact that most of the organization's officers and membership continued to be Puerto Rican and that the two Latino ethnic feast days commemorated Puerto Rican national holidays, continued to create resentments.

An external constraint imposed on HUP that contributed to these tensions was the fact that DOCS policies limited the number of members in formal prisoner organizations at Green Haven to 125 (later to 150). This meant that at most only 150 Latino prisoners could potentially participate in, and invite friends and family members to ethnic and family day events organized by HUP. However, by 1982, there were over 500 Latino prisoners at the institution (see Table 7). The resentment against HUP leaders was intensified by the fact that they frequently invited African-American and white prisoners to take part in the events. Though this was done as an expression of solidarity or in exchange for favors it further decreased the number of slots available to Latinos.

The combination of personal and political rivalries, coupled with DOCS' policies and the multiple interests of Latino prisoners produced a situation in which Dominican, Cuban, South and Central American, and even Puerto Rican prisoners began to form ad hoc committees to address particular interests. Ironically, because only formal prisoner organizations were allowed to have a meeting space, invite third parties to their activities, etc., these ad hoc committees were forced to seek the sponsorship of HUP. The reaction of HUP's leaders to these organizing efforts was conflicted. While some were supportive of these initiatives, others argued they were "divisive." The latter feared that the ability of Latino prisoners to secure concessions from DOCS would be weakened if Latinos subdivided along nationality lines and made autonomous calls for changes. This fear was heightened by the fact that some of the ad hoc committees, did in fact, seek DOCS' authorization to create another formal Latino prisoner group based on nationality. In spite of these fears, however, HUP leaders agreed to officially sponsor the activities of the Dominican, the Cuban, and the South and Central American ad hoc committees. For HUP to have denied these requests would have invited further criticism and led to the increasing isolation of its leaders. The goals the ad hoc committees pursued and the types of events they organized are considered below.

At the beginning of 1983, the Dominican Committee was formed. One of its stated objectives was to hold yearly seminars on Dominican culture to which civic leaders and community organizations would be invited. A second goal was to organize a family day event to commemorate Dominican Independence Day. In February 1983, the first event commemorating the independence of the Dominican Republic was held in the Latin American Culture classroom located in the school building.[29] In June 1983, the Dominican Culture class met for the first time.[30] During the second half of the 1980s, the committee continued to meet and sponsor educational and cultural activities.[31] However, its ability to invite outside community members to participate in its activities was hindered by the fact that it was not a formal prisoner group, and as such, was not authorized to hold major events. As a result, most of those who attended its activities were either other prisoners or Latino institutional personnel.

Requests by the Dominican Committee during the mid-1980s to be recognized as a formal prisoner organization were denied by DOCS on the basis that there was already one formal Latino prisoner group at Green Haven and most Dominican prisoners were not United States citizens. The fact that Dominicans (and other Central and South Americans) were not citizens also meant that they could not enroll in higher educational programs because they were ineligible to participate in federal tuition assistance programs.

Another group of prisoners that formed an ad hoc committee during the first half of the 1980s were Cubans. The aims of the Cuban Committee were to provide economic and social orientation to the recently arrived "marielitos," that is, those who left Cuba in 1980 through the port of Mariel. In May 1985, under the auspices of HUP, the committee held its first Cuban Day celebration.[32]

During the second half of the 1980s, a South and Central American Committee was also formed.[33] The committee, dominated by Colombians, was created to deal primarily with the immigration problems confronted by prisoners from Central and South America. Its main goal was to hold cultural seminars with civic leaders and experts in immigration who could assist them with their immigration cases. The committee also sought to organize a family day event commemorating the independence of each one of the South American nations. As in the case of the Cuban and Dominican committees, the ability to hold the desired events and invite the widespread participation of third parties was limited by DOCS' restrictions which allowed only formal prisoner organizations to organize major events.

Denied formal organizational recognition by DOCS, these ad hoc committees continued to use HUP's structure to gain access to meeting space and other resources. However, the ad hoc committees also continued to criticize HUP. In reply to the criticisms leveled against it, HUP published an article in the February 1985 issue of the *Green Haven Monthly*,[34] stating its aims and accomplishments up until that time. HUP's accomplishments included: organizing the yearly ethnic and family day events; patronizing sports teams (i.e., football, softball, soccer); and sponsoring educational courses (i.e., Latin American Culture Class,[35] Life Skills Class,[36] Análisis Conciliatorio/Transactional Analysis Class[37]). The article reiterated that HUP was basically an educational organization, although it sponsored other activities.

In 1985, as an expression of growing discontent with both HUP and the other nationality-based committees, a handful of Puerto Rican prisoners formed Puertorriqueños Unidos en Estados Unidos de América (Puerto Ricans United in United States of America, PUEDA). The origin of PUEDA can be traced to June 1983, when a member of HUP argued in an article written for the *Green Haven Monthly* for the need to create another formal Latino prisoner organization to meet the needs of the growing Latino prisoner population.[38] PUEDA's founders maintained that, as United States citizens, Puerto Ricans faced a number of distinct problems. Underlying the formation of PUEDA was the fact that many Puerto Rican prisoners felt alienated from their non-Puerto Rican peers because they were resented by the latter for being United States citizens by birth and also looked down upon because Puerto Rico is a United States colony.[39]

In 1986, PUEDA submitted a proposal to DOCS addressed to the Petrita Hernández-Rojas, director of the Division of Hispanic and Cultural Affairs (DHCA), and Hector de la Concha, coordinator of Hispanic programs. (The creation of the DHCA will be discussed shortly). In the proposal, PUEDA sought recognition as a formal Latino prisoner group. The request was denied by DOCS on the grounds that there was already a formal Latino prisoner organization at the facility. A PUEDA document written a year later demanded: the right of PUEDA to have an office and a meeting space; federal funding to implement the organization's cultural and educational programs; the establishment of PUEDA in all state facilities; the extension of the Marist Bilingual College program from one to two years; additional bilingual counselors, academic, and vocational teachers; two additional Latino feast days; and seminars on Puerto Rican history and culture.

The changes that had taken place in PUEDA since its creation were reflected in its documents. The original proposals, written in Spanish, appear to have been translated by the same prisoner who wrote them. They reflected his limited knowledge of the English language and, perhaps, his limited access to sympathetic Puerto Rican bilingual prisoners. However, the subsequent drafting of PUEDA's constitution and its statutes in English, and the signatures of 192 prisoners requesting permission to create a new formal organization, showed that support for the group had grown to include bilingual members. Nevertheless, some of PUEDA's critics argued that the signatures did not mean much because, "People get signatures for a lot of things, but even them people are not down with that. They'll just sign their names."[40] Moreover, tensions did exist within PUEDA between the Spanish-monolingual prisoners and those who felt they should be the leaders of the organization because they knew English.[41] However, the inclusion of both sectors of the Puerto Rican prisoner population in PUEDA increased the potential for unity, as well as the access of non-English speaking prisoners to penal authorities.

The response of HUP leaders to PUEDA's efforts was generally anger or ridicule. Some felt the group had been created by former HUP members who had become resentful after being voted out of their leadership positions. In any event, the creation of PUEDA as well as the other ad hoc committees demonstrated a continued discontent both with penal policies toward Latino prisoners as well as with the manner in which HUP responded to such treatment.

In spite of the multiple criticisms directed at HUP, there remained a sector within the Latino prisoner population that believed that it would not be in the best interest of Latino prisoners to form a rival formal prisoner organization. These men felt it would be wiser to join HUP and change its "social" orientation in order to make it more responsive to the concerns of all Latinos. Their ultimate goal was to reduce the support within the general Latino prisoner population for those who favored the creation of another formal Latino prisoner group. It was feared that the creation of the latter would result in the further dilution of Latino prisoner unity. This point of view was represented by Domingo Morales:

> I said, "We've already got an organization in existence. We make that work and we make it see . . . our needs, not try to get another organization . . . Why split up, you know, the brain power and the things that need to be done like that?" I thought it would be better to become members and work your way [to] become executive board members.[42]

Prior to these efforts to subvert HUP's leadership, HUP leaders had made another major attempt to dispel the criticisms leveled against it. In April 1986, the organization sponsored a seminar to discuss the conditions Latino prisoners encountered within the state penal system and the services available to them. Topics of discussion included prison conditions, the family reunion program, bilingual and educational programs available at the facility, and parole.[43] Participants included Latino prisoners, institutional and central office personnel, members of Hunter College, and representatives of Caribe Village, a community organization that in 1984 had agreed to act as HUP's outside liaison. While the event provided valuable information, HUP's lack of significant sources of third party and penal support meant that by the end of 1987, the organization had been unable to secure major concessions from penal elites. The unavailability of primary forms of support had plagued Latino prisoners since the dissolution of PUL.

Courting Third Party Support

One of the problems that besieged HUP was the difficulty it had in convincing outside community groups to act as its sponsor. Lacking such support, HUP was left without any non-penal sources of support for long periods of time. While in 1984 Caribe Village had agreed to act as HUP's community liaison, the former was limited in terms of the types of support it could provide. Its initial commitment to HUP was to sponsor social activities such as softball games, theater, and musical groups.[44] Although all of these activities were of significant value to Latino prisoners, they did not address other core concerns such as the need for more bilingual staff and services.

While individual members of the outside Latino community made their presence felt from time to time, their involvement with Latino prisoners at Green Haven tended to be inconsistent and/or temporary. Even in those cases where volunteers made themselves available, they were limited with respect to the types of support they could provide because, according to Palma, ". . . to be able to keep coming, they have to . . . be in good graces with the administration."[45] That is, their ability to provide services lasted only as long as penal authorities did not see them as threatening the status quo. The fact that many outside volunteers were themselves isolated from significant sources of third party support meant they were devoid of significant means of counteracting the decisions of penal authorities.

During 1987, HUP sought the support of Diana Correa, who had been hired that year to act as the director of the newly created and short-lived Latino Prisoners' Project of the Correctional Association of New York (CANY). The purpose of the project was to, "assess the conditions for Latino inmates located or incarcerated in the New York State prison system."[46] According to Correa, some of the major barriers to obtaining third party support for Latino prisoners during the 1980s were similar to those of the 1970s: the lack of knowledge about the extent of Latina(o) imprisonment; worsening economic conditions that forced individuals in the community to concentrate on day-to-day survival issues; and the lack of community resources that would allow organizations to cover the costs entailed in prisoners' rights work. According to Correa, "We've got community groups who are doing work in other areas and to try to get . . . support for something outside of what they directly do, it's almost impossible because they're barely, you know, keeping their heads above water . . . because they're not getting the kind of federal money that they used to get."[47] While Correa was available to meet with Latino prisoners at Green Haven, the amount of support she could provide was limited by the fact that the project she directed was itself dependent for its existence on the availability of small donations from foundations.[48]

As a result of the factors discussed above, family members, a few Latino legislators such as Olga Méndez, and church groups seem to have been the most consistent sources of support available to Latino prisoners during the 1977–1987 period. However, even in the case of religious organizations, Latino prisoners frequently had to struggle with religious leaders in order to have Latina(o) clergy made accessible to them. According to Domingo Morales, "They have services in Spanish. But again, the presos had to fight for that . . . Because they might say "Spanish services" but they might not have a Spanish minister . . . it was the presos that said . . . 'Wait a minute, we need a Spanish minister or Spanish people coming from . . . the outside'."[49]

It was within this context that the few Latinas(os) hired in DOCS during the late 1970s and early 1980s attempted to address some of the concerns of Latino prisoners. The increase, albeit modest, in the number of Latina(o) personnel at both the institutional and central office levels had been a response to the lobbying efforts of groups such as the Ad Hoc Committee for Hispanic Inmates during the late 1970s, the persistent demands of Latino prisoners for Latina(o) bilingual programs and personnel, the alarming growth in the state's Latina(o) prisoner population, and Latino prisoner willingness to engage in coalition-building efforts.

DOCS Policies Towards Latino Prisoners and The Role of Latina(o) Staff

There were times in which Latino prisoners were able to mobilize the support of sympathetic Latina(o) as well as non-Latina(o) penal personnel. However, the type of support provided by staff was influenced by several factors. One was the harassment staff members were frequently subjected to by both co-workers and supervisors who felt they sympathized too much with prisoners. As Morales explained, "If they went a little bit too far, then they would have to stop because they were getting paid by the state. So they only went, you know, to a certain extent . . . They didn't want to go out in the parking lot and see their tires blown or get threatened. . . . 'Don't bite the hand that feeds you,' so to speak."[50]

Asked which staff members would harass their peers and how, Domingo Morales stated that, "Los blancos que son racistas. . . . if you got a car they might just make a hole in your tire or they might threaten you or ostracize you or mock you and make their jobs difficult."[51] In spite of the threat of such reprisals a few staff members supported Latino prisoners in a number of ways. "They would like give them the opportunity to . . . make calls to outside agencies that could assist the prisoners. They might do a little bit of footwork or they would become like staff advisor . . . but again, it was only to a certain extent."[52]

Other staff members were willing to go as far as to deliver or mail out information that prisoners did not want the administration to know about.

> They would mail what's going on in the prison, like si hay abusos. If there's abuses and there's a certain cop that's has always been harassing the Latinos, been abusive, they would like maybe send these names . . . to an outside watchdog agency. Because if you send it through the regular mail, it always gets scrutinized, it might never go where it's supposed to go.[53]

With each one of these actions, however, sympathetic personnel took the additional chance of being set up by co-workers and fired or being let go for "unprofessional behavior" during their probationary period. Few staff members were willing to take these chances.

Other staff resisted becoming deeply involved with Latino prisoner efforts because they were afraid, as discussed by Eddie Rosa in chapter 7, that their offices and the programs they sponsored, would be used by opportunistic prisoners to pursue their own ends (e.g., drug trafficking). The fact that there were prisoners who were willing to set-up staff members for prison administrators made such fears more real.

However, there were also Latina(o) staff members who would not advocate on behalf of Latino prisoners because they clearly identified with custody-oriented goals. Although Latino prisoner leaders also took advantage of the services provided by these staff members (e.g., educational, counselling), they did not seek the latter's support for politically sensitive matters such as leaking information out to the media.

Within this context, the ability of sympathetic Latina(o) institutional personnel to bring about a significant and permanent change in penal policy towards Latino prisoners was hindered by the fact that the former did not occupy significant positions of power within the institutional hierarchy. The isolation of Latino prisoners within the institutional context was further compounded by the fact that between 1977 and 1987 there were few, if any, Green Haven administrators who were supportive of Latino prisoner goals.

Interestingly, a brief but perceptible change in penal policy toward Latino prisoners did occur at the end of the 1980s.[54] This change was primarily the result of the transformation occurring in the composition of the Latino prisoner population and the increase in Latino prisoner discontent throughout the state during the 1980s. Such discontent was expressed in a number of ways. One was the growth in the num-

ber of confrontations between Latino prisoners and custodial personnel.[55] Second, were the continuing demands of Latino prisoners for the
hiring of more bilingual personnel, the implementation of additional
bilingual programs, and, as shown in the case of Green Haven, the
authorization to form other Latino formal prisoner groups. Perhaps,
most importantly was the continued willingness of a number of Latino
prisoner leaders to participate in underground reform-oriented coalition-building efforts. In fact, as the 1980s wore on, DOCS' apprehen-
sions about the potential for Latinos to engage in collective acts of
resistance were intensified by the fact that both Latina and Latino
prisoners frequently played leadership roles in helping organize mul-
tiracial/multiethnic prisoner coalitions throughout the state.[56] The fear
of Latino prisoner organizing was further deepened by the fact that
because only a small number of staff spoke Spanish, it would make it
more difficult for DOCS to keep abreast of organizing efforts among
Latino prisoners. It was this combinations of factors which led DOCS
Commissioner Coughlin to state:

> The New York State Department of Correctional Services made a
> mistake in the 60s and 70s. The inmate population was changing
> from white to black and the Department did not adjust accordingly.
> Now, in the 80s, the inmate population is changing again. This time
> it is becoming Hispanic. Not only is there a change in culture as has
> occurred in the 60s and 70s, there is also a change in language.[57]

The implications of this statement were clear. DOCS could not
afford to ignore indefinitely the growing concerns of Latino prisoners
if it was to avoid future major prisoner outbreaks such as the Attica
Rebellion. It was the combination of these factors coupled with the
calls of Latinas(os) working within the DOCS institutional and central
office bureaucracy that motivated Commissioner Coughlin to support
the creation in 1984 of the Division of Hispanic and Cultural Affairs
and the subsequent establishment of more programs geared towards
meeting the concerns of Spanish-speaking prisoners.[58] The person
named by Commissioner Coughlin as DHCA's director was Petrita
Hernández-Rojas, a Puerto Rican woman working at DOCS' central
office since 1977. Hernández-Rojas was one of the bilingual staff persons hired as a result of the pressures exerted by the Ad Hoc
Committee for Hispanic Inmates.[59]

    According to DHCA's statement of purpose, the goal of the divi-
sion was:

. . . to serve as a resource and liaison for the Department's staff and inmates in the delivery of programs and services for the Hispanic inmate population and other limited English-speaking inmate groups. The Division operates in coordination with Guidance, which is under the supervision of Program Services which reports to the Deputy Commissioner for Programs.[60]

The importance of Latino prisoner activism in helping establish the DHCA was stressed by former prisoner Domingo Morales:

The prisoners were asking for it . . . the population in prison was getting larger . . . and there was special needs—the language barriers, the education, the immigration things—and, you know, the reason you see Black and Latino guards is because the Blacks and Latinos asked for them. The reason why you see Black and Latino personnel is because they asked for them. So when they started the . . . Hispanic Cultural Affairs, it's because the Latinos . . . asked for it.[61]

Despite the DHCA's stated objectives and Latino prisoner support for its creation, Hernández-Rojas' primary concern was security not programs.[62]

While the creation of the DHCA was supported by Commissioner Coughlin, its founding was resisted by other members of the penal bureaucracy. As a result, the financial resources as well as the staff made available to it were inadequate from its inception.[63] In part, the DHCA's difficulties in securing appropriate support were due to the fact that the area of programs under which the division falls, as well as the concerns of Latina(o) prisoners and staff members, were not budgetary priorities of either DOCS or other governmental elites responsible for drafting the state's budget. The lack of budgetary support for the DHCA created a situation in which Hernández-Rojas had little clout within the department, despite Commissioner Coughlin's support. In fact, according to a source in DOCS, the naming of Hernández-Rojas as director of DHCA was itself an attempt to reduce the limited clout and visibility she had acquired in the department while working as director of education from 1980 to 1985. The objections to Hernández-Rojas occupying the latter position resulted primarily from the fact that she was a woman, a Puerto Rican, and "a new kid on the block." In fact, she was the first woman to hold that position.

In spite of these difficulties, however, Commissioner Coughlin's support as well as that of a few other central office personnel, made it possible for the DHCA to secure the creation of over one hundred new bilingual positions during the second half of the 1980s. However, even these positions were insufficient to meet the needs of Latino prisoners. This was so because the number of Latina and Latino prisoners at each facility far surpassed the number of positions created to address their concerns.

At the same time that the DHCA lobbied for the creation of new bilingual positions, it also became immersed in gathering data on the composition of the Latina(o) prisoner population. In order to achieve its goal, the DHCA first had to design a more adequate system for classifying Latina(o) prisoners and then update statistical data using the new categories developed.[64] The importance of designing a more effective way of identifying who was a Latina(o) prisoner lay in the fact that programs, both at the central office and institutional levels, were funded according to the perceived need for them. Thus, by traditionally undercounting (see Appendix A) the number of Latinas(os) in New York State prisons, DOCS had underestimated the amount and types of programs and resources needed to address their concerns as well as the number of bilingual Latina(o) staff necessary to provide services. Furthermore, as the Latina(o) prisoner population became more diverse during the 1980s, the need arose to identify them by nationality since diverse groups had different experiences with the United States criminal justice system and, hence, different concerns.

In order to gather further data on the conditions encountered by and the concerns of Latina(o) prisoners, the DHCA established the Hispanic Inmate Needs Task Force (HINTF) in 1985. The HINTF was given the additional responsibility of writing a report based on its findings and of making recommendations to DOCS. The HINTF was composed primarily of Latinas(o) who worked for DOCS and/or who had worked with Latina(o) prisoners at some point. It also included some ex-prisoners as well as African-American and white staff who had worked closely with Latina(o) prisoners.[65]

In 1986, the findings of the HINTF were published as a report to Commissioner Coughlin.[66] While several Latina(o) prisoner leaders throughout the state mailed their input to the HINTF, only Latino prisoners at Green Haven, meeting under the auspices of HUP, submitted a formal report to the HINTF. Several reasons accounted for this. Some Latina(o) prisoners were indifferent to DOCS initiatives that did not address their immediate interests. Others did not believe the DHCA would ultimately do anything for them. Still others simply did not trust the DHCA's intentions, seeing the division's main function as troubleshooting for DOCS and keeping the department abreast of Latino prisoner organizing efforts.

One of the most interesting observations made in the HINTF's report concerned the role played by Latina(o) prisoner leaders in encouraging their peers to develop educational and other rehabilitation programs.

> Hispanic inmate leaders encourage group members to get involved in education programs and counseling. The Hispanics have been instrumental in developing rehabilitation programs and in moving the administration to provide educational programs. In fact, Hispanics participate in education and other rehabilitation programs to a significantly greater degree than other inmate groups, doing so despite racial and cultural barriers.[67]

As a result of the above, the HINTF recommended that DOCS should work closely with Latina(o) leaders to encourage Latinas(os) continued involvement in such activities. These were, of course, some of the areas that were the least threatening to penal hegemony. The HINTF report also indicated that Latino prisoners exhibited a, "high degree of aggressiveness."[68] This was reflected in the increasing number of violent confrontations between Latino prisoners and guards. Controlling this aggressiveness seemed to be one of the main concerns of the DHCA. While the HINTF report was the result of a combination of sometimes contradictory philosophies, there appeared to be an underlying agreement that the aggressiveness of Latino prisoners was caused by a combination of factors which included the conditions of imprisonment and the lack of personnel knowledgeable about Latina(o) culture and cultural values that, if ignored by staff, could cause Latinos to become violent (e.g., concern with loyalty, respect, machismo, shame).[69] One of the recommended ways to reduce Latino prisoner aggressiveness was to assign Latina(o) bilingual personnel knowledgeable about Latina(o) culture to each facility.

In 1986, DHCA began to implement the recommendations of the HINTF. At the time, the DHCA was authorized by Governor Mario Cuomo's Executive Budget of 1985–1986 to conduct a pilot project whereby six Spanish-speaking counsellors, called Hispanic Inmate Needs Coordinators (HINCs), were assigned to work at six male facilities (including Green Haven) with large numbers of Latino prisoners.[70] The primary objective of the Hispanic Inmate Needs Program under which they operated was, "to improve institutional adjustment of Hispanic inmates with inadequate language skills by assisting and representing them at all formal facility proceedings."[71] Such services were expected to reduce the discriminatory treatment encountered by

Latino prisoners as a result of staff prejudices and language barriers, and as a consequence, reduce both Latino prisoner discontent and the number of violent incidents between guards and Latino prisoners.

At Green Haven, the two HINCs hired at the beginning of 1986[72] were laden with a number of responsibilities that included: implementing programs for the Spanish monolingual population; counselling Latino prisoners individually and collectively; acting as liaisons between Latino prisoners and staff; translating DOCS literature (e.g., rules and regulations); participating in institutional committees; seeking community support for Latino prisoners; and keeping the DHCA abreast of developments within the Latino prisoner body.[73] In practice, a large part of the coordinators' time was spent in troubleshooting, translating, and working as counsellors.[74]

How effective HINCs were in addressing the concerns of Latino prisoners depended on the individual's personality, the skills he/she brought to the job, and the openness of facility administrators to what he/she could offer. Administrators' resistance to the presence of the HINCs was partially reflected in the high turnover rate among the latter. Between 1986 and 1987 alone, Green Haven had at least four HINCs assigned to it.[75] One of the motivations for leaving was the frustrations encountered when having to deal with unsympathetic institutional personnel. While the HINCs were initially assigned to the facility to address collective, not individual problems, institutional administrators generally resisted any attempts by HINCs to act as ombudsmen or spokespersons for the Latino prisoner population. In spite of administrative resistance, the HINCs worked closely with HUP. In fact, several of the HINCs became HUP's staff advisors.[76] Gregorio Palma discussed some of the positive contributions of Carmelo Marín, one of Green Haven's HINCs.

> He tried to fight for . . . things that we needed. You know, when we had our festivals, when we had desires and needs in commissary and other places, he would champion our cause . . . it was someone of your culture who understood why at a festival you wanted to get Latin food.

> With the cultural food, they didn't know where to purchase the stuff a lot of times. He would come down to the city and find vendors that sold the yuca and the . . . bacalao sin espina and, you know, aguacate . . . We needed special seasonings so that the cooks could make our food taste like Latino food. And he would go out and get the "Accent" and "Sazón" and all these things for us. When Latinos were in trouble, if they were in the box, he would go and see them . . ."[77]

Moreover, Marín encouraged Latino prisoners to translate institutional material, particularly DOCS rules and regulations. With his assistance, a translation committee was established under the auspices of HUP. In addition, with the support of Marín and DHCA, Latino prisoners were able to have translation services recognized as a distinctive employment category for which prisoners could get paid.

The close association between the HINCs and HUP, however, caused a number of prisoners who were not part of HUP to distrust the former. Moreover, some saw the HINCs as being in the facility primarily to "troubleshoot" for DOCS, that is, to keep the department abreast of what Latino prisoners were doing, particularly those who sought to create alternative formal Latino prisoner organizations and/or engage in coalition-building efforts. The fact that HINCs were both bilingual and Latinas(os) did, in fact, facilitate the surveillance by DOCS of the Latino prisoner population.

In addition to the complaints voiced by Latino prisoners concerning the ambivalent role played by HINCs at the facility, the DHCA was also criticized because it frequently paid only token attention to Latino prisoners' requests for support. Such was the case when Latino prisoners, working in Green Haven's industrial program, complained of being harassed by supervisors for speaking in Spanish. Although the DHCA sympathized with prisoners' complaints, it was not able to effectively resolve their dilemma. There were also times that Latino prisoners sought financial support from the DHCA that was not forthcoming due to DHCA's limited budget. The DHCA was quick, however, to take credit for the creation and/or administration of a number of programs between 1985 and 1987. These included:

Prevención de Alcoholismo (Alcoholism Prevention)
Bilingual Vocational
Compadre Helper Program (Peer Counseling)[78]
Consejería Especializada (Specialized Counselling)
Creando Conciencia (Self-Awareness)
Diálogos Con Mi Gente (Dialogues with My People)
Prevención del Abuso de Drogas (Drug Abuse Prevention)
Mejorando la Familia (Family Enrichment)
Cultura Hispánica (Hispanic Culture)
Desarrollo Integral (Holistic Development)
Como Empezar su Propio Negocio (Minority Entrepreneurship)
Más Personalidad (Personality Plus)
Resocialización (Resocialization)
Realidad y Responsabilidad (Reality and Responsibility)[79]

Entrenamiento para el Personal en Diferencias Culturales
(Ethnic Awareness)

These programs, most of which were offered only a few days a year, were conducted on an ad hoc basis depending on the availability of Latina(o) staff to facilitate them and the initiative of Latino prisoners. The programs were generally designed to provide prisoners with life skills that would allow them to change self-destructive behaviors and facilitate their reentry into the outside community. One of the programs offered, Ethnic Awareness, was devised to educate non-Latino staff about Latina(o) cultural values. Participation in the latter program was voluntary which reduced its impact among staff members who were most in need of it.

It is interesting to note that while some of the prisoner-initiated programs were offered at the facility on a regular basis (e.g., Compadre Helper) none were recognized by DOCS as being "inmate programs." The latter designation, as mentioned previously, would have allowed them access to additional resources and the ability to organize major events to which outside community members could be invited.

At Green Haven, the programs were generally sponsored by HUP and/or the HINCs. It is important to stress that despite the fact that DHCA claimed to administer all the programs listed above, the fact was that some of these had been formed by Latino prisoners or their supporters prior to the creation of the DHCA. While the DHCA and the HINCs worked closely with HUP, some Latino ex-prisoners interviewed felt that DHCA's exaggerated claims of stewardship were geared to reduce Latino prisoner autonomy within these programs. Examples of programs developed at the initiative of prisoners included: Bilingual Tutor Services; Compadre Helper;[80] Diálogos Con Mi Gente; Más Personalidad; and Resocialización.[81] In any case, by stating that it had created and/or was administering the programs listed above, the DHCA was centralizing in one DOCS' division Latino prisoner-initiated as well as DHCA-initiated programs.

By the end of its first three years of existence, the DHCA claimed to have accomplished several of the goals it had set out for itself despite the limited resources assigned to it. Achievements included the hiring of additional bilingual personnel throughout the state penal system, the sponsoring of a number of new programs aimed at meeting the needs of the Spanish-monolingual population, and the establishment of consistent relationships with formal Latino prisoner organizations. Other accomplishments were the creation of the Hispanic Inmate Needs

Task Force and the publication of the task force's report on Latina(o) prisoners in New York State. However, the most interesting claim made by DHCA was that the presence of HINCs at the facilities helped maintain security by reducing the number of violent incidents between Latino prisoners and guards.

The concern with preserving security motivated DHCA's Director Hernández-Rojas to ask Pedro Cortijo a former Cuban HUP leader, to create a program specifically tailored for Mariel Cubans. The request came after the 1987 Cuban prisoner rebellions in Louisiana and Georgia.[82] In response to Hernández-Rojas' request, Cortijo created the Cuban and Hispanic Assimilation of New Cultural Economies Project (CHANCE Project).

> CHANCE . . . was geared toward Mariel Cubans, who did not understand the American system, and also Dominicans, Colombians, other individuals who came from other cultures who were Hispanic and did not really assimilate into the system very well. My intent was to . . . help them assimilate into the American system . . . A lot of them got arrested shortly after coming from Cuba because they went amuck. They didn't understand the system so they found themselves really alienated. And what my attempt was just to kind of give them . . . an overview of what the American family was all about, the American dream, what were the concepts in America, how to buy a car, how to buy a house . . . Just sort of like an overview of the entire American perspective on things and . . . you know, an overview of the law, of how the American justice system works and what place they had in the justice system.[83]

Notwithstanding Cortijo's broad objectives, the request by Hernández-Rojas was motivated by security interests aimed at avoiding the same kinds of outbreaks occurring in New York State prisons as a result of Cuban prisoner discontent.

In summary, despite its accomplishments, however, DHCA was unable to quell for long the growing discontent of Cuban, Puerto Rican, Dominican, and other Latino prisoners. Such discontent persisted for several reasons. One was that by the end of 1987, the DHCA had been unable to obtain from DOCS more than the assignment of two HINCs at Green Haven. This was so despite the fact that the Latino prisoner population at the time numbered 582 prisoners. The lack of an adequate number of Latina(o) bilingual personnel meant that many Latino prisoners were not able to participate in a variety of programs necessary to achieve a successful parole review. This situation was compounded by the fact that Latino prisoners continued to be subjected to discriminatory treatment by the overwhelmingly white staff. Moreover, Latino prisoner requests for authorization to create other formal Latino prisoner groups were continually resisted by DOCS despite the persistent growth in the Latino prisoner population throughout the 1980s. Latino prisoners continued to respond to these circumstances in a myriad of ways.

Life Goes On

The average preso would go to the yard and exercise. . . . Morning, afternoon . . . and even in evenings . . . Most of them would try to get a job in industry because a lot of times they did not get no support from their family . . . Some of them went to school to get their GED or bilingual GED . . . that was all. It was either you work, you go to school or you hang out in the yard . . . or you got porter jobs . . . or you work in the mess hall.

. . . everyday life it's boring, okay. It's a lot of loneliness. There's a lot of madness. You could either go to the yard, si tienes un programa, vas pal' programa. You spend most of your time in you cell hoping that somebody writes or you spend maybe some time waiting for a visit. You might use the phone . . . a lot of people watch a lot of TV or they listen to the radio plugs, you know. You eat. Some of the brothers get together and cook together . . . They play sports and that's it, you know. The majority of the time is a lot of time in your cell, in the solitude, with a lot of loneliness . . .

[The guards] . . . they harass in a sense, for any little thing. They'll harass you for maybe not dressing a particular way . . . or . . . when you're supposed to go to a program and a certain classroom is supposed to be open they don't open it. They don't let you go somewhere because you might not have a call out. They might not even crack your cell, you know . . .
                              —Domingo Morales, interview with author (1993)

In addition to the informal and formal groups Latino prisoners created, during the period studied, a few Latino prisoners survived imprisonment by becoming active in a number of formal interracial and interethnic prisoner and administrative groups available at the facility throughout much of the period studied. These included the Pre-Release Center, the Inmate Liaison Committee, the Inmate Grievance Resolution Committee, the *Open Gate*,[84] and, its successor, the *Green Haven*

Monthly.[85] Other Latino prisoners, particularly during the 1980s, were active in the Peregrine Jaycees, the Law Library, and in various religious (e.g., Catholic, Protestant) and self-help programs (e.g., Veterans Self-Help, Alcoholics Anonymous, and HIV/AIDS support groups). The level of Latino prisoner participation in these groups was generally determined by their knowledge of the English language, as few of the programs were offered in Spanish.

As always, when any coalition-building efforts became too threatening to prison authorities group members were subjected to harassment. For example, during the 1980s, Latino and African-American prisoners became the overwhelming number of those active in the Peregrine Jaycees. In addition to sponsoring African-American and Latino classes, the Jaycees sought to bring prisoners of color together to pursue a number of common interests.

> We were taking over Black and Latino artists in the prison and encouraging them on doing ethnic pieces . . . it was basically designed to kind of bring some unity in, some culture, and to be able to study Egyptian art. The individuals that were in the groups were very political . . . And John Peters[86] knew a lot about law . . . so he applied the legal concepts that he knew to make our chapter work . . . to find out what we could demand from the administration . . .[87]

The administration's response to these coalition-building efforts soon made itself felt.

> . . . they would stop the call-outs. They would write guys up that were coming to this group. They would, you know, try to infiltrate our group and listen to what we were doing and try to get our material. And in prison you find that they can justify anything they want. They'll find a reason for saying that you shouldn't meet anymore. . . . Then they call you a communist without having any proof. And that's it, you're through.[88]

The group's effectiveness eventually decreased both as a result of administrative actions and the fact that it received only token support from its parent organization on the outside.

Faced with continued harassment and discrimination, a number of Latino prisoner leaders attempted to organize their peers in political underground prisoner groups to demand collective reforms. Many of the difficulties encountered by Latino leaders seeking to politicize their peers during the 1980s were similar to those encountered during the 1970s. The difference was that prisoners were increasingly more hesitant to engage in reform-oriented activities because of the fear of losing the privileges they had gained after the Attica Rebellion. By the end of the 1980s, these included not only those benefits accruing from participation in formal prisoner and administrative organizations, but also the privilege to participate in trailer visits,[89] and other programs which reduced the time prisoners spent within the facility (e.g., work release and educational release, furloughs).

Green Haven's reputation for being more lax than other maximum security prisons where violence from both guards and other prisoners was more pervasive (e.g., Comstock, Clinton) also made many Latino prisoners hesitant to engage in reform-oriented efforts that could result in their being transferred. Gregorio Palma describes his first impression on arriving at Green Haven, after having been imprisoned in several other state facilities.

> I never knew until I got to Green Haven that I was living in so much tension because when I got off the bus . . . I felt a relief . . . There were guys running around doing all kinds of things. I saw guys in full length leathers . . . and these guys had hats from the street . . . In Green Haven all you had to wear was the green pants . . . I remember going to the bathroom in the yard and there were a couple of guys standing by the bathroom. They had these big yards . . . and it was very loose. There was a lot of recreation. A lot of guys playing dominoes. They were gambling. And one guy said, "I got the loose. I got the loose," and he was taking about loose joints, marijuana joints. And he said, "I got coke too and I got . . . dime bags," and he had dope too . . . I couldn't believe it! It was like in the street.[90]

Ironically, Green Haven's reputation for being a liberal institution was the result of its having been the state facility where the most experimentation with post-Attica Rebellion reforms was carried out, particularly in the form of prisoner organizations and other programs.

Other barriers to organizing Latino prisoners included the perennial interpersonal rivalries. "Sometimes if the person that's bringing on a challenge is someone that Latino does not get along with due to a personal grudge, it will keep him from rallying and sometimes calling his other friends not to rally."[91]

Political naiveté as well as the lack of trust in the ability of prisoners to achieve changes through organizing also hindered attempts by Latino prisoners to build unity. "Some brothers cannot see the need for any kind of unity. They really never thought that there would be any kind of changes in prison and they didn't believe in that 'knowing-your-culture-stuff.' And they . . . really thought that this country was the greatest and most beautiful . . ."[92]

In spite of these barriers, Latino prisoner leaders continually sought to politicize their peers through one-to-one contact and group discussions carried out under the cover of the new formal prisoner organizations. Political discussions resembled those of the late 1960s and early 1970s which sought to make the connections between Latino oppression inside and outside the walls.

> . . . we learn about our ancestors and leaders that tried to change con-
> ditions in the community and how they were like ostracized or named
> terrorists or communists. And then from there on we look at the pre-
> sent conditions of our communities and how it's been existing and
> how we have fell into this trap that they have set for us because
> prison is a business . . . It's a multi-billion dollar business . . . And as
> long as we keep feeding into the racist attitudes that they have, we
> start feeding into the drugs and the alcohol and we start robbing and
> killing each other, you're going to continue to go to prison.[93]

Once Latino prisoners became politicized they were more likely to engage in organizing activities at other institutions to which they were transferred.

> I had a best friend that I knew from Green Haven . . . when I asked
> him to be vice-president he said, "Nah, I'm not down with that shit,
> bro. I'm tired of organizations. All they do is collect money. They don't
> do shit. I said, "Yo bro, . . . what we learned in Green Haven we got a
> chance to put it into practice." Now, he's somewhere in Attica and he
> thanks me for that because he saw how you learn 'cause you're forced
> to speak to people . . . now you got an opportunity to change things. . ."[94]

The ultimate goals of Latino prisoner leaders during the 1980s were also similar to those of their predecessors. Once released, Latino prisoners could both educate the Latina(o) community about the penal system and challenge oppressive conditions on the outside.

> And then the thing is that the community is not educated about us
> being in prisons. . . . they ostracize us, too, okay? So the key thing is
> . . . to educate the community. But you got to educate the presos
> because . . . 95 percent of them go out. They're gonna come out but
> they're going to come back to the same conditions . . . but you got to

teach them to sense what's really going on, the conditions of the community, that they're not powerless, that we could change the conditions if we put our minds to it.[95]

These attempts to politicize Latino prisoners were made simultaneously with the efforts of a number of Latino prisoner leaders to form
reform-oriented coalitions with their African-American and white
peers. For example, at the end of 1987, Latino, African-American, and
white prisoners working in the kitchen refused to leave their cells
protesting work conditions and the abusive treatment they received at
the hands of a staff member. The administration's response was, on the
one hand, to transfer two hundred of the protesting prisoners. On the
other hand, prison administrators used prisoners who were locked in
segregation as strikebreakers. "They went in the box and told everybody, 'We will cut you loose and let you out of the box if you go down-
stairs to the mess hall and serve the food.' And they did, a whole bunch
of them."[96]

In spite of these setbacks, Latino prisoners continued using a myriad of tactics to make their grievances known. These included creating
both formal and informal Latino prisoner groups and interracial
reform-oriented coalitions, filing complains with administrative groups,
the DHCA, the commissioner of corrections, and other state agencies
(e.g., governor's office, legislature). From time to time, individual Latino
prisoners as well as HUP sought the assistance of Prisoners Legal
Services.[97] Latino prisoners also sought the support of third parties, particularly family, friends, community organizations, and Latinos working in New York City radio stations (e.g., WBAI, WKCR-FM).[98]

Conclusion

The post-Attica Rebellion reforms allowed Latino prisoners and
their allies inside and outside the penal establishment, to experiment
with a number of innovative programs in spite of the resistance of the
overwhelmingly white civilian and custodial staff. Nevertheless,
throughout the 1970–1987 period studied, the calls of Latino prisoners
for an end to discriminatory treatment, the hiring of additional bilingual personnel, and the implementation of bilingual programs, key
beginnings to any real reform, went basically unheeded. As a result,
the post-Attica Rebellion concessions failed to significantly reduce
Latino prisoner discontent for long.

The response of Latino prisoners to this situation varied depending
on their political consciousness and their commitment to reforming

prison conditions. While a few Latino prisoners preferred to "do their time" in isolation, many participated in a number of Latino and/or multiracial/multiethnic formal and informal prisoner groups and administrative organizations with the objective of promoting both individual and collective interests.

Within this context, the role played by reform-oriented Latino prisoner leaders was to help Latino prisoners change those behaviors which led them to victimize members of their own community and to point out how Latinas(os) were oppressed by the dominant white/ European power structure inside and outside the walls. The ultimate objective was to produce politicized men who upon release from the institution would contribute to their community's multiple struggles against oppression. Another aim of reform-oriented Latino prisoner leaders was to foster the creation of unity between Latino, African-American, and white prisoners for the purpose of demanding penal and other criminal justice reforms.

Major obstacles to the building of Latino prisoner solidarity were the continued harassment of prisoners by prison personnel, personal rivalries within the Latino prisoner population, and the conflict between those who favored pursuing "Latino" goals through formal prisoner and administrative groups and those who felt the organization needed to pursue larger goals through additional means. Added to this were the frictions caused by the emergence of nationality-based cleavages within the Latino prisoner population particularly as of the first half of the 1980s. Despite such divisions, however, as the 1980s wore on, a significant number of Puerto Rican prisoners joined their Spanish-speaking Caribbean and Central and South American peers to voice their concerns regarding discriminatory penal policies as well as the lack of an adequate number of bilingual services, programs, and Latina(o) personnel.

One of the difficulties encountered by Latino prisoners after the withdrawal of the CPRS Prison Task Force from Green Haven at the end of the 1970s, was their inability to mobilize consistent sources of third party support despite the fact that they continually sought such patronage. Throughout the period studied, third party support for Latina(o) prisoners came primarily from the outside Latina(o) community—through family, friends, religious organizations, and community activists involved in various struggles of the Latino community. While the support for Latino prisoners was most keenly felt within the outside Latina(o) community during the years immediately following the Attica Rebellion, as the mid-1970s wore on and economic conditions began to worsen, the support of third parties lessened community efforts increasingly turned towards dealing with day-to-day survival issues.

The ability of third parties to consistently support Latino prisoners was hindered by the fact that the community groups most likely to
support prisoners were also the ones most likely to be engaged in a
number of other community struggles that made equal demands for
time, energy, and resources. Thus, the 1977–1987 period found Latino
prisoners unable to mobilize significant sources of third party support
outside of family members and religious groups. Consequently, Latino
prisoners were left with few sources of third party support which could
be used to counter the actions of penal elites.

The lack of non-penal sources of support was paralleled by the
inability of the few Latinas(os) working at the institutional level to
effectively address the concerns of Latino prisoners for the hiring of an
adequate number of bilingual personnel, the permanent implementation of bilingual programs, an end to discriminatory treatment, and the
formation of additional formal Latino prisoner organizations. While following the Attica Rebellion Latino prisoners had been able to muster
the patronage of civilian penal administrators for the implementation
of a number of bilingual programs and the hiring of some bilingual
Latina(o) personnel, by the mid-1970s, Latino prisoners had lost these
significant sources of institutional support. Though during the 1977–
1987 period Latino prisoners continued to solicit the support of the few
available Latina(o) line staff, the ability of the latter to help bring about
significant changes in penal policy towards Latino prisoners was limited by the fact that they did not occupy significant positions of power
within the penal hierarchy. Faced with this situation, during the mid-
1980s, Latino prisoners increasingly sought the support of Latinas(os)
working within the Division of Hispanic and Cultural Affairs.

The creation of DHCA in 1984, was DOCS' response to the increase
in the Latino prisoner population, continuing Latino prisoner discontent, and the calls of Latino prisoners, third parties, and Latina(o) staff
at the institutional and central office levels for the hiring of more bilingual personnel and the implementation of bilingual programs. DHCA's
primary goals were to maintain security, conduct research on Latina(o)
prisoners, secure the hiring of additional bilingual personnel, and
implement bilingual programs designed primarily to meet the needs of
those Latinas(os) with few or no English language skills.

While the DHCA was able to achieve some of its goals and provide Latino prisoners with a number of bilingual personnel and services, its efforts on behalf of Latino prisoners and staff were,
nevertheless, hindered by the limited resources made available to it
by state elites and the fact that security remained its priority. The

DHCA's inability to secure additional funding was primarily due to the fact that neither the area of programs nor Latina(o) prisoner and staff concerns have historically been considered priorities within DOCS. The DHCA's preoccupation with security explained its attempts to reduce prisoner/guard violence, centralize DHCA-initiated as well as prisoner-initiated programs under its wing, and establish close relations with leaders of formal Latino prisoner organizations. Ultimately, DHCA's primary goal was to prevent the occurrence of another major prisoner rebellion, such as Attica.

Latino prisoner reaction to the creation of DHCA and the presence of its representatives in the facility was a combination of indifference, support, and distrust. While some welcomed the efforts of DHCA and the presence of Hispanic Inmate Needs Coordinators at the facility, others saw it as yet another attempt by DOCS to monitor the actions of Latino prisoners, particularly those Latinos involved in carrying out coalition-building efforts. Thus, by the end of 1987, DHCA had been unable to win the trust of Latino prisoners.

Notes: Chapter 8

1. Entertainment was provided by the band "Inspiración Latina" and a group of guitarists called "Los Amigos." See Angel Ramos y John [Flaco] Rivera, "Conmemoración del Descubrimiento de Puerto Rico (1493)," *Green Haven Monthly* (hereafter cited as *GHM*) (January 1979): 19; and El "Salserito" Raúl Rodríguez, "Rincón Salsero," *GHM* 2, No. 2 (February 1979): 21–22.

2. Luis Lozano, "Monthly Profile," *GHM* 3, Nos. 3/4 (March/April 1980): 21.

3. Robert Maldonado, "Latin Group Organizes," *GHM* 2, No. 6 (May/June 1979): 19.

4. G. Ryder, "La Fiesta," *GHM* 2, No. 8 (August 1979): 17. Entertainment at the event was provided by a Latino prisoner band called "Le-Lo-Lai."

5. Bob Maldonado, "Descubrimiento de P.R.," *GHM* 2, No. 11 (November 1979): 20.

6. Idem, "In Search of New Horizons," *GHM* 2, No. 6 (May/June 1979]): 13–14.

7. Sally Stein, interview with author, Ritchie, Md., 13 February 1989.

8. Castro had been the Director of Public Relations for the New York City Department of Correction during the 1970 New York City jail rebellions.

9. Robert Maldonado, "Latin Group Organizes," *GHM* 2 No. 6 (May/June 1979): 19.

10. Another way in which Latino prisoner concerns were ignored was the fact that the musical instruments used by Latino prisoners had been allowed to deteriorate (Ibid.).

11. Harris had been named warden of Green Haven in 1977. In April 1979, he was the state's only African-American prison warden (UPI Team, "Overcrowding No Threat," *GHM* 2, No. 4 [April 1979]: 5).

12. L. Lozano, "Hispanos Forman Comité," *GHM* 3, Nos. 3 and 4 (March/April 1980): 26.

13. For a list of the names of founding members, see G. Ryder traducción Bob Maldonado, "Latino Americanos Unidos, "La Fiesta," *GHM* 2, No. 8 (August 1979): 17; and L. Lozano, "Hispanos Forman Comité," *GHM* 3, Nos. 3 and 4 (March/April 1980): 26.

14. The need for coalition-building efforts became particularly urgent after a violent confrontation took place between over 100 Latino and African-American prisoners during November 1979 ("7 Inmates Hurt in Melee at Green Haven Prison," *New York Times* [hereafter cited as *N.Y. Times*], 5 November 1979, IV, 7; and *N.Y. Times*, 6 November 1979, II, 2).

15. In February of 1980, administrators at Green Haven found themselves increasingly engaged in conflict with the Creative Communications Committee (CCC), the prisoners' long-termers' committee. Harris claimed that the organization had become "radical" and was not engaging in "constructive" activities. The blame for the radicalization of the Committee was placed on Uhuru, the group's community liaison at the time. The CCC was ordered by prison officials to find another community organization to serve as its sponsor (Thomas A. Johnson, "A Prisoner, 24, Slain in Corridor at Green Haven," *N.Y. Times,* 28 February 1980, II, 2).

16. L. Lozano, "Hispanos Forman Comité," *GHM* 3, Nos. 3 and 4 (March/April 1980): 26.

17. For example, while some Latino prisoners supported United States intervention in Latin America and the policies pursued by Latin American military regimes, others supported the Cuban and Nicaraguan revolutions, Puerto Rican independence, and the El Salvadoran guerrilla struggle.

18. Such support was made even more evident on April 19, 1986, when HUP co-sponsored an event organized by the Comité Albizu Campos. The event commemorated the birth of the Puerto Rican nationalist leaders. Participants included Latino prisoners and staff and at least one member of the outside Latina(o) community (Bomexi Iztaccihualt, "Reflexiones sobre una visita a Green Haven," *GHM* 8, No. 6 [July/August 1985]: 19).

19. Paul L. Montgomery, "Unrest Reported at Green Haven Prison," *N.Y. Times,* 23 July 1980, II, 2.

20. Ibid.

21."Editorial Comment: Charles Scully," *GHM* 3, No. 8 (August/ September 1980): 3. One of Scully's first actions was to order all prisoners locked in their cells until a CERT Team of 130 guards searched the facility for contraband (Paul L. Montgomery, "Unrest Reported at Green Haven Prison," *N.Y. Times,* 23 July 1980, II, 2).

22. See "Inmates Are Confined to Cells After Protests in Green Haven Prison," *N.Y. Times,* 29 July, 1980, II, 2; and "Green Haven 'Strike' Is Losing Support," *N.Y. Times,* 30 July 1980, II, 2.

23. In 1980, following these incidents, 15 prisoners filed a class action suit against Commissioner Coughlin and Green Haven Warden Scully. In 1987, a U.S. District Court civil jury ordered Coughlin and Scully to pay damages to the prisoners because they had violated prisoners' "constitutional rights to free speech and due process . . . and the constitutional prohibition against cruel and unusual punishment." ("Prison Officials are Ordered to Pay $750,000," *GHM* 9, No. 4 [Summer Edition: July, August, September 1987]: 5). Moreover, "The federal jury found 15 prisoners were beaten by officers at Green Haven before being transferred and later at Great Meadow prison" (Ibid.).

24. Cervantes Hernández, "El comité hispano (H.U.P.) y los hispanos," *GHM* 5, No. 1 (January/February 1982): 18.

25. Comité, Hispanos Unidos Para el Progreso 1982, "¡Atención, Hispanos!," *GHM* 5, No. 1 (January/February 1982): 15. Author's translation: "The central objective of H.U.P. has always been to promote the integration of Hispanics in the educational field . . . H.U.P. is an apolitical organization, structured with the objective of helping the Hispanic to find an appropriate solution to his basic needs: bilingual education; bilingual legal orientation; English-as-a-second-language education; counselling services for our brothers who do not speak English; high school equivalency classes. These orientations encompass from serving as interpreters to preparing you for your appointment with the parole board."

26. L. Lozano, "Hispanos Forman Comité," *GHM* 3, Nos. 3 and 4 (March/ April 1980): 26.

27. Hernández, "El comité hispano (H.U.P.) y los hispanos, *GHM* 5, No. 1 (January/February 1982): 18.

28. Comité, Hispanos Unidos Para el Progreso 1982, "¡Atención, Hispanos!," *GHM* 5, No. 1 (January/February 1982): 15.

29. José Rodríguez, "Independencia de la República Dominicana, *GHM* 6, No. 3 (March 1983): 13.

30. Pablo de Jesús, "Compañeros," *GHM* 7, No. 5 (June/July 1983): 14.

31. Joe Torres, "142 Aniversario de la Independencia de la República Dominicana," *GHM* 8, No. 13 (June/July 1986): 21.

32. "Latin Communications," *GHM* 8, No. 6 (July/August 1985): 21.

33. José Rodríguez, "H.U.P. se reune con Diana Correa," *GHM* 10, No. 2 (March 1988): 17–19.

34. HUP, "H.U.P. . . . ¿que es de mi dólar?," *GHM* 8, No. 3 (March 1985): 14.

35. The Latin American Culture class was begun on November 2, 1980 (José R. Rodríguez, "Plantando Bandera," *GHM* 5, No. 1 [January/ February 1982]: 16).

36. This class taught skills on how to write resumes, how to conduct oneself during a job interview, how to fill out tax forms, etc.

37. The Transactional Analysis class was a course in self-awareness initiated in 1983 (Angel Herrera, "Tercer Aniversario Análisis Conciliatorio," *GHM* 8, No. 15 [October 1986]: 15–16).

38. Pablo de Jesús, "Compañeros," *GHM* 7, No. 5 (June/July 1983): 14.

39. During both 1984 and 1985, the requests of PUEDA members to be allowed to celebrate an additional Latino feast day, "Three Kings' Day," was rejected by DOCS (Puertorriqueños Unidos en Estados Unidos de América [P.U.E.D.A.], "Programa Resumen," New York, 1988).

40. Domingo Morales [pseud.], interview with author, New York, N.Y., 6 April 1993.

41. Israel Ruíz Jr., "New York State Department of Correctional Services Hispanic Needs: Employment and Inmate Programs Report, February 29, 1988 (xeroxed manuscript).

42. Morales, interview with author, 1993. While the post-1987 period is outside the scope of this project, by the end of the 1980s prisoners holding the above opinion had been able to carry out their objective of replacing HUP's moderate leadership with another one more inclined to foster the building of solidarity among Latino prisoners and between Latino and non-Latino prisoners.

43. Darío Lora, "Seminario de Nuestra Organización, H.U.P.," *GHM* 8, No. 12 (April/May 1986): 19.

44. Pablo de Jesús, "Caribe Village Nos Visita," *GHM* 7, No. 8 (October 1984): 14. According to de Jesús, Caribe Village had also sponsored PUL.

45. Gregorio Palma [pseud.], interview with author, New York, N.Y., 16 April and 1 May 1993.

46. Diana Correa, interview with author, New York, N.Y., 31 January 1989. The project's primary areas of research were: medical services; immigration issues; bilingual vocational and academic training programs; and recruitment of more bilingual personnel. In addition to these areas, the project was concerned with the harassment of Latino prisoners that resulted from the racist attitudes of penal staff. Another major preoccupation was the fact that

as late as 1989, DOCS, departmental and institutional literature was generally written only in English. According to Correa, "It depends on what facility you go. If you got a superintendent who's more sensitive to the issues, knowing that he has a very large Latino inmate population, there may be more of an attempt to try to take all the literature that goes out to inmates and that's posted, will be done both in English and Spanish" (Ibid.). Correa was also responsible for doing community outreach and lobbying legislators.

47. Ibid.

48. In 1990, the Latino Prisoners' Project was discontinued as a result of the lack of funding. On the basis of Diana Correa's research, 10 July 1992, the Correctional Association of New York subsequently published a report entitled, *Not Simply a Matter of Words: Academic and Vocational Programs for Latino Lnmates in New York State Prisons*.

49. Morales, interview with author, 1993.

50. Ibid.

51. Ibid. Author's translation: "The whites that are racist . . ."

52. Ibid.

53. Ibid.

54. This change lasted until 1990 when DOCS began to increasingly withdraw the limited financial support it had offered to the Division of Hispanic and Cultural Affairs.

55. Petrita Hernández-Rojas, interview with author, Albany, N.Y., 14 February 1989.

56. Correa, interview with author, 1989; and Hernández-Rojas, interview with author, 1989.

57. New York State Department of Correctional Services (hereafter cited as NYSDOCS), Division of Hispanic and Cultural Affairs, Hispanic Inmate Needs Task Force, Final Report, *"A Meeting of the Minds, An Encounter of Hearts,"* 1986 (*Action Plan*), Albany 1986, 1. This excerpt was taken from an address by Coughlin to criminal justice officials and others on May 2, 1985.

58. "Hispanic Ratio Rises in State's Prisons," *N.Y. Times*, 4 February 1987, II, 6.

59. Stein, interview with author, 1989. Hernández-Rojas began working for DOCS during the summer of 1976.

60. NYSDOCS, Division of Hispanic and Cultural Affairs, Hispanic Inmate Needs Task Force, *Report 1985* (*Draft Action Plan for Hispanic Inmate Needs Programming*), Albany, November 20, 1985, 2.

61. Morales, interview with author, 1993.

62. Hernández-Rojas, interview with author, 1989.

63. According to Diana Correa of the Latino Prisoners' Project, ". . . what they [DOCS] often do in a lot of similar circumstances is that they hire a skeleton staff and give them an enormous amount of work. . . . And when that happens . . . people overwork and ultimately are not as effective as they'd like to be because it's too few people to do the amount of work necessary. So that they make it not the best working situation for the people who have taken on this kind of work" (Correa, interview with author, 1989).

64. For more information on the problems encountered when attempting to identify the Latina(o) prisoner population, see Appendix A.

65. The first meeting of the HINTF took place on May 3, 1985. The second meeting was held on November 20–22, 1985. Although members of various Latina(o) community and educational organizations and Latin American consulates were invited to attend these meetings, only a few of the former and none of the latter attended. Moreover, while at least two Latina(os) legislators sent representatives to its deliberations, only Olga Méndez was personally involved throughout the HINTF's brief existence.

66. NYSDOCS, Division of Hispanic and Cultural Affairs, Hispanic Inmate Needs Task Force, *Final Report,* 1986.

67. Ibid., 53.

68. Ibid., 56.

69. Ibid., 19–52. This author wants to call attention to the racist implications of this argument for it ignores the manner in which other ethnic/racial groups may be equally as aggressive though this aggression might be expressed differently.

70. The other facilities were Clinton, Eastern, Fishkill, Great Meadow, and Sing Sing.

71. NYSDOCS, Division of Hispanic and Cultural Affairs, Hispanic Inmate Needs Task Force, *Final Report,* 5.

72. See de Armas, "Programa de Necesidades Hispanas," *GHM* 8, No. 1 (February/March 1986): 12.

73. Carmelo Marín [pseud.], interview with author, Beacon, N.Y., 2 February 1990; and Hernández-Rojas, interview with author, 1989.

74. Other services provided by HINCs during 1986 and 1987 included: teaching a relaxation class (de Armas, "Programa de Necesidades Hispanas," *GHM* 8, No. 1 [February/March 1986]: 12); collecting the names of Latino prisoners interested in taking a course on legal research in Spanish (Ibid.); attending events organized by HUP subcommittees (Joe Torres, "142 Aniversario de la Independencia de la República Dominicana," *GHM* 8, No. 13 [June/July 1986]: 21); arranging for prisoners to visit families at times of death (Jesús de

Armas, "Entrevista: Necesidades Hispanas," *GHM* 9, No. 1 [January/February 1987]: 16–17); and helping form Latino prisoner groups in some state facilities (e.g., Adirondack) (Ibid.).

75. de Armas, "Programa de Necesidades Hispanas," GHM 8, No. 1 (February/March 1986): 12; and Idem, "Entrevista: Necesidades Hispanas," *GHM* 9, No. 1 (January/February 1987): 16.

76. Carmelo Marín [pseud.], interview with author, Beacon, N.Y., 2 February 1990; and Jesús de Armas, "Entrevista: Necesidades Hispanas," *GHM* 9, No. 1 (January/February 1987): 16–17.

77. Palma, interview with author, 1993.

78. According to Hernández-Rojas, the Compadre Helper program was, "Peer counselling . . . con los valores hispanos, con el compadrazgo, con la familia extendida, con el "¡Ay, bendito!" (Hernández-Rojas, interview with author, 1989).

79. NYSDOCS, Division of Hispanic and Cultural Affairs, Hispanic Inmate Needs Task Force, *Final Report*, 7.

80. The Spanish Compadre Helper program was established at Green Haven at the end of 1979 (George A. Saninocencio, "Tooting the Horn for Petrita Hernández," *GHM* 3, No. 1 [January 1980]: 23). At the beginning of 1980, prior to the creation of the DHCA, Hernández-Rojas offered a six day training in Spanish for forty bilingual peer counsellors at Green Haven (Luis Lozano, "Compadre Helper Graduation," *GHM* [February 1980]: 19). At the time, the program had been offered at Woodbourne, Bedford Hills, Fishkill, Eastern, and Wallkill prisons (Ibid.). At the end of 1986, the English Compadre Helper program was established at Green Haven ("Better Late Than Never, English Compadre," *GHM* 8, No. 15 [November/December 1985]: 18–19).

81. Ibid., 54.

82. Pedro Cortijo [pseud.], interview with author, New York, N.Y., 4 February 1993. For an account of the rebellions and the conditions faced by Mariel Cubans imprisoned in federal detention centers and state prisons see, The Commission Pro-Justice Mariel Prisoners, *The Mariel Injustice In the Bicentennial of the United States Constitution* (Coral Gables, Fla.: The Commission Pro-Justice Mariel Prisoners, 1987).

83. Cortijo, interview with author, 1993.

84. The *Open Gate* was Green Haven's prisoner newspaper until at least 1976. At that time, Salvador Agrón was one of the collective's members. Agrón had also been active in the Think Tank Concept, the Latino Think Tank Concept, and PUL (Vincent A. Hall, "September 1971," *GHM* 2, No. 9 [September 1979]: 9).

85. Latino prisoners made their presence visible within the paper in a number of ways: they formed part of the paper's collective; published poetry

and wrote articles in Spanish and/or English concerning events taking place on an institutional and statewide level; interviewed Latina(o) staff and third parties; took photographs; and translated institutional information of interest to the Latino prisoner population.

86. Pseudonym.

87. Palma, interview with author, 1993.

88. Ibid.

89. Trailer visits were begun at Green Haven during the spring of 1980 as part of the Family Reunion Program. Trailer visits allowed prisoners to spend several days with immediate family members (excluding non-legal spouses) in a mobile home or trailer located within the prison grounds (Richard Akbar Salahuddin, "Family Reunion Program," *GHM* 3, No. 1 [January 1980]: 8).

90. Palma, interview with author, 1993.

91. Ibid.

92. Morales, interview with author, 1993.

93. Ibid.

94. Ibid.

95. Ibid.

96. Palma, interview with author, 1993.

97. "Comunidad Hispana en Acción," *GHM* 3, No. 10 (October/November 1980): 13.

98. José Torres, "Día del Descubrimiento de Puerto Rico," *GHM* 9, No. 1 (January/February 1987): 19.

PART III

LATINA PRISONERS: BEDFORD HILLS CORRECTIONAL FACILITY

9

Latina Prisoners and the
Institutional Context

The conditions encountered by women prisoners at Bedford Hills at the beginning of the 1970s precluded their ability to achieve a redefinition of the conditions of their imprisonment for a full decade longer than their male counterparts at Green Haven. This was the case for several reasons. First was the fact that DOCS generally prioritized the needs and concerns of male prisoners. Secondly, despite the implementation of the post-Attica Rebellion reforms that allowed women prisoners to create formal prisoner groups, Bedford Hills' administration remained firmly custody-oriented, flagrantly ignoring not only court mandated changes, but DOCS' own reform-oriented directives. As a result, the few liberal administrators at Bedford Hills were not allowed the same freedom to work with prisoners and experiment with new programs that their counterparts had enjoyed at Green Haven. Moreover, unlike the case of PUL at Green Haven, which was able to mobilize the support of penal administrators at the institutional and central office levels during the early 1970s, Latina prisoners at Bedford Hills did not have any significant sources of support within the penal bureaucracy until the early 1980s.

An equally important factor affecting women's ability to secure a redefinition of the conditions of their imprisonment during the 1970s was that third parties involved in the prisoners' rights movement of the 1960s and 1970s, with few exceptions, also prioritized the concerns of male prisoners. This resulted partially from the fact that, as Erika Anne Kates[1] has noted, what constitutes prison "activism" has been framed by the actions of male prisoners.[2] Women prisoners were not generally considered "activists" because they did not always prioritize the same concerns or organize in the same manner as their male counterparts. For example, women prisoners frequently prioritized family matters over other concerns considered to be of a more political nature. Moreover, they did not engage in riots/rebellions, work strikes, or widespread litigation efforts on the scale or with the same frequency

271

as their male counterparts during the late 1960s and early 1970s. This meant that they did not generally call attention to their plight through means deemed significant by the mass media, third parties, DOCS personnel, and other state elites. As a result, women prisoners were defined as "apolitical" and, therefore, not deserving of the types of support offered male prisoners. Such beliefs were not only based on sexist assumptions but also on ignorance about the severity of repression imprisoned women were exposed to in comparison to male prisoners.

The fact that the women's prison population was small meant that their collective actions were easily quelled and/or ignored by penal authorities. Moreover, the fact that 70 to 80 percent of women in prison were mothers, many of them single heads of households prior to their imprisonment, also affected the manner in which they organized and the issues they prioritized at any given point in time.[3] Strategies women devised to pursue their concerns were, therefore, tailored to suit their particular organizing dilemmas. Notwithstanding, the 1970s were to show that women prisoners across the country were interested in litigation[4] and were able to organize collective acts of resistance despite brutality on the part of male guards.[5]

This chapter challenges commonly held assumptions about the lack of activism among women prisoners. It also shows how women's vulnerability, through lack of numbers and penal system repression, combined to make a different organizing style imperative for them. It emphasizes that women's concerns as heads of households provided penal personnel extra leverage with which to control them and attempt to thwart their reform efforts. We will see that under the pressure of brutal repression, Latina (and non-Latina) prisoner leaders were forced to depend primarily on a combination of interracial /interethnic political underground coalitions, pseudo-family kinship alliances, and the support of third parties, and a few trusted staff, to pursue prison reform efforts. The major questions guiding the chapters in this part of the book were: What types of informal and formal groups and networks did Latina prisoners create to pursue their concerns? What were the conditions under which they sought to wrest concessions from the state? What was the response of third parties and penal personnel to their calls for support? How did the types of third party and penal support available affect the formulation of Latina prisoner goals and the tactics and strategies used?

Before expanding on the points mentioned above, it will be necessary to discuss the institutional context Latina prisoners encountered during the 1970–1987 period studied. This will allow us to gain a fuller understanding of the constraints under which Latina prisoners and their allies operated.

The Prison, the Keepers, and the Kept

Bedford Hills Correctional Facility is located fifty miles north of New York City in Westchester County. Until 1970, it consisted of a reformatory wing and a prison wing.[6] That year, the institution's prison side was transformed into a male division and its female occupants were transferred to the reformatory side across the street. The male and female divisions shared one superintendent until 1972, when the men's side became a separate male facility. In 1970, Albion Correctional Facility, located in upstate New York, was closed and its female guards and prisoners were transferred to Bedford Hills. This left Bedford Hills as the only state facility for women until December 1979, when Bayview Correctional Facility was opened in New York City.

Bedford Hills was classified as a medium security facility until the first half of the 1980s, when it became the state's only maximum-security prison for women. In 1977, women at Bedford Hills were "housed primarily in three residence buildings known as '112,' '113,' and '114'."[7] There was also a "Hospital" building which housed some prisoners, "a segregation and reception building, an administration building, and an industry building."[8] While on December 31, 1970, the institution was underutilized with 219 prisoners, by May 5, 1986, the prisoner population had more than doubled, topping 513 women (see Table 10). This led DOCS to add a 200 bed expansion to the facility.[9] Moreover, the overcrowding experienced at Bedford Hills was one of the major reasons cited by state elites for establishing several other women's prisons during the 1980s. The opening of these facilities gradually affected Bedford Hills' daily prisoner composition as the institution became the state's classification center for women. As of the early-1980s, all new prisoners were sent to Bedford Hills where they were classified and dispatched to various women's facilities. This practice led to a high turnover rate in the institution's prisoner population.

Between 1970 and 1986, about two-fifths of the Bedford Hills prisoner population was being held for murder and/or attempted murder; one quarter was imprisoned for drug-related offenses (see Table 11). The largest overall change during the period studied occurred in the area of economic crimes. While in 1970, about one quarter of the women were imprisoned for economic crimes, by 1986, this number had increased to almost one third (see Table 11).

In comparison to their African-American and white counterparts, Latinas held in New York State prisons at the end of 1985 tended to be imprisoned more for drug-related offenses and less for violent and economic crimes.[10] However, while a distinction has been made here between economic and drug-related crimes, it is widely accepted among criminal justice personnel that many of the drug-related crimes committed by Latinas were, in fact, economically motivated. That is, many were not using drugs but engaging in the importation and distribution of illegal drugs to meet economic needs within a deteriorating national and international economy.

The increase in drug-related activities among the outside population coincided with changes in sentencing laws[11] and with ethnic discrimination to produce a situation in which, as of the early 1980s, a significant shift began taking place in the ethnic/racial composition of the prisoner population at Bedford Hills. The greatest percent of increase occurred in the Latina prisoner group. While in 1970, Latinas comprised 12.3 percent of all prisoners at the facility (i.e. 27 women),[12] by 1986, they constituted 25.0 percent of the total (i.e., 128 women) (see Table 10).[13] The most rapid growth among Latina prisoners occurred among immigrants from the Dominican Republic and Colombia. Many of these women were both Spanish monolingual and undocumented.

As at Green Haven, in 1972, Bedford Hills' position of Deputy Superintendent was replaced by the three newly created positions of Deputy Superintendent of Administration, Deputy Superintendent of Security, and Deputy Superintendent of Programs. As stated in chapter 4, the objective of this administrative reorganization was to decentralize administrative responsibilities and deemphasize security concerns. However, unlike the case of Green Haven, where Leon Vincent replaced a custody-oriented superintendent who refused to carry out the post-Attica Rebellion reforms, at Bedford Hills a custody-oriented superintendent was replaced in 1972 by Janice Warne who was similarly custody-oriented.[14] In fact, a study conducted by James G. Fox[15] comparing the management style at Bedford Hills with that found in five men's prisons, concluded that during the 1970s, the primary management style used by Bedford Hills administrators was a "restrictive management style."

> Restrictive management followed traditional custody-oriented policies and practices, emphasized loyalty and conformity to organizational norms, used autocratic or power-based methods to insure achievement of goals, were basically unreceptive to change, and had information flow downward from higher members in the form of directives.[16]

Restrictive management characterized Bedford Hills' administrative policies until at least until 1982.

The post-Attica Rebellion reforms, as will be shown, did allow both an increase in the number of volunteers who had access to the facility (albeit under the constant surveillance of security personnel), and the creation of a small number of formal prisoner and administrative groups. In 1972 a coordinator of volunteer services was added to the administrative staff.

As in the case of Green Haven, civilian employees tended to be outnumbered by security staff, sometimes by over twice as much (see Table 8). During the period studied, most civilians were employed as kitchen or clerical workers. A small number worked as teachers, chaplains, counselors, parole officers, medical staff, and administrators. The number of Latina(o) civilians working at the facility between 1970 and 1986 was minimal. As late as 1986, only 6.4 percent (i.e., 11) of the 172 civilian staff were Latinas(os) (see Table 8).

During the first half of the 1970s, the custodial staff was changing from a predominantly white female to a predominantly African-American female guard force. By 1978, 69.2 percent of the guards were classified as African-American. At the time, another 15.4 percent were classified as "White," 3.8 percent as "Hispanic," and 11.5 percent as "Others."[17] Until at least 1978, there were only two Latina guards working at the facility.[18] By May 1986, the number of Latina(o) guards had increased to thirty-nine. However, this represented only 12.5 percent of the total guard force of 312 (see Table 8).

In 1978, the guard force was overwhelmingly female (97.7 percent).[19] While 40.4 percent of the guards were between the ages of 31 and 40, another 38.3 percent were over 40 years of age.[20] Almost one-third of the guards had been at the facility for over ten years.[21] The latter phenomenon was primarily due to the fact that until October 1977, women guards were not allowed to work in male facilities.[22] At the beginning of 1977, however, the facility began to undergo a transformation in terms of the sexual composition of its guard force, as male officers were increasingly assigned to work in all areas of the facility. This transformation was accelerated during the 1980s as Bedford Hills, like Green Haven, became a "training facility" for guards. Trainees tended to be young white men from rural upstate areas. The average time they spent training in the facility was between one and two months.[23] By the end of the 1980s, only about 20 percent of the guards assigned to Bedford Hills were experienced; 60 percent tended to have less than one year's experience.[24]

The nature of the duties assigned to guards also underwent a significant transformation during the period studied. Until 1977, the responsibilities assigned guards were determined by their sex. Male guards were assigned to the storehouse, the front gate, to patrol the prison's perimeters, and to work as roundsmen.[25] Because of the nature of these responsibilities they were the only ones who carried weapons. Additionally, until the end of the 1970s, male guards made up the CERT teams responsible for quelling prison disturbances and subduing prisoners presumed to be violent and/or troublesome.[26] Women guards were responsible for monitoring the rest of the institution. Both male and female guards resented the restrictions which accompanied such division of labor. However, because the nature of the work assignments performed by male guards implied that women guards were ill-equipped to handle "high-level" responsibilities, such as physically subduing women prisoners, women guards often complained of discriminatory treatment.

As of February 1977, both male and female officers were assigned to work in all areas of the facility. According to DOCS and Council 82 (the guards' union),[27] this change in policy was supported by Title VII of the 1964 Civil Rights Act (as amended in 1972), which mandated nondiscriminatory work assignments.

Despite a DOCS' 1977 directive stating that only one-third of the guards in any facility could be of the opposite sex,[28] the growth in the number of male guards exacerbated existing tensions between them and the female guard force. Women guards contended that their male peers were continually given preferential treatment in the assignment of posts and positions. Such preferential treatment led the former to file a suit in October 1975, alleging sex discrimination in that, "they had not been allowed to take an examination to qualify as permanent employees."[29] When, through the collective bargaining agreement, male guards were granted the ability to bid for positions in women's institutions on the basis of seniority, women guards found themselves at a further disadvantage. The latter, restricted until 1977 to working in a few women's facilities, now found themselves having to compete for positions at Bedford Hills with their male counterparts. Male guards argued that as heads of households they should be given priority in job assignments, ignoring the fact that women guards, like women prisoners, tended to be single heads of households.[30]

The discrimination experienced by women guards throughout the 1970s, was not only apparent in the nature of their work assignments, but also in the manner in which their behavior, language, and dress were scrutinized by their superiors. Ironically, such close supervision of women staff by prison administrators resembled the type of surveillance to which women prisoners were subjected by staff.

Big Sister is Watching: Encouraging Docility, Femininity, and Domesticity

Overall administrative goals during the 1970-1987 period were similar to those of nineteenth century prison reformers and administrators: to instill femininity, domesticity, and docility in women prisoners.[31] These preoccupations were based on the assumption that women who broke the law did so because they rejected or were unable to fulfill their socially-prescribed roles of obedient wife and mother. In either case, their actions were seen as threatening the very foundation of the family, and as a result, the socio-economic and political order itself. Within this context, the goals of prison reformers and administrators were to help women prisoners accept the traditional gender roles assigned to them. While current prison administrators may recognize even more clearly than those of the past that women who break the law generally do so for economic reasons, in practicality, as will be shown throughout this chapter, the treatment accorded women prisoners is very much still designed to maintain security and socialize women prisoners into socially acceptable gender roles. The concern with these issues meant that women prisoners were often disciplined for behavior deemed acceptable in their male counterparts such as using "profane, vulgar or obscene language," "rough housing,"[32] and talking back to staff.

The responsibility for teaching women prisoners to be good wives and mothers, was left to female staff, particularly guards. The latter were expected to provide "good feminine examples." As a result, particularly during the 1970s, the behavior and dress of guards were strictly monitored by supervisors lest officers look or behave too much like prisoners. The fact that both the overwhelming number of women prisoners and guards were African-American, single heads of households, and tended to come from the same neighborhoods in New York City, made administrators fear the development of familiarity between the two groups. Such familiarity could lead to prisoner disrespect for security personnel and/or guard identification with prisoners. The latter could further result in guards becoming emotionally and/or sexually involved with prisoners.[33] Such relationships could, in turn, lead guards not only to ignore rule violations by preferred prisoners but also to support prisoners' unity efforts and calls for reforms.

The fear of guard/prisoner familiarity was one of the excuses used throughout the 1970s to chastise Latina guards and further penalize Latina prisoners caught speaking in Spanish without authorization. The restriction was also motivated by the fact that the overwhelmingly English-speaking staff was otherwise unable to monitor the actions of Latina guards and prisoners. According to Diana Jiménez, a former Bedford Hills guard:

> A lot of women would try to talk to me in Spanish and that was against the rules. So I was reprimanded a few times . . . on the basis that . . . English was the only language to be spoken there. That it could be considered a form of manipulation. That the inmates [would] be talking to me about how they felt about the non-English speaking personnel or . . . other inmates . . .[34]

In an attempt to prevent the development of guard/prisoner solidarity, administrators continually reminded guards that it was "Them and Us."[35] The proof that guards were, not only different but superior, was the fact that they were the keepers. It was this assumed superiority that entitled guards to act as role models for women prisoners. Guards who attempted to establish amicable relationships with prisoners, despite administrators' warnings, were continually harassed by both peers and superiors.[36]

Ultimately, the development of guard/prisoner solidarity on a massive scale was precluded by the fact that a guard's primary responsibilities were to maintain security, surveillance, and control. Jiménez described her duties as being to:

> . . . keep law and order. To make sure that. . . I knew where every woman was on that ward . . . I had to learn to recognize all of them. . . . If I saw you over there a little while ago and I don't see you anywhere on the unit, then I have to find out where you are. It was just strictly . . . by the book. We were there to control the behavior. We weren't there to socialize with them. We weren't there to be of any . . . support.[37]

A review of the prisoners' weekday scheduled during the late 1970s will give a better idea of just how closely prisoners were monitored by staff.

6:15 A.M.   — Mess Hall workers report to Mess Hall for assignments.

6:25 A.M.	— Population notified to prepare for lock-in standing count.
6:30 A.M.	— Lock-in standing count.
6:45 A.M.	— Sears' [work training program] participants report to Mess Hall. After breakfast, report to Sears' office in 114 lobby.
	— 114 C&D (Honor Floor) and 112 C&D (Network) unlock to prepare for breakfast at 7:15.
	— Stoves turned on from 7:00 to 7:45 A.M. on galleries to boil water only.
7:00 A.M.	— 114 A&B, 112 A&B, 113 building unlock to prepare for breakfast at 7:30 A.M.
7:30 A.M.	— Medication will continue to be dispensed from 7:30 A.M. to 8 A.M. in Satellite Clinic in 113 Lobby . . .
8:15 to 9:15 A.M.	— All doors locked. Inmates have option of remaining in cells or in recreation area.
9:15 to 9:30 A.M.	— Doors unlocked. Inmates may enter their rooms at this time to get what they need and return to the recreation area. Those inmates who are locked in their rooms may come out at this time unless on cell confinement status.
9:30 to 11:15 A.M.	— All doors locked.
11:15 to 12:30 P.M.	— Doors locked.
12:30 to 1:00 P.M.	— Institution Count—doors locked.
1:15 to 2:15 P.M.	— Doors locked.
2:15 to 2:30 P.M.	— Doors unlocked for inmates to have access to personals.
3:30 to 5:30 P.M.	— Doors unlocked.
5:30 to 6:00 P.M.	— Institution Count—doors locked.
6:00 to Count	— Honor Floor exempt from remainder of locking procedure.
6:00 to 6:30 P.M.	— When count cleared, school call-outs let out of their cells. Then school call-outs cleared of unit, all other call-outs.
6:30 to 6:35 P.M.	— Doors open for five (5) minutes, for access to personals.
7:30 to 7:35 P.M.	— Doors open for five (5) minutes, for access to personals.
8:30 to 8:35 P.M.	— Doors open for five (5) minutes, for access to personals.
9:00 to 9:30 P.M.	— Doors open for showers and personal needs.
9:30 to 9:35 P.M.	— Doors open for five (5) minutes for access to personals.[38]

As in the case of male prisoners, the concern with security led penal personnel to subject prisoners' rooms to constant "raids." These raids involved searching prisoners' rooms and belongings and confiscating any items considered dangerous or illegal. The types of contraband most frequently found in women's rooms were: jars (predominantly used to store personal belongings); scissors (to cut hair); knives (for protection); drugs; and food taken from the lunch room.[39] Because these raids could take place at any time of the day or night, both prisoners and guards were kept in a constant state of apprehension.

Constant surveillance served several functions, two of which were to prevent escapes and deter prisoners from engaging in behavior not legally sanctioned by institutional personnel. The latter included a wide range of activities such as drug trafficking, reform-oriented activities, and sexual relationships between prisoners. The prohibition against consensual lesbian relationships among peers was not only the result of heterosexual biases, but was designed to prevent the formation of bonds between prisoners that could lead to their forming alliances to counter the actions of their keepers both at a personal and a political level.[40]

As in the case of male prisoners at Green Haven, a graded system of penalties, coupled with continual surveillance, was intended to create fear in prisoners and instill in them the belief that they were completely powerless to change the conditions of their imprisonment. This process of intimidation began the day a woman entered the facility. It initially entailed isolating incoming prisoners from the general prisoner population for a period of two weeks.[41] During this quarantine period, prisoners were kept in cells resembling those in segregation while they underwent physical examinations and/or psychological evaluations. Prisoners frequently complained that this isolation was meant to illustrate the conditions they would encounter in segregation lock-up if they did not obey prison rules.[42] Once released from quarantine, new prisoners were assigned to "an introductory period (six weeks) of cleaning or 'the mop' intended to instruct new arrivals in institutional control and inducement."[43] This period was later extended to seven weeks.[44]

During the first part of the 1970s, a woman's introduction to the facility also entailed the issuance of color-coded uniforms. New arrivals wore pink and were assigned the least desirable jobs. They were teased and tested by guards and other prisoners to see what their weaknesses were.[45] Continual attempts were made to break down their integrity and test their resistance to institutional rules.

As women prisoners adapted to the facility's rules and regulations, their uniforms were changed from pink to brown, to green, and ultimately to blue. As the colors changed, the harassment lessened. The system of color-coded uniforms symbolized the stages prisoners were intended to go through during their period of socialization into the institution. Because women prisoners were seen as not only having broken the law, but as having violated gender-determined norms, the use of different colored uniforms was intended to serve a dual function: to punish women for their crimes (also understood as gender role transgressions) and to "resocialize" them into behavior acceptable for their sex. As Jiménez explained:

> ... they have to be taught a lesson. They have to be corrected. And the way . . . that you would do that is to start with these uniforms. . . . They took the model . . . of parenting . . . We are the parents, the . . . authority and they are the child. And how do you get a grown woman who has been convicted of any crime, who's going to spend the next ten years in prison, how do you contain that woman? What do you reduce her to? You reduce her to a little helpless kid in order to control her . . . you had to break down her dignity . . . The uniform of pink made you a little girl. And then you gradually start working away from that.[46]

The psychologically intimidating use of such infantalizing control methods as the color-coded uniform system gave a blatantly sexist edge to the domination techniques used by Bedford Hills staff. Although the uniform system was not used during the 1980s, elements of such color coding as a way of indicating differential institutional privileges still remained. For example, prisoners (and visitors) authorized to walk within the facility unescorted were given blue passes, the others, pink passes.

As in the case of male prisoners at Green Haven, women prisoners who broke institutional rules were subject to a series of penalties starting with verbal reprimand and/or "write-ups" by civilian and security personnel. According to Marta Flores, a former guard at Bedford Hills, "It generally starts out with a correction officer, but teachers, secretaries, everybody could write an inmate up for an infraction."[47] Being written up meant that a prisoner's behavior was formally recorded in writing and a penalty for the infraction was prescribed. Rule violations would go in the prisoner's file where they would be seen by the Parole Board when reviewing the prisoner's case for release. Along with the write-up, privileges were also frequently taken away. According to Flores, privileges included, "things which could be taken away through the disciplinary process."[48] These included: particular work assignments; program participation; yard time; television; radio; packages; commissary; and more than one hour's recreation a day. Privileges were differentiated from rights that were granted by New York State Corrections Law 139 and included such things as: visiting; correspondence; food; clothing; shelter; medical care; one hour of recreation a day; limited calls to the outside; at least two showers a week; magazines, books, and newspapers (subject to "Media Review"); and filing grievances within the institution.[49] Additionally, the courts granted prisoners the right to litigate.

According to James G. Fox, during the 1970s, an additional means used by Bedford Hills authorities to discipline prisoners was to appoint those considered "disruptive"[50] to kitchen, laundry, and sewing assignments. Clearly, these were also duties traditionally designated as "women's work." In any event, these assignments were also meant to keep prisoners away from housing areas and other facilities during much of the day. Likewise, Fox argues that the few educational, vocational, and industrial training programs available at the facility at the time, in fact, "primarily served institutional maintenance and control interests."[51] These areas also overwhelmingly fell into the category of traditional women's work.

Prisoners accused of breaking institutional rules and regulations could be further penalized by being placed in keeplock or segregation and/or being transferred out of the institution for indefinite periods of time. During the 1970s, transfers were made to the Matteawan State Hospital for the Criminally Insane. The conditions under which such transfers took place and prisoners' responses to them will be discussed later in the chapter.[52] However, it should be mentioned here that a related way in which institutional personnel sought to regulate prisoners' behavior was through the use of prescription drugs such as tranquilizers. In fact, it was frequently argued by prisoners and their supporters that one of the common ways prison staff sought to control the behavior of women prisoners was by making tranquilizers easily accessible to them.

Perhaps the most physically intimidating method used to control prisoners' behavior was the use of CERT teams. As will be discussed in chapter 11, throughout the 1970s, prisoners who challenged institutional rules and regulations were frequently physically assaulted by CERT teams composed of male guards called in from men's prisons. This was so until Bedford Hills established its own mixed CERT teams.

As shown above, throughout the period studied, prison administrators at Bedford Hills used a combination of psychological and
physical methods designed to control the behavior of prisoners,
enforce traditional gender roles, and hinder the development of solidarity among prisoners and between prisoners and staff. However,
the process of intimidating women prisoners into accepting traditional, subservient gender roles must also be seen in light of the fact
that the overwhelming number of prisoners were of poor and working-class extraction. By examining the types of work assignments and
educational and industrial training programs available to imprisoned
women, one sees that, overall, assignments centered on traditionally
female-dominated, low-paying, low-skilled occupations in the service
sector. Prisoners thus continued to be socialized into behavior deemed
"appropriate" for both their gender and class.

Work, Education, and Industry

Women prisoners frequently pointed out that male prisoners had
access to a greater number of vocational and industrial programs that
allowed them to leave prison with marketable skills.[53] Academic
courses offered at Bedford Hills during the 1970s included high school
equivalency, English, typing, Black Studies, and a basic bilingual program for women working toward their high school equivalency.
Throughout the 1970s, prisoners who requested the implementation
of college programs such as those available at Green Haven as of the
early 1970s, were told by prison administrators and school personnel
that there were not enough prisoners who were college eligible. In
spite of this, Latina, African-American, and white prisoners were
able, with the help of Mercy Sanders, the staff person for the South
Forty Corporation[54] at the institution, to mobilize outside support
that allowed prisoners to earn college credit through the New York
State Regents External Degree Program. In 1978, partly as a result
of these efforts and partly as a result of a change in educational personnel at Bedford Hills, DOCS allowed Mercy College to institute a
college program at the prison.[55] However, as of 1987, there were still
no bilingual education programs beyond the high school level available to non-English speaking prisoners. During the 1980s, academic
training included: Adult Basic Education-Reading/Math; General
Equivalency Diploma, Title 1 (limited to under 21); English-as-a-
Second Language (ESL); Pre-College; and College. Other courses
taught included: Music; Physical Education; Arts and Crafts; and
Handicrafts.[56]

Vocational courses offered during the 1970s included IBM data processing and cosmetology. During the 1980s, vocational programs expanded to include: general business education; data processing/ computer programming; electronics; building maintenance; cosmetology; commercial art; food service; and printing. From time to time, attempts were made to introduce training in non-traditional jobs for women but these programs generally did not last long as a result of staff resistance to them, loss of interest on the part of prisoners, and/or the inability to place prisoners in these work areas upon release from prison.[57] Moreover, such programs tended to compete for support with similar ones established at male institutions.

Job assignments at Bedford Hills included the laundry room, waitressing, maintenance work, working as a clerk for staff, and sewing. Sewing assignments, performed on outdated equipment, were of two types: the needle trade section that made clothing for prisoners and the industry section, that made clothes for outside institutions. During the late 1970s, the "incentive wage" given to prisoners who had work "assignments" started at 45 cents per day. Those prisoners housed in reception prior to being classified received 35 cents per day.[58]

Throughout the period studied, many Latinas were unable to participate in educational programs because, according to former Latina prisoner leader Tita Puente, ". . . if the person was able to speak it [English] but they weren't able to read, they couldn't follow the text. No efforts were made to get the text in Spanish."[59] Latina prisoners were further handicapped by the fact that vocational programs generally required an eighth grade English reading level to participate.[60] Latinas who did not understand English were frequently assigned jobs where little verbal communication was needed, such as maintenance work or the laundry room.[61] Those who did not speak English were sometimes able to participate in certain work assignments and courses if there was another Spanish-speaking prisoner available to train her. According to Puente, the few successes that educational personnel had with non-English speaking Latinas, ". . . came about as a movement organized by the Hispanic Committee . . . you know, a person showed high motivation participating in something and we would coordinate them with a . . . Latino peer in that classroom who would translate the information for them . . ."[62]

Women prisoners were also discriminated against in the provision of work release programs. Work release programs allowed soon-to-be-released prisoners to work outside the prison during the day.

However, although such programs existed throughout the state, rarely were they open to women. Furthermore, a *New York Times* article indicated that even in Nassau County Correctional Facility[63] where women had been allowed to participate in a work release program, some of the criteria used to determine eligibility specifically discriminated against them. For example, "Because the county required that they take an experimental drug antagonist, Naltrexone, and birth control devices for which the state refuses to pay, none of these Nassau women, upstate can be eligible."[64]

During the first half of the 1970s, Bedford Hills experimented with work release and study release programs. However, as a result of bureaucratic red tape and security concerns, very few prisoners were allowed to participate in them.[65] In spite of the fact that during the 1970s the institution was the only women's prison in the state, in 1978 it had no work release program. This led prisoners to file a class action suit in October of that year charging, according to a *New York Times* article, that "the Department of Corrections had failed to provide community-based work release programs for women like those provided for men."[66] While women prisoners also had the legal right to participate in a variety of other types of release programs, such as Temporary Release,[67] these were not made accessible to prisoners at Bedford Hills during the 1970s.[68]

In summary, the lack of adequate educational and work programs meant that women prisoners were not only being resocialized into accepting traditional gender roles and traditional women's work, but also traditional low-paying, low-status jobs. This was so despite the fact that, upon their release, the overwhelming majority of prisoners was expected to continue fulfilling their pre-prison responsibilities as single heads of households. Latinas suffered additional discriminatory treatment due to staff biases, the lack of bilingual programs and staff, and the fact that until at least 1978 Latinas were severely penalized for speaking in Spanish.[69] The lack of adequate educational, vocational, and work programs was complemented by the lack of adequate medical, mental health, and dental services.

Who Needs Medical Care Anyway?

During the 1970s, it could take as long as a week to see a doctor. Nurses were separated from prisoners by a barred window; saving DOCS a pay differential nurses received for direct physical contact with prisoners. Prisoners were often given inappropriate medication by nurses not authorized to dispense them. Medication prescribed prior to incarceration was frequently terminated and not replaced, depriving prisoners of necessary medicine such as insulin, for long periods of time.

In numerous cases, prisoners were diagnosed with serious medical problems and/or lab tests were conducted, but proper medical follow-up was not provided. At times, this resulted in severe damage to prisoners' health. Many prisoners were also subjected to unnecessary gynecological examinations by a doctor who was not a gynecologist.[70] Moreover, prisoners who were seriously ill were frequently left unattended in an infirmary which had no lights or call bell. The cells in the sick wing lacked toilet facilities.

There were also occasions when the hospital area was used to house prisoners labelled "incorrigible." Once there, prisoners could be subjected to further abuse. According to former prisoner leader Luz Santana:

> . . . the general Hospital area was used as Observation Units for what was then termed as "incorrigible." In actuality, it was for women who would not submit to the atrocities that surrounded them. Stripped bare of clothing, furnishings, and pride, these women were checked every hour on the hour, occasionally a cigarette was given to the inmate, which she had to smoke in the presence of the officer. It was there that I witnessed my first death at Bedford Hills. In the middle of the night, after days of dealing with the cold of winter and the torment of futility, an inmate was found hanging from a blanket in a cell, her name was Billy Jean. I still own some of her poetry, and to this day, I cannot understand how she managed to receive the blanket, since we were not allowed anything but a paper gown and paper sheets, nor have I ever understood how she managed to tie the blanket up in an absolutely bare cell.[71]

In view of the conditions described above, in 1975 a group of Latina, African-American, and white prisoners asked the New York City Legal Aid Society Prisoners' Rights Project to file a class action suit to redress medical conditions at the facility.[72] The support among prisoners for *Todaro v. Ward*, 74 Civ. 4581, 431 F. Supp. 1129 (1977) was evidenced by the fact that at least 64 of the 380 women imprisoned at the time gave medical releases to allow their records to be used by prisoners' attorneys. Others testified about medical conditions at the facility in the court hearings held from January 12 through February 1976. In 1977, the District Court found that:

. . . the medical system was unconstitutionally defective in relying on a dangerous x-ray machine, in denying or substantially delaying access to primary care physicians as a result of lobby clinic procedures for screening and record keeping, in failing to provide adequate communication with patients in sick wing, and in failing to provide adequate follow-up laboratory services and medical appointments.[73]

. . . the Court has found that the laboratory technician is not informed of test orders, lab results are not brought to a physician's attention, inmates are not informed of laboratory tests, test results, or physician appointments, and physician appointments are either not scheduled or scheduled at times which conflict with inmate commitments. These failures in turn result in inefficient use of physician staff and failure to comply with physician orders.[74]

The court decision instructed DOCS authorities and prisoners' attorneys to meet within forty days and report on what steps were being taken to ensure compliance with the court order.[75] Nevertheless, despite widespread evidence of negligence on the part of medical personnel, the District Court avoided the issue of malpractice.[76]

On October 31, 1977, the state's appeal, *Todaro v. Ward*, 565 F.2d 48 (1977), was also decided on behalf of prisoners. As a result, the Court of Appeals continued to support temporary court monitoring of medical services at the facility. Interestingly, the court's decision to interfere in penal affairs was based on the belief that it did not have to defer to prison officials on the matter of the administration of medical care since issues of prison discipline and security were not at stake.

Despite the *Todaro v. Ward* decision, Latinas continued to be affected by discriminatory treatment. Although, as a result of the original decision, prisoners who were bilingual were authorized to act as translators during medical discussions, the medical staff frequently did not allow translators to be present. This was so despite the fact that as of November 1985 there were still no bilingual medical personnel employed at the facility. According to Luz Santana, the lack of adequate medical care and the lack of bilingual personnel produced a situation in which at least 50 percent of the prisoners who died at Bedford Hills for medical reasons between 1977 and 1985 were Latinas.[77]

As shown in this chapter, the lack of bilingual personnel in the area of medical services was complemented by the lack of bilingual personnel, programs, and services throughout the facility. This created a situation in which many Latinas prisoners were unable to receive even the basic, though inadequate, care and services provided to their African-American and white peers. Within this setting, Latina prisoners suffered further discriminatory treatment as a result of institutional policies which prohibited them to speak in Spanish.

It was within the context of the foregoing conditions that Latina prisoners created informal and formal prisoner groups and networks to pursue individual and collective goals that would allow them greater control over the conditions of their imprisonment. It is the nature of these groups, their goals, and the tactics and strategies they employed that will be addressed in the following chapter.

Notes: Chapter 9

1. See Erika Anne Kates, "Litigation As a Means of Achieving Social Change: A Case Study of Women in Prison," (Ph.d. diss., Brandeis University, 1984).

2. Kates challenges feminist criminologists to redefine what activism means using women as a frame of reference for themselves. That is, she urges them to, "undertake research which takes into account problems of women *defined in women's terms*, (underlined in original) especially since the ways in which women define power appear to differ from those of men . . ." (Ibid., 154–155). Moveover, "The ways in which women solve moral dilemmas may also differ from men. The relative creativeness in problem-solving of women may not so much resemble indecisiveness, or lack of logical thinking, but rather a desire to reconcile different, but equally important values . . ." (Ibid., 156).

3. A DOCS survey carried out on December 31, 1985, showed that over two-thirds (77.4 percent) of all Latinas were mothers, many of them single heads of households prior to their imprisonment (New York State Department of Correctional Services [hereafter cited as NYSDOCS], Division of Hispanic and Cultural Affairs, Hispanic Inmate Needs Task Force, *Final Report, "A Meeting of Minds, An Encounter of Hearts" 1986 (Action Plan)*, Albany, 1986, 157).

4. According to Kates, between 1970 and 1980, women prisoners across the country became increasingly interested in their legal rights (Kates, "Litigation As a Means," 1984). Women's legal activism was evident in a number of ways. More women engaged in litigation, made use of prison law libraries, filed formal grievance procedures, and wrote petitions and complaint letters to penal and other state elites. There was also an increase in the number of women asking for legal advice as well as in the number of jailhouse lawyers. For a more detailed discussion of legal activism among women

prisoners as well as the institutional and structural barriers hindering their litigation efforts, see Anna Aylward and Jim Thomas, "Quiescence in Women's Prison Litigation: Some Exploratory Issues," *Justice Quarterly* 1, No. 1 (March 1984) 253–276; Kates, "Litigation As a Means," 1984; and Idella Serna, *Locked Down: A Woman's Life in Prison, The Story of Mary (Lee) Dortch* (Norwich, Vt.: New Victoria Publishers, 1992).

5. For a discussion of rebellions at women's penal institutions during the early 1970s see Phyllis Jo Baunach and Thomas Murton, "Women in Prison: An Awakening Minority," *Crime and Corrections* (Fall 1973): 4–12; Joyce Ann Brown with Jay Gaines, *Joyce Ann Brown: Justice Denied* (Chicago: The Noble Press, Inc., 1990); Kathryn Watterson Burkhart, *Women in Prison* (New York: Doubleday, 1973); Jean Harris, *They Always Call Us Ladies: Stories from Prison* (New York: McMillan Publishing Co., 1988); *Midnight Special: Prisoners' News* (New York): *New York Times* (hereafter cited as *N.Y. Times*), 14 January 1973; Idem, 28 June 1973; Idem, 7, 20 June 1975; *No More Cages: A Bi-Monthly Women's Prison Newsletter* (New York); and Assata Shakur, *Assata: An Autobiography* (Westport: Lawrence Hill and Co., 1987).

6. For an early history of the evolution of Bedford Hills see Estelle Freedman, *Their Sisters' Keepers: Women's Prison Reform in America, 1830–1930* (Ann Arbor: University of Michigan Press, 1981); and Nicole Hahn Rafter, *Partial Justice: Women in State Prisons, 1800–1935* (Boston: Northeastern University Press, 1985).

7. *Todaro v. Ward*, 431 F.Supp. 1129 (1977).

8. Ibid.

9. Milena Jovanovitch, "Concern on Prison Expansion," *N.Y. Times*, 4 May 1986, XXII, 8.

10. On December 31, 1985, 46.4 percent of the Latinas, 12. 5 percent of the African-American, and 18.4 percent of the white prisoners in New York State were being held for drug-related offenses (NYSDOCS, Division of Hispanic and Cultural Affairs, Hispanic Inmate Needs Task Force, *Final Report*, 158). While the observations made in this paragraph are inclusive of other women's facilities in addition to Bedford Hills, they are representative of the general trend in Bedford Hills commitments.

11. Such laws included the Rockefeller Drug Laws (1973), the Second Felony Offender Law (1973), the Violent Felony Offender Law (1978), and changes in Consecutive Sentence Provisions (1978). For a discussion of the impact of these laws on the women's prison population in New York State, see NYSDOCS, Division of Program Planning, Research and Evaluation, *Characteristics of Female Inmates Held Under Custody, 1975–1985*, by Kathy Canestrini, September 1986.

12. DOCS figures before 1983 were kept only for Latinas(os) of Puerto Rican birth or parentage.

13. While the percent of increase in the number of Latinos at Green Haven was offset basically by a decrease in the white male population, the increase in the Latina prisoner population at Bedford Hills was offset by a decrease in the African-American prisoner population (see Table 10).

14. Janice Warne had been the warden of Albion Correctional Facility from 1968 to 1970. During the period covered by this research, Bedford Hills had at least six superintendents. Top administrators, with the exception of the first two coordinators of volunteer services, tended to have prior experience working either for DOCS and/or parole before being assigned to Bedford Hills.

15. James G. Fox, *Organizational and Racial Conflict in Maximum Security Prisons* (Lexington, Mass.: D.C. Heath and Co., 1982).

16. Ibid., 24.

17. Ibid., 38.

18. Ibid.

19. Ibid.

20. Ibid.

21. Ibid., 39.

22. "Woman Guard Attacked by Inmate in Attica," *N.Y. Times*, 30 March 1977, 22.

23. Elaine Lord, interview with author, Bedford Hills, N.Y., 7 March 1989.

24. Ibid.

25. Roundsmen served as messengers for watch commanders.

26. For other examples of how male guards have been used to repress women prisoners, see "Women Prisoners Sue on 'Beatings'," *N.Y. Times*, 28 June 1973, 18; and "Officers Charge Women Inmates Staging North Carolina Protest," *N.Y. Times*, 20 June 1975, 32).

27. Security Unit Employees Council 82, American Federation of State, County and Municipal Employees, AFL-CIO ("Council 82").

28. "New York Prisons Curb 'Opposite Sex' Guards," *N.Y. Times*, 22 May 1977, 43.

29. Lena Williams, "New Prison Warden Bars the Old Stereotype," *N.Y. Times*, 28 May 1978, XXII, 2.

30. Fox, *Organizational and Racial Conflict*, 66. Interestingly, the resentment of women guards to the presence of male guards in women's facilities was less than the resentment felt by male guards toward women guards assigned to work in male facilities.

31. According to Estelle Freedman, women prison reformers argued that these goals would be best accomplished by the women staff and administrators responsible for overseeing the running of the newly created separate facilities for women offenders. For a more detailed discussion of these issues, see Freedman, *Their Sisters' Keepers*, 1981.

32. See NYSDOCS, Bedford Hills Correctional Facility, *Inmate Orientation Book*.

33. Such relationships between women prisoners and guards did, of course, take place throughout the period studied.

34. Diana Jiménez [pseud.], interview with author, New York, N.Y., 12 December 1988.

35. Ibid. In his essay, "Characteristics of Total Institutions," Erving Goffman described this "split" between supervisory staff and inmates in which, "Each grouping tends to conceive of the other in terms of narrow hostile stereotypes, staff often seeing inmates as bitter, secretive and untrustworthy, while inmates often see staff as condescending, highhanded, and mean. Staff tends to feel superior and righteous; inmates tend in some ways at least, to feel inferior, weak, blame-worthy, and guilty" (Erving Goffman, *Asylums* [Garden City: Doubleday, 1961], 7). While some prisoners and guards at Bedford Hills were able to transcend the stereotypes described above, Goffman's description tends to provide an accurate picture of the overall attitudes of guards and prisoners toward one another at Bedford Hills during the period studied.

36. Such attempts to prevent the development of prisoner/guard solidarity were also observed by Elouise Junius Spencer in her study of a midwest women's prison. Guards deemed to identify with prisoners, particularly African-Americans, were subject to a series of reprisals including, among others: discriminatory work and shift assignments; denial of promotion; demotion; and being accused of wrongdoing, including having lesbian relationships with prisoners (Elouise Junius Spencer, "The Social System of a Medium Security Women's Prison," [Ph.D. diss., University of Kansas, 1977]).

37. Jiménez, interview with author, 1988.

38. NYSDOCS, Bedford Hills Correctional Facility, *Inmate Orientation Book*.

39. Jiménez, interview with author, 1988.

40. Spencer's study found that authorities used a number of additional means to prevent the development of intra-prisoner solidarity. These included, among others: interpreting non-racial incidents as racial; giving white prisoners preferential treatment in work and housing assignments; prohibiting African-American prisoners from forming groups based on racial identification; and granting prisoner leaders special privileges (Spencer, "The

Social System," 1977). The discriminatory treatment given African-American prisoners was also replicated in the case of African-American staff.

41. Goffman calls this process of initiation "the welcome" (Goffman, *Asylums,* 18).

42. New York, Advisory Committee Report, *Visit to Bedford Hills Correctional Facility,* March 12–13, 1972.

43. James G. Fox, "Women's Prison Policy, Prisoner Activism, and the Impact of the Contemporary Feminist Movement: A Case Study," *The Prison Journal* 64 (March 1984): 25.

44. NYSDOCS, Bedford Hills Correctional Facility, *Inmate Orientation Book.*

45. Jiménez, interview with author, 1988.

46. Ibid.

47. Marta Flores [pseud.], interview with author, Albany, N.Y., 18 March 1989.

48. Ibid.

49. Ibid.

50. Fox, "Women's Prison Policy," 25.

51. Ibid.

52. See Two Sisters, Bedford Hills, "Dear Sir," *Midnight Special* 4, No. 8 (October/November 1974): 1; "Carol Crooks," *Midnight Special* 4, No. 8 (October/November 1974): 22; "cheaper than chimps," *Midnight Special* 5, No. 3 (May 1975): 10; and "Inquiry Pressed on Tranquilizers at Bedford Hills Women's Prison," *N.Y. Times,* 21 November 1976, 58.

53. In 1976, male prisoners at Green Haven had access to eleven vocational courses, including printing, drafting, welding, motorcycle repair, electronics, building maintenance, carpentry, and major appliances. Industrial training included a knit shop, an upholstery shop, a furniture shop, and an optical shop (Susan Sheehan, *A Prison and a Prisoner* [Boston: Houghton Mifflin Co., 1978], 25, 122–125.) However, as indicated in chapter 4, the access of Latino prisoners to such vocational training was limited by the fact that the courses were offered in English and that non-Latino prisoners were often given preference in job assignments.

54. In April 1981, South Forty offered "workshops in art and creative writing; a biology class taught through the State University of New York at New Paltz and college correspondence courses" (Lynne Ames, "Mrs. Harris Begins As Prison Teacher's Aide," *N.Y. Times,* 12 April 1981, XXII, 1).

55. During the late 1970s, the degrees offered were a, "One year Certificate in Personnel Administration, Mental Health and Family Development. An Associate Degree in Science or Arts, and a Bachelor's Degree in

Behavioral Science" (NYSDOCS, Bedford Hills Correctional Facility, *Inmate Orientation Book*.

56. Bedford Hills Correctional Facility, Coordinator of Volunteer Services, *Bedford Hills Correctional Facility Tour Brochure*, 1989. See also Liana MacKinnon, "Prison Offers Women Industrial Skills," *N.Y. Times*, 13 April 1980, XXII, 13.

57. For example, in 1976, Sears, Roebuck and Co., began an automobile repair program at Bedford Hills where women prisoners were taught to service and repair cars. In 1980, there were only twelve women in the program (Lena Williams, "New Prison Warden Bars the Old Stereotype," *N.Y. Times*, 28 May 1978, XXII, 2).

58. NYSDOCS, Bedford Hills Correctional Facility, *Inmate Orientation Book*.

59. Tita Puente [pseud.], interview with author, Bronx, N.Y., 21 March 1989.

60. Mirna González [pseud.], interview with author, New York, N.Y., 22 March 1989.

61. Mercy Sanders [pseud.], interview with author, Boston, Mass., 1 February 1990.

62. Puente, interview with author, 1989.

63. Between 1969 and November 1976 only 5 of the 570 prisoners served by the work release program had been women at Nassau Community Correctional Facility. The justification given for this was that "there are not enough women with vocational skills to warrant providing a staff" (Ellen O'Meara, "In the Slammer, It's Still a Man's World," *N.Y. Times*, 14 November 1976, XXI, 24). On November 1976, there were 30 women and 500 men being held at the Nassau County facility. The discrimination women prisoners experienced at the Nassau facility went beyond being denied access to work release programs. According to Ellen O'Meara, "Programs depend on the availability of space—and for women, space isn't available. While the men exercise in the gym and a regular recreation yard, the women are relegated to the roof in the summer, and in the winter there are no facilities at all. The women's vocational programming consists of sewing with obsolete machines and working in the kitchen or laundry—even though they already know how to sew, cook, and clean . . ." (Ibid.).

64. Ibid.

65. One of the reasons why few women participated in work release and study release programs was because participants had to be unanimously approved by a committee of seven persons. The committee's decision could be vetoed by the warden.

66. Lena Williams, "New Prison Warden Bars the Old Stereotype," *N.Y. Times*, 28 May 1978, XXII, 2.

67. According to DOCS Directive #7001, Temporary Release programs during the late 1970s, allowed prisoners to be furloughed to the community for up to seven days. Prisoners had to be within one year of release.

68. González, interview with author, 1989.

69. Harris, *They Always Call Us Ladies*, 1988.

70. See *Todaro v. Ward*, No. 74 Civ. 4581, 431 F. Supp. 1129 (1977), 565 F. 2d 48 (1977).

71. Luz Santana, "Address Before the Hispanic Inmate Needs Task Force," Hispanic Inmate Needs Task Force Awards Banquet, Albany, N.Y., November 20, 1985 (xeroxed copy).

72. At the time of the trial there were, "eight nurses, the nurse administrator, one full-time physician, one part-time gynecologist, a laboratory technician, a part-time pharmacist, and a part-time x-ray technician" responsible for providing services to 380 prisoners" (*Todaro v. Ward*, 431 F. Supp. 1129 [1977]).

73. Ibid.

74. Ibid.

75. Defendants and plaintiffs were instructed by the court to report on procedures for, "1. Providing better access to medical providers by inmates in sick wing; 2. Conducting sick call which provides adequate nurse screening and reasonably prompt access to a physician; 3. Insuring that ordered laboratory work is reported and followed-up and medical reappointments are scheduled; 4. Periodic self-audits of the performance of the medical care delivery system, and record keeping procedures conducive to such audits" (Ibid.).

76. The District Court's decision stated that, "It is important to note at this juncture that the Court has made its findings of fact solely with reference to the constitutional standards. Whether the treatment provided these women would constitute malpractice is not before the court." (Ibid.)

77. Luz Santana, "Address Before the Hispanic Inmate Needs Task Force," 1985.

10

Latina Participation in Informal Groups and Networks and the Formation of Formal Prisoner Groups

Latinas at Bedford Hills created formal and informal prisoner groups for the same reasons Latino prisoners did so at Green Haven. They sought to reform prison conditions, protect themselves from other prisoners and staff members, secure emotional, social, cultural, and economic support, and increase their access to family members. They also strove to: mobilize the support of third parties, penal personnel, and non-Latina prisoners for both Latina-oriented and general prisoner concerns; obtain equal access to rehabilitation programs through the hiring of bilingual personnel and the implementation of bilingual programs; and increase their chances of leaving the institution as well as reduce their chances of returning to the facility. The major differences between Latina and Latino prisoners lay in how diverse concerns were prioritized at any given point in time and the tactics and strategies pursued. As in the case of their male counterparts, the activities of informal and formal Latina prisoner groups tended to overlap and encompass actions that were both sanctioned and proscribed by prison authorities.

Other considerations which affected the manner in which Latina and Latino prisoners framed their concerns were the differences in the treatment accorded male and female prisoners by penal personnel, the type of penal and third party support available to male and female prisoners, and prisoners' experiences prior to incarceration.

Informal Latina Prisoner Groups and Networks

Women prisoners generally formed informal groups based on housing assignments, race and ethnicity, homegirl networks, social and recreational activities, prison family/ kinship networks, and political underground reform-oriented activities.[1] (This will be discussed in subsequent chapters). Latinas further subdivided according to nationality and language spoken.

295

The main functions of groups formed by women who lived in the same housing unit were to provide protection, share resources, and reduce the isolation of their members by furnishing various types of support. Each housing unit had a recreation room where prisoners played board games, danced, and listened to the radio. Movies were offered in a separate building. There was a gym where basketball and handball were played. The range of recreational sports activities around which Latinas formed groups was much more limited than in the case of Latino prisoners. The main reasons for this were that most women prisoners were either not interested in the types of sports male prisoners were or, more importantly, they were not allowed to play "male" sports by prison personnel. As a result, women prisoners were not provided the same sports equipment and facilities as their male counterparts.[2]

Racial and Ethnic Cleavages

Much of the day-to-day group socializing took place in the housing units, the yard, and the dining room. It was in these areas that divisions based on race and ethnicity were most apparent. According to former prison guard Diana Jiménez: ". . . the women would . . . split up into their own little communities and networks. The Hispanic women stuck together in one section. The Black women in another section. The white women in another . . . section. The only time that they mingled together was either at recreation or in the dining hall . . ."[3]

While it was not uncommon for prisoners to have interracial/ interethnic personal and sexual relationships, divisions based on race and ethnicity were entrenched enough to make the formation of coalitions among large numbers of prisoners difficult. During the 1970s, intra-prisoner attempts at unity were additionally hindered by the frequent verbal and physical confrontations that took place between Latina and African-American prisoners. According to both prisoners and third parties, prison authorities were aware of these confrontations and did nothing to discourage them because such conflicts made it more difficult for prisoners to jointly challenge institutional authority.[4]

Ironically, the racism of some Latina prisoners coupled with racial polarization within and outside the prison led a small number of Latinas to subdivide along color lines. As Paloma Román, a former Latina prisoner at Bedford Hills explained, "Black Latinas usually end up with the Black community. . . . They feel more at ease with their own color."[5]

Latina prisoners further subdivided according to nationality, class, and language spoken. During the 1970s, the overwhelming majority of the Latina prisoner population was comprised of poor and working-class Puerto Rican women. However, by the early 1980s, a significant number of Latina immigrants from Colombia, the Dominican Republic, and Cuba began to enter the facility. This influx led to the deepening of cleavages along nationality and class lines. Dominican and Puerto Rican prisoners tended to intermingle because of their similar cultural, racial, and economic backgrounds. South American prisoners, primarily Colombian, tended to form their own subgroups. Colombian prisoners, particularly those who entered the facility during the 1980s, were seen by Puerto Rican and Dominican prisoners as being "stuck up" and "middle-class," due to the higher standard of living they were perceived to have gained through their involvement in larger scale drug-related enterprises.

Cuban prisoners who had arrived in the United States after April 1980 as a result of the "Mariel Boatlift" also formed a distinct subgroup primarily due to their common experience as refugees and former citizens of a communist government. The latter prisoners were the most isolated of the Latina prisoner population. They tended to be perceived as being too "pushy," "critical," and/or "radical" by other prisoners. Despite these cleavages, however, Latina prisoners unlike Latinos at Green Haven, did not go so far as to form nationality-based committees to pursue special interests. Language differences further led Latinas who were Spanish-monolingual to associate with one another most often. Those who were English dominant, for the most part Puerto Ricans, formed their own subgroups.

Despite such cleavages among the Latina prisoner population, the support Latinas offered one another was apparent in several ways. Latinas were generally willing to support their peers whenever they were physically threatened by non-Latina prisoners. Moreover, despite prison regulations throughout the 1970s which prohibited prisoners from speaking in Spanish unless authorized by a staff member, Latina prisoners frequently taught one another how to read and/or write in Spanish and/or English. Latinas who were English-dominant also helped their Spanish-monolingual peers with the translation of significant documents (e.g., misbehavior reports, letters). Such support, particularly during the 1970s, was given in the yards, the housing units, and the recreation areas. Furthermore, Latina prisoners who were bilingual were frequently asked by staff members to translate for their non-English-speaking peers.

Two additonal ways in which prisoners subdivided to support one another were homegirl networks and prison family/kinship networks.

Latina homegirl networks were generally comprised of prisoners who had lived in the same neighborhoods in New York City. As such, it was not unusual for these groups to include African-American and white prisoners. Other homegirl networks were comprised of prisoners whose family came from the same towns in Puerto Rico or from the same Latin American country.

Prison Family/Kinship Networks

One of the ways in which Latina (and non-Latina) prisoners supported one another was through the creation of prison family/kinship networks.[6] Prison family/kinship networks involved the formation of relationships in which prisoners adopted the roles of husband, wife, mother, father, sister, brother, etc. They included heterosexual, bisexual, and lesbian-identified prisoners. They encompassed anywhere from two women to an extended family unit. In many ways, prison family/kinship networks recreated the dynamics of heterosexual families.

Latina prisoners, like their African-American and white counterparts, formed family groups to provide the same economic, social, cultural, emotional, and sexual services families were designed to provide on the outside. For example, prison mothers were expected to give their daughters advice when they had a problem. Fathers, other male relatives, and sometimes mothers, were expected to provide protection from other prisoners. Companionship, and sometimes sex, were other benefits obtained from such ties. Individual goods and services were frequently shared, thus guaranteeing that those with less financial and material resources were provided for. Moreover, individual members frequently passed on their contacts and "opened doors" to family members within the prisoner and institutional structure. Prison families also helped new prisoners become acquainted with institutional rules and regulations as well as a number of prisoner codes.[7] Thus, the primary function of prison family/kinship networks was to provide stable groups on which prisoners could depend while incarcerated.

An additional motivation for becoming part of a prison family/kinship network was the fact that such affiliations reduced prisoners' chances of being economically exploited and/or physically victimized by other prisoners. Clara Toro, formerly imprisoned at Bedford Hills, described some of the ways in which prisoners who were alone and not able to take care of themselves were exploited by peers. "Say you go in there with jewelry . . . if I wanted to take it from you and you let me take it from you, you'd be mine. I could make you do anything for me. I could make you wash my underwear, wash my clothes, do this, do that. You'd be my gofer . . . I could sell you, prostitute you off or sell you to somebody else."[8]

To avoid being taken advantage of Toro argued, ". . . either she has to fight it out or . . . her aggressive attitude has to be strong enough where she's not going to be put in that position where she can be taken advantage of."[9] Thus, one of the motivations that led prisoners to adopt an "aggressive" or "masculine" role was to protect themselves from other prisoners or at least give the impression that they could take care of themselves physically. As a result, it was not uncommon for prisoners who identified as heterosexual on the outside to adopt "male" roles in prison. Lesbian-identified prisoners called these women "flippers" because they frequently reverted back to traditionally prescribed "feminine" gender roles on their release and/or whenever their boyfriends or husbands visited them in prison. According to Clara Toro, other prisoners adopted masculine roles because, "A lot of it is from loneliness, too, but the only way they know that they're going to get over and not be hit on and be in control is if they play the aggressive role."[10]

While prison family/kinship networks were designed to protect prisoners from exploitation, some aspects of the families themselves could be deemed exploitative because they reproduced subordinate gender roles. These were evident in relationships in which prisoners who adopted the "male" role provided sexual services and/or protection for one or more prisoners in exchange for services and privileges traditionally accorded men on the outside (e.g., cooking, cleaning, laundry, drugs).

When asked how Latina prisoners choose family members, Paloma Román, explained, ". . . when somebody does something extraordinary for you or you've become emotionally connected in one way or another. Nothing stupendous has to happen. It's just an attraction that automatically formulates."[11] Interestingly, this description of how Latina prisoners pick their family members is similar to Piri Thomas' description of how Latino prisoners form prison "cliques."[12] When asked what a prisoner would do if another prisoner cast her in a role she did not feel comfortable in, such as that of mother, Román stated, "Then I would tell you, 'You're not fit to be my mother. You're fit to be my sister, so I will call you, 'Sis'."[13] However, once a prisoner had been chosen by another to play a role within a particular family it was difficult for the one chosen to reject the role because it would mean that, "Then you can't fit in with my other people that surround me."[14] The implication being that one took the chance of alienating oneself, not only from an individual, but from a group of prisoners one might need support from in the future.

While family kinship networks tended to form along ethnic/racial lines, there were times when Latina family groups included white and African-American prisoners.[15] Family members might live in the same housing unit or in different areas of the facility. Various families were often interrelated by overlapping relatives. Family groups with no relatives in common were frequently referred to as "neighbors."[16]

Although staff members generally frowned on prison families, they were aware of their existence. This was so because prisoners frequently tended to be open about their participation in such groups. In this manner, they consciously challenged institutional regulations condemning such types of relationships. There were also times when staff members became aware of such ties after a verbal and/or physical confrontation had taken place by women involved in such relationships (e.g., lover's quarrels). According to James G. Fox at Bedford Hills, "The kinship system had informal recognition (and acceptance) from correctional officers for a substantial period of time—dating back to the early years of the institution."[17] Such acceptance was shown by the fact that, ". . . many correctional officers would elect to approach the maternal head of the respective "family" and request that the "mother" counsel her "daughter" out of disruptive behavior, thus avoiding direct confrontations and the imposition of formal sanctions and controls."[18]

While prison staff opposed to kinship networks could do little to eliminate them, prisoners who were caught engaging in sexual relationships with one another ran the risk of being subjected to further punishment, depending on the personal beliefs of the staff member and the nature of the sexual activity they were caught performing. That is, two women caught kissing would be penalized less severely than two women who were caught engaging in a more intimate sexual act. Moreover, not all members of prison families ran the same risk of being punished. For example, a relationship between a "mother" and a "son" might be frowned upon by staff but might not be penalized as a rule infraction, while one between a "mother" and a "father" might be, because it frequently involved physical contact between women.

According to Fox, overall prisoner involvement in prison family groups at Bedford Hills decreased as the 1970s wore on. Fox found that while two-thirds of the prisoners in 1972–1974 reported being involved in such relationships, by 1977–1978, the number had decreased to one-fourth.[19] According to former prisoner Jean Harris, by the end of the 1980s, these relationships were even less common.[20] However, she commented that Puerto Rican prisoners relied on them more heavily than either their African-American or white peers. It is unclear whether

Harris is using the term Puerto Rican to encompass all Latinas. In any case, it appears that the number of prison family/kinship networks decreased as the number of formal prisoner and administrative groups increased. One could thus speculate that the participation of prisoners in the informal networks decreased as formal prisoner and administrative groups began to fulfill some of the functions of prison family groups. The fact that prisoners could now address some of their concerns in organizations that were sanctioned by penal authorities meant that they did not have to risk penalties imposed for participation in prison familie/kinship networks. An additional factor contributing to the decrease in women's participation in prison family groups and networks could have been prisoners' increasing access to family, friends, and outside volunteers, as a result of changes in visiting policies after the post-Attica Rebellion reforms began to take effect. Yet a third explanation for the decrease in prison families could be the impact of the women's rights movement with its questioning of gender roles and the subordination of women to others. It is possible, of course, that all three influences made themselves felt at the same time.

In any event, the importance of Latina family groups for the purpose of the current research is that they at times facilitated the reform-oriented activities of group members. This assertion contradicts the contentions of social scientists such as Rose Giallombardo who argued that:

> . . . by forming exclusive family groups and by relating all meaningful interaction and functions to those inmates who are linked by kinship bonds, the Alderson inmates have in effect created a social structure which deters the possibility of a leadership emerging that could unite the many prison families. Causes which would require a united inmate body are not likely to meet with success in the Alderson inmate community. Paradoxically, the kinship network which integrates the inmates by innate social bonds and serves to maintain the internal equilibrium of the inmate social system is the very structure which also functions to keep the inmates forever divided into small family units.[21]

In spite of Giallombardo's statement that the existence of prison families would hinder the emergence of political leadership among women prisoners, throughout the 20th century women in prison have joined together to protest treatment in numerous penal facilities throughout the United States. In all of these facilities prison family/kinship networks existed at the time. In fact, in 1971, five years after

Giallombardo published her study of Alderson, women prisoners there organized a four-day rebellion in which they protested the "Attica Holocaust" and presented prison authorities with forty-two demands.[22] Thus, the structure of prison families did not necessarily hinder prisoners' politicization and coalition-building potential. Other factors, such as the fear of reprisal from prison authorities, the availability of third party support, and internalized racism were more important in determining whether women prisoners united to pursue common goals.

In fact, one of the major findings of this research was that the hierarchical nature of the family structure and the emotional bonds that existed among group members ensured that Latina (and non-Latina) prisoners would support the reform-oriented activities engaged in by other family members, especially those involving "heads of households." Hence, while individual prisoners might not care much about organizing to reform prison conditions, when requested to do so by family members, they typed petitions, translated grievances, collected evidence of guard abuses, and passed messages to prisoners in other housing areas. This support was given even though these otherwise "apolitical" prisoners risked being penalized for such actions.[23]

The existence of family groups also facilitated political underground activities because they allowed group members to circulate information and other materials (e.g., petitions) to family members, neighbors, etc., throughout the facility. In a setting where movement between buildings was rigidly monitored and restricted, such networks played an invaluable role.

Moreover, during the late 1970s, Latina, African-American, and white prisoners "heads of households" at Bedford Hills did, in fact, unite to pursue coalition-building efforts. Interestingly, while Latino prisoner leaders were not allowed by their peers to be openly gay, in the case of women prisoners, a leader could be involved in an open lesbian relationship and command the respect of both prisoners and staff. This was so regardless of whether the woman was perceived as being "butch" or "femme." Equally important was the fact that there were times when members of a prison family became the most active in a particular formal prisoner organization.[24]

As discussed above, prison family/kinship networks were created to address a wide range of prisoner concerns. While the politicizing capability of such groups has generally been denied or ignored by social scientists, their structure included the potential for contributing to prisoner politicization and reform-oriented organizing. In fact, prison family/kinship networks were created to address a number of prisoner concerns and facilitate, along other informal prisoner groups such as homegirl networks, prisoner involvement in numerous activities throughout the prison.

The Underground Prison Market

As in the case of Latino prisoners, the material deprivations[25] suffered by women prisoners and the fact that institutional regulations made even small interchanges of personal goods illicit meant that it was almost impossible for Latina prisoners not to engage in activities proscribed by prison personnel. As a result, prisoners at Bedford Hills like their male counterparts at Green Haven, also developed an underground "prisoner market economy" that involved bartering, gambling, the sale of information, the distribution and sale of drugs and stolen goods, and the provision of personalized services. The manner in which this economy worked was described by Clara Toro:

> The population within the prison system is a community. It's a community within a community. So, it's like a little New York . . . So if I need a new pair of pants and I work in the commissary then you'd say, "I need this." . . . It depends [on] the area of work that you're at . . . And it was all very . . . confidential. You only knew key people and those names were never divulged . . .[26]

The sale of drugs was one of the activities that required the most secretive and intricate networks. These networks included not only prisoners, but staff and outsiders. Drugs entered the facility in two major ways. One was through visitors. As Toro explained, "You have a lot of drugs in there. I mean you have visitors bringing it in there. . . . You can put it up your legs. You can swallow a balloon. You can just drop it off at some point or you could drop it off to another inmate."[27] "Drop off" points included places of employment and areas of the facility least likely to be searched by guards. However, as in the case of men's prisons, the most effective manner in which drugs entered the facility was through staff, particularly guards. According to Toro, ". . . it's no secret that officers themselves have relationships with inmates or brought them drugs."[28] Thus, as in the case of male prisons, some staff formed part of the underground prison economy.

Participation in underground economic networks tended to run along ethnic and racial lines although it was not infrequent for prisoners from one ethnic or racial group to buy supplies outside their group if they ran out. This process entailed sending a messenger to a few trusted prisoners in the other group asking, "Look, we're short of this supply, who can you recommend? This is the amount of money we have. Where can we get the best buy?"[29] Marta Flores, a former guard at Bedford Hills, summarizes prisoner participation in underground economic activities as follows:

> There's always some kind of illegal stuff going on throughout the facility. And people, inmates, they float in and out of those activities as their survival trip takes them. Sometimes an inmate can get involved in something that's illegal, not so much because they're going to personally benefit from it but because it's . . . an activity that their friend or their group is involved in, in that moment . . . The rule is survival and they do whatever they got to do. Even some of your leader-inmates who have access, you know, to the administration via ILC, and whatever other groups, even they too get involved in the illegal activities. Maybe not as bad as . . . drug-running and stuff, but there's . . . always the exchange of commodities, either personally or stolen . . .[30]

In spite of the participation of Latina prisoners in underground economic networks, Latina political leaders tended to discourage their participation in activities involving the large-scale distribution of drugs and/or stolen property. However, aside from ostracizing prisoners who participated in such ventures, there was little Latina leaders could do to prevent it, short of notifying penal authorities. That option was not generally employed because it could result in the informer being physically assaulted and/or "squealed on" in turn. In fact, during the late 1970s, as prisoners began solidifying the interethnic/interracial coalition that developed during the early part of the decade to challenge the actions and policies of prison administrators, it became necessary for Latina leaders to form alliances with non-Latina prison leaders who dominated those parts of the underground economic networks. This alliance was essential because the latter represented a significant prisoner constituency that could not be excluded from such coalition-building efforts without increasing intra-prisoner rivalries and hostilities. Moreover, prisoners involved in activities, such as the distribution of drugs, had established ties with staff members that allowed them access to information they would otherwise not have had, for example, impending raids.

In addition to the activities described above, there were times when prisoners received certain services from one another according to a prisoner "code" shared by most prisoners.

Usually if you have counselling you don't have to pay for that. If you need translation, you don't have to pay for that . . . It's like a code, like your ethics, your morals and your values. We have a value system. . . . Our value system of women is that we don't do sexual pay. Like if you need help from me, I don't take advantage of you sexually. I don't ask you for drugs, if the issue is behind drugs. If it's a legal matter I don't more or less charge you. I may ask you, if I'm good at legal stuff and you're a painter, and you're coming to me with legal issues for me to research, I might research it for you and at a later date ask you to paint my room, okay.[31]

Women prisoners, then, like their male counterparts, created a number of overlapping informal prisoner groups and networks to address a wide range of concerns. At times, prisoner networks included staff. The greatest strength of informal prisoner groups was that they allowed prisoners to meet each other's needs largely independently of the actions of prison personnel. While during the period studied, Latina prisoners continued to address most of their concerns through informal prisoner groups, once DOCS authorized the creation of formal prisoner and administrative organizations Latina prisoners also used these groups to pursue a number of interests. Thus, membership in informal and formal prisoner groups frequently overlapped.

Creating Formal Prisoner Groups

At Bedford Hills, unlike Green Haven, the formation of formal prisoner groups at the beginning of the 1970s, does not seem to have been immediately preceded by the creation of political underground prisoner groups. That is, at the time of the Attica Rebellion, Bedford Hills had no visible informal prisoner group seeking to reform prison conditions. The lack of political underground prisoner groups does not mean, however, that prisoners did not openly question institutional rules and regulations as well as the treatment received from penal staff. According to Fox, "between 1970 and 1973, the number of disciplinary reports related to prisoner challenges to authority, e.g., insubordination, disrespect, verbal abuse, increased by over 200 percent."[32] Fox attributes such challenges to the influx of younger prisoners[33] as well as "a small number of prisoners who were active feminists and political radicals prior to their imprisonment."[34] Nevertheless, despite the presence of such prisoners, there does not seem to have been any coordinated efforts on the part of Latina, African-American, and Latina prisoners to challenge prison authorities during that period of time.

There were several primary reasons for this. For one, most prisoners were short-termers, that is, women who had a minimum sentence
of less than four years. As a result, many did not have a great deal of
incentive to engage in activities geared toward reforming prison conditions, activities that could lead to their being denied parole or further
penalized. Secondly, the psychological and physical repression exercised by custodial personnel seems to have been more severe in the case
of women prisoners than in the case of their male counterparts. The
fact that until the end of the 1970s it was male guards and state troopers in full riot gear who were responsible for quashing any type of disturbance at Bedford Hills deterred many prisoners from engaging in
reform-oriented actions. Coalition efforts were also hindered by the
intense rivalries which existed among Latina and African-American
prisoners and the lack of third party support women prisoners could
call upon if they attempted to collectively pursue their reform-oriented
concerns. Once such support was available, as will be shown in the following chapters, women prisoners participated in the formation of
political underground prisoner groups to demand prison reforms. These
efforts, however, came after prison administrators began to implement
some of the post-Attica Rebellion reforms and allow prisoners to create
a number of formal prisoner groups.

Once the post-Attica reforms were implemented and prisoners
throughout the state were authorized to create formal groups, Bedford
Hills prisoners did so. At the same time, more volunteers were being
given access to the facility under the supervision of the newly-hired
coordinator of volunteer services. Volunteers helped expand existing
programs as well as develop new ones.[35] The effect of these initiatives
was to make prisoners feel somewhat more empowered and less isolated from the outside. All of these developments were closely monitored by prison administrators who, until then, had severely restricted
both prisoners' organizing activities and their contact with outsiders.
While during the 1980s, a more liberal administration somewhat facilitated prisoners' access to volunteers, these contacts were still met
with distrust, and hence, resisted by custodial personnel.

Prison administrators' resistance to legislative and central office
mandated changes after the Attica Rebellion was also reflected in the
fact that it took a while before the role of the coordinator of volunteer
services was clearly established.[36] Moreover, while in the case of Green
Haven civilian administrators were influential in helping prisoners
challenge security-oriented policies during the early 1970s, the activities pursued by Bedford Hills' volunteer services coordinators focused

on such things as: bringing fashion shows and dance groups to the facility; seeking donations of supplies (e.g., fabric) from local merchants; and recruiting local volunteers to tutor prisoners.[37] Despite the fact that by the end of the 1970s, the coordinators were responsible for overseeing a wide variety of activities (i.e., volunteers, prisoners organizations, legal services to prisoners, ethnic feast days and family day events),[38] their role continued to be more of a supervisory one than one seeking to challenge custody-oriented administrators. Likewise, throughout the 1980s, by the close supervision of prisoner activities, the coordinator of volunteer services played a central role in helping reinforce security interests.

A brief list of the formal prisoner and administrative groups created between 1972 and 1987 will give a better idea of what types of prisoner concerns administrators were most open to addressing. As in the case of male prisoners, DOCS' guidelines divided prisoner organizations into two major categories "inmate organizations" and "inmate programs." For the purpose of the current research they have been divided below into: (a) Ethnic/Racial and Special Interest groups; and (b) Self-Help and Religious programs. Ethnic/Racial groups formed between 1970 and 1987 included:

> Movimiento Unido de Mujeres Latinas/Hispanic Committee (1973–present)
>
> National Association for the Advancement of Colored People Chapter (NAACP, 1979–1987)[39]

Special Interest groups included:

> Long-Termers' Committee (1973–present)
> Upstate Committee (early 1970s?)[40]
> Legislative Action Committee (1975–1979?)[41]
> Women Helping Other Women (1987–present, formerly NAACP)
> Committee Against Life for Drugs (1978?–1982?)[42]

The most important Self-Help programs existing between 1971 and 1987 included:

> Parent Awareness (1970s?)[43]
> New Directions (late 1970?–1988?)[44]
> Reality House (1977?–1985?)[45]
> Money Addiction (1980s?)

Down on Violence/Alternatives to Violence Programs[46] (early 1980s)
Sister Sisters (1985?–present)[47]
Alcoholics Anonymous (1970s–present)
Al-Anon (1970s?-1980s?)[48]
Violence Alternative (late 1970s–1980s?)

Special Interest groups consisted of:

Youth Assistance Program (1983?–1987?)[49]
Facility Photography Program (1978?–present)[50]

Religious Programs included:

Catholic
Jewish
Seventh Day Adventist
Pentecostal
Protestant
Muslim (1977–?)

Prisoner groups and programs existing at the end of 1987 were:[51]

Hispanic Committee
Long Termers' Committee
Women Helping Other Women
Facility Photography Program

Administrative groups encompassed:

Inmate Liaison Committee (1972–present)
Inmate Grievance Resolution Committee (1976–present)

A review of the organizations listed above reveals that prisoners seem to have participated most often in self-help organizations. In fact, at the end of 1978, according to James G. Fox, ". . . over 43 percent of all Bedford Hills affiliated prisoners held membership in one or more self-help organizations . . ."[52]

Prisoners also participated in the activities sponsored by the South Forty Corporation. By the end of the 1970s, South Forty staff, in conjunction with prisoners and outside volunteers, sponsored programs in basic math, reading, "creative writing, college proficiency, external degree, pottery, poetry, health, art, and correspondence courses."[53] Perhaps one of the most important aspects of South Forty's work at Bedford Hills was that in addition to sponsoring programs, it provided a meeting place for long-termers (i.e., prisoners with sentences of four years minimum to a maximum of life). This was so because South Forty's civilian program manager at Bedford Hills, Mercy Sanders, was particularly interested in the plight of women with long sentences. Sanders' interest led her to become volunteer staff adviser for the Long-Termers' Committee (LTC) between 1979 and 1986. Moreover, because the programs sponsored by South Forty needed a stable staff, many of them came to be staffed by long-termers. Interestingly, the most politicized prisoners also tended to be long-termers. It was long-termers who were the first to create formal prisoner groups.

The LTC and the Movimiento Unido de Mujeres Latinas (MUML), also known since the late 1970s as the Hispanic Committee, seem to have been the first formal prisoner organizations created at Bedford Hills. The LTC was founded by Latina, African-American, and white prisoners. LTC advocated the passage of law reforms that would allow long-termers to work time off their minimum sentences, have their cases reviewed periodically by the parole board, and allow greater contact with family members through the expansion of temporary release and family furlough programs.[54] The LTC eventually sponsored a business called Tender Loving Crafts, designed to help members achieve financial independence. This was done through the sale of crafts (e.g., knitted sweaters, pottery) made by prisoners and sold inside and outside the institution.[55] One of the advantages enjoyed by the LTC, was that because of its affiliation with South Forty, it was the only prisoner organization which was assured a permanent meeting space within the facility.[56] That is, as long as South Forty continued to offer its services at Bedford Hills.

According to Susan Hallett, imprisoned at Bedford Hills during the 1970s and 1980s, until the mid-1980s the LTC had a "more political viewpoint" in that its members "were really trying to change laws and make things easier for long-termers."[57] However, by the mid-1980s, partly in response to its failure to achieve legislative reforms and partly as a result of member "burn out," the LTC became "more focused on helping people help themselves while in prison."[58]

While the LTC was founded by women of color and its staff and membership were interracial/interethnic, the fact that within a few years after its founding both the LTC chair and staff advisor were white and that white prisoners gradually came to comprise a significant component of the group, led to its gradually becoming identified as a white prisoner organization. During the first half of the 1970s, however, the LTC was dominated by African-American prisoners. It was partly as a result of tensions between them and Latina prisoner leaders in the group that the Movimiento Unido de Mujeres Latinas was created.

Movimiento Unido de Mujeres Latinas (MUML) and Third Party Support

MUML (also known as the Hispanic Committee), was the only formal Latina prisoner organization at Bedford Hills during the period covered by this research. It was also the only ethnic/racial prisoner organization at the facility until 1979, when a chapter of the NAACP was formed.[59] MUML was created to pursue the implementation of policies that specifically addressed the particular concerns of Latina prisoners. These included securing bilingual services and staff persons, promoting the Latina(o) culture, and ending discriminatory treatment, including language policies. An additional motivation for MUML's creation was that the LTC's African-American leadership was not seriously committed to addressing Latina prisoner concerns.

Notwithstanding the fact that MUML was the only Latina prisoner group, the organization was not very active during its first three years of existence. The lack of support from Latina prisoners for the creation of a formal prisoner group led MUML's leaders to participate in the creation of a parallel Latina ad hoc committee. It was this ad hoc committee which asked the Prison Task Force (PTF) of the Center for Puerto Rican Studies to help them organize ethnic and family day events, implement basic reading and writing classes in Spanish and English, and conduct seminars regarding family problems. During the first half of the 1970s, the ad hoc committee was able to mobilize more prisoners than MUML. In fact, MUML did not establish a stable presence as a formal prisoner organization until the mid-1970s.

There were several reasons Latina prisoner leaders had difficulty sustaining a formal Latina prisoner group. According to Haydé Ortega, coordinator of the PTF, Latina (and non-Latina) prisoners seemed to be "more isolated in the prison structurally than the men. . . . In their daily activities they didn't get that much group interaction as the men did."[60] Thus, it was harder for women prisoners to come together as a group, particularly during the period when the post-Attica reforms were first being implemented. This was so because institutional administrators kept a close watch over any organizing activity among prisoners, even when these were authorized by DOCS' central office. Hence, prisoners were hesitant to engage in endeavors not clearly sanctioned by prison personnel.

Another variable influencing Latina prisoners' willingness to participate in a formal Latina prisoner organization was the fact that between 70 and 80 percent of Bedford Hills' prisoners were mothers. This made them more vulnerable to reprisals by custody-oriented administrators who could deny them the ability to see their children. Furthermore, the fact that the women's prison population was comprised mainly of short-termers meant that many of them were not willing to challenge custody-oriented staff in order to pursue activities from which they were not going to receive immediate benefits.

Equally important was the fact that, in an atmosphere in which prison personnel reprimanded and further penalized Latina prisoners for speaking in Spanish without authorization, Latina prisoners were hesitant to join an ethnic-identified organization whose status within the prison was still unclear. Within this context it was easier to create ad hoc committees to pursue goals that already had the approval of institutional administrators.

As a result of the circumstances described above, when PTF volunteers began working with Latina prisoners at Bedford Hills, they were confronted by a different set of structural circumstances and prisoner priorities than at Green Haven. During the 1973–1975 period, the PTF heard of the existence of MUML, but never met with it formally. During that period of time, PTF interaction with Latina prisoners took place only through a parallel Latina ad hoc committee formed by MUML leaders and other Latina prisoners. Through the ad hoc committee, the PTF offered literacy classes in Spanish and English and helped Latina prisoners organize ethnic and family day events. The former involved such things as finding instructors and providing educational materials. The latter, as in the case of Latino prisoners at Green Haven, involved providing resources, securing speakers and entertainers, bringing in family members for the event, and negotiating with prison administrators at various points. There were also times when PTF members brought in the children of individual prisoners to visit them.

Asked why the PTF did not help develop and implement the same types of higher education and study release programs at Bedford Hills that it did at Green Haven, Haydé Ortega commented that conditions did not exist at Bedford Hills that would have allowed the PTF to play a similar role.[61] While Latina prisoner leaders supported the creation of bilingual college education programs it was not until the end of the 1970s that prison administrators and educational personnel supported the establishment of a permanent higher education program at the facility. As the case of Green Haven demonstrated, without the support of penal bureaucrats it was difficult for prisoners and third parties to counteract the opposition of white custodial and civilian personnel to the implementation of such programs.

Moreover, the general Latina prisoner population did not see the implementation of bilingual college education programs as an immediate priority. Latina prisoners, as stated earlier, sought the assistance of the PTF primarily to organize ethnic and family day events, conduct seminars regarding family problems, and provide basic literacy classes in English and Spanish. In fact, according to Ortega, "Muchas de las clases were en español porque era el lenguage que más entendían."[62] The classes offered by the PTF were also generally given in Spanish because this was one area in which institutional services was most lacking. Hence, the priorities of Latina prisoners were directly related to the composition of the Latina prisoner population. The fact that a significant number of Latina prisoners were elementary or high school drop-outs meant that they prioritized the development of basic reading and writing skills. Because of the short sentences most Latina prisoners were serving and the fact that many of them had little or no English language skills, many of them would not have been able to take immediate advantage of higher education courses. Hence the feeling, why fight for the implementation of programs that would remain inaccessible to most Latinas especially when they were not likely to be offered in Spanish?

Another factor which differentiated Latina prisoners from their male counterparts was the manner in which they tended to prioritize family-related concerns. This resulted from the fact that a significant number of Latinas were mothers and generally single heads of households prior to their incarceration. In fact, one of the motivations for learning to read and write was to facilitate contact between prisoners and their children and families. As Ortega explained, "They wanted to be able to write letters" back home.[63] For some, imprisonment meant losing custody of their children and/or the right to see them while in prison. For others, it meant not being able to see their children often because the cost of travelling to and from the facility was prohibitive for family members. Moreover, even those prisoners whose families could bring their children to visit were often prevented from seeing their offspring due to excessive bureaucratic regulations and difficult visiting policies.

Janice Warne, former warden at Bedford Hills, described visiting policies at the facility in December 1972.

> At present, the prison has no special programs dealing with the problems of inmate mothers . . . As it is now, the prisoners are not allowed to show affection to their families during the visit, on the grounds that narcotics or weapons could be exchanged during the embrace. And during the visits, the inmates must sit on one side of a very wide table . . . while their families sit on the other side.[64]

Given these conditions, when visiting policies were liberalized after the Attica Rebellion and prisoners were allowed to form groups to organize "Children's Day," "Family Day," and ethnic day events to which children and other family members could be invited, one of the main priorities of Latina (and non-Latina) prisoners became organizing these events. According to Ortega, "They perceived the Latin festival as a way in which they could bring their children, in a more intimate setting, than the visiting room, where there was a table, where they couldn't touch the kids . . . They saw the Latin festival as a more intimate way of connecting to family and to their children."[65]

Thus, when PTF volunteers first came in contact with Latina prisoners at Bedford Hills they were asked to support the work of the Latina ad hoc committee created for the purpose of organizing the San Juan Bautista event in June of that year. The event sought to bring together prisoners, family members, friends, and other outside community members. Members of the ad hoc committee had already participated, along with their African-American and white counterparts, in organizing the first "Children's Day" event. The latter was held on April 19, 1973, around the time that the PTF was first becoming acquainted with Latina prisoners at Bedford Hills.[66] The Children's Day event was held on the prison grounds rather than in the visiting room, where prisoners were not allowed to hold their children in their laps and the interaction between them and their offspring was closely monitored.[67]

The Children's Day event was the first major prisonwide activity organized by Latina, African-American, and white prisoners. The successful organizing of the activity allowed prisoners to see that they could effectively join forces to achieve common goals despite the existence of deep cleavages among them. It also demonstrated the potential for women prisoners to create alliances with one another based on common concerns. One of the repercussions of holding the festivity was that it gave prisoners a stake in organizing similar events. Hence, many prisoners became even more hesitant to challenge prison policies if it interfered with their ability to see their children and families. Prison authorities were aware both of the importance of family ties to imprisoned women and of the ability of prisoners to join together to pursue common goals. Hence, throughout the period studied, they continued their attempts to intimidate prisoners into not challenging prison conditions and abusive treatment by threatening to interfere and actually interfering with prisoners' visiting "privileges" and activities.

As shown above, when DOCS authorized prisoners to create formal prisoner groups, Latina prisoner leaders participated both in the creation of interracial/interethnic prisoner organizations (e.g., LTC) and in the creation of a formal Latina prisoner group. Once the latter was unable to win the widespread support of Latina prisoners, however, Latina prisoner leaders joined in the formation of a parallel Latina ad hoc committee. The ad hoc committee was able to bring together more Latina prisoners than was possible for MUML at the time. This was due to the fact that the former both addressed concerns shared by an overwhelming number of Latina prisoners and issues sanctioned by institutional personnel.

Within the context described above, PTF members did not feel it was their responsibility to try to convince Latina prisoners that it was in their best interest to pursue the same goals Latino prisoners were pursuing at Green Haven. According to Ortega, "We felt that . . . it wasn't our role to dictate what was needed from within. [The women] knew the conditions . . . We would . . . support [them] when they defined how they wanted the support, but we didn't go in and say, 'You should do this,' or, 'This is what you should ask [for].'"[68] Furthermore, according to Frank Bonilla, former director of the Center for Puerto Rican Studies and member of the PTF:

> It should be made clearer that both at Green Haven and Bedford Hills, the task force made it a condition for its involvement to work directly with an inmate organization that was a going concern. We did not go in to organize inmates or tell them what to do . . . The difference in level of organization and politicization between Bedford Hills and Green Haven had to do with the pace and nature of the collaboration with the Centro task force and other outsiders.[69]

According to Ortega and Bonilla, the ability of PTF volunteers to further pressure prison administrators to implement bilingual programs and services on behalf of Latina prisoners was hampered both by the lack of a strong Latina prisoner group and the lack of solid demand among Latina prisoners for such programs.

In spite of the collaborative efforts between the PTF and the Latina ad hoc committee, the former's ability to provide support to Latina prisoners was hindered by several additional factors, some of them internal to the task force, others external. For one, the work with Latino prisoners at Green Haven took up a lot of the PTF's time, energy, and resources,[70] leaving less for work with women prisoners. Secondly, from several interviews conducted with former PTF volunteers, it is clear that some of them did not think Latina prisoners were as organized or as politicized as their male counterparts because the overwhelming number of Latina prisoners did not prioritize the formation of an ethnic prisoner organization or bilingual higher education. Thus, the lack of understanding concerning the different but yet equally significant ways in which Latina and Latino prisoners organized and the concerns they prioritized at any given point in time made PTF members less enthusiastic about working with women prisoners.

A third factor influencing the task force's work was that PTF volunteers faced a greater degree of resistance from Bedford Hills administrators than from those at male institutions. According to Ortega, compared to Green Haven, PTF volunteers, "got harassed a lot . . . It was a lot stricter. For instance, I was called in and didn't get allowed in because I wore a turtle neck . . . According to them that encouraged homosexuality."[71]

Last but not least, one of the strengths of the PTF at Green Haven had been its ability to form loose alliances with third parties to pursue goals beneficial to Latino prisoners such as bilingual college education. However, at Bedford Hills, the PTF did not establish a working relationship with other third parties. This was partly due to the nature of the support the PTF was willing and able to offer Latina prisoners and partly a result of the nature of third party support available to women prisoners.[72]

It was previously mentioned that through the office of Volunteer Services a larger number of volunteers began to make their presence felt at Bedford Hills during the early 1970s. These volunteers generally provided a number of educational courses and helped prisoners develop artistic skills. However, as in the case of PTF members, the actions of these outside volunteers were closely monitored by penal administrators who worried about the impact outsiders would have on prisoners' compliance with institutional policies. Notwithstanding the above preoccupations, the primary source of third party support for women prisoners during the early 1970s, as will be discussed in the following chapter, became the faculty and students of New York University's Women's Law Project and the attorneys, paralegals, and community activists who began to work with prisoners in 1974 primarily through Bronx Legal Services and the Prisoners' Rights Project of the Legal Aid Society. Although the PTF was aware of the work of the Women's Law Project at the institution, it does not appear to have established any direct links to it. This was primarily due to the fact that prisoner litigation was not one of the strategies the PTF pursued. When Latina prisoners had legal concerns, PTF members referred them to legal institutions such as the Legal Aid Society and the Puerto Rican Legal Defense and Education Fund. PTF members shied away from litigation because, according to Ortega, ". . . it becomes real massive. That becomes a full-time job, to follow and monitor the legal proceedings."[73] Moreover, ". . . you need to know what you're doing."[74] Added to this was the fact that prisoner litigation required both a great deal of time and resource investment, both of which the PTF increasingly lacked.

As demonstrated in this chapter, the beginning of the 1970s, found Latina prisoner forming a number of formal and informal prisoner groups and networks for the purpose of addressing a wide range of concerns. Faced with institutional policies which targeted Latina prisoners for discriminatory treatment, as well as the opportunity to see their children in a more open setting, Latina prisoners opted to form an ad hoc committee for the purpose of organizing family day events to which children and family members could be invited. While a few Latina prisoner leaders created a formal Latina prisoner organization in 1973, the organization had not established its presence at the facility by the end of 1975. Latina prisoner leaders were, nevertheless, able to mobilize the support of the PTF.

While the PTF provided Latina prisoners at Bedford Hills support on a number of family and educational issues, its ability to provide additional support was hampered by discriminatory penal policies towards Latina (as well as non-Latina prisoners), the lack of both institutional and other sources of third party support for specific Latina prisoner concerns, and the prioritizing of Latino prisoner interests by PTF members. Ironically, at the time the PTF began winding down its work with Latina prisoners, the facility began experiencing a series of changes that led to the blossoming of MUML and a subsequent change in its leadership and goals. In order to understand this transformation it is necessary to discuss other events that were taking place at the facility between 1973 and 1977.

Notes: Chapter 10

1. Diana Jiménez [pseud.], interview with author, New York, N.Y., 1988; Marta Flores [pseud.], interview with author, Albany, N.Y., 18 March 1989; Clara Toro [pseud.], interview with author, New York, N.Y., 9 April 1989; and Mercy Sanders [pseud.], interview with author, Boston, Mass., 1 February 1990.

2. Barbara Cole [pseud.], interview with author, New York, N.Y., 15 May 1993.

3. Jiménez, interview with author, 1988.

4. Spencer's study of a medium security women's prison also found that interracial bonding among women prisoners was as threatening to administrators in women's institutions as that of men in male prisons. See Elouise Junius Spencer, "The Social System of a Medium Security Women's Prison," (Ph.D. diss., University of Kansas, 1977).

5. Paloma Román [pseud.], interview with author, New York, N.Y., 10 December 1989.

6. For a description of the internal dynamics of family and kinship networks groups, see Joyce Ann Brown with Jay Gaines, *Joyce Ann Brown: Justice Denied* (Chicago: The Noble Press, Inc., 1990); Kathryn Watterson Burkhart, *Women in Prison* (New York: Doubleday, 1973); Charles A. Ford, "Homosexual Practices of Institutionalized Females," *Journal of Abnormal and Social Psychology* 23 (January/March 1929): 442–444; Rose Giallombardo, *Society of Women: A Study of a Women's Prison* (New York: John Wiley and Sons, 1966); Jean Harris, *They Always Call Us Ladies: Stories from Prison* (New York: McMillan Publishing Co., 1988); Margaret Otis, "A Perversion Not Commonly Known," *Journal of Abnormal Psychology* 8 (June/July 1913): 112–114; Idella Serna, *Locked Down: A Woman's Life in Prison, The Story of Mary (Lee) Dortch* (Norwich, Vt., New Victoria Publishers, 1992); and David A. Ward and Gene G. Kassebaum, *Women's Prisons* (London: Weidenfeld and Nicolson, 1965).

7. Román, interview with author, 1989.

8. Toro, interview with author, 1989.

9. Ibid.

10. Ibid.

11. Román, interview with author, 1989.

12. Piri Thomas, *Seven Long Times* (New York: Praeger Publishers, 1974).

13. Román, interview with author, 1989.

14. Ibid.

15. In fact, interracial lesbian relationships were so common at Bedford Hills at the beginning of the 20th century that they were used as an excuse to racially segregate prisoners until the 1950s. See Ford, "Homosexual Practices of Institutionalized Females," 1929; Otis, "A Sexual Perversion Not Commonly Noted," 1913; and Estelle Freeman, *Their Sisters' Keepers: Women's Prison Reform in America, 1830–1930* (Ann Arbor: University of Michigan Press, 1981). For social scientists who discuss interracial relationships among women prisoners, see Candance Kruttschnitt, "Race Relations and the Federal Inmate," *Crime and Delinquency* 29 (October 1983): 577–592; and Spencer, "The Social System," 1977. Spencer found that interracial bonding among prisoners was as threatening to prison authorities in women's facilities as it was in men's.

16. Mirna González [pseud.], interview with author, New York, N.Y., 22 March 1989.

17. James G. Fox, "Women's Prison Policy, Prisoner Activism, and the Impact of the Contemporary Feminist Movement: A Case Study," *The Prison Journal* 64 (March 1984): 25.

18. Ibid.

19. James G. Fox, *Organizational and Racial Conflict in Maximum Security Prisons* (Lexington, Mass.: D.C. Heath and Co., 1982), 131n23.

20. Harris, *They Always Call Us Ladies*, 1988.

21. Giallombardo, *Society of Women*, 175–176. Giallombardo did concede that the creation of prison families was "an attempt to resist the destructive effects of imprisonment" (Ibid., 103).

22. Phyllis Jo Baunach and Thomas Murton, "Women in Prison: An Awakening Minority," *Crime and Corrections* (Fall 1973): 7. In addition to Alderson, prison disturbances occurred in other facilities throughout the country in which prison family groups and networks existed. Between 1969 and 1973, there were four "disturbances" at the women's prison in Milledgeville, Georgia (Ibid., 5). In October 1971 and February 1973, rebellions broke out in Tennessee's State Prison for Women and at the Philadelphia House of Correction, respectively (Ibid., 8). In 1973, 90 percent of the prisoners at the California Institution for Women in Clinton, N.J., also organized a three day work stoppage. Grievances "centered on mail distribution, food and medical care. Prisoners also have complained that privileges granted under the honor system are not given promptly enough . . ." ("Women Inmates Also Have Grievances," *New York Times* (hereafter cited as *N.Y. Times*), 14 January 1973, 80). In May 1975 prisoners at the Clinton Reformatory for Women participated in a "disturbance" which was put down by male guards and state troopers. Prisoners responded to the physical repression which ensued with a class action suit filed by the New Jersey chapter of the American Civil Liberties Union ("Women Prisoners Sue on 'Beatings'," *N.Y. Times*, 28 June 1973, 18). In 1974, North Carolina Women's Prison in Raleigh experienced five

days of protests. Prison authorities responded by sending an estimated 125 "helmeted guards and highway patrolmen" to subdue prisoners. Prisoners' grievances included "poor medical and counselling services. They also demanded that the prison laundry be closed" ("Officers Charge Women Inmates Staging North Carolina Protest," *N.Y. Times,* 20 June 1975, 32).

23. González, interview with author, 1989.

24. Flores, interview with author, 1989.

25. During the late 1970s, women entering Bedford Hills were issued: three jumpers; six blouses; one all-weather coat; six bras; six pairs of panties; two half-slips; two sleeping apparel; two sweaters; one bathrobe; one pair of boots; two pairs shoes; one rain hat; two pairs of slacks; six handkerchiefs; one pair of sneakers; six kneesocks; two pairs of snuggies (outside work detail only); one pair of scuffs; and one pair of gloves (New York State Department of Correctional Services [hereafter cited as NYSDOCS], Bedford Hills Correctional Facility, *Inmate Orientation Book.*

26. Toro, interview with author, 1989.

27. Ibid.

28. Ibid.

29. Ibid.

30. Flores, interview with author, 1989.

31. Toro, interview with author, 1989.

32. Fox, "Women's Prison Policy," 23.

33. According to Fox, younger prisoners were more likely to respond to stress and staff provocation with physical and emotional outbursts (Ibid., 24).

34. Ibid., 23.

35. Ibid., 27. During the late 1970s, volunteers offered evening classes (i.e., between 6:10 P.M. and 8:30 P.M.), which included, "High School Equivalency, Typing, Video Music and various therapeutic programs" (NYSDOCS, Bedford Hills Correctional Facility, *Inmate Orientation Book.*

36. Fox, "Women's Prison Policy," 26.

37. González, interview with author, 1989; and Sanders, interview with author, 1989.

38. NYSDOCS, Bedford Hills Correctional Facility, *Inmate Orientation Book.*

39. The NAACP sought to encourage prisoners to strengthen their self-esteem and to participate in educational and vocational programs within the facility. It also sought to help soon to be released members to find work, housing, and re-enter into the outside community.

40. The Upstate Committee was created primarily by white prisoners who came from the northwestern part of New York State. The committee sought to mobilize the support of third parties and penal personnel for the establishment in upstate areas of work release programs and the development of community programs to assist prisoners upon release. The committee's legacy was the establishment of monthly bus transportation services that allowed the relatives of upstate women to visit them free of charge.

41. The Legislative Action Committee sought to influence the development of sentencing statutes by holding seminars, forums, workshops, and legal discussions aimed at educating both the inside and outside communities concerning sentencing policies.

42. The Committee Against Life for Drugs met with third parties in an attempt to change New York State's drug laws. It also sought to educate the outside community about these laws.

43. Parent Awareness sought to strengthen the parenting skills of imprisoned mothers.

44. New Directions was sponsored by South Forty and aimed to improve women's coping skills in a wide range of areas.

45. Counselors from the Reality House agency conducted drug therapy sessions for prisoners with drug-related problems. The Reality House program at Bedford Hills was an offshoot of Reality House outside the walls.

46. Down on Violence involved having outside professionals (e.g., psychiatrists, clergy, heads of organizations) conduct seminars on alternatives to violence for prisoners committed for violence-related crimes.

47. Sister Sisters was created to provide support to women survivors of domestic abuse.

48. Al-Anon is a program for relatives and friends of alcoholics.

49. The Youth Assistance Program sought to steer young women away from criminal activity. Prisoners conducted workshops with adolescent girls brought in by outside social agencies.

50. This program allowed individual prisoners and their visitors to be photographed in the Visiting Room during regular visiting hours (9:00 A.M. to 3:30 P.M.). During the late 1970s, this program was run by the Hispanic Committee (NYSDOCS, Bedford Hills Correctional Facility, *Inmate Orientation Book.*

51. NYSDOCS, Bedford Hills Correctional Facility, *The Office of Volunteer Services.*

52. Fox, *Organizational and Racial Conflict*, 1982, 148. Fox speculated that the high rate of Bedford Hills' prisoner participation in self-help groups, as compared to the male prisoners he studied, was caused by the fact that, "either the opportunity for participation in self-help programs was substantially greater

at Bedford Hills or that female prisoners were more likely than males to view self-help organizations as being a legitimate means of fulfilling personal needs and interests" (Ibid.). Fox concluded that both the opportunities available for participation in such groups and prisoners' personal preferences accounted for the different rate of participation of women and men in self-help groups.

53. NYSDOCS, Bedford Hills Correctional Facility, *Inmate Orientation Book*. During the beginning of the 1980s, prisoners active in South Forty worked in two main programs. One was Crafts, in which prisoners learned to make sweaters and ceramics as well as help each other sell their products. The other was Career Awareness Program, Bedford Hill's pre-release program.

54. At the time, the few vocational, educational, furlough, work release, and study release programs available to prisoners in New York State were geared toward meeting the needs of short-termers. Legislation passed after the Attica Rebellion required prisoners applying for participation in these programs to be within one year of eligibility for release on parole. According to a *N.Y. Times* article, one of the things the LTC worked for, "was the establishment of a review process, allowing inmates to become eligible for parole before completing their minimum sentence. Another was having 'good time'— participation in certain prison programs and having a good institutional record—used to reduce the time of the minimum sentence instead of just the maximum sentence as is now the case" (Gary Kriss, "Prison Group Honored for Criminal-Justice Work," *N.Y. Times,* 9 June 1985, XXII, 29).

55. Ibid. The women's products were also sold "at a shop that the committee pays someone to run in Long Beach, L.I., or at a private party. The committee receives 20 percent of the selling price, the inmate the rest . . . the committee has made donations to the prison for . . . 'little extras that the facility wasn't budgeted for.' It has also made contributions outside of the prison to organizations such as the Muscular Dystrophy Association. And it purchases equipment used for the program of crafts instruction . . . The committee also has people come in once a month to give talks on subjects as diverse as world affairs and vegetarianism" (Ibid.).

56. González, interview with author, 1989.

57. Gary Kriss, "Prison Group Honored for Criminal-Justice Work," *N.Y. Times,* 9 June 1985, XXII, 29.

58. Ibid. In June 1985, the LTC's work was publicly recognized through an award received for its "notable contributions to criminal justice" from the Westchester Council on Crime and Delinquency (Ibid.).

59. In 1987, the Bedford Hills' NAACP chapter was disbanded and its $9,000 treasury was confiscated by DOCS (Carl Walker, interview with author, New York, N.Y., 28 February 1990).

60. Haydé Ortega [pseud.], interview with author, New York, N.Y., 12 and 28 February and 17 March 1989.

61. Ibid.

62. Ibid. Author's translation: "A lot of the classes were in Spanish because it was the language they most understood."

63. Ibid.

64. Judy Klemesrud, "At Prison, a Season to Be Especially Sad," *N.Y. Times,* 22 December 1972, 26.

65. Ortega, interview with author, 1989.

66. Judy Klemesrud, "Children's Day at Prison: Mother's . . .", *N.Y. Times,* 20 April 1973, 22.

67. One of the drawbacks of participating in the event, however, was that a new policy was instituted, "whereby a mother has to strip for a body search (for drugs and weapons) before and after a visit with her family" (Ibid.). As a result of these policies, some prisoners chose not to participate in the event in order to avoid being subjected to such humiliation.

68. Ortega, interview with author, 1989.

69. Letter from Frank Bonilla to Juanita Díaz, 8 June 1993.

70. According to Ortega, most of the PTF work with prisoners took place with PUL at Green Haven. However, the PTF also maintained contact and from time to time visited Latino prisoners in other state prisons, such as Comstock (Ortega, interview with author, 1989).

71. Ibid.

72. As we saw in chapter 7, at Green Haven, PTF members, at the request of PUL, contacted colleges interested in providing Latinos higher education both inside and outside the prison. Together, they pressured DOCS administrators to allow the implementation of educational programs.

73. Ortega, interview with author, 1989.

74. Ibid.

11

Litigation, Third Party Support, and Prisoner Politicization

With the implementation of the post-Attica Rebellion reforms, Bedford Hills' custody-oriented administrators were forced to allow an increasing number of volunteers to enter the facility. One of the most significant sectors to become involved with women prisoners at Bedford Hills after the Attica Rebellion were attorneys, law students, and paralegals. In 1972, Marilyn Haft and Michelle Herman, attorneys working at the Women's Law Project (WLP) of New York University's Law School began, with some of their students, to provide legal assistance as well as a course in criminal and constitutional law to prisoners at Bedford Hills. The first year the class was offered at least fifty prisoners attended. The WLP assisted prisoners primarily with cases pertaining to criminal law, family law, and prisoners' rights. The WLP was instrumental in getting the prison to open a law library and taught prisoners how to use it.[1] However, the WLP had been allowed into Bedford Hills only after project directors signed a contract with DOCS agreeing that its members would not litigate against the institution.

WLP's presence in the facility helped increase prisoners' awareness of their legal rights. With the project's assistance, "several prisoners attempted to file or reinstate appeals."[2] Others began to question court and social service agency decisions involving child custody cases. The law students were themselves, "impressed by the legal expertise of the prisoners who had taken the course"[3] that year. Equally important, as shall be shown subsequently, was the fact that the students' exposure to imprisoned women motivated at least one of them, Elizabeth Koob, to pursue litigation on behalf of women prisoners at Bedford Hills during the late 1970s and 1980s.[4] Such initiatives were vital because while women prisoners became more aware of their rights through the courses offered by WLP, the fact that the project could not sue the institution on behalf of prisoners, still left the prisoners' with no source of third party support through which to file grievances against institutional administrators. Before long, however, services offered by attorneys, paralegals, law students, and community activists affiliated with Bronx Legal Services filled the gap.

In February 1974, an African-American prisoner, Carol Crooks, was confined to segregation indefinitely following an incident in which institutional authorities accused her of attacking and injuring five guards. Crooks herself was severely beaten during the confrontation. According to an article that appeared in *Midnight Special,* a prisoners' rights newsletter, "The incident between Crooksie and the guards occurred last February, when the guards refused to let Crooksie receive medical treatment, since that time, Crooksie has been confined in segregation which she has been fighting in the courts."[5] According to Crooks, this incident had been only one of several similar ones in which:

> They would use male officers from other facilities to come in my room . . . I would be stripped down and they would beat me . . . in my cell. . . . They would keep me handcuffed in my cell. They would keep me in my own . . . waste. And for days they wouldn't feed me or they would try to feed me and I wouldn't eat. I would only eat from inmates. I wouldn't take nothing from them because I felt that sometimes they would put stuff in my milk or my water or my food and it would make me drug-out where I couldn't function for days and days.[6]

Once Crooks was sent to segregation, a defense committee comprised primarily of Black nationalist women and radical white (primarily lesbian) feminists, was formed to call attention to Crooks' case and to secure her release from segregation. As part of its efforts, the committee asked Bronx Legal Services' attorney Stephen M. Latimer, to represent Crooks.[7] The *Crooks v. Warne,* 74 Civ. 2351 (S.D.N.Y. 1974) suit that ensued represented the first time, at least since the Attica Rebellion, that third parties had been willing to litigate against Bedford Hills administrators. As other prisoners learned of Latimer's efforts on behalf of Crooks, they began to flood his office with letters seeking his support.

Latimer's support of Crooks proved worthwhile when, during the early part of August 1974, the court ruled in *Crooks v. Warne,* that Crooks' rights had been violated. It found prison authorities in violation of the United States Supreme Court decision in *Wolff v. McDonnell,* 94 S.Ct. 2963 (1974), 41 L.Ed.2d 935 (1974).[8] As a result, the judge issued a court injunction ruling that Crooks be released from segregation.[9] However, on August 28, 1974, a few days after the court issued the injunction, Crooks was once again beaten by guards and sent to segregation by the institution's Adjustment Committee. This time a number of prisoners who witnessed the incident responded with a rebellion in support of Crooks.

> On August 28, 1974—we the inmates of 112D housing unit witnessed the brutal beating of one Carol Crooks by 5 male officers. On August 29, 1974, we ask [sic] for an explanation of the insodent [sic] prior. None was given. We at the hour of 7 o'clock were told to lock in. Lock in is promptly at 10 P.M. Again no reason was given. We started a non-violent demonstration at which time over 200 male guards, armed were called on us.[10]

During the Rebellion, prisoners held seven staff members hostage for two and one-half hours.[11] Male state troopers and guards were called in from Green Haven, Taconic, and Wallkill men's prisons to subdue prisoners. As a result, several of the protesters were injured and put in segregation.

> On August 28, 1974, myself and many of your sisters and mine, witnessed the inhuman treatment of a fellow comrade, Sister Jermilla (slave name carol crooks). She was dragged, beaten bloody, bruised, and almost crippled by male pigs, one sister with no fighting chance against 20 male watch dogs . . . We could no longer allow all this, so we choose to unite and prevent the pigs from taking these severe actions. . . . We too then were beaten, cut, punched, bones were broken, stomachs, arms, faces and hands were lacerated. Noses were broken, head [sic] were clubbed, blood was severely shed, yes, comrades this was done to twenty-eight women by three hundred men.[12]

Prisoners' willingness to participate in the August Rebellion was important for several reasons. Through the publicity generated, the incident called attention to the plight of women prisoners. The incident also demonstrated the willingness of women prisoners following the Attica Rebellion to engage in collective acts of resistance to protest penal abuses. The reaction of penal authorities to the rebellion illustrated the manner in which male guards were used to physically subdue and intimidate women prisoners.

At a press conference held by prisoners' attorneys Latimer and Florence Kennedy in October 1974, it was alleged that twenty-five prisoners had been injured during the rebellion and twenty-eight prisoners put in segregation following the incident.[13] Several prisoners described the type of treatment to which they were subjected while in solitary confinement.

> Since August 30, 1974, we have been subjected to all types of inhumane treatments. Food pushed under the door, no showers for 7 days. No beds, we are presently sleeping on mattrisses [*sic*] on the floor. I have never seen such disgust in my intire [*sic*] 27 yrs. of living. We are neglected mentical [*sic*] attention properly. We need "help" desperately. All legal information, stamps (etc.) will be gratefully appreciated.[14]

> On August 29, 1974 a disturbance took place at Bedford Correctional Facilities [sic] which we were involved in. On August 30, 1974, we were brought to segregation and locked until seen by the adjustment clinic. During our segregation lock for 7 days we were unable to take showers, we had our food shoved underneath our doors like we were some type of animals. We had our beds taken from us, we did not receive clean linen or cleaning utensils to clean our cells out nor do we have proper writing utensils as you can see. We have been harassed by officers and haven't received proper medical attention. We feel we have been subjected to cruel and unhuman [sic] treatment.[15]

Two days after the Rebellion, Crooks was transferred to the Matteawan Complex for the Criminally Insane in Beacon, New York. According to a prisoner locked in segregation with Crooks.

> On September 1, 1974, an inmate who was in segregation with us whose name is Carol Crooks was called for a visit which was supposed to be with her mother. There was no such visit. They called 5 to 8 men to escort her on this so called visit with belts and gas pellets in their hands. They took her and put her in a car bodily and transferred her to Matawan [sic]. Which there is nothing wrong with her mentally at all . . . We were seen by the adjustment clinic twice. Each time no charges were presented to us. . . . I feel our Constitutional rights have been violated. . . .[16]

Once at Matteawan, Crooks was once again placed in solitary confinement.[17] In addition to Crooks, twenty-two other prisoners were transferred to Matteawan following the rebellion. The reason given by prison authorities for the transfer was that the latter prisoners were "slow learners."[18] The transfers took place without the required commitment hearings. While held at Matteawan, the women were forced to take high doses of behavior modifying drugs such as Thorazine and

Prolixin even though the medical records of the women were not available to Matteawan doctors at the time.[19] Prisoners, represented by Latimer, responded by filing a suit in federal court seeking their transfer back to Bedford Hills. As a result of the suit, hearings were held in court on February 18, 19, and 20, 1975, and all but two of the prisoners were returned to Bedford Hills.[20] Shortly after, however, a Latina prisoner was severely abused by guards. According to one report, ". . . on Friday, Feb. 28th, papers were submitted protesting that 30 guards had been sent to hold down Daisy García to give her a shot of Prolixin. The guards had also kicked her in the stomach.[21]

As shown heretofore, during the period preceding and following the Attica Rebellion women prisoners at Bedford Hills found themselves confronting a custody-oriented prison administration willing to use undue physical force to subdue prisoners. Prisoners' attempts to empower themselves, challenge authority, and/or protect themselves and their peers from physical violence at the hands of male guards, were met with further physical abuse. This situation helps explain some of the hesitancy Latina prisoners demonstrated to building a formal Latina prisoner group within an environment in which they were already targeted for discriminatory treatment. The abuse by male guards was at times complemented by that received at the hands of medical personnel at Bedford Hills and other state institutions. The medical establishment not only stigmatized women who rebelled as being mentally ill but also perpetrated further psychological and physical abuse through forced medication.

Without the availability of significant sources of third party and penal support there was little women prisoners could do to collectively counteract the actions of custody-oriented prison personnel. However, once third party support was made available in the form of prisoners' rights attorneys, law students, paralegals, and women community activists, women prisoners were more than amenable to take advantage of such support. The increasing willingness of prisoners to collectively challenge administrative policies was demonstrated by the August Rebellion and the fact that, as shall be shown in this and the following chapter, the *Crooks v. Warne* suit became the first in a series of suits challenging penal practices and prison conditions at the facility.

Prisoners and their advocates responded to the treatment received by prisoners during and following the August rebellion with *Powell v. Ward,* 74 Civ. 4628, 392 F. Supp. 628 (1975), a class action suit. The suit addressed the fact that twenty-eight prisoners had been placed in segregation by the Adjustment Committee[22] following the incident for as long as four weeks "pending investigation" of the charges against them. While in solitary confinement women remained locked in their cells twenty-three hours a day. They were not given written notification of the charges against them, nor were they provided explanations for the disciplinary actions taken or the evidence used against them. These violations of prisoners' rights occurred despite previous rulings by the United States Supreme Court,[23] DOCS directives (e.g, October 1970), and the August *Crooks v. Warne* decision detailing procedures to be followed by prison authorities conducting disciplinary procedures. The suit alleged that the treatment accorded prisoners in August was common procedure at Bedford Hills. That is, it was common for prison personnel to violate prisoners' due process rights while conducting disciplinary procedures. As a response to these violations Latimer also filed a preliminary injunction requesting that prison administrators refrain from enforcing disciplinary procedures until they began to comply with due process.[24]

In the meantime, Carol Crooks was convicted of five counts of assault on guards. At the time of her conviction on October 1974, she was being held in segregation. Once again, Latimer sought to secure Crooks' release from solitary confinement. As a part of Crooks' defense, prisoners were given the opportunity to testify on her behalf. Consequently, during November and December of 1974, African-American, Latina, and white prisoners testified before the District Court about the various ways in which prison personnel violated their rights. The fact that Latina and white prisoners were willing to testify on behalf of an African-American prisoner, despite existing racial/ethnic rivalries, is a testament to the severe repression to which all prisoners were subjected by custodial personnel. It also indicated prisoners' awareness that only by uniting could they counter the actions of penal administrators. Such awareness, in fact, led a small group of Latina, African-American, and white prisoners to form a political underground prisoner group at the end of 1974 for the purpose of gathering information concerning the violation of prisoners' rights by staff. The information compiled was then passed on to attorneys, paralegals, and community activists who used it to support litigation efforts and to educate the general public about events taking place at the facility.[25]

Four months after hearing prisoners' testimony, the District Court noted in its *Powell v. Ward* decision of April 23, 1975, that the actions taken by prison administrators after the August Rebellion were, as prisoners' had argued, "not peculiar to the August 29 disturbance."[26]

That is, penal personnel frequently violated prisoners due process rights. Such violations took several forms. At times, prisoners were kept in segregation more than the seventy-two hours legally mandated before a hearing was held. At other times, the hearings were held within the prescribed period of time but prisoners were not told how long they would be held in segregation. The Adjustment Committee would then review cases on a weekly basis to determine if prisoners' behavior merited their release into the general population. Sentences could vary greatly from prisoner to prisoner for the same rule infractions. Many prisoners were not informed of their right to present witnesses on their behalf. The requests of those who were aware of such rights were often ignored. Furthermore, prisoners were confined in the same special housing units regardless of whether they were subject to Adjustment Committee Proceedings or Superintendent's Proceedings. Prisoners so placed were locked in their cells twenty-three hours a day. The District Court also found that guards and/or administrators who had either witnessed or participated as investigating officers for the August 29 Rebellion or who had conflicts of interest due to the nature of their responsibilities at the facility, had been allowed to preside over the disciplinary hearings. This deprived prisoners of the right to an impartial hearing.[27]

One of the drawbacks of the *Powell v. Ward* (1975) decision was that it mandated prisoners who had complaints concerning violations of their due process rights to file a grievance with the institution's Inmate Grievance Resolution Committee before they sought court relief. That is, the court mandated prisoners to file complaints against the guards who had violated their rights through a mechanism supervised by custody-oriented personnel. The repercussions of this stipulation will be explored further along in the chapter.

Interestingly, while the *Powell v. Ward* (1975) litigation was still in progress DOCS' reaction was to issue a statewide directive on March 12, 1975, instructing all of its institutions to grant prisoners an Adjustment Committee hearing within three days after being placed in segregation or Special Housing and "a Superintendent's Proceeding within seven days of such special confinement."[28] The directive was one of DOCS' attempts to avoid an unfavorable court decision.

The state's response to the court's decision was twofold. DOCS appealed the ruling, but also replaced Warden Janice Warne (who at the time had twenty years experience working for DOCS) as warden in August, 1975. Her replacement, Frances Clement, was the institution's deputy superintendent for security at the time of the August

Rebellion.[29] Clement's response to the *Powell v. Ward* (1975) decision was to ignore it while awaiting the Appellate Court's ruling.

On September 17, 1976, the Second Circuit issued *Powell v. Ward,* 542 F.2d 101 (1976). While the circuit court reaffirmed the lower court's decision mandating Bedford Hills administrators to observe due process in disciplinary hearings, it reversed the lower court's decision on two other counts. The court ruled that, "Prison officials responsible for maintaining security are not disqualified by the Due Process Clause from adjudicating allegations of breaches of prison security solely by the nature of their positions."[30]

Furthermore, the court allowed prison administrators to keep prisoners in segregation or special housing confinement over seven days, without holding the required hearings, though only under "truly exigent circumstances." Hence, while the *Powell v. Ward* (1975) decision sought to curtail the arbitrary actions of penal personnel, the Court of Appeals ultimately reinforced the power of custody-oriented sectors. Notwithstanding, the response of institutional administrators to the court's due process decision was to continue ignoring it for at least another six years.

In the meantime, Bedford Hills administrators continued to use a number of means to try to discourage prisoners from filing litigation and openly demanding reforms. Tactics included labelling prisoners who sought reforms as "disruptive," "violent," and "troublemakers," threatening prisoners with reprisals if they challenged institutional rules and regulations or participated as plaintiffs in the law suits, and promising additional "privileges" to prisoners who informed on their peers.[31] Initially, such pressures led a small number of prisoners to speak out in the media against the lawsuits. The reasons were explained by Barbara Cole, a former African-American prisoner at Bedford Hills: "Cause they told them they wouldn't give them this [or that] . . . they'd lock them down, they'd take their privileges from them. And the reason why they couldn't give no movies and the reason why it's slow for the visiting room is because they have to use officers because [of] this disruptive inmate . . . this disruptive group . . ."[32] The fact that prisoners saw male officers in full riot gear assault their peers was another factor that kept many prisoners uninvolved.

Despite the retaliatory actions of Bedford Hills' personnel there continued to be enough unrest at the facility and enough prisoner determination to change conditions that DOCS administrators felt it necessary to take additional steps to curtail reform-oriented activities. One solution, supported by DOCS, was proposed by a Westchester

County grand jury which conducted an investigation of Bedford Hills from March through May 1976. That solution was to open a second women's prison. According to the grand jury report made public on July 29, 1976, the "inability to transfer incorrigible prisoners to another facility for security reasons or for an inmate's protection creates a myriad of problems."[33] This was so because prisoners labelled incorrigible or violent were frequently able to continue their organizing activities even while they were in solitary confinement. According to the report, "Women guilty of violent behavior within the Bedford facility are segregated in a building at the center of the prison complex . . . where they are able to exchange messages and maintain their roles as ringleaders or instigators."[34] In view of the fact that Bedford Hills had been sued by prisoners labelled instigators by prison personnel, it is clear the report blamed the unrest at the institution on prisoners.

Furthermore, while during the *Powell v. Ward* (1975) suit, prisoners had testified about the ways that they were physically abused by male guards, the grand jury concluded that not only was the facility understaffed and the guards inadequately trained,[35] but administrators failed "to punish violent inmates adequately."[36] In effect, the grand jury seemed to be condoning Bedford Hills administrators' continued violation of prisoners' rights. Such abuses continued to occur even as the grand jury was writing its report.

On July 23, six days before the grand jury report was made public, Warden Clement transferred seven prisoners from Bedford Hills' segregation unit to Matteawan without granting them a judicial hearing. The seven prisoners subsequently filed a lawsuit charging that "they were illegally confined to a mental hospital, forcibly injected with drugs, and compelled to participate in a behavior modification program."[37] They were returned to Bedford Hills only when so ordered by a federal judge.

Continued charges by prisoners of staff misuse of medication led the State Commission of Corrections in November 1976 to investigate reports of rampant use of tranquilizers at the institution. Commission investigators contended that "tranquilizers had been indiscriminately distributed to prisoners, causing some to become dependent on drugs."[38] The response of Warden Clement was that "the responsibility for taking care of health needs lies with the physicians."[39] The psychiatrists, penal authorities argued, were staff of the State Department of Mental Hygiene not DOCS. However, while penal administrators argued that they were not responsible for the over-medication of prisoners, prisoner leaders and prisoners' rights advocates continued to charge that the widespread distribution of tranquilizers was one of the primary ways in which prison authorities sought to maintain the submissiveness of women prisoners.

Yet, there was another way prisoners claimed their rights were being violated and that was through the assignment of male officers to work in all areas of the facility. The conflicts created by the increasing presence of male guards led ten prisoners to file *Forts v. Ward,* No. 77 Civ. 1560, 434 F. Supp. 946 (S.D.N.Y. 1977), a class action suit, on April 1, 1977. Prisoners were represented once again by Stephen M. Latimer. The guards and DOCS were represented by attorneys for the state and Council 82. The suit alleged "that assignment of male officers to the housing units deprived appellees of their constitutionally guaranteed right to privacy by causing them to be 'involuntarily exposed' to the officers."[40] According to one prisoner, "Men guards have come into the shower room while I am drying myself and watched as I dried and dressed myself."[41] Moreover, male guards, who frequently walked throughout the housing corridors unannounced, often observed prisoners while they were using the toilet. As another prisoner claimed, "The men correction officers look over the curtains which we use to cover the doorways to our cells when we are on the toilet. They pull these curtains down for no good reason . . ."[42]

> It is also embarrassing that male guards are sent around to take the 6:30 A.M. count. I am usually asleep, and I feel very awkward about being awakened and peered at by these men guards when I am completely unable to control what position they observe me sleeping in.[43]

> Finally, I feel very awkward that men are assigned as C.O.'s at the hospital. One time. . . . I went to the hospital and was describing to the nurse what my problem which was of a personal female nature. There was a man guard directly in front of the medications window, where the nurse was. I was very embarrassed to have to describe the problem in front of the man guard.[44]

In June 1977, the District Court of New York granted prisoners' request for a preliminary injunction temporarily banning male guards from being assigned to those areas of the housing and hospital units which contained living quarters, toilets, or shower facilities. The court ruled that, "such assignments invaded inmates' constitutional rights to privacy without serving legitimate and compelling state interests, and were not required by the Civil Rights Act of 1964."[45] However, the state's appeal, *Forts v. Ward,* 566 F.2d 849 (1977), supported by the American Civil Liberties Union,[46] reversed the lower court's ruling. The Court of Appeal's decision had been influenced by a May 9, 1977, DOCS' directive issued in response to the lawsuit. The directive stated that, "correction officers of the opposite sex shall announce their presence in housing areas . . ."[47] The court agreed with DOCS' proposed solution that prisoners could dress in the shower stall and request guards to close their door slots for fifteen minutes while they were using the toilets. At the time of the decision, one out of every four guards at the facility, or 45 out of 130, were men.[48] Neither decision addressed the widespread fear among women prisoners that the increasing presence of male guards would lead to greater sexual and other types of physical abuse of prisoners.

Soon after the court's decision in *Forts v. Ward* (1977), prisoners' litigation efforts received further encouragement by the court's finding in *Todaro v. Ward* (1977) (discussed in chapter 9) that the provision of medical services at the facility was severely inadequate. In December 1977, as a response to the widespread publicity concerning prison conditions at Bedford Hills, as well as the *Forts v. Ward* and the *Todaro v. Ward* medical suits, Frances Clement was replaced as warden by Phyllis Curry. Prior to her assignment to Bedford Hills, Curry was deputy superintendent at Eastern Correctional Facility for Men. At the time she had eighteen years' experience in the criminal justice system. Her view of women prisoners was that, "Women have always acted as if they had basic rights as inmates. They wanted to know, 'Why can't we have this or that.' Even when you told them why they couldn't, they would retort, 'But I don't understand why we can't have this'."[49] In view of such opinions, it should not be surprising that under Curry, penal personnel at Bedford Hills continued to ignore state and federal court decisions as well as DOCS' directives (i.e., October 1970, March 1975) mandating that prisoners be accorded due process in disciplinary hearings.

By the second half of the 1970s, it was clear to a number of Latina, African-American, and white prisoners, that institutional administrators were not going to implement reforms nor carry out judicial decisions unless they were further coerced into doing so by the courts. The fact that the courts mandated prisoners to first file grievances through the institution's Inmate Grievance Resolution Committee before they could recur to litigation once again, meant that prisoners were right back where they started before they filed the *Powell v. Ward* suit.

Confronted with the fact that prisoners who openly challenged abusive penal policies were severely penalized by institutional administrators, a number of Latina, African-American, and white prisoners decided to revitalize the political underground coalition formed during the mid-1970s to document the widespread violation of prisoners' due process rights. Prisoners hoped this information could be used by prisoners' rights attorneys to file further litigation.

The revitalization of the political underground prisoner coalition at the end of the 1970s, was the result of the realization by various prisoner leaders, that they needed to put aside personal rivalries in order to build a broader-base of support within the prisoner population that would facilitate the documentation of prisoner abuses. The coalition was also designed to provide support to those prisoners who took on the responsibility for openly demanding reform of prison conditions.

Although the political underground coalition had existed since the mid-1970s, and had complemented the litigation efforts of third parties during the *Powell v. Ward* litigation, its activities had been limited by the lack of an organizational structure that could secure and coordinate the assistance of prisoners who were members of formal, informal, and administrative groups. Without such coordination, prison authorities could use one group of prisoners against another as it had done when the initial lawsuits had been filed.

An underground network was also needed because prisoner leaders felt that if existing formal prisoner organizations were used to openly challenge penal authorities the groups would be disbanded. Former African-American prisoner leader Barbara Cole clearly expressed the limitations placed on formal prisoner groups, "That's all right for communication but they give them guidelines, okay? And if they jeopardize those guidelines, they ice them or they ice the program itself."[50] The need for an underground structure was also made apparent by the harsh reaction prison authorities had to prisoners who openly sought reforms.

The revitalization of the underground coalition during 1978 was fostered by the emergence in 1977 of Tita Puente as MUML's president. It was Puente's visibility within the Latina prisoner population that motivated the African-American prisoners, who had dominated the underground network since 1974, to include her in the group. Puente's willingness to mobilize Latina prisoners in support of diverse types of coalition-building efforts increased the scope of Latina prisoner participation in such activities. Puente's emergence as MUML's leader reflected the transformation the organization had undergone since the mid-1970s.

Changes in MUML's Leadership

During the time that the major class action suits of the 1970s were being filed (1974-1977), the primary concern of most Latina prisoners continued to be organizing the yearly ethnic and family day events. However, by the mid-1970s the responsibility for organizing such activities had passed on to MUML. As a result, more Latinas joined the organization to help plan the events. Others saw MUML meetings as a place where they could go to receive emotional and cultural support and speak in Spanish. Still others went to obtain information about prison programs and events as well as institutional rules and regulations. MUML's founders, nevertheless, continued to see the organization as a means to advocate for a number of collective Latina concerns.

Despite the diverse interests apparent within MUML, by the end of 1975 the organization had established a visible presence within the facility. MUML's consolidation became evident in March 1976, when the organization issued a "Position Paper" addressing the immediate need to implement bilingual educational and vocational programs and to hire additional bilingual personnel, particularly guidance counselors, parole officers, doctors, and nurses.[51] Moreover, the organization called for the creation of "a follow-up program on the outside for job sponsorship, training programs, housing, family ties, and educational programs for women upon their release."[52] These concerns demonstrated the increasing preoccupation among Latina prisoners with mobilizing third party support to address a number of non-family related issues.

Interestingly, MUML's "Position Paper" seems to have been heavily influenced by Martín Sosa, co-coordinator of the Center for Puerto Rican Studies' Prison Task Force, and PUL, Green Haven's Latino prisoner organization, with which he worked closely. MUML was receptive to such influences precisely because Latina and Latino prisoners were experiencing the same concerns about the need to implement bilingual programs, hire additional bilingual personnel, and secure the support of the outside Latina(o) community in order to ensure a successful reentry of Latina(o) prisoners into the community upon release.

An important contributing factor to changes in MUML's political orientation was the fact that between 1972 and 1975 the number of Latinas within the state's prison system doubled.[53] This led to a growth in the number of prisoners needing bilingual programs and services. The fact that few bilingual staff and programs were available to meet the needs of Latina prisoners encouraged MUML leaders to redouble their efforts to secure such services. Luz Santana, ex-prisoner leader at Bedford Hills, described the conditions and treatment Latinas, particularly those who were Spanish-monolingual, were exposed to during the 1970s. While Santana's narrative begins in 1977, it similarly describes the conditions encountered by Latina prisoners during the early 1970s. Because this is the only available account of the conditions encountered by Latina prisoners at Bedford Hills, the following section of the speech is quoted at length.

> 1977 was not a very good year. Hispanics coming into Bedford Hills Correctional Facility had less choices than other women arriving, in terms of obtaining rehabilitative programming. There were many openings for menial and maintenance assignments. There was one bilingual Basic Education class which accommodated fifteen women per day. Women who applied for certain vocational programs were interviewed and judged by their Hispanic accents, and often prejudice disqualified them from participating in the educational programs . . .
>
> There were three Spanish-speaking officers who were kept off the unit areas, often kept at the front gate. There was one Spanish-speaking counsellor who was so bogged down with caseloads, that he was unable to meet the needs of those Hispanic women who required his cultural logistics in dealing with their needs. In addition to the fact that there were very few Hispanic personnel at this facility, they were discouraged from speaking their native language, unless a supervisor considered it "absolutely necessary". Administrators appeared to fear what was being said, if it was not in their language, even if it was their own staff that was speaking. . . . Hispanic women were ordered not to speak Spanish, and if they did, punishment was often received for it. It was easy for those who knew English to comply with these regulations, but those who knew no English at all were expected to remain mute. Occasionally, we could interact, hidden in one of our cells or at the Hispanic Committee meetings held once a week.
>
> There were no bilingual officers working around inmates. There were no bilingual personnel in any of the special service areas, such as: Parole, Medical Department, Mental Hygiene, Inmate Grievance Resolution Committee, Law Library, Vocational, Educational or in the administrative areas. There were no Hispanic Group Therapy programs and this caused many of the Hispanic women to be excluded from adequate services in all areas of the facility. This situation also hindered the release of these women to parole. Many parole release decisions were based upon the fact that these Hispanic inmates had not participated actively in the precise services the Parole Board required to determine their eligibility for release.[54]

One area in which the lack of bilingual personnel was most clearly evident was the fact that until the end of the 1970s, the prisoner rule book was written only in English. Moreover, disciplinary hearings and documents were not translated into Spanish. This meant that Latina prisoners who were not fluent in English had to depend on the services of their peers to translate such documents. In fact, it was only as a result of the *Powell v. Ward* (1976) litigation (to be discussed) that DOCS was forced as of the early 1980s, to make translations of disciplinary documents available.[55]

Faced with these circumstances, it became clearer to more Latina prisoners that in order to compel prison administrators to address their concerns, they needed a permanent organization that could make collective demands and mobilize third parties and penal personnel on their behalf. As a result, more Latina prisoners became willing to join MUML. However, as with most organizations, the number of members who participated in organizing any one event fluctuated depending on prisoners' interests in that area. For example, more prisoners continued to participate in the organizing of family day events than in the planning of educational workshops or the filing of class action suits. However, while during the 1973-1975 period, the number of prisoners active in the organization on a regular basis fluctuated between three and four, by 1976, it fluctuated between six and twelve.[56]

An additional factor contributing to MUML's change in orientation was the fact that several Latina prisoners who had been involved in the 1974 August Rebellion and had participated as witnesses in the *Powell v. Ward* (1975) suit, joined the organization. These Latinas were willing to confront institutional policies openly, and along with their non-Latina peers, could mobilize third party support for collective concerns. Their actions increased the hope of other Latina prisoners that changes in prison policies toward them could be achieved if MUML was able to mobilize outside sources of third party support particularly within the Latina(o) community.

In spite of such expectations, however, MUML's leaders were unable to mobilize consistent sources of support within the Latina(o) community. While the Prison Task Force had begun to work with Latina prisoners at Bedford Hills in the middle of 1973, as its focus began to change away from prisoners' rights work in 1975, its ability to provide support to Latina prisoners dwindled. In 1976, MUML leaders were able to secure the sponsorship of Martín Sosa, co-coordinator of the PTF, and Women United for Struggle, a student group from Hostos Community College, for the celebration of the yearly San Juan Bautista Feast Day event. In 1977, the support for the event was provided, once again by Sosa, and the newly-created "Ad Hoc Committee in Support of Hispanic Women at Bedford Hills."[57]

The importance of third party support was demonstrated when the Ad Hoc Committee was able to successfully intervene on behalf of Latina prisoners when Warden Curry tried to prevent MUML from inviting family members to the event that year. However, these Latina(o) community activists were unable to provide MUML the ongoing support needed to achieve a substantial change in institutional policies toward Latina prisoners. In both years, the supporters promised MUML that they would continue to lobby central office and institutional personnel on their behalf. However, following each feast day event, long periods of time elapsed before members of the groups visited the facility again. One of the limitations of the Ad Hoc Committee, for example, was precisely that it was a committee, not an organization. In fact, the group was made up of Puerto Rican community activists who used the names of organizations they belonged to (e.g., Concerned Boricua Committee, Young Film Makers) to gain credibility with prison authorities. They could not count fully on the resources of these organizations which in turn had limited resources and were undergoing financial difficulties. As the 1980s approached, Latina prisoners, like their male counterparts, found themselves without any significant sources of third party support within the Latina(o) community.

As MUML's leadership tried unsuccessfully to mobilize sustained third party support in the Latina(o) community during the late 1970s, it was confronted by Latina prisoners who questioned the leaders' capabilities and tactics. This was so despite the fact that two of MUML leaders had been main plaintiffs in the *Todaro v. Ward* medical suit. Some prisoners felt that the organization's main approach of writing letters to institutional and central office personnel was ineffective and insufficient. It was argued that while MUML wrote letters, other Latina prisoners were being physically abused by guards because they openly challenged the abuses by institutional personnel. Luz Santana recounted the type of treatment received by Latina, African-American, and white prisoners who openly demanded reforms at the end of the 1970s and/or became involved in verbal confrontations with guards.

> 1977–1978: There were some women at Bedford Hills who had the foresight and education to speak out against these inequalities, not only for Hispanics, but for all women. For this, they were labeled as "defiant troublemakers." Per administrative policies, fraternizing or congregating was seen as a breach of security, and stiff penalties were imposed . . .

Every inmate was viewed as "criminal", first and foremost. There was no such thing as an attempt at interpersonal communication between a staff person and an inmate in order to resolve critical problems. It was a frequent sight to see a CERT Team of twenty (20) officers, in full gear, with helmets, vests, and nightstick, arrive at a unit to beat and pummel a single female into unconsciousness, then drag her off to a Special Housing Unit. Often, this occurred simply when women were running off at the mouth behind some frustrating and painful problem. In some instances, it happened due to a personality clash between the inmates, often the Hispanic inmates who were impeded from expressing thoughts, ideas, anxieties, etc.[58]

Within the Latina prisoner population there were women like Tita Puente who refused to bow to institutional personnel and responded to guards' verbal and physical provocations and abuse with a like response. These prisoners, some of whom later became MUML members, were feared by some of MUML's leaders who, ironically, also considered them "rabblerousers."[59] In fact, the latter prisoners were also the most likely to form part of the political underground prisoner network. At the center of MUML's disagreements, however, was the age old controversy between those Latina prisoners who felt the formal Latina organization should concentrate on demanding reforms through formal prisoner and administrative groups and those who felt it was necessary to use all available methods to counter the actions of penal personnel. Ultimately, MUML leaders feared that if group members went "too far" in terms of the methods they used to demand changes, the organization would be disbanded and Latina prisoners would lose the little they had gained (e.g., the ability to meet as a group and hold meetings, organize ethnic and family day events).

Despite these conflicting viewpoints an accord was reached whereby the more traditional MUML leaders agreed not to interfere with the efforts of those Latina prisoners who wanted to challenge prison policies in other ways. Latina leaders involved in the political underground prisoner coalition agreed, in turn, not to compromise the existence of MUML by using its name when demanding reforms unless the organization agreed to it. This accord was similar to one reached by prisoner leaders involved in the political underground coalition and those involved in other formal prisoner and administrative organizations. According to Barbara Cole, an African-American prisoner active in the political underground network throughout the 1970s, such understandings were made possible because the leaders of formal and administrative groups also favored reforms. However, they did not want to risk the existence of the groups to achieve them. According to Cole, the agreement reached was that, "They didn't want to lose what they had . . . but they would not stand in our way and they wouldn't speak against us."[60] Such agreements were facilitated by the fact that, on occasion, membership in formal and informal groups overlapped.

In 1977, Puente was elected president of MUML. Perhaps as a symbol of this change in orientation, MUML became increasingly referred to as the Hispanic Committee. With the election of Puente as MUML's president, the organization's balance of power shifted toward those Latina prisoners who endorsed the use of a wider range of tactics. Puente favored the strengthening of the political underground coalition and the use of other informal as well as formal prisoner and administrative groups to lobby for prison reforms and the implementation of more bilingual services, the hiring of additional bilingual personnel, and an end to the discriminatory treatment to which Latina prisoners were subjected. Puente herself was not only a member of the Hispanic Committee, but at different times she also formed part of the Long-Termers' Committee, the ILC, and the IGRC. Equally important was the fact that Puente favored cultivating the support of institutional personnel who were disaffected with prison authorities and might, therefore, be sympathetic to prisoner demands for reforms. Thus, under Puente's leadership, Latina prisoners participated simultaneously in formal and informal prisoner and administrative groups and coalitions in the hopes of forcing prison administrators to carry out much needed reforms. Such combined tactics were necessary in view of the limits of litigation to ensure a prompt change in prison conditions. Prisoners' rights activists, nevertheless, continued to support the efforts of women prisoners seeking redress through litigation.

Third Party Support and the Limits of Litigation

The indifference of penal administrators to court mandates was countered by prisoners' continued willingness to challenge administrative policies. Summarizing the change in women's approach to litigation between 1974 and 1979, Latimer stated:

> Back then [1974] women were just starting. So in terms of development, of using the legal process, they were behind in that . . . When I was there they were just figuring it out, what it was all about and how to do it . . . By the time I left, by '79, they had . . . a couple of really

good people in the law library that were doing a lot of work. . . . pulling
a lot of stuff in the law library together . . . and filing cases for people.[61]

Prisoners litigation efforts were complemented by the willingness
of third parties to advocate on their behalf. Although prison personnel
continued to ignore court decisions favorable to prisoners, the fact that
prisoners and their advocates were able to win some of the suits
increased prisoners' hopes that conditions within the institution would
eventually change for the better. The support of third parties in the
form of prisoners' rights attorneys, law students, paralegals, and community activists was evident in a number of ways. During the early
1970s, the WLP offered courses and legal assistance to prisoners.
Starting in 1974, prisoners' rights attorneys affiliated with Bronx Legal
Services and later the Prisoners' Rights Project of the Legal Aid Society
filed a number of class action suits challenging penal policies and practices. Moreover, attorneys made their presence felt within the facility
whenever they visited Bedford Hills to interview prisoners involved in
the lawsuits. They also supported prisoners by holding press conferences and by participating in community events designed to educate
the outside community about women in prison. Such events were often
planned by grassroots women community activists, some of whom
worked as paralegals with Latimer particularly during the mid-1970s.
    Women community activists, predominantly radical white and
Jewish (primarily lesbian) feminists and African-American women
identified with Black nationalist movements of the times such as the
Black Panther Party, were fundamental sources of support for women
imprisoned at Bedford Hills during the 1970s. While some of these
activists were known to prisoners such as Carol Crooks, prior to their
incarceration, most had been attracted to prisoner support work by outside political affiliations and the concern for the welfare of women who
were victims of state violence. Some of these women had themselves
experienced incarceration as a result of having been set-up by the government for their involvement in grassroots community activities.
    The support women community activists offered Bedford Hills'
prisoners varied. Some, particularly law students and paralegals, visited prisoners involved in litigation to compile data for the lawsuits.
Others put themselves on the visiting lists of individual prisoners.
This allowed them to keep abreast of events taking place at the facility. Community activists also made their presence felt during court
hearings. This let prisoners, DOCS' personnel, and the court know
that prisoners' claims were being supported on the outside. Women

community activists held demonstrations outside prison grounds protesting penal policies and regulations. They sent out mailings, organized teach-ins and fundraising drives, and publicized in the media
the plight of prisoners.

In spite of the support offered by prisoners' rights attorneys and
other community activists, the effectiveness of litigation to relieve the
overall conditions of imprisoned women was limited. For example, it
could take six months or longer from the moment prisoners first filed
a class action suit for the lower court to issue a decision. In the meantime, prison administrators continued violating prisoners' rights. Decisions favorable to prisoners were immediately appealed by DOCS. It
then took the Court of Appeals anywhere from six months to a year to
issue its decision. Sometimes, as in *Fort v. Ward,* the lower court's ruling in favor of prisoners was overturned by a higher court. At other
times, as in the *Powell v. Ward* suit, the Court of Appeals ratified the
lower court's overall decision but reversed some of its findings. The
fact that the *Powell v. Ward* decision continued to be ignored by penal
authorities was what motivated prisoners to redouble the efforts of the
political underground prisoner coalition created at the end of 1974.

Organizing Underground and Litigating for Reforms

Between 1974 and 1978, several elements converged that made it
possible for Latina, African-American, and white prisoner leaders at
Bedford Hills to increasingly confront the actions of prison administrators. First, women began to realize that unless they united as prisoners there was little they could do to secure institutional reforms.
Moreover, without some measure of unity, administrators could always
use existing ethnic and racial cleavages against them. Second, a small
but significant number of prisoners' rights attorneys, paralegals, and
women community activists supportive of prisoners' demands for
reforms surfaced. These third parties refrained from becoming involved
in intra-prisoner conflicts and rivalries, thus contributing to the creation of unity among prisoners. Third, prisoners had learned that they
needed to use all existing organizations (e.g., informal, formal prisoner,
and administrative) simultaneously to challenge penal policies and
practices. Equally important was the formation of a multiracial/multi-
ethnic underground prisoner coalition designed to document the abuses
of prisoners by institutional personnel. Its creation was the result of the
realization that reforms could not be accomplished merely through the
use of existing formal prisoner and administrative organizations

because these groups could be disbanded if administrators felt they had gone too far in demanding reforms. Thus, ironically, prison authorities had left prisoners little alternative but to create a political underground coalition aimed at achieving a redefinition of the conditions of imprisonment. How did the political underground coalition pursue its goals? How successful was it in generating penal and third party support? And what impact did its activities have on the conditions encountered by Latina prisoners?

The interracial/interethnic underground network that gelled at Bedford Hills at the end of the 1970s, used organizing tactics which included rotating leadership among a core group of primarily long-termers housed in different sections of the institution. Having leaders in the various housing units was essential because, as former underground leader Mirna González stated:

> . . . the units were separated and . . . if you lived in 113 Building, you were not supposed to go to 114 Building or 112 Building, alright? The only time that we really had to organize and to discuss . . . were during our leisure hours. On our leisure hours we were subject to remaining in our housing unit or we would get an hour recreation in the yard. But . . . they had the yards divided, 114 had their own yard, 13 and 12 shared another one. And in terms of getting like the petition signed and getting the women mobilized, I would not be able to go . . . from one building to another but I had somebody there that would handle it and bring it back, the finished work, you know, and I would compile it . . .[62]

Issues around which prisoners organized depended on what was happening at the facility at the time. According to González, "Whatever was the most oppressive situation at the moment would become an issue. . . . Everything from conditions on the living units to education to recreation to medical to disciplinary to therapeutic."[63] Open discussions of concerns took place among prisoners in areas of the facility where they were allowed to congregate in groups. Sometimes a handful of prisoners were able to meet and discuss strategies while participating in programs and/or classes.

Prisoners learned to identify staff members, particularly guards, who were sympathetic enough to reform efforts to allow discussion in "public" places without reporting participants to administrative personnel. According to Pamela Santiago, former underground leader:

> Like if there was an officer on the unit that was racist and we knew that he was KKK ('cause a lot of them flashed their KKK rings) we

wouldn't even discuss . . . a thing. But if the officer that was on the
unit was, maybe not partisan but . . . understood or sympathized . . .
we would go ahead and do our work because they wouldn't call the
forces on us."[64]

These discussions would continue in the housing units where
more support for reform efforts was gathered and prisoners were
recruited for various tasks.

> It's like I would speak . . . whether it was in the yard, in the restroom.
> We would throw out the subject, discuss it, open discussion, okay?
> Out of that, then it would go into the other floors. They would pass it
> on, okay? Out of that there was always a group of women that would
> approach me to get further information and to express their wanting
> . . . to become involved, you know, just to help bring about the situa-
> tion. Some of them remained in the dark and some of them . . . you
> know, stood by me.[65]

According to Santiago, prisoners' efforts were coordinated by, ". . .
a congregate group, you know, from throughout the institution . . . who
were not afraid to take a stand. Black, white, and Latina. We even had
a Chinese girl with us at one point."[66] When coordinating the functions
of the underground network, the core group would take into account
the fact that prisoners' willingness to participate in various aspects of
organizing varied. According to former African-American underground
prisoner leader Barbara Cole:

> What we did is we used everybody in the institution that wanted to
> take part . . . There was some women that did not want to go to court,
> did not want their name down, but they would do research or they
> would do the typing, okay, or they would sneak the information out
> of the administration or give us the scuttlebutt . . . what the officers
> or the commanding officers was getting ready to do or talking about
> . . . or directors or whatever . . .[67]

Some prisoners gathered, translated, and documented information
about prison conditions and/or abuse of prisoners by staff members.
Others wrote letters and petitions addressed to institutional administrators requesting reforms in various issue areas. According to Mirna
González:

> We used to draft . . .petitions . . . and take a section at a time, you
> know, . . . per area, what was needed in the hospital. What was

needed in the parole area. What was needed in the unit. What was needed as part of recreation. What was needed as part of education. What was needed for the Latino community.[68]

Prisoners typed and photocopied petitions and other documents to protect themselves against guard raids that could result in the destruction of the material gathered and the imposition of severe penalties for those caught with it. Once the final version of a document was drafted, it was circulated throughout the facility and signed by prisoners who were willing to visibly support reform measures. Documents would then be forwarded, either through formal prisoner or administrative organizations, to administrators at both the institutional and central office levels.

> It would be directed to [the] Administration . . . We would cc it to anybody hoping that somebody would come . . . to review things . . . to [meet] with a particular group or through ILC . . . We would try to get them to resolve some of the situations. We were trying to get them to be accountable . . . for the women they had in their custody . . . If we didn't get a . . . favorable response within the facility . . . then we would make a copy of what we had submitted to the . . . . Administration . . . . and [mail it] to Coughlin with a cc to all his subordinates . . . And then we would make him accountable . . .[69]

Prisoners' documents were also forwarded to third parties.

> It was a conscious strategy because we knew that we had to get the information out of the prison . . . When we found that [outside agencies] responded to that, then we knew that was . . . the key . . . Everything needed to be documented and at times had to be remembered. And people had to remember who was there and what it was about . . . specifics . . . And we had to help each other. The ones who weren't able to write, somebody else would write it for them . . . There was . . . an organization and documentation of fact. And this kept going to the outside agencies . . .[70]

Prisoners knew that third parties were interested in receiving information concerning prison conditions and the treatment given prisoners by staff because they could use it to publicize events taking place within the institution and/or to litigate against prison administrators. As Santiago described:

> I'm in the rec and . . . we're talking about something and we're watching the news. And all of a sudden, you know, somebody would comment about some officer stifling their phone call, alright? Then I would speak on it, you know. Then a few others would start and it would become . . . an issue of debate. Then we would go out and find out who else was suffering that same type of bias . . . and document it and present it and get copies to outside organizations. That was . . . the focal point of [it].[71]

Getting the information out to third parties was also important for another reason.

> Because anything that happened internally . . . would get squashed internally, right? But if we were working on something and we were making a presentation . . . to DOCS, we made sure that there was outside groups who had copies of everything that we were doing in case they came in the middle of the night and kicked your ass and dragged you into solitary or you were transferred to another facility or you were stuck up in Mental Hygiene to be vegetableized, you know, . . . or they gave you the wrong medication at the dispensary, okay? By having an outside group having copies of what was going on, set up a safety mechanism for the individuals that were doing the work. It wasn't total safety but it was more than none.[72]

Prisoners who acted as the visible spokespersons were the ones most often exposed to retaliation by prison authorities. Retaliations took several forms.

> . . . the floor officer would go and search your room and be specific in their search, okay. . . . The women were, in fact, violating the rules in many instances, not all, okay? Hey, you know, like bringing up an egg or sugar from the cafeteria to have in your room. You'd have coffee upstairs or you decide to skip dinner meal because you didn't like what was on the menu. You took the egg you got in the morning and scrambled it with a piece of toast and you had it with a cup of coffee and that was your dinner, alright? Since the rule was that you couldn't have eggs, they could use something like that. If an officer has an argument with you today, tomorrow they could go in your cell and toss and come up with any given thing to cause you to be disciplined. And if you protest then they would say that you were disobeying a direct order and you were assaultive. And then they would bring up a CERT Team of twenty officers with head gear and nightsticks and . . . vests and . . . beat you unconscious and drag you into solitary.[73]

Charges could include anything from:

> "improper behavior towards officer" . . . "verbal abusive," "assault,"
> "fighting," "disobeying direct orders," "out of bounds." They would
> charge me with shit like that, "out of bounds." I was walking three feet
> away from an area and . . . they would use something like that to put
> me out of circulation."[74]

Another way to intimidate and/or further penalize prisoners was
to interfere with their visits.

> They would attack people through their emotions. You know, like
> the family would come in to visit somebody and they wouldn't find
> the inmate's chart and [they'd] tell the family they weren't there and
> turn the family away at the gate, okay? . . . And the inmate would
> go off because their family came and they weren't able to see them,
> you know. And then like . . . an officer would come back . . . and shoot
> at the side of their mouth, "Yeah, bitch . . . you got yours!" You know,
> like that, letting them know that it was purposely done, and push-
> ing people over the edge.[75]

Prisoners who went "over the edge" tended to become involved in
physical confrontations with guards. Such confrontations frequently
resulted in the former being locked in segregation.

In view of the various actions taken by personnel to interfere with
prisoners' reform-oriented actions, one of the motivations for the creation of the underground network was to prevent institutional personnel from stopping "the movement before it started."[76] This could be done:

> By coming onto the [housing] unit and tearing up people's documents
> . . . and intimidating. By penalizing you . . . through your mail, losing
> your mail, not giving you your mail. Especially . . . if the officer was
> very accurate and his reporting said, "So and so was leading a topic of
> discussion around ta-ta-ta-ta," that person would be harassed, and sit-
> uations would be set up so that, that person would be provoked into
> doing something wrong or . . . going off. And then they would remove
> them from the unit into segregation. And when they came . . . out . . .
> they would place them on a whole different housing unit. So it dis-
> rupted the communication or the . . . . alliance that [existed] . . .
> amongst that group of women.[77]

Prisoners involved in the underground network also had to protect
themselves from the actions of their peers who were willing to provide

prison officials with information concerning the organizers in exchange for additional privileges. As it was mentioned earlier, when the first class actions suits were filed some prisoners came out against them before the mass media. The reaction of underground prisoner leaders to this turn of events was to ask those prisoners who did not want to be involved with litigation to remain neutral. They were told, "If you don't want to work with us, just don't stand in our way and say nothing against us . . ."[78] As stated earlier, a similar agreement had been made between leaders of the underground network and those involved in formal prisoner and administrative organizations.

In exchange for such neutrality, members of the underground network agreed not to use the names of any of the formal prisoner organizations in their endeavors lest that be used by prison administrators as an excuse to disband the groups. This agreement was maintained even when membership in the underground network and in the formal organizations overlapped and even in those cases in which underground prisoner leaders had joined and/or created specific formal prisoner groups to pursue the agenda of the underground coalition.

Prisoners who "squealed" on their peers were dealt with in different ways by prisoner leaders. Some believed they should merely be ostracized, others felt they needed to be punished in additional ways, including physical retaliation.

Prisoners organizing underground also sought to mobilize the support of a few trusted staff who might be willing to mail documents or make phone calls to third parties to publicize what was happening in the facility. Underground leaders were aware that there were some guards and civilian personnel who favored reforms. However, because staff members who were openly sympathetic to prisoners could themselves be subject to retaliation by administrative personnel or co-workers,[79] they overwhelmingly chose to stay on the outskirts of what was happening at the facility, "They wouldn't . . . turn us in, but they wouldn't participate."[80]

One of the ways Latina leaders won the support of penal personnel was by refraining from criticizing any one sector of the institutional staff or any one ethnic/racial group. Latina prisoner leaders recognized that Latina and African-American guards and civilian employees were also victims of discriminatory racial/ethnic policies. They emphasized the need for bilingual services as well as an end to the discriminatory policies to which both Latina prisoners and staff were subjected. These requests were supported by African-American and white prisoners both in the underground network[81] and in the formal organizations.

As discussed in this section, during the late 1970s, Bedford Hills prisoners revitalized the multiracial/ multiethnic political underground coalition created in 1974 to coordinate prisoners' efforts to document abuse of prisoners by institutional personnel. The revitalization allowed the African-American-dominated coalition to expand its support among the prisoner population, particularly among Latina prisoners. African-American prisoner leaders became more open to including Latinas in coalition-building efforts, not only because of the increasing numbers and distinct language needs of Latinas, but because administrators were arguing that the demands for reforms were only being made by a few prisoners. According to Barbara Cole, "The people from . . . Albany was trying to say that it was only the Blacks or it was only one group of people."[82] Thus, ironically, coalition-building efforts were encouraged by DOCS' own reactions to prisoners' attempts to achieve reforms.

The participation of Latinas in the political underground network served to politicize prisoners who had not been politically active before their incarceration. Some gained a clearer understanding of what their rights as prisoners were. Others came to understand that collectively they might be able to achieve what none of the groups could achieve alone: a change in penal policies. By forming a coalition with African-American and white prisoners, Latinas were also able to see that they could struggle for specific Latina concerns (e.g., bilingual education) at the same time that they worked to achieve collective prisoner goals (e.g., better medical conditions).

Moreover, the political underground coalition was able to continue mobilizing the support of third parties and a few staff members. Prison authorities responded to prisoners' reform efforts by severely penalizing those prisoners involved in such activities. While such repression alienated some prisoners from the political underground coalition, they succeeded in convincing others that reforms could only come about through the efforts of informal political prisoner groups. By the end of the 1970s, the efforts of the underground coalition to document the abuse of prisoners by institutional personnel allowed prisoners' rights attorneys access to information and documents that were then used to charge prison authorities with continued violation of prisoners' due process rights.

Resistance, Litigation, and Changes in Prison Administration

In late 1978, Elizabeth Koob (then working at Bronx Legal Services) filed a contempt motion to get Carol Crooks, once again, out of solitary

confinement. Crooks had already spent over four months in segregation, though prison authorities had never conducted the required disciplinary hearing. Soon after filing the motion on behalf of Crooks,
attorneys at Bronx Legal Services began receiving letters from other
prisoners informing them that their due process rights had also been
violated. According to Koob, "We received letters from . . . about ten or
fifteen women complaining about their hearing. And we contacted
them and met with them. And they told us about other women . . . "[83]
Oftentimes, this information was forwarded to the attorneys as a
result of the efforts of the political underground coalition. These documents revealed the gross pattern of violation of prisoners' rights that
took place at the facility despite the 1975 *Powell v. Ward* decision.

Following the court decision, the judge had instructed prisoners
who felt their due process rights were being violated to seek redress
by filing grievances with the institution's IGRC. Prisoners' use of the
IGRC (for those who dared complained about the actions of prison
personnel openly), soon proved ineffective in curtailing abuses of their
rights. It was the continued violations of prisoners' rights, combined
with the ineffectiveness of the grievance mechanism to stop such
abuses, that had prompted prisoners to renew their reform efforts
through the underground coalition and prisoners' rights advocates.
According to Mirna González, "The legal cases came out of the organizing that was going on, trying to bring the Administration to concur,
you know, on what was needed. And then as a result of all the . . .
abuse and everything that went on behind that, their trying to stifle
us, to stop us, that's where the legal cases emerged."[84]

Upon realizing that prison authorities had not been implementing
the *Powell v. Ward* decision, prisoners' attorneys decided to convert the
motion to get Crooks out of segregation into a motion for the class. This
time the contempt motion also included a demand that for those prisoners who only read Spanish, "all disciplinary records . . . charges and
everything, had to be given to them in Spanish."[85] Latina prisoners also
alluded to, "the bias and the prejudice of not allowing the women to
speak in their own native language, the bias of not allowing the Latino
officers to speak in Spanish . . ."[86]

In the period between 1979, when hearings were being held in
court, and 1980, when the final decision on the contempt motion was
made by the judge,[87] prison authorities continued to violate prisoners'
rights and penalize those who called for reforms. During the hearings,
prisoners testifying before the court, ". . . had to show that . . . the times
that they [the guards] utilized "use of force" and the times they came in

and raided . . . were not necessarily "security-wise" but prejudice-wise and biased-wise . . . It was meant to subjugate the individual, you know, that was their means of stifling situations."[88]

In 1980, the contempt motion was decided in favor of Bedford Hills prisoners and Judge Charles E. Stewart, Jr. appointed Attorney, Linda Singer as a "Special Master"[89] to oversee compliance with the 1975 *Powell v. Ward* decision. According to Elizabeth Koob:

> The Judge found: the defendants to be in contempt of his prior orders which he now made into a permanent injunction, and ordered the Superintendent to comply within a set period or be subjected to a fine for each day thereafter of noncompliance. Additionally, the Court added further protections, most significantly, an order that non-English, Spanish speaking inmates be provided disciplinary documents in Spanish, a translator at their hearing, and a Spanish speaking assistant if they were entitled to an assistant. The Judge also ordered that past violative hearings be expunged from the inmate's records, and that a Special Master be appointed to supervise compliance with the Court Orders and to report findings and recommendations to the Court.[90]

DOCS' response was to appeal the court's decree. However, in 1981, the Appellate Court reaffirmed the lower court's ruling. DOCS authorities at the institutional and central office levels responded by ignoring the court decisions once again. Finally, in February 1981, six years after the filing of the original *Powell v. Ward* decision, DOCS, confronted with the dilemma of having to pay a $1,000 a day fine for each day of noncompliance with the court order, negotiated an agreement with the prisoners' attorneys and Linda Singer. In the agreement, DOCS conceded to observe due process in carrying out disciplinary procedures and established a "settlement fund" of $125,000 to be spent by prisoners for improvements they wanted to make at Bedford Hills.[91] At the time, prisoners' attorneys also requested that a series of manuals be produced by DOCS indicating the procedures to follow in disciplinary cases, the responsibilities of guards, and the rights of prisoners.

Once the settlement fund was allotted to prisoners at Bedford Hills, prisoners used all existing formal prisoner and administrative groups as well as formed additional ad hoc committees (e.g., Education Committee, Recreation Committee) to discuss the manner in which the $125,000 should be spent. For the first time, as part of the discussions, attorneys were allowed to have group meetings with prisoners in the housing units. Luz Santana and Carol Crooks were chosen by their peers to represent them in the ensuing negotiations with DOCS to discuss how the allotted fund should be spent.[92] This decision was then forwarded to administrators through the Inmate Liaison Committee.[93] The court allowed Santana to act as one of the two class representatives primarily because Latina prisoners were the fastest growing group within the prisoner population and had additional language needs.

As prisoner representatives, Santana and Crooks were authorized to "investigate sources for products and meet with consultants to determine how best the money could be spent in certain areas, for example, to improve the educational program at the facility."[94] One of the most important aspects of the negotiation was that, it was the prisoners, not DOCS, who determined how the money should be spent. This was so despite the fact that, "The Special Master had the authority to rule whether or not a purchase chosen by plaintiffs was for the benefit of the plaintiff-class and whether any objections by defendants to a purchase was reasonable."[95] According to Carol Crooks:

> We had to get a poll. We wrote up a sheet and we . . . sent it out. We talked to all the community and we asked them to give us an agenda of things that we should ask the inmates . . . to vote on . . . We had already made an overall decision about what we should look forward to but we wanted to know exactly what we should itemize to, okay? And the way we itemized was we took it to the population, let them make the decision, okay.[96]

Part of the funds awarded prisoners was used to expand the library collection, buy books on African-American history, hire an educational consultant, and buy computers for business classes. Other funds were used to address various concerns raised by Spanish-speaking prisoners. According to Luz Santana:

> The funds were used to enhance the educational, vocational, legal, recreational, and living conditions at the facility for women. In addition, Spanish literature was provided for the circulating Library, added materials were brought into the bilingual classroom, and some materials were found for several of the vocational classes in Spanish.[97]

Thus, Latinas were able to obtain a number of services, albeit limited, as a result of their participation in coalition-building and litigation efforts.

The negotiations that produced the settlement above were facilitated by a change in Bedford Hill's administration, which took place in

April 1982. Once it became clear that DOCS could no longer afford to ignore court orders, central office personnel responded by replacing the Superintendent, the Deputy Superintendent for Programs, the Deputy Superintendent for Administration, and the Deputy Superintendent for Security with a number of liberal administrators. DOCS' action was motivated, not only by financial considerations, but by the fact that prisoners' rights attorneys had already asked the court to take such action.

As has been demonstrated in this chapter, in spite of the implementation of post-Attica Rebellion reforms, throughout the 1970s, Bedford Hills continued to be managed by custody-oriented personnel who harshly resisted prisoners' attempts to achieve a redefinition in the conditions and terms of their imprisonment. Moreover, until the beginning of the 1980s, institutional administrators defied implementing both unfavorable court decisions and DOCS' central office directives mandating reforms in penal policies and procedures.

In spite of such obstacles, however, Latina, African-American, and white prisoners were able to create a small number of formal prisoner and administrative groups as well as ad hoc committees to address a number of concerns. Membership in these groups overlapped with that in informal prisoner groups and networks.

While successive custody-oriented prison administrations limited both the extent of prisoner organizing and the support they could wrest from the few liberal administrators assigned to the facility, with the creation of the position of Coordinator of Volunteer Services in 1972, women prisoners gradually gained access to a wider range of outside volunteers. The latter helped prisoners become more aware of their rights, provided a number of much needed services and programs, and facilitated conditions under which prisoners could meet and discuss common concerns.

Whereas during the first half of the 1970s, Latina prisoner leaders were not successful in their efforts to build a stable Latina prisoner organization, they were able to form a parallel ad hoc committee for the purpose of organizing family and feast day events and mobilizing the support of outside Latinas(os) for a number of educational and family-oriented goals. Nevertheless, while by the mid-1970s, the formal Latina prisoner organization had established a solid presence within the facility, by the end of the 1970s it had been unable to secure the hiring of additional bilingual personnel, the implementation of additional bilingual programs or to change discriminatory policies toward Latina prisoners. The organization's efforts were hindered, on the one hand, by the absence of institutional and central office support for specific Latina prisoner concerns, and on the other hand, by the lack of consistent sources of third party support. The latter was primarily the result of the prioritizing of male prisoners' concerns, the lack of adequate resources to sustain ongoing prisoner support work, and distorted views about what constituted prisoner activism.

Faced with constant harassment by penal personnel and the inability to generate significant sources of third party and penal support for specific Latina concerns, a number of Latina prisoners became more willing during the late 1970s to participate in the activities of a political underground prisoner coalition created to demand changes in institutional policies and conditions and support third party litigation efforts on behalf of women prisoners.

What role did Latina prisoners play in the activities of the political underground coalition? It is clear that Latina prisoners were indispensable participants in the activities sponsored by the coalition—compiling data, translating and distributing materials, typing petitions, participating as witnesses and/or defendants in class actions suits, negotiating with prisoner leaders of other informal and formal prisoner and administrative groups, openly questioning institutional policies, lobbying supportive personnel, and negotiating with penal authorities.

What impact did the activities of the coalition have on the conditions encountered by Latina prisoners? As a result of the combined efforts of the political underground prisoner coalition and third parties, Latina, African-American, and white prisoners were able to win a number of concessions from DOCS. These included a damages award of $125,000 to prisoners, documentation of prisoner abuse at the hands of custodial personnel, the removal of security-oriented administrators, and further court intervention in Bedford Hills' affairs. These concessions were complemented by others which included the right of non-English speaking prisoners to have translators present during disciplinary hearings and the right to have disciplinary charges translated into Spanish. Such policy changes, carried out by a newly appointed liberal prison administration, were aimed at reducing prisoner discontent and, ultimately prisoner political activism. How effective they were in accomplishing their goals will be explored in the following chapter.

Notes: Chapter 11

1. "Women N.Y.U. Law Students and 2 Professors Teach Course to Bedford Hills Prisoners," *New York Times* (hereafter cited as *N.Y. Times*), 14 October 1973, 58.

2. Ibid.

3. Ibid.

4. Another significant prisoners' rights attorney which began her involvement with women prisoners through the New York University Women's Law Project was Ellen Barry, Director of Legal Services for Prisoners with Children based in San Francisco, Calif.

5. "Carol Crooks," *Midnight Special* 4, No. 8 (October/November 1974): 22.

6. Carol Crooks, interview with author, Brooklyn, N.Y., 18 May 1993. For references concerning the use of male guards to subdue women prisoners, see Rose Giallombardo, *Society of Women: A Study of a Women's Prison* (New York: John Wiley and Sons, 1966; *N.Y. Times,* 14 January 1973; Idem, 28 June 1973; Idem, 7, 20 June 1975; and Idella Serna, *Locked Down: A Woman's Life in Prison, The Story of Mary (Lee) Dortch* (Norwich, Vt.: New Victoria Publishers, 1992).

7. Stephen Latimer, interview with author, New York, N.Y., 24 March 1989.

8. On June 26, 1974 the Supreme Court's *Wolff v. McDonnell,* 94 S.Ct. 2963 (1974), 41 L.Ed.2d 935 (1974) decision ruled that, "prisoners subject to disciplinary proceedings must be accorded the following rights: advance written notice of charges to be given at least 24 hours before a hearing, a written statement by the fact-finders of the evidence relied on and the reasons for disciplinary action, the right to call witnesses and present documentary evidence when doing so does not jeopardize institutional safety or correctional goals, and the right to counsel where the inmate is illiterate or where the issues are unusually complex" (*Powell v. Ward,* 392 F.Supp. 628 [1975]).

9. "Carol Crooks," *Midnight Special* 4, No. 6 (August/September 1974): 23.

10. Sister from Bedford Hills, "Dear Sirs," *Midnight Special* 4, No. 8 (October/November 1974): 1.

11. "45 Women Inmates in Disturbance," *N.Y. Times,* 30 August 1974, 33.

12. Bedford # 28, "Sisters Fight On," *Midnight Special* 5, No. 4 (January 1975): 1, 2.

13. "Abuse of Women Convicts Charged," *N.Y. Times,* 9 October 1974, 47. Spokespersons for DOCS denied the allegation claiming only one woman had been injured ("State Denies Injuries At Women's Prison," *N.Y. Times,* 10 October 1974, 51).

14. Sister from Bedford Hills, "Dear Sirs," *Midnight Special* 4, No. 8 (October/ November 1974): 1.

15. Ibid.

16. Ibid.

17. "Carol Crooks," *Midnight Special* 4, No. 8 (October/November 1974): 22.

18. "cheaper than chimps," *Midnight Special* 5, No. 3 (May 1975): 10.

19. Ibid. Prolixin was described by E.R. Squibb, its manufacturer, as "a highly potent behavior modifier with a markedly extended duration of effect. Adverse side effects include: catatonic-like like [sic] state, nausea, headache, blurred vision, glaucoma, impotency, liver damage, hypertension, palsy like syndrome, facial grimaces like encephalitis . . . The symptoms persist, and in some patients appear to be irreversible" (Ibid.).

20. "Trial Briefs: Bedford Hills Sisters," *Midnight Special* 5, No. 2 (March 1975): 20.

21. Ibid.

22. Both the Adjustment Committee and the Superintendent's Proceedings could lead to confinement in special housing or segregation units where prisoners were kept separate from the general population. Prisoners in special housing were allowed to commingle with each other but those in segregation were not. However, in 1974, according to the court, Bedford Hills had, ". . . only one facility euphemistically denominated 'Special Housing' wherein all discipline inmates are kept under the same conditions of punitive segregation, without regard to the diverse causes and commitment procedures whereby they may be placed there, or the nature of the misconduct involved . . . Inmates placed in Special Housing are locked 23 hours a day, whether committed for punitive, protective or administrative confinements. The rigors are the same" (*Crooks v. Warne*, 74 Civ. 2351 [S.D.N.Y. 1974]).

23. *Wolff v. McDonnell*, 418 U.S. 539, 94 S.Ct. 2963, 41 L.Ed.2d 935 (1974).

24. *Powell v. Ward*, 392 F.Supp. 628 (1975).

25. Barbara Cole [pseud.], interview with author, New York, N.Y., 15 May 1993.

26. *Powell v. Ward*, 392 F. Supp. 628 (1975).

27. The Deputy Superintendent of Security, for example, was allowed to sit in as a hearing officer in the Superintendent Proceedings, of prisoners involved, although the incident included behavior which threatened institutional security (Ibid.).

28. *Powell v. Ward*, 542 F.2d 101 (1976).

29. "Men's Prison Gets a Woman Warden in State Shake-Up," *N.Y. Times*, 22 August 1975, 33.

30. *Powell v. Ward*, 542 F. 2d 101 (1976).

31. Cole, interview with author, 1993.

32. Ibid.

33. James Feron, "2d Prison Urged to House Women," *N.Y. Times*, 30 July 1976, II, 3.

34. Ibid. A second problem was that prisoners who needed protection from other prisoners were transferred to the hospital's maternity ward but once there they could not participate in any prison programs.

35. Ibid. The grand jury found that only one in every six guards had completed the state's 90-day training program.

36. Ibid.

37. "Inquiry Pressed on Tranquilizers at Bedford Hills Women's Prison," *N.Y. Times,* 21 November 1976, 58.

38. Ibid.

39. Ibid.

40. *Forts v. Ward,* 566 F.2d 849 (1977).

41. Ibid. quoting "Affidavit of Carol Crooks sworn to on May 3, 1977."

42. Ibid. quoting "Affidavit of Bernidienne Watkins sworn to on May 3, 1977."

43. Ibid., quoting, "Affidavit of Yvonne Lee sworn on May 3, 1977."

44. Ibid.

45. *Forts v. Ward,* 434 F.Supp. 946 (S.D.N.Y. 1977).

46. The American Civil Liberties Union filed a "Friend of the Court Brief" alleging that it was discriminatory to distribute job assignments on the basis of sex.

47. *Forts v. Ward,* 434 F.Supp. 946 (S.D.N.Y. 1977).

48. "New York Prisons Curb 'Opposite Sex' Guards," *N.Y. Times,* 22 May 1977, 43.

49. Lena Williams, "New Prison Warden Bars the Old Stereotype," *N.Y. Times,* 28 May 1978, XXII, 2.

50. Cole, interview with author, 1993.

51. Movimiento Unido de Mujeres Latinas, "Position Paper," Bedford Hills Correctional Facility, New York, 1976.

52. Ibid., 2.

53. While in December 1972 there were thirty Latinas in prison, by December 1975 the number had increased to sixty-one (NYSDOCS, Division of Program Planning, Research and Evaluation, "Female Inmate Population Ethnic Distribution on December 31: 1960–1988," [loose sheet], Albany, N.Y., May 1989).

54. Luz Santana, "Address Before the Hispanic Inmate Needs Task Force," Hispanic Inmate Needs Task Force Awards Banquet, Albany, N.Y., November 20, 1985 (xeroxed copy).

55. *Powell v. Ward*, No. 74 Civ. 4628, 392 F.Supp 628 (1975), *Powell v. Ward*, 542 F.2d 101 (1976).

56. MUML, "Position Paper," 1976.

57. Georgina Castro [pseud.], interview with author, Brooklyn, N.Y., 27 February 1990.

58. Santana, "Address Before the Hispanic Inmate Needs Task Force," 1985.

59. Tita Puente spent all but sixty-seven days of her first two and a half years at Bedford Hills in keeplock or segregation for both organizing prisoners and becoming involved in physical confrontations with guards (Tita Puente [pseud.], interview with author, Bronx, N.Y., 21 March 1989).

60. Cole, interview with author, 1993.

61. Latimer, interview with author, 1989.

62. Mirna González [pseud.], interview with author, New York, N.Y., 22 March 1989.

63. Ibid.

64. Pamela Santiago [pseud.], interview with author, New York, N.Y., 15 April 1989.

65. Ibid.

66. Ibid.

67. Cole, interview with author, 1993.

68. González, interview with author, 1989.

69. Ibid.

70. Ibid.

71. Santiago, interview with author, 1989.

72. Ibid.

73. Ibid.

74. Ibid.

75. Ibid.

76. González, interview with author, 1989.

77. Ibid.

78. Cole, interview with author, 1993.

79. As in the case of male prisons, retaliatory action against employees perceived to be sympathetic to prisoners included being demoted, transferred, harassed, and/or "set up" by co-workers.

80. González, interview with author, 1989.

81. Cole, interview with author, 1993.

82. Ibid.

83. Elizabeth Koob, interview with author, New York, N.Y., 12 April and 11 May 1989.

84. González, interview with author, 1989.

85. Koob, interview with author, 1989.

86. González, interview with author, 1989.

87. "Jail Superintendent Held in Contempt," *N.Y. Times,* 1 March 1980, 24.

88. González, interview with author, 1989.

89. As Koob noted, "Special Masters are appointed to assist Judges in complex litigation. Their role is to make findings and recommendations which are then submitted to the Judge who then issues orders which may or may not be recommended by the Special Master. In this case, the Special Master reviewed individual disciplinary hearings for violations and expungement; she also reviewed the facility's disciplinary procedures. She made regular findings on defendants' compliance and made recommendations as to further monitoring and additional orders concerning the conduct of hearings. She held hearings on compliance. After the state's continued noncompliance, the Court granted plaintiffs' request for individual damage awards for illegal confinements to solitary and the Special Master held hearings and made findings and recommendations on these individual damage claims. She also supervised the spending of the settlement fund. The Special Master in this case is Linda Singer . . . Ms. Singer is still monitoring compliance because the Court has not been satisfied that the facility has sufficiently institutionalized compliance with the Court's orders. Although Ms. Singer is an attorney, this is not a requirement for being a Special Master" (Elizabeth Koob, "Letter to Juanita Díaz," 9 August 1990).

90. Koob, "Letter to Juanita Díaz," 1990. "The defendants also petitioned the Supreme Court for review, but were denied" (Ibid.). Prison administrators were also imposed a fine of $5,000 and an additional fine of $1,000 a day was imposed on Superintendent Curry. The court gave the institution thirty days to implement the decision and indicated he would revoke the fines if prison authorities adopted the required disciplinary procedures in the meantime ("Jail Superintendent Held in Contempt," *N.Y. Times,* 1 March 1980, 24).

91. Prisoner attorneys also filed for individual damages. As a result, about twenty prisoners whose convictions were reversed by the Special Master after they had been released from segregation received individual damages. Prisoners received a per diem amount for each day spent in solitary. They also

received compensation for wages lost during their time in segregation. Individual damages were awarded only until 1984. Prisoners who wanted to file for damages after 1984 had to do so through the court of claims or start their own suit (Koob, interview with author, 1989).

92. The negotiations, according to Koob, took place, "between the plaintiff-class, as represented by two class representatives and their attorney, and the defendants and their attorneys" (Koob, "Letter to Juanita Díaz," 1990). Singer engaged a mediator who conducted the negotiations.

93. Luz Santana, interview with author, New York, N.Y., 20 March and 4 April 1989.

94. Koob, "Letter to Juanita Díaz," 1990.

95. Ibid.

96. Crooks, interview with author, 1993.

97. Santana, "Address Before the Hispanic Inmate Needs Task Force," 1985.

12

Liberalization: The Other Side of Security, Bedford Hills 1982–1987

The replacement of custody-oriented administrators at Bedford Hills by liberal ones in 1982 was seen by some observers as marking the end of an era in which wardens ruled women's prisons like private fiefdoms. While it was true that DOCS central office administrators allowed the facility to ignore court orders because of the department's own resistance to court interference in penal affairs, the fact that Bedford Hill's administrators also failed to obey departmental directives mandating the observance of due process in disciplinary hearings indicated the extent to which security-oriented sectors were able to exert almost complete hegemony over women's prisons and the extent to which they were allowed to continue implementing policies that had been somewhat modified in male facilities. The changes that took place at the administrative level in 1982 brought the institution increasingly under the aegis of DOCS' central office.

The change from a custody-oriented to a reform-oriented administration, brought about in part by prisoners' political underground organizing and litigation efforts, also reflected the new manner in which penal authorities sought to exercise control over women prisoners. Summarizing the impact the 1982 administrative changes had on the way in which business was conducted at the facility between 1982 and 1987, Mirna González stated:

> The attitude may remain the same, okay . . . If some people were acting on their racism . . . we may not have changed their attitude, okay, but we've changed their strategy. They can't do things the way they used to do. Now they do it with a lot of precaution. And they have to . . . answer to other people, other than their little "cliques," in terms of implementing things or doing things.[1]

The immediate impact of replacing Warden Curry with Frank R. Headly[2] was that prisoners and their attorneys were able to conduct

361

negotiations with DOCS personnel in a more open fashion than would have been possible only months before. Moreover, Headly was willing to meet with formal prisoner organizations and with prisoner representatives in administrative organizations. According to González, ". . . none of the prior wardens met with the groups."[3]

The primary aim of liberal administrators was, nevertheless, to reduce overall prisoner discontent and, thereby, reduce prisoner involvement in litigation. It was primarily as a result of such motivations that liberal administrators supported both Latina prisoners' calls for additional bilingual services and personnel and overall prisoners' efforts to create a number of self-help groups. However, as will be shown in this chapter, administrators continued to resist prisoners' attempts at self-empowerment if they were seen as threatening custody-oriented interests. In fact, the process of liberalization was accompanied by a series of actions designed to reaffirm administrative control over prisoner initiatives.

Despite the efforts by liberal administrators to reduce prisoner discontent and litigation efforts, the facility continued to experience increasing tensions, particularly between the growing Latina prisoner population and the increasing number of white male guards assigned to the facility as the 1980s progressed. It is the conditions contributing to overall prisoner/staff tensions as well as the response of prisoners and administrators that will be explored in this chapter. The major questions guiding the discussion are: What combination of tactics did liberal administrators use in their attempts to reduce prisoner discontent and political activism? How did prisoners respond to such policies? What sources of support were Latina prisoners able to mobilize during the 1982–1987 period? What concessions were Latina prisoners able to win from penal elites?

Growing Tensions Within a Changing Institutional Context

The ability of prison managers to reduce prisoner discontent was hindered by several factors, some of which were not under the direct control of institutional administrators. During the beginning of the 1980s, the women's prisoner population increased by 25 percent.[4] DOCS' response was to re-open Albion Correctional Facility as a women's prison and add a 200-bed expansion to Bedford Hills.[5] By May 1985, Bedford Hills had 578 prisoners, 350 staff persons, and a budget of $8 million.[6] Overcrowding increased prisoner idleness and taxed the ability of prison officials to provide adequate medical, educational, and nutritional services. Overcrowding also aggravated prisoners' emotional and psychological difficulties existing prior to imprisonment or resulting from the experience of institutionalization itself. The fact that staff members were expected to work overtime and provide services to an ever increasing number of prisoners, also exacerbated any emotional and psychological problems they brought with them to work. These conditions led to higher levels of tension among prisoners and staff and contributed to violence among prisoners and between prisoners and staff. Moreover, in the view of security personnel, overcrowding reduced the staff's ability to control prisoners' behavior. As former Bedford Hills guard Marta Flores explained, ". . . it's very hard for a prison when you don't have the space to move your inmates around. Moving inmates from one building to another and breaking up gangs and all of that is part of control. It's a control factor."[7]

Tensions between prisoners and staff were further exacerbated by the fact that while a significant number of the new guards assigned to the facility during the early 1980s were white males with little or no previous guard experience, a growing number of new prisoners during the same period of time were Latinas, many of whom had little or no knowledge of the English language. As Bedford Hills became a "training facility" for new guards during the second half of the 1980s guard/prisoner tensions continued to rise. Such tensions were not only caused by language barriers but also by the racism of white guards. According to Clara Toro, a former Bedford Hills prisoner, there was a marked difference in the manner in which white and Puerto Rican male guards treated prisoners. Puerto Rican male guards seemed to be:

> . . . wanting to help encourage a woman that is serving time, not looking down on her like she only has a number and she's an animal in a cage, you know. Not trying to put that macho image on them that now, ". . . because I'm wearing blue and you're wearing green, you're a slave and I'm the master.". . . A lot of white correctional officers abuse their rights against Black and Hispanic women in prison and they carry that attitude.[8]

The growth in the number of male guards assigned to the facility also led to an increase in the number of women prisoners who were sexually and/or physically abused by guards. While in some cases prisoners offered to "barter" sexual favors in exchange for goods and services (e.g., drugs, extra clothes, extra food), there were many other instances in which sexual favors were coerced. Moreover, according to several sources, there were several occasions in which male guards have not only raped prisoners but have simultaneously fathered the children of both women prisoners and women guards. The latter situation led to occasions in which the presence of male guards increased the tensions not between them and women prisoners, but between the women prisoners and the women guards who competed for their attention. It was within this institutional context that liberal administrators introduced a number of reforms.

"Good Programs Mean Good Security"

Both Warden Headly and Elaine Lord, the deputy superintendent for programs, supported the implementation of a series of reforms designed to reduce prisoner discontent and political activism. Reforms included allowing prisoners to make collect phone calls every day[9] and opening Fiske Cottage, the first self-governing prisoner unit in the state system.[10] While the new phone privileges allowed the larger prisoner population to have greater access to family members and friends, participation in Fiske, considered a "superhonor" building,[11] was a privilege reserved for "model prisoners," many of whom worked as clerks for staff members. The twenty-six prisoners who lived in Fiske had access to a vegetable garden, their own separate yard, and enjoyed more freedom of movement within their housing unit. Moreover, prisoners were not locked in their cells. The building, according to former prisoner Jean Harris, ". . . has terrazzo floors, marble showers, and lovely hand-hammered down-spouts . . ."[12]

With the opening of Fiske and the special privileges accorded prisoners housed in the unit, prison administrators sought to attract the attention of various prisoner leaders. It was hoped that the latter's relocation to Fiske would discourage them from engaging in further reform-oriented activities. The divide and conquer tactics of prison managers were so apparent that some Latina prisoner leaders refused to apply to live in Fiske even when encouraged to do so by administrative staff. These leaders felt that prisoners who lived in Fiske became more and more isolated from the general prisoner population and, hence, lost their ability to act as effective leaders. This was particularly so because Fiske participants were often seen by their peers as catering to prison administrators.

In addition to these reforms, under both Headly and Lord the institution was made more accessible to outside volunteers. Interestingly, according to a top Bedford Hills administrator who wishes to remain anonymous, one of the motivations liberal administrators had for courting greater community involvement at the facility was because, "They represent the women. They vote. They provide services. They write letters. They lobby. . . . Community people, together with the superintendent, can get the needs of women met." Thus, third parties were also significant sources of support for liberal administrators wishing to carry out changes in light of continuing resistance to prison reforms by custodial sectors.

An area of particular concern to both Headly and Lord was the expansion of old programs and the creation of new programs and self-help groups designed to address a number of prisoner concerns. It was hoped that these activities would reduce prisoner discontent. Such views had been succinctly expressed by Headly when he stated that, "Good programs mean good security."[13] These views were supported by Headly's successor, Elaine Lord. Lord herself, had helped "develop prison programs statewide in the aftermath of the Attica Prison riot."[14]

In July 1984, Lord replaced Headly as warden.[15] Lord's appointment had the support of a number of prisoner leaders involved in the political underground coalition as well as leaders of formal prisoner and administrative organizations because she had been supportive of prisoners' claims during the *Powell v. Ward* negotiations.[16] It was under Lord, in 1985, that the facility first made available a "policy-procedure manual."[17] The release of the manual had been partially a response to the demands of prisoners and their attorneys for the production by DOCS of a series of manuals outlining the responsibilities of guards and the rights of prisoners during disciplinary procedures.

After Lord was named warden, a number of programs designed to address the concerns of imprisoned mothers (70 percent to 85 percent of the prisoners) were instituted or expanded. These "family programs," sought to strengthen mother-child relations. They included: a nursery, where children born to mothers in prison could live with their mothers generally until they were one year of age;[18] a parenting center, known as The Children's Center located in the prison's visiting room, where mothers and children could meet in private without interruption;[19] and a Sesame Street Room, where children visiting their mothers could play.[20] Day-to-day activities in these programs were overseen by a group of prisoner volunteers who were allowed to work only if there was a non-prisoner supervisor present in the room.[21] During the second half of the 1980s, the Family Reunion Program, first implemented in Bedford Hills in 1977, was modified. The program allowed prisoners to spend several days with immediate family members (e.g., legal spouses, children, parents, stepparents, grandparents, siblings) in a trailer on prison grounds.[22]

One of the advantages of these diverse programs was that they were able to mobilize the support of outside volunteers and sometimes other sectors of the state. For example, The Children's Center was supported by the New York State Division for Women. However, one of the handicaps of these diverse family programs was that participation in them was considered a privilege and not a right. Oftentimes, participation was determined by the whims of prison administrators. The programs themselves were coordinated by a Catholic Charities liaison working at the facility.[23] According to María Rodríguez, a former participant in the nursery program:

> "It is difficult," said María Rodríguez, as she watched her 3-month-old son, Alfredo . . . "They feel this is a privilege and you shouldn't complain. Sometimes I feel disgusted about it because there are a lot of things they don't let you do with your baby."

> "If the baby has to go outside to a hospital, we're not allowed to go. We're not allowed to bring the babies into our room. We can't take out own baby's temperature or feed them the food we want to feed them," she said.[24]

Mirna González explained how participation in the Family Reunion program depended on how prisoners' behaved while in the facility.

> The Family Reunion Program is a privilege, okay? . . . Anything you have to "earn" through a "point system" or through "brown-nosing" with the Administration is a privilege . . . They have a point system criteria based on your program participation . . . your institutional adjustment . . . And when you get up to thirty-something points . . . and you fall within the . . . two year guideline now, that's recent too because it used to be a one year guideline prior to release, then you would apply and they would review...and determine if you could participate or not.[25]

Because participation in these programs was considered a privilege, prisoners were kept in a constant state of apprehension about whether or not they would be allowed to participate. According to González, it was not uncommon for prisoners who publicly criticized institutional personnel to be denied participation in the programs.[26] Despite such obstacles, however, the existence of these family programs addressed the concerns of many women prisoners to have increased access to their children and family members and to be able to interact with them in more relaxed environments.

In addition to the family programs described above, penal administrators oversaw the creation of self-help groups in other areas such as domestic violence, traditionally seen as being of particular concern to women. These programs, which have included Sister Sisters, Down on Violence, and Alternatives to Violence were designed to empower women prisoners by helping them recover from domestic violence.[27] The fact that empowerment could lead women to individually and collectively question their traditional roles of wives, mothers, and dutiful daughters, and as a result, to question prison policies deemed discriminatory towards women prisoners did not escape security-oriented sectors within DOCS who resisted their implementation. Such resistance was so intense that the first support group for battered women imprisoned for killing their barterers had to keep its existence semi-clandestine. The group called Women Against Injustice and Violence (WAIV) was facilitated by outside women community activists between 1981 and 1983. While WAIV was never a formal prisoner group or program, it was in fact, the forerunner of all the other domestic violence programs created at the facility. As the mid-1980s approached, however, and the dilemmas encountered by battered women on the outside began to make headlines, women imprisoned at Bedford Hills for killing their batterers were able to gather enough support from third parties, liberals within DOCS, professional women on the outside, and other sectors of the state bureaucracy, to have hearings on domestic violence held at Bedford Hills during September 1985.[28] The hearings sought to call attention to the plight of battered women and also change New York State laws which penalize women who kill their batterers more harshly than men who kill the women they batter. Such patronage helped counter the resistance of custody-oriented sectors to the implementation of the programs.

Both the family programs and the new self-help groups had the support of Latina, African-American, and white prisoners. In fact, the development of the domestic violence programs and the organizing of the legislative hearings on battered women was spearheaded by Tita Puente, president of the Hispanic Committee.[29] Ironically, participation by non-English speaking Latinas in these diverse groups and programs was limited by the fact that they were, with few exceptions, conducted in English.

As demonstrated above, as a result of a change in Bedford Hills's administration from a security-oriented to a more liberal one, women prisoners were increasingly able to participate in a number of groups and programs created to address some of their concerns. Administrators' willingness to allow the expansion or creation of these programs stemmed from the belief that their existence would help reduce prisoner discontent. Ironically, by encouraging women prisoners to focus on "family issues," liberal administrators were reinforcing prisoners' investment in precisely those types of concerns that had traditionally made them more vulnerable to reprisals if they engaged in reform-oriented activities. This latter point was illustrated by the fact that participation in family programs was contingent upon how far prisoners went in criticizing penal policies and regulations. Furthermore, the liberalization that took place at the facility during the first half of the 1980s, was accompanied by a series of measures aimed at strengthening the institution's security apparatus and reducing prisoners litigation efforts.

Tightening the Screws

One of the ways in which liberal administrators sought to hinder prisoners' litigation efforts was by thwarting prisoners' access to the law library. Admission to the library was hindered by restricting the number of days and hours prisoners could use it. Moreover, while ill-prepared law clerks were assigned to work in the law library, other prisoners more knowledgeable about legal matters were either continually harassed by personnel or reassigned to work in other areas of the facility. Legal materials were also frequently outdated and prisoners were not allowed to use an available computer specifically designed to facilitate prisoners' access to legal material.[30]

Moreover, Bedford Hills' personnel continued violating prisoners' due process rights while conducting disciplinary procedures. Prisoners, in turn, persevered in filing complaints with the Special Master appointed by the court to oversee institutional compliance with disciplinary procedures.[31]

During this time, Bedford Hills' classification was also being changed from a medium security prison to that of the state's only maximum security prison for women. During the early 1980s, the security system also underwent "a general upgrading."[32] Part of the upgrading included the placement of a third fence around the facility. Some observers speculated that the motivation behind these actions was the transfer of political radicals Kathy Boudin and Judith Clark to Bedford Hills.[33] Both federal and New York State authorities frequently claimed that members of political groups with whom Boudin and Clark were affiliated might try to help them escape from prison, hence, the need to take additional security measures.[34] Other observers claimed that the tightening of security was because the state was finally beginning to take the reform efforts of women prisoners as seriously as those of their male counterparts. As a result, the state was preparing itself to meet future challenges by women prisoners accordingly.

Whatever DOCS' motivations were, the transfers of Clark and Boudin were used as a justification to restrict the movement of other prisoners within the facility. Prisoners were frequently told by staff that their movements were being restrained because the guards who would normally be used to escort them to their programs and work assignments were needed to guard Clark and Boudin.[35] While some prisoners blamed the latter for the inconveniences they suffered, Latina, African-American, and white prisoner leaders soon began circulating a petition to have Clark and Boudin released into the general population. This action, which proved successful, allowed guards to be reassigned to their regular duties. The petition had been motivated by the desire of prisoner leaders to eliminate administrative restrictions on prisoner movements and by the fact that prisoner leaders considered the isolation of Clark and Boudin from the general population as a violation of those prisoners' human rights.[36] Soon after her release into general population, however, Clark was sentenced by prison authorities to spend two years in segregation for an alleged escape plot.[37]

As both the cases of Green Haven and Bedford Hills have shown, one of the state's primary goals has always been to reduce or eradicate the impact politically conscious prisoners have had on the general prisoner population. In the case of Bedford Hills during the 1980s, federal and state authorities sought to isolate prisoners who were politically active in revolutionary groups prior to their imprisonment from those prisoners who had for years, through their organizing and litigation efforts, demonstrated their willingness to struggle for their rights. It was this preoccupation with monitoring the political awareness of women prisoners that accounted for the increasing surveillance to which prisoners who associated with Clark and Boudin were subjected. There were times when a prisoner's security status was changed because Clark and Boudin were housed near them. In spite of these obstacles, several prisoner leaders continued to associate with Clark and Boudin and sought their advice and support in organizing various activities and prisoner groups within the facility. One such group was AIDS Counselling and Education Program (ACE). A discussion of the difficulties prisoners encountered while forming ACE will allow us to better understand the obstacles prisoners encountered, even under a more liberal administration, in organizing formal prisoner groups, particularly if Clark or Boudin sought to actively participate in them.

Creating AIDS Counselling and Education Program (ACE)

In 1985, Boudin and Clark approached prison administrators about forming a group to educate their peers about HIV/AIDS. Their requests were ignored. As several Latina and African-American prisoners became more aware of the increase in the number of AIDS-related deaths at Bedford Hills,[38] they, along with Boudin, decided to approach prison administrators once again. By this time, the outside community had become more knowledgeable about the spread of HIV/AIDS and DOCS administrators were under increasing pressure to attend the needs of prisoners with HIV/AIDS. Until then, ignorance concerning how the disease was transmitted had led DOCS' administrators to keep prisoners diagnosed with HIV/AIDS isolated from other prisoners.

In the meantime, the overall prisoner population, ignorant about how HIV/AIDS was spread, was reluctant to talk about such issues lest their peers think they had AIDS and ostracize them. Concerned prisoners, nevertheless, afraid that the disease would continue to spread within the facility through needle exchanges and/or sexual acts between prisoners and between prisoners and staff members, continued to pressure prison administrators to be allowed to form a formal prisoner organization for the purpose of educating both prisoners and staff about the disease.

The women who formed ACE between 1986 and 1987 had already been somewhat educated about HIV/AIDS through contact with a volunteer from the Mid-Hudson AIDS Task Force who frequently visited prisoners with AIDS and conducted support groups for them. Once prisoners decided to create ACE, they wrote a proposal to prison administrators requesting that outside educators and medical personnel be sent to Bedford Hills to train them to do HIV/AIDS counseling and to provide support to ill prisoners. ACE founders also asked for changes in the manner in which hospital personnel at the institution handled HIV/AIDS cases. The latter, "weren't doing anything except putting them away, you know, isolating them."[39]

Once institutional administrators accepted the need for such services, they met with ACE founders and third parties to discuss how the group would be structured. This included observing DOCS' guidelines mandating formal prisoner groups to write a constitution, designate officers, and appoint a group advisor.[40] Administrators, prisoners, and third parties also discussed how ACE should advertise its existence to other prisoners and the type of training group members would receive from outside medical personnel. The group's long-term goal was to train other prisoners to act as peer counsellors who would provide one-to-one counseling to prisoners before and after they had been tested for HIV.

Although prison administrators favored ACE's educational goals, they, along with security personnel, feared and resisted several of the group's other goals, particularly the one-to-one aspect of the counselling. While the peer counselling component of ACE was not implemented until the second half of 1988, a brief discussion of this facet of the program will illustrate both the reasons for and the type of opposition ACE participants encountered from staff, particularly guards. According to former Bedford Hills prisoner Paloma Román, peer counselling was resisted, "Because it's a one-to-one and they can't control what goes on. You always have to have either a civilian or somebody with you if you're organizing, but on a one-to-one basis it's very personal. And they don't know what you're talking about. . . ."[41] Thus, administrators and guards feared that such types of unsupervised contact between prisoners would be used to organize reform-oriented activities. Such organizing would be further facilitated by the fact that peer counsellors would have direct access to prisoners housed throughout the facility. Moreover, unsupervised contact between prisoners could also facilitate the circulation of a wide range of contraband.

Custody-oriented personnel also resented the fact that in order to effectively implement the peer counseling aspect of ACE, prisoners would have to fulfill some of the functions reserved solely for staff. "It's very uncomfortable to the correctional officers because they seen that the inmates have the power to call down such and such an inmate . . . to be able to interview or counsel."[42] It was feared that this "power" would blur some of the distinctions between prisoners and staff members.

The fact that Boudin, whose movements were recorded every fifteen minutes as a result of federal regulations, was a member of ACE,
increased some staff fears that the group would be used to further
politicize prisoners.[43] Guards also resented the fact that the close surveillance to which Boudin was subjected meant they had to assume
additional responsibilities which restricted their own freedom of movement during their work shifts. Moreover, because Boudin was part of
the group, other ACE members also had to be closely monitored.

In addition to what has been discussed above, there were also
guards who rejected the work being done by ACE because they feared
"catching" AIDS and/or felt contempt for prisoners with HIV/AIDS.
Whatever their motivations, guards' resistance to ACE's activities
was expressed in a number of ways. Prisoners who showed willingness to work with Boudin were at first labelled "revolutionaries" in
the hopes of discouraging such types of close associations and dis-
crediting ACE. At times, guards would not allow prisoners to go for
peer counseling, claiming that there were not enough guards on duty
to escort them to the counseling area. At other times, they would
reveal the identity of those being counselled to other prisoners.

> If they know that . . . one of us is a peer counsellor, right, that deals
> with people that have AIDS or teach people about AIDS, and they
> see your name on a list, automatically they assume that you have
> AIDS. So they'll spread it around that this person is going to meet-
> ings or that you're meeting this person. They can be very vicious
> that way.[44]

These types of rumors created dissension among prisoners and made
it more difficult for ACE to conduct its educational and counselling
activities.

In order to counteract the resistance of prisoners to HIV/AIDS
education work, ACE members began an advertising campaign
designed to educate prisoners about the group's functions. This was
done by, ". . .talking their language, putting up flyers that they understood, videos. We did a play on AIDS. We invited people to an open
house . . . to know what . . . ACE was all about."[45]

Despite the numerous obstacles encountered by ACE founders,
they not only established a peer counselling program, but also began
a "buddy system" whereby ACE members took care of prisoners who
were already ill. According to Román, "You take care of the women
that have AIDS, you know, you take care of their needs . . . You keep

them company. You talk to them. You know, you just give them support. Sometimes you bathe them . . . You write their letters. You read their cards."[46]

To summarize, while liberal administrators were more open than their predecessors to prisoners forming groups and programs, concerns with security issues continued to dominate administrative decision-making and guard actions. Such preoccupations led Bedford Hills' managers to increasingly restrict prisoners' access to the institution's Law Library and to attempt to discourage prisoners from forming ties with peers who had been politically active in radical movements prior to their incarceration. In spite of such obstacles, Latina, African-American, and white prisoners continued to collaborate in the creation of a number of prisoner groups and programs in order to help one another meet needs not addressed by DOCS personnel. Román clearly expressed the attitude of prisoner leaders faced with institutional resistance to the formation of prisoner groups. "We service our own needs. We don't need your services . . . It would be nice if we could get this together and it would be easier to organize, but if you don't want to give it to us, we're still going to do it anyway."[47]

The difficulties encountered by ACE while trying to establish an official presence within the facility also reflected DOCS' resistance to carrying out much needed reforms in various health care programs at Bedford Hills. DOCS' resistance led prisoners and their attorneys to renew their litigation efforts. At the same time, prisoners sought to establish new groups and programs within the facility. In fact, ACE's official recognition by DOCS was partly due to the pressures exerted on penal administrators by prisoners' renewed litigation efforts and the department's fears that prisoners might resort to litigation if services to prisoners with HIV/AIDS continued to be denied.

Picking Up the Banner of Litigation Once Again

In 1984, as a response to the lack of adequate medical care and the unwillingness of penal authorities to remedy the situation, prisoners and their attorneys filed two class action suits that sought to change the delivery of dental and psychological services at the facility. In both of these cases, Latina prisoners participated as plaintiffs and/or witnesses. *Dean v. Coughlin*, No. 84 Civ. 1528 (SWK), 623 F. Supp. 392 (D.C.N.Y. 1985), was filed by the Prisoners' Rights Project of the Legal Aid Society on March 2, 1984, six and one-half years after the Court of Appeals issued its *Todaro v. Ward* (1977) decision mandating improved medical services at Bedford Hills (Discussed in chapter 9). Through *Dean v. Coughlin* (1985), prisoners sought "a preliminary injunction ordering defendants to provide adequate dental care . . ."[48] At the time of the District Court's decision on December 3, 1985, there were one full-time and two part-time temporary dentists, and one dental hygienist to care for up to 600 prisoners. The court found that there was a "total breakdown in the provision of dental care" at the institution and that "inmates with serious dental problems at Bedford Hills were in immediate danger of irreparable harm to their health."[49] Proof of irreparable harm included, ". . . pain, loss of teeth, discomfort, weight loss, and infection."[50] The court instructed DOCS to "provide adequate dental care to inmates with serious dental needs"[51] and to make necessary changes to improve dental services. DOCS' response was to ignore the court's ruling.

The District Court's response to DOCS' defiance came on April 1, 1986, when it issued "a more detailed order implementing the injunction."[52] In *Dean v. Coughlin*, 633 F. Supp. 308 (S.D.N.Y. 1986), the court stated that:

> Defendants' attitude about this litigation has . . . been problematic . . . the Court has entered a preliminary injunction ordering them to institute an appropriate dental care system. Instead, defendants have refused to enter into settlement negotiations as the court has urged. They have fiercely resisted plaintiffs' legitimate discovery requests, requiring intervention by the Court on a number of occasions. . . . Even more disturbing to the Court has been the defendants' failure even to attempt to improve dental services at Bedford Hills as ordered.[53]

As a solution, the District Court provided a detailed system of how dental care should be provided at the facility and gave the institution a timetable in which to do it. It also ordered that prisoners be notified of the court's decision in a language they could understand. The state's response to the District Court was to appeal the decision.

On October 28, 1986, the United States Court of Appeals filed its decision in *Dean v. Coughlin*, 804 F.2d 207 (2nd Cir. 1986). While the Court of Appeals agreed that DOCS needed to improve its delivery of dental services to prisoners at Bedford Hills, it also chastised the District Court and vacated its injunction claiming that the latter should have shown deference to penal authorities.

Restraint and initial deference to state institutional authorities in curing unconstitutional conditions are furthermore advisable as a matter of realism; federal courts lack the facilities or expertise needed for the formulation and day-to-day administration of detailed plans designed to insure that a state will provide constitutionally acceptable prison services.[54]

Moreover, according to the Court of Appeals:

. . . the State is not constitutionally obligated, much as it may be desired by the inmates, to construct a perfect plan for dental care that exceeds what the average reasonable person would expect or avail herself of in life outside the prison walls. The Bedford Hills correctional facility is not a health spa, but a prison in which convicted felons are incarcerated. Common experience indicates that the majority of Bedford Hills prisoners would not in freedom or on parole enjoy the excellence in dental care which the plaintiffs understandably seek on their behalf.[55]

Hence, the Court of Appeals' decision not only showed judicial deference to penal authorities but also demonstrated judicial bias against prisoners. In the end, the court accepted DOCS' proposed timetable for carrying out reforms in the prison's dental care system. In view of the fact that the case had originally been filed in March 1984, and that DOCS had continued to defy the court's ruling at least until the October 28, 1986 decision, it is clear that neither the health needs of prisoners nor compliance with judicial decisions was a priority of DOCS' institutional or central office administrators whether liberal or conservative.

DOCS' continued resistance to court rulings was exemplified by its handling of another class action suit, also filed in 1984. On July 31, 1984, attorneys Elizabeth Koob and Joan Magoolaghan filed *Langley v. Coughlin*, 84 Civ. 5431 (LBS), 83 Civ. 7172 (LBS), 709 F. Supp. 482 (S.D.N.Y. 1989),[56] a class action suit seeking to improve the conditions and mental health care provided to prisoners held in solitary confinement. While the District Court's decision, *Langley v. Coughlin*, 715 F. Supp. 522 (S.D.N.Y. 1989), was not filed until June 8, 1989, the case is discussed here because the plaintiff class was comprised of 250 prisoners held in Building 118 (Special Housing Unit, SHU or "solitary") between August 31, 1981, and August 20, 1987. According to former prisoner Jean Harris:

... the prison's SHU ... looks ... quite ugly, a small, unimaginative cinder-block box with twelve cells for solitary confinement on one side and twelve cells for protective custody on the other. The cells are small, the furniture minimal, the beds permanently attached to cement floors, and inmates locked down twenty-three hours a day.[57]

Prisoners placed in the SHU between 1981 and 1987 were frequently held in segregation for extended periods of time without being given either an initial mental health evaluation or follow-up treatment. However, some of the prisoners had been isolated because they were considered mentally ill and a threat to their own physical well-being. In the suit, prisoners charged that:

... until September 1987 New York State Correction Department officials routinely placed severely mentally ill inmates on SHU and that in so doing they failed to conduct any screening of these inmates, failed to provide even marginally adequate treatment for their mental condition while they were on SHU, and failed to protect the other inmates in SHU from the conditions that resulted from the presence of these disturbed inmates—including filth, noisome odor, deafening noise, fire and smoke, and the sight and sound of prisoners engaging in such ... behavior as attempted suicide, self-mutilation, and hallucination.[58]

Between 1984 and 1989, the District Court "visited the site, held hearings, decided motions, and supervised a Consent Decree"[59] pertaining to the case. However, between 1984 and 1987, Bedford Hills and DOCS central office administrators continued to ignore court stipulations. One of the solutions proposed by Warden Lord, that the cells in the SHU should be made soundproof, illustrated the harsh attitude of penal administrators toward the conditions encountered by prisoners locked in segregation.[60] It was not until August 20, 1987, when the court approved a settlement reached by prisoners' attorneys and DOCS, that changes began to take place in the mental health care provided at the institution. The changes were made possible because the parties had agreed to the appointment of a psychiatrist to act as a court monitor to oversee both DOCS' compliance with the agreement and mental health care at the facility for a minimum of two years.[61]

In view of the testimonies of women housed in SHU between 1981 and 1987, and in the view of the experts called in to testify before the court, on June 8, 1989, the District Court issued *Langley v. Coughlin*, 715 F. Supp. 522 (S.D.N.Y. 1989). The decision stated that prison authorities had exhibited "deliberate indifference" to the medical needs of women housed in SHU. Moreover the court found that:

> Record in class-action was adequate to find that correctional and mental hygiene officials violated prisoners' substantive due process rights, on basis that psychiatric treatment constituted substantial departure from accepted professional judgment, practices, or standards; there was evidence that many decisions were made by untrained personnel, that decisions were arguably motivated by personal hostility, that decisions might represent substantial deviations from any defensible professional standards, and that professional credentials of unit chief of mental hygiene unit at correctional facility were questionable.[62]

Equally important was the court's finding that, ". . . to the extent that some of the evidence could be viewed as reflecting significant hostility by treating psychiatrists at Bedford Hills to the SHU inmates in need of care, a trier of fact could even conclude that the failures of treatment were in fact motivated by a desire to punish . . ."[63] Within this context, prisoners engaged in reform-oriented efforts were always aware that prison authorities could ultimately use isolation and segregation as means of separating politically active prisoners from their peers. In fact, both prisoner leaders and prisoners' rights attorneys argued that that was exactly what had taken place when institutional administrators sentenced Judith Clark to spend two years in segregation.

As a result of the lawsuit, the facility's mental health staff was replaced and, "Plaintiff's damage claims were settled for $350,000, placed in a fund administered by Koob and Magoolaghan, and distributed on a formula based on degree of need for psychiatric care and number of days spent in SHU between 1981 and 1987."[64]

As discussed above, despite the replacement of security-oriented administrators by liberal administrators at Bedford Hills during the first half of the 1980s, institutional and central office personnel continued to resist the implementation of court mandated changes that supported prisoners' claims. In the meantime, prisoners' rights to adequate medical services continued to be violated. The ambivalent attitude of the courts concerning the degree of deference the judicial branch should observe with respect to penal affairs, not only reflected the bias and conflicting opinions of state elites concerning the degree of autonomy to be granted penal administrators, but contributed to the delay in the implementation of court decisions.

The importance of these court cases for the purposes of the current research lies not only in the fact that they illustrate the context in which prisoners argued for the implementation of various programs, but demonstrate the willingness of Latina prisoners to unite with their African-American and white peers to demand changes in prison conditions. In fact, faced with the lack of significant sources of third party support during the 1982–1987 period, the lawsuits and the prisoner-initiated groups and self-help programs that Latina prisoners helped create during the 1980s, remained the primary means through which they were able to impact on the conditions of their imprisonment. The sources of third party support Latina prisoners had access to during the 1980s will be discussed below.

Latina(o) Sources of Third Party and Non-Penal Support

The reasons for the lack of consistent sources of third party support for Latina prisoners within the Latina(o) community have been mentioned previously: prejudice against persons who have "victimized" their own community; the lack of resources among those community organizations most likely to support prisoner issues; the prioritizing of male prisoner concerns; and distorted views concerning the lack of "activism" among women prisoners. The fact that women prisoners were seen as having violated gender norms of how mothers, wives, and daughters ought to behave meant that they were less likely than their male counterparts to be supported by the Latina(o) community-at-large.

This is not to say, however, that Latina prisoners were not able to mobilize any sources of support from the outside Latina(o) community between 1977, when the Ad Hoc Committee in Support of Hispanic Women at Bedford Hills helped Latinas plan their ethnic feast day event, and 1987, when the current research project ended. However, the types of support mustered tended to be offered on an individual and/or an ad hoc basis, the latter usually for the organization of the yearly ethnic and feast day events. Latinas(os) who supported Latina prisoners during the 1977–1987 period tended to be family members and friends, attorneys working on individual cases, a few Latina(o) legislators, and religious organizations, women's prisoner support groups, and progressive grassroots organizations.

While religious denominations had the potential, if they offered services in Spanish, to provide the most consistent presence within the institution, these groups also tended to see imprisoned women as morally inferior. As a result of such attitudes, Latina (as well as non-Latina) prisoners were less likely than their male counterparts to take part in religious services.

Family members and friends tended to be the most constant sources of support for Latina prisoners. The former were most likely to provide bail money, secure attorneys, take care of the children left behind, provide emotional and financial support once women were imprisoned as well as take children to visit their mothers. However, the ability to provide such assistance was often limited by the fact that many of the families from which imprisoned women came had few financial resources to cover such expenses.

There were times in which members of multiracial/multiethnic women's prisoner support groups or other progressive organizations offered assistance to imprisoned women. The support women community activists offered Bedford Hills' prisoners during the 1980s resembled those offered a decade before. Such assistance included visiting individual prisoners, facilitating workshops inside the walls, and compiling information for attorneys as well as prisoners' rights newsletters. Outside community activists also organized teach-ins and fundraising drives, and publicized the plight of imprisoned women in the media. It was the commitment to educating the outside community about prison conditions as well as their desire to reduce the isolation of women prisoners that prompted a group of primarily lesbian-feminist grassroots activists to form Women Free Women in Prison (WFWP), a women's prisoner support group. The group's statement of purpose summarized the conditions and neglect confronting women prisoners on a national level.

First, there are problems special to women in prison, distinguished from the oppression faced by all those in prison: the presence and physical threat of male guards, the overall sexism of the prison system, the lack of specialized training which leads to fewer available jobs, the tragedy of mothers separated from their children, the assault on the women's reproductive organs and much more. Second, though women in prison are among the most oppressed of all women, they certainly have not received much support from the women's movement. . . . Third, because of the invisibility which male supremacy in our society bestows on women everywhere, women in

prison have not so far received much support from the prison movement either . . ."[65]

Soon after it was created, WFWP began publishing *No More
Cages: A Bi-Monthly Women's Prison Newsletter*. The purpose of the
newsletter was stated as, "We hope this newsletter will fight against
that isolation by providing a forum where women inside can speak,
and through which they can learn of the similar experiences of women
in other prisons . . ."[66] At its peak, *No More Cages*, which was published
between 1979 and 1984, was distributed in over twenty women's facilities throughout the country, despite constant attempts by prison
administrators to thwart its dissemination. The newsletter frequently
included articles written by Bedford Hills prisoners and outside volunteers concerning prison conditions and treatment by staff.

Nonetheless, while the support these political activists offered
prisoners at Bedford Hills was significant, the fact that such groups
did not have access to permanent sources of financial support meant
that they existed only as long as the individual members and/or organizations could afford to cover the costs of prison support work.

There were also times when a few Latina(o) attorneys visited the
facility, but they tended to be there to meet with individual clients.
During the 1980s, a few Latina(o) legislators such as Olga Méndez,
Israel Ruiz, and Robert García made their support of Latina prisoners
known. According to Mirna González, "They did write letters and . . .
request explanations and information and do inquiries . . . They supported the administration holding negotiations with inmates . . ."[67]
Politicians also stressed the need to hire more bilingual personnel and
implement additional bilingual programs. Inquiries were frequently
made at the behest of the institution's Hispanic Committee. While
there was not much individual Latina(o) legislators could accomplish
without the support of their colleagues, they did let DOCS' know that
their actions were being monitored by other members of the state
bureaucracy. Legislators also provided letters of support for prisoners
seeking parole. In addition to the assistance, albeit limited, offered
Latina prisoners by the various sources discussed above, during the
1980s, Latina prisoners received some measure of support from penal
staff at the institutional and central office levels.

Latina Prisoners and Penal Sources of Support

With the naming of Elaine Lord as Deputy Warden for Programs
under Headly, however, bilingualism came to be looked upon more

favorably. This was partly the result of the fact that Lord had been raised in a bilingual home and understood the cultural and linguistic dilemma in which non-English-speaking prisoners found themselves.[68] According to Lord, "Society needs to learn to define things differently. Programs in Spanish should not be considered 'special needs.' " It is a legitimate thing. You have a need not for the language you speak but to be legitimately recognized as coming from that culture."[69]

Lord was also aware of the administrative and security concerns inherent in overseeing a growing prisoner population whose language was not understood by the greatest number of staff. According to Lord, "If you can't talk with someone, it is difficult to manage things."[70] In response to this situation, Lord had a Latina prisoner assigned to tutor her in Spanish. The growing number of Latina prisoners was also of concern to Bedford Hills administrators because, as one administrator explained, "If the Hispanic Committee makes proposals and represents significant numbers of women, it is going to be heard differently than if it was just one Hispanic prisoner. There is strength in numbers. Common interests are being put forth." Ultimately, "The increase in the number of Hispanic women is important because you now have a group. Prison managers are managing groups and they have to recognize shuffles of power among the groups." The implication of this statement was that as the ratio of Latinas to African-American and white prisoners increased, the ability of Latinas to make their concerns heard would grow.

While during the 1970s, the support Latina prisoners had received from other administrators such as the deputy superintendent for programs and the coordinator of volunteer services had been almost nil, during the 1982–1987 period, Latina prisoners, primarily through Tita Puente, the president of the Hispanic Committee, gained direct access to these administrators. Puente's initial ability to establish direct contact with institutional bureaucrats resulted from the fact that she had been a prisoner leader in various informal and formal prisoner and administrative groups throughout the years and had been at the forefront of prison reform and litigation endeavors during the late 1970s and early 1980s. As a result of her involvement in these activities, she had also worked closely with liberal administrators during the *Powell v. Ward* negotiations and the establishment of a higher education program at the facility. The fact that for over five years Puente worked as one of the clerks for the coordinator of volunteer services[71] not only facilitated her access to prison managers, but also to outside community groups. It was this position that made it possible for Puente to cultivate relationships with third parties who were willing to assist with the organization of Latina cultural and educational events, the facilitating of various multiracial/multiethnic support groups, and the implementation of new programs.

Interestingly, interviews conducted with several Bedford Hills staff members who wish to remain anonymous indicated that there were times when Latina prisoners were preferred as clerks over African-American prisoners because the latter were seen as being more manageable and "ladylike." The underlying racist and sexist assumptions of such views were quite apparent. The attempts to co-opt Latina prisoner leaders and the "divide and conquer" implications of such tactics were also quite evident.[72] While the favoritism showed Latina prisoner leaders by some administrators no doubt helped deepen ethnic and racial rivalries between prisoners, we have seen how, during the 1980s, prisoners continued to join together to participate in class action suits and pressure penal administrators to allow the formation of new prisoner groups and programs.

In spite of Puente's access to various administrators, the gains made by Latina prisoners, as a whole, were modest. Although Warden Lord supported Latina calls for the hiring of more bilingual staff, the assignment of such personnel was contingent upon the budgetary priorities of state elites. Due to the fact that programs, women prisoners, Latina(o) prisoners, and bilingual concerns were never a priority of DOCS, in 1985, Bedford Hills still lacked adequate bilingual personnel and services particularly in the areas of parole, legal assistance, medical, mental hygiene, and drug therapy.[73] Moreover, even in those areas in which bilingual personnel had been hired (e.g., educational and vocational programs, counselling, reception, classification, Inmate Grievance Resolution Committee), the numbers employed continued to be grossly inadequate to meet the growing demands of the Latina prisoner population. The discrepancy in the Latina prisoner/Latina(o) staff ratio continued to present a problem, particularly as the institution experienced a significant increase in the number of Latina immigrants, many of them Spanish monolingual, during the 1980's (see Table 10). The support of prison administrators did, nevertheless, allow Latina prisoners to have some breathing room from previous institutional policies that specifically targeted them for harassment.

Budgetary considerations, the influx of prisoners who were not United States citizens, and the low priority given both women prisoners and bilingual concerns collided in the area of higher education, producing a situation in which Latina prisoners fared worse in comparison to their English-speaking peers and their male counterparts. For example, while a one year bilingual college education program was available to Latino prisoners at Green Haven by 1979, as late as 1985, according to Luz Santana:

> . . . there is no college level education for non-English speaking Hispanic women who attain their High School Equivalency in this facility. The Hispanic population has inquired repeatedly into obtaining bilingual college education and continuously has run into obstacles which have to do with insufficient numbers of participants, most importantly, a great portion of the Hispanic women who have High School diplomas are illegal aliens, and this factor makes them ineligible for grant funding.[74]

Thus, while the population of non-English-speaking Latina prisoners continued to rise and become more diverse during the 1980s, DOCS was unwilling to meet their requests for educational services already available to other prisoners.

While during the 1980s, a small number of Latina(o) staff provided a series of valuable services to Latina prisoners (e.g., teaching, counselling, translating), these services were few in number to meet the needs of the Latina prisoner population. The inaccessibility of Spanish-monolingual prisoners to a series of educational, vocational, and rehabilitation programs meant that Latinas had fewer chances of being released on early parole than their African-American and white peers, as participation in these programs was oftentimes deemed necessary for early parole consideration.

Faced with this condition, Latina prisoners sought the support of Latina(o) institutional penal personnel in pressuring state elites to implement the necessary programs and end discriminatory policies encountered at the hands of white and African-American personnel. However, because Latina(o) staff tended to occupy lower level positions within the prison hierarchy, they were hesitant to engage in activities that would endanger their employment. As a result, few were willing to forcefully confront the discriminatory treatment to which they, as well as Latina prisoners, were frequently subjected.

Perhaps one of the most significant changes that took place within the institution's administrative hierarchy was the 1984 naming of Sergia León as Inmate Grievance Supervisor. León, a Puerto Rican, had been working as a guard at Bedford Hills since 1974. As one of the few Latina guards working at the facility during the 1970s, she had been directly affected by the administration's discriminatory language policies toward Latina staff and prisoners. Ironically, she was also expected to act as a liaison between prison administrators and Latina prisoners, primarily by providing translating services when requested by her superiors.

Interestingly, while León's priority was security, there were also times when Latina prisoner leaders sought her assistance to accomplish a number of goals. For example, there was a short period of time in which León acted as the unofficial staff advisor of the Hispanic Committee because the committee was unable to get an outside organization or a civilian employee to sponsor the group. Without such sponsorship, the committee would have been unable to meet. Once she was named inmate grievance supervisor, the fact that León was Latina and bilingual led some Latina prisoners to seek her out for personal, not just official, counsel. For example, there were Latina prisoners, particularly among the new immigrant population, who were not willing to file official grievances against staff but who felt comfortable discussing such issues with León.

However, the responsibilities León fulfilled, first as a guard and then as Inmate Grievance Supervisor, illustrated the manner in which Latina(o) staff frequently helped to uphold DOCS' long-range security interests. As inmate grievance supervisor, León reported directly to the superintendent and/or the first deputy. Her responsibilities included participating in supervisors' meetings and meeting with the executive team on occasion. Most importantly, one of her functions was to alert prison administrators of particular patterns in areas that were problematic.[75] That is, she also acted as a "troubleshooter" for DOCS. This was an important function in an institution in which only a few trusted staff members spoke Spanish, the Latina prisoner population was increasing, and Latina prisoner leaders were at the forefront of prison reform efforts.

The ambivalent role played by León and other Latina(o) institutional personnel was also reflected in the conflicting roles played by Latinas(os) working at DOCS' central office.[76] Such conflicts were created by the fact that, on the one hand, Latina(o) staff, like Latina prisoners, continued to experience discrimination at the hands of white and African-American institutional and central office personnel. They could, therefore, identify with many of the concerns of Latina prisoners. As a result, they attempted to provide a small number of bilingual programs to Latina prisoners throughout the 1980s. On the other hand, the primary concern of Latina(o) central office personnel was to maintain security. The fact that Latina prisoners had played key roles in helping build prisoner unity did not escape them. Consequently, the small number of programs they introduced to the facility were aimed both at providing services to Latina prisoners and reducing Latina prisoner discontent.

In 1979, Petrita Hernández-Rojas, working at DOCS' central office, had introduced the Compadre Helper Program (Peer Counselling) to Bedford Hills. While Compadre Helper had been designed for Latino prisoners, it was adapted to meet the needs of Latinas. The program was offered once a year in Spanish to about forty to fifty prisoners by Hernández-Rojas and a few of her aides. During the second half of the 1980s, Hernández-Rojas, by then Director of the Division of the Hispanic and Cultural Affairs (DHCA), introduced two additional programs to Bedford Hills namely, Diálogos Con Mi Gente and Más Personalidad. Diálogos Con Mi Gente sought to motivate Latina prisoners to participate in existing programs at the facility, aid in the reorientation to society of women being released from prison, and contribute to the development of a positive self-image. Más Personalidad was geared toward helping prisoners strengthen their etiquette and self-esteem. Both programs were offered for only a few days, once a year. These programs, together with Compadre Helper, were the few bilingual programs available to Latina prisoners throughout the 1980s.

Thus, while Latinas(os) within the DOCS bureaucracy took some steps to address the needs of Latina prisoners, the support they offered was minimal. Their efforts were hampered by the fact that neither Latina prisoners nor the programs they advocated for were considered DOCS' budgetary priorities. As a result, the programs provided by the DHCA were few in number and limited in scope. In fact, at the end of 1987, DHCA had not yet been allowed to appoint a full-time Hispanic Inmate Needs Coordinator to Bedford Hills, although they had been appointed at male facilities such as Green Haven as of 1986. How did the Hispanic Committee respond to the lack of significant sources of third party support and the lack of adequate bilingual staff and services?

The Hispanic Committee (HC)

Throughout the late 1970s and early 1980s, Latina prisoners, through the Hispanic Committee (HC), continued organizing the yearly ethnic and family day events. The committee also provided Latina prisoners cultural, emotional, and social support as well as information and orientation concerning a wide range of penal policies and regulations. On occasion, HC members took responsibility for translating institutional material of particular concern to Latina prisoners. Moreover, HC members made sure that there was always at least one bilingual prisoner available to translate for newly arriving prisoners during the initial period of orientation. These services were particularly important as the number of Spanish-monolingual prisoners continued to increase during the 1980s.

HC representatives also actively sought the support of third parties and other members of the state bureaucracy, particularly Latina(o) politicians and professional staff working in other state agencies such as universities and the New York State Division for Women. In addition, the HC continued lobbying DOCS managers to hire more bilingual personnel, implement additional bilingual programs, and end discriminatory policies against Latinas. These concerns were supported by Latina, African-American and white prisoner leaders active in the political underground coalition as well as in other informal and formal prisoner and administrative groups. The support for Latina prisoner concerns within these groups was facilitated by the fact that membership in the HC frequently overlapped with membership in other groups.

Equally important was the fact that HC, such as Tita Puente, members were instrumental in helping organize coalition-building efforts centered both around the creation of a number of prisoner groups and self-help programs[77] as well as successful litigation efforts. Luz Santana, as shown in chapter 10, was instrumental in representing the interests of Latina prisoners during the *Powell v. Ward* negotiations discussed in the previous chapter. It was as a result of those negotiations that Latina prisoners were able to secure a number of educational and vocational materials as well as the right to have Spanish translations of disciplinary charges and to have translators present during disciplinary hearings.

As the end of the 1980s approached, the ability of Latina prisoners to mobilize significant sources of institutional, central office, and third party support was, nevertheless, hindered by the fact that Tita Puente, HC's president was released from Bedford Hills. As a result of Puente's release, the HC found itself in the midst of a power struggle among prisoners seeking control of the organization. Personal and political differences as well as cleavages based on nationality seemed to have been at the root of these conflicts as more Latinas, other than Puerto Ricans, entered the prison population during the second half of the 1980s. Although such cleavages had existed prior to 1987, they were contained by the ability of Puente to address the concerns of both the "new" Latin American immigrants and the "old" Puerto Rican prisoner population.

As in the case of the Latino prisoner population at Green Haven, Puerto Rican prisoners at Bedford Hills were the ones most likely to occupy leadership positions within the HC. They were also the Latinas most likely to occupy leadership positions within other formal prisoner and administrative organizations. This was the result of several factors. Puerto Ricans comprised the majority of Latina prisoners. They also had the longest history of imprisonment of any Latina group statewide. Moreover, many were bilingual. The latter allowed them greater access to third parties, institutional personnel, and African-American and white prisoners.

By the end of the 1980s, it was not unusual to hear some of the new Cuban and Colombian immigrants criticize Puerto Rican leaders within the HC. The inability of non-English-speaking Latinas, many of whom were not United States citizens, to directly communicate their needs and make themselves heard by prison authorities, increased their resentment toward those Latinas who did. By the end of 1987, these conflicts coupled with the lack of a Latina leadership who could reconcile such differences, had almost halted the work of the HC. However, Latina prisoners unlike their male counterparts, did not go as far as to form nationality-based ad hoc committees.

The Hispanic Committee also ran into difficulties after Puente's departure because its work and initiatives were heavily dependent upon the actions of Puente, who at the time of her release, had been HC president for at least nine years. In fact, the contacts that the HC had with third parties were basically Puente's contacts cultivated through her years of working as a clerk for the coordinator of volunteer services and through organizing prisoner groups and events at the facility. After Puente's departure, the HC was left with few sources of third party support, although some of its members had access, primarily through their work assignments, to a number of administrators. The influence HC's new leadership had over penal administrators was, nevertheless, limited by the fact that they did not have the history of resistance and activism Puente was known and feared for by DOCS' personnel. As one former Bedford Hills prisoner put it, "[At times] it all boils down to chain of command and where your representatives are at."[78] At other times, "It doesn't matter where you're at. It doesn't matter what you're trying to organize per se. It's the power that person has to attract other people to organize."[79] Those other people could include prisoners, penal personnel, or third parties. In the case of Puente, these two tendencies converged strongly.

In spite of the lack of significant sources of third party and penal as well as the internal difficulties discussed above, at the end of 1987, the HC was still able to obtain enough support, particularly within the Puerto Rican and Dominican prisoner population, to continue organizing the yearly ethnic and family day events. HC members also continued participating in other informal and formal prisoner and administrative organizations and programs.

Conclusion

Despite the period of liberalization that took place in men's facilities such as Green Haven, following the 1971 Attica Rebellion, Bedford Hills continued to be administered by custody-oriented personnel who rigidly monitored the actions of both women prisoners and women guards for another decade. Moreover, until the end of the 1970s, Latina prisoners and staff were reprimanded for speaking in Spanish without the authorization of institutional administrators. Latina prisoners were also negatively affected by the lack of an adequate number of bilingual personnel and programs. The unavailability of such services prevented many Latina prisoners from participating in educational and vocational programs deemed necessary for successful early parole revision. It also prevented Latinas from participating in formal prisoner and administrative groups, and hindered their ability to receive even minimal medical care and other basic services. Latina prisoners were further negatively affected by the sexism of and sexual harassment by male guards and the prejudice of the overwhelmingly African-American and white staff. Moreover, tensions between Latina prisoners and guards at times led to the former being physically assulted by the latter.

The response of Latina prisoners to these circumstances varied depending on the availability of third party support, the openness of prison administrators to the creation of formal prisoner groups, and their relationship with non-Latina prisoners. Initially, Latina prisoners were cautious about forming a formal Latina prisoner organization in an environment in which they were specifically targeted for discrimination. Thus, in spite of the efforts of various Latina prisoner leaders to recruit members for the formal Latina prisoner organization created in 1973, the majority of Latina prisoners during the first half of the 1970s, opted to create a Latina ad hoc committee which solicited and received the support of third parties in the Latina(o) community, such as the Prison Task Force of the Center for Puerto Rican Studies. The PTF provided Latina prisoners assistance with a number of educational and family issues as well as the planning of family day events. However, its ability to provide further support was thwarted by the lack of penal as well as other third party support for specific Latina concerns, discriminatory institutional policies towards Latinas, the lack of adequate resources, the prioritizing of Latino prisoner interests, and stereotypes concerning what constituted appropriate prisoner activism.

Ironically, as the PTF was winding down its work with Latina prisoners, Movimiento Unido de Mujeres Latinas, the formal Latina prisoner organization, was stabilizing its presence within Bedford Hills. MUML's transformation was partly due to the growth in its membership as a result of the increase in the Latina prisoner population. The latter growth led to increasing Latina prisoner demands for additional bilingual personnel, services, and programs. MUML's transformation also reflected the influence of Latina prisoner participation in other formal prisoner and administrative organizations, and the impact on prisoners of the availability of third party support in the form of prisoners' rights attorneys, other legal workers, and women community activists. Faced with the availability of such sources of third party support, continued discrimination and harassment by penal administrators, and deteriorating prison conditions, a number of Latina prisoners active in larger prisoner struggles, joined MUML in order to use the organization to demand changes in institutional policies toward Latinas. At the same time they participated as litigants and witnesses in a number of lawsuits designed to force prison administrators to change their practices.

The response of Bedford Hills managers to prisoners' activism in the form of litigation was to repeatedly ignore unfavorable court decisions as well as DOCS' regulations mandating institutional administrators to observe due process while conducting disciplinary hearings. The defiance of Bedford Hills managers was accompanied by the beating and segregation of prisoners, their transfer to a state mental facility, the forced medication of prisoners, and the interference with prisoners' visits and correspondence, among others.

In response to the continued violation of prisoners' rights, during the mid-1970s, several Latina, African-American, and white prisoner leaders formed a political underground prisoner coalition to document the abuses of penal personnel and force the courts to take further actions against Bedford Hills administrators. The result of such efforts was the awarding of $125,000 to prisoners, the assignment of a Special Master to oversee compliance with certain areas of administration, and the replacement of custody-oriented administrators by liberal managers in 1982. As a result of these litigation efforts, as of the early 1980s, prison administrators were also required to provide translators as well as translations of disciplinary charges to Latina prisoners undergoing the disciplinary process. Additional litigation forced prison administrators to change the manner in which they provided medical services to prisoners and mandated that prisoners be provided with translators during medical examinations.

After the replacement of custody-oriented administrators in 1982, liberal administrators used a combination of methods in an attempt to reduce prisoner discontent and political activism at Bedford Hills. Such methods included the carrying out of a small number of reforms and the tightening of security control. Thus, while, on the one hand, prison managers supported prisoners' efforts to create a number of prisoner groups and programs, on the other hand, they restricted prisoners' access to the law library and resisted prisoners' attempts to create formal prisoner organizations which threatened security interests. Prisoners responded to administrative restrictions and the lack of adequate health care services not only by creating new prisoner groups to address their concerns but also by renewing their litigation efforts. Latina prisoners were a fundamental component of such organizing endeavors.

While the change in prison administration in 1982 brought a measure of support for Latina prisoner concerns from institutional administrators, such support was motivated by both the personal idiosyncrasies on the part of penal administrators and security concerns which sought to reduce prisoner activism and litigation. While during the 1982–1987 period Latina prisoners also had access to Bedford Hills administrators through Tita Puente, the president of the Hispanic Committee, the support administrators could offer was limited by the budgetary priorities of DOCS and other state elites responsible for setting the state's budget.

During the 1980s, the HC was able to gain a minimal amount of support from Latinas(os) working at the institutional office level. However, as in the case of Latino prisoners, the support institutional personnel could offer was limited by their fears of reprisal from both their co-workers and also by the fact that they did not occupy significant positions of power within the institutional hierarchy. Moreover, even when a Latina was named the institution's inmate grievance supervisor, her primary responsibility was security. The limited assistance offered by Latinas(os) working at the Division of Hispanic and Cultural Affairs was also limited by the lack of adequate financial resources and DHCA's concern with defusing Latina prisoner discontent and political activism.

Throughout the 1980s, the HC continued to seek the patronage of third parties in the Latina(o) community. While from time to time such support was forthcoming, particularly from family members, a few Latina(o) legislators, and Latina(o) community activists, the limited resources available to these advocates made it difficult for them to engage consistently in prisoner support work.

At the beginning of 1987, the work of the HC was further hindered by the release on parole of Tita Puente, the committee's president. Upon Puente's release the HC underwent a series of internal conflicts between Latina prisoners vying for control of the organization. The changes in the Latina prisoner population caused by the increase in the number of non-Puerto Rican prisoners, also produced a situation in which the HC's predominant Puerto Rican leadership was often challenged by the newly arriving Colombian, Dominican, and Cuban prisoners.

Within this context, the lack of major sources of penal and third party support for Latina prisoners, combined with internal conflicts, limited the HC's ability to lobby penal administrators on behalf of Latina prisoners. Nevertheless, the HC continued to lobby DOCS for the assignment of bilingual personnel, the provision of bilingual programs, and an end to the discriminatory treatment encountered from the predominantly African-American and white institutional staff. While the new liberal administration, as well as the small number of Latina(o) staff within DOCS, supported the calls of Latina prisoners for additional bilingual personnel and programs, the impact these forces had on the conditions confronting Latina prisoners was limited by the fact that neither women, Latina(o) prisoners, nor the area of programs were budgetary priorities of state elites. Within this context, the limited gains made by Latina prisoners during the period studied were to a great extent the result of pressures exerted on DOCS by successful prisoner litigation efforts supported by Latina prisoners, their African-American and white peers, and third parties.

Notes: Chapter 12

1. Mirna González [pseud.], interview with author, New York, N.Y., 22 March 1989.

2. Headly was the first male warden appointed to the facility in sixty years. In May 1985, there were forty-seven prisons in New York State, of which five were administrated by women (Milena Jovanovitch, "Warden Assesses Her Bedford Hills Job," *New York Times* (hereafter cited as *N.Y. Times*), 12 May 1985, XXII, 10).

3. González, interview with author, 1989.

4. The average prisoner at the time was 24 years old. Approximately 70 percent of them were mothers (Milena Jovanovitch, "Warden Assesses Her Bedford Hills Job," *N.Y. Times*, 12 May 1985, 10).

5. Milena Jovanovitch, "Concern Over Prison Expansion," *N.Y. Times*, 4 May 1986, XXII, 8. For a discussion of some of the causes of the increase in the women's prison population, see Department of Correctional Services, Division of Program Planning, Research and Evaluation (hereafter cited as NYSDOCS), *Characteristics of Female Inmates Held Under Custody, 1975–1985* by Kathy Canestrini, September 1986, and Juanita Díaz-Cotto, "Women and Crime in the United States," eds. Chandra Talpade Mohanty, Ann Russo, and Lourdes Torres, *Third World Women and the Politics of Feminism* (Bloomington: Indiana University Press, 1991).

6. Milena Jovanovitch, "Warden Assesses Her Bedford Hills Job," *N.Y. Times*, 12 May 1985, XXII, 10.

7. Marta Flores [pseud.], interview with author, Albany, N.Y., 18 March 1989.

8. Clara Toro [pseud.], interview with author, New York, N.Y., 9 April 1989.

9. Until then, prisoners could only make two five-minute calls a month.

10. Ironically, Fiske originally served as the institution's Special Housing Unit (Jean Harris, *They Always Call Us Ladies: Stories from Prison* (New York: McMillan Publishing Co., 1988), 19. The prison also had an "honor's floor" open to prisoners who had been in the facility at least six months and "demonstrated very good behavior." (Lynne Ames, "Bedford Hills Prison, Mixed Emotions on Jean Harris," *N.Y. Times*, 22 March 1981, XXII, 1).

11. Lena Williams, "Measuring Success at Bedford Hills," *N.Y. Times*, 5 February 1984, XXII, 1, 7.

12. Harris, *They Always Call Us Ladies*, 20.

13. Lena Williams, "Measuring Success at Bedford Hills," *N.Y. Times*, 5 February 1984, XXII, 1, 7.

14. Milena Jovanovitch, "Warden Assesses Her Bedford Hills Job," *N.Y. Times*, 12 May 1985, XXII, 10.

15. During the early part of 1984, Bedford Hills administrators had come under criticism from the State Comptroller's office which had conducted an audit of the facility during the 1981–1982 fiscal year. The Comptroller argued that the facility had "exorbitant overtime costs" for guards and that prisoners were consuming more food than allowed by DOCS guidelines. Perhaps more important, was the fact that the facility was considered a security and fire risk (Lena Williams, "Measuring Success at Bedford Hills," *N.Y. Times*, 5 February 1984, XXII, 1). Interestingly, one of the ways state officials defended their expenses for food was by indicating that in previous audits, "Bedford Hills had been cited as one of two facilities that had spent the lowest percentage or money on food services" (Ibid.).

16. González, interview with author, 1989.

17. Milena Jovanovitch, "Warden Assesses Her Bedford Hills Job," *N.Y. Times*, 12 May 1985, XXII, 10.

18. Prisoners who were within eighteen months of their parole release date were allowed to keep their children until then. While the nursery allowed prisoners to live in the same building as their babies, they were the only prisoners who were housed two, sometimes three to a cell (Harris, *They Always Call Us Ladies*, 179, 180).

19. The Children's Center also organized children's summer, Christmas, and Hanukkah programs, taught prisoners how to sew clothes for their babies, sponsored a parenting class for prisoners living in the nursery, and paid for four free buses per month from New York City (Ibid., 15, 266).

20. Joan Potter, "Child-Care Is a Release for Women in Prison," *N.Y. Times*, 3 December 1978, XXII, 2; and Sheila Rule, "A Prison is 'Home' to Babies," *N.Y. Times*, 31 July 1981, II, 1.

21. Joan Potter, "Child-Care Is a Release for Women in Prison," *N.Y. Times*, 3 December 1978, XXII, 2.

22. Trailer visits for prisoners were first experimented with in California. The first trailer visit program in New York State was instituted at Wallkill in June 1976. Bedford Hills was the third state facility to take part in the program. When first instituted, only those prisoners having a year to serve before parole eligibility could participate in the program. In 1977, only 115 of the 420 prisoners at Bedford Hills met this requirement. Moreover, prisoners had to be legally married for their partners to participate in the program. At the time, only 7 of the 115 prisoners otherwise eligible met this requirement (Edward Hudson, "Prison Starts 30 Hour Family Visits," *N.Y. Times*, 3 September 1977, 29). During the 1980s, the qualifications for program participation changed so that prisoners with only two years left before parole eligibility could participate.

23. Bedford Hills' family programs were administered by Sister Elaine Roulet, the Catholic Charities family liaison at Bedford Hills. Technically, Sister Roulet was not a DOCS' employee.

24. Sheila Rule, "A Prison is 'Home' to Babies," *N.Y. Times*, 31 July 1981, II, 1, B7.

25. González, interview with author, 1989.

26. Ibid.

27. Domestic violence includes incest and other forms of childhood sexual abuse as well as battering. At least one informal prisoner group sought to provide support to women imprisoned for offenses against their children.

28. The hearings were held before a "blue-ribbon panel of state legislators, social service and correction system officials" (Nadine Brozan, "Women in Prison Say Abuse Led Them to Crime," *N. Y. Times*, 28 September 1985, I, 30). The hearings were organized by DOCS, the Governor's Commission on Domestic Violence, and the New York State Division for Women.

29. Previous to the hearings, Tita Puente had conducted a poll of Bedford Hills prisoners to measure the extent of domestic violence in prisoners' lives prior to imprisonment. The poll subsequently "became a key element in 'Battered Women and Criminal Justice,' a study by the statewide Committee on Domestic Violence and Incarcerated Women" (*New York Newsday*, 10 June 1987, 2, 17). The 35-page report released on June 9, 1987, was prepared by a "coalition of attorneys, women's, and victim's-rights groups and inmates" and "questions jailing women who have killed abusive husbands and parents" (Ibid.).

30. González, interview with author, 1989.

31. It was not until 1995 that Linda Singer, the Special Master, ruled that prison personnel were finally complying with the court's mandates issued twenty years before.

32. Milena Jovanovitch, "Warden Assesses Her Bedford Hills Job," *N.Y. Times*, 12 May 1985, XXII, 10.

33. Kathy Boudin and Judith Clark had been sentenced to prison for their role in the theft of $1.6 million from a Brink's truck on October 20, 1981, in Nanuet, New York ("Escape Plot Laid to Brink's Convict," *N.Y. Times*, 12 September 1985, II, 9). According to state authorities, both women were part of the Weather Underground (Ibid.). Boudin was transferred to Bedford Hills in May 1984 (*Dean v. Coughlin*, 623 F.Supp. 392 [D.C.N.Y.] 1985).

34. Milena Jovanovitch, "Warden Assesses Her Bedford Hills Job," *N.Y. Times*, 12 May 1985, XXII, 10.

35. González, interview with author, 1989.

36. Ibid.

37. Attorney Judith Holmes indicated that Clark was not allowed to be represented by an attorney during the administrative hearing which made the decision to place her in segregation. Clark was also denied the right to see the letter supposedly related to the escape plot ("Escape Plot Laid to Brink's Convict," *N.Y. Times*, 12 September 1985, II, 9). At the time, the sentence imposed on Clark was the longest sentence to solitary confinement ever given at Bedford Hills. Clark was subsequently released from segregation due to an investigation by Linda Singer, who found that her due process rights had been violated. Clark was also awarded damages as a result of the *Powell v. Ward* litigation.

38. Some of the deaths had resulted from the sharing of a needle by women shooting heroin within the facility. According to an article that appeared in the *Green Haven Monthly* (hereafter cited as *GHM*), a former Bedford Hills prisoner reported that, "she and several other inmates, whom she declined to name, had been shooting heroin all during 1983 and 1984. But when the AIDS scare became headlines in 1985 they all panicked, she said, and gave up the habit. However, she hinted that they used crack and cocaine at various times" ("Women Gets AIDS in Jail," *GHM* 9, No. 4 [Summer Edition: July, August, September 1987]: 26).

39. Paloma Román [pseud.], interview with author, New York, N.Y, 10 December 1989.

40. Interestingly, once ACE was firmly established its classification was changed by DOCS from a formal prisoner group to a program.

41. Román, interview with author, 1989.

42. Ibid.

43. One of the sources interviewed indicated that it was federal agencies such as the Attorney General's office and the Federal Bureau of Investigations, not Bedford Hills administrators, who most feared the close association of Clark and Boudin with other prisoners.

44. Román, interview with author, 1989.

45. Ibid.

46. Ibid.

47. Román, interview with author, 1989.

48. *Dean v. Coughlin*, 623 F. Supp. 392 (D.C.N.Y. 1985).

49. Ibid.

50. Ibid.

51. Ibid.

52. *Dean v. Coughlin*, 633 F.Supp 308 (S.D.N.Y. 1986).

53. Ibid.

54. *Dean v. Coughlin*, 804 F.2d 207 (2nd Cir. 1986).

55. Ibid.

56. In 1983, a single prisoner had filed a lawsuit alleging similar conditions at Bedford Hills' SHU. Her complaint was subsequently consolidated with *Langley v. Coughlin* (*Langley v. Coughlin*, 715 F.Supp. 522 [S.D.N.Y. 1989]).

57. Harris, *They Always Call Us Ladies*, 19-20.

58. *Langley v. Coughlin*, 715 F.Supp. 522 (S.D.N.Y. 1989).

59. *Langley v. Coughlin*, 709 F.Supp. 482 (S.D.N.Y. 1989).

60. *Langley v. Coughlin*, 715 F. Supp. 522 (S.D.N.Y. 1989), Plaintiffs' Exh. 26 (December 31, 1985), Lord memo to Coombe.

61. *Langley v. Coughlin*, 715 F. Supp. 522 (S.D.N.Y. 1989). As a result of the settlement, a mental health review of all women sent to SHU must now be conducted. Also, the Office of Mental Health (OMH) is responsible for informing the warden if confinement in SHU is detrimental to the mental health of a particular prisoner. While the "settlement was for injunctive relief, litigation continued for damages" (Elizabeth Koob, "Notes to Juanita Díaz," 1994).

62. Ibid. Earlier on March 31, 1989, the District Court's decision in *Langley v. Coughlin*, 709 F.Supp. 482 (S.D.N.Y. 1989), had dismissed DOCS' request for "summary judgement on grounds of qualified immunity." That is, the court denied DOCS' allegations that central office and Bedford Hills' administrators were immune from litigation because of the nature of their duties. On October 25, 1989, the Court of Appeals' *Langley v. Coughlin*, 888 F.2d 252 (2nd. Cir. 1989) decision, dismissed DOCS' claim that its officials were immune from litigation.

63. Ibid.

64. Elizabeth Koob, "Notes to Juanita Díaz," 1994.

65. Women Free Women in Prison, Untitled, *No More Cage: A Bi-Monthly Women's Prison Newsletter* 1, No. 4 (September/October 1979): 1.

66. Ibid.

67. González, interview with author, 1989.

68. Elaine Lord, interview with author, Bedford Hills, N.Y., 7 March 1989.

69. Ibid.

70. Ibid.

71. During the 1980s, Bedford Hills' coordinator of volunteer services fulfilled a greater number of functions and enjoyed a greater degree of auton-

omy than any of her predecessors. As such, she: supervised all prisoner organizations; coordinated all family and ethnic feast day events and prisoner entertainment; recruited and oriented volunteers; sought outside donations for the facility; represented the facility before the media; conducted tours of the prison; represented the deputy superintendent for programs at certain staff meetings; kept accounts of prisoner funds and exercised control over prisoner profits; established an indigent prisoner fund; and oversaw the functioning of the Youth Assistance Program.

72. Such attempts to co-opt prisoner leaders were also observed by Spencer in her study of a women's medium security prison. See Elouise Junius Spencer, "The Social System of a Medium Security Women's Prison," (Ph.D. diss., University of Kansas, 1977).

73. Luz Santana, "Address Before the Hispanic Inmate Needs Task Force," Hispanic Inmate Needs Task Force Awards Banquet, Albany, N.Y., November 20, 1985 (xeroxed document).

74. Ibid.

75. Other responsibilities fulfilled by León were: supervising the election of prisoner representatives to the IGRC every six months; record keeping; supervising prisoners working for the committee; translating; and escorting members of the Latina(o) mass media around the facility (Sergia León, [pseud.], interview with author, Albany, N.Y., 16 March 1989).

76. In fact, during the *Powell v. Ward* negotiations, one of the Latino attorneys representing DOCS supported prisoners' claims. His support was, nonetheless, offered with the understanding that it was to be kept confidential.

77. In addition to the programs described in the text, the HC was also responsible for the introduction in 1978 and administration of the photography program. The program allowed prisoners and their visitors to be photographed together in the visiting room.

78. González, interview with author, 1989.

79. Ibid.

13

Conclusion: Two Steps Forward, One Step Back

This project examines the ways in which Latinas and Latinos in New York State experienced and responded to imprisonment between 1970 and 1987. It also considers the manner in which penal elites and third parties responded to Latina(o) prisoner calls for support. One major objective was to study the conditions under which successful coalitions among prisoners and their allies could be forged in the effort to win concessions from custody-oriented state sectors.

There has been much debate within the social science literature about whether prisoner society is the result of endogenous or exogenous factors. The Latina(o) prisoner experience described in this text confirms that the manner in which Latina(o) prisoners responded to their imprisonment was the result of the interaction of the conditions they faced while imprisoned, behavior patterns imported into the prison, their continuous interaction with individuals inside and outside the walls, and their exposure to the various sociopolitical movements.

As this book demonstrates, prisoner activism and the reforms carried out after the 1971 Attica Prison Rebellion changed the terms and conditions of imprisonment. That is, while custody-oriented sectors remained in firm control of the penal establishment throughout the period studied, no longer could they ignore prisoner demands for reforms, greater access to outside community members, the ability to create formal prisoner groups, and the establishment of a wider range of programs and services. However, these same organizations soon became the new instruments through which penal authorities sought to reestablish custodial hegemony. By pursuing a number of policies which decreed the manner in which such organizations should conduct themselves and the interests they should pursue, and by holding the power to withdraw privileges associated with having such organizations, DOCS fostered within the prisoner population the development of pursuits which subdued reform-oriented activities. Moreover, prison authorities benefited from prisoners' competition with one another for a number of scarce resources. Such competition helped undermine prisoner solidarity.

However, while it is true that the creation of a host of formal prisoner groups and administrative organizations disrupted prisoners' coalition-building efforts, DOCS' attempts to subvert prisoners' solidarity was diffused by the fact that the new organizations existed alongside a number of political underground interethnic/interracial (reform-oriented) prisoner groups. To this end, the strategies pursued by both male and female prisoner leaders varied. At times, prisoner leaders created formal prisoner groups or programs to pursue reform-oriented interests. At other times, leaders of political underground prisoner groups operated within an existing organization to pursue the same interests. In some cases, prisoner leaders of informal and formal prisoner and administrative groups cooperated by agreeing not to interfere with each other's goals nor compromise the existence of one another's groups. On occasion, formal prisoner organizations were used openly to promote prisoner coalitions. Ultimately, reform-oriented prisoner leaders were able to influence other prisoners to engage in coalition-building efforts because membership in formal and informal prisoner groups and administrative organizations overlapped tending to reinforce one another. Hence, while DOCS benefited from the increasing diversification of prisoner interests, prisoner leaders continued to resist DOCS' attempts to divide them in order to lessen their ability to challenge custodial hegemony.

One of the targets for this study was to examine the tactics and strategies pursued by the New York State Department of Correctional Services regarding Latina(o) prisoners between 1970 and 1987. Such policies, however, cannot be separated from the interests federal and non-penal governmental elites had in reducing the threat to the status quo posed by the prisoners' rights and other social protest movements. The concerns of government elites became particularly evident in the period immediately preceding and following the Attica Prison Rebellion when federal and state authorities around the country decried the relationship that existed between the radicalization of male prisoners and the political ideologies espoused by leftist and progressive social movements on the outside. While *Gender, Ethnicity, and the State* does not examine the impact such governmental views had on the outside Latina(o) community, the threat of and the widespread imprisonment of Latinas(os) was one of the primary means used by state elites to reduce outside Latina(o) community discontent and political activism. The fears of social upheaval, fueled by the realization of the role played by imprisonment in subduing social discontent and maintaining societal inequalities, led President Nixon to commend New York State Governor Rockefeller and DOCS Commissioner Oswald for their handling of the Attica Prison Rebellion and their quashing of "radical" elements within the prisons; those prisoners who demanded reforms and challenged custodial hegemony primarily through rebellions, work strikes, and litigation.

Faced with unremitting discontent and activism on the part of both male and female prisoners during the 1970–1987 period, penal elites continued to balance reforms with repression. The use of a combination of repression and reforms by New York State elites was a result of conflicting opinions concerning the manner in which state sectors should respond to challenges by both individuals and social protest movements. Between 1970 and 1987, these conflicts led to the development of significant rifts between and within state sectors concerned about penal policy. These cleavages were charted on a continuum of struggles for power between upper and lower courts, judicial and penal sectors, institutional and central office DOCS bureaucrats, civilian and custody-oriented personnel, Latina(o) staff and white staff, guards' union versus DOCS, and so forth.

However, such conflicts were not fundamentally of an ideological nature, as all parties involved concurred that the status quo must be maintained. Nevertheless, there were times in which the conflicts were so profound that custody-oriented sectors were forced to carry out reforms they deeply feared and resented. For example, the 1970 and 1971 New York City jail and upstate male prison rebellions, and the public support for prison reform they generated, allowed reform-oriented penal elites to implement a number of statewide reforms despite the resistance of custody-oriented sectors. Likewise, litigation efforts pursued by women prisoners during the 1970s and 1980s, and supported by prisoners' rights attorneys and other community activists, led several judges to issue decisions favorable to prisoners; a blow to custody-oriented keepers. However, these "rifts" or "openings" within the state which allowed the implementation of reforms demanded by prisoners and their allies, were brief.

The impact of cleavages within and between state sectors, coupled with the fears of prisoner unrest and activism, made itself felt at both Green Haven and Bedford Hills. At Green Haven, central office administrators supported the implementation of a study release program proposed by Latino prisoners, third parties, and civilian institutional administrators which was opposed by custody-oriented guards and administrators. At Bedford Hills, several court decisions mandated changes in prison conditions and institutional policies. Through these decisions Latina prisoners were able to obtain a few concessions from penal elites. However, continuing conflicts between penal and judicial sectors led DOCS administrators to repeatedly ignore decisions unfavorable to it. The latter were implemented only after penal elites were forced to do so by the imposition of monetary penalties by the courts. The rift between judicial and penal elites, in turn, led DOCS' central office to substitute Bedford Hills' custody-oriented administrators with liberal ones a decade after the Attica Rebellion.

Within this context, the goals of DOCS during the 1970–1987 period were to reduce prisoner discontent and political activism. It was expected that the decrease in prisoner activism would diminish court and legislative interference in penal affairs and public support for prisoners. Opinions on how these goals should be accomplished, and what the balance should be between the use of reforms and repression, was what differentiated custody-oriented from reform-oriented penal sectors. While the primary concern of DOCS elites was to reduce male prisoner discontent, once women prisoners began to pursue successful litigation, penal authorities also sought ways in which to reduce activism at Bedford Hills.

Despite the ground covered by all parties in the past two decades, conditions which prisoners challenged prior to the Attica Rebellion continued to exist at the end of 1987, fueling prisoner discontent and activism. Prisoners continued to strike and file litigation to demand criminal justice reforms, better conditions, services, treatment, and the right to have input to determine penal policies. Moreover, prisoners demanded an end to physical abuse by guards.

How effective were the state's tactics of combining repression and reform in reducing Latina(o) prisoner discontent and activism following the Attica Rebellion? The ability of the post-Attica Rebellion reforms to reduce Latina(a) prisoner discontent was limited because the reforms themselves were considered superficial by most prisoners. This was particularly so in the case of Bedford Hills where custody-oriented personnel were entrenched long after the Attica Rebellion. In addition, the reforms failed to effectively address concerns specific to Latina(o) prisoners.

Latina(o) response to DOCS' overall policies, discriminatory treatment, and the conditions of imprisonment was to form and participate in a number of overlapping informal and formal prisoner groups. Other Latinas(os) also participated in administrative organizations, such as the ILCs and the IGRCs. Within these multiple groups, Latinas and Latinos pursued a number of similar concerns. These included improving their immediate living conditions, protecting themselves from other prisoners and staff, increasing their chances of early release and reducing their chances of returning to prison. Latina(o) prisoners also sought to obtain emotional support from peers, maintain and promote their language and culture, as well as increase their access to family members and friends.

Additional goals included mobilizing the support of non-Latino prisoners, third parties, and penal staff on their behalf, reforming penal policies and practices, and acquiring a wide range of range of goods and services. Latina(o) prisoners were equally concerned with the hiring of additional bilingual personnel, the implementation of additional bilingual programs, and an end to discriminatory treatment encountered at the hands of white and African-American staff. The provision of bilingual programs and services, they hoped would allow Latina(o) prisoners equal access to educational, vocational, and other programs available to the English-speaking population. Such access would, in turn, increase Latina(o) prisoners' chances for early parole and success in the outside community.

The basic difference between the goals pursued by Latinos and those pursued by Latinas was the extent to which Latinas prioritized having access to visits by family members over other concerns. Such prioritizing resulted primarily from the fact that, prior to incarceration, the overwhelming number of Latinas were single heads of households. Once imprisoned, bureaucratic regulations and the costs of travelling made it difficult for their children and other relatives to visit them. The men, on the other hand, usually had women on the outside who were taking care of their children.

Interestingly, the overwhelming concern of Latina (and non-Latina) prisoners with pursuing reforms which would allow them increasing access to their children and families was one of the reasons some third parties within the Latina(o) community considered Latinas to be less political than their male counterparts. Ironically, penal elites, recognizing the political implications of such concerns, were able to use women's interests in their families, in an attempt to thwart organizing efforts among women prisoners.

The ability of Latina(o) prisoners to gain ground in their struggles was affected by their level of unity and organization and their ability to mobilize third party and penal sources of support. The level of unity was, in turn, affected by institutional constraints and by factors internal to the Latina(o) prisoner population. Internal factors included personal rivalries, political differences, and the subdivision of Latina(o) prisoners into a host of informal and formal groups and networks.

One of the most serious internal barriers to the formation of Latina(o) prisoner unity was the fact that once formal Latina(o) prisoner organizations were created Latina(o) prisoners became divided between those who wanted to focus on Latina(o) concerns pursued through formal prisoner and administrative groups, and those who favored openly using the organization to pursue coalition-building efforts with African-American and white prisoners. One of the reasons some Latina(o) prisoners were hesitant to engage in coalition-building efforts was because involvement in such activities could lead to the harassment of group members by institutional personnel and the dissolution of the organization. In spite of these fears, however, during the second half of the 1970s, the leadership of the formal Latina(o) prisoner organizations both at Green Haven and Bedford Hills underwent changes which led them to support the efforts of political underground prisoner groups. However, while at Green Haven, PUL leaders supported these efforts openly, at Bedford Hills, Latina prisoner leaders were careful not to compromise the name and the existence of the formal Latina prisoner organization.

Another significant internal threat to Latina(o) prisoner unity during the 1980s, was posed by the development of cleavages along nationality lines. These divisions emerged with the increasing incarceration of non-Puerto Rican prisoners and the subsequent broadening of Latina(o) prisoner concerns. While in the case of Latino prisoners such cleavages led to the creation of Dominican, Cuban, Central and South American, and Puerto Rican ad hoc committees who competed with the formal prisoner organization for membership, in the case of Latina prisoners such differences did not lead to the creation of separate entities. Despite the existence of such polarization, common ethnic concerns combined with the discrimination suffered by Latinas(os) at the hands of white and African-American prisoners and staff, insured that Latina(o) prisoners continued to be one another's main source of support.

Institutional administrators also created constraints which hindered the ability of Latina(o) prisoners to organize to pursue reforms. Latino(a) prisoners, like their African-American and white counterparts, had to get permission whenever they were going to meet. They could not meet in groups larger than twelve for organizational meetings. Their organizations could not have more than 125 (Bedford Hills) to 150 (Green Haven) members. The names of all members attending meetings and events were logged. They could not make phone calls or write letters to the outside without being subjected to censorship and monitoring.

Whenever Latino leaders were seen as being too strong and/or independent of institutional authorities their leaders and members ran the risk of being physically assaulted by guards, transferred to less desirable facilities, and/or put in segregation. This made it difficult to build a stable and consistent organizational leadership with whom third parties and/or sympathetic correctional personnel could work with over long periods of time. For Latinas, the risks of organizing carried with it the threat of losing access to their children, forced drugging, being transferred to a mental institution, and/or being beaten by male guards.

Prison authorities raided prisoners' rooms and tore up legal documents. At times informants were used to set-up prisoner leaders for further reprisals. In some cases, prisoners were reassigned to less desirable work areas or lost the ability to participate in certain groups and programs. On occasion, prison authorities attempted to interfere with the organizing of Latina(o) social and cultural events. While in some instances prisoners who participated in reform-oriented activities were labelled "disruptive," "violent," "revolutionaries," and "troublemakers," in others, the same prisoners were released on parole to eliminate their influence over the prisoner population.

There were also times when penal administrators targeted Latina(o) prisoners for further differential treatment. For example, in both male and female facilities Latinas(os) were penalized for speaking in Spanish, particularly during the 1970s. Moreover, penal concern about the leadership role Latino prisoners played in various work strikes and rebellions during the second half of the 1970s, led in the case of administrators at Green Haven, to disband the formal Latino prisoner organization and to prohibit Latino prisoners from forming another formal prisoner organization for over two years.

While both at Green Haven and Bedford Hills, Latina(o) prisoners were able to mobilize the support of institutional, primarily Latina(o) personnel to pursue their concerns, the ability of the latter to help produce long-term changes in penal policies toward Latina(o) prisoners was hindered by the fact that overall Latina(o) staff members did not occupy significant positions of power within the institutional hierarchy. Moreover, the behavior of line staff was strictly monitored by their superiors and peers, making them more hesitant to become involved in prisoners reform-oriented efforts.

During the first half of the 1980s, it became clear to DOCS that it had been unable to quell Latina(o) prisoner activism as evidenced by the leadership role they played in rebellions (Latinos) and class actions suits (Latinas) during the late 1970s and 1980s. In response, DOCS created the Division of Hispanic and Cultural Affairs, the Hispanic Inmate Needs Task Force, and assigned Hispanic Inmate Needs Coordinators to work at various state penitentiaries; first with Latino and subsequently with Latina prisoners. The creation of these entities had also been the result of the demands by Latina(o) prisoners and their allies within the Center for Puerto Rican Studies and the CPRS–affiliated Ad Hoc Committee for Hispanic Inmates, for an increase in the number of Latina(o) staff at a state level.

However, the ability of these bodies to reduce Latina(o) prisoner discontent was limited by the fact that state elites never gave budgetary priority to the area of programs, bilingual services, Latina(o) prisoners, nor the concerns of women in prison. Thus, ethnocentrism and sexism colluded with unbalanced fiscal management to hinder the ability of Latina(o) institutional and central office personnel to "deliver" bilingual programs and services to Latina(o) prisoners.

The degree and type of support Latina(o) staff gave Latina(o) prisoners also depended on the level of their preoccupation with upholding security concerns and maintaining their employment. While Latina(o) line staff generally feared losing their employment or being harassed by co-workers and superiors if they seemed too sympathetic to prisoner concerns, a primary interest of Latina(o) central office personnel were to keep abreast of Latina(o) prisoner organizing efforts, reduce the number of violent incidents between Latino prisoners and guards, and monitor both prisoner-initiated as well as DHCA-initiated bilingual programs.

While by the end of 1987, the DHCA had been able to place a number of bilingual counsellors in facilities with large numbers of Latino(a) prisoners and had been able to provide a number of bilingual programs, the problem still remained that the DHCA had neither been able to gain credibility within the mass of the Latino(a) prisoner population nor quell their discontent. In spite of these considerations, the probability that Latino(a) prisoner concerns would be addressed by the penal bureaucracy increased when there were more Latino(a) personnel working at the institutional and central office level.

The fact that Latina(o) prisoners lacked significant sources of institutional and central office support made it imperative for them to build alliances with third parties who could intercede with penal and other state elites on their behalf. Both at Green Haven and Bedford Hills, the most consistent sources of outside Latina(o) community support during the period studied were family members and a few Latina(o) legislators and religious organizations.

Family members provided financial as well as emotional support. Moreover, prisoners' families frequently acted as liaisons between prisoners, attorneys and the mass media. However, the ability of family members to influence penal policies on behalf of prisoners was limited by the fact that they lacked the monetary resources to conduct ongoing prisoner support work. Family members also often lacked knowledge of the criminal justice system and the English language making it difficult to further support imprisoned relatives. While a few Latina(o) legislators provided support throughout the years, their ability to help Latina(o) prisoners was hampered by the lack of wider legislative support for their efforts.

Both Latina and Latino prisoners mobilized the support of the Prison Task Force of the Center for Puerto Rican Studies during the 1973–1977 period. PTF members lobbied institutional authorities on behalf of Latina(o) prisoners, helped plan family and ethnic day events, brought the children of prisoners to visit their parents, and offered educational programs. Such services helped legitimize the activities pursued by Latina(o) prisoners and let institutional personnel know that its actions were being monitored by outside community members.

However, the ability of the PTF to provide support to Latino prisoners at Green Haven was hindered by the lack of sufficient resources and personnel with which to continue prisoner support work, the fact that PUL's leadership was continually being recreated, and barriers placed on outside volunteers by institutional personnel. In the case of Latina prisoners, the PTF's ability to provide support was also hampered by the task force's prioritizing of Latino male concerns. Such prioritizing was partly the result of stereotypes concerning what types of activities constituted prisoner "activism."

By ignoring the various ways in which prison authorities hindered women's ability to organize themselves to pursue reforms, such as the use of male guards to physically subdue women prisoners, and by ultimately devaluing as less political the concerns women prisoners considered priorities, male-oriented third parties, like mainstream social scientists, distorted the prison experiences of women and ignored important ways in which state sectors sought to maintain their continued subordination. The current research has shown that the attempts by women prisoners to empower themselves were primarily thwarted, not by their passivity, their apolitical stance, or the existence of prison families and networks, as some social scientists have argued, but by structural barriers created by penal personnel and the lack of third party support. As this study shows, Latina prisoners (as well as their non-Latina counterparts), resisted traditionally-imposed gender roles and oppressive penal policies by creating a number of informal and formal prisoner groups and networks, filing petitions and class action suits, and by forming political underground prisoner groups.

It was in an attempt to counter widely held stereotypes about the lack of activism among women prisoners, that Black nationalist women and radical white (predominantly lesbian) feminists supported the efforts by women prisoners to empower themselves. These community activists publicized the conditions encountered by prisoners at Bedford Hills, monitored the actions of the penal bureaucracy and the courts, wrote letters and petitions, and interviewed women involved in class-action suits. This type of assistance was important because it provided prisoners much needed emotional and political support as well as encouraged prisoners to pursue coalition-building efforts to demand reforms. However, in itself, this aid was not sufficient to help Latina prisoners acquire access to bilingual programs and staff personnel.

Latina prisoners, along with their African-American and white peers, also received significant support throughout the period studied from prisoners' rights attorneys, and other legal workers. Such assistance helped women prisoners bring about changes in medical as well as disciplinary policies at Bedford Hills. Prisoners' successful litigation efforts also led to the replacement of custody-oriented administrators by liberal administrators. However, the impact of such support was limited by the fact that penal elites could afford to ignore unfavorable court decisions for long periods of time. Such delays were, in part, the result of the continued judicial deference to prison administrators. The courts showed such deference by forcing prisoners to follow institutional grievance processes even though litigation had been won and by allowing DOCS a large latitude of time in which to implement court decision.

In the final analysis, what was important was not only whether there was third party support available but what kind of support was offered and what resources and time commitments third parties were able and willing to devote to prisoners. Thus, for example, the implementation of the Green Haven Study Release Program illustrated that Latino prisoners secured the most from DOCS when they were organized into a mass Latino prisoner organization and mobilized the support of DOCS central office institutional personnel, non-Latino prisoner leaders, and third parties in the Latina(o) community. The experiment with the Study Release Program also showed that it was when the penal bureaucracy was weakened by internal conflicts (e.g., reform versus custody-oriented sectors, central office versus institutional administrators), that an opportunity or "opening" was created for Latino prisoners and their allies to achieve a number of limited goals. Ultimately, such experiments were short-lived because both institutional and central office personnel prioritized security concerns.

In the case of Bedford Hills, Latina prisoners were able to win a limited amount of concessions from penal elites as a result of political underground activities which helped bolster litigation efforts by prisoners' rights attorneys. Such reform-efforts were supported by a few staff members at the institutional level and by women prisoner rights activists on the outside. In the end, litigation, combined with Latina prisoner activism, led to the hiring of a small number of bilingual personnel, put an end to discriminatory language policies, and won Latina prisoners the right to have translations during both medical and disciplinary proceedings.

Interestingly, the type of support offered by third parties influenced both the formulation of Latina(o) prisoner goals and the strategies pursued by the formal Latina(o) prisoner organization. For example, at Green Haven, where the Prison Task Force emphasized educational and cultural concerns, PUL pursued the implementation of bilingual higher educational programs through formal channels. At Bedford Hills, where the most consistent type of non-family third party support came out of the legal community, one of the priorities of women prisoners became to bolster the lawsuits documenting prisoners' abuse. Furthermore, the fact that attorneys, other legal workers, and community activists emphasized the need for unity among women prisoners, encouraged the latter to put their differences aside to pursue collective goals.

Within this setting, liberal administrators also needed the support of third parties in order to be able to carry out reform-oriented efforts in the face of widespread resistance from custody-oriented penal sectors. Third parties, in turn, could not operate successfully without the support of custody-oriented personnel occupying significant positions of power within the penal bureaucracy.

In summary, during most of the period, women prisoners lacked significant sources of both central office and institutional support for their concerns. As a result, it was not until a decade after the Attica

Rebellion, and only after a number of lawsuits had been decided against DOCS and monetary penalties imposed, that prison administrators addressed some of the basic concerns of women prisoners. As such, because women and men are perceived and treated differently in this society, Latinas and Latinos did not receive the same response from penal personnel and third parties, and hence, could not possibly experience imprisonment nor respond to such experiences in the same way.

Thus while Latina and Latino prisoners tended to share the same concerns, substantial gender differences existed with respect to the manner in which they organized. The variation in organizing tactics was conditioned not only by the priority they assigned to diverse interests but also by the disparate treatment male and female prisoners have historically received from both penal personnel and third parties. Furthermore, the study concludes that the ability of Latina(o) prisoners to have their concerns addressed was affected by their level of organization and unity, the degree to which they were able to mobilize penal and third party support on their behalf, and their ability to secure the support of non-Latina(o) prisoners, or at least, neutralize their resistance to Latina(o) prisoner concerns.

APPENDICES

Appendix A:
Latinas(os) and Criminal Justice Statistics

It is difficult to know exactly what portion of the nation's Latina(o) population comes into contact with the criminal justice system. The reasons for this are numerous. In some cases, statistical data may not include a breakdown by racial and/or ethnic composition. In others, data may be compiled but not released by the agency in question.[1] According to Jerry Mandel,[2] Latina(o) background is rarely included in any of the six major sources of criminal justice statistics (e.g., arrest[3] and prisoner[4] statistics, court and juvenile delinquency data, victimization studies, and public surveys). When such a breakdown is given, Latinas(os) are frequently classified as "Black", "White" or "Other" depending on the color of their skin or their surnames. The "Other" category may include non-Latinas(os) as well.

Using color as a criteria of ethnicity can be misleading because members of the same ethnic group may be of different colors. Moreover, the designation of "Hispanic" may include persons who have a Spanish surname, whether they are Latinas(os) or not, while excluding Latinas(os) who do not have Spanish surnames.[5] Using the term "Hispanic" to refer to people from different countries is also problematic because it does not differentiate among Latina(o) groups whose experience with the criminal justice system varies, depending, for example, on whether they are living in the United States as citizens, refugees, documented or undocumented workers. Moreover, not all Latinas(os) are "involved in the same type of criminal activity, not at the same level."[6] At times all Latinas(os) have been classified as "Puerto Ricans." Agencies define who is "Puerto Rican" either by birth or parentage. In some cases, "Puerto Ricans" and "Hispanics" have been listed separately. In others, "Puerto Ricans" are listed as a separate category and other Hispanics are included with "whites."[7]

Problems also arise when one uses language and self-identification as criteria for ethnic identification. Large numbers of Latinas(os), particularly those born and raised in the United States, do not know Spanish.[8] And while some Latinas(os) may hide their Latina(o) identity for fear of being deported,[9] others will do so because they feel ashamed of being Latinas(os). Additional problems ensue when one is gathering data about the composition of penal populations:

> The population for which data on inmate ethnicity are available is frequently defined differently, making comparative analysis difficult. The population may be defined either as the total population of the correctional system on a given day, or as the average daily population for the year, or as the number of new commitments in a specific month or year. All states use a combination of these reporting methods and provide different types of data in different reports.[10]

Finally, some statistics include racial and/or ethnic data but not information about the sex of the persons studied. The lack of interest nationally on the part of social scientists and government personnel about the fate of women in prison has led to the existence of widespread inconsistencies in government data on women prisoners.[11] The result is that it is even more difficult to obtain data on the experience of Latinas within the criminal justice system because they tend to be overlooked, both as a result of their ethnicity and their gender.

In 1986, the Division of Hispanic and Cultural Affairs of the New York State Department of Correctional Services sought to remedy the scarcity of information on Latina(o) prisoners by publishing, through its Hispanic Inmate Needs Task Force, the first extensive report on Latinas(os) in state facilities.[12] What have various types of New York State penal sources said about the experiences of Latina(o) prisoners? The information provided by DOCS personnel can be summarized into three major types. One describes the major problems encountered by Latina(o) prisoners as a result of discriminatory treatment and the lack of bilingual personnel and services. The second provides information about the sociodemographic characteristics of the Latina(o) prisoner population. The third discusses briefly the nature and goals of Latino prisoner groups, the role Latino prisoner leaders can play to help reduce tensions between their peers and the predominantly white staff, and reactions of penal staff to Latino prisoner groups. Although it is clear that the latter of these observations was made with Latino prisoners in mind, this researcher argues that many of them could easily have been made about Latina prisoners.

The Division of Program Planning, Research, and Evaluation of DOCS defined as Latinas(os) those prisoners "identified as Hispanic by classification personnel at departmental reception or determined to have been born in a Spanish-speaking country."[13]. The data included in Table 4 reveals that between 1970 and 1986 Latinos comprised between 98.2 and 96.6 percent of the Latina(o) prisoner population, although the percentage of Latina prisoners has been increasing. In fact, Latinas have been experiencing a faster rate of increase than have Latinos.[14]

As of January 1986, 77.8 percent of Latina(o) prisoners were still Puerto Rican (see Table 5), although during the 1980's increasing numbers of Dominican, Cuban, Colombian, and other South American immigrants entered the system (see Table 5). In fact, the greatest rate of increase among the Latina(o) prisoner population has been taking place among non-Puerto Rican and foreign-born Latinas(os). The growth in the number of Latina(o) prisoners who were immigrants meant that, by 1986, 11 percent of all Latina(o) prisoners were Spanish monolingual and another 33 percent exhibited limited English proficiency (see Table 6).

The available data for 1986 indicated that Latina(o) prisoners (91.0 percent) were more likely to come from New York City and its suburbs (5.7 percent) than African-American and white prisoners.[15] Most Latinas(os) came from New York and Bronx counties. Only 3.3 percent were living in upstate New York at the time of their arrest. Both Latinas and Latinos were more likely than African-Americans and whites to be imprisoned for drug-related crimes (24.3 percent) and less likely to be imprisoned for property (6.9 percent) and violent/coercive offenses (68.1 percent).[16] Latinas (45.9 percent) were less likely to be imprisoned for violent/coercive crimes than Latinos (68.7 percent), more likely to be imprisoned for drug-related offenses (47.0 percent compared to 23.6 percent), and equally likely to be imprisoned for property crimes (6.3 percent compared to 7.0 percent for Latinos).[17]

Latina(o) prisoners tended to come from poor and working-class families. Few had graduated from high school (13.3 percent of the men and 16.7 percent of the women).[18] As a result, they were "the most educationally disadvantaged"[19] prisoners in the system. Those employed at the time of their arrest tended to be blue collar workers, although Latinas were more likely to be employed (i.e., three-fourths)[20] than Latinos (i.e., two-thirds). Interestingly, the Latina prisoner population was older than their male counterparts, with Latinos under 29 years of age being at a greater risk of imprisonment than Latinas.[21]

In 1986, 45.9 percent of all Latina(o) prisoners were either married (18.8 percent) or living in common-law marriages (27.1 percent) at the time of their arrest,[22] although it appears that Latinas were less likely to be married (16.9 percent) or living in common-law marriages (3.5 percent) than Latinos.[23]

Latina(o) prisoners were more likely than non-Latinas(os) to have been diagnosed with AIDS. In fact, between 1976 and 1985, they made up 48 percent of those so diagnosed.[24] Latinas(os) were also overrepresented among those attempting suicide, assaulting other prisoners, and self-mutilators. However, they were as likely as African-American and white prisoners to assault guards and to use drugs.

Several factors have contributed to the rise in the number of Latina(o) prisoners in New York State. Perhaps, most important, the increase has been primarily caused by drug-related and mandatory sentencing laws passed during the 1970s. Such laws included the Rockefeller Drug Laws (1973),[25] the Second Felony Offender Law (1973)[26], the Violent Felony Offender Law (1978),[27] and changes in Consecutive Sentence Provisions (1978).[28] These laws made imprisonment mandatory for certain crimes, increased the sentence length for others, and reduced the ability to plea bargain. The result was to increase the number of men and women sentenced to prison[29] and the length of their stay there.[30]

The fact that Latinas(os) are increasingly being arrested for drug-related offenses, which are among the most harshly punished, means that they have been particularly adversely affected by the passage of such laws in comparison with white and African-Americans.[31] However, the fact that during the 1976 to 1984 period, "a notably higher percentage of female new commitments were sentenced for drug crimes than male new commitments"[32] would indicate that Latinas may have been disproportionately affected by the passage of these laws. In fact, a January 1, 1986, DOCS survey found that, although Latinas and Latinos are *more* likely to be imprisoned for drug-related offenses than are African-Americans and whites, "Hispanic females are more likely to be under custody for drug offenses (47.0 percent) than are male Hispanics (23.6 percent).[33]

Once Latinas(os) in New York State come in contact with the criminal justice system they have a greater chance of being convicted and imprisoned than whites,[34] receive harsher sentences than whites for similar crimes and/or criminal records[35], and are not as likely to receive early parole.[36] Moreover, Latino(a) prisoners, particularly Latinas,[37] have higher rates of recidivism compared to African-American and white prisoners[38] partly due to the lack of bilingual personnel that could provide supportive programs and services while imprisoned. Perhaps sadder still is the fact that a review of the number of Mexican-Americans executed in the southwestern United States between 1890 and 1986 revealed that they were the least likely of any racial/ethnic group to file an appeal of their conviction before their execution.[39]

As a result of the factors discussed above, in 1985, Latinas(os) comprised approximately 16 percent of the prisoners in adult federal institutions and 9 percent of those in adult state facilities throughout the country.[40] In addition, large numbers of Latinas(os) were confined in "county workhouses, municipal jails or precincts,"[41] awaiting trial or sentencing or already serving sentences. This increase in the Latina(o) adult prisoner population has been paralleled by a similar growth among the Latina(o) adolescent population held in juvenile detention centers and jails or under the supervision of probation officers.[42] The states with the largest numbers of Latina(o) prisoners also include those with the largest number of Latinas(os) within the general population (i.e., Arizona, California, Colorado, New York, and Texas). In all those states Latina(o) prisoners are overrepresented[43] and their numbers are likely to continue increasing in the future.[44]

Appendix B:
Tables

Table 1

PERSONS HELD UNDER CUSTODY OF NEW YORK STATE
DEPARTMENT OF CORRECTIONAL SERVICES, BY ETHNICITY/RACE,
DECEMBER 31: 1960; 1970; 1980; AND 1986.

Year	Total	White	Black	Hispanic*	Other/Not Stated
1960	19,213 (100.0) **	9,156 (47.7)	7,932 (41.3)	1,952 (10.2)	173 (0.9)
1970	12,579 (100.0)	4,146 (33.0)	6,735 (53.5)	1,639 (13.0)	59 (0.5)
1980**	21,548 (100.0)	5,929 (27.5)	11,260 (52.3)	4,149 (19.3)	210 (1.0)
1986	38,488 (100.0)	8,006 (20.8)	19,243 (50.0)	10,975 (28.5)	264 (0.7)

SOURCE: Adapted from State of New York, Department of Correctional Services, Division of Program Planning, Research, and Evaluation, New York State Department of Correctional Services, *Ethnic Distribution of Inmate Population on December 31: 1960–1988* (May 4, 1989).

NOTE: Figures for 1976 onward taken from preliminary reports. May differ slightly from final population. Figures exclude detainees.

*Figures before 1983 were kept only for Hispanics of Puerto Rican birth or parentage.

**Percentages may not add to 100 due to rounding.

Table 2
MEN HELD UNDER CUSTODY OF NEW YORK STATE DEPARTMENT
OF CORRECTIONAL SERVICES, BY ETHNICITY/RACE,
DECEMBER 31: 1960; 1970; 1980; AND 1986.

Year	Total	White	Black	Hispanic*	Other/Not Stated
1960	18,097	8,721	7,383	1,832	161
	(100.0) **	(48.2)	(40.8)	(10.1)	(0.9)
1970	12,210	4,024	6,521	1,609	56
	(100.0)	(33.0)	(53.4)	(13.2)	(0.4)
1980**	20,938	5,764	10,902	4,062	210
	(100.0)	(27.5)	(52.1)	(19.4)	(1.0)
1986	37,165	7,759	18,561	10,607	238
	(100.0)	(20.9)	(49.9)	(28.5)	(0.6)

SOURCE: Adapted from State of New York, Department of Correctional Services, Division of Program Planning, Research, and Evaluation, New York State Department of Correctional Services, *Male Inmate Population Ethnic Distribution on December 31: 1960–1988* (May 4, 1989).

NOTE: Figures for 1976 onward taken from preliminary reports. May differ slightly from final population. Figures exclude detainees.

*Figures before 1983 were kept only for Hispanics of Puerto Rican birth or parentage.

**Percentages may not add to 100 due to rounding.

Table 3

WOMEN HELD UNDER CUSTODY OF NEW YORK STATE
DEPARTMENT OF CORRECTIONAL SERVICES,
BY ETHNICITY/RACE,
DECEMBER 31: 1960; 1970; 1980; AND 1986.

Year	Total	White	Black	Hispanic*	Other/Not Stated
1960	1,116	435	549	120	12
	(100.0) **	(39.0)	(49.2)	(10.8)	(1.0)
1970	369	122	214	30	3
	(100.0)	(33.1)	(58.0)	(8.1)	(0.8)
1980**	610	165	358	87	0
	(100.0)	(27.0)	(58.7)	(14.3)	(0.0)
1986	1,323	247	682	368	26
	(100.0)	(18.7)	(51.5)	(27.8)	(2.0)

SOURCE: Adapted from State of New York, Department of Correctional Services, Division of Program Planning, Research, and Evaluation, New York State Department of Correctional Services, *Female Inmate Population Ethnic Distribution on December 31: 1960–1988* (May 4, 1989).

NOTE: Figures for 1976 onward taken from preliminary reports. May differ slightly from final population. Figures exclude detainees.

*Figures before 1983 were kept only for Hispanics of Puerto Rican birth or parentage.

**Percentages may not add to 100 due to rounding.

Table 4
LATINAS(OS) HELD UNDER CUSTODY OF NEW YORK STATE
DEPARTMENT OF CORRECTIONAL SERVICES, BY GENDER,
DECEMBER 31: 1960; 1970; 1980; AND 1986.

Year	Total	Men	Women
1960	1,952	1,832	120
	(100.0) **	(93.9)	(6.1)
1970	1,639	1,609	30
	(100.0)	(98.2)	(1.8)
1980**	4,149	4,062	87
	(100.0)	(97.9)	(2.1)
1986	10,975	10,607	368
	(100.0)	(96.6)	(3.4)

SOURCE: Adapted from State of New York, Department of Correctional Services, Division of Program Planning, Research, and Evaluation, New York State Department of Correctional Services, *Ethnic Distribution of Inmate Population on December 31: 1960–1988* (May 4, 1989).

NOTE: Figures for 1976 onward taken from preliminary reports. May differ slightly from final population. Figures exclude detainees.

*Figures before 1983 were kept only for Hispanics of Puerto Rican birth or parentage.

**Percentages may not add to 100 due to rounding.

Table 5

PERSONS HELD UNDER CUSTODY OF NEW YORK STATE
DEPARTMENT OF CORRECTIONAL SERVICES,
BY ETHNIC STATUS IDENTIFIED AT RECEPTION OR BY
SPANISH-SPEAKING PLACE OF BIRTH, JANUARY 1, 1986

Place of birth	Total	White	Black	Hispanic	Other
Total	34,734	7,693	17,511	9,381	149
New York State	21,147	6,259	11,491	3,345	52
(P.R. Parentage				(3,069)	
(P.R. Born)*				(101)	
(Other Hispanic)				(175)	
Other States and U.S. Possessions	6,092	915	5,015	149	13
Puerto Rico	4,129	0	0	4,129	0
Dominican Rep.	614	0	0	614	0
Cuba	456	0	0	456	0
Colombia	275	0	0	275	0
Panama	107	0	0	107	0
Ecuador	48	0	0	48	0
Mexico	19	0	0	19	0
Other Central/ South American Countries	223	10	47	165	1
Other Countries	1,255	370	780	29	76
Unknown	369	139	178	45	7

SOURCE: Adapted from State of New York, Department of Correctional Services, Division of Program Planning, Research, and Evaluation, *Selected Characteristics of the Department's Hispanic Inmate Population* (December 1986): 9-11, Tables 2 and 3.

*It is not clear who this category is referring to.

Table 6
LANGUAGE DOMINANCE AND PROFICIENCY OF HISPANIC
PRISONERS HELD UNDER CUSTODY OF THE NEW YORK STATE
DEPARTMENT OF CORRECTIONAL SERVICES,
DECEMBER 1985 AND MAY 1986

	12/85	5/86
Total Population	34,872	35,547
Number of English Dominant	31,037	31,636
Hispanic Population	9,343	9,701
Number of Spanish Dominant (Bilingual Program Eligible)	3,835	3,910
Number with limited English Proficiency	3,000 (32.1)	3,199 (33.0)
Number of Spanish Monolingual	1,050 (11.2)	1,066 (11.0)

SOURCE: Adapted from State of New York, Department of Correctional Services, Division of Hispanic and Cultural Affairs, Hispanic Inmate Needs Task Force, *Final Report, "A Meeting of Minds, An Encounter of Hearts" 1986 (Action Plan)*, 111, Table 3.

Table 7
MEN HELD UNDER CUSTODY OF NEW YORK STATE
DEPARTMENT OF CORRECTIONAL SERVICES IN
ALL INSTITUTIONS AND AT GREEN HAVEN
CORRECTIONAL FACILITY, BY RACE/ETHNICITY,
DECEMBER 31, 1970; SEPTEMBER 1, 1982; AND MAY 5, 1986.

Date	Total	White	Black	Hispanic*	Other
Total	12,210	4,024	6,521	1,609	56
12/31/70	(100.0) *	(33.0)	(53.4)	(13.2)	(0.4)
GH	1,919	482	1,076	358	3
	(100.0)	(25.1)	(56.1)	(18.7)	(0.2)
Total	26,102	6,865	13,645	5,378	214
9/1/82	(100.0)	(26.3)	(52.3)	(20.6)	(0.8)
GH	2,067	413	1,122	523	9
	(100.0)	(20.0)	(54.3)	(25.3)	(0.4)
Total	34,004	7,393	17,074	9,325	212
5/5/86	(100.3)	(21.7)	(50.2)	(27.4)	(0.6)
GH	2,075	355	1,128	582	10
	(100.0)	(17.1)	(54.4)	(28.0)	(0.5)

SOURCE: Adapted from State of New York, Department of Correctional Services: Division of Program Planning and Evaluation, *Characteristics of Inmates Under Custody 1970*, Vol. VI, No. 3 (July 1972): 10, Table Iva; Ibid., *Ethnic Distribution of Inmates Under Custody in New York State Correctional Facilities as of 9/1/82* (Loose sheet); Idem., Division of Hispanic and Cultural Affairs, Hispanic Inmate Needs Task Force, *Final Report, "A Meeting of Minds, An Encounter of Hearts" 1986 (Action Plan)*, 205-206.

NOTE: Figures for 1976 onward taken from preliminary reports. Figures exclude detainees.

*Figures before 1983 were kept only for Hispanics of Puerto Rican birth or parentage.

**Percentages may not add to 100 due to rounding off.

Table 8

TOTAL BILINGUAL OR HISPANIC SECURITY AND CIVILIAN STAFF
IN ALL NEW YORK STATE CORRECTIONAL INSTITUTIONS AND
AT BEDFORD HILLS AND GREEN HAVEN CORRECTIONAL
FACILITIES, AUGUST 1986.

Facility	Total Popu.	Total Hisp. Popu.	Total	Staff	Total Bil. or Hisp. Staff	
			Sec.	Civ.	Sec.	Civ.
GH	2084	556 (26.7)	632	257	3 (0.5)	11 (4.3)
BH	530	127 (24.0)	312	172	39 (12.5)	11 (6.4)
Total All Inst.	—	—	13,489	6,951	469 (3.5)	270 (3.9)

SOURCE: Adapted from Susan Sheehan, *A Prison and a Prisoner* (Boston: Houghton Mifflin Co., 1978), 43, 479; and State of New York, Department of Correctional Services, Division of Hispanic and Cultural Affairs, Hispanic Inmate Needs Task Force, *Final Report, "A Meeting of Minds, An Encounter of Hearts"* 1986 (Action Plan), 77-84.

Table 9
MEN HELD AT GREEN HAVEN CORRECTIONAL FACILITY,
BY SELECTED SOCIODEMOGRAPHIC CHARACTERISTICS,
DECEMBER 31: 1970 AND 1986.

| Characteristic | Green Haven | |
	12/31/70	12/31/86
Total	1,919	2,075
Ethnicity/Race		
White	482	339
	(25.1) *	(16.3)
Black	1,076	1,129
	(56.1)	(54.4)
Puerto Rican	358	596
	(18.7)	(28.7)
Other	3	11
	(0.2)	(0.5)
County of Commitment		
NYC	78.4	
Upstate	21.6	
Age		3/31/86
16-18	0.0	0.0
19-20	1.6	0.2
21-29	37.8	34.7
30-39	37.9	41.1
40 and over	22.7	23.9
Education		
College or Vocational	2.9	
H.S.	14.4	
Less than H.S.	82.8	
Prior Adult Criminal Record		(Universe=1961)
No Prior Record	9.7	No Prior Arrest/Conviction 33.3
Prior Record	90.3	66.7
Prior Institutional Commitment		
No Prior Commitment	21.1	67.2
Local Institution Only	24.4	9.0
State/Fed Institution	54.5	23.8

Table 9 (continued)

Characteristic	12/31/70	Green Haven	12/31/86
Minimum Sentence			(Universe=2069)
No Minimum	7.5	No Minimum	0.0
Less than 29 months	35.8	less than 24	2.2
30-119	36.1	24-119	35.5
120 and over	20.7	120 and over	62.3
Maximum Sentence			
Less than 36 months	0.9	Less than 36	0.0
36 months	15.5	36 months	1.4
37-48 months	14.4	37-53 months	1.1
49-60 months	15.8	54-71 months	1.7
61-120 months	22.5	72-107 months	5.2
121 and over	30.8	108 and over	90.6
Second Felony Status			
1st Felony			65.3
2nd Felony			30.6
Persistent Felony			4.1
Felony Offenses			
Murder/homicide	22.5		46.1
Felonious Ass.	6.9	Att. Murder/Assault	6.3
Rape/Other Sex Off.	4.0		7.0
Robbery	31.6		21.0
Burglary	9.1		5.1
Grand Larceny	5.9		0.5
Forgery	0.9		0.1
Dangerous Drugs	13.4		9.6
Dangerous Weapons	3.2		1.2
All other Felonies	2.0		3.3
Misdemeanors & Violations in 552 CCP**	0.3		0.0
Other Misdemeanors & Violations	0.4		0.0
Youthful Offenses	0.8		0.0
Wayward Minors & Juvenile Delinquents	0.0		0.0

SOURCE: Adapted from Department of Correctional Services, Division of Program Planning and Evaluation, *Characteristics of Inmates Under*

Table 9 (continued)

Custody 1970, Vol. VI, No. 3 (July 1972): 7-12; Idem., Green Haven Correctional Facility, December 31, 1986: Commitment Offense Type by Current Age by Ethnicity, Persons Under Custody; Offense Type by First or Second Felony Status; Offense Type by Ethnic Status; Offense Type by Prior Criminal Record; Offense Type by Minimum Sentence Length; Offense Type by Maximum Sentence Length; Ibid, March 1, 1986: Offense Type by Current Age.

*Percentages may not add to 100 due to rounding.

**Section 552 of the Code of Criminal Procedure.

Table 10
WOMEN HELD UNDER CUSTODY OF NEW YORK STATE
DEPARTMENT OF CORRECTIONAL SERVICES IN ALL
INSTITUTIONS AND AT BEDFORD HILLS CORRECTIONAL
FACILITY, BY RACE/ETHNICITY,
DECEMBER 31, 1970; SEPTEMBER 1, 1982; AND MAY 5, 1986

Date	Total	White	Black	Hispanic*	Other
Total	369	122	214	30	3
12/31/70	(100.0) **	(33.1)	(58.0)	(8.1)	(0.8)
BH	219	48	144	27	0
	(100.0)	(21.9)	(65.8)	(12.3)	(0.0)
Total	788	190	463	129	6
9/1/82	(100.0)	(24.1)	(58.8)	(16.4)	(0.8)
BH	452	96	285	68	3
	(100.0)	(21.2)	(63.1)	(15.0)	(0.7)
Total	1,064	249	549	257	9
5/5/86	(100.0)	(23.4)	(51.6)	(24.2)	(0.8)
BH	513	123	258	128	4
	(100.0)	(24.0)	(50.3)	(25.0)	(0.8)

SOURCE: Adapted from State of New York, Department of Correctional Services, Division of Program Planning and Evaluation, *Characteristics of Inmates Under Custody 1970*, Vol. 6, No. 3 (July 1972): 10, Table Iva; Ibid., *Ethnic Distribution of Inmates Under Custody in New York State Correctional Facilities as of 9/1/82* (Loose sheet); Idem., Division of Hispanic and Cultural Affairs, Hispanic Inmate Needs Task Force, *Final Report,* "A Meeting of Minds, An Encounter of Hearts" 1986 (Action Plan), 205-206.

NOTE: Figures for 1976 onward taken from preliminary reports. Figures exclude detainees.

*Figures before 1983 were kept only for Hispanics of Puerto Rican birth or parentage.

**Percentages may not add to 100 due to rounding.

Table 11
WOMEN HELD AT BEDFORD HILLS CORRECTIONAL FACILITY,
BY SELECTED SOCIODEMOGRAPHIC CHARACTERISTICS,
DECEMBER 31: 1970 AND 1986

	Bedford Hills	
Characteristic	12/31/70	12/31/86
Total	219	599
Ethnicity/Race		
White	48	116
	(21.9) *	(19.4)
Black	144	297
	(65.8)	(49.6)
Puerto Rican	27	182
	(12.3)	(30.4)
Other	0	4
	(00.0)	(0.6)
County of Commitment		
NYC	72.6	
Upstate	27.4	
Age		(3/1/86: Universe=600)
16-18	4.6	0.8
19-20	11.4	2.2
21-29	36.1	40.6
30-39	23.3	38.5
40 and over	24.7	17.7
Education		
College or Vocational	1.8	
H.S.	11.4	
Less than H.S.	86.8	
No Prior Adult Criminal		
Record		(Universe=487)
No Prior	32.9	No Prior Arrest/Conviction 46.8
Prior Record	67.1	53.2
Prior Institutional		
Commitment		(Universe=487)
No Prior Commitment	46.3	73.3
Local Institution Only	23.8	14.8
State/Fed Institution	29.9	11.9

Table 11 (continued)

Characteristic	12/31/70	Bedford Hills	12/31/86
Minimum Sentence			(Universe=598)
No Minimum	16.9	No Minimum	00.0
12-29 months	56.6	Less than 24	20.4
30-119	17.8	24-119	60.2
120 and over	8.6	120 and over	19.4
Maximum Sentence			(Universe=600)
Less than 36 months	0.9	Less than 36	0.0
36 months	32.9	36 months	14.5
37-48 months	27.4	37-53 months	10.0
49-60 months	10.9	54-71 months	6.3
61-120 months	14.2	72-107 months	10.8
121 and over	13.7	108 and more	58.3
Second Felony Status			
1st Felony			67.8
2nd Felony			30.7
Persistent Felony			1.5
Felony Offenses			(Universe=600)
Murder/homicide	36.1		32.2
Felonious Ass.	4.6	Att. Murder/Assault	5.7
Rape/Other Sex Off.	0.0		1.5
Robbery	11.4		16.2
Burglary	0.5		5.0
Grand Larceny	8.7		6.7
Forgery	0.9		4.5
Dangerous Drugs	20.5		22.7
Dangerous Weapons	0.9		1.0
All other Felonies	2.3		4.3
Misdemeanors & Violations in 552 CCP**	2.3		0.0
Other Misdemeanors & Violations	3.2		0.0
Youthful Offenses	5.9		0.3
Wayward Minors & Juvenile Delinquents	2.7		0.0

SOURCE: Adapted from Department of Correctional Services, Division of Program Planning and Evaluation, *Characteristics of Inmates Under*

Table 11 (continued)

Custody 1970, Vol. VI, No. 3 (July 1972): 7-12; Idem, Bedford Hills Correctional Facility, December 31, 1986: Commitment Offense Type by Current Age by Ethnicity, Persons Under Custody; Offense Type by First or Second Felony Status; Offense Type by Ethnic Status; Offense Type by Prior Criminal Record; Offense Type by Minimum Sentence Length; Offense Type by Maximum Sentence Length; Ibid., March 1, 1986: Offense Type by Current Age.

*Percentages may not add to 100 due to rounding off.

**Section 552 of the Code of Criminal Procedure.

Appendix C:
Relevant Court Cases

Sostre, Pierce, SaMarion v. Lavallee, 293 F.2d 233 (1961)

Sostre v. Mcginnis, 334 F. 2d 906 (1964)

Sostre v. Otis, 330 F. Supp. 941 (1971).

Sostre v. Rockefeller, 312 F. Supp. 863 (S.D.N.Y. 1970), modified sub-nom *Sostre v. McGinnis*, 442 F.2d 178, 193 n. 23 (2d Cir. 1971), cert. denied, 404 U.S. 1049, 92 S.Ct. 719, 30 L.Ed.2d 740 (1972)

Wolff v. Mcdonnell, 418 U.S. 539, 94 S.Ct 2963, 41 L.Ed.2d 935 (1974)

Crooks v. Warne, 74 Civ. 2351 (S.D.N.Y. 1974)

Powell v. Ward, 74 Civ. 4628

Powell v. Ward, 392 F. Supp. 628 (1975)

Powell v. Ward, 542 F.2d 101 (1976)

Todaro v. Ward, 74 Civ. 4581

Todaro v. Ward, 431 F. Supp. 1129 (1977)

Todaro v. Ward, 565 F.2d 48 (1977)

Forts v. Ward, 77 Civ. 1560

Forts v. Ward, 434 F. Supp. 946 (S.D.N.Y. 1977)

Forts v. Ward, 566 F.2d 849 (1977)

Dean v. Coughlin, 84 Civ. 1528 (SWK)

Dean v. Coughlin, 623 F. Supp 392 (D.C.N.Y. 1985).

Dean v. Coughlin, 633 F. Supp 308 (S.D.N.Y. 1986)

Dean v. Coughlin, 804 F.2d 207 (2nd Cir. 1986)

Langley v. Coughlin, 84 Civ. 5431 (LBS)

Langley v. Coughlin, 83 Civ. 7172 (LBS)

Langley v. Coughlin, 709 F. Supp. 482 (S.D.N.Y. 1989)

Langley v. Coughlin, 715 F. Supp. 522 (S.D.N.Y. 1989)

Langley v. Coughlin, 888 F.2d 252 (2nd. Cir. 1989)

Appendix D:
The Folsom Prisoners' Manifesto of
Demands and Anti-Oppression Platform

DUE TO THE CONDITIONAL FACT THAT FOLSOM PRISON IS ONE OF THE MOST CLASSIC INSTITUTIONS OF AUTHORITATIVE INHUMANITY UPON MEN, THE FOLLOWING MANIFESTO OF DEMANDS IS BEING SUBMITTED:

1. *We demand* the constitutional rights of legal representation at the time of all Adult Authority hearings, and the protection from the procedures of the Adult Authority whereby they permit no procedural safeguards such as an attorney for cross examination of witnesses, witnesses in behalf of the parolee, at parole revocation hearings.

2. *We demand* a change in medical staff and medical policy and procedure. The Folsom Prison Hospital is totally inadequate, understaffed, prejudicial in the treatment of inmates. There are numerous "mistakes" made many times, improper and erroneous medication is given by untrained personnel. The emergency procedures for serious injury are totally absent in that they have no emergency room whatsoever; no recovery room following surgery, which is performed by practitioners rather than board member surgeons. They are assisted by inmate help neither qualified, licensed, nor certified to function in operating rooms. Several instances have occurred where multiple injuries have happened to a number of inmates at the same time. A random decision was made by the M.D. in charge as to which patient was the most serious and needed the one surgical room available. Results were fatal to one of the men waiting to be operated upon. This is virtually a death sentence to such a man who might have otherwise lived.

3. *We demand* adequate visiting conditions and facilities for the inmates and families of Folsom prisoners. The visiting facilities at this prison are such as to preclude adequate visiting for the inmates

437

and their families. As a result the inmates are permitted two hours, two times per month to visit with family and friends which of course has to be divided between these people. We ask for additional officers to man the visiting room five days per week, so that everyone may have at least four hours visiting per month. The administration has refused to provide or consider their request in prior appeals using the grounds of denial that they cannot afford the cost of the (extra) officers needed for such a change. However, they have been able to provide twelve new correctional officers to walk the gun rails of this prison, armed with rifles and shotguns during the daytime hours when most of the prison population is at work or attending other assignments. This is a waste of the taxpayers' money, and a totally unnecessary security precaution.

4. *We demand* that each man presently held in the Adjustment Center be given a written notice with the Warden of Custody's signature on it explaining the exact reason for his placement in the severely restrictive confines of the Adjustment Center.

5. *We demand* an immediate end to indeterminate Adjustment Center terms to be replaced by fixed terms with the length of time to be served being terminated by good conduct and according to the nature of the charges, for which men are presently being warehoused indefinitely without explanation.

6. *We demand* an end to the segregation of prisoners from the mainline population because of their political beliefs. Some of the men in the Adjustment Center are confined there solely for political reasons and their segregation from other inmates is indefinite.

7. *We demand* an end to political persecution, racial persecution, and the denial of prisoners' right to subscribe to political papers, books, or any other educational and current media chronicles that are forwarded through the United States Mail.

8. *We demand* an end to the persecution and punishment of prisoners who practice the constitutional right of peaceful dissent. Prisoners at Folsom and San Quentin Prisons, according to the California State Penal Code, cannot be compelled to work, as these two prisons were built for the purpose of housing prisoners and there is no mention of prisoners being required to work on prison jobs in order to remain on the mainline and/or be considered for release. Many prisoners believe their labor power is being exploited in order for the State to increase its economic power and continue to expand its correctional industries which are million dollar complexes, yet do not develop working skills acceptable for employment in the outside

society, and which do not pay the prisoner more than the maximum sixteen cents per hour wage. Most prisoners never make more than six or eight cents per hour. Prisoners who refuse to work for the two to sixteen cent pay rate, or who strike, are punished and segregated without the access to privileges shared by those who work. This is class legislation, class division, and creates class hostilities within the prison.

9. *We demand* an end to the tear-gassing of prisoners who are locked in their cells. Such action led to the death of Willie Powell in Soledad Prison in 1968, and of Fred Billings on February 25, 1970 at San Quentin Prison. It is cruel and unnecessary.

10. *We demand* the passing of a minimum and maximum term bill which calls for an end to indeterminate sentences whereby a man can be warehoused indefinitely, rehabilitated or not. That all prisoners have the right to be paroled after serving their minimum term instead of the cruel and unusual punishment of being confined beyond his minimum eligibility for parole, and never knowing the reason for the extension of time, nor when his time is completed. The maximum term bill eliminates indefinite life time imprisonment where it is unnecessary and cruel. Life sentences should not confine a man for longer than ten years, as seven years is the statute for a considered lifetime out of circulation and if a man cannot be rehabilitated after a maximum of ten years of constructive programs, etc., then he belongs in a mental hygiene center, not a prison. Rescind Adult Authority Resolution 171, arbitrary fixing of prison terms.

11. *We demand* that industries be allowed to enter the Institutions and employ inmates to work eight hours a day and fit into the category of workers for scale wages. The working conditions in prisons do not develop working incentives parallel to the money jobs in the outside society, and a paroled prisoner faces many contradictions on the job that adds to his difficulty to adjust. Those industries outside who desire to enter prisons should be allowed to enter for the purpose of employment placement.

12. *We demand* that inmates be allowed to form or join Labor Unions.

13. *We demand* that inmates be granted the right to support their own families. At present thousands of welfare recipients have to divide their checks to support their imprisoned relatives who without the outside support could not even buy toilet articles or food. Men working on scale wages could support themselves and families while in prison.

14. *We demand* that correctional officers be prosecuted as a matter of law for shooting inmates, around inmates, or any act of cruel and unusual punishment where it is not a matter of life or death.

15. *We demand* that all institutions that use inmate labor be made to conform with the state and federal minimum wage laws.

16. *We demand* that all condemned prisoners, avowed revolutionaries and prisoners of war be granted political asylum in the countries under the Free World Revolutionary Solidarity Pact, such as Algeria, Russia, Cuba, Latin America, North Korea, North Vietnam, etc., and that prisoners confined for political reasons in this country, until they can be exchanged for prisoners of war held by America, be treated in accord with the 1954 Geneva Convention; that they and their personal property be respected, that they be permitted to retain possession of personal property and that they not be manacled.

17. *We demand* an end to trials being held on the premises of San Quentin Prison, or any other prison without a jury of peers—as required by the United States Constitution—being picked from the country of the trial proceedings; peers in this instance being other prisoners as the selected jurors.

18. *We demand* an end to the escalating practice of physical brutality being perpetrated upon the inmates of California State Prisons at San Quentin, Folsom, and Soledad prisons in particular.

19. *We demand* that such celebrated and prominent political prisoners as Reis Tijerina, Ahmad Evans, Bobby Seale, Chip Fitzgerald, Los Siete, David Harris, and the Soledad Brothers, be given political asylum outside this country as the outrageous slandering of the mass media has made it impossible either for a fair trail or for a safe term to be served in case of conviction, as the forces of reactions and repressions will be forever submitting them to threats of cruel and unusual punishment and death wherever they are confined and throughout the length of their confinement.

20. *We demand* appointment of three lawyers from the California Bar Association for full time positions to provide legal assistance for inmates seeking post-conviction relief, and to act as liaison between the administration and inmates for bringing inmate complaints to the attention of the administration.

21. *We demand* update of industry working conditions to standards as provided for under California law.

22. *We demand* establishment of inmate workers insurance plan to provide compensation for work related accidents.

23. *We demand* establishment of unionized vocational training program comparable to that of the Federal Prison System which provides for union instructors, union pay scale, and union membership upon completion of the vocational training course.

24. *We demand* annual accounting of Inmate Welfare Fund and formulation of an inmate committee to give inmates a voice as to how such funds are used.

25. *We demand* that the Adult Authority Board appointed by the Governor be eradicated and replaced by a parole board elected by popular vote of the people. In a world where many crimes are punished by indeterminate sentences, where authority acts with secrecy and vast discretion and gives heavy weight to accusations by prison employees against inmates, inmates feel trapped unless they are willing to abandon their desire to be independent men.

26. We strongly demand that the State and Prison Authorities, conform to recommendation #1 of the "Soledad Caucus Report," to wit,

> "That the State Legislature create a fulltime salaried board of overseers for the State Prisons. The board would be responsible for evaluating allegations made by inmates, their families, friends, and lawyers against employees charged with acting inhumanely, illegally, or unreasonably. The board should include people nominated by a psychological or psychiatric association, by the State Bar Association or by the Public Defenders Association, and by groups of concerned, involved laymen."

27. *We demand* that prison authorities conform to the conditional requirements and needs as described in the recently released Manifesto from the Folsom Adjustment Center.

28. *We demand* an immediate end to the agitation of race relations by the prison administrations of this state.

29. *We demand* that the California Prison System furnish Folsom Prison with the services of Ethnic counselors for the needed special services of the Brown and Black population of this prison.

30. *We demand* an end to the discrimination in the judgement and quota of parole for Black and Brown People.

31. *We demand* that all prisoners be present at the time that their cells and property are being searched by the correctional officers of state prisons.

We the men of Folsom Prison have been committed to the State Correctional Authorities by the people of this society for the purpose of correcting what has been deemed as social errors in behavior, errors which have classified us as socially unacceptable until re-programmed with new values and a more thorough understanding of our roles and responsibilities as members of the outside community. The structure and conditions of the Folsom Prison program have been engraved on the pages of this manifesto of demands with the blood, sweat, and tears of the inmates of this prison.

The program which we are committed to under the ridiculous title of rehabilitation is likened to the ancient stupidity of pouring water on the drowning man, in as much as our program administrators respond to our hostilities with their own.

In our efforts to comprehend on a feeling level an existence contrary to violence, we are confronted by our captors with violence. In our effort to comprehend society's code of ethics concerning what is fair and just, we are victimized by exploitation and the denial of the celebrated due process of law.

In our peaceful efforts to assemble in dissent as provided under the nation's United States Constitution, we are in turn murdered, brutalized, and framed on various criminal charges because we seek the rights and privileges of *all american people.*

In our efforts to keep abreast of the outside world, through all categories of news media, we are systematically restricted and punished by isolation when we insist on our human rights to the wisdom of awareness.[45]

Appendix E:
Observers' Proposals
(Based on the Attica Prisoners' Demands)

1. Provide adequate food and water and shelter for this group.

2. Replace Superintendent Mancusi immediately.

3. Grant complete administrative and legal amnesty to all persons associated with this matter.

4. Place this institution under federal jurisdiction.

5. Apply the New York State minimum wage law to all work done by inmates. STOP SLAVE LABOR.

6. Allow all New York State prisoners to be politically active, without intimidation or reprisal.

7. Allow true religious freedom.

8. End all censorship of newspaper, magazines, letters, and other publications from publishers.

9. Allow all inmates on their own to communicate with anyone they please.

10. When an inmate reaches conditional release, give him a full release without parole.

11. Institute realistic, effective rehabilitation programs for all inmates according to their offense and personal needs.

12. Modernize the inmate education system.

13. Provide a narcotics treatment program that is effective.

14. Provide adequate legal assistance to all inmates requesting it.

15. Provide a healthy diet; reduce the number of pork dishes; serve fresh fruit daily.

16. Reduce cell time, increase recreation time, and provide better recreation facilities and equipment.

17. Provide adequate medical treatment for every inmate, engage either a Spanish-speaking doctor or interpreters who will accompany Spanish-speaking inmates to medical interviews.

18. Provide a complete Spanish library.

19. Educate all correction officers in the needs of inmates.

20. Institute a program for the employment of significant number of black and Spanish-speaking officers.

21. Establish an inmate grievance delegation comprised of one elected inmate from each company which is authorized to speak to the administration concerning grievances, and develop other procedures for community control of the institution.

22. Conduct a grand-jury investigation of the expropriation of inmate funds and the use of profits from the metal and other shops.

23. Cease administrative resentencing of inmates returned for parole violation.

24. Conduct Menechino hearings in a fair manner.

25. Permit other inmates in C block and the box to join this group.

26. Arrange flights out of this country to nonimperialist nations for those inmates desiring to leave the country.

27. Remove inside walls, making one open yard and no more segregation or punishment.

28. Expansion of work-release program.

29. End approved lists for visiting and correspondence.

30. Remove screens in visitation rooms as soon as possible.

31. Institute parole violation changes—revocation of parole shall not be for vehicle and traffic violation.

32. Due process hearing for all disciplinary proceedings with 30-day maximum.

33. Access to facility for outside dentists and doctors at inmates' expense.[46]

Appendix F:
Latino Prisoner Organizations

The Concerned Puerto Rican Committee
(Great Meadow Correctional Facility)

The Concerned Puerto Rican Committee (CPRC) at Great Meadow Correctional Facility had been in existence at least as of September 9, 1972, when it petitioned the governor, the warden and the DOCS' Commissioner for "seventeen badly needed reforms for the Spanish-speaking inmates to be implemented."[47] The petition was ignored by DOCS' administrators.

The CPRC then requested DOCS to recognize November 19 as "Puerto Rican Discovery Day" in all state facilities. On November 8, 1972, Deputy Commissioner Edward Edwin informed the CPRC that their request had been granted. However, institutional opposition to the event led to its initial cancellation. The celebration was subsequently held on December 17, 1972, with the assistance of Latino legislators such as Herman Badillo and Robert García, community organizers like Genoveva Clemente and the Committee to Defend Pancho Cruz.

As a response both to the problems encountered while trying to organize the above event and the discriminatory conditions faced by Puerto Rican prisoners at Great Meadow, the CPRC, along with the institution's Young Lords Party, filed a "civil rights action against the administration because of its discriminatory policies against their community."[48] In the suit filed at the end of 1972, "The explicit conditions which were exposed were the lack of medical attention because of the absence of interpreters, also in the parole hearings, the long delay in mail, because of language, fact, non-existing educational programs. Theres [sic] no means of recreation to [sic] them to release the psychological tension built up. Due to the fact of a different language, they are forced to live in a total alienated world, since everything is written or spoken in English. During the past decades, they have been subjected to exist in a state of a cruel and unusual punishment, because of the administrators' neglect to the law, and their nationality."[49] The prison administration responded to the suit by increasing their harassment of Latino prisoners.

On May 14, 1973, the CPRC petitioned the governor "for the recognition of June 24, 1973, as a religious holiday for all Puerto Rican inmates to celebrate the day in their native tongue."[50] The festivities would observe June 23, 1974, in honor of Saint John the Baptist, the patron saint of Puerto Rico. On May 31, 1973, Herman Badillo informed the organization that the request had been granted. Latina(o) honored guests present at the event, which was held on June 23, included Tamarra and López Ferrer from *Claridad* newspaper, Tom Soto of the Prisoners Solidarity, Alfredo López, secretary of community affairs of the Socialist Party, and Federico Velez of the Puerto Rican Legal Defense and Education Fund.[51] At the time of the June 23 celebration, the class action suit filed at the end of 1972 was still pending.

Concerned Puerto Rican Committee, Chapter II (Attica Correctional Facility)

The purpose of the Concerned Puerto Rican Committee, Chapter II (CPRC II) created at Attica in 1973 was, "the involvement and participation of the Spanish-speaking residents at this institution."[52] According to the CPRC II, its major objective was:

> . . . to speed up and smooth out the adjustment process. To accomplish this, it works both with the prisoner and with the community, which he has made his new home. The following services are rendered:
>
> Employment Service: Helps find jobs and gives vocational guidance through an employment program which collaborates with organizations in the community.
>
> Social Service: Provides professional orientation in the use of institution resources and outside agencies and offers consultations on personal problems, legal aid, and community relations.
>
> Education Program: Provides information about correctional programs such as English classes, guidance and orientation on vocational courses, and higher education. Works with community groups and agencies.
>
> Community Organization Program: Offers technical assistance to all Puerto Rican prisoners, collaborating in the organization and

development of self-help programs and community improvement campaigns.

Information and Public Relations Program: Disseminates information about Puerto Rico and Puerto Ricans in the United States. The committee will distribute publications and will try to establish in this institution a research library and coordinate cultural projects.[53]

El Partido Nacionalista Revolucionario Boricua de la República Socialista de Boriquen (Attica)

Coexisting with the CPRC II at Attica was an informal Puerto Rican prisoner group called El Partido Nacionalista Revolucionario Boricua de la Republica Socialista de Boriquen. El Partido identified itself as being of "Marxist-Albizuista-Maoista" leanings. In a letter to its members, it mentioned the placement of ten Puerto Rican/Latino prisoners in segregation. It also chastised party members for not continuing to organize Latino prisoners upon being transferred to other facilities.[54]

Subsequently, El Partido subscribed to the eleven programmatic principles of the Puerto Rican Socialist Party (PRSP). El Partido was first exposed to the PRSP principles at its first party congress held at Green Haven Correctional Facility on August 9, 1972.[55]

Latinos Unidos (Eastern Correctional Facility)

According to an announcement that appeared in the *Midnight Special*:

> The aims and goals contemplated by Latinos Unidos shall be: (a) to improve the political, educational, social and economical [*sic*] conditions of the Latin population confined in correctional Institutions of the State of New York; (b) to establish a sincere and effective system of communication and mutual help between the Internal and external communities for the better understanding of both sides, enabling the internal community to function and share its constructive qualities within the external community; (c) all aims and goals shall be geared to improve the conditions and relations between the Internal and external communities.[56]

Shortly after its creation, Latinos Unidos, along with representatives of the African-American prisoner population, issued an open letter in which they listed fourteen grievances. The list of grievances given below was forwarded to DOCS administrators, the Commission on Crime and Correction, newspapers, prisoners' newsletters, and community leaders throughout the state, in hopes of promoting changes in conditions at the institution.

1) There are no civilian personnel at this facility functioning within the capacities of vocational instructors, correctional and educational counselors, parole, medical or psychiatric officers who can communicate in Spanish. As a result of the existing language barriers at this facility, the majority of the Latin prisoners are victimized by administrative deficiencies which perpetuate a condition and atmosphere of frustration and alienation.

2) There are no civilian and/or correctional personnel assigned to the Temporary Release Committee, Time Allowance Committee, Adjustment Committee, etc. who can communicate in Spanish, nor are there any Latins and/or Blacks on such committees.

3) It is our contention that stringent measures must be undertaken by the correctional hierarchy in an effort to remedy and curtail the pathological pattern of dereliction by departmental recruiting agencies which discriminate and facilitate the racist exclusion of non-white civilian personnel from these positions . . .

4) A disproportionately few Latin prisoners at this facility are approved for participation in the several temporary release programs. For example, there are currently seven men involved in the educational release programs, none of which are of Latin extraction and notwithstanding the fact that Latin prisoners meet the criteria and have applied for such programs.

5) While from time to time, ethnic and/or culturally oriented courses are part of the college curriculum at this facility, there has never been a Latin cultural course, notwithstanding the expressed interest in such a course by any given number of Latin prisoners.

6) There is a need today, just as there has always been a need where minority groups have been, discriminately, denied their mobility, to ascertain equal and qualitative education that would promote higher socio-economic stations in life for Third World people. There is a need today, for the radicalization of educational programs within the New York State Correctional system. The introduction of bilingual and bicultural courses of study would re-define our experiences in the context of our cultural and social well being an d improve the overall education of the interned Latin and Black Community.

7) It is our contention that just as all other ethnic groups prior to migration of Latin-Americans which had resisted the so-called North American melting pot so have Latin Americans of Puerto Rican nationality, especially in the case of the Latin prisoner. It is

paramount and must be clearly understood that no groups and/or race of people have ever consciously consented to assimilation wherein the benefits of such dehumanizing process meant the decimation of their cultural identity. Undoubtedly, this systemic pattern of cultural aggression victimizes the Latin prisoners and it is one of the many contributing factors that facilitate and promote such a high influx of Latin prisoners into North America's prisons.

8) The institution's prison library has been the meagerest selection of books written in Spanish and/or English concerning the spectrum of "Third World" studies, notwithstanding the fact that Latin and Black prisoners comprise eighty-five (85%) percent of the total imprisoned populace at this facility.

9) Institutional job assignments reflect discrimination against Latin and Black prisoners both with regard to preferred positions and rates of compensation.

10) The institutions' commissary has no visible selection of Goya, Progresso, and/or Shabazz food products which are normally consumed by Latins, Italians, and Blacks, not withstanding the fact that these food products are sold at other correctional facilities through the State of New York.

11) None of the weekend or holiday movies, plays, and musicals, shown from time to time at this facility are of Latino origin, nor do any reflect our cultural preferences . . .

12) Our annual preparations for the forthcoming Puerto Rican Discovery Day and Black Solidarity Day festivities have been wantonly degenerated to a complete spectacle by this already questionable and unpopular administration (e.g., our immediate families have been excluded from participating in these events, despite the unsurmountable wave of prisoner discontent and departmental policies which dictate and encourage the strengthening of family and social ties, as a humane approach toward rehabilitative experiences, that are conducive to the constructive process of rehabilitation).

13) Latinos Unidos, as a recently formed Spanish-speaking prisoners' organization at this facility, has met with continued resistance, abortive administrative attempts and successes to suppresses our efforts in establishing rapports and links of communication with outside community leaders, civil organizations and cultural institutions (e.g., outgoing organizational and/or related correspondences aspirating to create relationships and mediums for the exchange of ideas, expressions, and experiences of both internal and external communities are callously returned and/or deliberately confiscated, withheld, and possibly destroyed).

14) There are no Latin or Black prison guards at this facility holding the rank of sergeant or higher, in spite of the fact that

eighty-five percent of the total imprisoned population are comprised of Latin and Black prisoners. Nor do these prison guards reflect the racial composition of the interned Latin and Black community. Needless to say, this is one of the many grievances brought to the public light during the Attica Uprising and which, though the State concurred to rectify, still remains unremedied.[57]

Notes: Appendixes

1. See Peter L. Sissons, *The Hispanic Experience of Criminal Justice* (New York: Hispanic Research Center, Fordham University, Monograph No. 3, 1979), 14–15.

2. See Jerry Mandel, *Police Use of Deadly Force: Los Angeles* (Washington, D.C.: National Council of la Raza, 1981).

3. The major national source of arrest statistics is that compiled by the Federal Bureau of Investigation Uniform Crime Reports (UCR) section and published annually in *Crime in America*. Until 1980, Latinas(os) were classified as "White," although separate statistics were kept for Indians, Chinese, and Japanese persons. See Edward R. Roybal, Untitled, *National Hispanic Conference on Law Enforcement and Criminal Justice*, U.S. Department of Justice, Law Enforcement Assistance Administration (Washington, D.C.: GPO, 1980), 39–44. As late as 1979, New York State did not report race to the UCR (Jerry Mandel, "Hispanics in the Criminal Justice System—the Nonexistent Problem," *Law and Justice*, No. 3 (May/June 1979): 16–20).

4. The major sources of prisoner statistics are: surveys of local, state, and federal facilities; reports gathered by individual state systems; and data periodically compiled by the Bureau of the Census. However, few states publish data on the ethnicity of their prisoners (Mandel, "Hispanics in the Criminal Justice System," 1979). The New Jersey Department of Corrections appears to be one of the few state systems that has allowed studies to be conducted of its Latino prisoner population. See Robert Joe Lee, *Hispanics—The Anonymous Prisoners* (Trenton: Department of Corrections, 1976); Idem, "Profile of Puerto Rican Prisoners in New Jersey and Its Implications for the Administration of Criminal Justice" (M.A. thesis, Rutgers University, 1977); Maggie Agüero, "An Exploratory Profile of Puerto Rican Prisoners in New Jersey" (M.A. thesis, John Jay College of Criminal Justice, 1980), and Idem, *Hispanics in New Jersey Adult Correctional Institutions: A Profile of Inmates, Staff, Services, and Recommendations* (Trenton: Department of Corrections, 1981). These reports, however, are limited to male prisoners. New York State did not publish any data on prisoners between 1975 and 1979 (Mandel, *Police Use of Deadly Force*, 1979). It was not until 1986 that the New York State Department of Correctional Services, through its Division of Hispanic and Cultural Affairs, published an extensive report on Latina(o) prisoners. See

New York State Department of Correctional Services (hereafter cited as NYSDOCS), Division of Hispanic and Cultural Affairs, Hispanic Inmate Needs Task Force, *Final Report, "A Meeting of Minds, An Encounter of Hearts" 1986 (Action Plan)*, Albany, 1986.

5. See Adalberto Aguirre, Jr. and David V. Baker, "A Descriptive Profile of the Hispanic Penal Population: Conceptual and Reliability Limitations in Public Use Data," *The Justice Professional* 3, No. 2 (1988): 189–200.

6. Ibid., 195.

7. NYSDOCS, Division of Program Planning, Research and Evaluation, *Characteristics of Female Inmates Held Under Custody, 1975–1985*, by Kathy Canestrini, Albany, September 1986.

8. See Aguirre Jr. and Baker, "A Descriptive Profile," 1988.

9. Agenor L. Castro, "Programming for Hispanic Inmates and Ex-Offenders," *Proceedings of the One Hundred and Eighth Annual Congress of Correction of the American Correctional Association*, Portland, Oreg., August 20–24, 1978 (College Park, Md.: American Correctional Association, 1979), 77–88.

10. Sissons, *The Hispanic Experience*, 15.

11. Erika Anne Kates, "Litigation As a Means of Achieving Social Change: A Case Study of Women in Prison" (Ph.D. diss., Brandeis University, 1984).

12. NYSDOCS, Division of Hispanic and Cultural Affairs, Hispanic Inmates Needs Task Force, *Final Report*, 1986.

13. NYSDOCS, Division of Program Planning, Research, and Evaluation, *Year-to-Year Changes in the Hispanic Under Custody Population 1986 and 1987*, by Charles H. Nygard, Albany, August 1987, 1.

14. One needs to be careful, however, when making such assertions because the number of Latinas has historically been so small that any increase in Latina imprisonment rates could result in a greater percentage of "rate of increase." The fact is that between 1970 and 1986 the number of Latina prisoners increased from 30 to 368, while that of Latinos increased from 1,609 to 10,607 (see Table 4). The same arguments concerning the misuse of statistical data have been made by feminist criminologists and social scientists who have analyzed rates of increase for male and female arrests during the past two decades. See Laura Crites, "Women Offenders: Myth vs. Reality," in Laura Crites, ed., *The Female Offender* (Lexington, D.C.: Heath and Co., Inc., 1976), 33–44; and Juanita Díaz-Cotto, "Women and Crime in the United States," in Chandra Talpade Mohanty, Ann Russo, and Lourdes Torres, *Third World Women and the Politics of Feminism* (Bloomington: Indiana University Press, 1991).

15. NYSDOCS, Department of Program Planning, Research, and Evaluation, *Selected Characteristics of the Department's Hispanic Inmate Population*, by Charles H. Nygard, Albany, December, 1986.

16. NYSDOCS, Division of Program Planning Research and Evaluation, *Characteristics of the Department's Hispanic Inmate Population*, 1986, 3–5, 12.

17. Ibid., 4–5.

18. NYSDOCS, Division of Hispanic and Cultural Affairs, Hispanic Inmate Needs Task Force, *Final Report*, 164.

19. Ibid., 244.

20. Ibid., 155.

21. Approximately 41.1 percent of Latina prisoners were under 29 years of age. Another 42.3 percent was between 30 and 39 years old and 16.5 percent were 40 years and over. For Latinos, the figures included: 56.1 percent under 29 years of age; 31.4 percent between 30 and 39 years old; and 12.6 percent 40 and over. The figures were arrived at by subtracting the number of Latinas in each age category given on page 160 of the Hispanic Inmate Needs Task Force Report from those given for the ages of all Latina(o) prisoners on page 214 of the same report (NYSDOCS, Division of Hispanic and Cultural Affairs, Hispanic Inmate Needs Task Force, *Final Report*, 1986). Although the Hispanic Inmate Needs Task Force took the figures from two different sources, the fact that the studies were conducted so close together (June 1985 and December 1985) makes my approximation quite realistic. The argument that Latina prisoners tend to be older than their male counterparts seems to be validated by a September 1986 DOCS' report which showed that, as a whole, "women held under custody in 1985 are slightly older, on average, than the women held in 1975" (NYSDOCS, Division of Program Planning, Research, and Evaluation, *Characteristics of Female Inmates*, 1986).

22. NYSDOCS, Division of Hispanic Affairs, Hispanic Inmate Needs Task Force, *Final Report*, 1986.

23. According to the Hispanic Inmate Needs Task Force Report, 55.0 percent of Latina prisoners were never married, 20.3 percent were separated or divorced, and 4.3 percent were widowed (Ibid., 156).

24. African-Americans made up 35 percent of prisoners diagnosed with AIDS. Whites and others accounted for 17.0 percent (Ibid., 225).

25. "The Meaning of the New Drug Bill," *Midnight Special* 3, No. 11 (November 1973): 21, 23.

26. "The second felony offender laws have contributed to increased population size through mandatory incarceration and by longer requirements for minimum sentences for second felony offenders" (NYSDOCS, Division of

Program Planning, Research, and Evaluation, *Characteristics of Female Inmates*, 28).

27. Violent Felony Offender Laws restricted certain plea negotiations, "increased the minimum period of imprisonment for persons convicted of Class B or Class C violent felony offenses," and "required judges to fix the minimum period of imprisonment at sentencing for Class B and Class C violent felony offenders" (Ibid., 29). As of 1980, the latter stipulation was extended to cover all felony offenders.

28. As of 1978, the legislature "required that the minimum terms of consecutive sentences be aggregated (or added together) as the method for establishing the minimum sentence that must be served prior to parole release consideration" (Ibid., 30). Prior to that the minimum was established by "serving the longest minimum period of the consecutive offenses" (Ibid.).

29. While in 1976, 15.1 percent of all women (new commitments) were sentenced under Second Felony Offender Laws, by 1984, the number had increased to 38.2 percent (NYSDOCS, Division of Program Planning, Research, and Evaluation, *An Examination of the Trend of Female New Commitments*, 1976–1984, by Kathy Canestrini, Albany, June 1986).

30. The Campaign for Common Sense in Criminal Justice, *Needless and Costly Incarceration: The Misguided Plan to Add 200 New Beds at Bedford Hills Correctional Facility*, Albany, N.Y., March 1986; and NYSDOCS, Division of Program Planning, Research and Evaluation, *An Examination of the Trend*, 1986. Both the average minimum sentence and the average time served by women increased between 1975 and 1985 (NYSDOCS, Division of Program Planning, Research, and Evaluation, *Characteristics of Female Inmates*, 1986).

31. Sissons, *The Hispanic Experience of Criminal Justice*, 1979; and Joan Moore and Harry Pachón, *Hispanics in the United States* (Englewood Cliffs: Prentice Hall, Inc., 1985).

32. NYSDOCS, Division of Program Planning, Research, and Evaluation, *An Examination of the Trend*, 19.

33. NYSDOCS, Division of Program, Planning, Research and Evaluation, *Selected Characteristics*, 5.

34. Robert García, Untitled, *National Hispanic Conference on Law Enforcement and Criminal Justice*, U.S. Department of Justice, Law Enforcement Assistance Administration (Washington, D.C.: GPO, 1980), 29-38.

35. Ibid.; and John Carro, "Impact of the Criminal Justice System on Hispanics," *National Hispanic Conference on Law Enforcement and Criminal Justice*, U.S. Department of Justice, Law Enforcement Assistance Administration (Washington, D.C.: GPO, 1980), 361–382. J. Petersilia's 1983 study of criminal justice practices in California, Texas, and Michigan revealed that

African-American and Latino male prisoners received and served longer sentences than whites (J. Petersilia, "Racial Disparities in the Criminal Justice System: A Summary," *Crime and Delinquency* 31 [1985]: 15–34).

36. New York Board of Correction, *Through a Veil of Partial Comprehension, 1973;* Sissons, *The Hispanic Experience of Criminal Justice,* 1979; García, Untitled, 1980; and Migdalia de Jesús-Torres, "Profile of Puerto Rican/Latino Women Offenders in New York State Correctional Institutions: Program, Policy and Statutory Changes," Somos Uno Conference, March 1988, New York State Assembly Puerto Rican/HSP Task Force, The Hispanic Woman: Issues and Legislative Concerns, Albany, N.Y. (unpublished paper).

37. NYSDOCS, Division of Hispanic and Cultural Affairs, Hispanic Inmate Needs Task Force, *Final Report,* 1986.

38. Ibid.

39. Adalbeto Aguirre, Jr. and David Baker, "The Execution of Mexican American Prisoners in the Southwest," *Social Justice* 16, No. 4 (Issue 38, Winter 1989): 150–161.

40. U.S. Department of Justice 1986, *Prisoners in 1985* (Washington, D.C.: U.S. GPO, 1986); and Aguirre, Jr. and Baker, "A Descriptive Profile," 1988.

41. Agenor L. Castro, "Bilingual Programming: A Viable Alternative in Corrections—Part A," *National Hispanic Conference on Law Enforcement and Criminal Justice,* U.S. Department of Justice, Law Enforcement Assistance Administration (Washington, D.C.: GPO, 1980), 87-119.

42. Ibid and New York, N.Y., Mayor's Commission on Hispanic Concern, *Report of the Mayor's Commission on Hispanic Concerns,* December 10, 1986.

43. According to Aguirre, Jr. and Baker, in 1985, the proportion of Latina(o) prisoners in these states was: Arizona, 23 percent; California, 25 percent; Colorado, 24 percent; New York, 20 percent; and Texas, 19 percent. (Aguirre, Jr., and Baker, "A Descriptive Profile, 1988). The history of Mexican-American overrepresentation in Arizona state prisons dates back to the end of the 19th century when the first penitentiaries were being established throughout the country. Paul Knepper's research on the history of the Arizona Territorial Prison at Yuma revealed that Mexicans composed over half of the prisoners confined there during the 1876-1909 period that the prison was in operation. Paul Knepper, "Southern-style Penal Repression: Ethnic Stratification, Economic Inequality, and Imprisonment in Territorial Arisona, *Social Justice* 16, No. 4 [Issue 38, Winter 1989]: 132–149. In 1969, Mexican-Americans composed at least 16.4 percent of California's prisoner population although they made up only 11 percent of the state population (Joan W. Moore, *Homeboys: Gangs, Drugs and Prison in the Barrios of Los Angeles* [Philadelphia: Temple University Press, 1978]). See also: Paul

Knepper, "Southern-Style Penal Repression: Ethnic Stratification, Economic Inequality, and Imprisonment in Territorial Arizona," *Social Justice* 16, No. 4 [Issue 38, Winter 1989]: 132–149).

44. Other demographic factors accounting for the growth in the Latina(o) prisoner population follow: First, Latinas(os) are one of the fastest growing groups in the country. Second, the Latina(o) population is a young population (NYSDOCS, Division of Hispanic and Cultural Affairs, Hispanic Inmate Needs Task Force, *Final Report*, 1976). The young are more likely to come in contact with the criminal justice system because they are more likely to be unemployed (Monica Hennera Smith, "Exploring the Re-entry and Support Services for Hispanic Offenders," *National Hispanic Conference on Law Enforcement and Criminal Justice*, U.S. Department of Justice, Law Enforcement Assistance Administration, [Washington, D.C.: GPO 1980], 147–148).

45. Compiled from Angela Y. Davis, Ruchell Magee, the Soledad Brothers, and Other Political Prisoners, *If They Come in the Morning: Voices of Resistance* (New York: Third Press Publishers, 1971), 57–63; and Ronald Berkman, *Opening the Gates: The Rise of the Prisoners' Movement* (Lexington, Mass.: D.C. Heath and Co., 1979), 183–186.

46. New York State Special Commission on Attica, *Attica: The Official Report of the New York State Special Commission on Attica* (New York: Bantam Books, Inc., 1972), 251–256.

47. The Concerned Puerto Rican Committee, Comstock, N.Y., "Vencer-emos: Puerto Rican Brothers Organize," *Midnight Special* 3, No. 3 (March 1973): 1–3.

48. Idem, "resocialization or dehumanization??," *Midnight Special* 3, No. 6 (June 1973): 2.

49. Ibid.

50. Ibid., "Revolutionary Festival," *Midnight Special* 3, No. 9 (September 1973): 8–9.

51. Ibid.

52. Central Committee, The Concerned Puerto Rican Committee, Chapter II, "Que Bonita Bandera," *Midnight Special* 3, No. 12 (December 1973): 8.

53. Ibid.

54. El Partido Nacionalista Revolucionario Boricua de la República Socialista de Boriquen, "Al Partido," *Midnight Special* 3, No. 8 (August 1973): 16.

55. Minister of Propaganda, "Communique of the B.R.N.P.," *Midnight Special* 3, No. 12 (December 1973): 9.

56. Latinos Unidos, "Latinos Unidos," *Midnight Special* 5, No. 5 (August/September 1975): 24.

57. El Comité, "The Harder They Come: Dear Brothers and Sisters," *Midnight Special* 5, No. 7 (December 1975/January 1976): 20–21.

About the Author

Juanita Díaz-Cotto is an Assistant Professor of Sociology, Women's Studies, and Latin American and Caribbean Studies at the State University of New York at Binghamton. She is also (under the pseudonym of Juanita Ramos) the editor of *Compañeras: Latina Lesbians (An Anthology)* (New York: Routledge, Chapman, and Hall, 1994), originally published in New York City by the Latina Lesbian History Project, 1987.

Index